# OXFORD–WARBURG STUDIES

*General Editors*

DENYS HAY *and* J. B. TRAPP

# OXFORD–WARBURG STUDIES

# THE
# ELECT NATION

## *The Savonarolan Movement in Florence 1494–1545*

LORENZO POLIZZOTTO

CLARENDON PRESS · OXFORD

1994

Oxford University Press, Walton Street, Oxford OX2 6DP

Oxford New York
Athens Auckland Bangkok Bombay
Calcutta Cape Town Dar es Salaam Delhi
Florence Hong Kong Istanbul Karachi
Kuala Lumpur Madras Madrid Melbourne
Mexico City Nairobi Paris Singapore
Taipei Tokyo Toronto
and associated companies in
Berlin Ibadan

Oxford is a trade mark of Oxford University Press

Published in the United States
by Oxford University Press Inc., New York

British Library Cataloguing in Publication Data
Data available

Library of Congress Cataloging in Publication Data
Polizzotto, Lorenzo.
The elect nation: the Savonarolan movement in Florence, 1494–1545
Lorenzo Polizzotto.
(Oxford–Warburg studies)
Includes bibliographical references.
1. Savonarola, Girolamo, 1452–1498—Political and social views.
2. Savonarola, Girolamo, 1452–1498—Influence. 3. Piagnoni
(Savonarolan movement) 4. Florence (Italy)—Politics and
government—1421–1737. I. Title. II. Series.
DG737.97.P58 1994 945'.5106—dc20 93–31942
ISBN 0–19–920600–7

1 3 5 7 9 10 8 6 4 2

Typeset by Best-set Typesetter Ltd., Hong Kong
Printed in Great Britain
on acid-free paper by
Biddles Ltd.,
Guildford and King's Lynn

For my parents

# PREFACE

The subject of this study is the followers of Girolamo Savonarola, who were known as the Piagnoni. Many Florentines were drawn to Savonarola during his lifetime by a programme of spiritual, political, and social renovation which corresponded very closely to their own aspirations. It was, indeed, largely inspired by them. Despite Savonarola's execution in 1498, the Piagnoni remained a powerful and fairly cohesive body. For the next fifty years or so they exercised a profound influence on ecclesiastical and civil affairs. In the process, they affected the whole course of Florentine history in the important period of the city's transition from a republic to a principate. This book examines their membership, ideology, and activity both before Savonarola's death and afterwards. What was the nature of the relationship between the Piagnoni and Savonarola? What was the essence of the ideology which they evolved and which, despite personal rivalries, ensured their cohesiveness, strength, and survival for over half a century?

Savonarola's influence during his lifetime and after his death was clearly immense. Throughout their history, the Piagnoni were to revere his memory above all else and to continue to be guided by his teaching. While Savonarola exerted a powerful influence over them, even from beyond the grave, this would not have been enough in itself to bind his followers together, nor to ensure them their all-important role in Florentine politics. Nor, finally, would it explain the sway of their message over their own and succeeding generations.

The explanation must be sought in the Piagnoni themselves. What emerges most clearly from an investigation of their activity is their remarkable ability to adapt to changing circumstances. Their very diversity was a source of strength. It allowed them not only to explore different avenues of ecclesiastical and political reform, in line with individual preference, but also to modify their responses in accordance with the sympathies of the prevailing political climate. In their versatility, it will be argued, lies one of the reasons for their long survival and for the power they were to wield until well into the period of the Medicean principate.

Even more important in explaining their influence and success in the face of the forces arrayed against them was the millenarianism which underpinned their whole ideology. By promising believers the certainty of divine election, with earthly gifts of wealth, empire, religious, and political supremacy, and perennial happiness, this ideology gratified Florentine pride and expectations. It did so, moreover, at a time when events over which the Florentines had no control seemed to be conspiring to deprive them of the cultural, economic, and political primacy to which they had long been accustomed and which they had expected to enjoy in perpetuity. While the ideology to which they were drawn was, arguably, both reactionary and anachronistic, this made it all the more attractive. By adapting Savonarola's ideology to changing conditions, the Piagnoni, paradoxically, elaborated an alternative view of man's role in religion and politics which ran counter to the prevailing headlong rush towards absolutism in both Church and State.

The debts which I have incurred in the long course of this study have been many and profound. Numerous friends and colleagues helped to smooth the path of my research, especially in Florence and London. It gives me great pleasure to thank Mrs Alison Brown, Dr Roslyn Pesman Cooper, Dr Robert Black, Dr H. C. Butters, Dr J. N. Stephens, and Ms Caroline Elam. Concerning likely sources of information, Professors Cesare Vasoli and Antonio Rotondò have been most forthcoming. In addition, the late Dr C. B. Schmitt was most generous with advice on the subject of Giovanfrancesco Pico della Mirandola and his works, and this study has benefited accordingly.

I wish also to express my gratitude to the following persons for their unstinting assistance and support throughout the various stages of research and composition. First and foremost, I thank Professor Nicolai Rubinstein, under whose supervision this study was originally begun. It was a privilege to work under his guidance and to continue to benefit from the inspiration which he has brought to the field of Renaissance history. I am also very grateful to Professor J. B. Trapp and Mrs Judith Ravenscroft for their careful reading of the typescript and for their expert advice. For their selfless assistance and most generous encouragement, especially during a time of personal hardship, my thanks go also to Professors F. W. Kent and Donald Weinstein. Professor Weinstein, in addition, has provided invaluable advice in the revision and preparation of the manuscript for publication. I hope that this book will reflect his inspiration.

I am most grateful to colleagues in the Department of Italian at the University of Western Australia for their understanding. In particular, I wish to thank Professor J. A. Scott for his support, friendship, and expert assistance in translating some of the more difficult Italian and Latin passages. I am also happy to express my gratitude to the personnel of the many institutions in Italy, England, and Australia who have facilitated the research for this book. I should like to make specific acknowledgement to the following: in Florence to the staff of the Archivio di Stato, and in particular to Signorina Paola Peruzzi; the staff of the Biblioteca Nazionale, the Biblioteca Medicea Laurenziana, and the Biblioteca Riccardiana; in London, to the staff of the Warburg Institute and the British Library; in Perth, to the staff of the Reid Library of the University of Western Australia and, in particular, to the late Mary Alexander and to Mrs En Kho. I should also like to acknowledge with gratitude assistance from the Erasmus Prize Fund towards the cost of compiling the index.

My warmest appreciation is extended also to the members of the confraternity of the Buonuomini of S. Martino in Florence for allowing me access to their archives; and to Professor Gino Corti for arranging my introduction to the Guicciardini Archives and for providing much needed specialized assistance whenever called upon. To the superiors of the Dominican Order go my thanks for the gracious welcome they gave me and for their permission to consult the archives of the convents of S. Marco, S. Domenico at Fiesole, and the Crocetta at Varlungo. To the communities of these convents, my deepest thanks for their hospitality. In particular I thank Suor Maria Osannna Gobbetto, Archivist at the Crocetta, and Fra Innocenzo Colosio, formerly Archivist of S. Domenico, Director of the Levasti Library of Spirituality at S. Marco, and factotum of the whole congregation in scholarly matters. Father

Colosio's congeniality, generosity, and unparalleled knowledge of
the archival holdings in S. Marco and S. Domenico have greatly
speeded my research, and for this I am profoundly grateful. Other
members of the Dominican Order, namely Fra Salvatore Camporeale, Fra Emilio Panella, Fra Armando Verde, and in particular
Fra Fausto Sbaffoni, provided all the assistance I could have
wished for. I have much pleasure in thanking them formally for
their courtesy and kindness.

For permission to reprint a portion of my article 'Prophecy,
Politics and History in Early Sixteenth-Century Florence: The
Admonitory Letters of Francesco d'Antonio de' Ricci' in P. Denley
and C. Elam (eds.), *Florence and Italy: Renaissance Studies in
Honour of Nicolai Rubinstein* (London, 1988), 107–31, I would like
to thank the Committee for Medieval Studies, Westfield College,
University of London. I am also grateful to the Frederick May
Foundation for Italian Studies for allowing me to reprint mate-
rial originally published in my article 'Domenico Benivieni and
the Radicalisation of the Savonarolan Movement', in C. Condren
and R. Pesman Cooper (eds.), *Altro Polo: A Volume of Italian
Renaissance Studies* (Sydney, 1982), 99–117.

During my various research trips to Italy, I have always been
most fortunate in being able to count on the extraordinarily warm
welcome of the whole extended Bussandri family. I am pleased here
to acknowledge my debt to them all but, in a special way, to Elvira
Bussandri, whose kindness, care, and generosity have provided the
pleasant and comfortable setting essential for study.

This book could not have been written without the constant
help, advice, and encouragement of my wife Carolyn Polizzotto. So
great has been her contribution that the book is as much hers as it
is mine. My debt to her can never be repaid.

Finally, I am proud to dedicate this book to my parents,
Antonino and Argilde Polizzotto Bussandri. They have stood beside me, through many vicissitudes, from the project's inception
and have seen to it, often at the cost of considerable sacrifice, that
it was brought to a successful conclusion.

# CONTENTS

# ABBREVIATIONS

| | |
|---|---|
| AAF | Archivio Arcivescovile di Firenze |
| ABSM | Archivio dei Buonuomini di S. Martino, Firenze |
| ACDC | Archivio del Convento Domenicano della Crocetta, Firenze |
| ACSL | Archivio Capitolare di S. Lorenzo, Firenze (Biblioteca Medicea Laurenziana) |
| ACSM | Archivio Provinciale del Convento di S. Marco, Firenze |
| *AFP* | *Archivum Fratrum Praedicatorum* |
| AGOP | Archivio Generale Ordine Domenicano, S. Sabina, Roma |
| ASF | Archivio di Stato, Firenze |
| *ASI* | *Archivio storico italiano* |
| ASM | Archivio di Stato, Milano |
| ASMO | Archivio di Stato, Modena |
| ASP | Archivio Salviati, Pisa |
| ASPI | Archivio di Stato, Pistoia |
| ASV | Archivio Segreto Vaticano |
| BAV | Biblioteca Apostolica Vaticana |
| BL | British Library |
| BMF | Biblioteca Marucelliana, Firenze |
| BMLF | Biblioteca Medicea Laurenziana, Firenze |
| BNF | Biblioteca Nazionale, Firenze |
| BPP | Biblioteca Palatina, Parma |
| BRF | Biblioteca Riccardiana, Firenze |
| Comp. Sopp. | Compagnie Soppresse |
| Conv. Sopp. | Conventi Soppressi |
| Copinger | W. A. Copinger, *Supplement to Hain's Repertorium Bibliographicum* (London, 1895–1902) |
| C. Strozz. | Carte Strozziane |
| *DBI* | *Dizionario Biografico degli Italiani* (Istituto della Enciclopedia Italiana; Rome, 1960–   ) |

| | |
|---|---|
| ENOS | Edizione Nazionale delle Opere di Girolamo Savonarola |
| Ep. Grand. | Epoca Granducale |
| Ep. Rep. | Epoca Repubblicana |
| *GW* | *Gesamtkatalog der Wiegendrucke* (Leipzig, 1925– ) |
| Hain | L. Hain, *Repertorium Bibliographicum* (Stuttgart, 1826–38) |
| Magl. | Magliabechiano |
| MAP | Archivio Mediceo avanti il Principato |
| MP | Monte di Pietà |
| Not. Ant. | Notarile Antecosimiano |
| Ord. Aut. | Ordinaria Autorità |
| Ottob. Lat. | Ottoboniano Latino |
| Pal. | Palatino |
| Panc. | Panciatichiano |
| Reichling | D. Reichling, *Appendices ad Hainii–Copingeri Repertorium Bibliographicum* (Munich, 1905–14) |
| Ricc. | Riccardiano |

# Introduction

*Piagnoni, Frateschi, Collitorti, Stropiccioni, Masticapaternostri, Pinzocheroni, Ierosomilitani, Hieronimini*: these and other names were applied with varying degrees of ferocity to the followers of Fra Girolamo Savonarola.[1] Whether clerics or laymen, Savonarola's followers were classed together by their enemies under one or other of these headings. Over time, the epithets dwindled in number until two of them, *Frateschi* and *Piagnoni*, came to the fore. But all were calculated to arouse a precisely calibrated range of emotions, from scorn at one extreme to fear at the other. They were intended to undermine the Savonarolans by calling into question their motives, their credibility, and even their sanity. Most were designed to stress the factionality of the Savonarolans and their divisive effects on society.

Though they responded with some imaginative name-calling of their own, the Savonarolans soon came to glory in these terms of abuse. They saw them, in fact, as a grudging admission of their strength and cohesiveness. Far from being disconcerted by the connotations of factionalism, they chose to interpret these instead as testimonial to their distinctiveness. Terms like *Frateschi* and *Piagnoni* were a confirmation that they were indeed the elect, destined to inherit the spiritual and material blessings promised by their prophet and guide.

Fra Girolamo Savonarola, the Ferrarese friar from whom they drew their strength and inspiration, was born in 1452 and had entered the Dominican Order in 1475.[2] He first visited Florence in

---

[1] Wailers, Followers of the Friar (Savonarola), Religious hypocrites, Humbugs, Zealots, Bigots, Partisans of Girolamo or Hieronimo Savonarola.

[2] The major biographical studies are: P. Villari, *La storia di Girolamo Savo-*

1482, when he became Reader at the convent of S. Marco, which was afterwards to become the headquarters of the movement of religious revival which he inaugurated in the city. At this time, however, he made little impression, and departed in 1487. Three years later, at the invitation of Lorenzo de' Medici, he returned to Florence to resume his post at S. Marco and almost immediately began to preach the sermons which, in series after series, were to have such momentous repercussions on Florentine religious and political life. Although he early assumed the prophetic mantle which was ever afterwards to clothe his utterances, at this stage his message, designed, by means of dire warnings of impending tribulations, to arouse the Florentines to a sense of their spiritual inadequacies and to prompt them to undertake a thoroughgoing moral and spiritual reformation, bore little that distinguished it from others of an apocalyptic sort. With the French invasion of 1494, however, there was a dramatic change.[3] Because this calamity appeared to be a confirmation of all that he had predicted concerning the trials to be visited upon Florence, Savonarola rose rapidly to a position of immense authority and prominence. Assured now of the attentiveness of those in high places, and enjoying great popularity and prestige amongst the populace in general, he began to develop a sweeping programme of religious and political reform, based upon his divinations of God's will.

Drawing upon widespread yearnings for some form of spiritual regeneration,[4] Savonarola refined and elaborated them into a fully

---

narola e de' suoi tempi (2 vols.; Florence, 1930); J. Schnitzer, Savonarola (2 vols.; Milan, 1931); and R. Ridolfi, Vita di Girolamo Savonarola (2 vols.; Rome, 1952). A useful, though extremely tendentious treatment of Savonarola is provided by F. Cordero, Savonarola (4 vols.; Bari, 1986–8).

[3] For the fullest exposition of this watershed in Savonarola's career, see D. Weinstein, Savonarola and Florence: Prophecy and Patriotism in the Renaissance (Princeton, NJ, 1970), in which his earlier, pioneering, articles on the subject are incorporated.

[4] D. Cantimori, 'Giuseppe Schnitzer: Savonarola', Annali della R. Scuola Normale Superiore di Pisa: Lettere, Storia e Filosofia, 2 (1932), 90–104. E. Garin, 'Desideri di riforma nell'oratoria del Quattrocento', Contributi alla storia del Concilio di Trento e della Controriforma (Quaderni di Belfagor; Florence, 1948), 1–11; id., 'Problemi di religione e filosofia nella cultura fiorentina del Quattrocento', Mélanges Renaudet (Bibliothèque d'Humanisme et Renaissance), 14 (1952), 70–

fledged millenarian scheme.[5] His fundamental message was that God was about to usher in a new Christian era which would be characterized by purity of faith and a spirit of complete unity and goodwill among men. Envisaging a society living in perfect harmony with the precepts of the Gospel, he demanded that the Church should be purged of its corruption, the vices of simony, nepotism, lust, and avarice being removed from all levels of the ecclesiastical hierarchy. In the universal renovation which would shortly overtake the whole of Christendom, Florence was marked out for a key role. Her past and present trials, Savonarola declared, were intended by God to befit her for the exalted post of harbinger of the coming changes; and her elect status had received confirmation in the fact that she had emerged unscathed from the recent invasion. First expressed in a series of sermons on Haggai, preached in November and December 1494, this message was developed in subsequent cycles in which the books of the Old Testament prophets—Amos, Micah, Zechariah, and Ezekiel—figured largely. His theories were put forward in written works as well: most notably the *Compendio di rivelazioni* of 1495, *De simplicitate christianae vitae*, published in 1496, and the *Triumphus Crucis* of 1497.

From the time of the expulsion of the Medici in November 1494, moreover, Savonarola had been calling also for reform of the Florentine political system. Having made a distinctive contribution to the governmental reforms which followed, he became thereafter a powerful force in Florentine politics. A political grouping devoted to the furtherance of the civic changes which he saw as a necessary preliminary to religious revival grew up around him, and was to play a crucial role in Florentine affairs in the following three years. As time wore on, however, his apostolate, which had been

---

82; id., 'Girolamo Savonarola', *Il Quattrocento* (Florence, 1954), 115–36; all repr. in id., *La cultura filosofica del Rinascimento italiano* (Florence, 1961). See also C. Vasoli, 'L'attesa della nuova era in ambienti e gruppi fiorentini del Quattrocento', *L'attesa dell'età nuova nella spiritualità della fine del medioevo* (Convegno del Centro di Studi sulla Spiritualità Medievale III: 16–19 Oct. 1962; Todi, 1970), 370–432. See also Chs. 3 and 4 below.

[5] Weinstein, *Savonarola and Florence*.

controversial from the beginning, came under increasingly severe attack, not least from Rome. By early 1498, the Florentine civil authorities had joined in the campaign of the ecclesiastical hierarchy against him, and they were ultimately successful. The man who, during the preceding few years, had played an unprecedented part in Florentine politics and religious life was arrested, tried, and condemned to death.

While originally aroused to a sense of their need for spiritual guidance and desire for reform by the teaching of Savonarola, the Piagnoni were not dependent upon his leadership for their survival. Far from depriving them of their identity or unity, his execution in May 1498 was actually to spur them on to ever greater efforts on behalf of the cause which he had championed. Prompted partly by a sense of outrage at what they interpreted as his martyrdom, and partly also by their absolute conviction, rendered even stronger by Savonarola's treatment at the hands of the civil and ecclesiastical authorities, that only through their efforts would the promised renovation occur, their activities were to be carried on well into the next century. It is the purpose of this study to trace these activities from 1494 to the 1540s, when the dramatically altered political and ecclesiastical situation put an end to their hopes. In order to do so, however, it is necessary to analyse, as far as it is possible, the Piagnoni's strength, their social composition, and their aspirations.

Of the multitudes who had flocked to hear Savonarola's sermons ever since his return to Florence in 1490, and who continued to support him even in his eclipse, little is known. Not much more than the plain fact of their vast numbers has come down to us. For more precise information concerning individual members of his following, it is necessary to rely on the writings, and especially the apologetic works, produced by professed Piagnoni, and on comments by contemporary and near-contemporary chroniclers, historians, and opponents. These are not, however, our only sources. Valuable additional information can be obtained from the records of the trials of Savonarola and his leading supporters in April and May 1498[6] and from the signatories of the Piagnone petition to

---

[6] Villari, *La storia di Girolamo Savonarola*, vol. ii, app., pp. cxlvii–cclxxxvi.

Alexander VI drawn up in June 1497 in an attempt to convince
the Pope to lift the excommunication which he had just imposed
upon the prophet.[7] Other official and semi-official records together
with private papers and correspondence provide further precious
information on lay and ecclesiastical Piagnoni.

The two initial chapters are devoted to an examination of their
emergence as a recognizable, ideologically distinct, and powerful
force in Florence. In the first of these two chapters their specifically
political emergence in the years between 1494 and Savonarola's
execution is discussed. Here particular attention will be given to
their strength, cohesion, ideology, and, above all, to the religious,
political, and social programme they pursued. The succeeding
chapter, covering the same period, analyses, in the context of the
pamphlet war raging during those years, the Piagnoni's elaboration
of the distinctive spiritual and religious positions which they were
to maintain thereafter. These two initial, parallel chapters, moreover, serve to highlight the complex symbiotic relationship between Savonarola and his 'followers'.

The next three chapters analyse the way in which the Piagnoni
attempted to implement their religious and political programmes
once Savonarola was no longer there to guide them. They were to
follow three main courses. Some, whose spiritual yearnings were of
a mystical bent, became increasingly certain that, in view of the
spiritual corruption and of the hostile climate which followed
Savonarola's fall, reform could best be achieved through individual
endeavour. Others continued to believe that the Church could still
be reformed under the direction of the hierarchy itself, and so
attempted to bring about the desired renovation by traditional
means. Others again of a more practical cast of mind reacted to
official inertia and hostility in a far less conservative manner. Believing the Church to be irredeemably hostile to change, these

---

[7] Three copies of the petition have been published: P. Emiliani-Giudici, *Storia
dei comuni italiani* (3 vols.; Florence, 1864–6), iii. 533–9; A. Portioli, 'Nuovi
documenti su Girolamo Savonarola', *Archivio storico lombardo*, 1st ser. 1 (1874),
341–5; P. Villari and E. Casanova (eds.), *Scelta di prediche e scritti di Fra Girolamo
Savonarola, con nuovi documenti intorno alla sua vita* (Florence, 1898), 514–18. See
Appendix.

Piagnoni abandoned all thought of reforming it from within and embarked instead upon a radical programme of independent religious reform in total disregard of official structures and hierarchies.

Because Savonarola's programme had been geared to a republican system of government, attention is also devoted to the Piagnoni's political activities and to the ways in which they sought to strengthen and preserve the Republic from internal and external enemies. An important preoccupation here is to show how the Piagnoni were instrumental in bringing about a major realignment of Florentine political factions by their formation of a coalition of the republican, anti-Medicean forces which they then proceeded to endow with their own ideology.

Piagnoni responses to the restored Medici regime are then examined, together with the gradual adoption by more and more of their number of an uncompromisingly radical stance. What this meant in practical terms is addressed in Chapter 7, which has as its focal point the Piagnoni's part in the last Florentine Republic, 1527–30. The triumph of the radicals made possible the inauguration of the divinely ordained regime which Savonarola had foretold. It also brought with it, however, an intolerance, both political and religious, an inflexibility and a vengefulness seldom witnessed in Florence. The full effects of this escalation of the conflict became evident after the capitulation of the Republic and the return of the Medici to Florence. The last chapter deals with the retribution visited by the Medici on their vanquished enemies and the steps they took to destroy the Piagnone movement, the major obstacle to their consolidation in power. Their success was undeniable, but not total. Though beaten, powerless, and dispersed, the Piagnoni were able none the less to bequeath some important elements of their vision to succeeding generations.

The predominant theme of this study is the resilience of the ideology which inspired the Piagnoni throughout the fifty years or so of their major activity. Evolved in the heat of controversy and drawing upon a mixture of humanist, Thomist, late scholastic, and conciliarist principles, this ideology was predicated on the conviction that government, whether lay or ecclesiastical, was the responsibility of the citizens or constituent members, and that it was in the exercise of this responsibility that individual members most perfectly fulfilled their own potential and the potential of the government or institution they served. It followed, therefore, that republican, popular, or collegiate systems of government were not only more lawful and just than oligarchic or despotic regimes but, because of this, also more efficient, responsive, and permanent.

This was an ideology which entailed a wholehearted commitment and a high degree of civic consciousness. On the other hand, the rewards for this commitment, in both this life and the next, were there for everyone to see. It was an ideology, furthermore, which ensured that as long as any Piagnoni survived, they would represent a force which civil and ecclesiastical authorities could disregard only at their peril. Finally, it was this ideology which inspired the Florentines to halt and even to reverse the general trend towards absolutism. When the transition to the principate took place, it did so not through the citizens' default and despite their heroic exercise of civic duties, through force of arms. By appealing to these principles, the Piagnoni and their republican allies ennobled a struggle which has all too often been seen exclusively in terms of a clash, totally devoid of ideological content, between powerful individuals and groups for the control of Florence.

# 1

## 'Holy Liberty': The Establishment of a Political Tradition, 1494–1498

I

The Savonarolan movement was born of a conflict that had its immediate origins in the collapse of Medici power in November 1494. The expulsion of the Medici released latent social, political, and religious rivalries which it proved impossible to resolve. Despite his and his followers' claims, Savonarola's intervention in politics was in the long run to harden divisions and to embitter the rivalries amongst the Florentines. There is no doubt that, as contemporary observers were already noting, Savonarola's personality together with his and his followers' propensity to justify on religious grounds even the most expedient political acts, accounted in part for the ensuing escalation of the conflict; but only in part. For both the conflict and the increasingly disruptive polarization of the Florentine polity had their origins in widely divergent views on the nature of politics and on the scope of political action which pre-dated Savonarola and the events of 1494. If at first, for a variety of reasons, these political principles remained in the background, with the passage of time and with the emergence of cohesive and active political groupings, they were thrust to the fore, becoming in the process more sharply defined. Only by analysing Savonarola's following, to determine its size and composition, the aspirations of its individual members, and the way they went about implementing them, can these underlying principles be discovered. It will then become possible not only to assess the exact nature of Savonarola's contribution to the Florentine political debate but also to proffer an explanation for the crisis afflicting the city.

To view the Florentine political struggle from this perspective can further enhance our understanding of Florentine society.[1] For, by canvassing and then appropriating various elements from the Florentine political tradition, Savonarola and his followers succeeded in forging a new ideology which in turn dramatically altered the terms and development of the traditional political conflict. Above all, at a time when the majority of Florentine *Ottimati* seemed to have thrown in their lot with the Medici, and to have become resigned to the gradual transformation of the republic into a principality, the Savonarolans stood out against the general trend. They became the rallying point for the opponents of the Medicean regime; they provided this opposition with the ideological justification for its stand; and, finally, when in 1527, the opportunity presented itself, they seized the initiative to overthrow an ungodly regime and to herald in a government which was to lead Florence and Christianity to the millennium.

## II

Neither contemporary observers nor modern historians have been able to agree on the composition, consistency, and strength of the Savonarolan political following. Indeed, whereas some historians cast doubts on the existence of a political movement owing its allegiance to Savonarola, others have no hesitation in both accepting its existence and in attributing to it all the characteristics — such as unity of leadership and of purpose, cohesiveness, and organization—of a modern political party.[2] The reasons for such

---

[1] See, however, the cautionary advice proffered by N. Rubinstein, 'Politics and Constitution in Florence at the End of the Fifteenth Century', in E. F. Jacob (ed.), *Italian Renaissance Studies* (London, 1960), 183.

[2] S. Bertelli, 'Embrioni di partiti alle soglie dell'età moderna', *Per Federico Chabod (1901–1960)*, i. *Lo stato e il potere nel Rinascimento* (Perugia, 1980–1), 17–35, presents the most trenchant argument for the existence of a Savonarolan party. Far more cautious in their assessments are N. Rubinstein, 'Politics and Constitution in Florence', 166–71, and H. C. Butters, *Governors and Government in Early Sixteenth-Century Florence, 1502–1519* (Oxford, 1985), 23–7.

disparity in assessment are to be sought, in the first instance, in the nature of the Florentine political system. As is well known, one of the central features of this system, both before and after the constitutional reforms of December 1494, was the elaborate mechanism set in place to prevent the formation of parties, lobby groups, and even covert allegiances or understandings between politically qualified citizens to influence voting patterns on either political issues or on the humdrum election of officials.[3] In the period of Medici ascendancy these laws had been disregarded to allow the manipulation of the system by the small ruling group. With their expulsion in 1494, and with memory of these manipulations still fresh in their minds, the representatives of the new regime renewed and strengthened the legislation on this matter.[4] Much of the subsequent political conflict was marked by highly damaging, and dangerous, accusation and counter-accusation that opponents were conspiring against the common good by organizing themselves along party lines and working for personal or factional interests.[5] To rely on these accusations, which occur in a variety of sources, private, historical, and judicial, tends to emphasize the 'party-like' character of the Savonarolan following and thus, by implication, of their opponents. Similarly, it tends to impose a rationality on the political divisions and struggles of the period which, patently, they often did not possess. Finally, it has the effect of inflating the size of Savonarola's following in, and therefore its influence on the policies of, the newly created Great Council. The situation

---

[3] N. Rubinstein, *The Government of Florence under the Medici* (Oxford, 1966), 118–19, 217–18, *et passim*.

[4] ASF Provvisioni, 185, fo. 6$^v$; ibid. 187, fo. 110$^{r-v}$; ibid., Signori e Collegi, Deliberazioni Ord. Aut. 96, fo. 123$^v$, where on 29 Dec. 1494 an extraordinary magistracy of ten citizens is created to see that political 'intelligenze' are not formed: 'Conciosiacosa che la casa de' Medici colle compagnie, intelligentie et conventicule anzi coniure contro la libertà habbino tiranneggiato la città anni sexanta'.

[5] See e.g. the accusations of the anti-Savonarolan Piero Parenti, *Istorie fiorentine*, ed. in part by J. Schnitzer, *Quellen und Forschungen zur Geschichte Savonarolas*, vol. i (Leipzig, 1910), 79, 135–6, 157, 201–3, *et passim* (hereafter this edition will be cited unless otherwise stated); and the counter-accusations of the Piagnone chronicler Giovanni Cambi, *Istorie*, ed. I. di San Luigi (Delizie degli Eruditi Toscani, 20–3; 4 vols.; Florence, 1785–6), ii. 105–6.

throughout this period was far less clear-cut than these sources suggest.

A more balanced view of the Savonarolan political following and of its influence is obtained if the information provided by these sources is compared with the archival records of the various legislative, administrative, and advisory bodies comprising the Florentine government. Admittedly, because of the constraining legislation already mentioned, this was not a setting in which to give full vent to individual or group interests. If the protocols of the *Consulte* and, to a lesser extent, the official correspondence of the Republic, are excepted, these documents record the decisions of the government rather than the process by which these decisions were reached. By their very nature, therefore, they are impersonal and normally devoid of all hints of controversy. More importantly, though recording the political divisions of the time, these documents are seldom so specific as to address the origins of these divisions or to permit us to identify the major individuals or groupings behind them. Despite these limitations, or rather because of them, their overall effect is to provide a much needed corrective to the often extreme impressions conveyed by the more personal, non-official, evidence.

One of the most important areas of disagreement concerns the strength of the Savonarolan following. The large contemporary estimates of the number of people attending Savonarola's sermons or participating in the processions organized in his name have often been taken as reliable indications of the strength of his following in Florence.[6] Any such equation is bound to mislead. In the first place, even accepting the estimates of numbers as accurate, it is obvious that one cannot assume that attendance at one of Savonarola's sermons or religious ceremonies entailed a specific political or even religious commitment on the part of the individual participants. One should remember, moreover, that the crowd was just as large on the occasion of the storming of S. Marco and of the execution of Savonarola. More pertinently, the crowd as such, though it might have influenced, indirectly and from a distance, the decisions of the

---

[6] R. Ridolfi, *Vita di Girolamo Savonarola* (2 vols.; Rome, 1952), i. 190, 241, 259.

government, did not have a political voice. What counted was the commitment of the politically qualified citizens of the city as represented in the Great Council. And here, for at least the first five years of its operation, the Savonarolans were never in the majority. Of the approximately 3,500 citizens rendered eligible for membership of the Great Council by the laws of 22–3 December 1494,[7] the Savonarolans numbered close to 400, that is a little better than one-ninth of the total.[8] Even on occasions of most pressing need, the Savonarolans do not seem to have been able to muster more adherents than this, as is attested by the city-wide petition of 1497 to Alexander VI which yields the names of 364 politically qualified citizens.[9]

Lack of numbers did not prevent the Savonarolans from steering through the Great Council many important items of legislation. That they were able to do so was due to a combination of factors. Early in the life of the Great Council they took advantage of the goodwill acquired by Savonarola as a result of the fulfilment of his prophecies and the role he had played in the establishment of the new regime. In those early months they could also count on the

[7] On the number of the *beneficiati* to the Council see N. Rubinstein, 'I primi anni del Consiglio Maggiore di Firenze (1494–99)', *ASI* 112 (1954), 181, 184; F. Gilbert, *Machiavelli and Guicciardini: Politics and History in Sixteenth Century Florence* (Princeton, NJ, 1965), 54; R. Pesman Cooper, 'The Florentine Ruling Group under the "Governo Popolare", 1494–1512', *Studies in Medieval and Renaissance History*, 7 (1985), 75.

[8] The most precise estimate is given by the opponent Fra Giovanni Caroli, 'De discretione vanitatum', MS BNF Conv. Sopp., D.9.278, fo. 61$^v$, where he states 'che sono in numero di quattrocento e più che pigliano il segno da llui [i.e. Savonarola] e tanto si fa quanto da llui è ordinato. E chi vuole una cosa bisogna far capo a llui altrimenti è ributtato colle fave . . . e che s'intendono insieme a uno accennare'.

[9] Once the three versions of the petition which have been published (see Introd., n. 7) are collated with two manuscript lists, BNF II.II.437, fos. 10$^r$–11$^r$, and ibid., Panc. 117, vol. i, fos. 382$^r$–387$^r$, a total of 364, verifiable, politically qualified citizens is obtained: see Appendix. The margin of error, however, is quite high. G. Guidi, who has subjected the three printed lists to an exhaustive analysis, identifies 267 politically qualified citizens, 245 of whom belonged to the arti maggiori and 22 to the arti minori: 'La corrente savonaroliana e la petizione al Papa del 1497', *ASI* 142 (1984), 41. That the Savonarolan component in the Great Council numbered from 300 to 400 members is attested by other sources, see for instance Ch. 5 below.

support of the erstwhile Mediceans who had escaped revenge from their enemies because of Savonarola's intervention and who realized that their safety was to depend for a while yet on their acquiescence in Savonarola's plans.[10] Equally as important in this initial stage was the Savonarolans' moderation and discretion.[11] They did not, on the whole, exploit their popularity by attempting to force the Great Council to vote in favour of sectional or highly controversial legislation. On the few occasions they did so, they were resoundingly defeated.[12] Finally, what must also be strongly emphasized, was the Savonarolans' good fortune in having in their ranks a number of exceptionally gifted and experienced politicians, men such as Domenico Bonsi, Lorenzo Lenzi, Jacopo Salviati, Giovanbattista Ridolfi, Paolantonio Soderini, Francesco Gualterotti, and, above all, Francesco Valori.[13] These were the men who dominated Florentine political life in the first few years of the newly established regime and who ensured with their expertise the initial successes of the Savonarolan movement.

Such an array of socially prominent names is in itself sufficient to dispel an influential contemporary *canard* circulated against the Savonarolan movement which held that it was exclusively composed of the newly enriched and politically enfranchised class (*gente nuova*) and of men belonging to the minor guilds.[14] But, on the other hand, neither should these names be taken as proof of the

---

[10] Parenti, *Istorie fiorentine*, 61, 98, 10; Rubinstein, 'Politics and Constitution in Florence', 171–2; Ridolfi, *Vita*, i. 161–2.

[11] At this early stage Savonarola insisted on forgiveness and on a *pace universale*. See his *Prediche sopra Aggeo con il Trattato circa il reggimento e governo della città di Firenze*, ed. L. Firpo (ENOS; Rome, 1965), 426–8; id., *Prediche sopra i Salmi*, ed. V. Romano (ENOS; 2 vols.; Rome, 1969–74), i. 8–15, 108, *et passim*.

[12] See below.

[13] A longer list of Piagnoni leaders in which all these names occur is to be found in Francesco Guicciardini, *Storie fiorentine del 1378 al 1509*, ed. R. Palmarocchi (Bari, 1931), 123–4. Those selected by me, however, were indeed the leading 'public' exponents, not least in the *pratiche*. Another list is to be found in the 'first trial' of Savonarola in P. Villari, *La storia di Girolamo Savonarola e de' suoi tempi* (2 vols.; Florence, 1930), vol. ii, app., p. clvii; it is advisable, however, to consult the MS of this trial in BNF Magl., XXXVII, 324, fo. 8ʳ, for some important alternative readings.

[14] See e.g. Parenti, *Istorie fiorentine*, 25, 36, *et passim*; Caroli, 'De discretione vanitatum', fos. 56ʳ, 61ᵛ.

aristocratic nature of the Savonarolan following as a whole, as apologists have done.[15] Socially, the Savonarolan following in the Great Council was neither wholly of middling to low extraction nor exclusively aristocratic. On this question, the petition of 1497 is misleading. As we know, in order to make a greater impact on Alexander VI, only socially prominent citizens were encouraged to sign; the others were either actively discouraged or for a while at least prevented from doing so.[16] The end result was a most impressive list of names in which major guildsmen outnumber minor guildsmen by a little over eight to one whereas the proportion in the city's councils and magistracies was somewhere between one to three and one to four.[17] There is one further point to be considered here. Fra Roberto Ubaldini of S. Marco, one of the men responsible for collecting the signatures for the petition, stated in his trial that Francesco Valori had recommended 'that it be burned, and care taken that no copy should ever be found and that on no account should it be sent to Rome'.[18] It could well be that his advice was acted upon, since the Florentine authorities had great difficulty obtaining a copy of the petition during Savonarola's trial and since

---

[15] See Girolamo Savonarola, *Lettere e scritti apologetici*, ed. R. Ridolfi, V. Romano, and A. Verde (ENOS; Rome, 1984), 244–5; Carlo da Firenzuola, 'Decennio delle cose seguite in Italia dal MCCCCLXXXXIIII al MDIII', MS BNF II.III.339, fo. 34, who, however, also claims that Savonarola favoured the plebs and was 'exoso alli grandi', fos. 29$^v$–30$^r$, 53$^r$. A similar interpretation is given by another Piagnone, the chronicler Giovanni Cambi, 'Libro dove sono scritti tutti gl'uomini e ciptadini abili al chonsiglio gienerale fattosi dopo l'anno 1494', MS BNF Manoscritti Passerini, 39, fo. [2$^r$], where he states that Savonarola was hated by 'e' ciptadini grandi, richi et potenti' because the Great Council 'metteva loro un freno in bocha'.

[16] Villari, *La storia di Girolamo Savonarola*, vol. ii, app., pp. cclv–cclvi.

[17] See Appendix. See also Rubinstein, *The Government of Florence under the Medici*, 8 n. 7; 148–9. The 'profile' of the Piagnoni subscribers has been discussed by G. Pampaloni, 'Il movimento Piagnone secondo la lista del 1497', in M. P. Gilmore (ed.), *Studies on Machiavelli* (Florence, 1972), 337–47, and by Guidi, 'La corrente savonaroliana e la petizione al Papa del 1497', who also notes, on p. 41, the discrepancy but assesses the proportion of minor to major guildsmen in the Great Council as 1:5 (20%).

[18] Villari, *La storia di Girolamo Savonarola*, vol. ii, app., p. cclvii: 'che la si ardessi, che mai non se ne trovassi copia alcuna, et per niente che la non si mandassi a Roma'.

none of the surviving copies can be dated any earlier than the trial.[19] The surviving lists, therefore, may have been drawn up, or rather reconstructed, by command of the civil authorities as a means of identifying Piagnoni so that proceedings could be initiated against them. Indeed, a *pratica* was held on 27 April 1498 to consider just what punishment should be meted out to the petitioners.[20] If this had been the case, that is if the surviving lists are merely a reconstruction of a lost master copy, then we have a further explanation for the disproportionately high number of major guildsmen in them, given that the tendency would have been to remember, or to select for punishment, the highly placed members of the movement. All in all there are no reasons to assume that the social composition of the Savonarolans varied substantially from that of the Great Council as a whole.

There is more to the question of composition than social standing. Even contemporaries were at a loss to explain the provenance of the individuals who had been attracted to the Savonarolan movement. Equally baffling were their motivations, interests, and aims. An example of the difficulty experienced in typifying them is provided by Guicciardini, who, unable to identify characteristics common to all, finally argues that they were an admixture of religious devotees, idealists, opportunists, and rogues. Some of the uncertainties inherent in this conclusion persist. It is now possible, however, to be more specific on some contentious issues. Little can be added to what has been said by Guicciardini regarding individual motivation for joining the Savonarolan movement. There is

---

[19] The copy published by P. Emiliani-Giudici, *Storia dei comuni italiani*, (3 vols.; Florence, 1864–6), iii. 533–9, occurs in the middle of the records of Savonarola's trial; that published by A. Portioli, 'Nuovi documenti su Girolamo Savonarola', *Archivio storico lombardo*, 1st ser. 1 (1874), 341–5, was sent, it has now been discovered, to the Marquis of Mantua on 7 May 1498: see G. Praticò, 'Spigolature Savonaroliane nell'Archivio di Mantova', *ASI* 110 (1952), 233; and although the provenance for that copy published by P. Villari and E. Casanova (eds.), *Scelta di prediche e scritti* (Florence, 1898), 514–18, is the Vatican Archives, where it is appended to the *Estratto della cronaca di Simone Filipepi*, it is clear that it too could not have been compiled before Savonarola's trial. The two MS copies used, see above n. 9, are of uncertain provenance, but undoubtedly issuing from the time of the trial.

[20] Guicciardini, *Storie fiorentine*, 123.

no doubt that some did so out of opportunism. The number of rogues and opportunists who fastened on to the movement for their own ends was, however, exceedingly small. Most importantly, there was not amongst them a single Piagnone notable despite the accusations levelled against such men as Francesco Valori and Jacopo Salviati.[21] The subsequent political careers of these men, their actions, and pronouncements, demonstrate unequivocally their devotion to Savonarola's cause and their determination to translate the religious and political ideals of their prophet into reality. In this context, a further consideration is in order. Partly because of its relatively small size, partly because of the concentration in it of a remarkable group of outstanding individuals, and partly because of the strictures continually uttered by Savonarola against personal ambition, the Savonarolan 'party' was hardly an ideal vehicle for personal political advancement. Nevertheless it was, because of its structural looseness and because of its ideological premiss, eminently suited to shelter individuals involved in continuing political activities in favour of the Medici, such as Giannozzo Pucci and Lorenzo Tornabuoni, two of the men who conspired for the return of Piero de' Medici in 1497 and who were made to pay with their lives for their betrayal of the cause.[22]

As the careers of these two conspirators suggest, the Savonarolan party in the Great Council was composed of individuals with the most disparate of political pasts. Some belonged, either personally or through close family association, to the anti-Medicean faction and had suffered banishment or proscription for their opposition.[23]

[21] On Francesco Valori see Silvano Razzi, *Vita di Francesco Valori il più vecchio*, in *Vite di cinque huomini illustri* (Florence, 1602), 181–98; and the sketch in G. Guidi, *Ciò che accadde al tempo della Signoria di novembre dicembre in Firenze l'anno 1494* (Florence, 1988), 189–90 and index; on Jacopo Salviati see Letter of Francesco Vettori to Paolo Vettori, 5 Aug. 1513, ASF C. Strozz., ser. I, 136, fos. 219[r-v].

[22] On the two see Guicciardini, *Storie fiorentine*, 139–43, and Villari, *La storia di Girolamo Savonarola*, vols. i and ii *passim*. Another equally notorious case of an individual joining the Savonarolans for his own ends is that of Ser Giuliano di Lorenzo da Ripa (*not* to be confused with the arch-Piagnone Ser Giuliano di Domenico da Ripa, on whom see below) who managed to obtain Savonarola's protection despite attacking one of his best known supporters: Parenti, *Istorie fiorentine*, 124–8.

[23] e.g. the Bartoli, Guadagni, and Gianfigliazzi.

It should not be assumed, however, that this was generally the case. Many anti-Mediceans with an equally impressive tradition of resistance and sacrifice for their beliefs, remained uncommitted or joined the anti-Savonarolan group of the *Arrabbiati* (the Enraged).[24] By far the largest number of Savonarolans in the Great Council, however, had willingly co-operated with the Medici during the latter's period of ascendancy. Some of them, including Francesco Valori, Piero Guicciardini, and Lorenzo de' Medici's son-in-law, Jacopo Salviati, had enjoyed prominent political careers and had even acquired some notoriety as reliable Medici partisans.

The initial fragmentation of the anti-Medicean forces has always defied explanation.[25] The problem is further complicated by the fact that one of the most significant events in the subsequent history of political alignments in Florence was the *rapprochement* between the Piagnoni and their enemies the *Arrabbiati* which occurred from 1500 onwards.[26] The removal of the controversial figure of Savonarola helps to explain this *rapprochement* and therefore, by implication, also the original hostility between the two groups. Other factors, however, were at play. Many anti-Mediceans disliked the conciliatory policies pursued by Savonarola and his supporters towards the exponents of the previous regime. Prevented by a foreigner from exacting the revenge they felt themselves entitled to, these anti-Mediceans turned in frustration against Savonarola and worked for his overthrow.[27]

If a Savonarolan spokesman, Lorenzo Lenzi, is to be believed, it was not merely unrequited desire for revenge which determined their opposition, but also disappointment at not being able exclusively to enjoy, after so many years in the wilderness, the spoils of government. They regarded themselves as the real exponents of the

[24] e.g. the Pazzi, Bardi, and Giugni.

[25] But see Rubinstein, 'Politics and Constitution in Florence', 170–5; Bertelli, 'Embrioni di partiti alle soglie dell'età moderna', 30–3.

[26] See below.

[27] This was Savonarola's and his followers' opinion, see e.g. Savonarola, *Prediche sopra i Salmi*, i. 26–7; ii. 212; Cambi, *Istorie*, iv. 7; Domenico Benivieni, *Tractato . . . in defensione et probatione della doctrina et prophetie predicate da Frate Hieronymo da Ferrara nella città di Firenze* (Florence, 1496) (Hain 2784), sigs. B7ʳ–C3ʳ.

regime of 1433 in both personnel and ideology: thus their refusal to brook compromise or to work with Savonarola when he was represented in the political sphere by men who had collaborated with the Medici from 1434 until their overthrow in 1494.[28] Only later, when the disappointment of having been deprived of the fruits of victory had worn off and when the man they viewed as primarily responsible for this had been executed, did the *Arrabbiati* relent and throw in their lot with the Piagnoni. By then it had also become evident to Piagnoni and *Arrabbiati* alike that to remain at loggerheads was playing into the hands of the Medici and facilitating their return to Florence. The process of *rapprochement*, set in motion by the leading figures in both groups, was slow, painful, and only partially successful.[29] But, if only in part, successful it was, as the Medici and their partisans were to learn in the stormy years of the last Florentine Republic.

An analysis of the 1497 petition and of other contemporary lists of Piagnoni reveals additional characteristics peculiar to the movement as a whole and important in shaping some of the policies it pursued. Though members came from all quarters of the city, the highest concentration of them was to be found in S. Giovanni.[30] Of the Piagnoni from S. Giovanni, a large proportion came, not surprisingly, from the districts (*gonfaloni*) of Drago and Lion d'oro, which incorporated the parish of S. Marco.[31] The convent, and the movement that drew strength and inspiration from it, benefited greatly from this parish-centred, local nucleus of supporters. In times of isolation and duress, and there were to be many such periods in the next half-century, the convent could count first and

---

[28] Reported in Giovanvettorio Soderini ['Ricordanze'], MS ASF Signori, Dieci di Balìa, Otto di Pratica, Legazioni e Commissarie, Missive e Responsive, 36, fo. 65ʳ; but cf. Bertelli, 'Embrioni di partiti alle soglie dell'età moderna', 32, who attributes the statement to Paolantonio Soderini. The assessment, however, holds regardless of the identity of the speaker.

[29] See below.

[30] Of the 364 Piagnoni whose provenance has been verified, 150 came from S. Giovanni, 92 from Sta Maria Novella, 76 from S. Spirito, and 46 from the Franciscan stronghold of Sta Croce. See Appendix.

[31] The *gonfalone* Drago provided 42 subscribers whereas Lion d'oro provided 57 subscribers.

foremost on its parishioners for financial help, moral support, and even armed protection.[32]

Equally significant was the high proportion of individuals who belonged to the cultural élite of Florence. The whole circle of literati, humanists, and philosophers who gathered round Lorenzo de' Medici seem to have joined *en bloc* the Savonarolan movement, even though it was from this group that a most damaging number of doubters and deserters was to come in later years.[33] Similarly high was the number of Piagnoni involved with the Florentine *Studio* either as teachers or as administrators.[34] What should also be remembered in this context is the fact that many of the lay members of these groups had already demonstrated an atypically high level of interest in religious discussion and activity in the period immediately preceding Savonarola's apostolate in Florence. For Savonarola and for his programme of reform, the backing of such men was invaluable, especially in the early years of his second apostolate. The long-term effects of their association with the Savonarolan movement, however, were not perhaps as beneficial as earlier assumed. They cultivated fastidiousness of thought as well as exclusiveness in association. Thus, apart from the damage caused by their public abjurations, with their attitude they also prevented the movement from gaining that unity of will and purpose it might otherwise have had.

Savonarola's apostolate did not destroy pre-existing cultural and social networks. On the contrary, as we have seen, some of these networks not only continued to exist but were incorporated into the Savonarolan movement. This is also true of other smaller, more local or personal, networks. An examination of the movement's membership reveals that many Piagnoni had close business, po-

---

[32] See below.

[33] On the Laurentian circle see D. Weinstein, *Savonarola and Florence: Prophecy and Patriotism in the Renaissance* (Princeton, NJ, 1970), ch. 6 (Savonarola and the Laurentians) and below, Chs. 2, 3, and 4.

[34] On these men, many of whom also belonged to the Laurentian circle and who comprised such important figures as Domenico Benivieni, Bartolomeo della Fonte, Ugolino Verino, Giorgio Benigno, etc., see A. Verde, *Lo studio fiorentino 1473–1503: Ricerche e documenti* (4 vols. in 7; Florence, 1973–85), *passim* (use indices) and see below.

litical, and social ties which pre-dated Savonarola's advent to Florence.[35] These connections continued to operate and were undoubtedly a source of strength to the movement by engendering cohesion and solidarity in after years. Similarly important was the group comprising Piagnoni who numbered one or more members of their families amongst the friars of S. Marco.[36] This was a most powerful network which often in the future was to spring to the defence of S. Marco, of its autonomy, and of its spiritual tradition.[37] Once again, however, it should not be assumed that a relative in S. Marco ensured a whole family's allegiance to Savonarola. For every family with friars in S. Marco and united in its devotion to Savonarola, like the Bettini, Cambini, or Tosinghi, there was an equal or larger number with divided loyalties, like the Soderini, Guidi, Strozzi, and Salviati. So numerous are the examples of similarly divided families that, far from sharing the shock of contemporary anti-Savonarolan publicists, one begins to wonder whether political diversification was not, in fact, a form of insurance, or protective device, in unsettled times against all future contingencies.[38]

With such a variety of individuals and interests represented, it would be unrealistic to expect the Piagnoni party to speak with one voice on all matters of policy. For the reasons already outlined, there was no opportunity for the members formally to meet to-

[35] A particularly important network, centred on the figure of Pandolfo Rucellai, who was later to become a friar in S. Marco, has been studied by R. Ristori, 'Un mercante savonaroliano, Pandolfo Rucellai', *Magia, astrologia e religione nel Rinascimento* (Convegno polacco-italiano, Warsaw, 25–7 Sept. 1972; Florence, n.d.), 30–47. Other pre-existing networks of importance were the Valori–Canigiani–Tosinghi, on which see ASF Dono Panciatichi, Patrimonio Valori, Libri d'azienda, 3, fos. 144b, 150b; Salviati-Valori, on which see Alamanno Salviati, 'Ricordi', MS ASP, ser. II, 22, fos. 79ᵛ, 80ᵛ, 83ʳ⁻ᵛ.

[36] On this see A. Verde, 'La congregazione di S. Marco dell'Ordine dei Frati Predicatori: Il "reale" della predicazione savonaroliana', *Memorie Domenicane*, NS 14 (1983), 151–237, and esp. Appendice I: 'La comunità di San Marco e la lista del 1497', 216–24; also P. Benelli, 'Catalogo dei frati di S. Marco, secoli XV e XVI', MS ACSM Miscellanea P. Benelli, inserto P, unpaginated.

[37] As occurred on the night of the siege of S. Marco, on 8 Apr. 1498 and on the occasion of the attempt to join S. Marco to the Lombard Congregation in 1503; on this see below, p. 186.

[38] As the Soderini were accused of doing: Soderini ['Ricordanze'], fo. 73ᵛ; see also Bertelli, 'Embrioni di partiti alle soglie dell'età moderna', 31–2.

gether to co-ordinate action or to plan future policies. The party drew its inspiration from Savonarola, who, as is well known, did not hesitate to address political issues in sermons and writings. On occasions he also spoke directly with the major Piagnoni spokesmen who attended his sermons or visited him in S. Marco.[39] But, as Savonarola admitted, he could provide only general guidelines. The details and implementation of policy were best left to the leaders of the Piagnoni in the Great Council, who he freely conceded were better versed in Florentine politics than he was.[40] To a certain extent, the very smallness of the party militated in the Piagnoni's favour because it meant they knew one another well; they were also personally known to Savonarola, and were able to congregate together at his sermons or at the religious ceremonies he organized, where, by Savonarola's own admission, some political consultation amongst them occurred despite the risk.[41]

None the less, to be effective the party needed a recognized political leader. Savonarola realized as much and tried to have Francesco Valori's leadership accepted by the other Piagnoni.[42] His efforts were not only unceremoniously rebuffed, but seem also to have brought to the surface latent rivalries and hostilities between the major exponents of the Piagnone party. In addition, they revealed the existence of three factions within the party headed by Francesco Valori, Paolantonio Soderini, and Giovan-

[39] See the depositions by him, his companions, and his followers at their trials in 1498: Villari, *La storia di Girolamo Savonarola*, vol. ii, app., pp. cxlvii–cclxxxvi.

[40] Ibid., p. clvi.

[41] Ibid.

[42] Ibid., p. cliv. There are some contradictions in Savonarola's deposition in that he states first that he wanted Francesco Valori as leader 'credendo non si potesse fare tyranno' but revealed later that he suspected Valori's intentions: 'Et hebbi già sospitione che Francesco Valori et altri di quelli che erano delli amici mei non si volesseno restringere et fare uno stato fra loro', ibid., pp. cliv–clv. Despite the excellent analysis of Savonarola's trials by R. Klein (*Il processo di Girolamo Savonarola* (Bologna, 1960)), and by R. Ridolfi ('I processi del Savonarola', *Bibliofilia*, 46 (1944), 3–41, and 'Ancora i processi del Savonarola', ibid. 47 (1945), 41–7), there is still the need to examine critically from both a philological and historical standpoint the various trials of Savonarola, of his two fellow Dominicans, and of his supporters with a view to their subsequent re-edition. Some very useful insights on these trials are provided by F. Cordero, *Savonarola*, (4 vols.; Bari, 1986–8), iv. 490–583.

battista Ridolfi.[43] Judging by Savonarola's depositions at his trials, it seems that a great deal of his political activity was devoted to the preservation of the party's unity which ensured the survival of the system of government on which his whole programme of reform was predicated.[44] The party owed its existence to Savonarola and to his doctrines; but, as this episode reveals, its members disagreed not only amongst themselves but even with Savonarola himself on how best to ensure the fulfilment of their prophet's vision.

This vision, though essentially religious, was founded on clear political premisses. As Professor Weinstein has already demonstrated, Savonarola's political tenets, in their general outline, were derived from traditional beliefs and aspirations long current in Florence.[45] Under Savonarola's urging, the Florentines' conviction in their city's divine election, in her political and religious primacy, and finally in her future and everlasting glory—a conviction which had long sustained them in times of calamity and duress—became the spur for present action. This message began to receive precise formulation in the wake of the expulsion of Piero de' Medici and of the departure of Charles VIII and his army from Florence. In the optimistic days that followed and while actively engaged in laying the foundations of the new government that was to replace the Medicean regime, Savonarola set forth the principles of the new political order which was to lead Florence to her pre-ordained inheritance.[46]

The details of the political settlement approved on 22–3 December 1494 need not detain us. The process by which they were

[43] Villari, *La storia di Girolamo Savonarola*, vol. ii, app., pp. cliv–clvi.

[44] Ibid., pp. cliv–clix. The divisions in the Piagnone party resulted in a dangerous, if short-term break at the end of 1497 when Paolantonio Soderini, Giovanbattista Ridolfi, and Piero Guicciardini dissociated themselves from Francesco Valori and his faction, comprising Domenico Bonsi, Antonio Canigiani, Francesco Gualterotti, and Bernardo Nasi: Parenti, *Istorie fiorentine*, 219–20, and p. 235 for eventual pacification. Ambiguous throughout these early years, too, was the conduct of another Piagnone leader, Lorenzo Lenzi, who, apart from continuing to keep very close ties with exponents of the *Arrabbiati*, like Giovanvettorio Soderini, seems also to have pursued policies at odds with those of the other Piagnoni leaders: Soderini ['Ricordanze'], fos. 65$^{r-v}$.

[45] Weinstein, *Savonarola and Florence*, ch. I; see also id., 'The Myth of Florence', in N. Rubinstein (ed.), *Florentine Studies: Politics and Society in Renaissance Florence* (London, 1968), 15–44.

[46] Weinstein, *Savonarola and Florence*, esp. chs. III–V.

arrived at, the part played in the process by Savonarola, the complexion of the new regime, and, finally, its operation till the end of 1499 have been closely analysed by Professor Rubinstein and lately also by G. Guidi.[47] Contemporary perceptions of what had occurred, however, differed considerably from the reality. To the Piagnoni there was no doubt that the newly instituted government was Savonarola's exclusive creation, his first, momentous achievement in pursuance of God's plans. He had been endowed by the Lord with the gift of prophecy to castigate and correct sinners and to predict the likely outcome of their obduracy. It was this prophesying, they argued, which had prepared the ground for the revolution of 8 November and for the overthrow of the ungodly tyranny of the Medici. Similarly, there was no doubt in their minds that the peaceful departure of the army of Charles VIII and the constitutional reforms of 22–3 December had been brought about by the intercession and the efforts of their prophet.[48]

Just as the expulsion of the Medici could not have been achieved by human endeavour, so the establishment of the new government could not have been effected without divine intervention. This new government as symbolized by its most characteristic institution, the Great Council, was, therefore, a divine creation and as such beyond political discussion or criticism. Those seeking to weaken it or destroy it were to be dealt with not solely as political but also as religious offenders and punished accordingly.[49] This veneration for the Great Council was soon extended to everything associated with

---

[47] Rubinstein, 'Politics and Constitution in Florence'; id., 'I primi anni del Consiglio Maggiore'; Guidi, Ciò che accadde al tempo della Signoria di novembre dicembre in Firenze l'anno 1494.

[48] Two typical examples are Placido Cinozzi, Estratto d'una epistola . . . de vita et moribus reverendi patris fratris Hieronimi Savonarole de Ferraria, fratri Iacobo Siculo, eiusdem Ordinis vicarius generalis [sic], post mortem dicti Prophete (hereafter cited as Epistola de vita et moribus Savonarole), in P. Villari and E. Casanova (eds.), Scelta di prediche e scritti di Fra Girolamo Savonarola, con nuovi documenti intorno alla sua vita (Florence, 1898), 18–23; P. Ginori Conti [and R. Ridolfi] (eds.), La vita del beato Ieronimo Savonarola, scritta da un anonimo del secolo XVI e già attribuita a fra Pacifico Burlamacchi (Florence, 1937 (hereafter this edition will be cited as Pseudo-Burlamacchi, La vita)), 73–8.

[49] See e.g. Savonarola's adjurations in Prediche sopra i Salmi, ii. 18, 57, 190–1, et passim; and in Prediche sopra Amos e Zaccaria, ed. P. Ghiglieri (ENOS; 3 vols.; Rome, 1971–2), i. 151–2.

it: to its deliberations, decisions, and, above all, to its meeting hall, the *Sala del Gran Consiglio*.[50] The continued existence of the Great Council was evidence of Florence's favoured status in the eyes of God and consequently of her acquisition of spiritual and temporal glory. Some minor modifications to its procedure and operations were countenanced by Savonarola and his followers in pursuit of greater efficiency. Nothing, however, was to be permitted that could undermine its authority or threaten its survival.

Within a remarkably short period of time the new system of government was invested with an ideology which it was to retain thereafter; an ideology which set forth a powerful alternative to contemporary trends towards absolutism and which, in the years 1527–30, provided the Florentines with the resolve to fight for their political freedom against overwhelming odds. Not surprisingly given Savonarola's role in its elaboration, this ideology was pervaded with religious elements and was all the more effective for it. In direct opposition to the tyranny that had preceded it and the oligarchy which some had wanted to put in its place, the newly instituted government was, Savonarola and his followers argued, 'popular' in both membership and orientation.[51] The term harked back to the distant but glorious Florentine political past

[50] Rubinstein, 'I primi anni del Consiglio Maggiore', 174–5; Villari, *La storia di Girolamo Savonarola*, i. 436; R. C. Trexler, *Public Life in Renaissance Florence* (New York, 1980), 469–70; R. M. Steinberg, *Fra Girolamo Savonarola, Florentine Art, and Renaissance Historiography* (Athens, Ga., 1977), 100–5; J. Wilde, 'The Hall of the Great Council of Florence', *Journal of the Warburg and Courtauld Institutes*, 7 (1944), 65–81.

[51] Savonarola, *Prediche sopra i Salmi*, ii. 117; id., *Trattato circa il reggimento e governo della città di Firenze*, edited in *Prediche sopra Aggeo*, 441, 448–50, 472–81; Lorenzo Violi, *Le Giornate*, ed. G. C. Garfagnini (Florence, 1986), 33; da Firenzuola, 'Decennio delle cose seguite in Italia', fo. 53ʳ; Cambi, *Istorie*, i. 90, 105, *et passim*. Indicative of how much Savonarola had absorbed of Florentine 'republican' ideology but how tied he still remained to Thomistic principles is the fact that throughout he equates 'governo popolare' to 'governo civile' and 'politico'. On this whole question see J. H. Whitfield, 'Savonarola and the Purpose of the "Prince"', in id., *Discourses on Machiavelli* (Cambridge, 1969), 87–110; D. Weinstein, 'Machiavelli and Savonarola', *Studies on Machiavelli* (above, n. 17), 251–64; id., *Savonarola and Florence*, ch. IX. More diffuse treatment of these concepts in J. G. A. Pocock, *The Machiavellian Moment: Florentine Political Thought and the Atlantic Republican Tradition* (Princeton, NJ, 1975), esp. chs. III and IV.

and because of that it was redolent with meaning and of great symbolic importance in conjuring up an antithesis to tyranny.[52] Surprise at the size of the Great Council, however, may also account for the currency of this argument despite the fact that the laws of 22–3 December, in which the criteria of membership had been set down, had consciously sought to establish a degree of continuity in membership with the recently overthrown Medicean regime.

The creation of the Great Council did not mark the emergence of a new social group in government.[53] Nor did it sanction the wholesale enfranchisement of hitherto politically unqualified citizens. Its unexpectedly large size was due, as Dr Pesman Cooper has clearly demonstrated, to two main factors. First, admission to it was opened at one and the same time to all men who had qualified to hold office in the past, establishing thereby continuity with the preceding, Medicean regime. Secondly, in order to associate the new government with the tradition of the pre-Medicean regimes and to recognize the claims of men who had been discriminated against by the Medici, membership was extended back over three generations, more specifically, to men whose ancestors had been politically qualified in the pre-1434 regimes.[54] Size and composition of the Great Council became important elements in the elaboration of the new ideology as did also the fact, more valid in theory than in practice, that access to offices and power was now open to all members and not restricted to a small élite.

In these elements lay the proof that in Florence there had been instituted a *vivere civile*, so called, Savonarola explained, because

[52] The term had its origins, of course, in the government of 'il primo popolo' but had been evolved and refined ever since. There is great need for an analysis of the political meaning of the term over this time; however, some preliminary, important observations are to be found in N. Ottokar, *Il comune di Firenze alla fine del Dugento* (Turin, 1962), esp. 97 ff.; H. Baron, *The Crisis of the Early Italian Renaissance* (Princeton, NJ, 1966), *passim*; and above all, N. Rubinstein, 'Florentine Constitutionalism and Medici Ascendancy in the Fifteenth Century', *Florentine Studies: Politics and Society in Renaissance Florence* (above, n. 45), 442–62; id., 'Florentina Libertas', *Rinascimento*, 26 (1986), 3–26, but esp. 7–9, 12–15.

[53] R. Pesman Cooper, 'The Florentine Ruling Group under the "Governo Popolare"', 89–90.

[54] Ibid. 75–6.

the government was 'in the hands of the whole population' and belonged 'to all citizens'.[55] However, important as institutions undoubtedly were, a true *vivere civile* was to be judged above all on its operations and on its effects.[56] As Savonarola never wearied of repeating, the newly established government had to reflect God's intentions and to engender His goodness in society. Political action by individual citizens was to be guided purely by considerations of common good, of reciprocal love, of natural and supernatural charity, of virtue, and of goodness.[57] In the fulfilment of his civic duties the citizen best expressed his love of God and also helped to bring the city closer to perfection.[58]

In addition, borrowing heavily from the rhetoric of the humanists, Savonarola and the apologists of the new regime argued that it was ideally suited to the preservation of individual and collective liberty, without which there could not be any spiritual amelioration.[59] In time, they came to argue that, unlike the Medici regime, a thinly veiled tyranny which had resulted in the enslavement of the Florentines, the new political order was equitable and just. Its institutions were now independent and not, as formerly, corruptly manipulated by the tyrant for his own and his followers' benefit.[60]

---

[55] Savonarola, *Trattato circa il reggimento e governo della città di Firenze*, 441, 472–3: 'nelle mani di tutto il popolo'; 'a tutti li cittadini'. Still missing is a comprehensive treatment of Florentine political terminology in this and earlier periods. Such terms as 'vivere civile', 'vivere politico', 'vivere libero', etc. acquired over time specific meanings which we are not as yet in a position fully to understand. Some discussion on these terms and others in N. Rubinstein, 'Politics and Constitution in Florence', 160; G. Bisaccia, *La 'Repubblica Fiorentina' di Donato Giannotti* (Florence, 1978); Pocock, *The Machiavellian Moment*; G. Silvano, *'Vivere Civile' e 'Governo Misto' a Firenze nel primo Cinquecento* (Bologna, 1985).

[56] Savonarola, *Trattato circa il reggimento e governo della città di Firenze*, 441–2.

[57] Ibid. 476–9; but see also *Prediche sopra i Salmi*, ii. 191–8, 208–19.

[58] *Trattato circa il reggimento e governo della città di Firenze*, 480–1.

[59] Ibid. 476–83; *Prediche sopra i Salmi*, ii. 213–16; see also *Prediche sopra Aggeo*, 144–6; Bartolomeo Redditi, *Breve compendio e sommario della verità predicata e profetata dal R.P. fra Girolamo da Ferrara*, ed. J. Schnitzer, *Quellen und Forschungen zur Geschichte Savonarolas*, i (Munich, 1902), 38–9; Domenico da Pescia, *Predica . . . facta in Sancta Reparata: A dì 29 di settembre 1495*, in Girolamo Savonarola, *Prediche sopra i Salmi* (Bologna, 1515), sigs. II2ᵛ–II3ᵛ.

[60] Id., *Trattato circa il reggimento e governo della città di Firenze*, 473–81.

They protected the citizens' rights as well as determining their duties. Justice was impartially administered with every citizen equal before the law. Taxes were fairly assessed and imposed. Unlike the past when the Medici tyrants had enriched themselves through the efforts of their subjects, now personal effort was encouraged and properly rewarded, contributing in turn to the prosperity of the whole city. There was no longer the need to seek approval for marriage and other contracts. Individuals could now dispose of their own affairs as they wished. In short, the new political order, in the opinion of its apologists, had created an environment in which the collective 'common good', rather than personal or factional interest, thrived.[61]

The contrast of political conditions was placed in even sharper relief by the juxtaposition of the moral and religious conditions obtaining under the old regime and those expected under the new dispensation. The tyranny of the Medici had led not only to the political but also to the moral enslavement of the Florentines. For, relying on arguments drawn from St Thomas Aquinas and from the humanist defenders of republican liberty, Savonarola and his followers stressed the fact that tyrants were motivated solely by the basest of instincts. Rapaciousness, lust, pride, and avarice were invariable concomitants of tyranny. The unfortunate subjects could not but be contaminated and corrupted by their all-pervasive sinfulness, which was consciously employed as an instrument of allure and control. Its moral effects were particularly destructive because the tyrants undermined the spiritual authority of the Church and regulated its activities to their own advantage.[62]

Under the new republican regime, on the other hand, conditions would be totally different. The citizens' participation in government would ensure a better, more efficient and stable government. Even more, by exercising their civic duties, the citizens would

---

[61] Ibid. 481–3; many of these concepts were first systematically expounded in *Prediche sopra Amos e Zaccaria*; see esp. sermons viii–ix. Redditi, *Breve compendio*, 49; Violi, *Le giornate*, 292.

[62] Savonarola, *Prediche sopra Amos e Zaccaria*, i. 216–30, 238–49; *Trattato circa il reggimento e governo della città di Firenze*, 456–66; Pseudo-Burlamacchi, *La vita*, 26, 32–3; and see below.

accrue virtue and merit as would also by extension their beloved Florence; so that, within a short period of time, the city would be like a terrestrial paradise.[63] Consciously harking back to, but turning on its head, a saying Cosimo de' Medici was fond of repeating, Savonarola and his followers with him argued that religious principles made, indeed, for a better and stronger government.[64]

The expulsion of the Medici tyrants and the institution of a *vivere civile* with the legislation of 22–3 December were the first steps in the sanctification of Florence. The city and the elect would henceforth grow in spiritual perfection until deemed fit by God to receive His promised blessings. This indissoluble link between politics and religion was strengthened further by the legislation promulgated by the new government and also by the language in which political decisions were justified. Thus, to cite but a few examples, on 2 December 1494 it was decided that henceforth in perpetuity the day God had delivered His city from the Medici tyranny, that is 9 November, should be celebrated as a solemn holy day, with appropriate thanksgiving ceremonies, processions, and distribution of alms to the poor.[65] Similarly, though not formally sanctioned by legislation, on Savonarola's urging, the citizens took Christ as their King and acknowledged the fact by popularly referring to the Hall of the Great Council as the Hall of Christ (*sala di Cristo*).[66] Political terminology changed accordingly. To empha-

---

[63] Savonarola, *Trattato circa il reggimento e governo della città di Firenze*, 482.

[64] Id., *Prediche sopra Aggeo*, 215.

[65] ASF Provvisioni, 185, fo. 51ʳ.

[66] Savonarola, *Prediche sopra Aggeo*, 422–3; *Prediche sopra i Salmi*, ii. 190–1. Within a short time the Virgin too was declared Queen of Florence, see e.g. ibid. 39, 87. Though unofficial, by the beginning of 1496 the dedication of the city to Christ began to be acknowledged in some of the records of the Republic, see e.g. ASF Camera del Comune, Deliberazioni dei Provveditori o Massai di Camera, 66, fo. 1ʳ, where the new book opens with the phrase: 'Jesus Christus Deus et Redemptor humani generis et Rex Florentie'. Only on 9 Feb. 1528 during the Second Republic and under the Gonfaloniership of Niccolò Capponi was the twin election formally enshrined in the legislation. The decree was promulgated once again on the following year under the Gonfaloniership of Francesco Carducci; texts of both decrees in V. Chiaroni, *Il Savonarola e la Repubblica Fiorentina eleggono Gesù Cristo re di Firenze* (Florence, 1952), and see also Ch. 7 below. For Savonarola's manipulation of other figures and symbols see A. Brown, 'Platonism in Fifteenth Century Florence', *Journal of Modern History*, 58 (1986), 403–4; ead.,

size the religious and moral effects resulting from the newly acquired political freedom, the government had no compunction in
referring to it as the holy liberty (*santa libertà*), a qualification
which the Piagnoni subsequently adopted as one of their catch-
phrases.[67] Conversely, in keeping with this religious outlook, subversive groups seeking to overthrow the new political order were
characterized as 'conventicles' or 'sects' and condemned as such.[68]

With the changed outlook went also a new approach to the
question of the government's duties and obligations. Savonarola
and his followers did not doubt that the government's duties
lay also in regulating more rigidly and more precisely than had
hitherto been the case the religious and moral life of the citizens. It
was the major task of government to create the conditions conducive to virtue by ensuring that the occasion for and temptation of
sin were removed. As envisaged, this entailed a twofold governmental commitment. On the one, more conventional level, the
government had to pass and enforce legislation against sin, against
activities which could lead to sin, and against persons or groups
who either by their actions or by their mere presence undermined
Christian living. This meant, in practice, immediate and strident
calls for government's intervention against sodomy, blasphemy,
gambling, lascivious literary and artistic works, obscene theatrical
representations, and excesses in dress, expenditure, and consumption.[69] It meant also calls for the expulsion of prostitutes and Jews.[70]

'Savonarola, Machiavelli and Moses: A Changing Model', in P. Denley and C.
Elam (eds.), *Florence and Italy: Renaissance Studies in Honour of Nicolai Rubinstein*
(London, 1988), 57–72.

[67] ASF Provvisioni, 186, fo. 85$^r$; Luca della Robbia, 'Vita di Bartolomeo (di
Niccolò di Taldo) Valori', *ASI* 1st ser. 4/1 (1843), 245–6.

[68] ASF Signori e Collegi, Deliberazioni Ord. Aut. 96, fo. 123$^r$; ibid. 97, fo. 59$^v$.

[69] Savonarola, *Prediche sopra Aggeo*, 220–1; *Prediche sopra i Salmi*, i. 156–7,
198; ii. 63, 100–1, 115–16, 124–5, 147–8, 168–9, *et passim*; *Prediche sopra Amos e
Zaccaria*, i. 148–50, 322–6; ii. 71; iii. 233; Cambi, *Istorie*, i. 105; da Firenzuola,
'Decennio delle cose seguite in Italia', fos. 34$^v$, 41$^v$; Domenico Cecchi, *Riforma
sancta et pretiosa*, ed. in U. Mazzone, *'El buon governo': Un progetto di riforma
generale nella Firenze Savonaroliana* (Florence, 1978), 194–7.

[70] Savonarola, *Prediche sopra i Salmi*, ii. 106–7, 169–70; Luca Landucci, *Diario
fiorentino dal 1450 al 1516 continuato da un anonimo fino al 1542*, ed. I. del Badia
(Florence, 1883; repr. 1969), 123–4; Cecchi, *Riforma sancta et pretiosa*, 194.
Savonarola's attitude towards prostitutes, however, was not as clear-cut as some of

On the other, more far-reaching and radical level, the government had to take an active role in initiating the moral and religious reform of its citizens. Religious practices had to be strengthened and moral behaviour encouraged in all sections of the population. Throughout, however, the dominant note of Savonarola's reforming message was Christian charity, understood as the tangible expression of love for one's neighbour. Pointing to Christ's sacrifice on the cross for erring mankind as the supreme example of this love, Savonarola asked for similar commitment from all the components of the Florentine polity: the government, the Church, and the people.[71] As he never tired of repeating, true Christian living, on which the blessings of Florence were stipulated, could not prosper in a polity in which large numbers of people were degraded and brutalized by poverty. It was beholden on the government and on the wealthier sections of the population, therefore, to act on behalf of the poor by providing alms and the means of employment and also by redirecting money now spent on other activities, like the *Studio*, to their sustenance. New institutions had to be created and old ones strengthened to minimize the effects of poverty on the moral life of the indigent and to guarantee a modicum of social justice to all Florentines.[72]

When the time came to translate these calls into the legislation needed to create a just and godly society, Savonarola and his followers had to contend with the reality of Florentine politics. Where

his sermons may lead one to believe. At times he seemed more concerned to keep them off the streets than to expel them, believing that their presence prevented a 'maggior male', meaning, perhaps, homosexuality: Savonarola, *Prediche sopra Giobbe*, ed. R. Ridolfi (ENOS; 2 vols.; Rome, 1957), ii. 66. This could explain why no legislation against them was passed or even contemplated at this time. On this whole question see R. C. Trexler, 'La Prostitution florentine au XV<sup>e</sup> siècle: Patronages et clientèles', *Annales ESC* 36 (1981), 983–1015.

[71] See e.g. Savonarola, *Trattato dell'amore di Gesù Cristo*, in *Operette spirituali* ed. M. Ferrara (ENOS; 2 vols.; Rome, 1976), i. 79–127; *Prediche sopra Aggeo*, 140–1, 343, 423; *Prediche sopra i Salmi*, ii. 27; *Prediche sopra Amos e Zaccaria*, ii. 144–21.

[72] Id., *Prediche sopra Aggeo*, 121–2, 131, 140–1, 151–3; *Prediche sopra i Salmi*, i. 16, 135–7; *Prediche sopra Giobbe*, i. 382–3; ii. 305–6; *et passim*; *De simplicitate christianae vitae*, ed. P. G. Ricci (ENOS; Rome, 1959), 206–28. Still useful is G. Gnerghi, 'Il Savonarola e i poveri', *La rassegna nazionale*, 119 (1901), 268–99.

some precedent existed for the legislation sought or where the measures proposed were perceived as moderate and beneficial, their passage was quick and uneventful. Where, however, no such precedent could be found or where doubts existed regarding the legislation's aims and possible effects on the balance of forces within Florentine politics, then the passage was slow and almost invariably destined to failure. Thus, legislation against sodomy was enacted with surprising speed and with overwhelming majorities on 28 December 1494.[73] The provisions of the law were extended and strengthened on four further occasions in 1495–7 with similar speed and agreement.[74] The reasons for this exemplary accord and efficiency are easily deduced. Despite the legislation's controversial preamble, in which, echoing Savonarola's sentiments, the blame for the prevalence of the vice in Florence was solely attributed to the preceding tyrannical regime,[75] there was little in it that could be construed as partisan or controversial. It was emphasized, in fact, that the legislation codified and rationalized the various, often conflicting, statutes on the matter. Most importantly, it laid down procedural guidelines for the prompt prosecution and exemplary sentencing of guilty parties.[76] Equally uneventful and for the same reasons was the passage of the law against gambling and games of chance on 1 February 1497, even though on this occasion there was a proportionately much higher negative vote in the Great Council, occasioned, perhaps, by the law's indiscriminate apportionment of guilt to gamblers and to householders who had permitted gambling on their property.[77]

Successful, too, were the campaigns, strongly advocated by Savonarola, to ameliorate by legislative and other practical means

[73] ASF Provvisioni, 185, fos. 17ʳ⁻ᵛ; ibid., Libri fabarum, 71, fos. 33ʳ, 34ᵛ. On this issue see the excellent preliminary work by M. J. Rocke, 'Il controllo dell'omosessualità a Firenze nel XV secolo: *Gli Ufficiali di notte*', *Quaderni storici*, 22 (1987), 701–23.

[74] ASF Provvisioni, 186, fos. 61ʳ⁻ᵛ, 159ʳ⁻ᵛ, 190ʳ⁻ᵛ; ibid. 187, fo. 121ᵛ; ibid., Libri fabarum, 71, fos. 57ʳ, 60ʳ⁻ᵛ.

[75] ASF Provvisioni, 185, fo. 17ʳ.

[76] Ibid. fo. 17ʳ⁻ᵛ.

[77] Ibid. 187, fos. 120ᵛ–121ʳ, citing the precedent decrees of 1473 and 1476; ibid., Libri fabarum, 71, fo. 83ᵛ (941 votes in favour; 274 against).

the lot of the poor and the sick in Florence. The activities of the Piagnoni were manifold, even though not all of them as thoroughly documented as one would wish. Where possible, they took over existing charitable institutions which had fallen on hard times. The most celebrated example of this process was their revitalization and subsequent take-over of the existing confraternity of the *Buonuomini di S. Martino*.[78] Originally instituted to aid the 'shamefaced poor' of Florence, that is those poor too ashamed to beg, the *Buonuomini*, under Savonarolan control and in line with trends already displayed, no longer restricted its ministrations to this category of indigents. At Savonarola's instigation, extraordinary allocations of money were made to the *Buonuomini* on at least three occasions in 1495–6.[79] Additional sums were provided then and later by Savonarolan *fanciulli* (children) who solicited alms throughout the city for the confraternity.[80] From this period onwards, moreover, committed Savonarolans began to take an active role in the administration of the *Buonuomini* and made endowments to it in their wills.[81] They became so influential in it that it was

---

[78] On this confraternity see A. Spicciani, 'The "Poveri Vergognosi" in Fifteenth Century Florence', in T. Riis (ed.), *Aspects of Poverty in Early Modern Europe* (Alphen, 1981), 119–82; id. 'Aspetti finanziari dell'assistenza e struttura cetuale dei poveri vergognosi fiorentini al tempo del Savonarola (1487–1498)', in *Studi di storia economica toscana nel medioevo e nel rinascimento in memoria di Federigo Melis* (Pisa, 1987), 320–46; R. C. Trexler, 'Charity and the Defense of Urban Elites in the Italian Communes', in F. C. Jaher (ed.), *The Rich, the Well Born and the Powerful: Elites and Upper Classes in History* (Urbana, 1973), 64–109; O. Zorzi Pugliese, 'Lo statuto "riformato" dei Buonomini di S. Martino: Riflessi del pensiero rinascimentale in un documento confraternale', *Rinascimento*, 31 (1991), 261–78; L. Passerini, *Storia degli stabilimenti di beneficenza e d'istruzione elementare gratuita della città di Firenze* (Florence, 1853), 501–15.

[79] ASF Provvisioni, 186, fos. 184ʳ–185ᵛ; ibid., Libri fabarum, 71, fos. 44ᵛ, 59ᵛ. On one of these occasions the *Buonuomini* were assigned the money originally raised for the *Studio*, just as Savonarola had suggested.

[80] Landucci, *Diario fiorentino*, 90, 124–6; Parenti, *Istorie fiorentine*, 23, 68, 93, 160.

[81] ABSM Capitoli e indulgenze dei Procuratori della Congregazione dei Buonuomini di S. Martino, 2 vols. (no location marks), vol. i, fos. 14ʳ–17ʳ, for list of officials to the year 1501; vol. ii, fos. 6ᵛ–13ᵛ, for list of officials from 1501 to c.1540. Amongst the recognizable Piagnoni names, some of whom had first served the confraternity before Savonarola's return to Florence, the following are particularly important: Pandolfo di Giovanni Rucellai, who was to become a friar of S. Marco, Domenico di Bernardo Mazzinghi, Carlo d' Aldighieri Biliotti,

suspected of having become an instrument of sectarian interest. As we shall see, in the aftermath of Savonarola's execution an attempt was made to render it independent of Piagnone control, but with disastrous results.

Less well known, but for this no less successful, was the Piagnone seizure of the confraternity of S. Michele Arcangelo. This company, founded it seems in an earlier period, had long ceased to meet or indeed to exist as a viable organization; so that, when the Piagnoni moved in and took it over early in 1493, it was natural for Florentines to regard it thereafter as a Savonarolan foundation.[82] Whatever its original purpose, once the Piagnoni seized it, the confraternity became exclusively concerned with charitable activities, and thereafter was to be known also as the Compagnia della Carità. As its statutes and other records of its operations indicate, its members had to visit the sick, take turns to watch over them at night, transport them to hospital if needed, and provide them with financial assistance. They took it upon themselves, moreover, to bury indigents who died alone.

Financial assistance, funded by a weekly tax imposed by the members upon themselves, was also given to deserving, God-fearing, poor; needy girls, too, were provided with a suitable dowry which would enable them either to marry or to enter a monastery.[83] The better to fulfil these aims and in pursuit of the 'simplicità' which, as Savonarola asserted, was the essence of Christian living, all other confraternal activities whether religious or ceremonial,

---

Francesco di Filippo Rinuccini, Bernardo d' Inghilese Ridolfi, Lionello di Giuliano Boni, Jacopo Salviati, Giovacchino Guasconi, and Piero d' Anfrione Lenzi. On the legacies to it by Piagnoni see my 'Dell'Arte del Ben Morire: The Piagnone Way of Death 1494–1545', I Tatti Studies: Essays in the Renaissance, 3 (1989), 51–3.

[82] On it see Marco della Casa, 'Vita del R.F. Girolamo Savonarola', MS BNF II.II.430, fo. 30$^r$; G. Richa, Notizie istoriche delle chiese fiorentine divise ne' suoi quartieri (10 vols.; Florence, 1754–62), viii. 261–70; F. L. Del Migliore, Firenze città nobilissima illustrata (Florence, 1684; repr. 1976), 402–6; R. F. E. Weissman, Ritual Brotherhood in Renaissance Florence (New York, 1982), 175–8.

[83] ASF Compagnie Religiose Soppresse, 1430, fo. 2$^r$; ibid., Capitoli delle Compagnie Religiose Soppresse, 18, fos. 1$^r$, 10$^r$; della Casa, 'Vita del R.F. Girolamo Savonarola', fo. 30$^r$; Villari, La storia di Girolamo Savonarola, vol. ii, app., p. cclxxxvi.

such as masses, self-flagellation, and processions, were expressly forbidden in the statutes.[84] The only exception was prayer. Again, so as to prevent the confusion which had undone so many confraternities, a limit of seventy-two was set on membership.[85]

From its inception, some well-known Piagnoni were associated with S. Michele Arcangelo.[86] Membership, however, was predominately drawn from the artisan classes. The confraternity was actively engaged in charitable work from the year of its refounding until the capture and execution of Savonarola in 1498.[87] Throughout this period and beyond, Savonarolan loyalties and aims were inculcated also by its spiritual guides, or correctors, who, by the terms of its statutes, had to be friars of S. Marco.[88] The connections with S. Marco were further strengthened by the convent's concession to the confraternity of a burial place for all its members in the main body of the church of S. Marco.[89] The confraternity of S. Michele Arcangelo thus became a significant element in the Piagnone-controlled system of welfare.

---

[84] ASF Capitoli delle Compagnie Religiose Soppresse, 18, fos. 3ᵛ–4ʳ. Neither the original statutes, if they ever existed, nor the statutes of 1493 have survived. This version of the statutes, undated but which from the handwriting should be dated to the early 16th cent., accords with the description of the statutes of 1506, revised in that year at the instigation of the corrector, Fra Cipriano di Pietro Cancelli da Pontassieve of S. Marco: ibid., Compagnie Religiose Soppresse, 1430, fos. 31ᵛ, 33ʳ.

[85] Ibid., Capitoli delle Compagnie Religiose Soppresse, 18, fos. 11ʳ⁻ᵛ.

[86] Such as Piero di Tommaso Salviati, Piero di Bernardo Mazzinghi, Bartolomeo di Antonio del Vantaggio, Girolamo di Gino Ginori, Girolamo d'Antonio Gondi, Giovanni di Banco degli Albizzi, Jacopo di Giovanni dell'Erede, Lorenzo Violi: ibid., Compagnie Religiose Soppresse, 1421, inserto 10, fo. 18ʳ, and inserto 11, index, fo. 39ʳ; ibid. 1431, fos. 2ʳ⁻ᵛ, 6ʳ, 11ʳ (continued to) 32ᵛ.

[87] Ibid., fos. 6ʳ–9ʳ. Weissman, *Ritual Brotherhood in Renaissance Florence*, 164, 173, 175, speaks of a 'Savonarolan' suppression of confraternities in 1494 which kept the confraternity closed until Feb. 1498 [*sic* 1499]. No such general closure occurred despite the legislation of 1494 and 1495 and indeed some of the evidence Prof. Weissman provides confirms as much. The closure of this and other companies by the *Otto di Guardia* to which the officials of S. Michele Arcangelo referred in their meeting of 24 Feb. 1499 was imposed on 17 Mar. 1498 on the same day in which Savonarola was ordered to stop preaching by the *Signoria*: ASF Compagnie Religiose Soppresse, 1430, fo. 9ʳ; ibid., Otto di Guardia, Ep. Rep. 109, fo. 136ᵛ.

[88] Ibid., Capitoli delle Compagnie Religiose Soppresse, 18, fo. 4ᵛ.

[89] Ibid., unfoliated paper folio at the beginning of the volume. Some of the members of the confraternity seem also to have provided armed escort for

At about the same time, the Piagnoni got hold of another important prize: the hospital of SS. Filippo e Iacopo, better known as the *Ospedale del Ceppo*. Pandolfo di Giovanni Rucellai, who had been a governor and benefactor of the hospital since 1476 and who was to become a friar of S. Marco in 1496, seems to have facilitated this take-over. By the mid-1490s the hospital was firmly in Piagnone hands.[90] The two largest Florentine hospitals, Sta Maria Nuova and Sta Maria degli Innocenti, came also within the orbit of Piagnone influence, although as organizations they were too large and too complex to fall under Savonarolan control. None the less, through the activities of the *spedalinghi* (hospitallers) of both institutions, the ecclesiastics Francesco di Cesare Petrucci and Leonardo Bonafé, both of whom were Savonarolan sympathizers, close contacts were established with the convent of S. Marco and with the Piagnoni.[91] All these institutions benefited greatly from Savonarola's injunctions and from his followers' subsequent contributions of personal effort, alms, and endowments.[92]

The Savonarolans' crowning achievement in social welfare, however, was their contribution to the foundation of the Florentine *Monte di Pietà*.[93] Here the Savonarolans were spurred on by the

---

Savonarola and to have defended the convent of S. Marco on 8 Apr. 1498: see deposition of Bartolommeo Mei in Villari, *La storia di Girolamo Savonarola*, vol. ii, app., pp. cclxxxiii–cclxxxvi.

[90] 'Ricordanze del Ceppo di Firenze', ASF Ospedale di S. Maria Nuova, Spedale degli Incurabili, 10, fos. 64ʳ–65ʳ. Apart from Pandolfo Rucellai, the following Piagnoni were amongst its governors: Neri di Filippo Rinuccini, Domenico di Bernardo Mazzinghi, Giovanni Bartoli, Girolamo Benivieni, and Bernardo di Carlo Gondi. These *Ricordanze*, transcribed in mid-16th century from older books which had been 'alluvionati', are unfortunately incomplete. More information in ibid. 11, 'Libro di dare ed avere di ser Ulivieri di Pagholo da Pescia', fos. 98ʳ–99ᵛ. See also Passerini, *Storia degli stabilimenti di beneficenza*, 188–97; some of the errors here contained have been rectified by L. Sebregondi Fiorentini, *La Compagnia e l'oratorio di San Niccolò del Ceppo* (Florence, 1985), 3–6.

[91] Polizzotto, *'Dell'Arte del Ben Morire'*, 49–50.

[92] Ibid. 50.

[93] On the *Monte di Pietà* see G. Pampaloni, 'Cenni storici sul Monte di Pietà di Firenze', *Archivi storici delle Aziende di credito* (2 vols.; Rome, 1956), i. 525–60; Mazzone, *'El buon governo'*, 127–43; Passerini, *Storia degli stabilimenti di beneficenza*, 501–15; M. Ciardini, *I banchieri ebrei in Firenze nel secolo XV e il Monte di Pietà fondato da Girolamo Savonarola* (Borgo S. Lorenzo, 1907; repr.

realization that its foundation could bring with it additional religious benefits since by removing the need to have recourse to Jewish money-lenders, it made possible their expulsion from God's city.[94] While Savonarola from the pulpit urged the authorities to act, his friend and follower Marco di Matteo Strozzi, a cathedral canon and Prior of the church of S. Miniato fra le Torri, led a riotous crowd to the Piazza della Signoria which demanded the expulsion of the Jews and the erection of a *Monte di Pietà*.[95] Both measures were adopted with large majorities in the Council of Eighty and in the Great Council and finally became law on 28 December 1495.[96]

Once again the opportunity was taken to score a political point off the Medici. The preamble makes it clear in fact that the religiously harmful practice of usurious lending had been introduced into the city sixty years earlier under the Medici, who had assigned the right to Jewish money-lenders. The preamble also acknowledged the contribution made by many devout clergymen and

Florence, 1975); F. R. Salter, 'The Jews in Fifteenth Century-Florence and Savonarola's Establishment of a "Mons Pietatis"', *Cambridge Historical Journal*, 5 (1935–7), 193–211; C. B. Menning, 'Loans and Favors, Kin and Clients: Cosimo de' Medici and the Monte di Pietà', *Journal of Modern History*, 61 (1989), 487–511.

[94] Cecchi, *Riforma sancta et pretiosa*, 194; ASF Consulte e Pratiche, 61, fo. 117ʳ (opinion of Domenico Bonsi) fo. 119ʳ (opinion expressed by Filippo Corsini); ibid. 62, fo. 79ʳ (opinion expressed by Enea della Stufa).

[95] Savonarola, *Prediche sopra Amos e Zaccaria*, ii. 106–7, 433, *et passim*; Pampaloni, 'Cenni storici sul Monte di Pietà di Firenze', 530. On Marco di Matteo Strozzi see 'Vita scritta da se stesso . . . con diverse particolari notizie attenenti a' suoi interessi', MS ASF C. Strozz., ser. III, 138, fos. 47ʳ–49ᵛ, but the whole volume should be consulted. See also Villari, *La storia di Girolamo Savonarola*, vol. ii, app., p. ccxxx, or P. Litta, *Famiglie celebri italiane* (10 vols.; Milan, 1819–74), iv, table ii; C. B. Menning, 'Loans and Favors, Kin and Clients', 487–91. None of these sources confirm Menning's assertion that he was a Franciscan; an assertion which may have originated in confusing the church of S. Miniato fra le Torri and the Franciscan convent of S. Salvatore al monte di S. Miniato.

[96] ASF Provvisioni, 186, fos. 167ʳ–168ᵛ; ibid., Libri fabarum, 71, fo. 58ʳ⁻ᵛ, with voting figures of 73:17 in the *Ottanta* and 603:56 in the Great Council. There were precedents for such a legislation since a *Monte di Pietà* had been approved in 1473 but never established: M. Ciardini, *I banchieri ebrei in Firenze*, 62–3.

preachers.[97] Eight citizens were appointed to draft the constitutions of the *Monte* and to see to its establishment, which was finally achieved on 21 April 1496.[98] Of these eight men five were committed Piagnoni.[99] There thus began an association between the *Monte* and the Piagnoni, which, as we shall see, was of great mutual benefit and was to last almost uninterruptedly till the final restoration of the Medici in 1530.

For the *Monte* too as for the *Buonuomini di S. Martino*, Savonarola launched from the pulpit an appeal for funds and organized at least one procession of children to collect alms from the population.[100] The decree of expulsion was not enforced at this time nor was the prohibition to stop Jewish money-lending since, as some Piagnoni admitted, to have done so while the *Monte di Pietà* was still not functional would have caused great hardship amongst the city's poor.[101] Indeed on 13 November 1496 it was formally quashed, despite strong opposition, in the Great Council, which had also rejected a first draft of the bill on 11 November.[102] If, as a contemporary suggests, Savonarola had a hand in bringing about this reversal of policy, then he was either more tolerant than some of his supporters—who were incensed by the turn of events and who continued to agitate for the expulsion of the Jews—or at the very least more realistic in view of the financial help the Jews were able to provide to the embattled republic.[103]

---

[97] ASF Provvisioni, 186, fo. 167[r].

[98] Ibid. 187, fos. 5[v]–11[v], obtaining votes of 72:12 in the *Ottanta* and 572:92 in the Great Council: ibid., Libri fabarum, 71, fos. 64[r], 64[v].

[99] These were: Piero d' Anfrione Lenzi, Piero Guicciardini, Bernardo di Stefano Segni, Jacopo Salviati, and Niccolò di Lorenzo Mannucci. For full list of names see ibid., Tratte, 83, fo. 35[r], and ibid., Provvisioni, 187, fo. 6[r].

[100] Savonarola, *Prediche sopra Amos e Zaccaria*, iii. 124, 153; Landucci, *Diario fiorentino*, 128. Governmental agencies, too, as Savonarola had urged began to donate money to the *Monte*: ASF Camera del Comune, Deliberazioni dei Provveditori o Massai di Camera, 66, fo. 45[r].

[101] ASF Consulte e Pratiche, 61, fo. 79[r–v].

[102] Ibid., Provvisioni, 187, fos. 81[v]–82[v]; ibid., Libri fabarum, 71, fos. 75[v] and 76[r], with voting figures of 807:383.

[103] On Savonarola's role in the stay of expulsion see U. Cassuto, *Gli Ebrei a Firenze nell'età del Rinascimento* (Florence, 1918), 76 n. 1; for an intolerant Piagnone reaction see Cecchi, *Riforma sancta et pretiosa*, 194.

More disturbing undercurrents in both the Piagnone camp and in the wider Florentine political stage were revealed by the long and only partially successful campaigns initiated by Savonarola to have the government legislate and thus assume responsibility for the reform of children and women. Disenchantment with the obduracy and procrastinations of the Florentines had prompted Savonarola and his closest collaborators to abandon hope of a sudden, total reform of the city and to seek the same end by the piecemeal reform of, and subsequent assistance by, certain key groups in society. The children ( *fanciulli*), for reasons that will be made clear later, were particularly important to Savonarola's vision of the future. They were to be protected from sin, spiritually nurtured, and carefully fitted for the great future that lay in store for them; for they were to receive the inheritance so disdainfully scorned by their elders. In fulfilment of these aims Savonarola and his trusted assistants had not hesitated in destroying a centuries' old pattern of decentralized confraternal associations. They had replaced it with a tightly knit, centrally directed, organization of children, which in its territorial deployment, consultative procedures, and governing methods reflected the political subdivisions and processes of Florence.[104]

Under the spiritual guidance of their elders, these children not only reformed their behaviour, but also enforced Savonarola's injunctions against sin and sinners. They enthusiastically participated in various campaigns designed to rid the city of 'vanities' and of other incitements to sin. Where political will was lacking they stepped in and, emboldened by the words of their spiritual guides, they hounded prostitutes and other women of dubious morals from the city streets.[105] With their carefully staged processions, accom-

---

[104] On all this see the seminal work of R. C. Trexler, 'Ritual in Florence: Adolescence and Salvation in the Renaissance', in C. Trinkaus and H. A. Oberman (eds.), *The Pursuit of Holiness in Late Medieval and Renaissance Religion* (Leiden, 1974), 200–65; now also expanded in Trexler, *Public Life in Renaissance Florence*, esp. 474–90; see also G. Gnerghi, 'Girolamo Savonarola e i fanciulli', *La rassegna nazionale*, 117 (1901), 345–70; and O. Niccoli, 'Compagnie di bambini nell'Italia del Rinascimento', *Rivista storica italiana*, 101 (1989), 346–74.

[105] Sympathetic descriptions of their activities in all Piagnoni sources, see e.g. Girolamo Benivieni, *Commento . . . sopra a più sue canzone et sonetti dello amore et della Belleza Divina* (Florence, 1500) (Hain 2788), fos. CXI$^r$–CXVI$^v$; Pseudo-Burlamacchi, *La vita*, 118–27.

panied by hymn-singing, sermons, and a final offering to God, these *fanciulli* provided a substitute for the customary revels, theatrical performances, and horse-races which had always been a feature of Florentine festivals but which had been suppressed on Savonarola's say-so. But, above all, they sought God's forgiveness and grace through prayer, exemplary Christian conduct, and processions; and finally, as we have seen, they became an important arm of the Savonarolan fight against poverty by gathering alms and offerings throughout the city. By all accounts, they were numerous, tenacious, single-minded, and extremely successful. Many Florentines, however, were horrified by the turn of events. They resented the degree of freedom the children were allowed and the influence they exercised. Anti-Savonarolans, in particular, asserted that the city was now ruled by children who had instituted a reign of terror. Far from rendering Florence glorious and revered as Savonarola had promised, these unnatural innovations, they argued, had made her the laughing-stock of Christendom.[106]

Such criticisms were widespread and they were voiced in such a way as to imply the government's collusion.[107] There was some truth in the assertion, though perhaps it would be more accurate to regard this collusion, if such it was, as unwitting, originating in the government's divisions and impotence. Savonarola and the Piagnoni, however, viewed the problem differently. They argued that the government was abdicating its responsibilities by failing to recognize and to regularize through legislation the organization of the *fanciulli*, which had already proved so beneficial to Florence.[108] This was the context in which the campaign was fought. On 21 June 1496 the government finally decided to act and passed in the Council of Eighty by a majority of 52 to 26 a reform law on the

[106] Apart from Giovanni Caroli, to be discussed in the next chapter, see Parenti, *Istorie fiorentine*, 95, 105–6, 112, *et passim*; Bartolomeo Cerretani, *Istoria fiorentina*, ed. in part by J. Schnitzer, *Quellen und Forschungen zur Geschichte Savonarolas*, iii (Munich, 1904), 39. (Hereafter this edition will be cited unless otherwise stated.)

[107] As in ibid. 38.

[108] Savonarola, *Prediche sopra Ruth e Michea*, ed. V. Romano (ENOS; 2 vols.; Rome, 1962), i. 96–7, 331–5; ii. 130; Parenti, *Istorie fiorentine*, 124, 155; Pseudo-Burlamacchi, *La vita*, 124–5.

*fanciulli*.[109] The following day, however, the Great Council failed to ratify the legislation, thus, in effect, rejecting it. The pattern was repeated on 11 July, 4 August, and 23 August.[110] Only at the beginning of the following year during the gonfaloniership of Francesco Valori and after a solemn petition and oration to the *Signoria* by the representatives of the *fanciulli*, followed by the *Signoria*'s formal consultation with Savonarola's spokesmen in S. Marco, was the legislation approved by both councils on 24 and 25 January 1497.[111] By then, however, the opposition both within and without the Great Council had taken its toll. Experience had shown that only a moderate, unexceptionable piece of legislation could hope to obtain the necessary majorities. Accordingly, the legislation as approved on 25 January was but a shadow of what had been sought by the Piagnoni and by the spokesmen of the *fanciulli* to the *Signoria*. They had sought formal approval and strengthening of the children's organization with, in addition, governmental authorization for the children to cleanse the city of the sinners who prevented the fulfilment of God's promises.[112] What they obtained, instead, was a traditional piece of legislation which regulated the dress and ornaments of children below the age of 14 and which was prefaced by a homily on the appropriateness of inculcating good habits in the young.[113]

However short of expectations, the government's intervention in favour of the children's reform was, none the less, a victory of sorts and as such a source of hope for the future. No such consolation could be drawn from the equally long, almost synchronous, campaign for the reform of women. Here Savonarola had to contend not only with opponents but with the misgivings of some of his conservative supporters, men and women alike. As F. W. Kent has

---

[109] ASF Libri fabarum, 71, fo. 67$^r$.

[110] Ibid., fos. 67$^r$, 69$^r$, 71$^r$, 72$^r$.

[111] Ibid., Provvisioni, 187, fos. 112$^r$–113$^r$, obtaining 69:25 votes in the *Ottanta* and 710:354 in the Great Council; see also ibid., *Libri fabarum*, 71, fo. 82$^r$. The oration is to be found in Pseudo-Burlamacchi, *La vita*, 125–6, whereas the petition and the consultative process are clearly set out in Roberto Ubaldini [*et al.*], 'Annalia Conventus Sancti Marci', MS BMLF S. Marco 370, fo. 18$^r$. Reports also in Cerretani, *Istoria fiorentina*, 38, and Parenti, *Istorie fiorentine*, 105–6.

[112] Pseudo-Burlamacchi, *La vita*, 125–6; Cerretani, *Istoria fiorentina*, 38.

[113] ASF Provvisioni, 187, fo. 112$^{r-v}$.

demonstrated, Savonarola had originally proposed on 18 March 1496 a reform of women along the lines already adopted unofficially for the *fanciulli*.[114] He had suggested, it seems, that women take the initiative in this reform by appointing small advisory committees from each of the quarters of the city. These committees of women were to meet together and decide upon the course of action to be adopted. Judging by the letter published by Professor Kent, the reaction to this proposal was so unfavourable as to compel Savonarola two days later to withdraw his suggestion.[115] While continuing to call for the reform of women, he seems thereafter to have sought refuge in the advocacy of sumptuary legislation to regulate their excesses in dress and ornaments (*ornamenta mulierum*).[116] The slide did not pass unremarked. A woman, Margarita di Martino, took him to task for it and accused him of having first fired women with enthusiasm and zeal for their own reform and then abandoned them to their own devices to concentrate exclusively on men and children.[117] In any case, even in such a diluted form, it proved impossible to muster a winning majority in the Great Council for the proposal. Despite majorities in the Council of Eighty, the legislation on *ornamenta mulierum* was rejected on 13 August and 24 August 1496 and also on 25 January 1497, the very sitting which passed the reform of the *fanciulli*. It was rejected once again the following day, 26 January, in a special sitting of the Great Council.[118] It was one of the worst failures of

---

[114] F. W. Kent, 'A Proposal by Savonarola for the Self-Reform of Florentine Women (March 1496)', *Memorie Domenicane*, NS 14 (1983), 334–41.

[115] Ibid. 336, 341.

[116] Savonarola, *Prediche sopra Amos e Zaccaria*, iii. 97, 121, 149, *et passim*; *Prediche sopra Ruth e Michea*, i. 96–7; Parenti, *Istorie fiorentine*, 124, 154.

[117] Letter of Margarita di Martino to Savonarola, 2 May 1496, BMLF Antinori 203, vol. ii, fo. 1ʳ. The letter has been published by G. Biagi, *Lettera di una monaca—Suor Margarita di Martino—a Fra Jeronimo Savonarola* (Nozze Carnesecchi-Bini; Florence, 1898); there is nothing in the letter which supports Biagi's assumption that Margarita di Martino was a nun. The letter was republished by I. Del Lungo, *La donna fiorentina del buon tempo antico* (Florence, 1926), 256–7.

[118] ASF Libri fabarum, 71, fos. 69ʳ, 71ʳ, 72ᵛ, 82ʳ; see also Guicciardini, *Storie fiorentine*, 158. A similar attempt to involve Florentine women in public affairs was made by Savonarola's opponent Angelo da Vallombrosa, *Epistole* [sic] *del venerabile heremita di valembrosa alle nobile matrone & pientissime donne fiorentine* (Florence, 1496).

Francesco Valori's gonfaloniership. Since sumptuary legislation could not have aroused such opposition, given the communal precedents for it, its rejection can only be explained by the lingering fears, caused by Savonarola's original proposal, that women were thereby to be given an unprecedented role in religious and political affairs.

Most of the legislation sought or policies pursued by the Piagnoni were not so controversial; they did not, therefore, encounter such massed opposition. It is obvious, however, that scorn of tactical considerations, derived from the conviction of the righteousness of their cause, the consequent reluctance to compromise, and a certain arrogance or lack of tact by some Piagnoni spokesmen, notably Francesco Valori, unnecessarily antagonized potential sympathizers, causing a gratuitous but none the less damaging isolation. For instance, there was general consensus on those measures designed to strengthen the new government and to protect it from the attacks of internal and external enemies. These measures, most vehemently, but not exclusively, proposed by the Piagnoni, obtained substantial majorities despite the fact that they would have been resented by the Mediceans, against whom they were primarily directed. Thus, bans against factional pacts (*intelligenze*) and the holding of popular assemblies (*parlamenti*) as well as the authorization to import arms into the city to defend freedom and to waive customary taxes on them were promulgated in the early months of the new regime with little opposition.[119] Only later when political differences had polarized did it prove impossible to bring the Great Council to pass more stringent legislation on *intelligenze*.[120]

Again, for the preservation of freedom, a long-standing statute forbidding the marriage of Florentines with foreign potentates or with *signori* not directly subjected to the authority of Florence was reissued with increased penalties for offenders. It was a piece of legislation which sought to prevent dangerous alliances, the importation of 'aristocratic' habits of mind and behaviour, and, not least,

---

[119] ASF Provvisioni, 185, fos. 18$^{r-v}$, 60$^r$; ibid., Signori e Collegi, Deliberazioni Ord. Aut. 96, fo. 123$^v$; ibid., Libri fabarum, 71, fo. 49$^{r-v}$.

[120] Ibid., fos. 67$^r$, 69$^r$, 71$^r$, 72$^v$.

the creation of a small élite which because of its wealth and standing was separate from the rest of the population. As the Medici's marriage policy had demonstrated, these were developments inimical to liberty and therefore a threat to the survival of the existing government. Despite the fact that the legislation curbed the real or potential ambitions of some important families, it was passed, although with lower than normal majority.[121] Nothing was done, however, to curb the cost of dowries. These escalating costs, Savonarola and some of his followers argued, were a threat both to the political and to the spiritual life of the city.[122] Savonarola had often raised the subject in his sermons. He argued for lower statutory limits on dowries and for the necessity of providing dowries for all girls of marriageable age. Failure to do so, he maintained, would force many girls to turn to sin or to enter convents against their wishes.[123] But not even these strictures could convince the Florentines to interfere with market forces, from fear, one suspects, of weakening, perhaps irreparably, the complex system of dowry funding in Florence.

Similarly, for most of the early years of the new government, there was general agreement that the survival of the new political order depended on the strict adherence to the terms of the recently concluded alliance with the French King, Charles VIII.[124] There were, of course, a number of sound commercial and diplomatic reasons for holding firm to this alliance.[125] For the Savonarolans,

---

[121] Ibid., Provvisioni, 185 fo. 40ᵛ; ibid., Libri fabarum, 71, fos. 36ᵛ, 37ʳ.

[122] See e.g. Cecchi, *Riforma sancta et pretiosa*, 190; R. de Roover, 'Il trattato di fra Santi Rucellai sul cambio, il monte comune e il monte delle doti', *ASI* 111 (1953), 38; now see, E. Fumagalli, 'I trattati di Fra Santi Rucellai', *Aevum*, 51 (1977), 328; Cambi, *Istorie*, ii. 253, 257.

[123] See e.g. Savonarola, *Prediche sopra Aggeo*, 153, 169, 224.

[124] Id., *Prediche sopra Giobbe*, i. 242–3; *Lettere e scritti apologetici*, 63–71, 97–100; *Compendio di rivelazioni e Dialogus de veritate prophetica*, ed. A. Crucitti (ENOS; Rome, 1974), 17–21; J. Schnitzer, *Savonarola* (2 vols.; Milan, 1931), i. 323–38; S. Bertelli, 'Machiavelli e la politica estera fiorentina', in M. P. Gilmore (ed.), *Studies on Machiavelli* (Florence, 1972), 31–72.

[125] An outline of them in Butters, *Governors and Government*, 27–30. Even Francesco Valori did not disdain to have recourse to economic reasons to advocate continuing adherence to the alliance. France, he argued, was the 'smaltitoio' of Florentine cloth and silk 'et per questo gli pare et per ogni altro rispecto di tenersi

however, there were additional, compelling considerations. They held the view that the new regime owed its origins to the French, thus giving more force to the legend of a special relationship between the two nations. After all, it had been Piero de' Medici's abandonment of the traditional French alliance which had contributed to his unpopularity and ultimately had led to his downfall. It was on this and on the deliverance of Florence from the threat posed by the French army that Savonarola had built his vision of reform and of Florentine glory. With the passage of time and with mounting evidence of French levity and greed, many Florentines, including leading exponents of the Piagnone movement and Savonarola himself, became disillusioned.[126] Some began to doubt the wisdom of continuing to subscribe to an alliance that isolated and endangered Florence and which called into question the Florentines' Italian patriotism. Not so Savonarola and the majority of Piagnoni, or at least not yet.[127]

On the three, perhaps most heatedly debated, issues of the time, namely electoral reform, fiscal policy, and the administration of justice it is often impossible to detect a unified front by the Piagnoni. Class interest and personal disposition often impinged on the way individuals reacted to these issues. Thus, despite Savonarola's firm advocacy of the preservation of the original system of election by voting, some of his partisans in the *pratiche* convoked to discuss this matter spoke in favour of election by lot. As Nicolai Rubinstein has already argued, Savonarola's stand was due partly to his refusal to countenance any alteration to the original law of 23 December 1494 and partly to his appreciation of the

---

fermamente colla Maestà sua et correre una medesima fortuna con sua Maestà': ASF Consulte e Pratiche, 62, fo. 260ᵛ.

[126] Schnitzer, *Savonarola*, i. 449.

[127] ASF Consulte e Pratiche, 62, fos. 218ʳ⁻ᵛ, 237ᵛ, 260ᵛ. On the Florentine awareness of betraying the Italian cause see comments of Bernardo Rucellai in a *pratica* of 16 June 1497: ibid. 63, fo. 44ʳ; see also the report of the 'embassy' of three principal Piagnoni, Giovanbattista Ridolfi, Paolantonio Soderini, and Pierfrancesco Tosinghi to Somenzi the Milanese ambassador made by Somenzi himself to the Duke of Milan. Although the embassy was made on behalf of the *Dieci*, it none the less reveals the beginnings of a Piagnone split over the French alliance: Bertelli, 'Machiavelli e la politica estera fiorentina', 43.

fact that the existing system could be more easily manipulated by him and by his supporters for their own ends.[128] By the same token, those of the Piagnoni who favoured electoral reform, including Francesco Valori, seem to have done so not on ideological but on tactical grounds.[129] They realized, in other words, that slavishly to follow Savonarola's injunctions and oppose a reform wanted by a 'popular' majority might have gained them short-term advantages but would in the long run have proved harmful to the cause.

A similar lack of agreement seems to characterize the Piagnoni response to taxation. It would be unrealistic to expect them to speak with one voice on such a vital matter, especially when one considers their different social and economic backgrounds. Like all Florentines they complained of the hardships caused by continual fiscal exactions, bewailed the government's wastefulness, questioned the uses to which the money was put, and demanded more accountability. Quite naturally, when asked their opinion on the measures to adopt in order to overcome the chronic financial crisis, they suggested those methods less onerous to themselves.[130] Seemingly more difficult to understand is their contradictory stance on justice. Like Savonarola they argued that the impartial administration of justice was the element which most clearly differentiated a *governo civile* from tyrannical rule.[131] When pressed

---

[128] Rubinstein, 'I primi anni del Consiglio Maggiore', 336–7.

[129] Francesco Valori almost stated as much in a *pratica* of 4 Apr. 1497; Amerigo Corsini was also for change whereas Jacopo Tedaldi, Francesco Rinuccini, and Bertoldo Corsini wanted things left as they were: ASF Consulte e Pratiche, 62, fos. 10$^{r-v}$, 11$^{r-v}$, 12$^v$, 17$^r$.

[130] See e.g. ibid., fos. 193$^r$–194$^v$, for disagreements between Francesco Valori and Piero Guicciardini, and fo. 207$^r$, for Giovanbattista Ridolfi's lamentation on how badly money had been spent to date, concluding with the words: 'et se noi non mutiamo modo et forma circa l'ordinarsi del danaro dubita non ci conduca a morte'; see also the opinion of Lorenzo Lenzi in ibid. 63, fo. 134$^{r-v}$. On fiscal policy at this time see L. F. Marks, 'La crisi finanziaria a Firenze dal 1494 al 1502', *ASI* 112 (1954), 40–72; Mazzone, '*El buon governo*', 53–87; Butters, *Governors and Government*, 37–42.

[131] For Savonarola see his *Trattato circa el reggimento e governo della città di Firenze*, 477–9; for a sampling of the opinions of his followers, and in particular Bernardo Ridolfi, Francesco Valori, Giovanni Dini, and Giovanbattista Ridolfi see ASF Consulte e Pratiche, 63, fos. 42$^v$, 43$^{r-v}$, 47$^r$–48$^r$.

for an opinion on the matter, they were all in agreement that observance of the law and the equality of citizens before it were principles which the government should always respect. Then civic harmony and final consolidation of the regime would naturally follow.[132] It might seem both hypocritical and contradictory, therefore, that some of the very people who had most insistently demanded the observance of the law, including Francesco Valori, should deny to the five conspirators who had plotted for the restoration of Piero de' Medici in 1497 the right to appeal against their sentence to the Great Council.[133] This volte-face may appear even more disturbing if it is remembered that Savonarola, Francesco Valori, and other leading exponents of the movement were amongst the strongest advocates of the promulgation of the right of appeal.[134]

Underlying these seemingly contradictory postures, however, was a coherence in political outlook and approach which subsumed and then nullified all individual disagreements and positions. Opinions amongst them might have differed, but consistent throughout was the Piagnoni's determination to pursue politics which safeguarded 'holy liberty' and strengthened the new government. As we have seen, like other citizens they resented the incessant round of taxes and forced loans which drained them of their resources. Unlike many of them, however, who had shown 'little

---

[132] Ibid., fos. 42$^v$, 43$^{r-v}$, 58$^{r-v}$, 59$^v$, 60$^r$.

[133] Ibid., fos. 83$^v$–87$^v$; Villari, *La storia di Girolamo Savonarola*, ii. 47–56 and app., pp. xlvi–xlviii. The denial, orchestrated by Francesco Valori, was undoubtedly motivated by the realization that the Piagnoni could not count on a majority in the Great Council especially as a result of the split in their ranks over the issue. See also the detailed account of Jacopo Pitti, *Dell'Istoria fiorentina*, *ASI*, 1st ser. I (1842), 42–50. Excellent discussion of the issues involved in L. Martines, *Lawyers and Statecraft in Renaissance Florence* (Princeton, NJ, 1968), 441–5; it should be noted, however, that Francesco Valori was not then *Gonfaloniere di Giustizia*.

[134] ASF Consulte e Pratiche, 61, fos. 3$^r$–4$^v$: *pratiche* of 6 and 15 Mar. 1495 on right of appeal in which Francesco Valori, Lorenzo Lenzi, Domenico Bonsi, and Francesco Gualterotti, amongst others, spoke in favour. See also Villari, *La storia di Girolamo Savonarola*, i. 294–304, and Savonarola, *Prediche sopra i Salmi*, i. 10–14, 32, 79–80.

love for their fatherland' (*patria*), they had always done their duty and paid all their taxes.[135] As Jacopo Salviati succintly put it:

And as far as money is concerned, he says that he and his clan have done so much to date (as may be seen) that they cannot do any more; nevertheless, he is ready—provided the others agree—to do all that is expected of him for what he owes, since he is prepared to sacrifice all that he has in order to safeguard freedom.[136]

If money was needed to defend the *patria*, then, Valori urged the government, do not stop at anything: vote in new and heavier taxes, tax the clergy, despoil the churches, show mercy to no one, 'because all our good comes to us from freedom and the republican government'.[137] Similar sentiments were echoed by other Piagnoni in the *pratiche* with such enthusiasm that on one occasion they fired the fastidious opponent and reluctant taxpayer Bernardo Rucellai to call for the urgent passing of a stronger tax bill.[138] In the circumstances, it is not surprising to see that one of the most impor-

---

[135] 'Poco amore alla patria': the phrase is Francesco Valori's: ASF Consulte e Pratiche, 62, fo. 205ʳ. Similar sentiments expressed by Lorenzo Lenzi, Giovanbattista Ridolfi, Piero Guicciardini, fos. 193ʳ–194ᵛ; all in turn echoed Savonarola's injunctions to aid the Republic with money, see for instance, *Prediche sopra Ruth e Michea*, ii. 324–5.

[136] ASF Consulte e Pratiche, 62, fo. 194ᵛ: 'Et quanto al facto del danaio lui et la casa sua per insino a hora dice hanno facto tanto quanto si può vedere che non possono più; pur tuctavolta lui con quello che gli resta è parato, quando gli altri converranno, a fare tanto quanto gli s'aspecta pel debito suo che per mantenere la libertà è apto a mectere ogni sua facultà'. Marks, 'La crisi finanziaria a Firenze', 65, cites only the first clause of Salviati's statement thus distorting his true position. Almost identical sentiments were expressed by Lorenzo Lenzi, who stated: 'Et lui vorrebbe essere più abbiente a fare el debito suo perchè havendo prestato più volte et pagato suo accatti non può più', none the less, 'egl'è parato, quando gl'altri cictadini concorrano, a non machare del debito suo et comenda molto la provisione': fos. 193ᵛ–194ʳ.

[137] Ibid., fo. 218ʳ, 'perchè dalla libertà et republica habbiamo ogni nostro bene'; but see also his opinion on fos. 193ʳ, 205ʳ, and ibid. 63, fo. 177ʳ⁻ᵛ.

[138] Ibid. 62, fo. 207ʳ⁻ᵛ, for Giovanbattista Ridolfi's appeal to vote in a tax bill 'celere, gagliarde et vive', and fo. 219ʳ, for Lorenzo Lenzi's appeal 'a ffare provisione grande, viva et gagliarda et con la celerità possibile'; see also fos. 194ʳ, 205ʳ, 221ʳ⁻ᵛ for further Piagnoni opinions and fo. 220ᵛ for Rucellai's statement; see also ibid. 63, fos. 117ᵛ, 121ᵛ for additional Piagnoni statements in favour of taxation.

tant money bills of the period, the *ventina*, was passed during the gonfaloniership of Francesco Valori, despite an initial rejection by the Great Council.[139]

Identical concerns inform the Piagnoni approach to the problem of justice. The fact they had argued for and obtained a general amnesty for all supporters of the Medici in January–February 1495 should not be mistaken for weakness; and, much less, should it be regarded as mawkish sentimentalism or a self-indulgent display of Christian mercy towards a vanquished enemy. As became clear, theirs was a deliberate policy of appeasement. They were sure in fact that immediate forgiveness and a guarantee against future reprisals through the promulgation of the law of appeal would reconcile erstwhile Mediceans to the new regime and eventually lead them to the full acceptance of all its institutions and aims.[140] It was the shock of betrayal as well as the realization of how close they had come to disaster that prompted the majority of Piagnoni to advise against granting the right of appeal. Even those in favour of observing the letter of the law, however, did so with the proviso that the appeal was to be granted only if the proceedings did not endanger the Republic.[141] Luca Corsini best summarized his fellow Piagnoni's intransigence at the evidence of a betrayal which 'since it had pleased God to bestow freedom on these people' was both religious and political, when he confessed to be astonished that the conspirators had not become reconciled with the new government despite having been forgiven for their Medicean past.[142]

The execution of the five conspirators did, indeed, as Professor Bertelli has argued, open an unbridgeable chasm between Mediceans and Piagnoni.[143] Yet, neither the conspirators nor the

---

[139] Ibid., Provvisioni, 187, fo. 104ʳ; ibid., Libri fabarum, 71, fos. 80ᵛ, 81ʳ: the bill was rejected in the Great Council on 4 Jan. 1497 but passed by 782:387 votes on the following day. On its importance see Marks, 'La crisi finanziaria a Firenze', 47.

[140] The best expression of the aims sought in Savonarola, *Prediche sopra i Salmi*, i. 9–13; see also ASF Consulte e Pratiche, 61, fo. 35ʳ⁻ᵛ for opinions of Lorenzo Lenzi and Luca Corsini.

[141] Ibid. 63, fos. 83ᵛ, 84ʳ, opinions of Bernardo di Inghilese di Schiatta Ridolfi and Francesco Gualterotti.

[142] Ibid., fo. 84ᵛ: 'da poi a Dio piacque di rendere la libertà a questo popolo'; see also Niccolò Valori, 'Ricordanze', MS BNF Panc. 134, fo. 17ʳ.

[143] Bertelli, 'Machiavelli e la politica estera fiorentina', 38.

Mediceans in general could claim not to have been forewarned of the likely punishment for any act of treachery against the Republic. On every suitable occasion from the foundation of the new regime, Savonarola and the Piagnoni had made it abundantly clear that they would show no mercy. They had invariably called for exemplary punishment of offenders against the state in deeds and words.[144] They were also the most insistent and vocal proponents of an increase in the number of officials entrusted with the maintenance of law and order. Greater vigilance ensured by, amongst other things, the posting of guards in public places and swift punishment, they believed, would rid the city of conspirators and malcontents.[145] As the normally conciliatory Domenico Mazzinghi advised in the discussion in March 1497 of a bread riot which had immediately assumed political overtones, offenders against the public peace should be left in no doubt that they would be cruelly punished.[146] There was far too much at stake for them personally and for their beloved city as a whole to show leniency to enemies and thus endanger their divine inheritance.

The special relationship between Florence and God, daily affirmed by Savonarola, vindicated, so they believed, the harsh treatment reserved for those who sought to undermine it. This special relationship, however, served also to justify acts and policies detrimental to the Holy See and to ecclesiastical authority in general.

---

[144] For Savonarola see *Prediche sopra i Salmi*, i. 179–80; *Prediche sopra Ezechiele*, ed. R. Ridolfi (ENOS; 2 vols.; Rome, 1955), i. 96–101; for a sampling of Piagnoni opinions see ASF Consulte e Pratiche, 61, fo. 35$^{r-v}$ (Lorenzo Lenzi and Luca Corsini); ibid. 62, fo. 380$^r$ (Francesco Valori); ibid. 63, fos. 42$^v$, 59$^v$ (Bernardo Ridolfi); 59$^v$–60$^r$ (Francesco Gualterotti). It should be emphasized that the records of these *pratiche* published by C. Lupi, 'Nuovi documenti intorno a Fra Girolamo Savonarola', *ASI*, 3rd ser. 3 (1866), 3–77, are incomplete.

[145] ASF Consulte e Pratiche, 63, fos. 69$^v$ (Francesco Gualterotti), 70$^{r-v}$ (Francesco Valori), 72$^{r-v}$ (Lorenzo Lenzi), 73$^v$ (Paolantonio Soderini). The *Arrabbiati*, on the other hand, argued that there was no danger to Florence from within and therefore opposed moves to increase the number of guards and to place a body of armed '*provisionati*' in the square: see, for instance, the opinion of Guidantonio Vespucci, ibid., fo. 74$^v$.

[146] Ibid. 62, fo. 384$^r$; agreement expressed by two other Piagnoni, Francesco Ambrogini, speaking for the *Otto di Guardia*, and Domenico Bonsi, fo. 384$^{r-v}$. On this riot see C. Carnesecchi, 'Un tumulto di donne', in I. Del Badia (ed.), *Miscellanea fiorentina di erudizione e storia* (2 vols.; Florence, 1502), ii. 45–7.

Already mentioned have been Francesco Valori's injunctions to raise money by taxing the clergy and by appropriating ecclesiastical goods. On diplomatic and military matters, too, Francesco Valori, Lorenzo Lenzi, and others had no hesitation, despite the threat of ecclesiastical censure, in recommending policies which defied direct papal commands.[147] In his usual direct style, Valori stated that:

As far as censures are concerned, he admits that he is no theologian; however, he knows well enough that all good citizens are obliged to defend their country and he does not believe that in doing this he may incur censure—although it is the duty of all good Christians to fear ecclesiastical censure.[148]

The normally conciliatory Lorenzo Lenzi went even further. Like Valori he did not believe in the validity of ecclesiastical censures incurred by defending one's freedom. In addition he contended that 'by defending yourselves, you could always be absolved in the future; but once you lose your freedom you have lost everything'.[149]

Even more defiant was the Piagnoni's attitude during the confrontation between Savonarola and Alexander VI. In the *pratiche* held to discuss how the government should react to Savonarola's excommunication and to the Pope's demands that he should be prevented from preaching, arrested, and sent to Rome, they unequivocally stood by their prophet even when Alexander threatened to place the city under an interdict. Neither the procedural constraints of the *pratiche* nor the personal animosity they aroused could prevent them from witnessing to their beliefs and speaking out in favour of their prophet. In a well-rehearsed series of argu-

---

[147] ASF Consulte e Pratiche, 62, fos. 235ᵛ–237ᵛ; ibid. 63, fo. 117ᵛ.

[148] Ibid. 62, fo. 236ʳ. 'Quanto al caso delle censure confessa lui non essere theologo ma ben cognosce che ogni buono cictadino è obligato difendere la patria sua et non crede facciendo questo che possa incorrere in censura benchè offitio di buon christiano sia el temere le censure.' On another occasion Francesco Valori urged the government to tax the clergy, preferably by obtaining a licence from ecclesiastical authorities; if, however, it was impossible to obtain it, he continued, Florence should act as if it had one 'per difendere una tanta republica. . . . Et circa questo . . . prego le Signorie Vostre non ci avere respecto alcuno', ibid. 63, fo. 117ᵛ.

[149] Ibid. 62, fo. 237ʳ: 'difendendosi potrete sempre essere absoluti, ma perdendo la libertà avete perduto ogni cosa'.

ments, in which they appealed constantly to Florentine patriotic pride and emphasized the city's indebtedness to Savonarola, they impugned the validity of the Pope's decision. They maintained, in particular, that the Pope's censures were not binding because he was acting contrary to the tenets of the faith; and more particularly because Savonarola had received his mandate directly from God. To comply with Alexander VI's commands, therefore, was equivalent to betraying Christ and to holding in contempt all that He, through Savonarola, had done in and for Florence; to do so, moreover, would undoubtedly have called down the wrath of God upon Florence.[150]

This is not to say that some Piagnoni were not frightened into submission nor that the majority of them had decided upon a course of open confrontation with the Pope and would reject a compromise if honourably attainable.[151] They were aware of the likely consequences of an interdict on their beloved city and on them personally. As their adversaries never tired of repeating, Florence courted political and military isolation as well as economic ruin.[152] If forced into a choice between Savonarola and Alexander VI then there was no alternative but to turn against Alexander VI, since as they averred it was preferable to obey God than the Pontiff. Furthermore, everything should be done to ensure 'that our freedom should not be yielded to a Pope'.[153] Only they, the Piagnoni, and the other Florentines of good intention, could decide on these matters because they alone could judge, on the basis of personal experience, the righteousness of Savonarola's cause and the worth of his apostolate. On the principles that the Pope could not be allowed to act against the well-being of the Church and that, conversely, the members of the Church Militant had the duty to ensure their salvation and should therefore have a say in matters pertaining to their spiritual well-being, leading Piagnoni backed Savonarola's calls for a General Council and worked for its

---

[150] Lupi. 'Nuovi documenti intorno a Fra Girolamo Savonarola', 30–53.
[151] See e.g. ibid. 43 and Landucci's own reactions, *Diario fiorentino*, 161–2.
[152] Lupi, 'Nuovi documenti intorno a Fra Girolamo Savonarola', 35, 43, 44.
[153] Ibid. 47, 53: 'che la libertà nostra non s'abbia a sottomectere a uno Pontefice'.

attainment.[154] Nothing came of the plan: not, however, because of the Piagnoni's lack of commitment since they fulfilled their part of the plan, but rather as a result of Savonarola's doubts and procrastination.

As their statement, and general attitude in the *pratiche* demonstrate, the Piagnoni brooked no interference, not even by God's representative on earth, in this special relationship between themselves and God and between God and the city. Advised by their prophet and inspired by prayer, they were the best interpreters of God's will and the best judges of which laws most closely conformed to it and thus contributed to speed the millennium on its way. Such convictions needed constant renewal and reinforcement, which took two main forms. There was, first, an increasing tendency by Piagnoni to have recourse to God, or to advocate such recourse by the whole city, before making important decisions. Speaker after speaker in the *pratiche* sought this divine assistance by counselling private and public prayer, processions, and alms.[155] As Lorenzo Lenzi admonished, recourse to God did not mean that the citizens could abdicate their responsibilities; it was essential 'first to have recourse to God with our prayers and then, on our own part, continually do our duty'.[156]

In the second place, it bound the Piagnoni even more closely to

---

[154] Lupi, 'Nuovi documenti intorno a Fra Girolamo Savonarola', 41–2, 43, 49, 52–3. On Savonarola and the Council see *Prediche sopra l'Esodo*, ed. P. G. Ricci (ENOS; 2 vols.; Rome, 1955–6), ii. 50–1; *Lettere e scritti apologetici*, 226–36. Some Piagnoni had been calling for a council and defending its authority *vis-à-vis* the Pope as revealed in Filippo Cioni and Paolo da Fucecchio, *Epistola di Philippo Cioni notario fiorentino in nelle conclusioni publicate contro al venerando padre frate Hieronymo da Ferrara in nome di frate Leonardo del ordine di Sancto Augustino, con le responsioni a quelle facte per maestro Paulo da Fucecchio del ordine de' frati minori, maestro in sancta theologia, et pel decto Philippo in vulgar lingua tradocte* [Florence, 1497] (Hain 5361), fos. 26ᵛ–27ʳ. For additional Piagnone involvement see Villari, *La storia di Girolamo Savonarola*, vol. ii, app., pp. lxviii–lxx, clxx–clxxi, *et passim*; see also next chapter.

[155] See e.g. ASF Consulte e Pratiche, 61, fo. 35ʳ (Lorenzo Lenzi); ibid. 62, fos. 194ʳ (Giovanbattista Ridolfi), 204ʳ (Francesco Valori), 207ʳ (Giovanbattista Ridolfi), 221ᵛ (Ubertino Risaliti); ibid. 63, fo. 59ᵛ (Bernardo di Inghilese di Schiatta Ridolfi).

[156] Ibid. 62, fo. 194ʳ: 'in primis ricorrer a Dio colle prece e di poi al continuo dalla parte nostra fare el debito nostro'.

Savonarola and S. Marco. From them, and exclusively from them, could they obtain knowledge of God's wishes and intentions. Only Savonarola and his friars could lead them to their glory, and they too, the Piagnoni believed, could best ensure personal salvation. Accordingly, they turned more and more to S. Marco for their spiritual needs and in turn benefited it greatly with alms and endowments.[157] So large was the number of Piagnoni both men and women who deserted their parish churches in favour of the spiritual ministrations of S. Marco that opponents felt duty-bound to condemn what they viewed as a deliberate policy of enticement dictated by greed.[158] Whatever the merits of their case, the influx of new spiritual charges was responsible for a stupendous increase in the wealth and prestige of the convent.[159] It was no doubt the mounting evidence of this prestige and concomitant political influence that caused the government to have discussed in a *practica* whether the convent should be closed or, at the very least, placed out of bounds to lay Florentines. Such was the indignation of the Piagnoni that nothing more was heard of the proposal.[160] Because of this new-found status, S. Marco was able to survive almost unscathed the arrest and execution of Savonarola and his two companions, the storming of its church and cloisters by armed opponents, and a number of legislative decrees seeking to humiliate it and to isolate it from the religious life of the city. Within a short period of time, as we shall see, it was to resume its position of eminence and to pursue an expansionist policy once again.

---

[157] Polizzotto, '*Dell'Arte del Ben Morire*', 56–7.

[158] Ibid. 57–8.

[159] Ibid. 65–6. Further evidence of this rise is to be found in the *Sepoltuari* which had to be purposely compiled by Fra Ruberto Ubaldini *et al.* from 1494 onwards: ACSM Sepoltuario di S. Marco dal 1494 al 1600 (no location number); and ibid. [Sepoltuario dal 1494 al 1605], Miscellanea P. Benelli, Inserto H.10. See also ASF Conv. Sopp. 103 (S. Marco), 73: Entrata e uscita di sagrestia, 1496–1541; BMLF S. Marco 902, Ricordanze A del Convento, 1445–1493; and ibid., S. Marco 903, Ricordanze B del Convento, 1493–1558.

[160] Lupi, 'Nuovi documenti intorno a Fra Girolamo Savonarola', 42, 44–5.

# 2

# *The Piagnoni and Religious Reform*

## I

In the summer of 1497, at the height of the pamphlet war, the Savonarolans' most formidable antagonist, Giovanni Caroli, issued a scathing denunciation of the doctrine they espoused. 'Full of nonsense, full of dreams', was his description of it. Considering Savonarola's teaching to be a farrago of mismatched notions, gleaned from a host of disparate sources, Caroli declared,

The varied nature of this teaching, therefore, gives rise to a whole variety of opinions, because it is — like all lies — all tangled up and turned upside-down, confused, unstable and founded on quicksand. At times it appears full of mercy, at others full of cruelty; sometimes full of good faith, at others full of treachery; . . . wholly dissembling, utterly false; full of nonsense, full of dreams; sometimes full of humility, sometimes puffed up with pride; sometimes pious, sometimes impious; sometimes full of hope, sometimes full of despair; sometimes totally sure, sometimes riddled with ambiguity.[1]

The theories voiced by Savonarola and defended by the Piagnoni during the controversy over his apostolate which raged from 1494

---

[1] Giovanni Caroli, 'Della verità della doctrina di fra Girolamo, e se è da Dio o no', MS BNF Conv. Sopp., D.9.278, fo. 154ʳ: 'La varietà addunque di questa doctrina è cagione di varie opinioni, perchè è tutta come la bugia aviluppata e rinvolta e inferma e instabile e in sull'acqua fondata. Alchuna volta par tutta misericordia, alchuna volta tutta crudeltà; alchuna volta piena di fede, alchuna volta infedelissima; . . . tutta simulata, tutta doppia; piena di fanfaluche, piena di sogni; alchuna volta piena d'humilità, alchuna volta emfiata di superbia; alchuna volta pia, alchuna volta impia; alchuna volta piena di speranza, alchuna volta di disperatione, alchuna volta tutta sicura, alchuna volta piena d'ambiguità.'

until 1498 were indeed diverse in origin.[2] Nothing so clearly illustrates the eclectic nature of Savonarola's doctrine as the fact that
many contemporary thinkers on Church reform, however much
differing in their respective approaches, found in him the answer
to their prayers. The result was, as Caroli saw, that the Savonarolan
religious ideology appeared to be an amalgam of vague, ill-assorted
arguments shaped by expediency. How far Caroli's view can be
accepted, and how far it falls short of a full assessment of Piagnone
ideology as it emerged during the pamphlet war, will be among
our preoccupations in this chapter. While it is true that the
Savonarolans' theories were to some extent lacking in unity, they
were by no means totally formless. A number of clearly defined, if
separate, strains were already becoming apparent, each of which
would afterwards dominate a particular current in Piagnone
thought. It was the pamphlet war which made this development
possible. As Savonarola's teaching came under attack, both from
spokesmen for the ecclesiastical hierarchy and from self-appointed
champions of the established order, those who believed in the truth
of his cause were obliged to take action.

The experience of public debate both spoken and written was,
moreover, to work its own changes upon them. The Piagnoni
polemicists were forced not only to articulate their beliefs, by
explaining what had attracted them, and ought to attract everyone, to Savonarola's cause, but also to defend those beliefs against
an attack of unexampled ferocity and skill. In four years of intensive controversy, the ideology which the Piagnoni were ever afterwards to uphold was hammered out. 'Full of nonsense, full of
dreams' it may have been, but these dreams of a better world were
far from insubstantial. Expressed in different ways, implemented
by varying means, they were to sustain the Piagnoni for fifty years
to come.

---

[2] The major studies on the pamphlet war are: J. Schnitzer, 'Die Flugschriften-
Literatur für und wider Girolamo Savonarola', *Festgabe Karl Theodor von Heigel*
(Munich, 1903), 196–235; id., *Savonarola* (2 vols.; Milan, 1931), i. 485–502; C.
Calogero, *Gli avversari religiosi di Girolamo Savonarola* (Rome, 1935); and D.
Weinstein, *Savonarola and Florence: Prophecy and Patriotism in the Renaissance*
(Princeton, NJ, 1970), 227–46.

## II

Although Savonarola's apostolate did not become the subject of a major controversy until 1494, it had been under sporadic attack for some time before then. The earliest outcry against him occurred on Ascension Day 1491, in a sermon by an Augustinian, Fra Mariano da Genazzano. Fra Mariano criticized Savonarola's calls for reform couched in prophetic terms chiefly on the grounds of their divisive effects upon Florence: an accusation which, in later years, would frequently be levelled against him.[3] Though calling for an all-embracing reform, Savonarola predicated this call on a violent criticism of the clergy, both secular and regular, and of the ecclesiastical hierarchy. It was the corruption of the clergy, stemming from its ignorance, its venality, and from the outright unsuitability of many of its members, which, he maintained, had both caused the present decline and also presented the major obstacle to reform.[4] To succeed, therefore, reform had to begin with the clergy. To this end, between 1491 and 1494 Savonarola engaged upon intense pastoral activity, often of a controversial kind, which aroused antagonism in many quarters. As the first step in a plan to found an independent Observant Congregation, headed by S. Marco, which would serve as the base for his programme of reform, he succeeded, with the

---

[3] Placido Cinozzi, *Epistola de vita et moribus Savonarole*, in P. Villari and E. Casanova (eds.), *Scelta di prediche e scritti di Fra Girolamo Savonarola* (Florence, 1898), 14–15; Pseudo-Burlamacchi, *La vita* (Florence, 1937), 28–9.

[4] P. Villari, *La storia di Girolamo Savonarola e de' suoi tempi* (2 vols.; Florence, 1930), i. 134 ff. and app., pp. xxviii–xxxviii; J. Schnitzer, *Savonarola*, i. 106 ff. Indispensable for the understanding of the conditions of the Church at the time are D. Hay, *The Church in Italy in the Fifteenth Century* (Cambridge, 1977) and R. Bizzocchi, *Chiesa e potere nella Toscana del Quattrocento* (Bologna, 1987). For a description of the state of the Florentine Church during the years closest to those covered by this book see AAF Visite Pastorali, Visita di Mons. Cosimo de' Pazzi alle chiese della diocesi fiorentina in città (1512); ibid., Atti della visita pastorale promossa dall'Arcivescovo Cardinale Giulio de' Medici (but undertaken by his Vicar Pietro Andrea Gammari, 1514); ibid., Visita diocesana (1537). The scandalized preamble by Gammari to the Acts of the visit of 1514 has been partially published by D. Moreni, *Notizie istoriche dei contorni di Firenze*, v (Florence, 1794; fac. repr. Rome, 1972), 23–6.

support of Piero de' Medici, in separating the convent of S. Marco from the Lombard Observant Congregation to which it had hitherto belonged. Further, by skilled manipulation of his political and ecclesiastical connections, he managed to bring the convents of Sta Caterina of Pisa and S. Domenico of Fiesole under the jurisdiction of S. Marco.[5]

Each move in this scheme of expansion was greeted with opposition and recrimination. The Dominicans of the Lombard Congregation and the Conventual Dominicans of Sta Maria Novella in Florence never forgave Savonarola: the Lombards, for the separation itself, and the Conventuals of Sta Maria Novella, for the reasons adduced to justify it, by which they felt personally insulted.[6] The friars of S. Spirito of Siena violently repulsed Savonarola's attempt to incorporate their convent into the newly formed Congregation of S. Marco; while those of Sta Caterina of Pisa, almost to a man, chose voluntary exile in preference to union.[7] Both within the new Congregation which it led and at S. Marco itself, moreover, there was opposition to his attempts to enforce a stricter code of conduct, in accordance with his interpretation of the Dominican Rule.[8] Similarly, by interfering in the internal affairs of the Camaldolese convent of Sta Maria degli Angeli[9] and, later, by giving his support to the separation of the convent of S. Salvi from the Vallumbrosan Congregation,[10] Savonarola

---

[5] Roberto Ubaldini, 'Annalia Conventus Sancti Marci', MS BMLF S. Marco 370, fos. 13ᵛ–14ᵛ; R. De Maio, *Savonarola e la Curia Romana* (Rome, 1969), 37–56; 177–81; A. Gherardi, *Nuovi documenti e studi intorno a Girolamo Savonarola* (Florence, 1887; fac. repr. 1972), 41–52; Villari, *Storia di Savonarola*, i., app., pp. xl–xliv; Convento di S. Domenico, Fiesole, 'Chronica Conventus Sancti Dominici de Fesulis', MS Fiesole convento P.P. Domenicani (no location number), fo. 5ʳ; F. Bonaini (ed.), 'Chronica antiqua Conventus Sanctae Catharinae de Pisis', *ASI*, 1st ser. 6/2 (1848), 604–7. D. Di Agresti, *Sviluppi della riforma monastica savonaroliana* (Florence, 1980), 12–13.

[6] Gherardi, *Nuovi documenti*, 52–4; and see below.

[7] R. Ridolfi, *Vita di Girolamo Savonarola* (2 vols.; Rome, 1952), i. 112–15; Bonaini (ed.), 'Chronica antiqua', 609–10.

[8] Pseudo-Burlamacchi, *La vita*, 151–4.

[9] J. Schnitzer, *Peter Delfin: Ein Beitrag zur Geschichte der Kirchenreform, Alexander VI und Savonarolas* (Munich, 1925), app., pp. 334–5; B. Ignesti, 'I Camaldolesi e il Savonarola', *Camaldoli*, 6 (1952), 139.

[10] De Maio, *Savonarola*, ch. 6; and app., 184–220.

provoked much resentment, even though his actions were conceived in pursuance of his reforming ideals.
Full-scale war began in January 1495. The timing is highly
significant: at the height of Savonarola's popularity and in a climate
of optimism engendered both by the recent political revolution
and by assurances that Florence was God's chosen city and was to
lead the imminent universal reform heralding the long-awaited
millennium.

Such an optimistic view of Florence's political and religious
future could not but antagonize men who, for various reasons,
resented the revolutionary developments of the previous two
months and who, as a consequence, refused to accept Savonarola's
vision of the future and the premisses on which it was predicated.
The first man publicly to voice criticism of Savonarola at this
juncture was the Franciscan Observant, Fra Domenico da Ponzo.
In a sermon preached early in January 1495, Domenico da Ponzo
queried, as Fra Mariano had done four years previously, the authenticity of Savonarola's prophetic claims. Since Savonarola's
whole programme of reform rested upon his assertion that he had
divined God's plans, this was a key issue and was to remain so
throughout the ensuing controversy. Fra Domenico attacked it fair
and square by declaring that prophecy had long ceased to be part of
divine revelation. Unlike Fra Mariano, who had done no more than
state that the prediction of future contingencies was not part of a
preacher's function, Fra Domenico contended that such predictions were nowadays impossible. He implied, further, that, since
God no longer appointed prophets to reveal His will to mankind,
Savonarola could not have received from Him the knowledge he
claimed to possess. His assertions and teaching, therefore, had to be
rejected as false and unchristian.[11]

---

[11] Piero Parenti, *Istorie fiorentine*, ed. J. Schnitzer (Leipzig, 1910), 6, 36–7. See
also A. Cappelli, 'Fra Girolamo Savonarola e notizie intorno il suo tempo', *Atti e
memorie delle RR. Deputazioni di Storia Patria per le provincie Modenesi e Parmensi*,
4 (1869), 339. For an account of Fra Domenico's spiritual zeal and preaching
activity, see L. Wadding, *Annales Minorum seu Trium Ordinum*, xiv (Rome, 1735),
244; and G. Sbaraglia, *Supplementum et castigatio ad Scriptores Trium Ordinum*
(3 vols.; Rome, 1908–36), i. 238.

With this attack, Fra Domenico set the tone for much of the anti-Savonarolan offensive to follow. The most immediate result of his sermon, however, was a public disputation on the truth of Savonarola's prophetic message. Convened by order of the Florentine *Signoria*, it was held in the Palazzo della Signoria on 18 January.[12] There is considerable disagreement in the sources regarding both the number of participants and the identity of the major anti-Savonarolan spokesmen in the disputation. The contemporary historian Piero Parenti plays down its importance and mentions the presence of only two clerics apart from Savonarola, these being Fra Domenico da Ponzo himself and Fra Tommaso da Rieti, Regent of Sta Maria Novella.[13] Savonarolan sources, on the other hand, concerned to emphasize their leader's role and the heroic virtues which enabled him to vanquish the opposition ranged against him, speak of a large 'council' comprising two representatives of all the religious orders and institutions in Florence, including Marsilio Ficino, and an indeterminate number of influential lay citizens.[14]

Even though little is known of the proceedings at the debate, it is evident that Savonarola came under fierce attack. Modern historians have conflated the various accounts of the debate and, misled by Parenti, have come to the conclusion that the ecclesiastic who led the attack against Savonarola was the Domenican Conventual from Sta Maria Novella, Fra Tommaso da Rieti.[15] There is no doubt, however, that the leading anti-Savonarolan spokesman was none other than Giovanni Caroli. The earliest, full-length, Latin biography of Savonarola, identifies him unequivocally as 'Magister Joannes Karolus', popularly known as 'Gherofanino', an identification with which the various, admittedly dependent, Italian bio-

---

[12] Parenti, *Istorie fiorentine*, 37–8.

[13] Ibid. 37.

[14] Cinozzi, *Epistola de vita et moribus Savonarole*, 22; Pseudo-Burlamacchi, *La vita*, 78–9.

[15] Schnitzer, *Savonarola*, i. 248; Calogero, *Gli avversari religiosi*, 106; Ridolfi, *Vita*, i. 164. Contrary to their assertions, moreover, Fra Tommaso da Rieti was never Prior of Sta Maria Novella though he had recently held the post of Regent of the *Studio* there: T. Kaeppeli, 'Il registro di Sebastiano Bontempi O.P. Priore Provinciale Romano (1510–1515)', AFP, 31 (1961), 311.

graphies of Savonarola, are in accord and which now, as we shall see, is also confirmed by Caroli himself.[16] The cleric chosen to mount the attack against Savonarola had necessarily to be a man of great standing whose opinions would carry considerable weight in the Florentine religious community: Caroli was just such a man. With the exception of Ficino, no other cleric in Florence enjoyed the necessary standing and reputation. Apart from filling various important administrative posts in the Conventual wing of the Dominican Order, Caroli had already served two terms as Prior of Sta Maria Novella, the later of these during the Interdict placed upon Florence by Sixtus IV in the aftermath of the Pazzi conspiracy, and was after the execution of Savonarola to be elected to yet a third. His contribution to learning also gave him prominence. Not only was he a renowned theologian and a reader at the theological faculty of the Florentine *Studio*, but also a prolific author of theological, devotional, biographical, and polemical tracts which, though not printed in his lifetime, are known to have circulated in manuscript.[17] Most pertinently, he also wrote a history of his times, of which only three books survive, entitled *Libri de temporibus suis*, in which a decidedly pro-Medicean interpretation of events was given even for such a controversial issue as the war against Sixtus IV and Ferdinand of Naples.[18]

At the disputation on 18 January Caroli spoke for many Florentine ecclesiastics when he opposed Savonarola on two

---

[16] 'Vita Beati Hieronymi, martiris, doctoris, virginis ac prophetae eximii', MS BNF Conv. Sopp., J.VII.28, fo. 18ᵛ (hereafter cited as *Vita latina*); Pacifico Burlamacchi, *La vita* (to distinguish it from the later edition published by Ginori Conti and Ridolfi); Pseudo-Burlamacchi, *La vita*, 79.

[17] On him see S. I. Camporeale, 'Giovanni Caroli e le "Vitae Fratrum S.M. Novellae": Umanesimo e crisi religiosa', *Memorie Domenicane*, NS 12 (1981), 141–267; id., 'Giovanni Caroli, Dal "Liber dierum" alle "Vite fratrum"', ibid. NS 16 (1985), 199–233; S. Orlandi, *Necrologio di S. Maria Novella* (2 vols.; Florence, 1955), i. 203–5; ii. 353–9; J. Quétif and J. Echard, *Scriptores Ordinis Praedicatorum recensiti* (2 vols.; Paris,1719–21), i. 898; L. G. Cerracchini, *Fasti Teologali ovvero notizie istoriche del Collegio de' Teologi della Sacra Università Fiorentina dalla sua fondazione fino all'anno 1738* (Florence, 1738), 147; for further biographical details, see Giovanni Caroli, 'Contra Iohannis Nesii Oraculum de novo seculo F[rater] I[ohannis] K[aroli] libellus', MS BNF Conv. Sopp., C.8.277, fo. 190ʳ; id., 'Dialogo della semplice verità', MS BNF Conv. Sopp., D.9.278, fo. 10ʳ.

[18] R. Hatfield, 'A Source for Machiavelli's Account of the Regime of Piero de' Medici', in M. P. Gilmore (ed.), *Studies on Machiavelli* (Florence, 1972), 319–33.

counts. Taking as his theme St Paul's words in 2 Tim. 2: 4—
'Nemo militans Deo implicat se negotiis saecularibus'—he condemned Savonarola both for the prophetic content of his sermons
and for his interference in the political affairs of Florence. Deeply
hurt by this attack from a member of his own Order, Savonarola
justified himself as best he could. An open discussion ensued and
the issues were put to the vote; but, since a clear-cut decision could
not be reached, the participants were given leave to go.[19]

Neither of the major antagonists could be satisfied with this
inconclusive result. Shortly afterwards, Caroli followed up his attack with an *Epistola . . . a uno amico suo sopra il detto dello Apostolo:
Nemo militans deum [sic] implicat se negotiis saecularibus.*[20] In the
*Epistola*, though never mentioning Savonarola specifically by name,
Caroli reiterates, elaborates, and clarifies arguments already levelled against his fellow Dominican at the debate in the Palazzo della
Signoria. The *Epistola*'s prevailing message was that the contemporary preacher who claimed to have prophetic powers forfeited
his appointment as a soldier of Christ.[21] While not denying, as Fra
Domenico da Ponzo had done, that prophets could exist at the

---

[19] Cinozzi, *Epistola de vita et moribus Savonarole*, 22; *Vita latina*, fo. 18ᵛ;
Pseudo-Burlamacchi, *La vita*, 79. To this *conciliabolo* may also be connected the
anti-Savonarolan treatise by the Benedictine Michele da Brescia entitled 'De
excellentia vite pure contemplative' in BNF Conv. Sopp., D.8.2738, on which see
B. Collett, *Italian Benedictine Scholars and the Reformation: The Congregation of
Santa Giustina of Padua* (Oxford, 1985), 57–61. I am most grateful to Dr Collett
for drawing my attention to this treatise.

[20] Giovanni Caroli, 'Epistola di frate Giovanni di Carlo . . . a uno amico suo
sopra il detto dello Apostolo: Nemo militans deum [*sic*] implicat se negotiis
saecularibus', MS BNF Conv. Sopp., D.9.278, fos. 46ʳ–53ᵛ. The manuscript is a
fair copy of some of Caroli's anti-Savonarolan tracts but they are not in chronological order. Whereas internal evidence shows that this *Epistola* must have been
composed shortly after Jan. 1495, for example, it occurs in the manuscript *after*
Caroli's 'Dialogo della semplice verità', which cannot have been composed until
the beginning of 1497 at the earliest. For a list of the manuscript's contents
(although incomplete and with errors in dating), see S. Orlandi, *Necrologio*, ii.
374–9. A bibliographical description of this and of the other codex of Caroli's
works to which we shall presently turn (C.8.277) in G. Pomaro, 'Censimento dei
manoscritti della Biblioteca di S. Maria Novella. Parte II: Secolo XV–XVI',
*Memorie Domenicane*, NS 13 (1982), 237–9, 253–5.

[21] Caroli, 'Epistola', fos. 48ʳ⁻ᵛ, 52ʳ⁻ᵛ. That the *Epistola* harks back to the discussion in the Palazzo della Signoria is also revealed by stylistic slips such as the
switch from the present to a past tense on fo. 47ʳ.

present day, the implications of Caroli's arguments were almost identical. Prophets, he claimed, were sent only rarely, at the last resort, when it was impossible by other means to apprise the faithful of God's will. Even then, true prophets had always produced undeniable proof of their divine appointment, either by the sanctity of their lives or by unequivocal signs from God. None of these conditions, he argued, obtained now. Modern pseudo-prophets had not, and could not, give proof of their appointment nor could they demonstrate that any religious benefits could be derived from their utterances. In the circumstances, all their claims of possessing prophetic powers were false and, what is more, harmful.[22]

Caroli has no hesitation in attributing these claims to personal ambition. By claiming to possess prophetic powers a preacher sought to acquire fame, following, and, therefore, personal authority. By thus attracting the enthusiasm of the vulgar multitude, a preacher betrayed the vows of his calling and interfered, in the worst possible way, in the affairs of the world. Becoming more and more pointed in his criticism until there could no longer be any doubt that Savonarola was the primary, if not the sole, target of the attack, Caroli went on to argue that these pseudo-prophets manipulated their credulous following in order to acquire authority in the state for their own ends. There could be no doubt that civil strife would inevitably result from the practice of allowing preachers to interfere in the state's political process at all levels and to posture afterwards as saviours of their countries.[23] Caroli admits of exceptions to the rule forbidding clerical interference in political affairs, but only in those rare cases in which such interference devolved from the clerical office or had been authorized by ecclesiastical superiors. In this context he cites the activities of saintly individuals in the past, such as Pope Gregory the Great, when still a cardinal, Fra Agnolo Acciaiuoli, Bishop of Florence, St Peter Martyr, Fra Antonino Pierozzi, Archbishop of Florence, Cardinal Latino Orsini and St Catherine of Siena, who had been forced to assume political and other worldly burdens.[24] Unlike modern

---

[22] Ibid., fos. 49ᵛ, 50ᵛ.          [23] Ibid., fos. 51ᵛ–52ʳ; 52ᵛ–53ʳ.
[24] Ibid., fo. 51ʳ⁻ᵛ.

pseudo-prophets, however, these saintly individuals had never exceeded the terms of their commission and, since they acted only for the common good, they had fulfilled their tasks through spiritual endeavours and sacrifice, spurning the facile and rabble-rousing resort to prophecy. By way of conclusion Caroli enjoins the erring clerics to abide by the spiritual essence of their calling: admonitory preaching, prayer, and meditation.[25]

The *Epistola* is undoubtedly Caroli's most moderate contribution to the anti-Savonarolan campaign. Savonarola is not mentioned by name and the attack against him is couched in general terms. Above all, and perhaps in deference to the assembly to which the arguments were first presented, it does not betray the personal animosity which in Caroli's later treatises often degenerates into open insults. Though by necessity very guarded, Caroli none the less raises issues and discloses concerns that inform all his later polemical works. First, he makes no secret of his contempt for the multitude and of his lack of esteem for its collective judgement.[26] Secondly, his arguments display an abiding conservatism not only in religious but also in social and political affairs. This innate personal conservatism influences the way in which he views religious and historical developments. Time and again, past and present are juxtaposed in order to bring into relief the contrast between past perfection and present decadence.[27]

Savonarola's public reply to Caroli's attack came on 20 January, two days after the debate in the Palazzo della Signoria. In a sermon delivered in the Florentine cathedral on the subject of truth and of the persecutions suffered by the just and by the prophets in particular, Savonarola answered Caroli's major charge, even though he too, for obvious reasons, did not identify his antagonist by name.[28] Though not addressing specifically the topic of prophecy, which is subsumed under the treatment of truth in general, Savonarola dwelt on Caroli's contention that ecclesiastics should not meddle in political affairs. He refers his fellow Dominican to the chronicles of their Order where he could apprise himself of S. Dominic's 'politi-

---

[25] Ibid., fo. 53[r-v].    [26] Ibid., fo. 50[r].    [27] Ibid., fos. 51[v], 53[r].
[28] Savonarola, *Prediche sopra i Salmi*, ed. V. Romano (ENOS; 2 vols.; Rome, 1969–74), i. 97–110.

cal' apostolate in Lombardy. Then, turning the very examples used by Caroli against him, Savonarola went on to mention in quick succession the activities of other saintly individuals who, like himself, had had to interfere in the affairs of the world for the welfare of the faithful. Who, he asks rhetorically, but a man of God, impartial and above factions, could undertake the task of pacifying the citizens and negotiating a political settlement for Florence? The man of God, far from having no warrant to intervene in the affairs of the world, was on the contrary duty-bound to do so.[29]

As this opening skirmish indicates, the religious debate was also influenced by other factors which, though subsidiary to the main arguments, were important because they impinged upon the protagonists' main religious positions. Of particular importance was the long-standing hostility between the reformed and unreformed branches of the Order. In Savonarola and Caroli the Observants and the Conventuals had found their respective champions. With this debate they were to rekindle a rivalry that was to flare up, periodically, until the middle of the next century. Likewise, the political element is not to be underestimated.

The concerted ecclesiastical campaign against Savonarola, of which the public debate in January 1495 was one of the earliest manifestations, swiftly gained momentum. In the early months of that year, Savonarola expressed his increasing concern: speaking, in a sermon of 4 April, of a secret meeting of Florentine ecclesiastics who were bent on plotting his downfall; and angrily refuting, four days later, the first precise charges of heresy circulated against him by his enemies. It was alleged that he advocated the ideal of monastic poverty, the special taxation of the clergy, and the spoliation of Church treasures: the *Fraticelli*, of dread memory, being cited as a basis of comparison, in an attempt to indicate the dimensions of the threat which Savonarola purportedly posed.[30] These accusations served both to condemn him on grounds which had already been anathematized by the Church and to arouse the resentment of clerics anxious to preserve their privileges.

The attack on Savonarola took a more public and more disturb-

---

[29]  Ibid., 107–8.
[30]  Savonarola, *Prediche sopra Giobbe*, ed. R. Ridolfi (ENOS; 2 vols.; Rome, 1957), ii. 149, 217–18; Ridolfi, *Vita*, i. 175–8.

ing turn with the publication of an anonymous commentary on Savonarola's letter of 26 May 1495 to Charles VIII, which it is believed one of his followers injudiciously had caused to be printed.[31] In the letter Savonarola had enjoined Charles VIII to prove himself worthy of having been chosen as God's instrument in the imminent renovation of the Church. Emphasizing his conviction that he was conveying God's will, Savonarola reminded Charles VIII of his duty to protect Florence because of the city's divine election and loyalty to France. Charles VIII's destiny, Savonarola asserted, depended entirely upon his response to God's injunctions.[32] The commentary, entitled *Epistola dell'Italia contro Frate Girolamo*, of which there survives only one copy from a second edition of 1496, was first published in July–August 1495 in Bologna.[33] Its alleged insulting tendentiousness, already condemned by the Savonarolan contemporary Domenico Benivieni, and its rarity has meant that apart from a few pertinent bibliographical remarks by its modern rediscoverer Ridolfi, it has been totally neglected by historians. On one level at least, this neglect is fully justifiable: the commentary is indeed an injurious piece of special pleading written and printed to discredit Savonarola and to advance the anti-French cause in Italy. On another level, however, it deserves the closest attention. Despite its obviously propagandistic purposes, the commentary airs some new and not irrelevant arguments against Savonarola and his programme of reform. From an examination of these arguments and of the style in which they are presented, it is clear that Caroli inspired its composition. The parallels between this work and Caroli's *Epistola* are too close to be fortuitous.

Caroli's arguments of 18 January are here restated but in a simpler and more forceful manner. Again, Savonarola is condemned for his unwarranted assumption of a prophet's mantle and for his meddling in Florentine politics.[34] With the safety provided by anonymity the author deals at length with the contrast between

[31] Ibid. 218–19.

[32] Savonarola, *Lettere e scritti apologetici*, ed. R. Ridolfi, V. Romano, and A. Verde (ENOS; Rome, 1984), 63–9.

[33] *Epistola dell'Italia contro Frate Girolamo* [Bologna after July–Aug. 1495] (Hain 14478); Ridolfi, *Vita*, ii. 157–8.

[34] *Epistola dell'Italia contro Frate Girolamo*, sigs. A^(r–v).

Florentine conditions under the Medici and 'under' Savonarola. Here, such a wealth of detail on Medici rule is given that one cannot but conclude that the author was a Florentine or, at the very least, someone who had lived there for a long time. The purpose of the contrast is obvious: it is drawn to show that Florence under Savonarola was weak, isolated, and despised, whereas under the Medici it had enjoyed the fame, prosperity, and the political, religious, and cultural leadership which were now merely promised her on the basis of a mendaciously prophesied role in the millennium.[35]

Mounting opposition of this kind was beginning to tell on Savonarola, if his sermons are a guide. He tried to circumvent the criticisms and machinations of his opponents partly by composing the *Compendio di rivelazioni*, an abstract of his prophetic message and reforming programme, and partly by a direct appeal to Pope Alexander VI, in which he acquainted him with the nature and object of his apostolate. The effects of both initiatives were not as he had hoped. The *Compendio di rivelazioni* presented his enemies with a great deal of additional ammunition which they could now aim back at him. Even more disastrous was Alexander VI's response to Savonarola's appeal. He first replied by inviting Savonarola to Rome to relate personally the content of his prophecies; when the latter, understandably alarmed, demurred and no threat could induce him to change his mind, Alexander VI quashed in effect the newly formed Congregation of S. Marco and, with the brief of 16 October 1495, commanded him to stop preaching forthwith.[36]

Savonarola's reaction was to publish his *Epistola a un amico*: an open letter of self-defence which was designed, as its three almost simultaneous editions attest, for widespread circulation.[37] Forbid-

---

[35] *Epistola dell' Italia contro Frate Girolamo*, sigs. b$^v$, bii$^{r-v}$. The north Italian 'flavour' of the expression—due perhaps to interference by the editor—should not be allowed to obscure the essentially Florentine character of the work.

[36] The entire correspondence has been published in one volume in *Alessandro VI e Savonarola (Brevi e lettere)* (Accademia d'Oropa; Turin, 1950). For an excellent discussion of the exchange see Ridolfi, *Vita*, i. 196 ff.

[37] Savonarola, *Le lettere*, ed. R. Ridolfi (Florence, 1933), Introd., pp. cxi–cxii; Ridolfi, *Vita*, i. 222–3.

den to preach, he chose the well-tried literary device of a letter to a vacillating friend as the means to air his views and grievances. He defended his teaching and justified his part in his dealings with the Pope; refuted his enemies' charges of heresy, disobedience to the Holy See, schism, and false prophecy; and gave his justification for his involvement in Florentine politics. Above all, the letter was employed to define the essentials of the reformed Church as he had outlined them in the *Compendio di rivelazioni* and in numerous sermons.[38]

The *Epistola a un amico* brought the issues surrounding Savonarola's apostolate into the arena of public debate, as it was undoubtedly designed to do now that the Friar's voice was silenced. Perhaps less intentionally, it accelerated the recourse, by both sides in the controversy, to printed polemic. Provided with another ready-made justification for attacking Savonarola in print, his opponents lost no time in taking advantage of it. The first tract to appear was an anonymous reply to Savonarola's *Epistola*, entitled *Epistola responsiva a frate Hieronymo*.[39] The tract took up Savonarola's literary device by purporting to be the reply from the still vacillating friend, who confessed himself unconvinced by Savonarola's arguments. Although simply a compilation of the various charges against him which were then current in Florence, the tract was evidently held in high esteem, being reprinted, together with the *Epistola dell'Italia contro Frate Girolamo*, within the next twelve months.[40]

Its author's main object was to show that Savonarola had deliberately placed himself outside the ambit of papal control. This he had done by refusing to go to Rome to submit his doctrines to the scrutiny of Alexander VI. He had thereby denied the plenitude of

---

[38] Savonarola, *Lettere e scritti apologetici*, 240–55.

[39] *Epistola responsiva a frate Hieronymo da Ferrara de' frati predicatori, da l'amico suo* (Florence, 1496) (Hain 6622). For dating of this work, see Ridolfi, *Vita*, ii. 158. A new edition of the *Epistola* is provided by Gian Carlo Garfagnini in *Rinascimento*, 31 (1991), 102–20.

[40] Domenico Benivieni, *Dialogo di maestro Domenico Benivieni Canonico di Sancto Lorenzo, della verità della doctrina predicata da frate Hieronymo da Ferrara nella ciptà di Firenze* [Florence, 1497] (*GW* 3846), sig. a5ᵛ.

papal authority in all matters of discipline and dogma: a denial also manifest in his condemnation of the corruption of the Papal Court, which was designed to cast its authority into question by discrediting it. His claim to preach only what was revealed to him, either directly from God or through the medium of Scripture, was a similar attempt to achieve independence of the ecclesiastical powers. While under the Old Covenant prophets had held a definite place in the divine plan—their most important function having been to foretell Christ's coming—their role had ceased with the birth of the Messiah. The author contended, further, that Savonarola could not be certain of the truth of the constructions which he put upon certain scriptural texts, because he had rejected the Church's mediatory role in the interpretation of the Bible.

The *Epistola responsiva a frate Hieronymo* heralded a new stage in the anti-Savonarolan polemic. It marked the beginning of the campaign to lay specific, rather than generic, charges of schism and heresy against Savonarola. Now the battle was well and truly joined. Domenico Benivieni, sometime lecturer in Logic at the *Studio* of Pisa, one of the most influential members of the Ficinian Circle and popularly known throughout Florence as 'Lo scotino' for his adherence to the doctrines of Duns Scotus, took upon himself the task of refutation.[41] He was one of the earliest representatives of the Florentine intellectual élite to espouse Savonarola's cause; and the fact that 'this gentle soul',[42] as his brother called him, 'totally disposed to goodness',[43] should have defended the prophet with such a venomous pamphlet as the *Epistola . . . a uno amico responsiva*[44] shows how high emotions were running over

---

[41] On these aspects of Domenico's career see A. Verde, *Lo studio fiorentino 1473–1503: Ricerche e documenti* (4 vols. in 7; Florence, 1973–85), i. 307, 311, 314; ii. 180–3; A. Della Torre, *Storia dell'Accademia Platonica di Firenze* (Florence, 1902), 771–2 *et passim*. More biographical details will be provided in the next chapter.

[42] 'Questa anima gentil': Girolamo Benivieni, *Opere* (Florence, 1519), fo. 115ᵛ, sonnet entitled 'Consolatoria a sè medesimo per la morte di Messer Domenico suo fratello'.

[43] Benedetto de' Riccardini, *Senecae Tragoediae*, Ep. ded. to Domenico Benivieni, in A. M. Bandini, *Iuntarum typographiae annales* (2 vols.; Lucca, 1791), ii. 20: 'propensa in omnia bonitate'.

[44] Domenico Benivieni, *Epistola di maestro Domenico Benivieni Fiorentino Canonico di Sancto Lorenzo a uno amico responsiva a certe obiectione et calumnie*

the contentious question of Savonarola's apostolate. The *Epistola
. . . a uno amico responsiva* was in fact an addendum to a pro-
Savonarolan work which Domenico Benivieni had published
several months before.[45] Entitled *Tractato . . . in defensione et
probatione della doctrina e prophetie predicate da Frate Hieronymo*,[46]
this was the clearest and most thorough statement of Savonarolan
reforming beliefs and aspirations that was to be produced throughout the pamphlet war. More than that, it was also the earliest
intimation of how, in the heat of the debate, some of Savonarola's
followers were forging new and largely independent notions of
reform.

An eloquent, and indeed poignant, personal testimony to the
truth of Savonarola's mission, the *Tractato* was very different
from the *Epistola . . . a uno amico responsiva* in style, though not in
substance. Both works were primarily conceived as defences of
Savonarola's apostolate. The first, however, addresses the more
generic attacks levelled at Savonarola and is, as a result, less polemical, more leisurely in treatment and as much an apologia as a
means of propagating the new concepts of reform. It is to this work
that we first turn.

In this exposition, Domenico's view of history held a pre-emi-
nent place. Unlike Savonarola, who placed the present decline of
the Church in a cyclical scheme in which respective phases of
decline and renewal had always succeeded one another, Domenico
created the impression of an age-old decline, of which the present
totally degenerate state of the Church was the nadir.[47] Before

---

*contra a frate Hieronymo da Ferrara* [Florence, 1496] (*GW* 3847). Since Domenico
stated here that the *Epistola responsiva*, published early in 1496, had just come into
his hands, it is likely that his answer would have been published in the same year,
and not in 1497, as suggested by C. Vasoli in his article on Domenico Benivieni in
the *DBI*.

[45] See his references to it in the *Epistola*, e.g. sigs. a2$^r$, a2$^v$.

[46] Domenico Benivieni, *Tractato di Maestro Domenico Benivieni prete fiorentino
in defensione et probatione della doctrina et prophetie predicate da Frate Hieronymo da
Ferrara nella città di Firenze* (Florence, 1496) (Hain 2784).

[47] For examples of Savonarola's view, see his *Prediche sopra i Salmi*, i. 48;
*Prediche sopra Aggeo*, ed. L. Firpo (ENOS; Rome, 1965), 234–8; *Prediche sopra
Amos e Zaccaria*, ed. P. Ghiglieri (ENOS; 3 vols.; Rome, 1971–2), i. 337. For
examples of Domenico's view, see his *Tractato*, sigs. a3$^{r-v}$, a8$^r$, e2$^r$; cf. his later
*Dialogo*, where the cyclical view, although stated, is belied by the subsequent

Savonarola's advent, he argued, the Christian faith had all but disappeared from Italy. The moral depravity of the clergy, the widespread denial of the word of God, the multiplication of pagan rites and the diffusion of superstitious beliefs were, he contended, glaring manifestations of the deeper and deadlier corruption that affected the whole Church. The hopelessness of the situation was best exemplified by the sinfulness of the keepers of the law, the lay and ecclesiastical leaders of Christendom. These leaders were no longer concerned with, or indeed capable of, providing the religious and moral guidance so sorely required by their charges. They had far too much to gain from the continuation of the status quo; thus their obduracy in sin and their rejection of all calls for reform. Because things had come to such a pass that the Church was incapable of reforming itself, he went on, God had been obliged to intervene directly in the affairs of men in order to have His Church restored. Upon this view of the past rested Savonarola's mandate: for he, according to Domenico, was God's chosen instrument of reform.[48]

The dark colours in which Domenico painted the world as it had been before Savonarola's advent led him to present his apostolate in even more glorious terms than did the prophet himself. From their basic agreement that God had bestowed the gift of prophetic illumination upon Savonarola, Domenico went on to claim for him achievements which he himself had never more than hinted at. He declared, for instance, that Savonarola's first task had been to demonstrate anew the truth of the Christian religion as a preliminary to evangelization. This extremely forceful affirmation of Savonarola's divine calling went far beyond a mere claim that he had commenced his apostolate simply by preaching the Word of God to a receptive audience already familiar with the tenets of the Christian faith.[49] It was, however, a clear foretaste of the exalted view of

---

analysis of the past: sig. a7$^r$. For an excellent discussion of Savonarola's view of history, see Weinstein, *Savonarola and Florence*, 159–63.

[48] Benivieni, *Tractato*, sigs. a3$^{r-v}$, a6$^r$, a8$^v$, b3$^v$, c3$^v$, e3$^v$.

[49] Ibid., sig. a3$^v$; cf. Savonarola's comment, 'E però predicando io la verità e la semplicità di Cristo, alcuni, quasi come da un profondissimo sonno pel suono delle mie parole svegliandosi, si sono constantissimamente a quella accostati', in his

Savonarola which was to become increasingly prevalent among his followers, especially after his death.

Having witnessed to the truth of the Christian religion, Savonarola's next task, Domenico went on to argue, had been to teach afresh the forgotten principles of the faith. He had shown that true Christian living consisted not in external works or empty ceremonies, but in man's perfect love for God and in his dedication of his life to the pursuit of this love.[50] There was nothing exceptional in all this: it accorded closely with Savonarola's own pronouncements on the subject in his sermons and, in particular, in his *De simplicitate christianae vitae*, the most recent and most accessible statement of his doctrinal views.[51] In the exposition of these concepts, however, Domenico, once again moved by enthusiasm, unwittingly altered the emphases of some arguments, thus in effect diverging from the teaching of his guide.

Departing from an unexceptional Thomistic position, Domenico argues that man inhabits a rationally ordered world which reflects, however imperfectly, the rationality of the divine mind which has created it. Since man's intellect was also created in God's likeness, it followed that it had the capacity to distinguish good from evil and to lead man to salvation. This process of salvation originates in God's gratuitous gift of grace; man, in turn, accepts this gift which frees him from the shackles of sin and contributes to his own salvation by his own strivings for perfection.[52] In explaining this process, however, Domenico relied almost exclusively on arguments derived from a synthesis of Scotist and Neoplatonist doctrines on divine illumination and love. While arguing that the soul ascends gradually through various stages of purification until final illumination and union with God, Domenico emphasized that the ascent, illumination, and union were occasioned by affective and other than intellectual responses. In other words, it was the

---

prefactory epistle to Benivieni's Italian translation of his *De simplicitate christianae vitae*.

[50] Benivieni, *Tractato*, sig. a3ᵛ.
[51] Savonarola, *De simplicitate christianae vitae*, ed. P. G. Ricci (ENOS; Rome, 1959), 150–3.
[52] Benivieni, *Tractato*, sigs. a3ᵛ, a5ʳ.

creature's innate love for the Creator that determined the progress and the direction of the soul's journey to God. It is this love, most perfectly expressed in the soul's endeavour to share the suffering of Christ on the cross, which enabled man to contribute through good works to the gradual achievement of his spiritual perfection and thus to his salvation.[53]

As it stands and by the liberal standards of the time, there is nothing suspect in this doctrinal synthesis. Domenico's presentation of his position, and the controversial context in which he placed it, however, had the effect of rendering it far more radical than he had, perhaps, intended it to be. The disquisition of God's gratuitous gift of grace to man, coming as it does immediately after the sombre 'historical' introduction and in the midst of strongly worded criticisms of the clergy, creates two strong impressions. It seems to suggest that salvation could best be achieved outside the normal channels of the Church, beyond the reach of the grasping and unworthy ecclesiastics who were a hindrance to it. Concomitantly, it instilled the belief that adherence to Savonarola's doctrines was the essential prerequisite for salvation, for the reception, that is, of the divine gift of Grace. Belief in Savonarola became, in effect, proof of election.[54]

Domenico's elucidation of how best to achieve a lasting religious reform could also be seen in a radical light. On the signs portending the inevitability of reform he reiterates the arguments proffered by Savonarola in the sermon of 13 January 1495,[55] but on the more specific question of the ways to bring it about Domenico differs substantially. Domenico's scheme emphasized the personal at the expense of the institutional approach to reform. For him mysticism was the surest path to spiritual regeneration, first of the individual and then, by extension, of the whole of society.[56] Savonarola's teaching had taken this element into account; none the less, it remained marginal to his message on reform. This, however, was

[53] Benivieni, *Tractato*, a4ʳ, a5ᵛ–a8ᵛ: cf. Savonarola, *De simplicitate christianae vitae*, esp. 154–71, where similar themes are raised (as acknowledged by Domenico) but are developed in a far more traditional way.

[54] Benivieni, *Tractato*, sigs. a3ᵛ, a7ʳ⁻ᵛ.

[55] Savonarola, *Prediche sopra i Salmi*, i. 37–62.

[56] Benivieni, *Tractato*, sigs. c3ʳ, e2ʳ⁻ᵛ.

the element which appealed most directly to Domenico and, not unnaturally, he therefore gave it pride of place. As expounded by Domenico, the gradual ascent of the soul to perfect union with God is tantalizingly accessible. All it requires is love and the will to seek God to the exclusion of everything else.[57]

Domenico's divergence from Savonarola's position becomes even more apparent in the later *Epistola . . . a uno amico responsiva*, in which he abandoned his customary restraint in argument, and sought to regain the initiative by counter-attack. He begins by accusing the anonymous author of cowardice, of sheltering, that is, behind anonymity so as not to have to stand by his arguments or to assume responsibility for the charges he was laying. He next approaches the delicate issue of Savonarola's failure to go to Rome when enjoined to do so by Alexander VI. Like Savonarola before him, Domenico argued that it had never been Savonarola's intention to defy papal authority; poor health had prevented him from undertaking the journey. In any case, Domenico continued, the Pope had not issued a command, which Savonarola would have been bound to obey, but merely extended an invitation which could be ignored without incurring ecclesiastical censures. Since they were based on false premisses, the arguments advanced by the *Epistola responsiva* were therefore false.[58]

Domenico next directed attention to Savonarola's prophetic mission. Though he has little of substance to add to what had already been said by Savonarola and also by himself in the *Tractato*, his arguments now display a few important refinements. In the first place, he emphasizes the obvious fact, purposely ignored by the *Epistola responsiva*, that the fulfilment of Savonarola's prophecies was conditional on a genuine reform on the part of the Florentines. Until such a reform had occurred, it was vain to expect the promised gifts. This observation enables Domenico to reject as tendentious all demands that Savonarola provide supernatural signs as validation of his mission.[59] It becomes increasingly evident, however, that Domenico was not comfortable with certain aspects

---

[57] Ibid., sigs. a5$^v$–a7$^r$, a8$^r$–b1$^r$, c2$^r$, c5$^{r-v}$.
[58] Benivieni, *Epistola*, sigs. a1$^v$, a2$^v$.
[59] Ibid., sig. a3$^v$.

of Savonarola's prophetic mission, and, in particular, with its millenarianism.

Despite indignantly rejecting as heretical the *Epistola responsiva*'s arguments that prophecy had ceased with the Incarnation, his reply demonstrates that he shared some of the author's main premisses. Prophecy is for him primarily an instrument of reform: the means by which God reveals to the elect His intentions regarding religious conduct and salvation. As he succinctly puts it, citing St Thomas, prophecy is bestowed on the Church not solely:

to make manifest the faith in the Son of God's incarnation; but in order to direct and govern human acts and works according to what is best at various times for the salvation of God's elect.[60]

Thus, while there could be no doubt that prophecy would continue to be an essential element in God's scheme for His Church, its significance, according to Domenico, was primarily spiritual and admonitory but only incidentally divinatory. In the circumstances there was no need to rely on eschatological arguments to justify Savonarola's interference in the political sphere since it was obvious that man's spiritual well-being depended also upon the political system by which he was governed and upon the nature of the society in which he lived.[61] Were this not sufficient, he distanced himself even further from Savonarola's conception of his own prophetic mission by refusing to be drawn into fruitless discussions on chronology once he had outlined his understanding of the causal sequence of future events. And finally he thoroughly undermined Savonarola's concept of an earthly millennium by asserting that his statements on the subject were to be understood not literally but figuratively. In a passage which, with others of the same tenor, was to exercise a profound effect upon the mystical strain in Piagnone ideology, Domenico declared that the enemies of Savonarola:

show that they do not understand what is meant by the reformation of the Church, because they have not truly noted the words of this father,

---

[60] Benivieni, *Epistola*, sigs. a6ᵛ–a7ʳ: 'per manifestare la fede della incharnatione del figliuolo di Dio: ma per directione et ghubernatione de gli acti et operatione humane secondo che in ciascheduno tempo è stato oportuno alla salute degli electi di Dio'.

[61] Ibid., sigs. a4ʳ–a5ᵛ.

or because they have quite perverted their meaning. They believe that
by renovation is meant the material construction of Jerusalem. This
would not be the case, if they did not choose to understand by this the
material physical walls of the Church . . . they have forgotten or perhaps
they have never known that the true temple of God, as the Apostle says,
is man's soul.[62]

While believing that the renewal of the Church was imminent, he
did not expatiate on the method by which this would be achieved,
or explain the form which the regeneration would take. He holds to
the views already expressed in the *Tractato* that reform is primarily
a personal matter to be achieved through mysticism. At the same
time, by positing a view of the Church in which not only the
distinction between laity and clergy but also the whole notion of an
ecclesiastical hierarchy are rejected, Domenico endowed his message with additional, revolutionary connotations.[63] In the following
chapter we shall see how these themes were developed.

Incensed by Domenico Benivieni's *Tractato*, Giovanni Caroli
returned to the fray. His tract, *Della verità della doctrina di fra
Girolamo*, aimed exclusively at the *Tractato*, was completed in the
summer of 1497.[64] Caroli was acutely aware of the radical implications of the concept of Savonarola's apostolate as Domenico expounded it. Apart from condemning as faulty the methods of
argumentation employed by the lesser Scotus ('il minor Scoto'), as
he derisively called him,[65] Caroli struck particularly at Domenico's

---

[62] Ibid., sigs. a7$^v$–a8$^r$: 'mostrono anchora non intendere che vogli dire
reformatione di Chiesa per non havere bene notate le parole di questo padre, o
vero retorquendole a perverso senso. Credono che la renovatione s'intenda la
hedificatione materiale di Hyerusalem. Il che non seguiterebbe se loro altro non
intendessino per la Chiesa che le mura materiale . . . si hanno sdimentichato o
forse non mai hanno saputo che el vero tempio di Dio, chome dice lo Apostolo, è
la anima dell'huomo'. Savonarola was himself to adopt this view in 1498, see his
*Prediche sopra l'Esodo*, ed. P. G. Ricci (ENOS; 2 vols.; Rome, 1956), i. 108.

[63] For additional arguments on the revolutionary import of such a view see V.
Marchetti, 'La formazione dei gruppi ereticali senesi del Cinquecento', in S.
Bertelli and G. Ramakus (eds.), *Essays Presented to Myron P. Gilmore* (2 vols.;
Florence, 1978), i. 126–7.

[64] Internal evidence would suggest that it was completed no later than Aug.
1497.

[65] Giovanni Caroli, 'Della verità della doctrina di fra Girolamo', fo. 126$^r$.

account of the black state of the Church prior to Savonarola's coming. To him, this account was highly inflammatory. Believing that Domenico, like Savonarola, was making a concerted effort to attract the Florentine rabble to the cause, since 'they are by nature ready and inclined to speak ill of the religious, both men and women', he contended that, with such arguments, they had succeeded in removing respect and devotion from all religious, thus weakening the bonds between people and clergy.[66] Nor was this the only consequence of their arguments. With devastating clarity, Caroli held up to them the true image of the new order for which they were supposedly striving. Interpreting Domenico's arguments concerning the corrupt state of the Church as an assertion that all religious were unworthy,[67] he contended that their real aim was to overturn the established order. The implication of such assertions, he maintained, was that the clergy was no longer fit to minister to Christians, who could, therefore, seek their own salvation by independent means. This, Caroli saw, was to deny the traditional distinction between clerics and laymen. By setting the Savonarolan view of the world in direct contrast to the existing structure, he showed that Savonarola's and Domenico's teaching would, in his vivid phrase, make 'the living die and the dead come to life':[68] that it would, in other words, turn the world upside-down.

In the period between the composition of his original *Epistola di frate Giovanni di Carlo*, early in 1495, and *Della verità della doctrina di fra Girolamo*, in mid-1497, Caroli had been far from idle. Among the works which he had produced in the cause of anti-Savonarolan propaganda during these years was the *Confutazione delle ragioni loro contra il comandamento del Pontefice*,[69] occasioned by the publication, by Savonarola and other friars of S. Marco, of an *Apologeticum* in which they sought to justify their refusal to obey Alexander VI's decree that a new Tusco-Roman Congregation

---

[66] Giovanni Caroli, fo. 130ᵛ: 'per lor medesimi prompti e inchinati a dir male de' religiosi e religiose'.

[67] Ibid., fo. 133ʳ.

[68] Ibid: 'de' vivi morti e de' morti vivi'.

[69] Giovanni Caroli, 'Confutazione delle ragioni loro contra il comandamento del Pontefice', MS BNF Conv. Sopp., D.9.278, fos. 156ʳ–170ᵛ; cf. another copy in MS BNF Conv. Sopp., C.8.277.

should be formed by combining the convents of the Congregation of S. Marco with other central Italian convents.[70] Another was the *Liber de discretione vanitatum*, written shortly after the great Florentine procession and public burning of vanities, inspired by Savonarola, which took place on 7 February 1497.[71] Yet a third was the essay *Contra la lamentatione della falsa sposa di Cristo e lamentatione dello sposo*,[72] provoked by the anonymous Savonarolan *Lamentatio sponsae Christi et exhortatio ad fideles*, published in 1497,[73] to whose highly coloured imagery and much inflated language Caroli responded with an amusing pastiche of this type of jeremiad.

Of these works, the *Confutazione* and the *Liber de discretione vanitatum* are undoubtedly the most significant: the first for the depth of animosity it revealed between the two wings of the Dominican Order, the second for the novelty of its arguments. In this latter work, moreover, Caroli attempted also to provide an assessment of both the composition and strength of Savonarola's following. He was in no doubt that the people who flocked to Savonarola belonged either to the *gente nuova* or to the lowest order of society, the plebs.[74] This in turn explained the nature of Savonarola's religious and political message: its attack on privi-

---

[70] Girolamo Savonarola *et al.*, *Apologeticum Fratrum Congregationis Sancti Marci Florentiae* [Florence, 1497] (Reichling 724). On the basis of the text of the *Apologeticum* transcribed by Caroli in C.8.277, fos. 133ʳ–139ʳ (old foliation used), Fr. A. Verde has demonstrated the existence of two versions of this important work: 'Dallo scrittoio savonaroliano del convento di S. Marco di Firenze', *Memorie Domenicane*, NS, 14 (1983), 342–5. He has now published this text in Girolamo Savonarola, *Lettere e scritti apologetici*, 418–29. For the papal decree, dated 7 Nov. 1496, see *Alessandro VI e Savonarola (Brevi e lettere)* (Turin, 1950), 101–6.

[71] Giovanni Caroli, 'Liber de discretione vanitatum', MS BNF Conv. Sopp., D.9.278, fos. 53ᵛ–108ʳ. This tract was composed after 7 Feb. 1497 but before the Ascension Day riot on 4 May.

[72] Giovanni Caroli, 'Contra la lamentatione della falsa sposa di Cristo e lamentatione dello sposo', MS BNF Conv. Sopp., D.9.278, fos. 171ʳ–178ʳ.

[73] *Lamentatio sponsae Christi et exhortatio ad fideles* (Florence, 1497) (Hain 14360). M. Ferrara has shown, on the evidence of Caroli's reply, that this work, although long attributed to Savonarola, was not in fact written by him: 'Indagini savonaroliane', *Memorie Domenicane*, NS 3 (1972), 120–5.

[74] Caroli, 'Liber de discretione vanitatum', fo. 56ʳ.

leges, and on superfluities, its defence of simplicity, its emphasis on
charity, its disregard for traditional, constituted authority, and,
finally, its pursuit of the new with the concomitant destruction of
the old and the traditional.[75] While praising some aspects of
Savonarola's doctrine and even admitting that, superficially at
least, one could notice a great improvement in Florentine religious
behaviour and morals,[76] Caroli none the less criticized the divisive,
sectarian, effects of Savonarola's apostolate on both Florence and
the Church.[77] From these premisses, he went on to condemn the
Savonarolan campaign against vanities and the role assigned to the
children in its implementation. In a series of arguments, remarkable for their directness and novelty, he took upon himself the task
of defending on religious, social, aesthetic, political, economic, and
psychological grounds the vanities attacked by Savonarola and his
*fanciulli*, from dances and horse-races to ornaments in women and
decoration in churches, from paintings and literary works to gambling, drinking, and polyphonic music.[78] Because of Savonarola's
superstition and sternness, he sadly concluded, the whole city
seemed dead.[79]

Controversy again flared up on the subject of Savonarola's
*Compendio di rivelazioni*, whose descriptions of an encounter between Savonarola and the Tempter and of a visionary embassy by
him to the Blessed Virgin made it a vulnerable target.[80] Although
the first Italian edition of this work had been published back in
1495, it did not become the object of a large-scale written offensive
until 1497. Once more, Caroli led the attack, this time with his
*Dialogo della semplice verità*, probably composed early in that year.[81]
Here too, as in the case of his essay *Contra la lamentatione della falsa
sposa di Cristo*, Caroli chose to fight fire with fire. As he observed,
the only way effectively to refute Savonarola's personal revelation

---

[75] Ibid., fo. 57ʳ.    [76] Ibid., fos. 57ʳ, 58ʳ.

[77] Ibid., fos. 57ʳ⁻ᵛ, 61ᵛ–62ʳ.    [78] Ibid., fos. 70ʳ ff.    [79] Ibid., fo. 80ᵛ.

[80] Girolamo Savonarola, *Compendio di rivelatione* (Florence, 1495) (Hain 14334)
and now ed. by A. Crucitti, *Compendio di rivelazioni e Dialogus de veritate
prophetica* (ENOS; Rome, 1974).

[81] Giovanni Caroli, 'Dialogo della semplice verità', MS BNF Conv. Sopp.,
D.9.278, fos. 3ʳ–45ᵛ.

was to counter it by means of another vision.[82] His chosen conceit was a dialogue between himself and Truth,[83] who, in answer to his heartfelt prayers, had appeared personified before him, willing and eager to resolve all his doubts concerning the veracity of Savonarola's prophecies on Church reform. Savonarola's prophetic stance, he contended, far from having been adopted at the behest of the Almighty, had been assumed through motives of simple opportunism. In response to the prevailing mood of disquiet, which had led people to anticipate an era of great change, Savonarola had ceased merely to preach upon the Apocalypse, as he had hitherto done, and had begun instead to prophesy, to growing acclaim, imminent disasters and the renovation of the Church. Eventually, as a sop to the Florentines' civic pride, he had incorporated into his message the notion that the city would play a leading role in the coming reform.[84] This devastating attack on Savonarola's purportedly divine mandate was rendered even more effective by the form in which it was couched. By putting forward his own vision, Caroli demonstrated how easily the invocation of a higher spiritual authority, which was the Savonarolans' all too frequent refuge when pressed, could be abused by charlatans.

Not long afterwards, another attack on the *Compendio di rivelazioni* appeared, this time in print. *De modo discernendi falsum prophetam*[85] was the work of another formidable polemicist, the Franciscan Observant Samuele Cascini, who seems to have specialized in polemical writings, especially against the Dominicans.[86] Like Caroli, Cascini appreciated that the feasibility of Savonarola's reforming programme depended on his claims to prophetic illumination; and like Caroli, therefore, he set out to refute them. Having subjected Savonarola's teaching to various criteria, most notably the rule of the Word, to determine its validity, Cascini concluded

---

[82] Ibid., fo. 4ʳ.    [83] Ibid., fo. 7ʳ.    [84] Ibid., fos. 10ᵛ, 19ᵛ.

[85] Samuele Cascini, *De modo discernendi falsum prophetam a vero propheta inter reprobandum falsam prophetiam atque visionem fratris Hieronimi* (Milan, 1497) (Hain 4566).

[86] L. Wadding, *Annales Minorum*, xv. 166; id., *Scriptores Ordinis Minorum* (Rome, 1906), 209; G. Sbaraglia, *Supplementum*, iii. 82–4; C. Ginzburg, *I Benandanti: Stregoneria e culti agrari tra Cinquecento e Seicento* (Turin, 1966), 34, n. 4; and 108 n. 10.

that it was the work of a false prophet who should be denounced as a heretic and schismatic.[87] Cascini further deplored the revolutionary import of Savonarola's condemnation of wicked prelates and his pleas for the renovation of the Church. In words reminiscent of Caroli's, he asserted that this teaching would, in effect, subvert the existing structure, for: 'You thereby establish a new church! You compose new Scriptures! You promulgate a new law!'[88]

Almost simultaneously with the composition of Caroli's work and the appearance of Cascini's, a pro-Savonarolan tract was published. Although not primarily conceived as a defence of the *Compendio di rivelazioni*, it nevertheless addressed the general issues which Caroli and Cascini had raised. Its author was Giorgio Benigno Salviati,[89] and it was entitled *Propheticae solutiones*.[90] At that time in exile from Florence in his native Ragusa, because he had been closely identified with the Medici, Benigno was one of the three leading figures to receive Guicciardini's accolade as the promoters of the study of philosophy and art in the flowering of scholarship which had occurred under the rule of Lorenzo il Magnifico, the others being Marsilio Ficino and Giovanni Pico della Mirandola.[91] To have won the allegiance of such a prominent personage was no mean achievement, and Savonarola was understandably gratified by his support.[92] This support was, however,

---

[87] Cascini, *De modo discernendi*, sigs. a1ᵛ–c1ʳ.

[88] Ibid., sig. c4ᵛ: 'Novam ergo condis ecclesiam! Novam scripturam ipse componis! Novam legem ipse promulgas!'

[89] C. Vasoli, 'Notizie su Giorgio Benigno Salviati (Juraj Dragisic)', *Studi storici in onore di Gabriele Pepe* (Bari, 1969), 429–98; C. Dionisotti, 'Umanisti dimenticati?', *Italia medioevale e umanistica*, 4 (1961), 288–321, which supplements and corrects F. Secret, 'Umanisti dimenticati: Georgius Benignus, il protetto del Bessarione', *Giornale storico della letteratura italiana*, 137 (1960), 218–27.

[90] Giorgio Benigno, *Propheticae solutiones* (Florence, 1497) (*GW* 3845). A new edition of this work with a most useful introduction has been published by G. C. Garfagnini, 'Giorgio Benigno Salviati e Girolamo Savonarola: Note per una lettura delle "Propheticae solutiones"', *Rinascimento*, 29 (1989), 81–123.

[91] Francesco Guicciardini, *Storie fiorentine dal 1378 al 1509*, ed. R. Palmarocchi (Bari, 1931; fac. repr. 1968), 76; Vasoli, 'Notizie su Giorgio Benigno Salviati (Juraj Dragisic)', 452–6.

[92] Savonarola, *Dyalogo della verità prophetica* [Florence, 1500] (1st Latin edn., 1497) (Hain 14341), sig. f5ᵛ; now ed. by A. Crucitti together with *Compendio di rivelazioni*, see above, n. 80.

rather cautious. Perhaps with an eye to his future preferment, Benigno carefully avoided such contentious issues as Savonarola's position *vis-à-vis* the ecclesiastical hierarchy, the desired reform as he himself envisaged it, and the precise time when Savonarola's millenarian promises could be expected to be consummated. Nevertheless, he did devote considerable attention to proving the truth of Savonarola's divine mission. Benigno was no less aware than the anti-Savonarolans of the crucial fact that the acceptability of Savonarola's teaching depended upon his claim to have received direct illumination from God; and so he did his utmost to testify to its truth. Addressing the well-known Piagnone, Ubertino Risaliti, his friend and fellow interlocutor in the *Propheticae solutiones*, which was in dialogue form, he contrasted his own previous scepticism with his present belief in Savonarola. His conversion to the cause, he declared, had been brought about by those very prophetic utterances whose origin was now in question. The French invasion, coming as Savonarola had foretold, had convinced him that Savonarola's mandate was indeed divine.[93]

The next polemicist to enter the lists in the prophet's defence was none other than Giovanfrancesco Pico della Mirandola,[94] who published an attack on Samuele Cascini's *De modo discernendi* some time in 1497. Entitled *Defensio Hieronymi Savonarolae Ferrariensis . . . adversus Samuelem Cassinensem*,[95] it added little to what had already been said on the subject of Savonarola's prophetic powers, but offered a novel answer to the oft-repeated argument, used by Cascini, that Savonarola's prophecies were not consonant with scriptural revelation. According to Giovanfrancesco, Scripture was no more than an adumbration of God's will regarding human redemption. The gap in man's knowledge on this vital matter had therefore to be filled by saints and prophets, whom God had appointed to give more precise information concerning His intentions.[96] One effect of Giovanfrancesco Pico's contribution was

[93] Benigno, *Propheticae solutiones*, sigs. c1$^v$–c2$^r$; cf. sigs. a1$^v$–a4$^r$; b6$^v$–b7$^r$; c6$^v$.

[94] See below.

[95] Giovanfrancesco Pico, *Defensio Hieronymi Savonarolae Ferrariensis ordinis praedicatorum adversus Samuelem Cassinensem*, in *Joannis Francisci Pici Mirandulae Opera* [Venice, 1503], sigs. CC4$^r$–FF2$^r$.

[96] Ibid., sigs. DD$^r$, DD3$^r$–DD4$^v$.

to force Cascini to clarify his stand on the Savonarolan programme of Church reform. In his reply, *Reseratio atque clarificatio falsarum solutionum ad argumenta Samuelis Cassinensis*,[97] Cascini explained that he was not opposed to ecclesiastical renovation as such, but to the Savonarolan concept of it, which would be likely to sow dissension among the faithful. The implication of the Savonarolans' denunciation of clerical corruption was that if Church prelates were not pure and in God's grace then they ceased to be prelates and the faithful were no longer subject to their administration. Even worse, they envisaged a reformation in which all prelates led the life and displayed the virtues of the Apostles and of primitive Christians: a dangerous, heretical, and schismatic proposition.[98] It is clear that Cascini feared that the privileged status and sacramental powers of the priesthood were threatened by Savonarola's call for a return to the virtues of the primitive Church.

Meanwhile, another debate was raging in Florence concerning a series of twelve propositions against Savonarola, which accused him of being a heretic, schismatic, false prophet, and an evil influence on the Florentines, published by an Augustinian friar, Leonardo da Fivizzano, in April 1497.[99] Their publication was the culmination of a mounting campaign against Savonarola which had been conducted by the Augustinians of the convent of S. Spirito ever since the appointment, as Vicar-General of the Order, of Fra Mariano da Genazzano, who had attacked Savonarola from the pulpit in 1491. Although Fra Leonardo's propositions have not survived, their gist can be ascertained from the Savonarolan refuta-

[97] Samuele Cascini, *Reseratio atque clarificatio falsarum solutionum ad argumenta Samuelis Cassinensis* (Milan, 1498) (Reichling 456). Reichling mistook this for another edition of *De modo discernendi*, and it has not since been treated as a work in its own right; see e.g. E. Valenziani, E. Cerulli, *et al.*, (eds.), *Indice generale degli incunaboli delle biblioteche d'Italia*, (6 vols.; Rome, 1948–82), ii. 38.

[98] Cascini, *Reseratio*, sig. b4ʳ.

[99] Parenti, *Istorie fiorentine*, 177. On Fra Leonardo, see Iacopo Gherardi da Volterra, *Diario Romano 1479–1482* (Rerum italicarum scriptores, Città di Castello, 1904), vol. XXXIII, part iii, pp. 100–1, 116; Cerracchini, *Fasti Teologali*, 208, 725; A. Neri, 'Un avversario di G. Savonarola', ASI, 4th ser. 5 (1880), 478–82; and esp. M. Petrocchi, *Una 'Devotio moderna' nel Quattrocento italiano?* (Florence, 1961), 37–8, 54–64.

tion of them. Apart from condemning Savonarola's presumptuous arrogation of prophetic powers and his equally insubstantial claim to be divinely elected, Fra Leonardo concentrated on two major issues. He argued, first, that Savonarola's projected reform could not take place before the Last Day; and took up the question, secondly, of where exactly Savonarola stood in relation to papal authority: a question which, in the near future, was to become pressing.

Fra Paolo da Fucecchio, Vicar of the Tuscan Province of the Franciscan Order,[100] took up the cudgels on Savonarola's behalf, producing a refutation of Fra Leonardo's propositions which was translated into Italian and published, with an introductory epistle, by Ser Filippo Cioni, a staunch Piagnone notary.[101] This refutation, known as the *Responsioni*, put forward views on the nature and composition of the true Christian Church which were in advance even of Domenico Benivieni's statements on the matter. In answer to Fra Leonardo's argument rejecting the prospect, foreseen by Savonarola, of a drastic cleansing of the Church, Fra Paolo declared unhesitatingly:

What is the Church if not the unity of the faithful and of those who live virtuously gathered together in praise of the Creator? Will you then say that the Church of Christ is the congregation of wicked and perverse men who lead evil lives and blaspheme the holy name of God? God forbid! In fact, they are members separated from the head in Christ and they do not receive the benign influence of God's grace. Hence, the Church of God must be the congregation of the just.[102]

---

[100] 'Consiglio dei Frati 1487–1566', MS ASF Conv. Sopp. 92, 360 (Santa Croce), fos. 19ʳ, 58ʳ; Cerracchini, *Fasti Teologali*, 187, 202; Dionisotti, 'Umanisti dimenticati?', 312.

[101] Filippo Cioni and Paolo da Fucecchio, *Epistola di Philippo Cioni notario fiorentino in nelle conclusioni publicate contro al venerando padre frate Hieronymo da Ferrara in nome di frate Leonardo del ordine di Sancto Augustino, con le responsioni a quelle facte per maestro Paulo da Fucecchio del ordine de' frati minori, maestro in sancta theologia, et pel decto Philippo in vulgar lingua tradocte* (see above, Ch. 1, n. 154). Ser Filippo, together with another notary Ser Benedetto di Paolo da Terrarossa, had played a prominent role in drawing up the petition of 1497.

[102] Ibid., sig. a7ᵛ: 'Che cosa è la Chiesa se non l'unità delli fedeli e di quelli che vivono bene congregati in laude del Creatore? Dirai tu che la Chiesa di Christo sia la congregatione delli iniqui e perversi huomini et che vivono male e blasfemano

As the anti-Savonarolans, Caroli and Cascini, had already shown themselves to be well aware, even the advocacy, much less the active pursuit, of this ideal posed a serious threat to the established order. If the enjoyment of God's grace was to be the chief criterion of membership in the true Church, then sinful men, whether clerical or lay, did not belong. Whether ordained members of the ecclesiastical hierarchy were truly Christian, therefore, depended on whether they were in a state of grace; and—what was worse— since the enjoyment of divine grace ensured a place in God's Church, salvation ceased to be dependent upon the intermediary role of the priesthood. It was dependent, however, on the belief in Savonarola's message and on the wholehearted commitment to his cause. This was a point which Ser Filippo Cioni too emphasized in his introductory epistle, where belief in Savonarola is equated to election.[103] A similar opinion, even more trenchantly expressed, was advanced by the Piagnone doctor Girolamo Cinozzi in an epistle to Taddeo Ugolini. Girolamo reiterates his conviction, already expressed vocally to Ugolini, that all those who believed in Savonarola's doctrine, regardless of whether they had led a sinful life in the past, were now to be deemed saints and would reap the rewards of saintliness.[104]

On 3 May 1497, in an endeavour to stop the situation deteriorating further, the Florentine *Signoria* decreed that after Ascension Day, which fell on 4 May, there was to be no further preaching in the city. Savonarola's Ascension Day sermon was disrupted by a riot; and he did not preach again for almost a year. In the interim, he resorted increasingly to the medium of pastoral letters in order to disseminate his ideas. The first of these, the *Epistola a tutti gli eletti di Dio*,[105] was published in the same month as the *Signoria*'s decree, and within days it had come under attack, again from Fra Leonardo da Fivizzano, in an *Epistola . . . a tutti e' veri amici di Iesu*

il sancto nome di Dio? Guarditene Idio: anzi sono membri separati dal capo di Christo: nè ricevano il benigno influxo della gratia di Dio. Adunque la Chiesa di Dio sarà la congregatione delli iusti.'

[103] Ibid., sigs. a8ʳ, a1ᵛ.
[104] Girolamo Cinozzi, *Epistola di Hieronymo Cinozzi phisicho in favore della verità predicata dal venerando padre frate Hieronymo da Ferrara* [Florence, 1497] (*GW* 7043), fo. [1ʳ⁻ᵛ]; see also DBI s.v.
[105] Savonarola, *Lettere e scritti apologetici*, 256–64.

*Cristo Crocifisso*.[106] Although a wholehearted champion of papal supremacy and ecclesiastical privilege, Fra Leonardo defended the decree — described by Savonarola as the work of Satan's followers[107] — even though it had been passed by a lay authority, on the grounds that, because preaching in Florence had become a means of fomenting discord, the civil powers had been obliged to intervene to preserve the peace.[108] Much the same point was made in another anti-Savonarolan tract prompted by the *Signoria*'s decree: the *Defensione contro all'archa di Fra Girolamo*, by Francesco Altoviti.[109] The ark of the title referred to Savonarola's frequent exhortations to his followers to enter the Ark so that they might be saved: an injunction which Altoviti interpreted as schismatic in import, since it appeared to suggest the foundation of a new sect.[110]

Loyally refusing to let the anti-Savonarolans have the last word, Domenico Benivieni took up arms again with his *Dialogo della verità della doctrina predicata da Frate Hieronymo*, published in the summer of 1497.[111] Apart from condemning Fra Leonardo da Fivizzano for his political motivation, his confusion of mind, and

---

[106] Leonardo da Fivizzano, *Epistola . . . a tutti e' veri amici di Iesu Cristo Crocifisso*, repr. by A. Neri in *Il Propugnatore*, 12/2 (1879), 230–40.

[107] Savonarola, *Lettere e scritti apologetici*, 259.

[108] Leonardo da Fivizzano, *Epistola*, 236.

[109] Francesco Altoviti, *Defensione contro all'archa di Fra Girolamo* [Florence, 1497] (Hain 885); also known by its subtitle, *In defensione de' magistrati et delle leggi et antiche cerimonie al culto divino della città di Firenze, contro alle invettive et offensione di fra Girolamo*, which reveals Altoviti's dislike of the religious ceremonies with which Savonarola had transformed the traditional Florentine festivals. Altoviti's claim that he had always opposed the Medici is cast into doubt by Giovanni de' Medici's recommendation of him to Piero as 'buono amicho': G. B. Picotti, *La giovinezza di Leone X* (Milan, 1927), 644. A modern edition of Altoviti's *Defensione* is provided by Gian Carlo Garfagnini in *Rinascimento*, 31 (1991), 121–30.

[110] Altoviti, *Defensione*, sig. a6ᵛ.

[111] Domenico Benivieni, *Dialogo della verità della doctrina predicata da Frate Hieronymo da Ferrara nella ciptà di Firenze* (Florence, 1497) (*GW* 3846). In his critical note to Girolamo Savonarola, *Triumphus Crucis* (ENOS; Rome, 1961), 554, M. Ferrara dates the *Dialogo* as late as autumn 1497. It must certainly have been published later than 12 May (when the *Epistola* of Fra Leonardo da Fivizzano, to which it refers, was published), but the likelihood is that it was published not long after that date, since Savonarola's *Epistola a tutti gli eletti di Dio*, which had been published on 8 May, is described as having appeared only days before; and since, also, the decree of excommunication against Savonarola, which was to be promulgated in Florence on 18 June, is not mentioned.

his downright ignorance,[112] Domenico did little more than restate Savonarola's message as he interpreted it, believing this to be the best way of disarming his detractors. As additional proof of its validity, however, he offered a new and interesting argument, which is a striking indication of the Piagnoni's burgeoning sense of their own identity. He pointed out how many great men had been drawn to Savonarola's cause, this being incontrovertible evidence of its truth and wisdom, and listed their names: Giorgio Benigno Salviati, Giovanfrancesco Pico, Paolo da Fucecchio, Giovanni Nesi, Bartolomeo della Fonte . . . an honour roll, in fact, of the Savonarolan stalwarts of the day.[113]

Benigno, Giovanfrancesco Pico, and Paolo da Fucecchio had already figured prominently in pro-Savonarolan polemic; and Giovanni Nesi was at the time following their example with his *Oraculum de novo saeculo*, published in May 1497.[114] A member of the Ficinian Circle since at least 1477, Nesi was one of Savonarola's most influential lay followers.[115] In his *Oraculum*, Savonarola was portrayed as a new Socrates, fulfilling the ideals of Neoplatonic syncretism: an incongruous guise,[116] but one which clearly shows wherein lay Savonarola's appeal to the Ficinians. While accepting and elaborating the familiar chiliastic themes of tribulation and renewal, and paying unquestioning homage to the role which Savonarola had allotted to Florence in the coming changes, Nesi envisaged the regeneration itself as no less a philosophical than

---

[112] Benivieni, *Dialogo*, sigs. a6ᵛ–b2ʳ.

[113] Ibid., sigs. a4ʳ–a5ᵛ. No apologetic works by Bartolomeo della Fonte have survived. Although C. Marchesi, *Bartolomeo della Fonte: Contributo alla storia degli studi classici in Firenze nella seconda metà del Quattrocento* (Catania, 1900), 4, denies him to have been a Piagnone, his Savonarolan sympathies are evident both from Domenico's comment and from his own letters, on which see below.

[114] Giovanni Nesi, *Oraculum de novo saeculo* (Florence, 1497) (Hain 11693). The second section of the *Oraculum* (ibid., sigs. b5ʳ–d4ᵛ) has been reprinted, with notes on its variations from the autograph MS of the work in BRF 384, by C. Vasoli, in 'Giovanni Nesi tra Donato Acciaiuoli e Girolamo Savonarola: Testi editi e inediti', *Memorie Domenicane*, NS 4 (1973), 161–79 (published separately under the title *Umanesimo e Teologia tra '400 e '500*).

[115] For a fuller discussion of Nesi and his works, see next chapter.

[116] Cf. D. P. Walker, *The Ancient Theology: Studies in Christian Platonism from the Fifteenth to the Eighteenth Century* (London, 1972), 51; Weinstein, *Savonarola and Florence*, 202–3; Verde, *Lo studio fiorentino*, iv/3: 1226–8.

a religious one.[117] Despite the fact, moreover, that the *Oraculum* appeared at a time when controversy concerning Savonarola and his apostolate had reached fever pitch, it evinced a strange detachment from these debates, touching only indirectly upon the issues to which others were devoting entire treatises. All this was grist to Giovanni Caroli's mill, and he lost no time in composing an answer, entitled *Contra Iohannis Nesii Oraculum de novo seculo*.[118] Confirmed in his conviction that Savonarola had adapted his message to accommodate the prevailing mood and that his teaching, consequently, had become all things to all men, Caroli reiterated, even more forcefully, the criticism he had levelled at the prophet in his *Della verità della doctrina di fra Girolamo*. He condemned the Savonarolan view of reform because of its destructive impact, countering with an appeal to tradition and traditional values. He was further incensed by what he regarded as Nesi's unjustifiable intrusion into a theological dispute. Such presumption by a layman, untrained in theology and ignorant of Scripture, was to be firmly discouraged. Thus, Nesi's fulsome praise of Savonarola's learning and achievements was dismissed on the grounds that he was totally unequipped to judge the rights and wrongs of Savonarola's apostolate.[119] The cobbler, Caroli argued, should stick to his last.[120]

From the middle of 1497 until Savonarola's arrest in April of the following year, one issue was to dominate all contributions to the pamphlet war. This was the validity of the bull of excommunication which Alexander VI sent forth against Savonarola on 13 May and which was promulgated in Florence on 18 June.[121] Issued because of Savonarola's alleged disobedience in failing to go to Rome;

---

[117] Nesi, *Oraculum*, sigs. b3$^v$, c2$^v$–c3$^r$, c5$^r$, c6$^v$, c8$^v$, d3$^{r-v}$.

[118] Giovanni Caroli, 'Contra Iohannis Nesii Oraculum de novo seculo F. I[ohanni] K[aroli] libellus . . . Editus MCCCCLXXXXVII', MS BNF Conv. Sopp., C.8.277, fos. 162$^r$–193$^v$; preceded by an epistle to Nesi, fos. 157$^r$–159$^v$.

[119] Caroli, 'Contra Iohannis Nesii Oraculum', fos. 157$^r$, 164$^r$, 178$^v$. See also Weinstein, *Savonarola and Florence*, 234–8.

[120] Caroli, 'Contra Iohannis Nesii Oraculum', fo. 163$^r$. Verde, *Lo studio fiorentino*, iv/3: 1288–91.

[121] Villari, *Storia di Savonarola*, vol. ii, app., pp. xxxix–xl; Parenti, *Istorie fiorentine*, 195.

his refusal, together with the other friars of S. Marco, to join the new Tusco-Roman Congregation; and his dissemination of false doctrine, the bull was to exercise a profound effect upon the controversy surrounding his apostolate. In the first place, this controversy ceased to be solely a Florentine concern, but was now elevated to a new level of importance. In the second, it brought the question of papal authority into even greater prominence; and in the third, it attracted the attention of many more polemicists than had hitherto contributed to the debate. But the effect of the excommunication upon Savonarola's following was even more profound. The Piagnoni were confronted with the undeniable fact, which was ever afterwards to dog their footsteps, that the ecclesiastical hierarchy had placed their leader and spiritual guide beyond the pale of the Church Militant. After Savonarola's excommunication, there could no longer be any doubt as to his position in the eyes of the ecclesiastical hierarchy. His followers were therefore forced to decide whether to abandon him and remain within the sheltering walls of orthodoxy or to continue faithful to him and disregard the risk of everlasting damnation.

Two days after the bull's promulgation in Florence, Savonarola proclaimed his defiance. In an open letter *A tutti li Christiani e diletti di Dio*, he protested that he was innocent of all charges made against him. Denying that he was guilty of the heresy and disobedience which were the grounds for his excommunication, he urged his readers not to believe in the validity of the excommunication, since it had been sought by evil men to undo God's work.[122] These reasons for disregarding the Pope's decree were taken up and developed by those of Savonarola's followers who continued unswerving in their devotion to him. Ser Filippo Cioni was among those Piagnoni who remained loyal. In the preface to his translation of Savonarola's apologetic letter *A un frate*, Cioni declared that the Florentines who were upholding the validity of the excommunication were doing so not on religious grounds, but for motives of political expediency.[123] While in many cases this accusation may

---

[122] Savonarola, *Lettere e scritti apologetici*, 273.
[123] Filippo Cioni, *Epistola . . . in nella traductione vulgare della epistola del Venerando Padre frate Hieronymo da Ferrara contro alla iniusta excomunicatione* [Florence, 1497] (Hain 14453), sig. a3ʳ.

well have been true, in others such considerations were not the decisive factor. For Angelo da Vallombrosa, for example, the excommunication of Savonarola was merely the last stage in his progression from guarded support of the prophet to total disenchantment with him.[124] Appalled by the rumours that Savonarola was advocating the spoliation of Church property,[125] soured by the battle to prevent him from achieving his aim of separating the convent of S. Salvi from the Vallumbrosan Order,[126] and outraged, above all, by his disregard for papal power and authority,[127] Angelo da Vallombrosa composed two fiery epistles on the subject of the excommunication. So vehement were his *Epistola a' frati usciti di Sancto Marcho* and *Replica . . . alla risposta de' frati di San Marco*,[128] in fact, that they provoked the physician Girolamo Cinozzi to address an open letter of protest to the General of the Vallumbrosan Order, in which he contended that the injustice of Angelo's charges was manifest from Savonarola's evident saintliness and the unmistakable signs portending the imminent fulfilment of his prophecies on reform.[129]

Where true loyalties lay was fast becoming apparent; Giovanfrancesco Pico now composed what was to become the standard Piagnone refutation of the bull of excommunication. Shortly after its promulgation, Savonarola had written to Giovanfrancesco, explaining his reasons for considering it invalid. 'First,' he wrote,

---

[124] See DBI; De Maio, *Savonarola*, 87 ff.; T. Sala, *Dizionario storico biografico di scrittori, letterati ed artisti dell'Ordine di Vallombrosa* (Florence, 1929), i. 327–33; Weinstein, *Savonarola and Florence*, 231–3.

[125] Angelo da Vallombrosa, *Epistole . . . alle nobili matrone et pientissime donne fiorentine* (Florence, 1496), sig. a4ᵛ.

[126] De Maio, *Savonarola*, 79–98.

[127] Angelo da Vallombrosa, *Epistola . . . dello stato della Chiesa et reformatione di Roma contra a' moderni propheti inscripta a Roma nel MCCCCLXXXXVI: In essa si pruova che fra Girolamo non può essere propheta et narrasi molti suoi errori* [Florence, 1496], sig. a4ʳ⁻ᵛ, cf. sigs. a1ᵛ, a5ʳ⁻ᵛ, a7ʳ.

[128] Angelo da Vallombrosa, *Epistola . . . a' frati usciti di Sancto Marcho confortatoria alle persechutioni dello excomunicato Frate Hyeronimo tanto si converta* [Florence, 1497], (*GW* 1913); id., *Risposta d'una lettera feciono e' frati di Sancto Marco a[l] Romito di Valenbrosa, replica del Romito di Valenbrosa alla risposta de' frati di San Marco* [Florence, 1497] (*GW* 1918).

[129] Girolamo Cinozzi, *Epistola . . . al P. Abbate et Generale di Valembrosa contra all'abate anachorita*, published together with his *Epistola del predecto Hieronymo a tucti i fideli et amatori della verità* [Florence, 1497] (*GW* 7044), fos. 3ᵛ, 4ᵛ.

'because it has been obtained by the entreaties of evil men; second, because it is full of false instigations; third, because it has been obtained in order to do evil; and therefore, having a bad beginning and a bad middle and a bad end, Your Lordship can imagine what it is worth.'[130] On these arguments, Giovanfrancesco was to base his impressive *In libros de iniusta excommunicatione pro Hieronimi Savonarolae innocentia.*[131] The tract was divided into two books, one theoretical, the other practical. The first book was devoted to proving that a sentence of excommunication could in certain circumstances be invalid. Arguing that the Church was infallible only in matters of faith, not discipline, and that many prelates were unfit to judge their inferiors, and so to pass sentence upon them, Giovanfrancesco Pico declared that an unjust or erroneous order, of whatever sort, from an ecclesiastical superior must be disregarded. Being invalid, it could not deprive a person of his membership of the Church or of his heavenly inheritance. A sentence of excommunication which came under this category should on no account be obeyed, because, in the observing of it, truth would be compromised.[132] In the second book, the author turned to an examination of the recent decree of excommunication against Savonarola. While taking great pains not to apply the general rules laid down in the previous book to this specific instance, he discussed the transgressions adduced by Alexander VI as the grounds for his excommunication of Savonarola, and showed them to have been unfairly levelled at the prophet. At the same time, he was most painstaking in his endeavour to absolve the Pope himself from all blame, using the time-hallowed argument that the fault lay in his advisers. Determined not to lay himself open to censure to exacerbate an already explosive situation, Giovanfrancesco asserted that the Pope had been completely innocent throughout the whole affair, having been misled by perfidious men who had insinuated

---

[130] Savonarola, *Lettere e scritti apologetici*, 163: 'Prima, perchè è impetrata da cattivi, secunda perchè è piena di false suggestioni, tertia perchè è impetrata per fare male; et ideo, havendo cattivo principio et cattivo mezo et cattivo fine, pensi la S.V. quanto vale.'

* [131] Giovanfrancesco Pico, *In libros de iniusta excommunicatione pro Hieronimi Savonarolae innocentia* (Wittemberg, 1521; 1st edn. Florence, 1497).

[132] Ibid., sigs. a4ʳ, bᵛ–b2ʳ, b3ᵛ–b4ʳ, c2ᵛ, c3ᵛ, dʳ, dᵛ–d2ᵛ.

themselves into his graces and extorted from him the bull of excommunication.[133]

The connection between the general arguments of the first book and the particular situation expounded in the second, although not made by Giovanfrancesco Pico, was nevertheless fully appreciated by his readers. The thesis that an unworthy prelate, issuing a judgement based on untrue allegations, was not to be obeyed became the foundation of the Savonarolans' polemical stance on the questions of the excommunication and, later, the execution of their leader. One Piagnone apologist after another would make his contribution to the accumulation of evidence showing that the charges upon which these sentences were based had been unjust and that Alexander VI, their perpetrator, had no right to have occupied S. Peter's throne, his title to the papacy having been defective. Meanwhile, the anti-Savonarolans showed by their response that they too were well aware of the import of the *In libros de iniusta excommunicatione*. The issue of the Pope's right to exercise untrammelled authority in disciplinary disputes was paramount in the three remaining anti-Savonarolan tracts to address the excommunication question. Although none of them referred directly to Giovanfrancesco's treatise, most of his arguments were refuted and, in one case, the texts which he had adduced in his support were re-worked to the disadvantage of the Savonarolans' cause.

Early in 1498, when it became known that Savonarola intended to begin preaching again in defiance of the bull, Angelo da Vallombrosa composed a letter to the Canons of Sta Maria del Fiore and to the Florentine clergy in general, castigating them for their failure to take up an unequivocally anti-Savonarolan stand.[134] Angelo struck particularly at the argument, put forward by Savonarola and voiced in chorus by his followers the 'hieronimiani', as Angelo called them, that Alexander VI's claim to the papacy was invalid because of his simoniacal election and scandal-

---

[133] Ibid., sig. d4ʳ; cf. sigs. d3ʳ–d4ʳ.

[134] Angelo da Vallombrosa, *[Epistola] Reverendis Patribus et Dominis Dominis praelatis capitulo et clero ecclesie florentine*, printed in E. Sanesi, *Vicari e canonici fiorentini e il 'caso Savonarola'* (Florence, 1932), 84–90.

ous life.[135] This he rightly saw as a move to circumvent the entire excommunication issue by subverting the authority of the Pope who had proclaimed it. He replied that, because the spiritual powers with which every Pope was invested by his election rendered him impervious to any charges of wrongdoing, there was no need to refute such accusations.[136] Giovanni Francesco Poggio Bracciolini, however, author of the next of these anti-Savonarolan tracts, was less unequivocal in his rejection of the Piagnone case against Alexander VI. A Canon of Sta Maria del Fiore,[137] Bracciolini may well have composed his epistle *Contra fratrem Hieronymum heresiarcam*[138] either at the Pope's request or as a means of gaining his favour. Its printing history is remarkable, and would suggest that the Papal Court used the work as a means of publicizing its stand on both sides of the Alps.[139] It is significant, further, that when the possibility of including Savonarola's works in the *Index librorum prohibitorum* came up for discussion many years later, during the pontificate of Paul IV, Bracciolini's tract was cited as

---

[135] Ibid., 85; cf. Savonarola, *Lettere e scritti apologetici*, 229, 232, 235.

[136] Angelo da Vallombrosa, *[Epistola] Reverendis Patribus*, 88–9.

[137] Bracciolini would seem to have been absent from Florence—and possibly in Rome, where his epistle was published—since his name is not listed among the participants in the stormy meetings held by the Chapter of Canons at this time: cf. Sanesi, *Vicari e canonici fiorentini*. He was back in Florence by 1500, however, when his name appears among the Canons for that year: Archivio del Capitolo di S. Maria del Fiore, Firenze, 'Libro dei Partiti A (1467–1504)', fo. 222ᵛ.

[138] Giovanni Francesco Poggio Bracciolini, *Contra fratrem Hieronymum heresiarcam* (Rome, [1498]) (Hain 13209), preceded by a letter *Fratri Hieronymo Savonarole Spiritum sanioris consilii*. In *Savonarola and Florence*, 229 n. 4, Weinstein, possibly misled by addenda in later editions, has dated the work to the period after Savonarola's imprisonment on 8 Apr., but in fact it must have been produced after 11 Feb., when Savonarola resumed preaching, and before his last sermon on 18 Mar.

[139] Within the next two years, the tract was twice reprinted, each time under a different title and with additions in the third edition. Identical to the first edition, but in black-letter, the second was entitled *Refutatorium errorum fratris Hieronymi Savonarolae* (Leipzig, 1498), (Copinger 13722). The third edition was *Contra fratrem Hieronymum heresiarcham libellus et processus* (Nuremberg, [1500]) (Hain 14478). To it were added the records of Savonarola's first trial, two papal bulls, and two poems, but the glosses to the canonical texts were removed.

damning evidence against them.[140] Considering the vindictiveness with which the Piagnoni were to proceed against Bracciolini in 1500, moreover, it would seem that they certainly were in no doubt of the ulterior motives which had led him to compose it.[141] Even so, Bracciolini's position, as expounded in his *Contra fratrem Hieronymum heresiarcam*, was more moderate than Angelo da Vallombrosa's. Unlike him, Bracciolini accepted the Savonarolans' premiss that orders from ecclesiastical superiors which were against charity, in opposition to the public good, or conducive to sin should be regarded as void.[142] He devoted his energies to demonstrating that none of these accusations could however be justly levelled at Alexander VI's excommunication of Savonarola, which, so far from promoting evil, had in fact forestalled it, by stopping him from disseminating false doctrine.[143]

Giovanni Caroli, on the other hand, categorically refused to concede even this much ground to the adversary. In his *Expositione del salmo 25 Iudica me domine*, he sternly resisted the temptation to be drawn into debate on his opponent's terms. Refusing to defend the sentence of excommunication, since this would be to defend what must not even be questioned, he contended that it was not for ordinary men to judge the rights and wrongs of the actions performed by Christ's Vicar on earth.[144] The refusal on the part of Savonarola and his followers to abide by the papal decree con-

---

[140] Vincenzo Ercolani, *Lettera del P. fra Vincenzo Ercolani Perugino dell'Ordine de' Predicatori, quando era Priore nella Minerva di Roma, scritta ai suoi frati di S. Marco di Firenze, dove si racconta l'esamina fatta sopra la dottrina di Girolamo Savonarola ed altre cose accadute a ciò*, in B. Aquarone, *Vita di fra Jeronimo Savonarola* (2 vols., Alessandria, 1857–8), vol. ii, app., p. xxxv.

[141] See below, pp. 212–13.

[142] Bracciolini, *Contra fratrem Hieronymum heresiarcam* (Rome, [1498]), sig. a1$^{r-v}$.

[143] Ibid., sigs. b4$^v$–b5$^r$.

[144] Giovanni Caroli, 'Expositione del salmo 25° Iudica me domine di F[rate] I[ohanni] K[aroli] contra le prediche fece ultimamente in Sancta Reparata per la LXXa [i.e., Septuagesima] e LXa [i.e., Sexagesima] frate Girolamo', MS BNF Conv. Sopp., C.8.277, fos. 196$^r$–231$^v$. The work is dated at the end to 16 Mar. 1496: clearly a *lapsus calami* for 1498, since reference is made to Savonarola's sermons on Exodus, which were delivered between 11 Feb. and 18 Mar. 1498. Although *Iudica me Domine* is given as Ps. 25, in the Vulgate it is Ps. 26.

firmed Caroli in his belief that they were prepared to stop at nothing. Since they clearly intended to pursue their notion of reform even to the lengths of disobeying an injunction from the Church whose renovation they purported to seek, he had no hesitation in declaring that their true object was not reform, but revolution. This aim, he declared, was implicit in the very term which they used to describe their desired end: 'to renew something means, when it is destroyed and in ruins, to build it up again'.[145] What the Savonarolans sought was to build a new Church. This view, which Caroli had maintained throughout the pamphlet war, was thus reasserted by him as it was coming to an end. For the decree of excommunication, although always to be a thorn in the Piagnoni's flesh, was shortly to be cast into the shade by the far more overwhelming reversal which they suffered early in 1498, when their leader was arrested, tried, and condemned to death. For a while, the very future of the Piagnoni was in doubt. By the time of Savonarola's execution in May, the crucial issue was no longer how best their cause of reform might be advanced in the present inauspicious circumstances, but whether it would continue to be advocated at all.


III


In defiance of the sentence of excommunication, Savonarola had resumed preaching in February 1498, to the fury of the ecclesiastical authorities in Rome. Under the impending threat of a papal interdict, the *Signoria* again ordered him to stop preaching, and he did so on 18 March with dire warnings to all those connected with the ban. Even after he had been silenced, however, the tension and discord in Florence did not cease. A trial by fire, designed to test the veracity of his message, was arranged for 7 April, but never actually took place, and this fiasco sealed Savonarola's fate. On the night of 8 April, the Convent of S. Marco was stormed and

---

[145] Caroli, 'Expositione del salmo 25° Iudica me domine', fo. 214ʳ: 'rinovar una cosa s'intende, quando ell' è disfatta e rovinata, rihedificarla di nuovo'. See also fos. 218ʳ, 224ʳ.

Savonarola and his two staunch companions Fra Domenico da Pescia and Fra Silvestro Maruffi were arrested. After a series of examination and trials, they were hanged and burned in the Piazza della Signoria on 23 May, their ashes being thrown into the Arno to prevent the Savonarolans from collecting and venerating them as relics.

The fear that the Savonarolan devotees, even though deprived of their prophet and guide, would continue to revere his memory and possibly also carry on his mission, was behind the spate of anti-Savonarolan works produced in the last months of Savonarola's life and shortly after his death. The most damaging were by two erstwhile admirers of Savonarola, Ugolino Verino and Marsilio Ficino, both of whom were now eager to dissociate themselves completely from the prophet in his eclipse. Addressed to the Florentine *Signoria* shortly after Savonarola's imprisonment, the letter by Verino was a blatant attempt to avoid involvement in Savonarola's fall.[146] Ficino, too, had been an enthusiastic early supporter,[147] but his letter, directed to the College of Cardinals in the weeks following Savonarola's execution, was not prompted merely by an instinct for self-preservation. There is no reason to doubt his statement that for three years past he had been disillusioned with Savonarola and had warned his friends against him in private and in public.[148] While Ficino may not have been fully aware of their ideological differences until Savonarola's message gained in confidence and precision in the aftermath of the French invasion, the ultimate break was nevertheless inevitable. The similarities between their thought had in fact been limited to their agreement that the recent history of the Church had been one of decline and to

[146] Ugolino Verino, *Magnificis et illustribus Dominis dominis Prioribus libertatis et Vexillifero Justitiae Populi Florentini: In Hyeronimum Savonarolam, archetypon filii perditionis Antichristi, Gratulatio Ugolino Verini*, in Gherardi, *Nuovi documenti*, 303–8. As late as July 1497, Verino had signed the Piagnone petition to Alexander VI. On Verino, see also A. Lazzari, *Ugolino e Michele Verino: Studi biografici e critici* (Turin, 1897), 127–35, 193–9.

[147] See R. Marcel, *Marsile Ficin (1433–1499)* (Paris, 1958), 555 ff.; and Weinstein, *Savonarola and Florence*, 185–90.

[148] Marsilio Ficino, *Apologia Marsilii Ficini pro multis Florentinis ab Antichristo Hieronymo Ferrariense Hypocritarum summo deceptis ad Collegium Cardinalium*, in P. O. Kristeller, *Supplementum Ficinianum* (2 vols.; Florence, 1937), ii. 77–8.

their common predilection for millenarian expectations. Whereas Ficino envisaged a gradual reform, to be achieved by an intellectual élite, Savonarola had seen it as sudden, violent, and universal. More importantly, Ficino's religious syncretism and his reliance on astrological and philosophical speculation contrasted dramatically with Savonarola's pietism, his suspicion of profane learning including Platonism, and his reliance on Scripture as the source of all knowledge.[149]

Pietro Delfin, the General of the Camaldolese Order, was another whose initial admiration for Savonarola had gradually turned to outright opposition. His *Dialogus in Hieronymum ferrariensem*[150] was the culminating point of this transformation; and it denounced in especially strong terms the disobedience towards the orders of his superiors of which Savonarola had been guilty.[151] Gabriele Biondo, on the other hand, had no taint of former allegiance for which to atone. The youngest son of Flavio Biondo and parish priest of Modigliana, a Florentine dependency in the Romagna, Gabriele had all along been an outspoken opponent of Savonarola.[152] He had condemned him from the pulpit and had caused to be distributed throughout Modigliana, in defiance of the local *Podestà*, a letter sent by the Florentine *Signoria* to acquaint the

---

[149] Marsilio Ficino, *Libro . . . della cristiana religione* [Florence, 1476] (Hain 7071), fos. 3$^{r-v}$, 22$^r$. For Ficino's first doubts concerning Savonarola, see his letter to Giovanni Cavalcanti, 20 Dec. 1494, in Marsilio Ficino, *Opera omnia* (Basle, 1576), i. 963–4. On Savonarola and profane learning see e.g. his *Apologeticus de ratione poeticae artis* and *Trattato contra li astrologi* in *Scritti filosofici*, ed. G. Garfagnini and E. Garin (ENOS; 2 vols.; Rome, 1982–8), i. 209–370; for his specific attacks on Plato see e.g. *Prediche sopra i Salmi*, ii. 24, 36, 64; *Prediche sopra Ezechiele*, ed. R. Ridolfi (ENOS; 2 vols.; Rome, 1955), i. 329–30, 343–4; *Prediche sopra l'Esodo*, ii. 291.

[150] Pietro Delfin, *Dialogus in Hieronymum ferrariensem*, in Schnitzer, *Peter Delfin*, app. II, pp. 366–99. Delfin's gradual disenchantment can be traced in his letters: cf. ibid., App. I.

[151] Delfin, *Dialogus in Hieronymum ferrariensem*, 374–85.

[152] C. Dionisotti, 'Resoconto di una ricerca interrotta', *Annali della Scuola Normale Superiore di Pisa: Lettere, storia, filosofia*, 2nd ser. 37 (1968), 259–69; C. Vasoli, 'A proposito di Gabriele Biondo, Francesco Giorgio Veneto e Giorgio Benigno Salviati', *Rinascimento*, 2nd ser. 9 (1969), 325–30. For Gabriele's opposition to Savonarola, see his letters to Strinato Strinati, 26 July 1495 to 28 Apr. 1498, BL MS Add. 14088, fos. 189$^v$–191$^r$.

people with Savonarola's crimes.[153] Gabriele's hostility found written expression in his *Commentarius*, composed apparently in 1498,[154] its purpose being, in his words, to vanquish and to destroy the poisonous doctrines of Savonarola and of his followers.[155]

Once Savonarola's execution was a foregone conclusion, there was no real need for fresh denunciations of his heretical and schismatic teaching unless the object was to restore his followers to the fold. That the anti-Savonarolan polemicists should have been concerned to convince the Piagnoni of their leader's errors shows how great an impression Piagnoni polemicists had made during the preceding years of controversy. By their writings, they had succeeded in demonstrating to their adversaries that they were not merely the prophet's mouthpieces, but an independent force for reform in their own right. Even though for the moment they were silent, harassed by the civil and ecclesiastical authorities and stunned by the sudden turn of events, they were still very much in the minds of Savonarola's adversaries.

How deeply Giovanni Caroli was preoccupied with them is evident from the treatise which he composed in thanksgiving to Providence, now that the long reign of darkness —as he saw the era of Savonarola's popularity—was over. Produced in the weeks between Savonarola's arrest and execution, Caroli's *Conclusione . . . come la scientia d'Iddio è cagione delle cose*[156] is remarkable for the moderation of its approach towards Savonarola's followers. Clearly hoping to bring them back into conformity with the traditional Church, Caroli presented a drastically revised interpretation of

[153] Biondo, letter to Strinato Strinati, 28 Apr. 1498, BL MS Add. 14088, fos. 190$^v$–191$^r$.

[154] Biondo, *Commentarius*, ibid., fos. 29$^r$–63$^v$. In the selection of anti-Savonarolan writings in MS BNF Magl., VIII, 1443, where the only copy of Ficino's *Apologia* is preserved, there is also an extract from the *Commentarius*: BL MS Add. 14088, fos. 62$^v$–63$^r$; cf. MS BNF Magl., VIII, 1443, fo. 147$^{r-v}$.

[155] Biondo, *Commentarius*, fo. 50$^r$. It has, however, been suggested that Gabriele's real purpose was to cloak the unorthodox nature of his own views and that the anti-Savonarolan polemic was intruded into the *Commentarius* to give the impression that its author was a faithful defender of the Church: see Dionisotti, 'Resoconto', 262–4.

[156] Giovanni Caroli, 'Conclusione di frate Giovanni di Carlo come la scientia d'Iddio è cagione delle cose', MS BNF Conv. Sopp., C.8.277, fos. 232$^r$–242$^r$.

their role in the turmoil of the previous four years. They were no longer to be allotted an equal share of blame with Savonarola because they had been the gullible prey of his wily enticements.[157] The same policy of conciliation informed the treatise *Contra delirantes qui volunt adhuc fratrem Hieronymum rite et recte damnatum defendere*,[158] composed after Savonarola's execution by Marco Bossio, the Milanese Prior of the Humiliati Convent of Ognissanti.[159] Bossio's declared object was to convince the Piagnoni—the 'delirantes' of his title—that they had been misguided in their allegiance to him and should now renounce him at all speed, in fear for their immortal souls.[160] The mixture of true and false doctrine in Savonarola's teaching had in itself been a trap to the unwary, Bossio argued, concluding that:

in my opinion it would be safer and healthier to burn all of his writings . . . in detestation of such a crime and so that the memory of this pestiferous man may be erased from this earth and his name cancelled out in one generation; and so that it may never return.[161]

That the Piagnoni did indeed remain, as these calculated and threatening phrases assumed, a force to be reckoned with is apparent from the single work which broke their silence in this time of sorrow and dread. From the haven of Mirandola, Giovanfrancesco Pico sent to the Florentines, a few days after Savonarola's arrest, an impassioned protest against the prophet's sufferings in his own land.[162] Entreating them to stand firm in their devotion to the friar, Giovanfrancesco strove to impress upon the Piagnoni that their present sufferings were in themselves positive proof of all that

---

[157] Ibid., fos. 233ᵛ ff.

[158] Marco Bossio, *Contra delirantes qui volunt adhuc fratrem Hieronymum rite et recte damnatum defendere* [Florence, 1498].

[159] G. Tiraboschi, *Vetera Humiliatorum monumenta* (Milan, 1766), i. 284–5; Schnitzer, *Peter Delfin*, 266; and app. I, p. 356.

[160] Bossio, *Contra delirantes*, sig. aʳ.

[161] Ibid., sig. a3ᵛ: 'consilio meo tutius esset et salubrius omnia istius opera igni tradere . . . in detestatione tanti sceleris et ut memoria ipsius pestiferi hominis de terra penitus eraderetur et in generatione una deleatur nomen eius: nec in memoriam redeat'.

[162] Giovanfrancesco Pico, *Epistola . . . in favore de fra Hieronymo da Ferrara dappoi la sua captura* [Modena, 1498] (Reichling 1321).

Savonarola had taught, since he had warned that Christ's kingdom could not be established upon earth without sacrifice. Giovanfrancesco's words of exhortation were in fact to herald a new phase in the Piagnone movement. As the anti-Savonarolans had foreseen, the contagion did not end with the casting of Savonarola's ashes into the Arno. Far from being cowed into submission by their persecution, the Piagnoni became more than ever convinced of the truth of their cause and assured that it would ultimately triumph.

# 3

# *The Mystical Path to Reform*

## I

Of the attacks levelled against Savonarola in the immediate aftermath of the pamphlet war, the *Apologia* of Marsilio Ficino was among the most virulent.[1] Representing a complete reversal of his former position, it was Ficino's public renunciation of Savonarola. Once the heaven-sent saviour of Florence, Savonarola was now the Antichrist, the dread *Saevus Nero* of Christianity.[2] Important as this personal act of renunciation undoubtedly was, the *Apologia* was intended by Ficino to have a far greater significance. For Ficino too looked upon himself as a religious guide and leader;[3] and he now spoke as though his influence over his followers had been unaffected by Savonarola's apostolate. Having made his own decision to renounce the prophet, he hoped, by his words, to enable his erstwhile disciples to do the same.

His impassioned appeal met with little response. Those of his followers who had been drawn into the ranks of the Piagnoni—men like Giovanni Nesi, Domenico and Girolamo Benivieni, Bartolomeo della Fonte, and, for a while at least, Paolo Orlandini[4]—ignored his entreaties and remained staunchly loyal to

---

[1] See above, pp. 95–6.

[2] Marsilio Ficino, *Apologia*, in P. O. Kristeller, *Supplementum Ficinianum* (2 vols.; Florence, 1937), ii. 77, where he states that Savonarola should more correctly be called 'Sevonerola': a play on *Saevus Nero*. For details of this figure, cf. R. De Maio, *Riforme e miti nella chiesa del Cinquecento* (Naples, 1973), 57.

[3] Cf. P. O. Kristeller, 'Lay Religious Traditions and Florentine Platonism', *Studies in Renaissance Thought and Letters* (Rome, 1956), 99–122.

[4] For the three last, see below.

Savonarola. Refusing to accept the dichotomy which Ficino had tried to establish between Savonarola's ideas and his own, they continued to owe allegiance to both. To their minds, such a stance entailed no conflict of loyalty or belief. What enabled them to maintain this position will be one of the main themes of the present chapter.

Since they provide the clearest indications of the reasons behind their decisions, and because their experiences were shared by many other Florentines who looked on Savonarola and Ficino as their religious guides, the careers and writings of Giovanni Nesi and Domenico Benivieni will be examined in detail. As we shall see, they were able to overcome the difficulties inherent in Ficino's renunciation of Savonarola for different reasons. Either because he failed to appreciate the full extent of the problem, or because it was immaterial to his chief concerns, Nesi continued to uphold the doctrines of both teachers. Benivieni, on the other hand, was—though never explicitly—to jettison certain aspects of Ficino's thought in favour of those elements in Savonarola's teaching which particularly attracted him.

An acute apprehensiveness concerning the radical import of Savonarolan ideology had permeated the *Apologia*. In Ficino's view, the prophet's appeal to the general populace was fraught with danger. Already, in *Della cristiana religione*, Ficino had made it plain that intellectual training, and especially philosophical knowledge, were essential prerequisites for religious reform. In fact, he attributed the Church's corruption to the separation of wisdom from faith and to the involvement of laymen in spiritual life: 'oftentimes the unworthy zeal of ignorant persons ought to be called superstition rather than religion.'[5] The danger of lay involvement in religion was to become ever greater as Savonarola's teaching spread. After his death, it became a prominent element in Piagnone activity, as is exemplified in the notorious career of Pietro Bernardino, called 'dei fanciulli', whose life will also be studied in

---

[5] Marsilio Ficino, *Libro . . . della cristiana religione* [Florence, 1476] (Hain 7071), fo. 3ᵛ: 'spesso le vile cure degli ingnoranti superstitione più tosto che religione chiamare si conviene'.

this chapter. Radical and uncompromising, he embodied the worst excesses which Ficino had envisaged and had sought—in vain, as it turned out—to forestall.

## II

Giovanni Nesi was born in 1456 into a well-to-do Florentine family. Nothing is known of his formal education, but, judging by his cultural pursuits and later appointments as *Officiale di Studio*, it can be assumed that he followed a course of studies, most probably in the humanities, at the *Studio*. Though not spectacular, his public career was moderately successful. On three separate occasions, in 1485, 1499, and 1503, he sat in the Priorate. He was created *Officiale di Studio* in 1497 and 1499; and, in 1505–6, was appointed *Podestà* of Prato. A further indication of his standing is that he was often requested to attend the meetings of the *pratiche*.[6]

The yearning for religious reform which engaged the attention of many Florentine minds in the second half of the fifteenth century is vividly epitomized in Nesi's spiritual journey. He first began to make a name for himself as a result of the religious orations which, as a member, he was required to preach in various youth confraternities in Florence during the 1470s.[7] To belong to several

---

[6] A. Della Torre, *Storia dell'Accademia Platonica di Firenze* (Florence, 1902), 422–5, 692–701; C. Vasoli, 'Giovanni Nesi tra Donato Acciaiuoli e Girolamo Savonarola: Testi editi e inediti', *Memorie Domenicane*, NS 4 (1973), 103–8; D. Weinstein, *Savonarola and Florence: Prophecy and Patriotism in the Renaissance* (Princeton, NJ, 1970), 192 ff.; A. Verde, *Lo studio fiorentino 1473–1530: Ricerche e documenti* (4 vols. in 7; Florence, 1973–85), i. 280; iv/3: 1226–8, 1327–31, *et passim*; R. Bonfanti, 'Su un dialogo filosofico del tardo '400: Il "De moribus" del fiorentino Giovanni Nesi (1456–1522?)', *Rinascimento*, 2nd ser. 11 (1971), 203–21, esp. 212 n. 5.

[7] Nesi's orations, only one of which was published during his lifetime, have survived in at least three manuscript collections and have recently been published: the first two, MS BRF 2204 and MS BNF Magl., XXXV, 211 by Vasoli, 'Giovanni Nesi tra Donato Acciaiuoli e Girolamo Savonarola', 123–52; the third, University of Pennsylvania Library, Medici–Gondi Archive II, Lea MS 481, by O. Zorzi Pugliese, 'Two Sermons by Giovanni Nesi and the Language of Spirituality in Late Fifteenth-Century Florence', *Bibliothèque d'Humanisme et Renaissance*, 42 (1980), 641–56. For a discussion of sermons preached before

confraternities at once in this way was rare and revealed Nesi's propensity for religious discussion, which was to be one of his most enduring qualities.

This interest was always to be combined with a fascination for philosophical issues. Also in the 1470s, and like so many promising youths of the period, including the future Piagnoni Bartolomeo della Fonte and Jacopo Salviati, Nesi came under the tutelage of the revered moralist educator and humanist Donato Acciaiuoli.[8] While his influence was considerable, however, he was not the only person to whom Nesi looked for guidance in the formative years of his youth. As a letter from Ficino to Nesi, dated 1 July 1477 and expounding the Platonist arguments pertaining to the soul's immortality, indicates, Nesi was also in close contact with this exponent of a philosophical scheme and theory of civil conduct which rivalled those of Acciaiuoli.[9]

A product of Nesi's youthful investigation of the intricacies of moral philosophy, the treatise *De moribus* is especially interesting as an example of his eclecticism. In dialogue form, it purports to summarize a discussion on the *Nicomachean Ethics* in 1477 between Acciaiuoli and various disciples, among them Jacopo Salviati and another future Piagnone, Filippo Valori. The treatise was conceived by Nesi as a practical guide for Florentine youths contemplating a career in public service. How this aim could be reconciled with the dedication to Piero de' Medici, representative of a regime which Aristotle would scarcely have envisaged as ideal, is not made clear. Perhaps it was not merely the changed political situation, but the realization of this incongruity, which prompted Nesi to dedicate a later edition, prepared for the press in 1503, to the youths of Florence.[10]

---

confraternities in this way, see Kristeller, 'Lay Religious Traditions and Florentine Platonism', 104–6, and G. M. Monti, *Le confraternite medievali dell'alta e media Italia* (2 vols.; Florence (Venice), 1927), i. 187 ff.

[8] See *DBI*; E. Garin, 'Donato Acciaiuoli cittadino fiorentino', *Medioevo e Rinascimento* (Bari, 1954), 211–87; C. Trinkaus, *In Our Image and Likeness: Humanity and Divinity in Italian Humanist Thought* (2 vols.; London, 1970), ii. 644–50.

[9] Marsilio Ficino, *Opera omnia* (Basle, 1576), i. 774–6.

[10] Bonfanti, 'Su un dialogo filosofico del tardo '400', 204–7.

Viewed in isolation, the first three books of the *De moribus*, which comprised four books in all, would appear to confirm Nesi's Aristotelianism and his commitment to the belief that the *summum bonum* could best be achieved by active participation in the affairs of the state. In the fourth book, however, political activism ceased to be an end in itself, now being praised solely because it afforded unequalled opportunities to master one's passions and to acquire the tranquillity of mind necessary for speculation on the divine. Much as Ficino had done in his *Theologia platonica* and *De amore*, Nesi presented contemplation as the loftiest of man's pursuits. Like Ficino, moreover, he asserted that the constant practice of contemplation enables man to achieve intuitive knowledge of God in this life. Using words and symbols which betrayed his direct dependence on the master, Nesi expounded this theme: expressing the desire for God, innate in all men, as the soul's natural appetite for its creator and opting for the superiority of love and will over intellect and knowledge as means to overcome the obstacles hindering man's efforts to rise above his fallen self.[11]

These Neoplatonic themes were to receive further elaboration and refinement in the sermon on charity which Nesi preached before the confraternity of the Magi in 1486. Expounding the Pauline concept of charity as presented by Ficino, Nesi showed this form of love to be the key which binds men together and to which everything else must be subordinated. By loving his neighbour, he argued, man participates in God's love, thus attaining communion with Him. This concept provided Nesi with the answer to his quest for salvation. As is evident in his use of the terms *sommo bene* and spiritual happiness, he held that the soul's ascent to God is possible not only in the afterlife but can be fully accomplished here on earth. With the articulation of this belief, his religious thought reached its apogee. While in subsequent works he was to develop this theme, he was never to progress beyond it.[12]

---

[11]  Giovanni Nesi, 'De moribus', MS BMLF Plut. LXXVII, 24, fos. 137ʳ–139ᵛ, 143ᵛ, 148ʳ, 149ᵛ.

[12]  Giovanni Nesi, *Oratio de charitate habita in Collegio Magorum*, (Florence, 1486) (Reichling 1005), sig. b1ʳ⁻ᵛ *et passim*; repr. in Vasoli, 'Giovanni Nesi tra Donato Acciaiuoli e Girolamo Savonarola', 152–60. For discussion of this work, together with a substantial extract, see R. Hatfield, 'The Compagnia de' Magi',

The next ten years of Nesi's life are cloaked in silence. Nothing relating to his cultural and religious activities has survived for the period 1486–97. It is nevertheless clear that during these years, if not before, he came under Savonarola's sway. The sermon of 1486 reveals no Savonarolan influence, but, in view of the connection between S. Marco and the confraternity of the Magi, which met in the convent's sacristy,[13] it would seem likely that Nesi had known Savonarola at the time of his visit to Florence in 1482–7. Be that as it may, in 1497 Nesi broke his long silence with the publication of the *Oraculum de novo saeculo*. His decision to publish this, his major and best-known work, at the height of the pamphlet war conveys as nothing else could the sincerity of his commitment to the prophet. A public profession of loyalty to Savonarola, it caused Nesi to be numbered thereafter among his staunchest followers.[14]

Nesi's ability to combine what he regarded as the best of both the Ficinian and the Savonarolan worlds is plainly evident in his *Oraculum*. From the Savonarolan doctrine of reform, he drew only those elements which confirmed his own position. The impact of Savonarola's ideas upon his thought was thus inevitably circumscribed. The notions of reform and renewal expressed by Savonarola were incorporated into the *Oraculum*, but his essentially mystical vision of the soul's ascent to God was not only reiterated, but expanded. In Nesi's hands, Savonarola became the medium by which this mystical path was to be made known to mankind. Because Savonarola alone had received those mysteries essential to salvation and inherent in all religious and philosophical systems, he alone could fulfil this role, and herein lay his attraction.[15]

The reception accorded to the *Oraculum* gives ample proof of the idiosyncratic nature of the synthesis which Nesi found satisfactory. Even Savonarola and his followers could not bring themselves to discuss, let alone endorse, the religious programme there set out.

*Journal of the Warburg and Courtauld Institutes*, 33 (1970), 107–61; see also Zorzi Pugliese, 'Two Sermons by Giovanni Nesi', 645–7, 653.

[13] Hatfield, 'The Compagnia de' Magi', 108–9.
[14] See above, pp. 86–7.
[15] Giovanni Nesi, *Oraculum de novo saeculo* (Florence, 1497) (Hain 11693), e.g. sigs. a2ᵛ, d3ʳ⁻ᵛ.

However gratified by Nesi's declaration of support, they could not but have been struck by its failure to reconcile divergent religious currents. While grateful to Nesi, and determined to make as much capital as they could out of his declaration, they did not really fathom it, or feel fully at ease with its arguments. They commended it for its elegance, enthused over its learning, but steered well clear of any assessment of its religious message.[16] The fact that Nesi's views were often at variance with Savonarola's was not lost on Giovanni Caroli. In his *Contra Iohannis Nesii Oraculum de novo seculo*, he exploited the discrepancies to the full, adding fuel to his argument that the Savonarolan movement was a medley of disparate elements.[17]

The vicissitudes of Savonarola's apostolate and his eventual death moved Nesi deeply. In a remarkable series of poems, he expressed his increasing concern at the signs which portended the end of his and Savonarola's dreams. Almost daily, from October 1497 onwards, he confided to his *canzoniere*, which hitherto had comprised only occasional pieces of dubious literary worth, his forebodings and his disillusionment. Their depth of emotion and incisiveness of expression rank them among the best examples of contemporary Florentine religious verse. They show him coming ever closer to the conclusion that the reversal in Savonarolan fortunes was to be laid at the Florentines' door. In their sinfulness, scepticism, and obduracy lay the reasons for the failure of Savonarola's apostolate. They had spurned his teaching, derided his prophecies, and, with the complicity of the new Babylon, caused his death. Not only banned forever from partaking in the benefits of the promised millennium, they were now also marked out by God for retribution, and would be consigned to perdition.[18]

---

[16] Savonarola praised the *Oraculum* as a 'libretto di elegante litteratura' by 'Uno laico ma principe di scientia et di costumi rarissimi'; Domenico Benivieni went no further, stating simply that it had been composed 'elegantamente et eruditamente': Girolamo Savonarola, *Dyalogo della verità prophetica* [Florence, 1500] (Hain 14341) sigs. f5ᵛ–f6ʳ; Domenico Benivieni, *Dialogo, della verità della doctrina predicata da Frate Hieronymo da Ferrara nella ciptà di Firenze* (Florence, 1497) (*GW* 3846), sigs, a4ᵛ–a5ʳ.

[17] See above, p. 87.

[18] MS BRF 2962, pp. 87, 137, 209, 278 (manuscript pagination used). On this *canzoniere* see Verde, *Lo studio fiorentino*, iv/3: 1327–30.

Even these sad events, however, did not shake Nesi's faith. Instead, their effect was to confirm him in his predilection for the contemplative life. Beset by doubts concerning the adequacy of his own contribution to Savonarola's apostolate, he searched his conscience, seeking to know whether he had done everything in his power to support the prophet and promote his cause. More importantly, he asked himself, had he taken full advantage of Savonarola's teaching?[19] It was only to be expected that Nesi should have looked inward for an answer. It was equally inevitable that, within himself, he should have found the answer. The quest for salvation through mysticism was to be the subject of his last extant work. Influenced partly by the *Divina Commedia* and partly also by Matteo Palmieri's *Città di vita*, it is known, from its opening line, as *La viva luce*. It was composed shortly after Ficino's death in 1499.

The recondite imagery and profuse classical allusions of this long allegorical poem render it difficult of interpretation. Nesi undertook to describe a twofold journey: a spiritual pilgrimage to the heavenly city, on the one hand, and the soul's endeavour to grasp the divine essence, and thus to enjoy communion with God, on the other. In striking contrast to the optimistic *Oraculum*, *La viva luce* was pervaded by gloom and uncertainty. Nesi's pessimism stemmed from his conviction that, by executing Savonarola, the Florentines had removed from their midst the very man whom God had chosen to turn their city into a community of saints. Although haunted by this vision of what might have been, Nesi did not surrender to despair. While the opportunity to transform Florence into a city of the elect was gone forever, the path to salvation which he had mapped out remained, he believed, still accessible to individuals. In his scheme, the unattainable and yet haunting dream of the heavenly Jerusalem was Savonarola's; the aim of personal salvation and the means by which it was to be achieved were Ficino's. Because Nesi kept their respective contributions separate in his mind, he was not swayed by Ficino's abjuration of

---

[19] MS BRF 2962, pp. 49, 51, 135.

Savonarola, but continued to look upon both men as his and Florence's spiritual guides. For him, there was no problem of conflicting ideals, and in *La viva luce* he mourned the loss of both with equal sincerity.[20]

Throughout his career, Nesi had addressed himself exclusively to an intellectual élite, believing, like Ficino, that only men of exceptional piety and learning could profit from his teaching. Like Ficino, too, he was out of touch with, if not actually mistrustful of, the religious aims and practices of the masses.[21] But not everyone belonging to the Ficinian circle shared the same prejudices. One whose intellectual gifts were in no way inferior to Nesi's and who believed, as he did, in the efficacy of contemplation and mysticism as pathways to salvation, was to devote his life to propagating this message among the masses. His name was Domenico Benivieni, and his achievement was to give to contemplation and mysticism a popular face which they had not hitherto possessed.

The youngest of three brothers, all of whom were to become Savonarolan stalwarts, Domenico Benivieni was born in 1460. Like his brothers, Antonio and Girolamo, he received a most thorough formal education, obtaining a doctorate in the liberal arts and medicine at an uncommonly early age. In 1479, he was appointed reader in Logic at the *Studio*, a post from which he resigned in 1481. From then little is known of his career until 28 April 1491, when, through the patronage of Lorenzo and Pierfrancesco de' Medici, he was nominated for membership in the Chapter of Canons in the church

---

[20] Giovanni Nesi, 'Poema (filosofico-morale)' [i.e. *La viva luce*], MS BRF 2750, e.g. fos. 20$^{r-v}$, 31$^r$, 48$^v$, 64$^r$, 70$^v$. While Vasoli relates how Nesi had begun composition of this poem *before* 1499 (the date assigned to it by Della Torre), the part which is relevant to our purposes could not have been written before this year: Vasoli, 'Giovanni Nesi tra Donato Acciaiuoli e Girolamo Savonarola', 106–7; Della Torre, *Storia dell'Accademia Platonica di Firenze*, 698. It should not be assumed that Nesi's attitude was perhaps due to his ignorance of Ficino's abjuration. Despite the assertions of some historians—such as R. Marcel, *Marsile Ficin* (Paris, 1958), 555 ff. and Kristeller, *Supplementum Ficinianum*, ii. 76—Ficino's abjuration was known to Florentine contemporaries; indeed, the Piagnoni took revenge on Ficino for this betrayal by casting into doubt his Christian faith, see Pseudo-Burlamacchi, *La vita*, ed. P. Ginori Conti and R. Ridolfi (Florence, 1937), 79 and the letter of Fra Ambrogio Caterini Politi to a cardinal, dated 6 Dec. 1548 published by R. Ridolfi, *Gli archivi delle famiglie fiorentine* (Florence, 1934), 70.

[21] e.g. Nesi, *Oraculum*, sigs. a2$^r$, b5$^r$.

of S. Lorenzo. It would appear that he left the *Studio* in order to become a friar; but he was never to be professed and at some time during the decade he became *Spedalingo* at Pescia: a position generally reserved to clerics and involving religious rather than administrative duties. In any case, he was to be a canon in the church of S. Lorenzo from the time of his appointment in 1491 until his death in 1507.[22]

Despite the lack of concrete evidence concerning his activities in the 1480s, it is clear that Domenico's intellectual gifts were greatly esteemed in those years as his nickname 'Lo scotino' attests.[23] Ficino dedicated to him his treatise *De rationibus musicae*, praising him for his learning and especially for his knowledge of Platonic philosophy; and, in a letter of 1485, addressed him as a respected colleague.[24] His standing is further affirmed by Giovanni Pico, who wrote advising him of his intention of composing a commentary on Plato's *Symposium* and who spoke, in the Proem to *De ente et uno*, of his learning and honesty.[25] Domenico's appointment to the

---

[22] For Domenico's life in general, see *DBI* and C. Re, *Girolamo Benivieni fiorentino* (Città di Castello, 1906), 46–54. For his scholastic career, see Verde, *Lo studio fiorentino*, ii. 180–3. The suggestion that he entered a monastic order after resigning from the *Studio* is made in a document cited by Verde, ibid. 181, and is corroborated by Giovanni Caroli, 'Della verità della doctrina di fra Girolamo', MS BNF Conv. Sopp., D.9.278, fo. 109ʳ. For his appointment to the Chapter of S. Lorenzo, see D. Moreni, *Continuazione delle memorie istoriche dell'Ambrosiana R. Basilica di S. Lorenzo* (2 vols.; Florence, 1804–17), ii. 198. He seems to have held the post of Canon and *Spedalingo* concurrently since in 1494 an unsuccessful attempt was made by the Pescia authorities to deprive him of the post of *Spedalingo*; Verde, *Lo studio fiorentino*, iv/3: 1494–5. See also L. Polizzotto, 'Domenico Benivieni and the Radicalisation of the Savonarolan Movement', in C. Condren and R. Pesman Cooper (eds.), *Altro Polo: A volume of Italian Renaissance Studies*, (Sydney, 1982), 99–117.

[23] For indications of the currency of this nickname and of Domenico's standing in the eyes of the anti-Savonarolans, see two poems by Giovanni sarto fiorentino: 'Dimmi, Ischotino, vuo' tu stare a schotto' and 'O Ischotino, dì a' tuo' Piagnoni', in R. Ridolfi, *Studi savonaroliani* (Florence, 1935), 230; cf. Caroli's derisive version of the nickname, above p. 75.

[24] Marsilio Ficino, *De rationibus musicae*, in P. O. Kristeller, *Supplementum Ficinianum*, i. 51–6; Marsilio Ficino, *Opera omnia*, i. 873–4.

[25] Giovanni Pico, *Opera omnia* (Basle, 1572), i. 382; id., *De hominis dignitate, Heptaplus, De ente et uno*, ed. E. Garin (Florence, 1942), 387. Similar attestations of esteem were made by the *Otto di Guardia* in a letter sent to the Vicar of Pescia on Domenico's behalf. In it he is described as 'certamente creatura di dDio et docta et honestissima et gentile persona': Verde, *Lo studio fiorentino*, iv/3: 1494.

Chapter of S. Lorenzo thus came as the crowning tribute to a decade's achievement.[26]

Much has been written, especially by Domenico's brother Girolamo, concerning Domenico's first encounters with Savonarola at about the time of his appointment at S. Lorenzo. In his account, Girolamo was at pains to emphasize Domenico's initial disappointment with Savonarola's preaching style, though he went on to underline his subsequent admiration for and complete acceptance of Savonarola's teaching.[27] While there is no reason to doubt the main thrust of Girolamo Benivieni's account, he exaggerated the extent of his brother's dependence on Savonarola. Surviving evidence suggests, in fact, that by the time they met Domenico had already evolved a highly sophisticated religious message of his own. There is no indication that he abandoned or even radically altered this message to conform with Savonarola's teaching. Rather, he incorporated into his own structure of salvation those of Savonarola's tenets which either complemented or confirmed his own message: most notably, Savonarola's indictment of the Church, his prophecies of imminent tribulation, and, later, with reservations as we have seen, his civic millenarianism. Just as importantly, his meeting with Savonarola and doubtless also the example he set in the pulpit led Domenico to adopt a more accessible method of expounding his ideas. Both by training and by inclination, Domenico favoured the logical presentation of argument, the stylistic conceit, the rhetorical flourish. Though he was never able to free himself entirely from these scholastic and Ficinian preoccupations, he none the less managed to achieve a directness of approach and a clarity of presentation which endeared him to a surprisingly wide audience. For his work as a spiritual counsellor, this was a vital development.

Domenico was active as a spiritual counsellor from the late 1480s until he died. He is known to have advised at least two convents:

---

[26] He was proposed for the post by Lorenzo di Piero and Lorenzo di Pierfrancesco de' Medici: ibid. 1495, and ACSL Libro di Partiti del Capitolo di S. Lorenzo, 2366, fo. 34ᵛ.

[27] Girolamo Benivieni, *Epistola . . . mandata a Papa Clemente VII*, in app. to B. Varchi, *Storia fiorentina*, ed. G. Milanesi (3 vols.; Florence, 1858), iii. 307–30.

the Murate in Florence and S. Michele Arcangelo in Pescia. In addition, he counselled the villagers of Calamecca, Lanciuole, and Crespole, near Pescia. Others who placed themselves under his spiritual wardship were Pietro Bernardino, to whom we shall return, and the Dominican tertiary, Domenica Narducci del Paradiso, a mystic, prophetess, and miracle-worker to whom we shall also refer.

In counselling Domenico found his true calling. We can learn much concerning the nature of his counselling from the letters which he sent to his spiritual charges. Fifty letters survive, all but one of them in manuscript. The earliest, addressed to the villagers near Pescia, was written while Domenico held the post of *Spedalingo* there.[28] The others were composed between 1492 and 1500: three addressed to one Suor Benigna of the Murate;[29] one, published almost immediately as the treatise *Scala della vita spirituale sopra el nome Maria*,[30] addressed to a certain Suor Maria of an unnamed convent; and the remainder to the nuns of the convent of S. Michele in Pescia.[31] In both form and content, Domenico's letters belong to the tradition of the *epistola spirituale*, designed primarily to provide spiritual guidance when circumstances prevented the counsellor from preaching and ministering directly to his charges.

Mainly through the influence of Ficino and Savonarola, the devotional letter was at this time undergoing a revival in Florence. It is important to appreciate, however, that in his letters, as well as in his apologetic writings, Domenico drew on sources other than their teaching. He relied heavily, for instance, on Nicholas of

---

[28] '[Epistola] A' dilecti in Christo fratelli et sorelle habitanti nelle terre di Chalamech, di Lanciuole e di Crespole', BRF, MS 2405, fos. 99$^r$–114$^v$.

[29] Ibid., fos. 29$^r$–53$^v$, 54$^v$–72$^r$, 73$^r$–84$^v$. The first of these epistles has also been transcribed in the collection of letters to the nuns of the convent of S. Michele in Pescia, MS BRF 4088, fos. 11$^v$–33$^r$.

[30] *Scala della vita spirituale sopra el nome Maria composta da Maestro Domenico Benivieni canonico di San Lorenzo* [Florence, 1495] (*GW* 3848).

[31] MS BRF 4088 'Devote epistole del Reverendo Padre Maestro Domenico Benivieni', which contains forty-six letters, the first of which, fos. 1$^v$–11$^r$, has also been copied in BRF 2405, fos. 85$^r$–98$^v$. The typed inventory appended to BRF 4088, which is based on the erroneous consecutive numbering of the letters in the MS, is unreliable.

Cusa's *Docta ignorantia* and on S. Bonaventure's *Itinerarium mentis ad Deum*.[32] He was strongly influenced too by the mystical treatises of Jean Gerson, especially *De mystica theologia* and *De elevatione mentis in Deum*, whose texts, included in the edition of Gerson's *Opera omnia* in Domenico's possession, are lovingly annotated in his hand.[33] Most significantly, there is strong evidence that the *Imitation of Christ* was among Domenico's sources.[34] The emphasis on a theology of the Cross, the rejection of intellectual speculation, and the pietism all argue familiarity with and reliance on the *Imitation of Christ*.

All these elements were developed by Domenico into a synthesis which was not only internally consistent but also accessible to his charges. The resulting personal message of salvation was undoubtedly his most significant contribution to the Piagnone movement. Like Ficino and, to a lesser extent, Nicholas of Cusa, Domenico placed great emphasis on the redemptive and transfiguring power of love, which he also saw as the means whereby men, through charity, could achieve perfect union with God. Like them, moreover, he regarded contemplation as the perfect vehicle for the expression and development of these virtues.[35] At this point, however, he parted company with Ficino and Neoplatonism. He was well aware that despite Ficino's aspirations to be taken seriously as

[32] References to both these writers or their works abound in Domenico's writings, see e.g. MS BRF 2405, fos. 40ᵛ–41ʳ, 55ᵛ; id., *Scala della vita spirituale sopra el nome Maria*, sig. b3ᵛ. As E. Wind has demonstrated, interest in Nicholas of Cusa's works was widespread in Italy even before their publication in Milan in 1502: *Pagan Mysteries in the Renaissance* (London, 1967), App. I.

[33] Domenico's copy of Gerson's *Opera omnia* is in BNF Incunab. H.5.8–9. He acknowledged his debt to Gerson in his *Tractato* (Florence, 1496) (Hain 2784); his esteem for Gerson was also mentioned by Giovanfrancesco Pico in *Operecta dello M. S. Johanfrancesco Pico della Mirandola in defentione della opera di Pietro Bernardo da Firenze servo di Jesu Cristo: Amico Domenicho Benivieni fiorentino amico suo mandato addì . . . di settembre 1501*, ed. P. Cherubelli (Florence, 1943), 21, where Gerson is referred to as 'quel pietoso et dotto theologo . . . il quale tanto s[t]imate'.

[34] M. Petrocchi, *Una 'Devotio moderna' nel Quattrocento italiano?* (Florence, 1961), 51–3.

[35] Domenico Benivieni, 'Hepistola [Ia] . . . a suor Benigna; Epistola IIa . . . alla suora Benigna; Epistola A'dilecti . . . habitanti . . . di Chalamech, di Lanciuole ed di Crespole', MS BRF 2405, fos. 31ʳ⁻ᵛ, 33ʳ⁻ᵛ, 41ʳ, 61ᵛ–62ʳ, 109ᵛ–110ʳ, 113ᵛ; 'Devote epistole', MS BRF 4088, fos. 35ᵛ–39ᵛ, 42ʳ⁻ᵛ, 46ᵛ–47ᵛ, *passim*.

a religious guide and reformer Neoplatonism was too intellectualized and exclusive to provide a general guide for religious renovation.[36] Domenico knew he could not expect specialized philosophical knowledge from his charges; he was also far more concerned than Ficino with practical issues of conversion and salvation. He was thus obliged to propose a religious programme which would be comprehensible to the humblest of his followers.

The path to perfection, as Domenico called it, was based not upon learning but upon commitment and effort. In his scheme, the example of Christ's suffering and self-denial upon the Cross was the central feature. The essence of the true Christian life, Domenico argued, lay in the determination to imitate Christ and to bear all mortifications as He had done.[37] He admitted that the individual Christian could do nothing without the gift of divine grace which enabled him to yearn for and to work towards a perfect Christian life. This gift could not be obtained through one's own efforts.[38] Domenico nevertheless felt free to reassure his audience that, as long as everything possible was done in the way of preparation, and proof given of the desire to follow Christ's example, then grace would unfailingly be bestowed. The first step on the ladder to perfection therefore involved meditation and penance. Meditation both upon the death of Christ and upon the individual's own end would provide a spur towards contrition. From contrition, he should progress to penance, in whose daily experience he would prepare himself to receive God's gift of grace. His perseverance met its reward when God, of His infinite mercy, finally bestowed this gift.[39]

The receipt of grace carried unmistakable signs by which the individual could recognize his new state. It was also proof of elec-

[36] On this whole issue see Kristeller, 'Lay Religious Traditions and Florentine Platonism', 99–122.

[37] Benivieni, 'Devote epistole', MS BRF 4088, fos. 35$^v$, 51$^{r-v}$, 59$^v$, 73$^r$–76, passim; 'Hepistola [Ia] . . . a suor Benigna', MS BRF 2405, fos. 30$^r$, 41$^r$; the best summary of his teaching is in Scala della vita spirituale sopra el nome Maria.

[38] This position is close to but not identical with Ficino's own later doctrines, expounded publicly in his lessons on the epistles of S. Paul: Verde, Lo studio fiorentino, iv/3: 1270–3.

[39] Benivieni, Scala della vita spirituale sopra el nome Maria, sigs. a3$^v$–a4$^v$; see also Tractato, sigs. a3$^v$, a5$^{r-v}$; 'Devote epistole', fos. 119$^{r-v}$, 134$^v$.

tion. Secure in the new-found conviction that he was numbered among the saved, the Christian pilgrim had now to enter, with contrite heart and an unshakeable will, upon the way of purgation. To tarry at this stage, Domenico repeatedly warned his charges, was highly dangerous. In the path to perfection, 'not to go forward is to go backwards'.[40] The member of the elect had therefore to resist the inclination to be dragged down by his human frailties and by his past habits of sinfulness. He must strengthen the as yet imperfect gift of grace by continuing to ascend the increasingly difficult path towards perfection. He must, accordingly, renounce all earthly goods and affections. He had then to abandon all self-respect and *amor proprio*, submerging himself in his work for the greater glory of God, mindful, however, not to fall into excesses.[41] Only in this way could true humility be acquired: this being the essential prerequisite for the divine illumination which would enable him to discern true teaching from false; to know divine revelation from diabolic illusion. This light would enable him to become conversant with things divine and, above all, to come closer to God. Taking this path, the true Christian was thus freed to achieve perfect union with God. While yet in this life, he would then be in the world but not of it.[42] Domenico did not underestimate the difficulties which his path presented. He warned his hearers of the worldly scorn which, as well as their own doubts and fears, could weaken the resolve of his pilgrims and force them back into sinful conformity.[43] All the more reason, therefore, that they should not slacken. Mindful of the scorn and self-doubt which had been part of Christ's sacrifice on the Cross, they must press forward undeterred.[44]

---

[40] Benivieni, *Scala della vita spirituale sopra el nome Maria*, sig. a3ᵛ: 'non andare innanzi è tornare indietro'; identical phrase in 'Devote epistole', fo. 119ʳ.

[41] Of this concern for moderation or 'discretione' the most telling evidence is his 'Ragione del corpo all'anima', MS ACDC, Codice O, fo. 120ʳ, sent to Domenica Narducci, known as Suor Domenica del Paradiso, in order to have her treat her own body more mercifully.

[42] Benivieni, *Scala della vita spirituale sopra el nome Maria*, sigs. a5ᵛ–a9ᵛ.

[43] Domenico's inner doubts regarding the possibility of union with God, expressed by the soul in ibid., sig. b4ᵛ, are dispelled by Domenico himself in sig. b5ʳ and by the Virgin Mary in a direct appeal to the soul in sigs. b9ʳ–b10ᵛ.

[44] Ibid., sig. a12ʳ⁻ᵛ; 'Hepistola [Ia] . . . a suor Benigna', fos. 40ʳ–42ᵛ; 'Devote epistole', fos. 65ʳ–66ᵛ, 126ʳ–129ʳ.

Domenico incorporated into his message the teaching of Savonarola regarding tribulation and renewal. As the controversy surrounding Savonarola's apostolate gathered momentum and as more and more ecclesiastics voiced their opposition to him, Domenico took up the task of Savonarola's defence. As we have seen, the experience of controversy had the effect of altering and even of radicalizing his message. The strength and virulence of the opposition he encountered caused him to temper his optimism that the restoration of the essential elements of true Christian living would shortly be achieved. He also came to the conclusion that the machinations of the opponents of Savonarola and of religious reform would prevent many individuals from heeding his call to personal salvation.[45]

Without hesitation, Domenico laid upon the clergy the responsibility for the worsening of conditions conducive to reform. Clerics both high and low, secular and regular, came under his attack. Instead of preaching the word of God, he argued, they spent their time discussing its purpose and relevance. No longer sustained by faith and refusing to be directed by the simple message of the Gospel, they strove to fathom the mysteries of Scripture by intellectual means alone. Worst of all, their pride and their submission to the enticements of profane learning caused them to dismiss as simpletons those who strove to live according to God's word. The clergy poured scorn on all who, believing that only through the 'folly of the Cross' (*stoltitia della Crocie*) could the highest knowledge of God be obtained, persisted in leading their lives in imitation of Christ. Notwithstanding his status, training, and background, Domenico was driven to the conclusion that his fellow clerics had caused the present degeneration of the Church Militant.[46] Where this conclusion would lead, he may not have foreseen. But the effect of his teaching upon his hearers was to offer them a path to salvation which was independent of the existing ecclesiastical hierarchy.

[45] Domenico Benivieni, '[Epistola] Alle dilecte suore di San Michele', MS BRF 2405, fos. 97ᵛ–98ᵛ; 'Devote epistole', fos. 150ᵛ–158ᵛ.

[46] Benivieni, 'Hepistola [Ia] . . . a suor Benigna', fos. 30ʳ, 32ᵛ–33ʳ, 34ʳ–37ʳ, quotation on fo. 40ʳ; *Dialogo della verità della doctrina predicata da Frate Hieronymo*, sigs. b1ʳ–b2ᵛ; and esp. *Tractato . . . in defensione et probatione della doctrina et prophetie predicate da Frate Hieronymo*, sigs. a3ʳ⁻ᵛ, b8ʳ⁻ᵛ.

Domenico contended that the clergy practised heinous misdeeds upon the faithful. Selfishly seeking to safeguard their own privileges and prerogatives, they had erected between God and man an impenetrable barrier of ritual and ceremony. Not content to decree what form devotion should take, they committed the further offence of presuming to assert that all devotion must be channelled through themselves. By restricting access to the Scriptures, opposing the practices of silent prayer and contemplation, and belittling the virtues of poverty, humility, chastity, and simplicity, they had succeeded in undermining the fundamental tenets of the Christian faith.[47]

Savonarola's trial and eventual execution in 1498 dashed Domenico's hopes. As he acknowledged in his letters to the nuns of S. Michele, the prospect of overthrowing the forces of evil was now remote, as was the instigation of a universal and lasting reform.[48] Savonarola's sufferings at the hands of the ecclesiastical hierarchy were shared by Domenico, who, because of his support for Savonarola and his advocacy of Church reform, also experienced the force of their antagonism. In the months preceding the execution of Savonarola, Domenico was suspended from the Chapter of Canons of S. Lorenzo.[49] Shortly after Savonarola's end, he was arraigned before an ecclesiastical tribunal, heavily fined, and commended to journey to Rome, covered by exorbitant securities, to account to the Pope for his actions.[50] The result, in terms of Domenico's theological programme, was to turn him to mysticism as never before. In this way, the effect of Savonarola's death was to underline Domenico's ultimate independence of him. It strengthened him in the conviction that salvation could best be achieved through one's own efforts, by seeking God in one's own heart and striving to share the sufferings of His Passion. In these times, marked by persecution and by a wilfully induced 'famine of the

---

[47] Benivieni, *Tractato*, sigs. a3$^v$, b8$^{r-v}$, c3$^v$.

[48] Benivieni, '[Epistola] Alle dilecte suore di San Michele', MS BRF 2405, fos. 85$^{r-v}$, 98$^v$; see also 'Devote epistole', fos. 160$^v$–161$^r$, 166$^v$–168$^r$.

[49] ACSL Libro di Partiti del Capitolo di S. Lorenzo, 2366, fo. 64$^r$; Moreni, *Continuazione delle memorie istoriche . . . di S. Lorenzo*, i. 154–5.

[50] Piero Parenti, *Istorie fiorentine*, ed. J. Schnitzer (Leipzig, 1910), 283–4. The surviving part of the warrant is printed in Verde, *Lo studio fiorentino*, ii. 182–3.

word of God',[51] the true Christian had to take refuge in the haven of the Cross. Only thus could salvation be assured. The words rang like a litany through his last epistles to the nuns of S. Michele: 'the loving Cross and tormented love. Love and the Cross. The Cross and love. That is the way.'[52]

So attractive was Domenico's message that he was soon to acquire a considerable popular following. The mystical strain in his teaching proved particularly enticing as demonstrated by the careers of a certain Dorotea di Lanciuole and of her small band of women followers from the same village. Domenico's influence is even clearer in the case of his spiritual ward and Dorotea's adversary, Domenica Narducci, whose visions, mystical transports, and victorious struggles over devils were to keep Florence in awe for years. Domenico's call for personal perfection combined as it was with a claim that this could be achieved without recourse to clerical assistance—or, worse, despite their interference—assumed, a yet more radical aspect in the hands of Pietro Bernardino. In Bernardino's writings and actions, Benivieni's views were invested with a purpose and significance which went far beyond their originator.

## III

In September 1501 Giovanfrancesco Pico della Mirandola wrote a long letter of commendation to Domenico Benivieni. Its subject was the Florentine Pietro Bernardino (or, Bernardo) dei fanciulli, who, with a small number of followers, had recently sought refuge in Mirandola. Giovanfrancesco Pico was extravagant in his praise. Emphasizing that he spoke not from hearsay, but from personal knowledge, he stated again and again that Bernardino's life and teaching were above reproach. Bernardino's doctrine, the letter emphasized, accorded fully with Scripture and with the reforming programme which Savonarola had advocated; and his divine man-

---

[51] Benivieni, '[Epistola] Alle dilecte suore di San Michele', MS BRF 2405, fos. 85ʳ, 98ʳ.

[52] Ibid., fo. 97ᵛ: 'la croce amorosa et l'amore cruciato. Amore et croce. Croce et amore. Questa è la via.'

date had been authenticated by numerous visions. Clearly, the charges of heresy now being levelled against him in Florence were baseless, and had been devised by the enemies of reform to discredit Bernardino in the eyes of his followers.[53]

The initial impression given by the letter—an impression which Giovanfrancesco did his utmost to encourage—is that nothing could be more natural than for him to come to the aid of a fellow Piagnone whose religious ideals had come under attack. On a second reading, however, this impression fades before a number of pressing questions. As the letter makes clear, Domenico Benivieni had been Bernardino's spiritual adviser before the flight from Florence.[54] No one, therefore, should have been less in need than he of an account, in minute detail, of his charge's views and activities. Why, then, should Giovanfrancesco have gone to such pains to give this account? Why, in addition, should he have insisted that Bernardino always spoke of his adviser with reverence, wished to remain in his charge, and promised to obey him in the future as he had done in the past? Above all, why should Giovanfrancesco have felt it necessary to labour the fact that Bernardino's doctrine was dependent both upon Scripture and upon the teaching of Savonarola before him?

It is clear that a breach must have occurred between Domenico Benivieni and Pietro Bernardino: a breach so severe as to warrant the intervention of Giovanfrancesco. To understand what had caused this rift within the Piagnoni's ranks, we must understand Bernardino's career in all its colourful phases. Complex as these were, they had as their unifying theme a preoccupation with the divine mission of the Florentine youth, or *fanciulli*. A refusal to be relieved of his duties towards the *fanciulli* was the one condition which Bernardino, using Giovanfrancesco as his mouthpiece, placed upon his request to be restored to Domenico Benivieni's care;[55] and the belief in their vital role, which he had long held, was never to desert him.

---

[53] Giovanfrancesco Pico, *Operecta . . . in defentione della opera di Pietro Bernardo da Firenze*, 9–10, 14, 15, 17, 18, 19–20, 23, 24.
[54] Ibid. 21, 25.          [55] Ibid. 21, 25.

A sculptor from the parish of S. Lorenzo,[56] Bernardino had taken the first steps in his career as a lay preacher in the recently reorganized youth confraternities of Florence. As we have seen, in order the better to fulfil Savonarola's religious programme, they had agreed to reorganize themselves radically, relinquishing, in the process, some of the privileges which they had hitherto jealously guarded. The regrouping was masterminded by Fra Domenico da Pescia, to whom Savonarola had delegated the reform of the Florentine *fanciulli*. The confraternities became a major instrument of Savonarolan reform, playing an especially important part in the charitable drives and campaigns against vanities.[57]

It is likely that, in keeping with the general practice, Bernardino had joined a confraternity in early adolescence.[58] In any case, by 1496, when he would have been about 21 years of age, he had risen to a position of some eminence in at least three: those of the Purification of the Virgin Mary and of S. Zanobi, the Archangel Raphael, and S. Giovanni Evangelista.[59] He was connected also with the adult Company of the Disciplinati della Cappella di S. Simone e S. Taddeo (also known as the Company of the Gesù Pellegrino), or, which is more likely, with a boys' confraternity

---

[56] On Bernardino, see Bartolomeo Cerretani, 'Istoria fiorentina', MS BNF II.III.74, fos. 274ᵛ–274ᵛ [*bis*]; Parenti, *Istorie fiorentine*, 292–3; ASF Signori, Carteggi, Missive Ia Cancelleria, 54, fos. 97ʳ⁻ᵛ, 105ʳ; J. Schnitzer, 'Pietro Bernardo il capo degli *Unti*', *Ricerche Religiose*, 4 (1930), 317–32; id., *Savonarola* (2 vols.; Milan, 1931), ii. 430, 444, *et passim*; Weinstein, *Savonarola and Florence*, 324–33; C. Vasoli, 'L'attesa della nuova era in ambienti e gruppi fiorentini del Quattrocento', *L'attesa dell'età nuova nella spiritualità della fine del medioevo* (Todi, 1962), 370–42; id., 'Pietro Bernardino e Gianfrancesco Pico', *L'opera e il pensiero di Giovanni Pico della Mirandola nella storia dell'Umanesimo* (Florence, 1965), ii. 281–99; id., 'Une secte hérétique florentine: Les *Oints*', *Hérésies et sociétés dans l'Europe pré-industrielle 11ᵉ–18ᵉ siècles*, (Paris, 1968), 259–71; *DBI*.

[57] Domenico da Pescia, *Epistola . . . mandata a' fanciulli fiorentini* (Florence, 1497) (*GW* 8636), fo. 1ᵛ; Girolamo Benivieni, *Commento . . . sopra a più sue canzone et sonetti dello amore et della Belleza Divina* (Florence, 1500) (Hain 2788), fos. 111ʳ–116ᵛ; Pseudo-Burlamacchi, *La vita*, 120–7; and see Ch. 1.

[58] R. C. Trexler, 'Ritual in Florence: Adolescence and Salvation in the Renaissance', in C. Trinkaus and H. A. Oberman (eds.), *The Pursuit of Holiness in Late Medieval and Renaissance Religion* (Leiden, 1974), 210.

[59] Pietro Bernardino, *Epistola di Bernardo de' fanciulli della città di Firenze mandata a epsi fanciulli el dì di sancto Bernaba apostolo adì XI di giugnio MCCCCLXXXXVII* [Florence, 1500] (*GW* 3896), sigs. a1ʳ–a3ʳ.

associated with it and sharing its meeting-place in the convent of Sta Maria Novella.[60] Two of these, the Company of S. Giovanni Evangelista and the Company of the Purification of the Virgin Mary and of S. Zanobi, were closely controlled from S. Marco. Savonarola himself preached to the former on many occasions;[61] and its members looked to him for guidance, often meeting at S. Marco to seek his advice.[62] The contacts with the Company of the Purification were even closer. From its very inception, it had been attached to S. Marco and had held all its meetings there.[63] Since, furthermore, it had been founded with the express purpose of encouraging youths to embrace a clerical vocation, it was the subject of special supervision and care.[64]

At this time, relations between the confraternity and S. Marco were strained because the friars wanted it to vacate its premises in order to enlarge the convent[65]—an expansion rendered necessary by the wondrous increase in the number of novices attracted to S. Marco by Savonarola.[66] None the less, relations between the offi-

---

[60] Pietro Bernardino, sigs. a2ʳ. a3ᵛ. Although the Company of the Gesù Pellegrino is not mentioned by name, this can be deduced from the fact that Bernardino preached in its meeting-place on many occasions, beginning on 28 Oct. 1496, the feast day of the company's patrons, S. Simone and S. Taddeo. It is likely that the boys' confraternity was that of the Purità, which is the only such adolescent confraternity known to have been meeting at Sta Maria Novella: see G. Aiazzi (ed.), *Ricordi storici di Filippo di Cino Rinuccini dal 1282 al 1460 colla continuazione di Alamanno e Neri suoi figli fino al 1506* (Florence, 1840), 246; Monti, *Le confraternite medievali dell'alta e media Italia*, i. 259.

[61] I. del Lungo, *Florentia: Uomini e cose del Quattrocento* (Florence, 1897), 194; Monti, *Le confraternite*, i. 189.

[62] I. G. da Hemso (ed.), 'La vita di Giovanni da Empoli, da che nacque a che morì, scritta da Girolamo da Empoli, suo zio', *ASI*, app. III (1846), 22–3.

[63] L. del Migliore, 'Zibaldone', MS BNF Magl., XXV, 418, fos. 35ʳ, 37ʳ; Monti, *Le confraternite*, i. 183–4; S. Loddi, 'Notizie del Convento di S. Marco', MS ACSM (no location number), fo. 32ʳ⁻ᵛ.

[64] L. del Migliore, 'Zibaldone', fo. 37ʳ; Loddi, 'Notizie del Convento di S. Marco', fo. 32ʳ; Monti, *Le confraternite*, i. 184. There is, however, no specific mention of this aim in the confraternity's statutes: MS BNF Magl., VIII, 1500.

[65] Roberto Ubaldini, 'Annalia Conventus Sancti Marci', MS BMLF S. Marco 370, fo. 17ʳ; Compagnia della Purificazione della Vergine e di S. Zanobi, 'Libro di Ricordi', 2 vols. bound together, MS ASF Comp. Sopp. 1646, vol. i (1501–25) fo. CCXLIIIIᵛ. The confraternity was first asked to vacate its meeting-place in 1496 for other premises, still in the convent's grounds.

[66] See below, Ch. 5, n. 72.

cials of the confraternity and the friars remained outwardly close with the friars regularly alternating with the monks of the Badia and of the Cestello as spiritual correctors and counsellors.[67] While it is likely that Pietro Bernardino's membership of the companies of S. Giovanni Evangelista, the Purification of the Virgin Mary and of S. Zanobi, and the Archangel Raphael pre-dated the reorganization of 1494–6, it is only for the subsequent period that we have a sufficiently detailed account of his activities to be able to draw firm conclusions concerning his status and influence. His main duty, and certainly the one to which he himself attached greatest importance, was to preach to the youths of these confraternities.[68] He was also charged with the responsibility of leading a certain number of youths in processions and, presumably, of organizing and deploying them for the various campaigns against sins and vanities.[69] These activities would seem consistent with the duties pertaining to the newly created office of custodian, at least as Fra Domenico da Pescia envisaged it.[70]

Although this may well have been Bernardino's official position, a closer examination of his activities reveals that he performed functions not easily reconcilable with that office. Unlike other custodians, for example, he did not confine his activities to any one of the four newly formed confraternal groups (which had been reorganized according to the four quarters of the city), but extended them over two: those of the quarters of Sta Maria Novella and S. Giovanni.[71] A similar freedom of action was enjoyed by the youths

---

[67] Compagnia della Purificazione della Vergine e di S. Zanobi, 'Libro di Ricordi', vol. i. fo. LX[r].

[68] Pietro Bernardino, *Epistola . . . a' fanciulli*, sigs. a1[v]–a3[v].

[69] Ibid., sigs. b1[v]–b2[r].

[70] Domenico da Pescia, *Epistola . . . mandata a' fanciulli fiorentini* f. [3][r]; Pseudo-Burlamacchi, *La vita*, 122.

[71] The companies with which Bernardino was associated were distributed in these quarters, as follows: the Purification of S. Zanobi met in S. Marco in the quarter of S. Giovanni; S. Giovanni Evangelista met in the Old Church of S. Trinita in the parish of S. Lorenzo in the same quarter; the remaining two were attached to the church of Sta Maria Novella and the Ospedale della Scala respectively, both situated in the quarter of Sta Maria Novella. That there was only one custodian for each quarter is confirmed by Filippo de' Nerli, *Commentari dei fatti civili occorsi dentro la città di Firenze dall'anno 1215 al 1537* (2 vols.; Trieste, 1859), i. 123.

in his care, who followed him in a body wherever he went, as though they belonged to no confraternity in particular.[72] The impression created is that of a small activist élite, freed from restrictions and thus able to go with Bernardino, like a task force, wherever he felt himself to be most needed. Unusual, too, was the number of sermons which he preached. As we have seen with Giovanni Nesi, members of some confraternities were required, as part of their training in religious doctrine, to preach to the assembled *confratelli*. Judging by the number of sermons preached by Nesi, the most active confraternal preacher of the pre-Savonarolan period, the members of the confraternities were seldom expected to preach more than once a year.[73] Bernardino, on the other hand, is known to have delivered sermons on at least seven occasions in the five months between 28 October 1496 and 26 March 1497.[74] That the real number was actually much greater is suggested by the fact that, of the seven sermons which Bernardino mentioned in the *Epistola* from which this information comes, five had been preached between the first Sunday in Lent and Easter Sunday 1497: that is, on each of the Sundays in Lent but two. It is highly probable, therefore, that he preached regularly every Sunday: if not throughout the year, then at least during such solemn liturgical seasons as Advent and Lent. The conclusion is inescapable that, far from being an ordinary member, however highly placed, of the Savonarolan confraternal structure, Bernardino occupied a peculiarly privileged position within it: a position, moreover, which was somewhat at odds with his youth and lay status.

He could only have achieved such a position with the protection and active support of Fra Domenico da Pescia. It would seem, from Bernardino's account of their relationship, that he had first come to Domenico da Pescia's attention when the confraternities were being reorganized. With disarming candour, Bernardino explains that

---

[72] Pietro Bernardino, *Epistola . . . a' . . . fanciulli*, sigs. a2ᵛ–a3ʳ.

[73] The five of Nesi's youthful sermons which have survived were preached in the period 1472–8. See above, p. 102.

[74] Pietro Bernardino, *Epistola . . . a' . . . fanciulli*, sigs. a1ᵛ–a3ᵛ; id., '[Epistola] Petrus Bernardus de Florentia inutilis et indignus servulus Jesus Christi et omnis puerorum bone voluntatis, veritatis amatoribus', MS BNF Magl., XXXV, 116, fo. 68ᵛ.

Domenico da Pescia was much struck by his piety and by the divine revelations which he had received. The import of these visions, which Bernardino had confided to Domenico da Pescia, was that he had been singled out by God to play a leading role in the reform of the *fanciulli*.[75] Fra Domenico—by all accounts 'a man of great purity, but truly obstinate, and far too ready to believe in revelation and the dreams of women and weak, addled brains'[76]—took heed of Bernardino's words, and afforded him the means to carry out the plans which God had revealed to him. For some time yet, even so, the relationship between the two remained that of master and disciple. But, soon after March 1497, when Bernardino had a vision in which he learned that God desired him to be of equal authority with Fra Domenico in reforming the Florentine *fanciulli*, this changed. Informed of the news, Fra Domenico da Pescia dutifully bowed his head to the will of God.[77]

Thereafter, while never denying his debt to Savonarola and to Fra Domenico in particular, Bernardino claimed, by virtue of his direct inspiration from God that he was beholden to no man for his doctrine or his actions. He was thus placed outside the existing structure of authority: a change exemplified in his changed status in relation to Domenico da Pescia. Their former relationship, of master and disciple, had ceased. Possessed now of a divine mandate, Bernardino set about fulfilling the duties which God had entrusted to him. Assuming a personal responsibility for the *fanciulli*, he addressed to them a letter of exhortation. Dated 11 June 1497, the *Epistola . . . a' . . . fanciulli* attests to the seriousness with which Bernardino approached his mission of instructing the Florentine youth in a Christian way of life. Written when famine and plague

---

[75] Bernardino, '[Epistola] . . . veritatis amatoribus', fos. 67ᵛ–68ᵛ; cf. Giovanfrancesco Pico, *Operecta*, 13–14, 17.

[76] P. Villari, *La storia di Girolamo Savonarola e de' suoi tempi* (2 vols.; Florence, 1930), vol. ii, app., p. cclix, deposition by Fra Roberto Ubaldini: 'huomo di buona purità, ma di dura cervice, et troppo credulo a revelatione et sogni di donne et di capi deboli et stolti'.

[77] In 'Pietro Bernardo', 319, J. Schnitzer states that the vision took place in 1496, but from the context in Bernardino's '[Epistola] . . . veritatis amatoribus', fo. 68ʳ, it is clear that the date is given in the Florentine style. Cf. also Pico, *Operecta*, 14.

were raging in Florence,[78] it urged the *fanciulli* to hold firm in their beliefs despite the present tribulations. This *Epistola* was the first of many works dedicated to Bernardino's reforming mission. During his career he was to attract a considerable number of adult followers, who attended his sermons and lent support to his activities.[79] He was always to maintain, however, that his primary duty was to the *fanciulli*. His sermons were addressed to them alone and his activities were wholly determined by their needs and aspirations. The *Epistola . . . a' . . . fanciulli* may be considered in conjunction with Bernardino's most ambitious work: the *Compendio di Contemplatione*, which was a synthesis of a series of sermons preached in the latter part of 1497 and in March 1498. The sermons had been delivered partly before the Company of S. Giovanni Evangelista and partly in a house belonging to the Martelli family and situated in the Florentine suburb of S. Gervasio.[80] Both works reveal Bernardino's concern for the moral and spiritual welfare of the *fanciulli*.

In the *Epistola . . . a' . . . fanciulli*, he accepted and reiterated Savonarola's message of tribulation and renewal, expressing it in almost identical terms and using examples which Savonarola had already made famous.[81] The hardships at present besetting Florence were taken as evidence that this message was true. Since the tribulations had come as foretold, Bernardino argued, then so would deliverance and the promised glory. The ark in which all the elect were to take refuge had been constructed; everything was in

---

[78] Luca Landucci, *Diario fiorentino dal 1450 al 1516 continuato da un anonimo fino al 1542*, ed. I. del Badia (Florence, 1883; repr. 1969), esp. 150, 152.

[79] Among Bernardino's adult followers were Rafaello di Corso della Colomba and Piero Temperani, for whom see Parenti, *Istorie fiorentine*, 293–4; and also Ser Giuliano da Ripa, for whom see below.

[80] Pietro Bernardino, *Compendio di Contemplatione nel quale si contenghono septe Contemplationi conforme a septe doni dello Spirito sancto: Ad inducere la universa età puerile al dispregio et odio delle cose del mondo et ad amore et desiderio delle cose del paradiso* [Florence, 1498] (*GW* 3895), sig. d6r.

[81] Bernardino's statement 'che la città di Firenze ha essere più riccha che mai, più potente che mai et più gloriosa che la fusse mai', for example, may be compared with Savonarola's 'che Firenze sarà più gloriosa, più ricca, più potente che mai fusse': Bernardino, *Epistola . . . a' . . . fanciulli*, sig. a1r, cf. Savonarola, *Prediche sopra Aggeo*, ed. L. Firpo (ENOS; Rome, 1965), 166.

readiness; and all that remained to be done was for the children of Florence to pray to God to make them worthy of partaking in the imminent rewards.[82] In one important respect, however, Bernardino was not content slavishly to follow the doctrine of Savonarola. He differed concerning the role which these children would have in the coming reform. Disillusioned by the unrepentant sinfulness of the Florentine populace, both Savonarola and Domenico da Pescia had come to believe that the adult population would be like those Israelites who had died in the desert.[83] Only their children would enter the Promised Land. Notwithstanding this conviction and their earlier intentions, Savonarola and Fra Domenico were forced by political opposition to conclude that the children would not take an active part in reform. Instead, they now argued, the children had to be carefully nursed along the way lest they stray from the paths of righteousness because of inexperience and lack of purpose.[84] By contrast, Pietro Bernardino remained convinced of the children's unlimited potential. He continued to believe that the tender age of the children, far from disqualifying them from a major role, was in fact their greatest asset. It meant that they had grown up under the new dispensation, and thus, being sheltered from corruption, had been able to preserve their innocence. Their virtue was a light to all. As Bernardino saw it, reform was not possible without them. 'Except ye . . . become as little children,' Christ had said, 'ye shall not enter into the kingdom of heaven' (Matt. 18: 3).[85] Unlike the sages of the world, the *fanciulli*, Bernardino maintained, were by their very innocence endowed with an intuitive knowledge of the divine will, and were thus able to put into effect God's plans for reform.[86]

---

[82] Bernardino, *Epistola . . . a' . . . fanciulli*, sigs. a1r–a3v, b4r.

[83] Savonarola, *Prediche sopra l'Esodo*, ed. P. G. Ricci (ENOS; 2 vols.; Rome, 1956), i, 120.

[84] Domenico da Pescia, *Epistola . . . mandata a' fanciulli fiorentini*, fo. 1v. On the children's reform, see Ch. 1 above.

[85] Bernardino, *Epistola . . . a' . . . fanciulli*, sigs. a7v, a8r–v. Fra Domenico da Pescia had preached a sermon on this text in 1495 but had not expounded it as radically as Pietro Bernardino was to do: see *Predica di fra Domenico da Pescia facta in Sancta Reparata: A dì 29 di settembre 1495*, in Savonarola, *Prediche sopra i Salmi* (Bologna, 1515), sigs. II2r–II4v.

[86] Bernardino, *Epistola . . . a' . . . fanciulli*, sigs. a5v, b1v.

In his discussion of the path to salvation in the *Epistola
. . . a' . . . fanciulli* and in the *Compendio di Contemplatione*, Bernardino used arguments which have no exact parallels in the writings either of Savonarola or of Domenico da Pescia. In contending that, in order to be saved, the true Christian must devote all his energies to loving God; in denying that this love could be acquired by mere theological and philosophical learning; in asserting that it could be attained only by following the example of Christ's sufferings; in emphasizing that the Bible was the only source of spiritual knowledge; and in extolling the benefits of contemplation as the sole way in which men could separate themselves from the temptations of the world,[87] Bernardino was drawing on the teaching of Domenico Benivieni. Although it is not known when the two men first came into contact with each other, they moved in the same circles—both being associated, for instance, with the Company of the Purification of the Virgin Mary and of S. Zanobi—and it is significant that, within these circles, Domenico Benivieni was the most articulate, if not the only, exponent of these tenets.

Giovanni Caroli, as we have seen, was one who failed signally to come under Pietro Bernardino's spell. He regarded the *fanciulli* with great suspicion: finding in their activities confirmation of his fears that the teachings of Savonarola and of Domenico Benivieni were bound to have destructive effects on the traditional structure of the Church, and especially on the relationship between clergy and laity. These fears were graphically expressed in his *Liber de discretione vanitatum*. In fact, his well-informed account of the *fanciulli*'s activities would suggest that he was among Bernardino's listeners during the sermons preached at Sta Maria Novella.[88] Whether he was or was not present, his forecast was extremely accurate. The very fact that Domenico Benivieni's doctrines, already controversial in themselves, were being restated by Pietro Bernardino, an unlettered layman, was

---

[87] Bernardino, sigs. a5ᵛ–a6ʳ, b1ʳ–b3ʳ; Bernardino, *Compendio di Contemplatione*, sigs. a2ʳ, a2ᵛ, a3ᵛ, b4ʳ⁻ᵛ, c5ʳ–c6ʳ, c7ᵛ.

[88] Giovanni Caroli, 'Liber de discretione vanitatum' MS BNF Conv. Sopp., D.9.278, fos. 62ʳ⁻ᵛ, 72ʳ⁻ᵛ.

enough to cause a stir. When Bernardino used them, together with his notions of the *fanciulli* as God's chosen instruments of reform, to mount a scathing attack on the clergy, the effect was very disruptive indeed.

Time and again, Bernardino contrasted the prelates' worldly wiles with the all-conquering innocence of the Florentine children. Untouched by worldly knowledge, unharmed by the world's temptations, they could know the ways of the Lord more intimately than any cleric. Insistently, he argued that the *fanciulli* must not be contaminated by prelates and other men in authority. They must show themselves worthy of their divine heritage by refusing all contact with such men and fleeing from their jurisdiction. Especially violent were Bernardino's denunciations of secular learning. Believing that such knowledge, so much vaunted by proud and vainglorious prelates, actually served as an obstacle in the path of divine knowledge because it prompted defiant questioning of the Almighty's plans, Bernardino went on to contend that anger, born of frustration, moved those in power to try to prevent true Christians from fulfilling God's will.[89] Despite these extremist utterances, however, Bernardino did not question the clergy's sacramental and mediatory powers in either the *Epistola . . . a' . . . fanciulli* or the *Compendio di Contemplatione*; and neither, when advising the *fanciulli* to confess and communicate as often as possible, did he raise the point which Savonarola had made, that they should consult only worthy priests.[90]

With Savonarola's trial and execution, Bernardino's career entered a new phase. Either because of his youth, or, more probably, because he was thought to have played only a minor role in the Savonarolan movement, he himself was untouched by the judicial authorities at this time. His name is absent from the numerous depositions requested by the *Signoria* in connection with the trials of Savonarola and his two fellow Dominicans; and he does not appear to have been among those Piagnoni who were tried and

---

[89] Bernardino, *Compendio di Contemplatione*, sig. a2ʳ.
[90] Bernardino, *Epistola . . . a' . . . fanciulli*, sigs. a2ʳ, a4ʳ, a5ʳ⁻ᵛ, b1ʳ, b4ʳ; id., *Compendio di Contemplatione*, sigs. a2ʳ, c7ᵛ, d2ᵛ.

sentenced after Savonarola's death. He must, nevertheless, have felt it prudent to withdraw from public view. For, although he continued to pursue his mission in the next two years, he did so in secret. With a hard core of stalwart followers, variously estimated at between twelve and thirty in number and apparently youths for the most part,[91] he held clandestine meetings: sometimes at his own house in the parish of S. Lorenzo, sometimes at the houses of his supporters, and once as far afield as Spagnuole in the Mugello.[92] It is interesting, moreover, that among Bernardino's followers at this time there were at least two ecclesiastics: Baldassarre da Pescia, a secular priest, and Amerigo de' Medici, the redoubtable Canon of Sta Maria del Fiore, who in March and April 1498 had been suspended from office, declared a rebel, deprived of his living, and otherwise heavily penalized by the Chapter for his partisanship of Savonarola's cause.[93] This phase in Bernardino's career is of paramount importance. Although the activities of his group—or, conventicle, as it should more properly be called—are necessarily hard to ascertain, it is clear, even so, that in the short space of two years, he progressed from a comparatively moderate position to one of unacceptable radicalism.

By far the most sensational information concerning the activities of Bernardino's conventicle comes from the pens of the contemporary observers Bartolomeo Cerretani and Piero Parenti. Both are agreed that Bernardino induced his followers to accept a variety of heretical positions. Among the most dramatic of his innovations was to anoint his followers. He also presided over them as an elected Pope and guided them by means of his heavenly visions. The members of the conventicle, according to Cerretani and

---

[91] The number was given by Giovanfrancesco Pico as twelve, by Cerretani as twenty, and by Bernardino himself as thirty: Pico, *Operecta*, 18; Cerretani, 'Istoria fiorentina', fo. 274ᵛ; Pietro Bernardino, '[Epistola] . . . veritatis amatoribus', fo. 67ᵛ.

[92] See below, n. 95.

[93] Bernadino, *Compendio di Contemplatione*, sig. d6ʳ, where it is also stated that 'molti cherici di sancta Reparata' had attended the sermons subsequently published in this collection. For an account of Amerigo de' Medici's controversy with the Chapter and with his brother Leonardo, Archdeacon and Vicar to the Florentine Archbishop, see E. Sanesi, *Vicari e canonici fiorentini e il 'caso Savonarola'* (Florence, 1932), 21–37.

Parenti, refused to partake in the sacraments, because they considered no priest to be worthy of administering them, and no longer attended mass, but fulfilled their religious duties by meditation, silent prayer, and fasting. They were also constantly on the watch for signs portending the fulfilment of Bernardino's prophecies regarding the tribulations that would destroy the present Church before its renovation.[94] It is clear that a number of these activities were the logical consequence of the beliefs which he had expressed in the earlier *Epistola . . . a' . . . fanciulli* and *Compendio di Contemplatione*. For additional evidence, we have two sermons preached by him early in 1500,[95] the first in his own home and the second in Spagnuole in the Mugello, which were published together later in the same year by one Antonio Buonsignori. As the publisher's propitiatory letters to the *Signoria*, prefacing the sermons, indicate, they were printed in Bernardino's defence.[96]

Since the sermons sought to scotch the various rumours which were by now circulating concerning Bernardino's heretical activities and to enlist the *Signoria*'s support for his mission, it is hardly to be expected that their contents would equal Cerretani's and Parenti's accounts in sensationalism. There is evidence to suggest, moreover, that an attempt was made to expunge controversial material from the sermons before their publication. Many arguments occur in a disjointed form, others have been radically abridged, and others again stop just short of their conclusion.[97] Enough remains, nevertheless, to show that the chroniclers' accounts were substantially true.

It is apparent, for instance, that the conventiclers had indeed decided to break all contacts with the existing ecclesiastical hierarchy. In both sermons, Bernardino advocated separation from the

---

[94] Cerretani, 'Istoria fiorentina', fos. 274ᵛ–274ᵛ [*bis*]; Parenti, *Istorie fiorentine*, 292–3.

[95] Pietro Bernardino, *Predica di Pietro Bernardo da Firenze inutile servulo di Iesu Christo et di tutti li fanciulli di buona voluntà. Facta nel populo di Sanc [sic] Lorenzo in chasa sua. Dove erono audienti huomini et fanciulli. Domenica prima Septuagesimae MCCCCLXXXXVIIII; Predica di Pietro Bernardo . . . Facta a Spugnole [sic] di Mugello loco di Giovanni Pepi. Adì II di Marzo MCCCCLXXXXIX circa hore una di nocte, ove erono presenti homini et fanciulli* (Florence, 1500) (*GW* 3898).

[96] Ibid., sigs. a2ʳ–a3ʳ, c5ᵛ–c8ʳ.      [97] Ibid., esp. sigs. b7ᵛ, c3ʳ.

clergy as the necessary condition for salvation and for the fulfilment of the conventicle's aspirations. Because the clergy no longer possessed the purity of intention or simplicity of spirit essential for receiving and preaching the Word of God, he maintained, their teachings were full of deceit, opposed both to the precepts of Scripture and to the example of Christ. There was thus no choice but to flee.[98] While Cerretani's report that the group had formed itself into a self-contained, quasi-monastic community is not borne out by the sermons, they contain enough evidence to suggest that its members had severed relations with the official hierarchy and were thus relying largely upon themselves.[99] Bernardino was their unchallenged leader and guide. Far from working to his disadvantage, the fact that he had received no formal religious training served as proof of his divine election.[100]

There were certain ecclesiastical prerogatives over which Bernardino did not dare to claim a definite competence. In his sermons, he still instructed his disciples to confess and to take communion as often as they thought necessary, in imitation of the early Christians. Like Savonarola and Domenico Benivieni, he held that it was thus possible to move closer to God.[101] Again, as in the *Compendio di Contemplatione*, he did not openly question the validity of the clergy's sacramental ministrations. But to have done so would have been not only foolhardy, but unnecessary. Bernardino had already made it abundantly clear that contact with the hierarchy was a danger to the soul and that his followers should therefore turn, for the fulfilment of their religious obligations, to priests who, by subscribing to the conventicle's tenets, had given proof of their holiness. As we have seen, there were at least two such ready to hand;[102] and it can safely be assumed that they served the conventiclers in this capacity. Thus, although Cerretani was wrong to state that Bernardino had persuaded his followers to abstain

---

[98]  Pietro Bernardino, sig. b3ʳ; cf. sigs. a8ʳ, c4ʳ, d8ʳ.

[99]  As admitted by Pietro Bernardino himself in his 'Epistola Venerabili viro et egregio decretorum doctoris Domino Iacobo Caniceo [*sic*] parmensis', MS BNF Magl., XXXV, 116, fos. 74ᵛ–75ʳ.

[100]  Bernardino, *Predica . . . facta in chasa sua . . . Predica . . . facta a Spugnole di Mugello*, sig. a6ʳ; cf. sig. a3ʳ⁻ᵛ.

[101]  Ibid., sigs. b4ʳ, c3ʳ⁻ᵛ.          [102]  Ibid., sigs. b3ʳ, d8ʳ, e1ᵛ; cf. above, p. 128.

from confession (and presumably also communion), because all clerics were spiritually lax (*tepidi*) and hence unworthy, it was, in substance, true that the conventicle had become a church within a church.[103]

It was not only independent of the existing ecclesiastical structure, moreover, but, in one way at least, competing with it. While Bernardino was never openly to acknowledge it, it would appear that he performed ritual anointings upon his followers. Both Cerretani and Parenti were convinced that he did, and convinced also that it was this peculiar ceremony which earned his group the name of the *Unti* (the Anointed). It is not easy to establish what significance Bernardino attached to this rite. According to Cerretani, he 'had a certain oil with which he anointed the temples of his followers, stating that it was the anointment of the Holy Ghost'.[104] And, on the one occasion in the sermons when Bernardino raised the subject of anointment, this was the significance which he accorded it.[105] Unfortunately, the passage is one of the most heavily emended in the sermons. Abounding in *non sequiturs*, it is cut short by a most uncharacteristic statement from Bernardino to the effect that he had no authority to proceed further.[106] Despite the difficulties, it is clear that, first and foremost, he applied the term 'anointed' to persons who had consecrated their lives to God and had received the manifold gifts of the Holy Ghost.[107] In possession of all fundamental truths, the anointed person was to use his knowledge of God's plans for the benefit of the faithful. These were all qualities which Bernardino believed himself to possess, so that he was hallowed by the Holy Spirit and raised above the elect.[108]

Whether he intended the ceremony of anointment to endow his disciples with these qualities as well is not clear. It may have been no more than a symbolic confirmation of the recipient's divine election and fitness to stand among Bernardino's supporters as part

---

[103] Cerretani, 'Istoria fiorentina', fo. 274 [*bis*].
[104] Ibid.: 'haveva certto olio del quale ugneva a' detti sua seghuaci le tempie, afermando essere l'untione dello Spirito Sancto'.
[105] Bernardino, *Predica . . . facta . . . in chasa sua . . . Predica . . . facta . . . a Spugnole di Mugello*, sigs. b6ʳ–b7ᵛ.
[106] Ibid.     [107] Ibid., sig. b7ʳ; cf. sig. a4ʳ⁻ᵛ.     [108] Ibid., sigs. b6ʳ, b7ᵛ.

of the select group which was to reform the Church. But in either case, he was intruding into a jealously guarded area of ecclesiastical privilege, overlaid with ritual and tradition. However he may have chosen to justify his ministrations, there can be no doubt that by them he was assuming sacerdotal powers. It is equally certain that, with the ceremony of anointment, he meant to formalize not only the conventicle's separation from the established Church hierarchy but also its right to be regarded as the nucleus of the renewed Church. In his conventicle alone, Bernardino now believed, there dwelt the Holy Ghost. Outside it, therefore, there could be no salvation. Despite his search in the outside Church at large, he had found no trace of divine grace.[109]

By the time these two sermons were published, Bernardino's career had entered upon its final phase. He had fled from Florence and was never to return. With some twelve of his followers, Amerigo de' Medici among them, he went, by way of Bologna, to Mirandola, where he was to meet his end.[110] The events which precipitated his flight from Florence are not clear. It would seem, however, that even before Antonio Buonsignori's decision to publish the sermons, Bernardino and his conventiclers had been arraigned before the *Otto di Guardia*.[111] Why the *Otto di Guardia* should have taken an interest is explained by the long-standing fear that confraternities and conventicles could serve as focuses of political discontent and even sedition.[112] Nevertheless, having made its investigations, it did not initiate formal proceedings against Bernardino and his *Unti*. According to Piero Parenti, this was because of Piagnone influence. It may well have been, as Parenti says, that the Piagnoni believed prosecution would redound to their own discredit. But Parenti also tells us that proceedings had first been instigated by those fearless upholders of Savonarola's memory and

---

[109] Bernardino, sig. b7ᵛ. Savonarola invested the term 'anointed' with an identical 'exclusive' meaning: *Prediche sopra i Salmi*, ed. V. Romano (ENOS; 2 vols.; Rome, 1969–74), ii. 74.

[110] Pico, *Operecta*, 16, 18, 22–3.

[111] Cerretani, 'Istoria fiorentina', fo. 274ʳ [*bis*]; Parenti, *Istorie fiorentine*, 293.

[112] N. Rubinstein, *The Government of Florence under the Medici* (Oxford, 1966), 39, 118–19; L. Mehus, *Dell'origine, progresso, abusi e riforma delle confraternite laicali* (Florence, 1785), 141–58.

of Piagnoni values: the friars of S. Marco. As Parenti implies, self-interest, rather than loyalty, had probably prompted some Piagnoni to intercede with the *Otto di Guardia* on Bernardino's behalf.[113] It is evident, at least, that the *Unti* had become an embarrassment to the Piagnoni and, at worst, that they had alienated an extremely influential section of Piagnone opinion: the friars of S. Marco. When next the *Unti* faced an official investigation, this time by the Archiepiscopal Curia, no one intervened in their favour. Anticipating arrest and torture, Bernardino and his followers made good their escape.[114]

In September 1500, writing from an unidentified 'Monte Olympa', Bernardino addressed to Jacopo Caviceo, the Florentine Archiepiscopal Vicar,[115] a letter of self-exoneration. Beginning with a lecture on the delicate issue of spiritual enlightenment, he patiently explained that worldly men were ill-equipped to comprehend his teaching or the purpose of his mission.[116] Lacking his own enlightenment, these men had persecuted Bernardino and had turned Caviceo against him. Asserting his willingness to accept whatever correction the Vicar might wish to administer, Bernardino offered to send him the statutes (*capituli*) of his congregation, so that Caviceo could decide for himself whether they contained anything contrary to the teachings of the Church.[117] It is doubtful, however, whether this offer was seriously meant. For Bernardino now wrote not as an individual, but as the spokesman of a divinely elected body of men, entrusted with a mission that no man could question and looking to him as 'chosen by God to guard the souls of the children not only of Florence and Italy, but of the

[113] Parenti, *Istorie fiorentine*, 293.

[114] Cerretani, 'Istoria fiorentina', fo. 274 [*bis*]; Pico, *Operecta*, 22–3.

[115] On Caviceo, see *DBI*; A. Ronchini, 'Iacopo Caviceo', *Atti e memorie delle RR. Deputazioni di Storia Patria per le Provincie Modenesi e Parmensi*, 4 (1868), 209–20; and the biographical note by Giorgio Anselmo prefacing Caviceo's *Libro del Peregrino* (Parma, 1523), fos. 1ʳ–5ᵛ. In addition to the information here contained, it may be noted that the *Signoria* thought highly of Caviceo, petitioning Archbishop Orsini to extend his period of tenure for another term in Jan. 1501: ASF Signori, Carteggi, Missive Ia Cancelleria, 52, fo. 132ᵛ.

[116] Bernardino, '[Epistola] Venerabili viro . . . Domino Iacobo Caniceo', fo. 74ʳ; cf. fo. 73ʳ⁻ᵛ.

[117] Ibid., fos. 74ᵛ–75ʳ.

whole world'.[118] Even their hurried departure from Florence became, in Bernardino's eyes, the fulfilment of God's will that, in order to pursue their mission more effectively, they should separate from evil-doers.[119]

At about the same time, Bernardino composed a second letter in his own defence. This was directed not to a hostile member of the ecclesiastical hierarchy, but to his erstwhile sympathizers: those lovers of truth mentioned in its title.[120] In other words, he was justifying his actions before the very men from whom he could surely have expected complete allegiance. This fact, together with the highly evocative nature of the text which he chose to expound in the letter, give it an unexpected poignancy. Taking as his theme S. Paul's diatribe against his calumniators in 2 Cor. 11 and 12, a passage fraught with pain and distress, Bernardino made S. Paul's lament his own. As S. Paul had done, he apologized for his lack of glib speech, recounted his sufferings in Christ's cause, and recalled the visions of heavenly glory which authenticated his mission. Maintaining, with S. Paul, that 'the truth of Christ is in me' (2 Cor. 11: 10), he expressed deep sorrow that, in order to defend himself, he should be obliged to boast of his divine revelations, since the reticence which had hitherto kept him from imparting them to anyone except Fra Domenico da Pescia was now being taken as an admission that his career as prophet and reformer was not divinely appointed.[121] He was driven, further, to underline the tribulations which his unqualified devotion to the Florentine *fanciulli* had brought him.[122] This was his final word to his detractors: that they remained in comfort while he endured the sufferings which marked him as God's servant.[123] But what hurt Bernardino most of all was that among his doubters must be included Domenico Benivieni, of whom he spoke, most movingly, as 'our beloved'.[124]

---

[118] Antonio Buonsignori, prefatory epistle to Bernardino, *Predica . . . facta . . . in chasa sua . . . Predica . . . facta . . . a Spugnole di Mugello*, sig. a2ʳ: 'da Dio electo alla custodia delle anime de' fanciulli non solo di Firenze et Italia, ma di tutto el mondo'.

[119] Bernardino, '[Epistola] Venerabili viro . . . Domino Iacobo Caniceo', fo. 74ᵛ; cf. id., '[Epistola] . . . veritatis amatoribus', fo. 61ᵛ.

[120] Bernardino, '[Epistola] . . . veritatis amatoribus'.

[121] Ibid., fos. 60ᵛ–63ᵛ; 67ᵛ–68ᵛ.     [122] Ibid., fo. 61ᵛ.

[123] Ibid., fo. 61ʳ.     [124] Ibid., fo. 63ʳ.

The letter is our clearest evidence that Bernardino was out of favour with certain sections of the Piagnone movement. For the explanation, we may look to his relationship with Domenico Benivieni. It is plain, for example, that the break between them could not have been caused by Bernardino's preaching. Lay preaching was then held in high esteem by the Piagnoni. As we have seen, Bernardino had been permitted to preach regularly in Piagnoni circles and had done so for a considerable period without apparent opposition. The reason for the rupture must be sought elsewhere. Something else must have led Domenico Benivieni to conclude that Bernardino had trespassed on forbidden ground by arrogating ecclesiastical privileges to himself. Given the timing of the break, moreover, the innovation must have been of recent adoption. All this would suggest that the controversial issues were Bernardino's organization of his followers into an independent community and his introduction of the ritual of anointment. Acceptance of these innovations would have required a total commitment to Bernardino's claims that he was divinely inspired and that there could be no salvation outside his conventicle. These claims could not be left unchallenged, not if the unity of the Piagnone movement was to be preserved.

In this letter to his Piagnoni brethren Bernardino showed himself aware, for the first time, that he had moved beyond positions which most of them found acceptable and that appeals to a higher authority were no longer enough to allay the doubts of his adversaries within the movement. He thus endeavoured to give his mission the endorsement of those men whose judgement they would not question. To this end, he cited Fra Domenico da Pescia as a witness to his claims. Learning of his visions, Fra Domenico had been struck with awe, Bernardino opportunely recalled, and had hailed him as 'the ambassador of Christ'.[125] In the *Operecta...in defentione della opera di Pietro Bernardo*, moreover, Giovanfrancesco Pico reiterated this point, asserting, at Bernardino's behest, that Fra Domenico had been fully aware of Bernardino's divine illumination and had revered it.[126] To this, Giovanfrancesco

---

[125] Ibid., fo. 65ʳ; cf. fo. 68ʳ⁻ᵛ.     [126] Pico, *Operecta*, 14, 17.

added the further dramatic disclosure that Savonarola himself, no less, had been the medium through whom Bernardino had received conclusive proof of his own mandate. A ray of light, Giovan-francesco recorded, had emanated from Savonarola's lips and had struck the youth, 'by whose ray P[ietro] B[ernardo] felt himself pierced and his head, chest and other limbs so set on fire that he could hardly bear to touch them with his hands; as a result, he says that ever since he has been more inspired towards heavenly things: and more profoundly enlightened to understand the meanings of Holy Scripture.'[127] By his recourse to the testimony of the two martyred leaders, Giovanfrancesco intended to place the legitimacy of Bernardino's calling beyond dispute. While admitting that, of late, his teaching had progressed beyond Savonarola's and had been the subject of violent attack, Giovanfrancesco begged Domenico Benivieni to realize that in fact it was so well founded as to compel belief. For his own part, he was convinced 'that one recognizes Savonarola in P[ietro] B[ernardo] as one does the master in his disciple'.[128]

Bernardino's period of refuge at Mirandola was short-lived. Less than a year after the composition of Giovanfrancesco's *Operecta*, and following a fierce siege which was marked by the fervour of the *Unti*, Mirandola fell to Lodovico Pico, Giovanfrancesco's brother, who had long contested Giovanfrancesco's title to Giovanni Pico's inheritance.[129] The *Unti* fell into the hands of Lodovico, who, according to Cerretani, 'had them tortured, and especially Pietro Bernardino, their leader, and having extracted from him an account of their way of life, customs, and behaviour, he condemned him to be burned with some others, since he found them riddled with heresies in their minds and full of filth and vices

---

[127] Pico, *Operecta*, 14: 'del cui lume P[ietro] B[ernardo] intrato si sentì scaldare il capo, il pecto et le membra che apena lo potea tochare con le mani, perchè lui dice essersi da poi più animato ad le cose divine: Et più profondamente illuminato a intendere li sensi delli sacri libri.'

[128] Ibid. 20: 'ch'el si chognioscha in P[ietro] B[ernardo] il padre frate Ieronimo come il maestro nel discepolo'. See also pp. 20–1, 24.

[129] 'Cronaca di Mirandola', MS Mirandola Biblioteca Comunale 12-A-7(4), no foliation; Cerretani, 'Istoria fiorentina', fo. 274ᵛ [*bis*].

in their bodies'.[130] In this passage, we have the first hint of the charge of unorthodox sexual practices which was to darken Pietro Bernardino's posthumous reputation.[131] As soon as the news of the imprisonment of the *Unti* reached Florence, influential voices were raised on their behalf. On three separate occasions, the *Signoria* petitioned Lodovico for the release of Amerigo de' Medici and Bernardino, expressing surprise at their arrest and belief in their innocence.[132] The intercession of the *Signoria* was instrumental in obtaining the release of Amerigo de' Medici and all the rest of the *Unti* save only their leader.[133] Writing on Lodovico's behalf to the *Signoria*, his mother Bianca Maria d'Este was at pains to emphasize that Bernardino would not have been detained without great and proper cause.[134] It seems that Lodovico not only considered him guilty of heresy but also, and more importantly, blamed him for causing the final rift that had led to the war against Giovanfrancesco. These, at any rate, were the reasons which Lodovico later gave to justify his decision to have Bernardino burned at the stake.[135]

Towards the end of 1502, Bernardino met a martyr's death.[136] His end closely paralleled that of Savonarola: even, it seems, down

[130] Ibid.: 'gli misse a martirii et maxime Pietro Bernardino, loro capo, et da lui ritratto il modo de loro vita et costumi e loro andamenti, lo chondannò con alquanti al fuocho, perchè gli trovò maculatissimi di molte heresie nello intellecto e del corpo spurcissimi et vitiosi'.

[131] See below.

[132] Letter of the *Signoria* to Lodovico Pico and Federico Pico, 17 Aug. 1502; letters of the *Signoria* to Lodovico Pico, 7 Sept. and 1 Oct. 1502, ASF Signori, Missive Ia Cancelleria, 54, fos. 94ᵛ, 97ʳ⁻ᵛ, 105ʳ. These letters and the reply below have now been published by C. Vasoli in an appendix to his 'Il notaio e il "Papa Angelico": Noterella su un episodio fiorentino del 1538–1540', *Religioni e civiltà: Scritti in memoria di Angelo Brelich* (Bari, 1982), 641–3.

[133] Cerretani, 'Istoria fiorentina', fo. 274 [*bis*].

[134] Letter of Bianca Maria d'Este to the Florentine *Signoria*, 11 Sept. 1502, ASF Signori, Responsive, 23, fo. 133ʳ.

[135] Francesco Vettori, *Viaggio in Alemagna*, in *Scritti storici e politici*, ed. F. Niccolini (Bari, 1972), 21.

[136] His death is reported as having occurred in the month of December by Piero Parenti, *Istorie fiorentine*, 293.

to the perfunctory trial and the manner of execution.[137] His career had epitomized the extremist tendencies in Savonarola's reforming programme. From the beginning, he had been attracted by the contemplative strain in Savonarola's thought, as it was given expression by Domenico Benivieni. In developing these Savonarolan themes, however, he had passed beyond the limits of what could be accepted as orthodox. In him, the radicalism which Marsilio Ficino had feared found its fullest embodiment.

Bernardino's inconstant brethren were to be the subject of an indictment from beyond the grave. While in prison awaiting execution, Bernardino composed, in imitation of Savonarola, a commentary on Psalm 69: 'Salvum me fac, Deus'.[138] In the spirit of that psalm, it was an angry and vengeful outcry against fate. No peaceful or resigned leave-taking of the world, the commentary dwelt long on the injustice perpetrated against God's chosen instrument. For the sake of the brethren who had now turned against him, Bernardino lamented, he had suffered persecution and insults; and was now, at the last, to forfeit his life. Although their interests had always been closest to his heart, in all he had done to lead them towards their inheritance, they had repulsed him as unworthy and had repaid his ministrations with calumny and derision.[139] But in the end, he was certain, victory would be his. In the rebellious spirit of a young man facing a tragically premature end, he declared that God would show his antagonists no mercy.[140] On the brink of death, Bernardino found consolation in the belief that God would never abandon the Church to His enemies. It would be saved; and renewed by just men who devoutly obeyed His word and fearlessly glorified His name. Theirs would be the kingdom of Heaven.[141]

---

[137] A. Giorgetti, 'Fra Luca Bettini e la sua difesa del Savonarola', *ASI* 7/2 (1919), 221–2.

[138] Pietro Bernardino, *Psalmo exposto per Pietro Bernardo da Firenze servo imprigionato di Christo alla Mirandola immentre era in prigione* [Florence, 1502] (incorrectly dated to 1500 in *GW* 3982).

[139] Ibid., sig. a3ʳ; cf. sig. a1ʳ⁻ᵛ.

[140] Ibid., sigs. a3ᵛ–a4ʳ.

[141] Ibid., sig. a4ᵛ.

# 4

# *Reform through the Conventional Channels of the Church: The Conservative Approach*

I

Our interest in this chapter is in the intellectual élite of Piagnone history: those persons who, having acquired considerable renown in the world of letters, found themselves attracted by the Savonarolan concept of reform and devoted their gifts to its advancement. Girolamo Benivieni, brother of Domenico, was one; Giovanfrancesco Pico another. The first was among the foremost Florentine poets of his generation; the second inherited the mantle of his illustrious uncle, Giovanni Pico della Mirandola, and was respected on both sides of the Alps as one of the foremost philosophers of the age. Although never to devote all their energies to the Savonarolan cause, which, while it was an important concern, always remained only one of several interests, they were never to renounce their allegiance to it. Faithful throughout their lives to the reforming ideal which Savonarola had advocated, they became identified with it and lent it their own particular aura of intellectual distinction. Even if their contribution to the movement was overshadowed by that of others more outspoken than they, the air of respectability with which they endowed it was of immeasurable benefit, and may indeed have helped to postpone its inevitable suppression.

The response of the literary world to Savonarola and his teaching had always been favourable. After a short period of coolness—caused, perhaps, by the directness of Savonarola's approach and

the absence from his sermons of any pretensions to eloquence—
men of letters had overcome their initial caution and had flocked to
hear him. They were led by Giovanni Pico, who was said to have
persuaded Lorenzo de' Medici to invite Savonarola back to Florence in 1490 and who was in any case to spend the remaining years
of his life, until his death in 1494, in close company with the
prophet.[1] Around the two men there gathered a group of literati
who carried on, and to some extent even rivalled, the traditions of
the Ficinian Circle. Domenico and Girolamo Benivieni, Pier
Crinito, Lorenzo Lorenzi, and Jacopo Salviati were among its
members.[2]

Others who had also been attracted to Savonarola from an early
stage in his apostolate included the notary and poet Ugolino
Verino,[3] the even more popular Castellano Castellani,[4] and the
most famous physician of his day, Antonio Benivieni, eldest of the
Benivieni brothers, who became especially interested in Fra
Domenico da Pescia as one whose miraculous powers could succeed where his own medical skills were defeated.[5] Some quickly
became disenchanted with Savonarola. Castellano Castellani's reversal, for example, was so complete that in 1498 he stood as one of
the witnesses at Savonarola's trial.[6] For Ugolino Verino, on the
other hand, the lapse was only momentary. Although he addressed
a letter of renunciation to the Florentine *Signoria* in 1498, he afterwards returned to the Piagnone fold.[7] Most, however, remained

---

[1] R. Ridolfi, *Vita di Girolamo Savonarola* (2 vols.; Rome, 1952), i. 18, 43–4, 59, 147–50.

[2] Pier Crinito, *De honesta disciplina libri XXV* (Basle, 1532), 80–1; G. Uzielli, 'Dialogo fra Girolamo Savonarola e Giovanni Pico della Mirandola narrato da Pier Crinito', *I centenari del 1898* (Florence, 1898), 46–8; C. Re, *Girolamo Benivieni fiorentino* (Città di Castello, 1906), 91–6. On all these and following men from the same academic background see A. Verde, *Lo studio fiorentino 1473–1503: Ricerche e documenti* (4 vols. in 7; Florence, 1973–85), index.

[3] See above, p. 95.

[4] G. Ponte, *Attorno al Savonarola: Castellano Castellani e la Sacra Rappresentazione in Firenze tra '400 e '500* (Genoa, 1969), esp. Chs. 1, 2.

[5] Antonio Benivieni, *De abditis nonnullis ac mirandis morborum et sanationum causis*, ed. Girolamo Benivieni (Florence, 1507), sigs. b2$^v$–b3$^v$, d$^{r-v}$; Verde, *Lo studio fiorentino*, iv/3: 1438–42.

[6] P. Villari, *La storia di Girolamo Savonarola e suoi tempi* (2 vols.; Florence, 1930), vol. ii, app., pp. clxxiv–clxxv.

[7] See below, p. 233.

unswervingly loyal to Savonarola, in whom they saw the solution to their deeply felt need for moral reform.

Although nurtured in the same cultural milieu as Domenico Benivieni and Giovanni Nesi, Girolamo Benivieni, Giovanfrancesco Pico, and their like were not to follow the same course. While sympathetic towards the aspirations of their near brethren, mysticism was not, for them, a viable path to reform. All those who have their place in the present chapter made a conscious decision to resist the allurements of the contemplative path, believing that it could be trodden only by individual believers of exceptional virtue rather than by the general mass of Christianity. Another reason for their rejection of the mystical solution was that they were, without exception, men who, so far as they were able, eschewed controversy. Since the pursuit of the contemplative life was sure to bring them into conflict with the ecclesiastical hierarchy, it was to be avoided. This hierarchy they viewed with a respect akin to reverence. Fully aware of the failings of certain of its members, they yet could not conceive of a reform of the Church which did not enjoy the approval of the hierarchy and take place under its direction. This idiosyncratic mixture of reforming ardour with an extremely strict notion of how to bring it about was always to characterize their endeavours and would, in the long run, severely limit their efficacy.

## II

Girolamo Benivieni, in his day one of the most famous Tuscan poets,[8] was born in 1453.[9] While not as precocious as Domenico, nor possessed of a comparable academic training, he had nevertheless a thorough grounding as a classical scholar and was to enjoy,

---

[8] G. Negri, *Istoria degli scrittori fiorentini* (Ferrara, 1722), 299.

[9] Antonio Benivieni, 'Vita di Girolamo Benivieni', MS BNF II.I.91, pp. 231–78; Re, *Girolamo Benivieni*; A. Pelizzari, *Un asceta del Rinascimento (Della vita e delle opere di Girolamo Benivieni)* (Genoa, 1906); *DBI*; O. Zorzi Pugliese, 'Girolamo Benivieni: Umanista riformatore (dalla corrispondenza inedita)', *La Bibliofilia*, 71 (1970), 253–88; S. Jayne (ed.), *Commentary on a Canzone of Benivieni* (New York, 1984); id., 'Benivieni's Christian Canzone', *Rinascimento*, 24 (1984), 153–79.

both during his lifetime and afterwards, well-deserved fame for his Italian poetic compositions. Like his brother, he soon came under the influence of Ficino and his friends, and enjoyed the protection of Giuliano and Lorenzo de' Medici, Poliziano, and Jacopo Salviati.[10] His earliest literary efforts, in fact, were Italian translations, usually in verse form, of the works of fellow members of the Ficinian Circle. Meanwhile, he was also producing occasional poetic pieces which, while evincing the same cultural preoccupations, nevertheless reveal the inclination towards vernacular literature which he was afterwards to follow. He first became known for a collection of bucolic poems[11] and for his rendering into verse of one of Boccaccio's tales.[12] His most ambitious project at this time was an exposition, in verse form, of Ficino's commentary on Plato's *Symposium*.[13] Both then and later, the influence of Dante was strongly felt in his poetry; and indeed Dante's work, to which he devoted much study, was always one of his greatest loves.[14]

Early in his career, Girolamo came into contact with the person who was to be one of the most important figures in his life: Giovanni Pico della Mirandola. Their meeting, which may have taken place as early as 1479, when Giovanni Pico made his first visit to Florence, was the prelude to an enduring friendship. While possibly more fervent on Girolamo's side—he requested, for example, that he should be buried beside Giovanni Pico[15]—the re-

---

[10]  Re, *Girolamo Benivieni*, 91–2, 96.

[11]  Girolamo Benivieni [*et al.*], *Bucoliche* (Florence, 1481).

[12]  Girolamo Benivieni, *Tancredi principe di Salerno: Novella in rima* (Scelta di curiosità letterarie inedite o rare dal secolo XIII al XIX: Dispensa XXVIII; Bologna, 1865).

[13]  Girolamo Benivieni, *Opere* (Florence, 1519), fos. 37ʳ–39ᵛ.

[14]  Girolamo Benivieni, *Dialogo di Antonio Manetti cittadino Fiorentino: Circa al sito, forma, et misure dello inferno di Dante Alighieri poeta excellentissimo* [Florence, 1510?]. Girolamo was an influential member of the 'Medici Academy' and took part in the attempts to have Dante's bones transferred from Ravenna to Florence in 1514–16: see P. O. Kristeller, 'Francesco da Diacceto and Florentine Platonism in the Sixteenth Century', *Studies in Renaissance Thought and Letters* (Rome, 1956), 301–3, and app., p. 329.

[15]  Antonio Benivieni, 'Vita di Girolamo Benivieni', 277; Re, *Girolamo Benivieni*, 380–1.

lationship was nevertheless based on a deeply felt mutual respect and affection. Giovanni Pico was greatly impressed, for instance, by Girolamo's poetic exposition of Ficino's commentary upon the *Symposium*, and wrote his own *Commento* upon it, which he completed in 1486.[16] When Giovanni Pico was in Florence, where he resided almost continuously after 1486, he and Girolamo were inseparable companions. Among other close friends who met with them in their tightly knit circle were Domenico Benivieni and Roberto and Jacopo Salviati.[17] The friendship between Girolamo Benivieni and Jacopo Salviati was particularly close, and was to last throughout their lives, with each giving invaluable assistance to the other on many occasions.[18] The group as a whole came under the spell of Savonarola almost from the commencement of his second apostolate. 'We frequently went to hear him', Girolamo recalled many years later, 'attracted by the truth and utility of his teachings, despite the fact that his way of preaching, his gestures, and his manner of speaking tended to offend our eyes and ears'.[19] Having overcome their initial irritation at his mannerisms, they became staunch devotees of Savonarola, accepting his teaching on the need for Church reform and casting about for ways in which they could be of greatest benefit to the cause. Savonarola was grateful for their support and welcomed them to S. Marco, where they met in the library for discussions on religious and philosophical subjects.[20] With the death of Giovanni Pico, however, which affected not only Girolamo Benivieni but also Savonarola himself very deeply the

---

[16] Giovanni Pico, *Commento delo Illustrissimo Signore Conte Iohanni Pico Mirandulano sopra una Canzona de Amore composta da Hieronymo Benivieni, ciptadino Fiorentino, secondo la mente et opinione de' Platonici*, in Girolamo Benivieni, *Opere*, fos. 1ʳ–67ᵛ; E. Garin, 'Marsilio Ficino, Girolamo Benivieni e Giovanni Pico', *Giornale critico della filosofia italiana*, 23 (1942), 94; Jayne, *Commentary on a Canzone of Benivieni*, esp. 4–5.

[17] Re, *Girolamo Benivieni*, 91–6.

[18] Ibid., app., pp. 348–54; and see below, pp. 275, 393 n. 26.

[19] Girolamo Benivieni, *Epistola . . . mandata a Papa Clemente VII*, in app. to Benedetto Varchi, *Storia fiorentina*, ed. G. Milanesi (3 vols.; Florence, 1858), iii. 313: 'Andavamo frequentemente a udirlo allettati dalla verità e utilità della sua dottrina, nonostante che il modo del suo predicare, i gesti, e la pronunzia in qualche modo gli occhi e gli orecchi ci offendessino'.

[20] See above, p. 19.

group lost its most cherished member. Ever afterwards, Girolamo Benivieni would look back upon this period before his friend's tragic end as the halcyon days of his past.[21]

Whether because of his distress at Giovanni Pico's death, or because of an innate reluctance to become involved in polemic, Girolamo Benivieni took no part at all in the pamphlet war. He was nevertheless of great assistance to Savonarola in other ways, most notably as a publicist for his theories. He translated many of Savonarola's works either into Italian or Latin: *De simplicitate christianae vitae*, for example, and many of his letters.[22] In 1496, he composed a preamble to the Latin edition of the *Compendio di rivelazioni*:[23] an undertaking which brought him closer to controversy than any of his other literary efforts of the time. In this preamble, he inveighed against those who opposed Savonarola's message of reform; and enjoined the faithful to resist their onslaught, comforting them with the promise that victory would be theirs in the end.[24] The activity which brought him greatest notoriety, however, was his composition of *canzoni* for Savonarola's festivals. Of these, his 'Viva ne' nostri cuori, viva o Florentia' ('Long may you live in our hearts! Long live Florence!'), extolling the power and happiness which would accrue to the city when the new age dawned, was the most famous.[25] It was sung during the Palm Sunday procession of 1496[26] and proved a lasting success. Girolamo's value as a publicist was well appreciated by the Florentine authorities, who, at Savonarola's fall, proceeded against him with considerable harshness. Like others who had come into prominence during Savonarola's ascendancy, he was barred from public office (*ammonito*) for two years.[27]

---

[21] See e.g. Girolamo Benivieni, *Commento . . . sopra a più sue canzone et sonetti dello amore et della Belleza Divina* (Florence, 1500) (Hain 2788), fo. 1$^{r-v}$.

[22] Savonarola, *Le lettere*, ed. R. Ridolfi (Florence, 1933), Introd., pp. clxxiv–clxxvii; *De simplicitate christianae vitae*, ed. P. C. Ricci (ENOS; Rome, 1959), critical note, p. 262; Ridolfi, *Vita*, ii. 202.

[23] Savonarola, *Compendium revelationum* (Ulm, 1496) (Hain 14333), sig. a2$^{r-v}$.

[24] Ibid.

[25] Girolamo Benivieni, *Commento . . . sopra a più sue canzone et sonetti dello amore et della Belleza Divina*, fos. CXII$^r$–CXV$^r$.

[26] Ibid., fo. CXI$^r$.

[27] Piero Parenti, 'Istorie fiorentine', MS BNF II.II.131, fo. 83$^{r-v}$.

Despite this experience, Girolamo's loyalty to the friar remained undiminished. Although silent for the next two years, in 1500 he published his *Commento . . . sopra a più sue canzone et sonetti dello amore et della Belleza Divina*, in which he expatiated upon the Savonarolan vision. In this work, which was always to be dearest to his heart, and which he revised many times during his life, he published the *canzoni* composed by him since 1476,[28] including those designed for the Florentine religious festivals. These were linked together by a prolix and often repetitive commentary. In the hostile climate which the Piagnoni suffered at this time, the publication of such a work was an act of bravery.[29] The *Commento* is interesting not only for its evidence of Girolamo's continuing adherence to the Savonarolan cause, but also for its revelation of the direction which his thought was taking. Apparent, in the first place, is a tension between the Neoplatonic ideals which had influenced him during his association with the Ficinian circle and the more sober vision of Christianity which Savonarola had imparted to him; and, in the second place, a clear indication that he would find the solution to this problem not in a mystical approach, as Domenico Benivieni had done, but in a wholehearted espousal of the Savonarolan notions of reform.

Already present in Girolamo's *Commento* are the scruples concerning the Neoplatonic view of divine love which he was later to elaborate much more fully in his *Opere* in 1519, believing its pagan elements to be a potential danger to Christians of a less philosophic bent.[30] These doubts can be traced back as far as 1494, when they had prompted him to replace all classical allusions in a new edition

[28] R. Ridolfi, 'Girolamo Benivieni e una sconosciuta revisione del suo Canzoniere', *La Bibliofilia*, 66 (1964), 213–34.

[29] It may, however, have been rather more prudently done than would at first appear. For, the most blatantly Savonarolan section of the *Commento*, included in the quire numbered 00 (fos. CXI$^r$–CXX$^v$) is missing from many copies of this work (cf. e.g. the copy in BL 82.g.12). Judging from the fact that the relevant quire is numbered according to a different sequence from those which precede and follow it, it would appear that it was added when the book was already completed, the foliation being added afterwards. The impression given is that Girolamo remained extremely cautious. On the peculiarities of the work, see also R. Ridolfi, 'Girolamo Benivieni e una sconosciuta revisione del suo Canzoniere', 218 n. 12.

[30] Benivieni, *Opere*, Ep. to Reader.

of his *Bucoliche* with scriptural terms,[31] and had prevented him, furthermore, from publishing his poetic exposition of the Ficinian *Symposium* and Giovanni Pico's commentary.[32] In the *Commento* of 1500, clearly disturbed by the Neoplatonic character of many of his early poems, Girolamo made every effort, in his accompanying exposition, to endow them with a Christian aspect: in order, as he put it, to 'turn away our souls from their inordinate attachment to creatures to the love of their Creator'.[33] The nature of this exposition is in itself an additional guide to the development of Girolamo's thought. An account of the soul's progress towards God, it seems at first sight, with its emphasis on the trials of the ascent and its reliance on S. Bonaventure's *Itinerarium mentis ad Deum*,[34] to be no different from the sort of mystical vision already expounded by his brother Domenico.[35] However, it becomes clear that Girolamo was in fact rejecting his brother's solution to the problem of the clash between Ficinian and Savonarolan ideals. For the soul's ultimate union with God depends not upon the development, through contemplative means, of its inner spiritual resources, but on the fulfilment of Savonarolan reforming ideals. To bring into existence in Florence the holy state which Savonarola had advocated, and whose first-fruits had been seen during his apostolate, would provide the conditions enabling men, Girolamo argued, to achieve perfect union with God.[36]

The *Commento* was dedicated to the nephew of Giovanni Pico, Giovanfrancesco, who, Girolamo Benivieni declared, had repeat-

---

[31]  Girolamo Benivieni [*et al.*], *Bucoliche* (Florence, 1494).

[32]  Benivieni, *Opere*, Ep. to Reader; but see also E. Garin, 'Marsilio Ficino, Girolamo Benivieni e Giovanni Pico', esp. 94–6; D. Weinstein, *Savonarola and Florence: Prophecy and Patriotism in the Renaissance* (Princeton, NJ), 207–9, 216–17.

[33]  Girolamo Benivieni, *Commento . . . sopra a più sue canzone et sonetti dello amore et della Belleza Divina*, fo. II[r]: 'revocare l'anima nostra dallo affecto inordinato delle creature allo amore del suo Creatore'. See also fo. III[r–v].

[34]  Ibid., fos. X[v]–XI[v], where this debt is acknowledged.

[35]  See above, Ch. 3.

[36]  Girolamo Benivieni, *Commento . . . sopra a più sue canzone et sonetti dello amore et della Belleza Divina*, Part iii ('Nella quale si tracta della revelatione della anima et della unione di qualla col suo fine, che è epso Dio'), fos. LXXIII[v]–CXXXVIII[v], esp. fos. CXI[r]–CXX[v]. See also Weinstein, *Savonarola and Florence*, 217–18.

edly urged him to publish it.[37] This was the first public acknowledgement of a friendship which had developed some years before
from their common devotion to Giovanni Pico and to Savonarola
and was fostered by their shared vision of how the Savonarolan
reformation should be achieved—involving, as it did, a rejection of
the pretensions of the so-called pagan philosophers. Born in about
1469, Giovanfrancesco Pico had purchased his uncle's title to
Mirandola in 1491.[38] It was perhaps through Giovanni Pico, with
whom he had always enjoyed an extremely close relationship, that
Giovanfrancesco met his Florentine acquaintances and came under
the influence of Savonarola. Contact with Savonarola had anyway
been made, according to Giovanfrancesco's *Vita Reverendi Patris
F. Hieronymi Savonarolae*, by 1492, and thereafter they enjoyed, in
his words, 'an uncommonly strong friendship': a friendship to
which he testified by his contributions to the Savonarolan cause
during the pamphlet war.[39] Giovanfrancesco was in fact one of the
first openly to defend Savonarola. In a letter to Girolamo Tornielli,
Vicar-General of the Franciscan Order, he fiercely attacked
Savonarola's detractors, condemning their mendacity and base-
ness.[40] His three polemical tracts written during the pamphlet war
added further weight to the Savonarolan stand. Giovanfrancesco
Pico, unlike Girolamo Benivieni, was prepared to engage in polemical warfare when he could see no alternative.[41]

His contribution was not, however, confined to this medium. In
1496, for example, he dedicated to Savonarola the treatise *De morte*

[37] Girolamo Benivieni, *Commento . . . sopra a più sue canzone et sonetti dello
amore et della Belleza Divina*, Ep. Ded.
[38] On Giovanfrancesco Pico, see C. B. Schmitt, *Gianfrancesco Pico della
Mirandola (1469–1533) and his Critique of Aristotle* (The Hague, 1967); id.,
'Gianfrancesco Pico's Attitude toward his Uncle', *L'opera e il pensiero di Giovanni
Pico della Mirandola nella storia dell'Umanesimo. Convegno internazionale,
Mirandola 15–18 September 1963* (Florence, 1965), ii. 305–13; C. Vasoli, 'Pietro
Bernardino e Gianfrancesco Pico', ibid., esp. 284, 287–8, 294–8; A. Corsano, *Il
pensiero religioso italiano* (Bari, 1937), 54–64.
[39] Giovanfrancesco Pico, *Vita Reverendi Patris F. Hieronymi Savonarolae*, ed.
J. Quétif (Paris, 1674), 2.
[40] Letter of Giovanfrancesco Pico to Girolamo Tornielli, 24 Dec. 1495, in
Giovanfrancesco Pico, *Opera omnia* (Basle, 1573) (vol. ii of edition uniform with
Giovanni Pico's *Opera omnia*, Basle, 1572), ii. 1322–3.
[41] See above, pp. 81–2, 90–1, 98–9.

*Christi et propria cogitanda.*[42] This work eschewed both the philosophical and mystical approaches to the subject of the Christian's moral improvement. Instead, it favoured an entirely conventional outlook: arguing that, by reflecting upon the Cross, man could be brought, through the contemplation of Christ's suffering and death in the past and his own in the future, to seek how best he might eliminate his vices and acquire greater virtue.[43] At about the same time, Giovanfrancesco also composed *De studio divinae et humanae philosophiae*:[44] a work which reveals that his thought was developing along lines very similar to Girolamo Benivieni's. As Girolamo was shortly to suggest in his *Commento* of 1500, so Giovanfrancesco here contended, that human philosophy was of little value to the Christian in his search for salvation and could, indeed, be of positive harm. More outspoken than Girolamo Benivieni, he delivered a scathing attack on the pretension of pagan philosophers: a theme which he would develop even more strongly in later works. Acknowledging debts to Giovanni Pico as well as to Savonarola, he declared that divine learning, which was to be contrasted with pagan knowledge and by which he apparently meant the study of Scripture, should be set before all else as the means by which man could best attain salvation.[45]

In his *De fide et ordine credendi*, written at roughly the same time, although not published for about ten years,[46] Giovanfrancesco again took issue with current philosophical trends. Like Savonarola's *Triumphus Crucis*, this was an apologetic work on behalf of the Christian faith, threatened, as it now was, by the incursions of contemporary philosophical schools, which were belittling the place of faith in human learning. Against the argument that knowledge must be based on rational thought, Giovanfrancesco attested

---

[42] Giovanfrancesco Pico, *De morte Christi et propria cogitanda*, in *Opera omnia*, ii. 40–106.

[43] Ibid., esp. 43–4, 47, 69–77; and the concluding exhortation to the reader, pp. 104–6.

[44] See Schmitt, *Gianfrancesco Pico della Mirandola*, 37–43; and app. A, p. 190.

[45] Corsano, *Il pensiero religioso italiano*, 56–9; Schmitt, *Gianfrancesco Pico della Mirandola*, 37–43.

[46] Giovanfrancesco Pico, *De fide et ordine credendi*, in *Opera omnia*, ii. 214–320; Schmitt, *Gianfrancesco Pico della Mirandola*, app. A, pp. 193–4.

the superiority of revealed truth over knowledge acquired by reason or experience.[47] In support of this contention, he cited the fact that theologians were in total accord on the tenets of the Christian faith. While the theological world might indeed be rent by dissension at the present day, this was to be attributed not to any disagreement on the nature of revealed truth but to the work of theologians who had fallen prey to the enticement of philosophical speculation.[48] Giovanfrancesco used his thesis concerning the importance of revealed knowledge as a basis for a further attack: this time on those who questioned the institution of the priesthood. In arguments closely akin to those put forward by Savonarola, and which could readily be turned to his defence, Giovanfrancesco maintained that the priesthood served as the mediator of divine revelation. To this traditional view, he added the less conventional assertion that prophets, too, fulfilled this essential need.[49] This argument, also put forward in his contemporaneous attacks on Savonarola's antagonists, was reiterated in his defence of Pietro Bernardino in 1501.[50] The pointed contrast between rationalist philosophers and those who trusted in faith above all else was to be made again, more forcefully still, in Giovanfrancesco's *Libro detto strega, o delle illusioni del Demonio*, first published in 1523.[51] Set here in the more precise context of an affirmation of the existence of witches and witchcraft, the argument that the testimony of faith and of general belief was sufficient to overturn objections based upon mere human reason was put forward more directly than ever before.[52]

Another Piagnone who took a firm stand against the pretensions of profane learning was Paolo Orlandini, a Camaldolese monk from

---

[47] Pico, *De fide et ordine credendi*, 216–19, 224–5, 271; Corsano, *Il pensiero religioso italiano*, 60–4.

[48] Pico, *De fide et ordine credendi*, 240–2, 247–8.

[49] Ibid. 216–18, 257, 285.

[50] See above, pp. 117–8, 135–6.

[51] Giovanfrancesco Pico, *Libro detto strega, o delle illusioni del Demonio*, tr. Fra Leandro degli Alberti (Bologna, 1524). For an excellent discussion of the treatise see P. Burke, 'Witchcraft and Magic in Renaissance Italy: Gianfrancesco Pico and his *Strix*', in S. Anglo (ed.), *The Damned Art: Essays in the Literature of Witchcraft* (London, 1977), 33–52.

[52] Pico, *Libro detto strega*, esp. fos. 8$^v$–19$^r$, 39$^v$–45$^r$.

the convent of Sta Maria degli Angeli in Florence.[53] A member of the Ficinian circle,[54] Orlandini had much the same cultural background as Girolamo and Domenico Benivieni. Among his friends and correspondents, he numbered Marsilio Ficino, Giovanni Pico, Giovanni Nesi, Ugolino Verino, and Pier Crinito.[55] While he would seem to have taken no active part in championing Savonarola's cause during the pamphlet war, Orlandini followed the controversy with great interest, passing on to Pietro Delfin, for example, the *Oraculum de novo saeculo* of 1497 which Nesi had forwarded to him.[56] In 1496, moreover, he had produced a dialogue dedicated to a certain Marco, Provost of Ognissanti, and entitled *Concordatio seu compositio quaedam super quibusdam Scripturae Sacrae locis*, where considerable weight was given to Savonarola's theories.[57] In this work, as in the collection of poems, *Epythoma super universam Bibliam*, which he produced in the early 1500s, Orlandini made much of the rival demands of philosophical and scriptural learning, and of his own resolution of the conflict in favour of the latter.[58]

[53] G. Farulli, *Istoria cronologica del nobile ed antico monastero degli Angioli di Firenze del sacro Ordine Camaldolese dal principio della sua fondazione al presente giorno* (Lucca, 1710), 69–71; G. B. Mittarelli and A. Costadoni, *Annales Camaldulenses Ordinis Sancti Benedicti*, vii–ix (Venice, 1762–73), vii. 416–17; viii. 11–12; ix. 119. See also E. Garin, 'Paolo Orlandini e il profeta Francesco da Meleto', *La cultura filosofica del Rinascimento italiano* (Florence, 1961), 213–23; Weinstein, *Savonarola and Florence*, 362–71.

[54] P. O. Kristeller, *Supplementum Ficinianum* (2 vols.; Florence, 1937), ii. 267–8, 348.

[55] Ibid.; Paolo Orlandini, 'Epythoma super universam Bibliam', MS BNF Conv. Sopp., D.5.827, fos. 313$^{r-v}$, 314$^r$, 320$^{r-v}$; id., 'De symbolo Nesiano' in *Eptathicum*, MS BNF II.I.158, fos. 270$^v$–280$^r$.

[56] Letter of Pietro Delfin to Paolo Orlandini, 9 Aug. 1497, in Pietro Delfin, *Epistolarum volumen* (Venice, 1524), sig. t$^r$; and also the letter of the same to Bernardino Gadolo, 4 Aug. 1497, in J. Schnitzer, *Peter Delfin* (Munich, 1925), app. I, p. 352.

[57] Paolo Orlandini, 'Concordatio seu compositio quaedam super quibusdam Scripturae Sacrae locis', MS BNF Magl., XL, 45. This Marco is to be identified with Marco Bossio, who was to write a treatise against Savonarola in 1498 and who was also implicated, with Bartolomeo Redditi, in an anti-Medicean plot in 1513: see above, p. 98, and below, pp. 261–2.

[58] Orlandini, 'Concordatio seu compositio quaedam super quibusdam Scripturae Sacrae locis', fos. 2$^{r-v}$, 27$^r$–28$^r$; id., 'Epythoma super universam Bibliam', fos. 329$^v$–332$^v$.

Following Savonarola's lead, he inveighed especially against the overweening vanity of astrologers:[59] a theme present also in Giovanfrancesco Pico's writings, and developed most fully in his *Quaestio de falsitate astrologiae in genethliacorum confutationem.*[60] Astrology, being contrary to Christian teaching, could offer no illumination whatever of the future, argued Orlandini in his poem 'De vanitate astrologiae' and elsewhere.[61] Future contingencies could be ascertained only by divine revelation and by the confluence of informed opinions. In the prediction of the future, he gave a key role to prophets. With Savonarola very much in mind, he defended prophetic utterances against the charge of imprecision, which had been levelled at Savonarola by his detractors. In the poem 'Contro quegli che pongono termini certi alle prophetiae' ('Against those who would set precise dates on prophecies'), for instance, he contended that, while God's prophet could foretell, in general outline, what was to take place, he could not be expected to put exact dates to coming events:[62] an argument put forward equally strongly in his 'Contra eos qui se putant plene nosse prophetarum mentem' (Against those who claim to have fully come to know the mind of the prophets).[63] Orlandini was later to renounce Savonarola,[64] and indeed to attack him in a major treatise of 1516,[65] but for the time being, his allegiance was total. It was also

[59] Orlandini, 'Concordatio seu compositio quaedam super quibusdam Scripturae Sacrae locis', fos. 28ʳ–30ʳ (29ʳ⁻ᵛ, in which Savonarola's theories were evidently discussed, has been removed); id., 'Epythoma super universam Bibliam', fo. 338ᵛ. Savonarola's views on astrology, greatly influenced by Giovanni Pico, were most fully developed in Girolamo Savonarola, *Trattato contra li astrologi* [Florence, 1497?] (Copinger 14378). See also Ridolfi, *Vita*, i. 150.

[60] Published by W. Cavini, 'Un inedito di Giovan Francesco Pico della Mirandola: La "Quaestio de falsitate astrologiae"', *Rinascimento*, 2nd ser. 13 (1973), 137–71; see esp. 139, 152–3, 158–63.

[61] Orlandini, 'Epythoma super universam Bibliam', fo. 338ᵛ; cf. poem to Piero Soderini on the stars' influence on men, ibid., fo. 339ᵛ.

[62] Ibid., fo. 333ʳ⁻ᵛ.    [63] Ibid., fo. 333ᵛ.

[64] Because of this later renunciation, the majority of the passages dealing with Savonarola in Orlandini's early works have been erased or removed and his name expunged: cf. e.g. Orlandini, 'Concordatio seu compositio quaedam super quibusdam Scripturae Sacris locis', fos. 28ʳ–30ʳ; 'Epythoma super universam Bibliam', fos. 319ʳ, 322ᵛ, 345ᵛ.

[65] See below, pp. 292–4.

unquestioning. Orlandini apparently found no difficulty, for example, in continuing to revere Ficino as his mentor as well as Savonarola, despite the divergences in their respective positions; he was, furthermore, unaware that it was inappropriate to hail Oliviero Arduini and the late Bernardino Gadolo in the same breath as Savonarola, as he did in his *Epythoma*, since both had already turned against him.[66]

This said, it must nevertheless be acknowledged that Orlandini's views on Church reform were in complete accord with Savonarola's. As well as composing resounding imprecations against the corruption which he found in Rome,[67] he took steps of a more practical kind, which brought him up against Pietro Delfin, General of the Camaldolese Order. In November 1499, preaching in the church of S. Ambrogio, Orlandini voiced criticism of the Pope, to which Delfin responded with a severe reprimand and a warning that such behaviour would not be tolerated.[68] Relations between the two men improved sufficiently for them to exchange, the following year, possible interpretations on an allegorical figure clearly alluding to the corrupt practices of Alexander VI.[69] But not for long; and in 1501, when Delfin forbade Orlandini to preach outside the convent, relations became much more strained. In a letter which plainly reveals the conflict of Savonarolan evangelical ideals with the traditional Benedictine concept of the monk's role, Delfin or-

---

[66] Orlandini, 'Epythoma super universam Bibliam', fos. 318ʳ–323ᵛ. On Oliviero Arduini, see E. Sanesi, *Vicari e canonici fiorentini e il 'caso Savonarola'* (Florence, 1932), 14–15, 26, 32; Simone Filipepi, *Estratto della cronaca*, in P. Villari and E. Casanova (eds.), *Scelta di prediche e scritti di Fra Girolamo Savonarola* (Florence, 1898), 509. On Bernardino Gadolo, sometime Prior of Sta Maria degli Angeli, see his letter acquainting certain Venetian patricians with the death of Savonarola, who is there condemned for heresy and schism, published in 'Supplizio di Girolamo Savonarola', *Camaldoli*, 6 (1952), 64–71.

[67] Orlandini, 'Epythoma super universam Bibliam', fo. 333ʳ. The poem is entitled 'Quando tornai amalato di Roma dove ero andato per conto della lite sopra la badia del Saxo'.

[68] Letter of Pietro Delfin to Paolo Orlandini, 29 Nov. 1499, in Schnitzer, *Peter Delfin*, app. I, p. 364.

[69] Letters from Pietro Delfin to Paolo Orlandini, 22 Oct. and 5 Nov. 1500, in Pietro Delfin, *Epistolarum volumen*, sigs. Z8ᵛ–&ʳ; G. B. Picotti, 'Un bue, ovvero di un disegno allegorico', *Studi Veneziani*, 10 (1968), 415–21.

dered him to remain in his cloister and to be content with his lot.[70] After a heated argument, Orlandini was forced to bow to his superior's wishes;[71] but he was later to have his revenge on Delfin. While it is not known how Orlandini had felt about Savonarola's support for the early attempt by the friars of Sta Maria degli Angeli to reform their convent,[72] it may be assumed that he was in favour of it, since he was later to take a leading part in the reform of the Camaldolese Order which was undertaken in spite of Delfin's resistance. Together with the Venetian friars, Vincenzo Quirini and Paolo Giustiniani, Orlandini succeeded in obtaining from Leo X in 1513 a bull which authorized the reorganization of the Order, strictly curtailing the General's power over the individual convents.[73]

In spearheading this reorganization of his Order, Orlandini was following notions of reform which accorded with Savonarolan ideals, but attempting to effect them from within the existing structure. His policy of using the available channels through which reform could be implemented with the approval of the hierarchy was to be adopted by other Piagnoni of similar outlook. Girolamo Benivieni, for one, was to devote the first decade of the new century to advocating such a course. In a series of letters to persons in holy orders, including Suor Benigna of the Murate, who had previously been under Domenico Benivieni's tutelage, Girolamo propounded his view that reform could successfully be accomplished by orthodox means.[74] In a society riddled by moral corruption—'the world is turned upside-down', he was to write in one of his sonnets—the role of the individual Christian, whether lay or religious,

---

[70] Letter of Pietro Delfin to Paolo Orlandini, 7 June 1501, in *Epistolarum volumen*, sig. & 8ᵛ.

[71] Letter of Pietro Delfin to Paolo Orlandini, 21 June 1501, in ibid., sig. ? [*sic*] verso. It was perhaps while smarting from this experience that Orlandini requested permission to retire to the hermitage of Camaldoli. He was, however, refused: see Mittarelli and Costadoni, *Annales Camaldulenses*, viii. 13.

[72] See above, p. 57.

[73] Mittarelli and Costadoni, *Annales Camaldulenses*, vii. 416–17, 436–8; Schnitzer, *Peter Delfin*, 166.

[74] Printed in Zorzi Pugliese, 'Girolamo Benivieni: Umanista riformatore', 264–72.

was vital.[75] Girolamo placed great emphasis upon true Christian living rather than outward forms. Each of his correspondents was exhorted to look to his own spiritual betterment instead of relying upon external observances such as prayers, fasting, or confession.[76] 'All we care about, all we strive and seek to do is to adorn ourselves externally with attractive ceremonies', he warned Suor Benigna, 'forgetting how we fare spiritually'.[77]

As a means towards true spiritual improvement, Girolamo advised, as did both his brother Domenico and Giovanfrancesco Pico, that the Cross should be the believer's guide. In his 'Laude dello Amore di Iesu Christo, chiamata la savia pazerella',[78] he wrote that the true Christian

Is simple as a dove
but prudent like the serpent.
He keeps one eye fixed on the grave
the other on You hanging on the cross.
His mind never thinks, desires, seeks, hopes for or loves aught else
except You, God, his true light
so blind is he to the world and foolish.[79]

His sentiments are as important for what they reject as for what they praise. In placing love of Christ above everything else, Girolamo sacrificed all earthly glory. More: he discounted the claims of secular learning and philosophical speculation, maintaining that Scripture alone was needed to direct the Christian on his way. In the Pauline concept of divine madness, Girolamo found substantiation for his view that nothing mattered but love for

---

[75] Girolamo Benivieni, 'Abhominatione delo amore carnale', *Opere*, fo. 123ᵛ.

[76] Zorzi Pugliese, 'Girolamo Benivieni: Umanista riformatore', 264–6, 269–72.

[77] Ibid. 271: 'Tutta la nostra cura, studio et diligentia è in ornare la casa nostra di fuori con belle cerimonie et a la parte di drento non si pensa come ella stia'.

[78] Girolamo Benivieni, 'Laude dello Amore di Iesu Christo, chiamata la savia pazerella', *Opere*, fos. 137ʳ–139ʳ.

[79] Ibid., fo. 138ʳ: 'Semplice è come colomba | Et prudentia ha di serpente. | L'uno occhio ha sempre alla tomba | L'altro a Te in croce pendente. | Mai nulla altro la sua mente | Pensa, vuol, cerca, ama et spera | Che Te Dio sua luce vera | Tanto è cieco al mondo et pazo'. See also, however, fos. 139ʳ–144ʳ, 145ᵛ–146ᵛ, 151ʳ–152ʳ, 187ʳ.

Christ: believing that to be God's fool was to cast aside all worldly knowledge, 'For human wisdom | Is folly in God's presence'.[80]

In the pursuit of his tenet that lack of learning should not be a bar to the Christian's understanding of the Word of God, Girolamo undertook the translation of the penitential Psalms into Italian. These were published in 1505, with a lengthy commentary, and dedicated to the nuns of the convent of the Murate.[81] In his preface, Girolamo explained that his object was to enable his readers, through the study of Scripture, to move closer to God.[82] In the commentary itself, he underlined the significance of God's infinite mercy: His willingness, in other words, to sustain the spiritual pilgrim upon his difficult journey and to forgive him his inevitable lapses from grace.[83] Given this, Girolamo argued, the faithful ought to be all the more earnest in their endeavours to tread the path to salvation. They ought to forsake the temptations of the world and keep fixed in their mind's eye the example of Christ's suffering.[84] These points were made with redoubled vigour in the *lettera spirituale* to an unknown nun which was appended to the *Psalmi penitentiali di David*.[85] Here, with acknowledgement to S. Bonaventure,[86] Girolamo set out in schematic form the steps to salvation. Twenty-four rules were enumerated, by which the aspiring member of the Church Triumphant must abide: their guiding principle being, once again, that outward observances counted as naught and that inward resolution was all-important.[87]

Both the *Psalmi penitentiali di David* and the attached letter show Girolamo to have been deeply perturbed by the present condition

---

[80] Ibid., fo. 138ᵛ: 'Ché la sapientia humana | E stultitia appresso a Dio'. Cf. fos. 136ʳ⁻ᵛ, 148ʳ–149ʳ, 172ᵛ–176ʳ.

[81] Girolamo Benivieni, *Psalmi penitentiali di David tradocti in lingua fiorentina et commentati per Hieronymo Benivieni* (Florence, 1505). Other Psalms translated by him are to be found in his *Opere*, fos. 125ʳ–129ʳ.

[82] Benivieni, *Psalmi penitentiali di David*, sig. a2ʳ⁻ᵛ.

[83] Ibid., sigs. a4ʳ, b2ʳ, c4ʳ⁻ᵛ, d1ʳ. See also O. Zorzi Pugliese, 'Girolamo Benivieni: Umanista riformatore', 265–6, 269, 272; and Benivieni, 'Laude dello Amore di Iesu', *Opere*, fos. 142ᵛ–143ᵛ.

[84] Benivieni, *Psalmi penitentiali di David*, sigs. a2ᵛ, d2ʳ, g4ᵛ.

[85] 'Hieronymo Benivieni alla dilecta in Christo sorella N. de B.' in Benivieni, *Psalmi penitentiali di David*, sigs. p1ʳ–r6ʳ.

[86] Ibid., sig. p1ʳ.      [87] Ibid., sigs. p1ᵛ–p2ʳ, q4ʳ.

of the Church Militant. He depicted it, using the biblical metaphor of Jerusalem, as a ravaged city, whose walls had been destroyed and were in sore need of rebuilding.[88] Even so, he made no fundamental criticism of the existing Church in terms of structure or organization, seeing its ills as the fault only of unworthy personnel. The remedy, therefore, lay in the replacement of its wicked prelates with worthy men: and it was his fervent plea to God that this should be accomplished.[89] Girolamo's own endeavours to improve the spiritual welfare of those persons in holy orders with whom he corresponded may be construed as an attempt to fulfil his reforming ideal. It was in the same spirit that he later wrote to Paolo Giustiniani, upon learning from a fellow Piagnone, Francesco Boni,[90] that he had entered the Camaldolese Order.[91] In his letter of 15 January 1511 he praised Giustiniani for this act of self-abnegation, which he saw to be a gift to the Church of precisely the sort of devout and scholarly person it so badly needed.[92]

But Girolamo would go no further than this. Ecclesiastical reform must wait upon God, and it must, moreover, be accomplished from within the existing hierarchy. The outlook of Girolamo Benivieni and of other conservative reformers is reflected in the activities of their various but overlapping circles. Francesco Boni was one of the links between Florentine Piagnoni like Girolamo, together with Fra Tommaso Strozzi and Fra Santi Pagnini, both of S. Marco, and the reformers within the Camaldolese Order, amongst whom Vincenzo Quirini and Paolo Giustiniani were prominent, and with whom Paolo Orlandini was to work in the reorganization of the Order.[93] Another link was Pier Francesco da

---

[88] 'Hieronymo Benivieni alla dilecta in Christo sorella N. de B.' in Benivieni, *Psalmi penitentiali di David*, sig. i4$^{r-v}$.

[89] Ibid.

[90] Pseudo-Burlamacchi, *La vita*, ed. P. Ginori Conti and R. Ridolfi (Florence, 1937), 19–20; Villari, *La storia di Girolamo Savonarola*, vol. ii, app., pp. ccii, ccxxviii, ccxxx, ccxxxiii, cclxi.

[91] Zorzi Pugliese, 'Girolamo Benivieni: Umanista riformatore', 272–4.

[92] Ibid., esp. 274.

[93] Ibid. 272–4; cf. also the letter of Pietro (formerly, in the secular life, Vincenzo) Quirini to Fra Tommaso Stoccio [i.e. Strozzi], 7 Sept. 1512, in Mittarelli and Costadoni, *Annales Camaldulenses*, vol. ix, app., cols. 571–3.

Gagliano,[94] who introduced Gasparo Contarini, close friend of Quirini and Giustiniani and later to be one of the key figures in the Catholic Reformation, to exponents of the Savonarolan cult in Florence.[95] The mutual respect between the groups must have been deep, since in 1512 Quirini extended a warm invitation to Tommaso Strozzi, Santi Pagnini, and two other friars of S. Marco to join the Camaldolese Order, assuring them that he would obtain full authorization from the Pope for the move.[96] Keeping in close contact, the various reformers encouraged each other in their efforts; suggested further worthwhile undertakings—Paolo Giustiniani, for example, urging upon Girolamo Benivieni the vital work of producing an Italian translation of the Bible[97]—and exchanged ideas on reform; but none of them was prepared to bypass the existing machinery or disregard the *magisterium* of the Church in order to achieve their aims.

For Girolamo Benivieni, renewed hope that the sort of reformation which he envisaged might yet be accomplished came with the election of Leo X to the papacy in 1513. In celebration of this event, which he saw as the inauguration of a new Christian era, Girolamo composed his *Frottola pro Papa Leone in renovatione ecclesiae*.[98] In this work, Leo X was hailed as the Angelic Pope who, elected by God, as Savonarola had foretold, would lead the Church into the dawning millennium.[99] Like the good shepherd, he would protect

---

[94] F. Gilbert, 'Contarini on Savonarola: An Unknown Document of 1516', *Archiv für Reformationsgeschichte*, 59 (1968), 146 n. 6.

[95] H. Jedin, 'Contarini und Camaldoli', *Archivio italiano per la storia della pietà*, 2 (1953), 99 n. 8, and 100, 101, 103–4, 108, 113. On the relations between certain Piagnoni, Contarini, and the Camaldolese friars, see also 'Copia d'una supplicatione . . . la quale Fra Pietro Quirino et Fra Paulo Iustiniano Veneti et Messer Pietro Bembo Secretario di Papa Leone feciono dare et signare da epso Papa Leone il secondo anno del suo Pontificato et mandaronla cosí signata a Fra Ruberto [Ubaldini]', in *Processo di S. Antonino*, MS BNF Conv. Sopp., J.I.51, fo. 84ᵛ; and J. B. Ross, 'Gasparo Contarini and his Friends', *Studies in the Renaissance*, 17 (1970), 192–232, and esp. 221–2; G. Fragnito, 'Cultura umanistica e riforma religiosa: Il "De officio boni viri ac probi episcopi" di Gasparo Contarini', *Studi Veneziani*, 11 (1969), 75–189, and esp. 119–25.

[96] Mittarelli and Costadoni, *Annales Camaldulenses*, vol. ix, app., cols. 571–3.

[97] Zorzi Pugliese, 'Girolamo Benivieni: Umanista riformatore', 276–8.

[98] Benivieni, *Opere*, fos. 196ᵛ–198ᵛ.

[99] Indeed, already in his lifetime, Savonarola had accepted, on the authority of

his flock against the ravages of despoilers. In his hands lay the future of the Church and the spiritual well-being of all its members, since without him, nothing could be achieved.[100] In a letter most likely written at about the same time, Girolamo gave a rather more down-to-earth account of the reform which it was the Pope's duty to initiate.[101] By contending that renovation was impossible without the head of the Church and its hierarchy, he implied that the Pope must ascertain whether the members of the hierarchy were adequate to fulfil this function. Above all, it was assumed that the promised reform and the present incumbent of S. Peter's Chair were indissolubly linked.[102] By favourably contrasting Leo X with his uniformly wicked and predatory predecessors, Girolamo much enhanced the overall impression of the *Frottola* that the present Pope had been specially selected by God for this role.[103]

In laying the Savonarolan dream at the feet of Leo X, Girolamo Benivieni was not alone among the conservative Piagnoni. Another to do so was Giovanfrancesco Pico, whom we last saw mounting a many-fronted attack on those who emphasized the importance of reason and experience in the acquisition of knowledge, at the expense of revealed truth. In August 1502, when his brother successfully stormed Mirandola,[104] Giovanfrancesco was forced to flee; and for the next eight or nine years he led a wandering existence, punctuated by sporadic attempts to wrest Mirandola from his

---

the visionary Suor Oretta da Ripoli, the Priest Giovanni Vitelli as the future Angelic Pope. Those of his friars who resisted this identification—an identification which, interestingly, Giovanni Vitelli himself was most reluctant to accept—were punished by Savonarola: see marginal annotation of Fra Giovanni Sinibaldi, one of the disgruntled friars, to Domenico Benivieni's, *Tractato . . . in defensione et probatione della doctrina et prophetie predicate da frate Hieronymo da Ferrara*, cit., in BNF Inc. Guicc. 3.7.91, sigs. e8ᵛ–f1ʳ.

[100] Ibid., esp. fos. 197ᵛ, 198ʳ.

[101] Zorzi Pugliese, 'Girolamo Benivieni: Umanista riformatore', 285–7. The letter is undated and the Pope to whom it was directed is not specified by name. In ibid. 285 n. 69, Zorzi Pugliese suggests that the addressee is more likely to have been Clement VII than Leo X, but, given the strong condemnations of preceding Popes which are made in the letter, it would seem unlikely that Girolamo was writing to Clement VII, since he would surely, if so, have exempted Leo X from these charges.

[102] Ibid. 285–6.      [103] Ibid. 286; cf. Benivieni, *Opere*, fo. 197ʳ.

[104] See above, p. 136.

mother's and brother's grasp. During this period, he took advantage, where occasion offered, of the opportunity to meet some of the foremost German humanists of the day: Willibald Pirckheimer and Johann Reuchlin, amongst others. With the assistance of Pope Julius II he recaptured Mirandola in January 1511, but Giovanfrancesco's success was short-lived, for by June he was once again in exile. In August 1514, however, Mirandola was once again restored to him.[105]

During these unsettled years, Giovanfrancesco continued to maintain his considerable literary output and to keep in touch with Florentine Piagnoni. Among those with whom he corresponded were two friars of S. Marco: Bartolomeo da Faenza, one of the great names in the Piagnone movement,[106] and Zanobi Acciaiuoli, through whom he kept up his contacts with Girolamo and Domenico Benivieni.[107] Fra Zanobi was a thinker very much after Giovanfrancesco's own heart. Although preoccupied with classical and patristic studies, he also gave his attention to the Church's pressing need for reform. The attractions of millenarian speculation were for him particularly strong: as early as 1495, for instance, he had importuned Pietro Delfin to obtain a treatise on the Angelic Pope for him from Venice.[108] From 1506 to 1510, he was engaged in spreading the Word of God, especially by preaching;[109] and in 1507 his *Oratio fratris Zenobii Acciaioli Florentini ordinis praedicatorum habita Romae coram Summo Pontifice* was published.[110] This work was an impassioned appeal for improvement in the spiritual ministrations of the Church. The need for reform was set firmly within a millenarian context:[111] the Papal Court was entreated, for exam-

---

[105] Schmitt, *Gianfrancesco Pico della Mirandola*, 18–26.

[106] Giovanfrancesco Pico, *Opera omnia*, ii. 1337. On Bartolomeo da Faenza, see *DBI* and below, pp. 200, 327, 341, 343, 400.

[107] Pico, *Opera omnia*, ii. 1274–8. On Zanobi Acciaiuoli, see *DBI*.

[108] Letter of Pietro Delfin 'Ad Hieronymum monachum', 14 Aug. 1495, in E. Martène and U. Durand (eds.), *Veterum scriptorum et monumentorum historicorum, dogmaticorum, moralium, amplissima collectio*, iii (Paris, 1734), cols. 1152–3.

[109] *DBI*.

[110] Zanobi Acciaiuoli, *Oratio fratris Zenobii Acciaioli Florentini ordinis praedicatorum habita Romae coram Summo Pontifice dominica prima Adventus MDVII* (Rome, 1507?).

[111] Ibid., sigs. a$^{r-v}$, a2$^{r-v}$, a3$^{r}$.

ple, to make the necessary changes before the coming judgement should overtake it. As part of the impending transformation of Christendom, Julius II was encouraged to expand its borders so that they should stretch even to the Orient, the eastward expansion of the Christian Church being a characteristically millenarian concept. Much was made, furthermore, of the wars and tribulations under which the Church was at present suffering, as these were taken as signs that the last days were indeed, as Fra Zanobi declared, truly imminent.[112]

Fra Vincenzo Mainardi da S. Gemignano, another friar of S. Marco, with whom Fra Zanobi had much in common and with whom in fact, during their frequent transfers, he kept up a regular correspondence, expressed similar but even more conservative views on reform.[113] A man renowned for his classical learning, but with only a middling knowledge of Holy Writ,[114] Fra Vincenzo was a favourite preacher of the Dominican hierarchy. He preached regularly to the synods of the Tusco-Roman Congregation.[115] Later, after the election of Leo X, he seems to have moved permanently to Rome, where he preached on a number of occasions before him and before Clement VII.[116] His letters show him to have been in contact not only with Fra Zanobi Acciaiuoli, but also with Fra Filippo Strozzi, Fra Giovanni Maria Canigiani, Fra Bartolomeo da Faenza, Fra Cherubino Primerani, Fra Lorenzo Macciagnini, and Pietro Quirini.[117] In these letters and in his sermons in particular, Fra Vincenzo demonstrates a genuine concern

---

[112] Zanobi Acciaiuoli, sigs. a2ᵛ–a3ʳ, a4ʳ⁻ᵛ, a5ᵛ–a6ᵛ. The text of the sermon was Luke 21: 25: 'Erunt signa in sole, et luna et stellis'.

[113] On him see Roberto Ubaldini, 'Annalia Conventus Sancti Marci', MS BMLF S. Marco 370, fo. 164ʳ.

[114] Ibid.

[115] Vincenzo Mainardi, 'Sermones et epistolae', MS BNF Magl., VI, 166, fos. 1ʳ–30ʳ: sermons preached in the convents of Pistoia, the Minerva at Rome, S. Spirito at Siena and Fiesole between 1505 and 1515.

[116] Ibid., fos. 30ᵛ–51ᵛ, dated between 1515 and 1526. These sermons, though not discussed by J. W. O'Malley, have many elements in common with those dealt with in his book *Praise and Blame in Renaissance Rome: Rhetoric, Doctrine, and Reform in the Sacred Orators of the Papal Court, c.1450–1521* (Durham, 1977).

[117] Vincenzo Mainardi, 'Sermones et epistolae', fos. 53ᵛ–91ᵛ; id., 'Epistolae', MS BNF Magl., XXXV, 225, fos. 64ʳ–89ᵛ.

for the state of the Church;[118] yet, when he comes to proffer his remedies, he has few original suggestions to make. Like the other conservative Piagnoni dealt with in this chapter, he too could not conceive of reform without Rome and the hierarchy. His concept of reform, moreover, is restricted purely to moral and disciplinary matters.

Not surprisingly, given his background, he attributes the present ills of the Church to a decline of learning and to the abandonment of virtues such as humility and charity so prized in previous generations.[119] He does not abstain from criticizing the clergy for its responsibility in the decline of Christian standards. Only the papacy and the Dominican Order are spared criticism. Indeed, his sermons show him to have been an apologist of both institutions. Dominican luminaries, but in particular Fra Antonino Pierozzi and S. Thomas Aquinas, are repeatedly praised for the reforms they introduced in the life and studies of the Order, reforms which brought about more effective preaching and thus the containment of corruption.[120] Their methods, he argues, had to be vigorously pursued in order to reform Christianity. Virtue had to be encouraged and proper study fostered. The pretensions of profane learning, and specifically astrology, classical poetry, and philosophy, had to be rejected so as to induce Christians to believe that salvation could be found only in Christ.[121] This simple message was none the less obscured by Fra Vincenzo's love of conceits and distorted by his readiness to show off the very profane learning he was condemning in others. The depth of his conservatism is most clearly evident in the sermons he preached before Leo X and Clement VII. In these sermons the whole of Christian history is viewed exclusively from the perspective of Rome and of the papacy. Rome and the papacy had been in the past and would continue to be in the future, the only fixed points in an ever-changing, troubled world, devoid of order and of peace.[122]

Disquiet and pessimism regarding the present turn of events were deep-seated and widespread. Among those voicing strong

---

[118] Ibid., fos. 59ᵛ–60ʳ; 'Sermones et epistolae', fos. 4ʳ, 5ᵛ, 16ʳ.
[119] Ibid., fos. 4ʳ, 7ᵛ, 9ᵛ.      [120] Ibid., fos. 4ᵛ, 7ᵛ, 8ᵛ.
[121] Ibid., fos. 9ᵛ–11ᵛ, 33ʳ.      [122] Ibid., fos. 33ʳ, 37ᵛ–40ʳ, 45ʳ⁻ᵛ.

concern about contemporary troubles was Giovanfrancesco Pico. Scorning as pagan the commonly held belief that this turmoil was the unavoidable consequence of an unfortunate conjunction of stars, he maintained it to be a sign of God's wrath. By its own sinful actions, Christendom had brought this suffering upon itself. This attitude was expressed with vehemence in his *Liber de veris calamitatum causis nostrorum temporum*, written in about 1515 and dedicated to Pope Leo X.[123] It was also an important ingredient in the *De reformandis moribus oratio* which Giovanfrancesco composed for presentation to the Fifth Lateran Council.[124] Addressed to Leo X and to the fathers of the Council, this treatise was the crowning achievement of Piagnone conservatism. Bringing to its fullest realization their concept of reform through existing channels, it bears comparison even with the masterly document produced for the same occasion by Quirini and Giustiniani and generally regarded as the summation of pre-Lutheran reforming thought.[125]

As with Savonarola himself, and indeed the majority of Giovanfrancesco's contemporaries who addressed themselves to the problem of ecclesiastical reform, the notion of a change in dogma was alien to Giovanfrancesco's vision of reform. In his *De reformandis moribus*, he gave no thought to it. Instead, in the programme which owed much to Savonarola's theories, he focused on the question of how far the Church was able to serve the religious needs of Christians. The problem which he considered to be the most cru-

---

[123] Giovanfrancesco Pico, *Liber de veris calamitatum causis nostrorum temporum ad Leonem X Pont. Max.*, ed. F. C. Cesio (Modena, 1860), 11–12, 22, 57–8, 61–8, 70–6. On this work, see C. E. Trinkaus, *Adversity's Noblemen: The Italian Humanists on Happiness* (New York, 1940), 130–2.

[124] Giovanfrancesco Pico, *Ad Leonem Decimum Pontificem Maximum et Concilium Lateranensem De reformandis moribus oratio*, in O. Gratius, *Fasciculus rerum expetendarum ac fugiendarum* (Cologne, 1535), fos. CCVIII^v–CCXV. On this work, see C. B. Schmitt, 'Gianfrancesco Pico della Mirandola and the Fifth Lateran Council', *Archiv für Reformationsgeschichte*, 61 (1970), 161–78; C. J. Hefele, J. Hergenröther, and H. Leclercq, *Histoire des Conciles*, viii (i) (Paris, 1917), 539–41; N. H. Minnich, 'Concepts of Reform proposed at the Fifth Lateran Council', *Archivum Historiae Pontificiae*, 7 (1969), 202–5.

[125] Paolo Giustiniani and Pietro (formerly Vincenzo) Quirini, *Libellus ad Leonem X*, in Mittarelli and Costadoni, *Annales Camaldulenses*, vol. ix, app., cols. 612–719. On this proposal, see H. Jedin, *Storia del Concilio di Trento* (4 vols. in 5; Brescia, 1973–81), i. 147–9 (hereafter cited as *Il Concilio di Trento*).

cial of those now confronting the Church was the abysmal deterioration in morals, especially those of the clergy, whose duty it should be to set an example to ordinary Christians.[126] To redeem Christendom, Giovanfrancesco proposed not a reform of existing laws, but their wholehearted implementation. Like his contemporaries who attended the Lateran Council, and Egidio da Viterbo especially, he believed that the legislation already in existence—based, as it was, on Scripture and the traditions of the primitive Church— was more than adequate, so long as it was properly enforced, to cope with even the present crisis.[127] The scriptural basis of these laws explains why Giovanfrancesco should have been as concerned as he was to see that the authenticity of biblical texts was established beyond dispute, and why he encouraged the work undertaken in this regard by Fra Santi Pagnini, who was engaged upon a new translation of the Bible from the Hebrew.[128] In common with Girolamo Benivieni and Paolo Giustiniani, Giovanfrancesco Pico argued that by making Scripture more readily available and more comprehensible great spiritual benefit would ensue and the worst moral abuses would be removed.[129] The blame for the fact that Christians had ceased to observe the laws of the Church, Giovanfrancesco asserted, was to be laid chiefly at the clergy's door. They had not only neglected to guide the laity in their charge but had

---

[126] Pico, *De reformandis moribus oratio*, fos. CCIX[r–v], CCX[r].

[127] Ibid., fos. CCVIII[v]–CCIX[r]. For the views of other prelates who addressed the Lateran Council on the subject of reform, see J. D. Mansi, *Sacrorum Conciliorum nova et amplissima collectio*, xxxii (Paris, 1902), esp. cols. 669–76, 719 ff., where the orations of Egidio da Viterbo and Tommaso de Vio Gaetano are printed; Minnich, 'Concepts of Reform proposed at the Fifth Lateran Council', esp. 233–4. On Egidio da Viterbo see J. W. O'Malley, 'Historical Thought and the Reform Crisis of the Early Sixteenth Century', *Theological Studies*, 28 (1967), 531–48; id., *Giles of Viterbo on Church and Reform: A Study in Renaissance Thought* (Leiden, 1968), esp. 2–3, 108–16, 139–48.

[128] See two letters from Giovanfrancesco Pico to Fra Santi Pagnini in 1518 and 1521, in Pico, *Opera omnia*, 1371–6. On Fra Santi Pagnini, see below, pp. 165, 247, 329, 376.

[129] Pico, *Opera omnia*, 1371–6. For Giustiniani's views, see his letter to Girolamo Benivieni, in Zorzi Pugliese, 'Girolamo Benivieni: Umanista riformatore', 277–8. See also Paolo Giustiniani and Pietro Quirini, *Libellus ad Leonem X*, cols. 682–3; F. Gilbert, 'Cristianesimo, umanesimo e la bolla "Apostolici Regiminis" del 1513', *Rivista storica italiana*, 79 (1967), 976–90.

failed to suppress their own baser instincts with respect to bene-
fices, indulgences, and the temptations of the flesh.[130] And the
result of their lack of self-restraint was that the Pope himself must
now shoulder the burdens of reform.

Here was the reason which, above all others, moved Giovanfrancesco Pico to lay his plans for reform before Leo X. If, as
Girolamo Benivieni maintained, Leo X had been appointed by God
to carry out the work of reformation,[131] this merely served to
highlight the desperate nature of the situation. It had come to such
a pass that, unless the Pope himself took charge, nothing could be
achieved. He must both initiate it and carry it through: directing
first the clergy, and then the people, to undertake a thorough moral
reformation and restore Christendom to the purity it had once
enjoyed.[132] To spur Leo X on to accomplish this mammoth task,
Giovanfrancesco made ominous reference to the tribulations under
which the Church was now suffering. These, clearly, were manifestations of God's wrath at the delay in renovation; equally clearly,
they were no more than a foretaste of the vengeance in store were
His will not immediately obeyed.[133] Speaking in the spirit of the
Piagnoni conservatives who had made it their creed, Giovanfrancesco declared, 'You can, Holy Father; nor can any one else do
so on earth; and since you are able to do it, you must.'[134]


## III


The achievements of the Lateran Council were to be cast into
abeyance by the sudden crisis of the Lutheran revolt late in 1517.
Almost before the constitutions of the Council were ratified, the
Church was thrown into confusion by this threat of a revolution
which proved to be far more radical than any hitherto contem-

---

[130] Pico, *De reformandis moribus oratio*, fos. CCIX$^r$–CCX$^r$.

[131] See above, p. 157. On the currency of this belief, see Paolo Giustiniani and
Pietro Quirini, *Libellus ad Leonem X*, col. 671, and below, p. 274.

[132] Pico, *De reformandis moribus oratio*, fos. CCIX$^v$, CCX$^v$.

[133] Ibid., fo. CCIX$^r$.

[134] Ibid., fo. CCIX$^v$: 'Potes, summe Pontifex, nec in terris alius potest, et quum
possis, debes.'

plated. Some Piagnoni extremists were apparently prepared to welcome the German reformer with open arms, regarding him as a fellow warrior in the crusade for ecclesiastical reform. The Piagnoni interlocutors in Bartolomeo Cerretani's *Storia in dialogo*, for example, were delighted at the news of Luther's stand on reform.[135] The majority of their brethren, however, were not. Iacopo Guicciardini, brother of the historian, looked askance upon the revolt;[136] while Fra Santi Pagnini of S. Marco, preaching in Lyons, carried on a campaign, by means of his sermons, to stop the spread of the infection through that city.[137] But the most outspoken opposition came from the conservatives, led, as always, by Girolamo Benivieni and Giovanfrancesco Pico. Girolamo Benivieni composed a prefatory letter to one of the earliest and most influential of the anti-Lutheran treatises: the *Apologia pro veritate catholice, et apostolice fidei, ac doctrine, adversus impia, ac valde pestifera Martini Lutheri dogmata*, by another Piagnone, Fra Ambrogio Caterino Politi of S. Marco.[138] In his epistle, Girolamo defended the unity of the Catholic Church and condemned Luther for creating schism by his pretended reformation. Giovanfrancesco

---

[135] Bartolomeo Cerretani, 'Storia in dialogo della mutatione di Firenze', MS BNF II.I.106, fo. 141ʳ. This enthusiasm was not as unqualified, however, nor as widespread among the Piagnoni as D. Cantimori has argued: D. Cantimori, 'Incontri italo-germanici nell'età della Riforma', *Studi Germanici*, 3 (1938), 67–70; id., *Eretici Italiani del Cinquecento* (Florence, 1939), 21–2. Cerretani's dialogue has been edited by R. Mordenti with the title *Dialogo della mutatione di Firenze* (Rome, 1990). I still refer, however, to the manuscript and to its original foliation.

[136] Letter of Iacopo Guicciardini to Niccolò Guicciardini, 10 June 1523, partially published in C. Guasti, *Le Carte Strozziane del R. Archivio di Stato in Firenze* (Inventario: 1st ser.) (2 vols.; Florence, 1884), i. 583–4. On Iacopo Guicciardini, see R. Ridolfi, *Gli archivi delle famiglie fiorentine*, i (Florence, 1934), 203; and below, p. 371.

[137] T. M. Centi, 'L'attività letteraria di Santi Pagnini (1470–1536) nel campo delle scienze bibliche', *AFP* 15 (1945), 20.

[138] Prefatory letter of Girolamo Benivieni to Antonio Negusantio in Ambrogio Caterino Politi, *Apologia pro veritate catholice, et apostolice fidei, ac doctrine, adversus impia, ac valde pestifera Martini Lutheri dommata*, ed. J. Schweizer (Corpus catholicorum, 27; Munster, 1956), 1. On Ambrogio Caterino Politi's Piagnoni sympathies at this time, see his *Discorso del Reverendo P. Frate Ambrosio Catharino Polito, Vescovo di Minori, contra la dottrina et le profetie di Fra Girolamo Savonarola* (Venice, 1548), fos. 1ʳ–2ᵛ; Benedetto Luschino, 'Vulnera diligentis', Part II, MS BNF Magl., XXXIV, 7, fo. 66ᵛ; Ridolfi, *Gli archivi delle famiglie fiorentine*, i. 70.

Pico took an even sterner line. His *Dialogus de adoratione*, written in 1524 and dedicated to Clement VII, inveighed against the Lutheran revolt because it had led Germany into impiety and, what was worse still, had rocked the foundations of divine worship throughout the whole of Christendom.[139] Calling Luther the worst of all heretics in all ages, Giovanfrancesco denounced him further for having transgressed all the canons of the Church, decreed by fathers and councils, in order to pursue his own course, contrary to the received tenets of the faith.[140] His sentiments were shared by Fra Vincenzo Mainardi, who, in addition, called on Clement VII to move against the schismatics and heretics who were destroying the Christian commonwealth (*respublica christiana*).[141]

Thus we find those in the vanguard of Catholic reform turning in outrage upon one with whom, at least for a time, they might have been expected to make common cause. Against Luther, Girolamo Benivieni and Giovanfrancesco Pico stood united with the most uncompromising defenders of the existing Church. Their own exhortations to reform temporarily forgotten, they closed ranks against an advocate of change far more extreme than they could bear to contemplate. The Lutheran revolt provides us with a new and illuminating perspective upon the moderate Piagnoni whose thought has been explored in this chapter. Luther completely overrode the sharply defined limits which hemmed in their own concept of reform. Fra Ambrogio Caterino Politi, in fact, who was later to renounce the Savonarolan cause completely, would seem to have traced his change of heart to the experience of the Lutheran revolt. With the destructiveness of this revolt in mind, he later denounced the Piagnone programme of reform, on the grounds that it could not be implemented without tearing the Church asunder.[142] Although Girolamo Benivieni and Giovanfrancesco Pico did not undergo such a reconversion, the Lutheran experience nevertheless

---

[139] Giovanfrancesco Pico, 'Dialogus de adoratione', MS BAV Vat. Lat. 3735, fos. 11ᵛ–14ʳ.

[140] Ibid.

[141] Mainardi, 'Sermones et epistolae', fos. 40ʳ–42ᵛ.

[142] Ambrogio Caterino Politi, *Discorso . . . contra la dottrina et le profetie di Fra Girolamo Savonarola*, fos. 36ᵛ–38ᵛ, 48ʳ.

changed them. Forced to reconsider their position, they became more cautious and, while not abandoning their Savonarolan sympathies, more alert to their possible consequences. The Lutheran revolt reveals how deeply conservative they were.

# 5

# *The Path to Radicalism*

## I

The intellectual luminaries of the last chapter have a vital place in the Piagnone legend. Their significance is reflected in Piagnone historiography, where, from the very first, they have been accorded pride of place.[1] While the importance of their contribution cannot be gainsaid, neither can it be allowed to overshadow the parts played by others who, in the first decade or so of the new century, were also devoting their every effort to the fulfilment of Savonarolan ideals. But not, however, by the same means. Theirs was not the conservative approach adopted by such Piagnoni as Girolamo Benivieni and Giovanfrancesco Pico; nor the radical, but limited, contemplative approach espoused by such Piagnoni as Domenico Benivieni and Pietro Bernardino. These Piagnoni wanted a root and branch ecclesiastical and social reform and set about implementing it independently of the existing ecclesiastical and civil hierarchies. Less learned, perhaps, than the conservatives, but no less forthright, these radicals imparted their own distinctive character to the movement. And the future, in fact, lay with them. The course of subsequent Piagnone history was largely determined by their activities.

'The more you kindle this fire', cried one of their number, addressing the Piagnoni's persecutors, 'the fiercer it will burn and

---

[1] See e.g. Pseudo-Burlamacchi, *La vita*, ed. P. Ginori Conti and R. Ridolfi (Florence, 1937), 12, 21, 28, 187, *et passim*; Serafino Razzi, 'Vita del Reverendo Padre Frate Girolamo da Ferrara', MS BRF 2012, fos. 36$^{r-v}$, 70$^{r-v}$; J. Schnitzer, *Savonarola* (2 vols.; Milan, 1931), i. 135–6, 158–61, 417, 420; ii. 517–19, 526–8, *et passim*.

spread throughout the world; moreover, although you have put the friar to death, this will not prevent his work from continuing: rather, this is the way to spread it even further.'[2] In these words, the spirit of Piagnone extremism is embodied. They epitomize the reaction of radicals both clerical and lay to all attempts to silence them. The more they were suppressed, the more fervent they became. Thus, the efforts of the ecclesiastical hierarchy, on the one hand, and the Florentine civil authorities, on the other, were long to prove self-defeating. Both powers were faced with a body of men and women who, inspired by Savonarola's teaching and outraged by his untimely end, relished persecution, reacting not with bowed heads, but with renewed endeavour, to whatever pressures were put upon them. Far from being passive in their response, the radicals welcomed the forces mounted against them, and their cause, in consequence, thrived.

The nature of their response, and its ideological origins, are explored in the present chapter. In the behaviour of Piagnoni clerics in the early years of the sixteenth century, we see this response at its most dramatic. Having come to the conclusion that the existing hierarchy was inimical to reform, they felt liberated from the ecclesiastical constraints which had hitherto limited their initiative. They were thus able to contemplate courses of action which would otherwise have been unthinkable. No longer bound by traditional ties, they were free to act independently of the Church and even, if necessary, in direct opposition to it. In these circumstances, their potential for radical activity was boundless. The corresponding behaviour of their lay counterparts, on the other hand, was neither as frenzied nor as extreme. While sharing the religious aspirations of their clerical brethren, lay Piagnoni did not take direct action against the government. There was no need, for in Savonarolan terms the government was sound, and was, indeed, the creation of the prophet himself. Room for improvement there certainly was, but this was less urgent than the pressing task of securing the system against the machinations of its

---

[2] See below, pp. 175–6: 'Quanto più stuzicherai questo fuoco . . . tanto più s'accenderà et dilaterà per tutto il mondo: et anchora, benchè tu habbi morto il frate, non impedirà che questa opera non vadi innanzi: anzi questa sia la via a dilatarla.'

adversaries. For the duration of the Florentine Republic, this was the end to which Piagnoni laymen, by and large, devoted their energies.

## II

In the early summer of 1498, Florence witnessed a curious procession. The great bell of the convent of S. Marco, known as the *Piagnona*, was publicly disgraced. Taken down from its tower, it was dragged through the streets of the city and, much to the delight, we are told, of the assembled throng, whipped all the way by the public executioner.[3] The *Piagnona* had been solemnly sentenced by the *Signoria* to suffer this indignity. Decrees of 29 and 30 June proclaimed that it was to be exiled to the convent of S. Salvatore al Monte, headquarters of the recently victorious campaign against Savonarola, and to remain there, in durance vile, for no fewer than fifty years.[4]

These proceedings, needless to say, were symbolic. How better to demonstrate to the Florentines that Savonarola's influence had come to an end than by silencing and degrading the voice which had called his supporters to worship and, when the convent was under siege on the night of 8 April last, to arms. The citizens, as the government well knew, were highly receptive to ceremonies of this sort, and quick to appreciate their purport. The Piagnoni, however, were no less averse than their now triumphant adversaries to utilizing symbols for their own purposes. And, in the present climate of anti-Savonarolan feeling, they had even more reason to do so. Calls to their fellow Savonarolans to remain faithful to the cause and to seek, at all costs, to promote it, could not be uttered openly without certain and immediate reprisal. These calls must therefore

---

[3] Schnitzer, *Savonarola*, ii. 432; L. Ferretti, 'Per la "Piagnona" di San Marco', *Memorie Domenicane*, 25 (1908), 375–8.

[4] ASF Signori e Collegi, Deliberazioni Ord. Aut. 100, fos. 68$^r$, 71$^v$, 74$^v$; P. Villari, *La storia di Girolamo Savonarola e de' suoi tempi* (2 vols.; Florence, 1930), vol. ii, app., pp. ccxci–ccxcii; A. Gherardi, *Nuovi documenti e studi intorno a Girolamo Savonarola* (Florence, 1887; fac. repr. 1972), 313–14.

be veiled; and veiled, to a considerable extent, they were. Using images from literature both sacred and profane; using extremely emotive scriptural texts; using, even, the very terms of abuse levelled at them by their opponents, militant Piagnoni clerics began, slowly but surely, to retrieve the ground they had lost and to marshal their scattered forces.

For nearly a year after Savonarola's execution, the Congregation of S. Marco would seem to have been cowed into submission. Even while Savonarola's trial was in progress, many friars, no doubt dismayed by the confessions extracted from him under torture, had wavered and abandoned their leader. On 21 April 1498 the convent of S. Marco had made a corporate act of submission to Alexander VI, abjectly begging absolution from the penalty of excommunication which it had incurred and solemnly abjuring Savonarola and his doctrines.[5] In May and June, for good measure, the *Signoria* exiled a number of friars from S. Marco, generally for a period of ten years but, in the case of Savonarola's brother Maurelio, for ever.[6] The *Signoria*'s acts of repression, among them the pillorying of the *Piagnona*, continued throughout 1498. The most effective steps to banish Savonarola's memory from S. Marco and to undo much of his work, however, were taken by the ecclesiastical hierarchy, acting through the superiors of the Dominican Order. On 23 May, the very day of Savonarola's execution, there was implemented the papal decree of 7 November 1496, quashing the independent Congregation of S. Marco and incorporating its four convents into a newly created Tusco-Roman Province, or Congregation, of sixteen convents, five of the remaining twelve being detached from the Lombard Congregation and seven from the Roman.[7] With the implementation of this decree, many of

---

[5] ASV, Politicorum, Arm, II.LV, for the letter of submission, of which there are two other copies in ibid., Arm. II.XX and CXXVIII, and a partial transcription in F. T. Perrens, *Jérome Savonarole, sa vie, ses prédications, ses éscrits* (2 vols.; Paris, 1856), i. 508–11, doc. XXI.

[6] ASF Signori e Collegi, Deliberazioni Ord. Aut. 100, fos. 52ᵛ–53ʳ, 55ᵛ, 57ᵛ, ibid. 101, fos. 23ᵛ, 68ʳ, 80ʳ, 81ᵛ, 85ʳ, 96ʳ⁻ᵛ, 102ᵛ, 105ʳ; Villari, *Storia di Girolamo Savonarola*, vol. ii, app., pp. cclxxviii–ccxc.

[7] For the decree, see above, p. 66. For its implementation, see Roberto Ubaldini, 'Annalia Conventus Sancti Marci', MS BMLF S. Marco 370, fo. 23ᵛ; R.

Savonarola's fears concerning what he had described as an unholy union were realized.[8] The unity of purpose which had been possible in a small, closely knit community was dispersed by incorporation into a large, heterogeneous unit. Independence of action was strictly curtailed, while interference from Rome became much harder to resist.

Both Gioacchino Torriani, the Master-General of the Dominican Order, and Francesco Mei, its Procurator, tried to prevent, when possible, the preferment of friars with known Savonarolan sympathies.[9] They were especially vigilant against signs of a resurgence of his ideals, and acted with uncompromising rigidity towards those customs and practices introduced by Savonarola and peculiar to the convents he had administered. For a while, it was not only impolitic, but also extremely foolhardy, to profess loyalty to Savonarola either in speech or in action. Not surprisingly, there were some notorious defections from the Savonarolan ranks.[10] More to the point, these ordinances had the effect of dividing the friars of the former Congregation of S. Marco. Even under Savonarola, there had been instances of discontent, and sometimes actual opposition to the policies pursued by the Congregation at his instigation. Now the hostility between the advocates of a stricter rule and the supporters of one more permissive, between the denigrators of hierarchical authority and its defenders—between, in short, the supporters of Savonarola and his adversaries—came to the surface. As well as their known enemies outside the convents, those friars who sought to continue Savonarola's work had also to beware of the brethren within their own communities who were embittered by past defeats and emboldened by the knowledge that

Creytens, 'Les Actes capitulaires de la Congrégation Toscano-Romaine O.P. (1496–1530)', *AFP* 40 (1970), 133. Despite the union, the newly created Congregation was often incorrectly called the Congregation of S. Marco by the authorities, see V. M. Fontana, *De Romana Provincia Ordinis Praedicatorum* (Rome, 1670), 23, 167.

[8] Girolamo Savonarola, *Apologeticum Fratrum Congregationis Sancti Marci Florentiae* [Florence, 1497] (Reichling 724), 300–1 and above, p. 76.

[9] e.g. the removal of Fra Jacopo da Sicilia from the post of Vicar of the Congregation by Mei, for which see Ubaldini, 'Annalia', fo. 25$^{r-v}$.

[10] Such as that by Fra Malatesta Sacramoro on whom see below, p. 180.

now their every complaint would find receptive ears in Rome. The internal peace of the convents was so threatened by the divisions that on 3 February 1499 Francesco Mei was forced to issue stringent orders for friars to refrain from mentioning Savonarola at all in their sermons and discussions, whether favourably or unfavourably, and to cease forthwith from using the pejorative terms *Piagnone* or *Compagnaccio*[11] to refer, respectively, to the pro- and to the anti-Savonarolan.

Other orders issued by Mei at the same time reveal further that the Piagnoni's spirit, although dimmed by the months of repression, was far from being extinguished. Despite the most severe ecclesiastical censures, some friars, according to Mei, were daring not only to venerate the relics of Savonarola and of his two companions executed with him, but also to resume the detestable practice of holding processions and singing the Psalm 'Ecce quam bonum', introduced by Savonarola and indissolubly linked with him and with his aspirations. Other friars were disseminating Savonarolan doctrine while ostensibly preaching the Word of God; others again had assumed the mantle of their dead leader and were claiming to enjoy heavenly visions and to be able to predict the future.[12] As a result, Mei was obliged to devise ways and means of stamping out these renewed manifestations of Savonarolan loyalty. Neither the threats of the penalties awaiting transgressors, however, nor the recommendations to superiors to increase their vigilance were to have any prompt effect. This was probably due to the fact that the Vicar-General of the new Tusco-Roman Congregation, Jacopo da Sicilia, especially appointed as a replacement for Savonarola, had turned out to be a crypto-Piagnone, more apt to encourage the cult than to suppress it.

In the middle of May 1499, little more than three months after the dispatch of Mei's instructions, the renewed Piagnone militancy at last broke the bounds of the Tusco-Roman Congregation. At this time, there was published an anonymous commentary on the Fifth

---

[11] For these orders, and for their ratification by Torriani, see Gherardi, *Nuovi documenti*, 329–30, 331–2.
[12] Ibid.

Psalm, 'Verba mea auribus percipe',[13] composed, as we now know, by Fra Simone Cinozzi of S. Marco.[14] Fra Simone was the son of Piero Cinozzi, who had been a signatory to the petition sent to Alexander VI in June 1497 and a stalwart defender on the night of 8 April 1498 of the convent of S. Marco, where, in addition to his son, he had two cousins and a nephew, among them Fra Placido Cinozzi, Savonarola's first biographer.[15]

In his commentary, Fra Simone carried on the family tradition, undertaking to exonerate Savonarola and to plead for the continued veneration of his name and doctrine. What made this commentary a milestone in Piagnone apologetics was the directness of its attack and its readiness to face delicate issues squarely. Unlike the Piagnoni polemicists who had contributed to the pamphlet war, for example, Fra Simone was not prepared to leave the question of papal responsibility for Savonarola's fate in abeyance, by resorting to the trite argument that Alexander VI had been wrongly advised. Nor did he shrink from calling the Florentine government to account for its part in the prophet's downfall. Both were roundly condemned: Florence as the perpetrator of the crime, the Pope as its mastermind.[16]

According to Fra Simone, the division separating those who supported Savonarola against all odds from those who contributed to his fall was the dividing line between the righteous and the unrighteous. Using a series of key phrases, which were to become

---

[13] [Simone Cinozzi], *Expositione sopra el psalmo 'Verba mea auribus percipe'* [Florence, 1499] (Hain 14409); Piero Parenti, *Istorie fiorentine*, ed. J. Schnitzer (Leipzig 1910), 288.

[14] G. C. Olschki, 'Un codice savonaroliano sconosciuto', *La Bibliofilia*, 23 (1921), 163–4; R. Ridolfi, *Vita di Girolamo Savonarola* (2 vols.; Rome, 1952), ii. 235. Additional evidence not cited by either is to be found in 'Registrum litterarum et actorum fr. Joachim Turriani, Mag, Gen, O.P.', AGOP, IV, 12, fo. 52ʳ. (Two brief extracts from the five registers of Torriani's letters and acts— AGOP, IV, 9–13—are printed in Gherardi, *Nuovi Documenti*, 332, 334.) For Fra Simone Cinozzi, see Convento di S. Marco, 'Liber vestitionum', MS ACSM (no location number), fo. 2ᵛ.

[15] For Piero Cinozzi, see Villari, *La storia di Girolamo Savonarola*, vol. ii, app., pp. ccxxxvii–ccxxxix; and Parenti, *Istorie fiorentine*, 273, 276.

[16] [Simone Cinozzi], *Expositione sopra el psalmo 'Verba mea auribus percipe'*, sigs. a2ʳ, a4ʳ⁻ᵛ, a5ʳ.

increasingly popular, he elaborated this point. Since Savonarola
had been God's chosen instrument of reform, he argued—the new
Moses, who was to lead the Chosen People into the Promised
Land—it followed that the anti-Savonarolans were the instruments of evil, as Pharaoh had been to the Israelites.[17] The corruption of the Church and of Florence herself confirmed Fra Simone
in his opinion, moving him to call down the wrath of Heaven upon
them. 'Woe,' he cried, 'woe, I say, to the prelates who have kept the
truth hidden from their charges. Woe to the confessors who have
not advised them properly and have not led them to a righteous
life, but instead have turned them away from it with their false
arguments'. 'Further, I say to you, Florence: woe, woe to you',
he continued, drawing now upon a text which was to become
the watchword of Piagnone militancy, 'because you killed the
prophet.'[18] Florence's fate was certain. Like those other cities of
iniquity, Sodom and Gomorrah, she would perish. The same end,
moreover, awaited all those who killed the prophets of the Lord.
Their hands 'stained with the blood of the three saints', prelates,
confessors, and the rest would suffer the vengeance of eternal fire.[19]
For those whom they oppressed, however, there was the promise of
heavenly glory.[20] This very persecution, in fact, was proof that God
numbered them amongst His chosen. This was a vital theme in Fra
Simone's commentary. When interceding with God on the
Piagnoni's behalf, for example, he spoke of them as 'Your elect'; he
thus equated espousal of the Savonarolan cause with the certainty
of eternal life and made the threat of persecution a trial of faith to
be welcomed with eagerness.[21] Moved by this belief, Fra Simone
could declare with utter conviction that a stronger movement
would emerge, phoenix-like, from the ashes of Savonarola's funeral
pyre. 'The more you kindle this fire', he declaimed to Florence,
'the fiercer it will burn and spread throughout the world; moreover,

---

[17] Ibid., sigs. a2$^v$, a4$^r$.

[18] Ibid., sig. a4$^r$: 'Guai, guai dico alli prelati che hanno tenuto ascoso la verità
alle pecorelle sue. Guai alli confessori che non l'hanno ben consigliate et ridocte al
ben vivere, ma da quello l'hanno rimosso con loro false persuasioni . . . Ancora
dico a te Firenze: guai guai a te qua re occidisti prophetam.'

[19] Ibid., sig. a4$^v$: 'macchiate . . . del sangue dei tre santi'; cf. sigs. a4$^{r–v}$, a5$^r$.

[20] Ibid., sig. a8$^r$.      [21] Ibid., sig. a7$^r$; cf. sigs. al$^{r–v}$, a2$^r$, a8$^{r–v}$.

although you have put the friar to death, this will not prevent his work from continuing: rather, this is the way to spread it even further.'[22]

Reaction was prompt. This defiant language, as Parenti tells us, infuriated many Florentines, who took steps to ensure that 'it should be punished as something irreligious and evil'.[23] Recognizing the dangers inherent in the sentiments which the commentary expressed, the civil and ecclesiastical authorities began an immediate witch hunt to discover its author. Copies were taken to the *Signoria* and to the *Otto di Guardia* and formal charges were laid against the unknown writer. Eventually, since the matter was deemed dangerous and concerned the Pope, it was decided to refer it to Rome.[24] The papal authorities needed no urging to act. As early as 24 May, Gioacchino Torriani had appointed a commission of three friars, headed by the redoubtable Giovanni Caroli, invested with plenipotentiary powers, to undertake a thorough investigation in the convents of S. Marco, S. Domenico at Fiesole, and S. Domenico at Prato, in order to seek out all those who had taken any part in the commentary's composition and publication.[25] Moving with impressive speed, the commission brought its inquiries to a successful conclusion, so that, by 8 June, Torriani was able to pass formal sentence on the culprits. As the commentary's author, Fra Simone Cinozzi was transferred from S. Marco to the Convent of the SS. Annunziata at S. Gimignano, deprived of his privileges, and otherwise sentenced to all the penalties prescribed

---

[22] [Simone Cinozzi], sig. a4ᵛ: 'Quanto, più stuzicherai questo fuoco . . . tanto più s'accenderà et dilaterà per tutto il mondo: et anchora, benchè tu habbi morto il frate, non impedirà che questa opera non vadi innanzi: anzi questa sia la via a dilatarla.'

[23] Parenti, *Istorie fiorentine*, 288–9: 'come cosa infedele et trista si dovessi gastigare'.

[24] Ibid. 289.

[25] Gioacchino Torriani, 'Registrum litterarum et actorum', AGOP, IV, 12, fo. 50ʳ. The transcription of this document in Gherardi, *Nuovi documenti*, 332, is wildly inaccurate, distorting, unrecognizably, Giovanni Caroli's name. The other two members of the commission, Mariano Vernaccia and Andrea Anselmi, were two of the oldest friars of S. Marco. I should like to thank Fr. Bernard Montagnes, formerly Archivist of AGOP for kindly checking the accuracy of my transcription.

for those found guilty of a major crime, which included a public act of repentance or submission and a diet of bread and water.[26] Fra Francesco de' Medici, one of Fra Simone's accomplices and a friar already notorious for his part in arming S. Marco on the night of 8 April,[27] was transferred to the convent of Sta Maria della Quercia at Viterbo, whence he was not to be moved without a special licence; and another accomplice, Fra Lorenzo da Uzzano, then Prior of S. Domenico at Fiesole, was relieved of his post.[28]

As Fra Simone had warned,[29] the authorities were to have cause to rue their actions. Only days after Torriani passed sentence on him and his accomplices, another friar of S. Marco, Fra Stefano da Codiponte, proclaimed his defiance in a sermon on Matt. 23: 37, a text which was rapidly gaining in popularity: 'O Jerusalem, Jerusalem, thou that killest the prophets and stonest them which are sent unto thee.'[30] The sermon was a vehement attack on the arguments adduced by the Church in defence of the execution of Savonarola and his two fellow Dominicans. Punitive action was forestalled by Fra Stefano's death; but his defiant mood had not gone unnoticed by Torriani, who said that, had he not died, he would have been burned at the stake, so incensed was the Apostolic See by his sermon.[31] Clearly, there were to be no half measures.

But railing against Piagnone obduracy was one thing; successfully quelling it was quite another. Informed that some convents had observed the anniversary of Savonarola's execution with ceremonies properly intended by the Church for the commemoration of martyred saints, Torriani wrote in fury to the priors of the Tusco-Roman Congregation that, by such demonstration, they threatened to make the whole Dominican Order the target of hatred and contempt.[32] Renewing his previous commands, he pro-

---

[26] Torriani, 'Registrum litterarum et actorum', AGOP, IV 12, fo. 52$^r$.

[27] Villari, *La storia di Girolamo Savonarola*, vol. ii, app., pp. ccxxxiii–ccxxxvi, ccxlv–ccxlvi.

[28] Torriani, 'Registrum litterarum et actorum', AGOP, IV, 12, fo. 52$^r$. For Fra Lorenzo, see Ubaldini, 'Annalia', fo. 167$^r$; and Convento di S. Domenico, Fiesole, 'Chronica Conventus Sancti Dominici de Fesulis', MS Archivio del convento di S. Domenico (no location number), fo. 50$^r$.

[29] See above, p.175.     [30] Gherardi, *Nuovi documenti*, 332–3.

[31] Ibid. 333.     [32] Ibid.

hibited the veneration of Savonarola or the discussion of his teaching; and went on to ban the introduction and performance of ceremonies not specified in the Constitutions of the Dominican Order.[33] Even so, a month later, they were to be renewed once more, and, before the year was out, yet again. The following year a similar fiat was issued to all convents of Dominican nuns in Florence.[34] Torriani's successors, Fra Vincenzo Bandelli and Fra Tommaso de Vio (better known as Gaetano or Cajetan), did no better. Equally numerous, and equally repetitious, injunctions and prohibitions are to be found in their registers also.[35] The Piagnoni could not be silenced by such means. As the anonymous tract, *Loqui prohibeor et tacere non possum*,[36] made clear, ecclesiastical prohibitions did not daunt them. In the presence of evil, the author maintained, the Christian could not remain silent if he valued his immortal soul. By suppressing dissident voices, princes and prelates were endeavouring to keep the truth hidden from those yearning for salvation. To obey their injunctions to silence, therefore, was to conspire with them in their deception and thus to contribute to the further diffusion of evil. Longingly, the anonymous Piagnone recalled Savonarola's day, when the faithful had experienced the sweetness of Christian living and had been drawn within reach of eternal life. Armed with this memory, he could not but bear witness as stridently as possible against the present spiritual tyranny.[37] 'Hence, I cannot be silent', he cried. 'Hence, I am compelled to speak and forced to cry out.'[38]

For this writer, mere belief in Savonarola and his teaching, which Fra Simone had considered sufficient to ensure membership of the elect, was not enough. To have any hope of salvation, the

---

[33] Ibid., 333–4; but see also Torriani, 'Registrum litterarum et actorum', AGOP, IV, 12, fo. 52ᵛ.

[34] Ibid., fo. 53ʳ; ibid., IV, 13, fo. 43ʳ; ibid., IV, 14, fo. 299ʳ; Gherardi, *Nuovi documenti*, 334–5.

[35] See below, pp. 185–6, 305–6.

[36] *Loqui prohibeor et tacere non possum* [n.p.n.d.]. On this work, long mistakenly attributed to Savonarola, see Villari, *La storia di Girolamo Savonarola*, ii. 63–4; and Schnitzer, *Savonarola*, ii. 465, 495 nn. 10 and 11.

[37] *Loqui prohibeor et tacere non possum*, sigs. a1ʳ–a4ᵛ.

[38] Ibid., sigs. a2ᵛ–a3ʳ, *et passim*: 'Ideo tacere non possum . . . Ideo loqui cogor et exclamare compellor'.

Piagnone had also to proclaim his beliefs in public, taking no heed of the powers massed against him. It is plain that the Piagnoni militants were demanding a progressively greater commitment from their supporters. The demand was to be further extended by yet another friar from S. Marco, Fra Giovanni da Pescia, in a treatise composed in the early months of 1500. His *Operecta interrogathoria*[39] reiterated the well-known arguments attesting the veracity of Savonarola's prophecies and the necessity for all Christians to follow his doctrine in order to earn the prize of eternal life. Fra Giovanni broke new ground, however, when he went on to assert that this prize would nevertheless be denied to the weak and timorous. To earn their heavenly crown, Christians had not only, as the author of the anonymous tract contended, to declare publicly their belief in Savonarola and to vindicate his conduct on every occasion: they had also to resist the sinners who attempted to expunge his memory and even, if called upon, to lay down their lives for him.[40]

In the latter part of his treatise, Fra Giovanni gave a striking example of the sort of commitment he required. He bent his vengeful gaze upon Fra Francesco Mei, the Procurator-General of the Dominican Order. To the Piagnoni, Mei was an apostate because he had turned against Savonarola, had contributed to his downfall, and was now determined to enforce Torriani's injunctions to the full.[41] Fra Giovanni was eloquent in his indictment. 'Come forward', he cried, addressing Fra Francesco, 'you who live constantly in Roman Babylon: you who after being appointed Procurator-General to the whole Dominican Order are now doing your utmost to procure the complete destruction of the seed sown by those who believe in the work foretold by Savonarola . . . Truly, you may well

---

[39] Giovanni da Pescia, 'Operecta interrogathoria fatta da un certo amico in chonsolatione di tutti e fedeli dell'opera di Frate Hieronymo da Ferrara: la quale demostra la malvagità e sciocchezza della chontraria parte: chon forte ragioni', MS BNF Magl., XXXV, 116, fos. 79^v–104^r (collated with another copy in BNF Magl., XXXVII, 65).

[40] Giovanni da Pescia, 'Operecta interrogathoria', fo. 85^{r-v}.

[41] P. Masetti, *Monumenta et antiquitates veteris disciplinae Ordinis Praedicatorum* (2 vols.; Rome, 1864), i. 471; Ridolfi, *Vita di Girolamo Savonarola*, i. 94, 113, 270; ii. 30.

boast that you have been one of the chief instruments to have appeared against that work.' To Fra Francesco, perhaps, this may have seemed a tribute; to Fra Giovanni, it was the greatest possible condemnation. For the seed, the *sementa*, that Fra Francesco persecuted was the seed of Christ Himself. 'As great as your efforts have been', Fra Giovanni continued, 'your present one is even greater in the way you persecute the poor seed in Jesus Christ; and even greater therefore will be the reward set up for you in hell.'[42]

The attack was resumed in a letter which Fra Giovanni sent on 10 May 1500 to the friars of the Tusco-Roman Congregation, then holding a Provincial Chapter in S. Domenico at Fiesole.[43] In the short interval between the composition of the *Operecta interrogathoria* and the dispatch of this letter, a considerable commotion had arisen. Fra Malatesta, another defector from Savonarolan ranks and newly created Vicar-General of the Order, had, inevitably, been informed of the general tenor of the treatise. Accordingly, while composing his letter, Fra Giovanni was expecting the imminent arrival either of the Vicar-General himself or of a specially deputized commission of friars to examine him on his views.[44] As he waited, he received a letter from a group of friars from S. Marco,

---

[42] Giovanni da Pescia, 'Operecta interrogathoria', fos. 95$^v$–97$^v$: 'Fatti un pocho innanzi tu el quale habiti de lo chontinuo nella romana babbilonia: El quale dopo l'essere creato prochuratore di tutto l'ordine di Sancto Domenicho t'ingegni etiam prochurare di volere pure mandare per terra totaliter tutta la sementa di chi crede la opera prenuntiata dal padre frate Ieronimo . . . Veramente tu ti poi vantare essere stato contro a questa opera uno dei principali instrumenti che appariscano. Grande è stata la tua fatica, maggiore è quella che al presente tu operi in persequitare la povera semente in Iesu Christo, maximo adunque sarà el premio riservatoti in inferno.'

[43] Giovanni da Pescia, 'Chopia d'una lettera di frate Giovanni da Pescia dell'ordine de' frati predicatori alli frati di decto ordine congregati a Sancto Domenico da Fiesole dove celebrorono el loro capitolo del mese di maggio proximo passato 1500', MS BNF Guicciardini 3.4.2. (This is a 19th-cent. transcript of the copy in MS BNF Magl., XXXV, 190, collated with copies in MS BNF Magl., XXXV, 116 and 205. In the Guicciardini catalogue, the work is incorrectly listed as *Operetta interrogatoria*.)

[44] The second possibility is more likely, since Fra Malatesta was still under the ban of exile from Florence and her territory, which had been imposed on 4 June 1498 and was not rescinded until 28 May 1500, eighteen days after Fra Giovanni wrote his letter. For the *Signoria*'s decree, pardoning all friars exiled in 1498, with the exception of Fra Maurelio Savonarola, see Gherardi, *Nuovi documenti*, 327–8.

at present in S. Domenico for the Chapter, who, at no small risk to their own safety, wrote urging him to hold fast to his convictions.[45] In his reply of 10 May, Fra Giovanni assured them that he had no intention of recanting, despite the 'monkish persecutions' to which he was subjected.[46] For him, the possibility of recanting or of equivocating did not exist. He could envisage no alternative to upholding the truth to the end. 'I cannot do otherwise', he declared simply: here he stood; he could do no other. Lamenting, indeed, that nothing had been done yet, he expressed his relish at the prospect of an encounter which would enable him to prove his devotion to the cause.[47]

'Monkish persecutions' was his term for the harassment to which he was now being subjected by his superiors in the Order. Coming from a professed Dominican, it strikes an oddly discordant note. Such a contemptuous phrase would surely have been more appropriate to the pen of an anti-clerical Machiavelli or Guicciardini than a friar who had taken solemn vows of obedience. It reveals, in fact, how far Fra Giovanni had travelled beyond the usual limits of acceptable conduct. The approval or disapproval of his ecclesiastical superiors had ceased to matter to him. Guided, as he believed, by a higher authority, he no longer owed allegiance to them. Answerable for his conduct to God alone, he was distanced from his formal superiors and thus able to judge them, and even the Vicar-General himself, with supreme detachment. Here we have the key to Piagnone radicalism. Savonarolans like Fra Giovanni were alienated, by their beliefs, from their lawfully constituted superiors, and, indeed, from all men. This gave them the freedom to stand out against powers both civil and ecclesiastical, to propose alternatives to the existing structure of society and, what is more, to set about putting them into effect. Understanding this, we may more fully understand the threat implicit in Fra Simone Cinozzi's words concerning the impossibility of quenching the fires of

For Fra Giovanni's comments on his situation at the time of his letter's composition, see 'Chopia d'una lettera', fos. 1ʳ⁻ᵛ.

[45] To protect them, he destroyed their letter: Giovanni da Pescia, 'Chopia d'una lettera', fo. 4ᵛ; cf. fo. 1ʳ.

[46] Ibid., fo. 1ᵛ: 'tribulationi fratesche'.           [47] Ibid., fo. 1ʳ.

Piagnone militancy:[48] words which Fra Giovanni, too, uttered. 'I cannot do otherwise', he began, 'for a flame is constantly gnawing at my heartstrings, and the more they try to extinguish it, the more it embraces my heart.'[49] Such was the path which the Piagnone militant trod. His purpose was single-minded and his policy uncompromising. In the world, but not of it, he steered an undeviating course towards his heavenly goal.

In his letter of 10 May, Fra Giovanni made intriguing reference to an accompanying treatise. 'I am sending you—enclosed in this letter—a strong defence which God in His goodness has inspired me to write and which proves', he told the friars, 'that Savonarola did not recant nor can he ever do so; have it copied for the whole of Florence and show it to anyone who wishes to see it.'[50] This treatise may now be identified as the *Argumentum eiusdem obiectione*.[51] In one of the manuscripts containing a copy of Fra Giovanni's letter, the opening lines of the *Argumentum* follow immediately;[52] in another—the only manuscript, moreover, in which the full text of the

---

[48] See above, p. 175.

[49] Giovanni da Pescia, 'Chopia d'una lettera', fo. 2ʳ: 'Altro non posso fare quoniam una fiamma mi mangi[a] continuo le medulla del core, et quanto più cerchano di spegnerla tanto maggiormente mi abbraccia il core.'

[50] Ibid., fo. 4ʳ: 'Mandovi una ragione fortissima la quale Iddio per sua bontà mi [ha] inspirato la quale prova che il padre frate Hieronimo non si è ridetto nè si può ridire inclusa in questa lettera nostra; fatela copiare a tutto Firenze et mostratela a chi la vuol vedere.'

[51] [Giovanni da Pescia], 'Argumentum eiusdem obiectione', MS BNF Magl., XXXV, 116, fos. 77ᵛ–79ʳ. Following the treatise are the words, 'Operecta dello M.S. Iohanfrancesco Pico', subsequently erased. Disregarding the erasure, Prof. Weinstein has concluded that Giovanfrancesco Pico della Mirandola was the author of the *Argumentum*, a conclusion for which P. Cherubelli's ambiguous description of the contents of MS BNF Magl., XXXV, 116, had left the way open: D. Weinstein, *Savonarola and Florence: Prophecy and Patriotism in the Renaissance* (Princeton, NJ, 1970), 242 n. 39; P. Cherubelli, 'Una miscellanea savonaroliana inedita del primo Cinquecento', *La Rinascita*, 4 (1941), 610. If the erasure is allowed to stand, however, an alternative explanation emerges. It is that the words were intended *not* to conclude the *Argumentum*, but to introduce another work, the *Operecta dello M. S. Johanfrancesco Pico della Mirandola in defentione della opera di Pietro Bernardo da Firenze* (for which see above, pp. 117–18) which follows later, on fos. 104ʳ–116ʳ. Clearly the transcriber, having first thought to copy this work immediately after the *Argumentum*, changed his mind, erased the words of the title already written, and placed it at a later and more appropriate point.

[52] MS BNF Guicciardini 3.4.2, fo. 5ʳ.

*Argumentum* survives—the entire treatise follows immediately upon the letter.[53] The likelihood that the *Argumentum* is, therefore, the work which Fra Giovanni described as 'enclosed in this letter'[54] is confirmed by its contents. It tackles the question of Savonarola's confession head-on, contending, as Fra Giovanni had outlined, 'that Savonarola has not recanted, nor can he ever do so'.[55] Whatever Savonarola had been forced to confess at his trial, Fra Giovanni asserted, nothing could diminish the truth of his diagnosis of the present corrupt state of the Church and the pressing need for its reform. To accept his recantation, extracted under duress by those who had a vested interest in maintaining the status quo, was tantamount to believing that the Church was neither corrupt nor in need of reform: and this was manifestly untrue. 'Who in our times will say—unless he be a fool—that the Church should not be flayed for its iniquities and filthy deeds? Who on earth will say if God cares and provides for the world that He will not reform Holy Mother Church, for whom He shed His precious blood?'[56]

To these fiery arguments, powerfully expressed, Fra Giovanni added the acumen of a practical and calculating campaigner. His inflammatory assertions were based on a careful assessment of the support he could command within the Tusco-Roman Congregation. In the *Operecta interrogathoria*, for instance, he had warned the anti-Savonarolan faction that they were outnumbered six to one by Piagnoni friars: a situation which, in the *Chopia duna lettera*, he implied had contributed to Fra Malatesta's delay in proceeding

---

[53] MS BNF Magl., XXXV, 116, fos. 77ᵛ–79ʳ.

[54] J. Schnitzer's conclusion that the work referred to was the *Operecta interrogathoria* (perhaps because the existence of the *Argumentum* was unknown to him) is unacceptable, since in the *Chopia d'una lettera* Fra Giovanni clearly states that the *Operecta interrogathoria* had been the cause of his present difficulties and that it was already known to the friars: Schnitzer, *Savonarola*, ii. 465; Giovanni da Pescia, 'Chopia d'una lettera', fo. 1ʳ.

[55] [Giovanni da Pescia], 'Argumentum eiusdem obiectione', MS BNF Magl., XXXV, 116, fo. 77ᵛ; cf. 'Chopia d'una lettera', MS BNF Guicciardini 3.4.2, fo. 5ʳ.

[56] [Giovanni da Pescia], 'Argumentum eiusdem obiectione', fo. 77ᵛ: 'Chi dirà mai alli tempi nostri se non hè [*sic*] già uno sciocho che la Chiesa non habbia a essere flagellata per le iniquità et spurcitie sue? Chi dirà mai . . . se Dio li ha providentia del mondo che non rinuova la Sancta Madre Ecclesia per la quale ha sparso il suo pretioso sangue?' See also fos. 77ᵛ–78ᵛ.

against him.[57] In the *Chopia duna lettera*, he also listed the names of certain friars, occupying senior positions, whose loyalty to the Savonarolan cause was unquestioned and who could therefore be counted upon in a crisis:[58] Fra Jacopo da Sicilia, late Vicar-General of the Congregation and now Prior of the convent of S. Romano in Lucca;[59] Fra Bartolomeo da Faenza, the most formidable theologian in the Congregation and Reader at the convent of S. Marco;[60] and Fra Giovanni Sinibaldi, former Master of Novices in the convent of S. Marco and about to be elected Prior of the convent of Sta Maria della Quercia.[61] Confident of the Savonarolans' strength, and exasperated by their failure so far to use it, Fra Giovanni pleaded with them to act. 'Use your power,' he urged in the *Argumentum eiusdem obiectione*, 'since the government is now in your hands, and assist the preachers who are ready to shed their blood and sacrifice their lives for this truth, which is not Savonarola's but God's.'[62]

Nothing more came from Fra Giovanni's pen. What fate befell him can only be surmised. There can be little doubt, however, that he was condemned to the maximum penalties laid down by Torriani for those who defied his orders.[63] Since, after May 1500,

[57] Giovanni da Pescia, 'Operecta interrogathoria', fos. 100ᵛ–101ʳ; 'Chopia d'una lettera', fos. 1ʳ, 4ᵛ.

[58] Ibid., fo. 4ʳ.

[59] Creytens, 'Les Actes capitulaires', 144–5 *et passim*; Ubaldini, 'Annalia', fo. 24ʳ *et passim*.

[60] Ibid., fo. 171ʳ; *DBI*.

[61] Ubaldini, 'Annalia', fos. 94ʳ, 166ᵛ; Villari, *La storia di Girolamo Savonarola*, vol. ii, app., pp. clxx, ccxx. Ridolfi, *Vita di Girolamo Savonarola*, i. 149, and ii. 104, 106, 133, 176, has recognized in the marginal annotations to a copy of Domenico Benivieni, *Tractato* (BNF Inc. Guicc. 3.7.91) Sinibaldi's hand. Given the tone of some of these annotations it would seem that Sinibaldi had by this time severe reservations about Savonarola.

[62] [Giovanni da Pescia], 'Argumentum eiusdem obiectione', fo. 78ʳ: 'Date adunque loco per la potentia vostra, havendo massime al presente il governo nelle mani, alli predicatori li quali per questa verità la quale non è di frate Hieronimo ma di Dio voglion spargere il proprio sangue e mettervi la vita.'

[63] The fact that Torriani died while the case of Fra Giovanni was under consideration, and that Fra Vincenzo Bandelli, while acting as Master-General thereafter in his stead, was not formally elected to the post until May 1501, may account for the absence of Fra Giovanni's name from the registers of either: D. A. Mortier, *Histoire des Maitres généraux de l'Ordre des Frères Precheurs*, v (Paris, 1911), 65–6.

his name disappears from the records of the Tusco-Roman Congregation, and since, at the time of his death, he held the office of Reader in a Conventual, not an Observant, convent at Cortona,[64] it would appear likely that his punishment was so severe as to include banishment from the Observant wing of the Dominican Order. The minutes of the Tusco-Roman Congregation's provincial Chapter at S. Domenico in Fiesole have not survived,[65] so that it is impossible to know whether the trial of strength which Fra Giovanni had eagerly envisaged between the Piagnoni and their opponents ever took place. Judging by the elections in 1500 and 1501, however, the Savonarolans seem to have suffered a serious reverse. With the exception of Fra Giovanni Sinibaldi, whose loyalty by this time was suspect, they lost their former positions of influence within the Congregation, which suggests that the Chapter was under considerable pressure not to elect candidates of known Piagnoni sympathies.[66] Meanwhile, with the full support of Fra Vincenzo Bandelli, who had succeeded Torriani as Master-General after his death in August 1500, Fra Malatesta proceeded to silence dissent within the Tusco-Roman Congregation. Not content merely to renew Torriani's measures, he and Fra Vincenzo commanded the friars to adhere strictly to the Rule of the Order in all matters pertaining to worship, discipline, and dress:[67] an attempt to suppress the customs which Savonarola had initiated and which his followers preserved as a means of demonstrating their loyalty to him and their contempt for the present superiors of the Order.[68]

---

[64] Ubaldini, 'Annalia'. fo. 168ᵛ.

[65] In 'Les Actes capitulaires', R. Creytens publishes only the decisions taken at the Chapters of the Tusco-Roman Congregation; and, since even these did not begin to be collected until the 1520s, they are very scanty for the early years of the Congregation's history.

[66] Creytens, 'Les Actes capitulaires', 150–2.

[67] Vincenzo Bandelli, 'Registrum litterarum et actorum', AGOP, IV, 15, fos. 65ᵛ, 66ᵛ, 67ʳ; Gherardi, *Nuovi documenti*, 335–6. Such prohibitions were usually extended to the Order as a whole at a subsequent general Chapter: see B. M. Reichert (ed.), *Acta Capitulorum Generalium Ordinis Praedicatorum*, iii and iv (Monumenta Ordinis Fratrum Praedicatorum Historica, 8 and 9; Rome, 1900–1), iii. 424–5; iv. 6, 40–1.

[68] Bartolomeo Cerretani, *Istoria fiorentina*, ed. J. Schnitzer, *Quellen und Forschungen zur Geschichte Savonarolas*, iii (Munich, 1904), 75.

Master- and Vicar-General together with the older friars at S. Marco, moreover, were behind the attempts to relax the austere conditions introduced by Savonarola and, above all, to unite the Tusco-Roman with the Lombard Congregation, in order to check the former's refractory and separatist tendencies.[69] Largely because of the intensive lobbying by the younger friars of S. Marco, their relatives and parishioners, however, which led the Florentine *Signoria*, via Francesco Pepi, Florentine ambassador in Rome, to petition Fra Vincenzo and Oliviero Caraffa, Cardinal Protector of the Order, on the convent's behalf, the attempted changes were strongly resisted. When put to a secret vote in January 1503, the proposals were rejected by an overwhelming majority of friars.[70]

After 1502, the Piagnoni's fortunes took a decided turn for the better. From that date until the fall of the last Florentine Republic in 1530, there was not a single year in which they did not number at least one sympathizer among the elected superiors of the Tusco-Roman Congregation. At one time or another, they held the priorates of all the reformed convents of the Congregation; and frequently, also, the office of Vicar-General: Fra Jacopo da Sicilia, Fra Bartolomeo da Faenza, and Fra Santi Pagnini being repeatedly appointed to this position.[71] Although the Savonarolans can be said to have achieved a certain degree of hegemony within the Congregation in this period, their position, even so, was never more than precarious. They had always to be on their guard against powerful enemies in the Roman Curia, the Dominican hierarchy, and the Congregation itself. Thus — warned, perhaps, by the punishment meted out to Fra Giovanni da Pescia, and fearful of the possibility of repressive measures, of which the project of union with the Lombard Congregation was a disquieting example — the

---

[69] Ubaldini, 'Annalia', fo. 26ʳ⁻ᵛ; Schnitzer, *Savonarola*, ii. 435. Though the *Annalia* seems to suggest that the whole Tusco-Roman Congregation was to be united with the Lombard Congregation, it is clear that the chronicler is using the term loosely to refer only to the convents of the old Congregation of S. Marco.

[70] *Signoria* to Francesco Pepi, 4 June 1501; to Caraffa, 4 June 1501; to Francesco Pepi, 12 Sept. 1502; to Caraffa, 20 Nov. 1502: ASF Signori, Missive Ia Cancelleria, 52, fos. 192ʳ–193ʳ; 53, fo. 43ʳ; 54, fos. 114ᵛ–115ʳ. Ubaldini, 'Annalia', fo. 26ᵛ.

[71] Creytens, 'Les Actes capitulaires', 152 ff.

Piagnoni now confined themselves to courses less confrontationalist than those which Fra Giovanni had advocated, but extreme nevertheless.

The incorporation of S. Marco and the three other convents of the Congregation into the purposely created Tusco-Roman province did not extinguish the friars' reforming zeal. Indeed, much as they resented the union, they came to look upon it as a challenge, an opportunity to broadcast more widely than had previously been the case the seeds of Savonarola's reform. The younger friars who had been attracted to the Order by Savonarola's preaching and who, in the majority of cases, had received the habit from him, were in the forefront of this movement of expansion. They had already given a demonstration of their strength by defeating the projected union with the Lombard Congregation. What should be realized was that theirs was a strength borne of commitment to the cause and of force of numbers. In the eight years of Savonarola's apostolate in Florence, no fewer than 143 friars were professed in S. Marco and in S. Domenico at Fiesole, the peak occurring in 1497 with an intake of 56 novices.[72] Fra Giovanni Sinibaldi was later to charge that Savonarola pursued a policy of active recruitment with little thought to the suitability of the men seeking admission.[73] But, as Savonarola often argued, these vocations were evidence of the achievements of his reforming programme to date and a guarantee of its continuation and expansion in the future.[74]

---

[72] Of these, 133 were professed in S. Marco: A. Verde, 'La congregazione di S. Marco dell'Ordine dei Frati Predicatori', *Memorie Domenicane*, NS 14 (1983), 175–98, 211–3. These figures do not include friars professed in the other convents of the Congregation and friars who, though professed elsewhere, asked to be transferred to S. Marco. The number of friars in S. Marco between 1497 and 1500 was close to 250 so that the younger friars represented a majority in their own right: ibid. 154 and V. Marchese, '*Cedrus Libani*, ossia vita di Fra Girolamo Savonarola scritta da Fra Benedetto da Firenze', *ASI*, app. 7 (1849), 84, n. 1. But T. Bottonio put the figure at 300, of whom only 60 were old friars (quoted in Masetti, *Monumenta et antiquitates*, i. 392).

[73] Marginal annotation to D. Benivieni, *Tractato* (BNF Inc. Guicc. 3.7.91), sig. e6ᵛ.

[74] Savonarola, *Prediche sopra Amos e Zaccaria*, ed. P. Ghiglieri (ENOS; 3 vols.; Rome, 1971–2), iii. 356–9; Verde, 'La congregazione di S. Marco dell'Ordine dei Frati Predicatori', 152–4.

These eager young men now ensured that the trust their martyred leader had placed in them would not be betrayed. Within a few years, as the chronicler of the convent of S. Marco noted with pride, they had risen to positions of prominence throughout the new Province.[75] They availed themselves of the opportunities thus presented to export to these convents the ideals of Savonarola's spiritual reform, in particular the stricter observance of the Dominican Rule, the scriptural emphasis in studies and preaching, and, finally, the overwhelmingly pastoral orientation in the friars' activities; all of this accompanied by an uncompromising militancy in the espousal of these ideals and in the pursuit of more converts to the cause. Some of these convents, especially those in Tuscany and S. Domenico in Perugia, became in turn reforming centres in their own right and renowned hotbeds of the Savonarolan cult.[76]

Though Savonarola had expressed a wish that the increase in male vocations would be accompanied by similar increases in female ones, he was prevented by the opposition he encountered and then by death from turning this wish into reality.[77] Despite the attention he bestowed on many convents of nuns, despite the inroads his doctrine made in them, and despite also overseeing the expansion of the Dominican convent of Sta Lucia and ensuring that its inmates were raised in status from tertiaries to fully professed nuns, during his lifetime he did not have the satisfaction of presiding over the creation of a wholly new foundation.[78] After his death, his fol-

---

[75] Ubaldini, 'Annalia', fo. 26ᵛ.

[76] Scrafino Razzi, 'Cronica della Provincia Romana dell'ordine de' frati predicatori', MS BMLF S. Marco 873, fos. 49ᵛ–154ʳ, where most convents are discussed; Masetti, *Monumenta et antiquitates*, i. 392–3; I. Taurisano, *I Domenicani in Lucca* (Lucca, 1914), 11–34, *et passim*; D. Di Agresti, *Sviluppi della riforma monastica savonaroliana* (Florence, 1980), esp. 122–33, 158–61, *et passim*; E. Ricci, 'Appunti Savonaroliani: Il P. Timoteo Bottonio', *Quarto centenario della morte di Fra Girolamo Savonarola* (Florence, 1898), 183–4, 192–3, 241–3, 294–6, 356–7.

[77] Ubaldini, 'Annalia', fo. 18ʳ, cf. Giovanni Sinibaldi in D. Benivieni, *Tractato*, sig. e8ʳ.

[78] Di Agresti, *Sviluppi della riforma monastica savonaroliana*, 18–22. On Sta Lucia and Savonarola's contacts with the nuns see Monastero di Sta Lucia, 'Estratti di cronaca', MS ACSM (no location number) no foliation but s.v.; G. Benelli, *Firenze nei monumenti domenicani: Guida storica* (Florence, 1913), 267–9; G. Richa, *Notizie istoriche delle chiese fiorentine* (10 vols.; Florence, 1754–62), viii.

lowers more than made up for lost time. New convents were founded and existing ones reformed under their direction in Prato, Lucca, and Pisa.[79] In Florence, too, apart from continuing with the wardship and expansion of Sta Lucia, two new convents were founded. In September 1500 Camilla Bartolini Rucellai, who had been attracted to the Order by Savonarola's sermons, becoming a tertiary and his spiritual ward, founded the convent of Sta Caterina.[80] In 1509 the convent received its rule, written by Fra Roberto Ubaldini, and a papal privilege which permitted the members of the community to take the solemn vows of professed nuns.[81] In 1508 the Canon Marco di Matteo Strozzi, whose activities in support of Savonarola's plans for a *Monte di Pietà* have already been discussed, saw to it that six Dominican tertiaries who had already joined together as a community were able to buy property on which to erect the convent of Sta Maria degli Angeli.[82]

Sta Lucia and Sta Caterina—both of which were dependent on S. Marco—became the two most important centres of female Savonarolan spirituality. They were both privileged by Piagnoni with alms and endowments. In addition, Piagnoni notables chose to place their daughters in them and also monopolized the lay func-

347–60; S. Loddi, 'Notizie del convento di S. Marco', MS ACSM Miscellanea Benelli H8, pp. 74–82.

[79] Di Agresti, *Sviluppi della riforma monastica savonaroliana*, 22 ff.

[80] Loddi, 'Notizie del convento di S. Marco', 86–92; 'Origine della fondazione et altre cose particolari appartenenti al Monastero di Santa Caterina da Siena in Firenze', MS AGOP, XIV, Liber O, pp. 192–226; Richa, *Notizie istoriche delle chiese fiorentine*, viii. 278–84; G. M. Brocchi, *Vite de'Santi e beati fiorentini* (2 vols.; Florence, 1742–61), ii/2. 339–47.

[81] Benelli, *Firenze nei monumenti domenicani*, 263; R. Creytens, 'Il direttorio di Roberto Ubaldini da Gagliano O.P. per le terziarie collegiate di S. Caterina da Siena in Firenze', *AFP* 39 (1969), 127–72. T. Ripoll and A. Brémond (eds.), *Bullarium Ordinis Praedicatorum* (8 vols.; Rome, 1729–40), iv. 395–6 for concession of the right to wear the scapular by Leo X in 1515. Fra Roberto Ubaldini, who had been one of Savonarola's closest collaborators, turned against him during the trials of 1498: Villari, *La storia di Girolamo Savonarola*, vol. ii, app., pp. ccliv–cclxii; see also his letter to Domenico Bonsi, dated 30 June 1498, in BNF Magl., XXXV, 190, fo. 88ʳ. By the time he began compiling the *Annalia* of S. Marco in 1505 he had returned to the Savonarolan fold, as the *Annalia* clearly attests.

[82] Richa, *Notizie istoriche delle chiese fiorentine*, ii. 276–87; Benelli, *Firenze nei monumenti domenicani*, 281–4.

tions of both convents.[83] Within a few years these convents were amongst the largest in Florence; by the middle of the century they had become, in terms of the number of nuns housed, the two largest.[84] From their success, S. Marco drew prestige, influence, and a great deal of money since it was to its friars that the nuns had to turn for their spiritual ministrations.[85] Above all, the relationship enabled the friars not only to continue the work begun by Savonarola but also to draw highly placed lay Piagnoni even closer to S. Marco.

An indication of the lengths to which the friars were prepared to go to increase the number of both male and female recruits to the Savonarolan cause is provided by two additional episodes. It is clear from the evidence that at about the time of the foundation of Sta Caterina the friars were also patronizing two other such informal groups of women with a view to enabling them to have their communities formally recognized and properly housed in new convents. The first group was led by one Dorotea da Lanciuole, a spiritual ward of Fra Tommaso Caiani; the second by Domenica Narducci del Paradiso, who was counselled by such well-known Piagnoni as Fra Silvestro da Marradi, Fra Jacopo da Sicilia, Fra Santi Pagnini, and Domenico Benivieni.[86] In 1506 Domenica began

[83] L. Polizzotto, 'Dell'Arte del Ben Morire': The Piagnone Way of Death 1494–1545', I Tatti Studies: Essays in the Renaissance, 3 (1989), 48 n. 52.

[84] Sta Lucia had 130 nuns in 1515 and 146 in mid-cent.; Sta Caterina had 55 in 1513, 80 in 1515, and 133 in mid-cent.: ibid.; C. Carnesecchi, 'Monache in Firenze nel 1515', in I. del Badia (ed.), Miscellanea fiorentina di erudizione e storia (2 vols.; Rome, 1902), ii. 29; G. Carocci, L'illustratore fiorentino: Anno 1909 (Florence, 1908), 60.

[85] It seems, in fact, that all funds, endowments, and alms had to go through S. Marco: Polizzotto, 'Dell'Arte del Ben Morire', 48 n. 52, for an example of the procedure followed. The nuns of Sta Caterina were eventually to seek relief from some of the financial exactions of S. Marco; see 'Notizie riguardanti il Monastero di S. Caterina da Siena in Firenze e il Convento di S. Marco', ACSM Miscellanea Pancani-Colosio (no location number, no foliation) for the 1629 controversy between the two convents finally resolved in favour of Sta Caterina.

[86] A. Moriconi, La venerabile Suor Domenica del Paradiso (Florence, 1943), 308, 324, 336, 343–4, 360; Sacra Rituum Congregatione excellentissimo et reverendissimo Domino Card. Guadagni Florentina beatificationis et canonizationis ven. ancillae Dei Sor. Dominicae a Paradiso Monialis professae et fundatricis monasterii Sanctissimae Crucis Florentiae Ordinis S. Dominici (Rome, 1755), Part ii, pp. 106–7.

THE PATH TO RADICALISM

even to wear publicly the habit of a Dominican tertiary.[87] Both women had by this time attracted a great deal of attention, Dorotea for her awe-inspiring fasts—she was reputed to draw nourishment solely from the consecrated Host—and Domenica for her equally astounding mystical gifts, divine revelations, and prophecies. Relations between the two seemed cordial until, early in 1506, Domenica was miraculously apprised in a vision with the knowledge that Dorotea was a fraud and, enjoined by Christ, took upon herself the task of unmasking her.[88]

There ensued a bitter controversy punctuated by accusations, counter-accusations, investigations, prophetic threats in which the fate of Pietro Bernardino figured largely, judicial depositions, and confrontations. The whole Piagnone hierarchy of S. Marco and lay notables outside—including such revered figures as Fra Bartolomeo da Faenza, Fra Silvestro da Marradi, Fra Santi Pagnini, Fra Simone Cinozzi, Domenico Benivieni, Girolamo Gondi—tried with all means available to bring the controversy to an end.[89] But all to no avail: Domenica would have none of it. She was convinced that Dorotea had been put up to her deceits by Fra Tommaso Caiani and by the other Piagnoni friars of S. Marco who sought thereby—or so Domenica inferred—to promote the construction of a convent at Lanciuole.[90] To the Piagnoni's deep embarrassment and mounting fury she rebuffed all overtures and attempts at arbitration, demanding nothing less than a full recanta-

---

[87] Ibid., Part iv, pp. 145 ff.; Fra Jacopo da Sicilia, Vicar-General of the Congregation gave her permission to wear the habit on 28 Apr. 1506: ACDC, 'Index litterarum seu brevium', MS (no location number), sig. A$^v$.

[88] Francesco Onesti da Castiglione, 'Persecutiones exagitate contra Venerabilem sponsam Jesu Christi S. Dominicam de Paradiso & ultiones divine contra persecutores', MS ACDC Codice F, fo. 11$^v$. For a full treatment of this whole issue see my 'When Saints Fall Out: Women and the Savonarolan Reform in Early Sixteenth-Century Florence', *Renaissance Quarterly*, 46 (1993) pp. 486–525.

[89] Francesco Onesti da Castiglione, 'Persecutiones exagitate contra Venerabilem sponsam Jesu Christi S. Dominicam de Paradiso', fos. 100$^r$, 111$^r$–112$^v$ (Domenica to Dorotea 27 Oct. 1507), 115$^v$–116$^v$ (Fra Bartolomeo da Faenza to Domenica, 11 Jan. 1508), 124$^{r-v}$ (Fra Tommaso Caiani to Girolamo Gondi, 29 Mar. 1506), 126$^{r-v}$ (Fra Santi Pagnini to Domenico Benivieni, undated), 124$^v$–126$^v$ (Fra Simone Cinozzi to Domenica, 18 July 1507), 129$^v$–130$^v$ (letters of Fra Simone to Domenica and Fra Tommaso dated 20 July and 28 Aug. 1507 respectively).

[90] Ibid., fo. 11$^{r-v}$.

tion by Dorotea and her accomplices. To stop the situation from deteriorating even further Fra Tommaso de Vio Gaetano, Master-General of the Dominican Order, was forced to intervene. On 22 October 1509 he issued a decree forbidding the friars of S. Marco to divulge prophecies, whether their own or other people's, whether in public or in private, for a period of ten years. For the same period, moreover, no friar was permitted to claim knowledge of the future. He concluded with the categorical injunction to the friars to break off relations with Domenica, to cease to minister the sacraments to her, and to exclude her from all convents in the Tusco-Roman Congregation.[91]

Dorotea and her four remaining followers were placed in the convent of Sta Caterina in Florence, where Dorotea, despite the ministrations of the convent's doctor Girolamo Buonagrazia, went into a melancholy decline from which she was never to recover.[92] Domenica, on the other hand, despite the hostility of the Order and despite the persecutions of the friars of S. Marco held out until she was finally able, under the restored Medici regime, to move into her recently built convent of the Crocetta, which was formally recognized by Leo X in 1515.[93] Not surprisingly, the convent and community were placed under the jurisdiction of the Archbishop. It is obvious that this was exactly the outcome Domenica had striven for throughout the controversy over Dorotea. Indeed, Domenica's conduct during the controversy, her inflexibility, her determination to wear the habit of a Dominican tertiary but refusing the formal vestition pressed upon her by the friars of S. Marco, becomes intelligible in the light of this outcome. She was determined to avail herself of the spiritual and moral teachings which only the convent of S. Marco could provide but was not prepared

---

[91] Tommaso de Vio Gaetano, *Registrum litterarum Fr. Thomae de Vio Caietani O.P. Magistri Ordinis 1508–1513*, ed. A. De Mayer (Rome, 1935), 122.

[92] Francesco Onesti da Castiglione, 'Ephemeris sive diarius vitae B.M. sor. Dominicae . . . ab anno 1473 ad anno 1542', MS ACDC Codice C, fo. 35ʳ; ASF Not. Ant., C555 (1511–14) (Ser Filippo Cioni), fo. 92ᵛ.

[93] B. M. Borghigiani, *Intera narrazione della vita, costumi e intelligenze spirituali della Venerabile sposa di Gesù, Suor Domenica del Paradiso* (2 vols.; Florence, 1719–1802), ii. 31–5; Papal bulls in ACDC *Index litterarium seu brevium*, sigs. Aᵛ–Aiʳ.

to pay the price which the friars exacted. In Domenica they had met their match.

As they did also with the six founding tertiaries of the convent of Sta Maria degli Angeli, who achieved the same ends with totally different means. In a letter dated 2 February 1505, one of their number, perhaps their leader Suor Vincenza Nemmi, relayed to Marco Strozzi the content of a vision she had just experienced. The Virgin Mary had appeared to her, so the writer relates, and had commanded her to urge Marco Strozzi, their spiritual guide and protector, to expedite the foundation of their convent dedicated to the Virgin. Though the convent was to be under Dominican rule, the Virgin enjoined that it be placed under the direct jurisdiction of the Ordinary, in imitation of the convent of Annalena. It was an injunction which Marco Strozzi could not ignore, despite his close contacts with S. Marco. By 1508, he succeeded in carrying out the Virgin's commands to the letter. In that year the tertiaries were given the habit by Archbishop Cosimo de' Pazzi and were formally placed under his jurisdiction.[94]

A further, far more successful undertaking in the Piagnoni strivings for vocations was S. Marco's virtual annexation of the confraternity of the Purification of the Virgin Mary and of S. Zanobi. As we have seen, relations between the convent and the confraternity were strained as a result of the friars' demand that the confraternity vacate its premises. In 1503, however, a first agreement notarized by Ser Lorenzo Violi was reached between them after negotiations led by Domenico Benivieni and Francesco di Cesare Petrucci. In 1505 the final contract was drawn up by another Piagnone notary, Ser Carlo da Firenzuola, its terms being guaranteed by Francesco del Pugliese and Niccolò del Nero.[95] When

---

[94] ASF C. Sopp., Ser. III, 138, fos. 70ʳ–71ᵛ, for the letter, and fo. 49ʳ, for Marco Strozzi's account of the foundation.

[95] Ubaldini, 'Annalia', fo. 25ᵛ; Compagnia della Purificazione della Vergine e di S. Zanobi, *Libro di Ricordi*, 2 vols.; MS ASF Comp. Sopp. 1646, vol. i, fos. ccxliiʳ⁻ᵛ. On Francesco del Pugliese a well-known Piagnone and Niccolò del Nero, whose loyalties cannot be ascertained despite the fact that he was contacted when ambassador in Spain by his brother on behalf of Savonarola for the Council, see Villari, *La storia di Girolamo Savonarola*, vol. ii, app., pp. lxviii, ccxxxii, *et passim*. Since the Medici were patrons of the confraternity a deputation of friars was sent

finally the new premises in the grounds of S. Marco were ready, the friars and the members of the confraternity, comprising children and also the adult officials, took possession of it on 1 May 1506 after a solemn procession. Fra Santi Pagnini, Prior of the convent, formally handed over the keys and then officiated at mass.[96] In the evening, after vespers, Fra Serafino Bellandini delivered, in the words of the astonished anonymous compiler of the confraternity's *Ricordi*, a 'great sermon' in which, in the name of all friars, 'he told us that the convent loved us greatly, so that everyone was amazed since for many years we had been at loggerheads over our refusal to give them our company's old meeting-place . . . they offered several times to be our advocates in anything we might need or want.'[97]

The reasons for these protestations of affection and offers of assistance soon became apparent. The friars had set out to win over the members of the confraternity and managed this so thoroughly that from 1507 onwards they virtually monopolized all its spiritual positions. For instance, on only one occasion in the following twenty-five years did they fail to secure the post of spiritual guide and corrector (*correttore*).[98] Once in control, moreover, the friars saw to it that the confraternity's procedures were changed so as to strengthen their hold over its members. In 1517 it was decided, in fact, that the *correttore* should confess all prospective members before a decision was made on their suitability. He and the guardian of the confraternity, moreover, were henceforth to have full authority in deciding whether members who had not attended meetings for a time should be readmitted. Finally, in a move obviously designed to prevent the contamination by harmful, competing influences, the children were forbidden to confess outside the confraternity without the express permission of the *correttore*.[99]

to Rome to Card. Giovanni to obtain his approval for the agreement: Ubaldini, 'Annalia', fo. 27[r-v].

[96] Compagnia della Purificazione della Vergine e di S. Zanobi, *Libro di Ricordi*, vol. i, fos. ccxliiii[v]–ccxliiii[r].

[97] Ibid., fo. ccxliiii[v]: 'magna predica', 'disseci el convento volerci tanto bene, per modo ognuno se ne maravigliava perché molt'anni era stata questa diferenzia di dare loro quella conpagnia vechia . . . offerissonsi più volte a essere sempre nostri prochuratori in ogni chosa quando bisognassi e noi volessimo'.

[98] Ibid., fo. ix[r].          [99] Ibid., fo. ccxlvii[r].

With these credentials it was not surprising that the confraternity should attract an increasing number of children of well-known Piagnoni.[100] These children, in turn, were spiritually nurtured and encouraged to embark on a religious career, preferably in the Dominican Order. The effects of this nurturing are graphically illustrated in the fact that, of the sixty-seven youths who left the company between 1501 and 1530 to undertake a religious career, sixty-three chose to enter either S. Marco or, more rarely, the dependent convents of S. Domenico at Fiesole and Sta Maria del Sasso near Bibbiena.[101]

While building for the future, Piagnoni friars did not neglect the present. Fra Giovanni's *Argumentum eiusdem obiectione* had regaled them with a vision of might and glory. 'And so', he had said, urging his course of immediate action upon them, 'for one Savonarola you would see ten preachers of the Holy Spirit, which would fill your city with consolation and both spiritual and temporal comforts.'[102] While his call to arms may have gone unheeded, his prophecy was proved correct. Piagnoni preachers came forth in their multitudes in the ensuing years. Florence, Tuscany, and the major centres of Florentine settlement in Italy and even in Europe reverberated to the sound of their trumpets.[103] Those of their sermons which have survived show that the ecclesiastical hierarchy had every reason to view them with dread. It was not merely the stridency of their demands for reform that rendered them suspect, nor even their propensity for circumventing the orders of their superiors and for

[100] To mention but a few names of Piagnoni notables with children in the confraternity: Zanobi Carnesecchi, Francesco Gualterotti (3 children of whom 1 became a friar in S. Marco), Ubertino Risaliti, Rinieri Tosinghi (2 children of whom 1 became a friar in S. Marco), Ulivieri Guadagni, Bernardo Guasconi, Antonio Benivieni, Maso degli Albizzi (4 children), Domenico Bonsi, Lorenzo Violi, Girolamo Gondi, Tommaso Soderini: ibid., vol. i, fos. i$^v$–viii$^r$; vol. ii, fos. 14$^r$–16$^v$ (second volume, unlike the first, is foliated in arabic numerals); see also ibid. 1650, *Debitori e creditori*, esp. vol. ii, fos. 73$^v$–103$^v$.

[101] Ibid. 1646, *Libro di Ricordi*, vol. i, fo. clx$^{r-v}$; vol. ii, fos. 200$^r$–202$^v$.

[102] [Giovanni da Pescia], 'Argumentum eiusdem obiectione', fo. 78$^{r-v}$: 'Così vederesti uscir fora per un frate Hieronimo dieci trombette di spirito sancto le quali riempirebbon la ciptà vostra di consolatione et remedii spirituali et temporali.'

[103] See below, pp. 196–202.

turning every sermon into a provocative indictment of the Papal Curia. It was, first and foremost, their insistence on the doctrine that salvation was impossible outside their ranks and that individual Christians, regardless of their status or condition, must work actively for reform. In arguing that the Piagnoni were the instruments of God's will and that they were therefore duty-bound to oppose evil at all costs, these preachers elaborated and extended the arguments which Fra Simone Cinozzi, Fra Stefano da Codiponte, and Fra Giovanni da Pescia had already put forward.

These themes were expressed with uncompromising firmness by three friars of S. Marco, Tommaso Caiani, Silvestro da Marradi, and Bartolomeo da Faenza in the district of Domenico Benivieni's early spiritual counselling, the villages of Calamecca, Lanciuole, and Crespole. Fra Tommaso's connection with the district dated back at least to 1495. Judging by a letter written in March or April 1496 to the villagers near Pescia, it would seem that he had taken over some of Domenico Benivieni's spiritual functions.[104] The district was at that time receiving a great deal of attention from the Piagnoni and, indeed, even Savonarola wrote to its inhabitants later in that year.[105] In any case, Fra Tommaso's wardship seems to have continued until Lent 1502, when, as a consequence of a controversial series of sermons, he was removed by his superiors and forbid-

---

[104] Tommaso Caiani, 'Hepistola di frate Thomaso dell'ordine di San Domenicho in San Marcho socto il priorato di frate Ieronimo da Ferrara Savonarola a lloro medesimi, cioè a quelli di montagnia', MS BRF 2405, fos. 117ʳ–122ᵛ. This epistle and the one following have been published by G. Benelli, 'Il S. Vincenzo Ferreri dipinto da Fra Bartolomeo (Due lettere inedite del P. Tommaso Caiani)', *Memorie Domenicane*, 34 (1917), 542–54. In the previous year an unsuccessful attempt had been made to deprive Domenico Benivieni of his post as *Spedalingo* at Pescia. Perhaps it was then that Fra Tommaso stepped in: see above, Ch. 3, n. 25. On Caiani's and Fra Silvestro da Marradi's apostolate in Pescia, see Giovanfrancesco Pico, *Vita Reverendi Patris F. Hieronymi Savonarolae*, ed. J. Quétif (Paris, 1674), 183–5; on Caiani's career in general: Villari, *La storia di Girolamo Savonarola*, vol. ii, app., p. ccxc; Ubaldini, 'Annalia', fo. 169ʳ; J. Quétif and J. Echard, *Scriptores Ordinis Praedicatorum recensiti* (2 vols.; Paris, 1719–21), ii. 77, and see below. Suor Domenica del Paradiso's followers spread some fanciful and scurrilous rumours about his subsequent career, see e.g. Francesco Onesti da Castiglione, 'Persecutiones', fos. 25–26ʳ, 131ʳ.

[105] L. Polizzotto, 'Una lettera inedita del Savonarola', *Rinascimento*, 24 (1984), 181–9.

den to return. Defiant and unrepentant, he kept in touch with his charges by letter, seeking to strengthen their spiritual resolve so that they could the better resist the persecution of their common enemies. One example, his *Hepistola . . . al populo di Pescia cioè agli helecti di Dio per conservarli nel bene fare nell'anno 1502*, survives.[106] Its object was to show the citizens the true nature of this persecution: that, in Fra Tommaso's words, 'it is not man persecuting man, but Satan in his members persecuting Christ in His members'.[107] Since their trials were thus a confirmation of their saintliness and elect status—a point which Fra Tommaso underlined when he addressed them as 'God's elect' (*helecti di Dio*)—they were an occasion not for sorrow, but for rejoicing.[108] Where he went furthest on the radical path, however, was in his comment on the citizens' relationship with their preachers. While advising patience and a certain degree of moderation, he expressed understanding of his charges' desire to be free to choose preachers who shared their beliefs and stated explicitly that any preacher sent to them who voiced opinions prejudicial to salvation and proved unresponsive to gentle admonition should be boycotted at all costs.[109] This was at least as revolutionary as anything Fra Giovanni had said. Although admitting of wider application, Fra Giovanni's call to arms had been directed primarily at clergymen, the struggle he envisaged being confined to the Dominican Order. Fra Tommaso, on the other hand, ignored the traditional distinction between clergy and laity. By acknowledging that the citizens of Pescia could judge their preachers, and even correct and censure them if they erred,[110] he

[106] Tommaso [Caiani], 'Hepistola la quale mandò al populo di Pescia cioè agli helecti di Dio per conservarli nel bene fare nell'anno 1502', MS BRF 2405, fos. 122ᵛ–128ᵛ. Since this was at the time when Fra Malatesta was Vicar-General of the Tusco-Roman Congregation, Fra Tommaso may well have been a victim of his repressive policy.

[107] Tommaso [Caiani], *Hepistola . . . al populo di Pescia*, fo. 123ᵛ: 'non è l'huomo che perseguiti l'altro huomo ma è el diavolo ne' sua membri che perseguita Christo ne' sua membri'.

[108] Ibid.   [109] Ibid., fos. 127ᵛ–128ᵛ.

[110] Here, it may be relevant to mention the incomplete and anonymous letter following Fra Tommaso's in MS BRF 2405, fo. 129ʳ. Since it advises parishioners to reject clerical appointees who are not to their liking, it may be connected with his apostolate in Pescia.

was assuming that the humblest Christian could possess greater knowledge of divine matters than an ordained cleric.

Six years after Fra Tommaso's silencing, Pescia was to resound to the discordant tones of Fra Silvestro da Marradi, who between 1508 and 1510 preached a series of sermons in the convent of S. Michele.[111] The sermons were just one episode in a career studded with sensational highlights, which caused Fra Silvestro to be revered as one of the greatest religious leaders of the Piagnone movement. Prophecies, miracles, and levitation were his stock-in-trade.[112] Although in his sermons at Pescia he addressed himself ostensibly to the nuns of S. Michele, it is clear from what he says that lay persons were also present in the congregation.[113] His diatribes against the existing Church hierarchy were heard by a mixed, if segregated, audience, accounting perhaps for their resonance and for the subsequent troubles he encountered. In characteristic Piagnone style, Fra Silvestro laid the blame for all the ills besetting Christendom upon the heads of worldly and sinful prelates, whose wickedness was nowhere more evident, as he constantly asserted, than in their treatment of Savonarola. Seizing upon the pejorative epithets 'piagnione' and 'hieronimine', used of the Savonarolan nuns by their opponents, Fra Silvestro exhorted his hearers to glory in these terms of abuse, which proclaimed their devotion to the cause and their election.[114] At first content that they should endeavour to redress existing wrongs by prayer and the exercise of virtue, he came gradually, as his sermons were attacked, to demand a far more active commitment from his audience. Humility and

---

[111] Silvestro da Marradi [*et al.*], 'Sermoni e prediche del Venerando fra Silvestro da Marradi dell'ordine de' Predicatori fatti alle monache di S. Michele fuori di Pescia nel 1508', MS BNF Magl., XXXV, 242 (foliation erratic after fo. 220ᵛ). The manuscript also contains spiritual letters by Fra Silvestro and other friars of S. Marco up to 1514.

[112] Convento di S. Domenico, Fiesole, 'Cronica Conventus Sancti Dominici de Fesulis', fos. 99ʳ, 147ᵛ; F. Bonaini (ed.), 'Chronica antiqua Conventus Sanctae Catharinae de Pisis', *ASI*, 1st ser. 6/2 (1848), 624; Pseudo-Burlamacchi, *La vita*, 246; Giovanfrancesco Pico, *Vita Reverendi Patris F. Hieronymi Savonarolae*, 183–5; S. Razzi, *Vita dei santi e beati del sacro ordine de' Frati Predicatori, così huomini come donne* (Palermo, 1605), 314–16; Quétif and Echard, *Scriptores*, i. 895.

[113] Silvestro da Marradi, 'Sermoni e prediche', fos. 1ʳ, 109ᵛ.

[114] Ibid., fos. 6ʳ, 30ᵛ, 46ʳ, 105ᵛ, 131ʳ, 167ᵛ–168ʳ, 177ʳ, 180ᵛ, 185ᵛ, 214ᵛ–215ʳ.

charity were no longer enough: the forces of evil must be shunned altogether if they were not to triumph.[115] 'Flee from them', he told his audience, recalling the exhortations of the Israelite prophets to their people, captive in Babylon, 'shun all evil company, wicked, lax and hypocritical religious, wicked friars, wicked nuns, wicked leaders who constantly say evil things and act in an even worse manner, because they are faint-hearted and lax hypocrites full of ill-humour and anger who lust after money . . . there is nothing, no vice of which they are not guilty; do not take pleasure in talking to them, because that would be the road to spiritual laxity and negligence.'[116]

Fra Silvestro's last sermon, in which this strident command was voiced, contains abundant hints that he, like Fra Tommaso before him, had incurred the displeasure of the ecclesiastical hierarchy and may, in fact, have been recalled as a result.[117] As his sermons and the letters which he wrote to the nuns and the villagers after his recall make clear, he had come under attack not only for his teaching but also for his active recruitment for the Savonarolan cause.[118] He rejected with indignation the attackers' charges that he had been trying to take over, on behalf of his Dominican Congregation, the convent of S. Michele. The very arguments used to reject these charges, however, suggest that there was some truth in the accusations.[119] The *affaire* of Dorotea da Lanciuole in which both he and Fra Tommaso Caiani were closely involved could not but have contributed to the acrimony and the accusations. Even at a distance, Fra Silvestro did not abandon his wards. He kept in touch with letters in which he reiterated his by now familiar message.[120]

---

[115] Ibid., fos. 6ʳ, 8ʳ–11ʳ, 25ᵛ ff.; cf. the changed approach in the sermons of 1509, e.g. fos. 177ʳ, 185ᵛ, 188ᵛ ff.

[116] Ibid., fo. 216ʳ: 'Fuggitele . . . fuggite le captive compagnie, captivi religiosi tiepidi et ipocriti, captivi frati, captive sorelle, captivi capi che sempre dicono male e fanno peggio perchè sono tiepidi ipocritoni pieni di stiza e di rabbia attendono a denari . . . non è cosa nè vitio che non conmectino; non vi dilectate di parlare con loro che voi intiepiderete e doventerete negligente.'

[117] Ibid., fos. 206ᵛ–216ʳ. That he had already been placed under a temporary ban on preaching, at an earlier stage, is suggested by the fact that in Nov. 1509 he was given permission to resume: see Tommaso de Vio Gaetano, *Registrum litterarum*, 126.

[118] Silvestro da Marradi, 'Sermoni e prediche', fos. 204ᵛ, 123ʳ–124ᵛ [bis].

[119] Ibid., fo. 204ᵛ.          [120] Ibid., fos. 217ʳ–119ᵛ [bis], 120ʳ–124ᵛ [bis].

He was assisted by other friars of S. Marco including the formidable Bartolomeo da Faenza. His surviving letter to the nuns of S. Michele —which he enjoined the nuns to burn once read—is an impassioned lesson on the essentials of the religious life as a Piagnone friar would conceive it. Dedication, love, and charity are the recurrent themes in these letters: but, through them all, there runs the polemic against spiritual decadence and corruption.[121]

While impossible to prevent, the delivery of such controversial sermons or the voicing of such unpalatable criticisms could, on the whole, be promptly suppressed by the officials of the Dominican Order. The hierarchy had considerable coercive powers at its disposal and, in the case of a recalcitrant offender, could call upon the secular arm to enforce its decisions.[122] Once the decision had been taken to proceed against a particular individual, he had little hope of continuing his activities unless, like Savonarola, he could count not only on the support of a united Congregation but also on the connivance of the secular authorities. If the dispute involved members of different Orders, however, or ranged the secular and regular clergy against one another, the prospects changed radically. The hapless Ordinary who wished to proceed against an offending regular in his diocese was faced with a host of privileges and dispensations, jealously guarded and readily invoked, which hampered him at every turn. Here was opportunity for the Piagnoni to turn ecclesiastical custom to their own advantage.

A typical example is the confrontation which took place in Florence early in 1509 between the newly appointed Archbishop, Cosimo de' Pazzi, and the Franciscan Amadeite, Fra Antonio da Cremona.[123] On 26 December 1508 Fra Antonio had preached a

---

[121] Silvestro da Marradi, fos. 134ʳ–141ᵛ [*bis*]. The codex contains also a sermon by an unnamed friar, fos. 127ᵛ–132ʳ [*bis*]; an incomplete exposition of the Ladder of Jacob by another anonymous person, fo. 132ʳ⁻ᵛ [*bis*]; and the opening line of a letter by Fra Zanobi de' Medici, fo. 141ᵛ [*bis*], on whom see Pseudo–Burlamacchi, *La vita*, 180 n. 1, and Ubaldini, 'Annalia', fo. 174ʳ, for the obituary in which his preaching is highly praised.

[122] e.g. the case of Fra Sante di Giovanni Cambi 'bonae arboris malus fructus & qui melius satisfecisset patri non nascendo' : Ubaldini, 'Annalia', fo. 163ʳ.

[123] G. Tognetti, 'Un episodio inedito di repressione della predicazione post-savonaroliana (Firenze 1509)', *Bibliothèque d'Humanisme et Renaissance*, 24 (1962),

sermon on that popular Piagnone text, 'O Jerusalem, Jerusalem, thou that killest the prophets'. After mounting the usual attacks on Florence and the Church for having executed Savonarola and his two companions, the sermon went on to proffer some acutely disquieting observations on the sensitive subject of divine retribution. The blood of those persecuted was crying out for vengeance, Fra Antonio luridly claimed, and only a terrible scourge could atone for the crime committed against God through His servants. Until she repented, Florence, which had received such an abundance of holy preachers without showing any noticeable spiritual improvement, would continue to suffer tribulation. Once she saw the error of her ways, however, the reform of the Church would ensue, under the guidance of a holy Pope (*pastore santo*).[124]

When summoned by the Archbishop on 13 January 1509, Fra Antonio was taxed with being a follower of Savonarola. Offered the choice of either substantiating his predictions or recanting, he denied the charge of being a Savonarolan, refused to provide the requisite proofs of his prophetic illumination, and reasserted the claims which he had made in his sermon. The situation was saved from degenerating into an obstinate and self-defeating trial of strength by a compromise proposed by Fra Antonio himself. Since his conscience did not permit him to recant, he explained, or to preach as the Archbishop wished, he would stop preaching altogether.[125] From the account of the dispute left by Fra Antonio, it would appear that fear of the effect of such sermons was foremost in Cosimo de' Pazzi's mind when he demanded a retraction. As well as being doctrinally unsound, their prophetic content was, above all, extremely dangerous, since it disquieted the listeners and made them predisposed to tolerate, and even to initiate, change. By scandalous sermons of this sort, Savonarola had almost brought the city to ruin.[126] The Archbishop's apprehension was well grounded. The proliferation of self-styled prophets, visionaries, and miracle-workers, all claiming to be able to trace their lineage to Savonarola and all commanding a ready following, combined with the ominous

190–9, where both Antonio da Cremona's sermon and his account of the subsequent dispute are printed.

[124] Ibid. 193–6.    [125] Ibid. 196–7.    [126] Ibid. 196.

rumblings of discontent issuing forth regularly from S. Marco, had kept Florence and the surrounding district in a state of constant turmoil for the past decade.

Preachers of a prophetic bent had appeared in the city every few years.[127] In 1500 and 1501 the inhabitants had witnessed the strange apostolate of the peasant Martino, better known as the 'madman from Brozzi', who, not content to presage the imminent Chastisement of Florence and Rome for their complicity in Savonarola's execution, had, further, attacked individual citizens by name. After twice being arrested, he was finally silenced by exile.[128] From the time of her move to Florence in December 1499, moreover, Domenica Narducci had startled the city with her prophecies of tribulation and renewal. In April 1501 she was tried before the Archiepiscopal Court for this and other suspect activities. Perhaps because of her large following and Piagnone backing, including at this time the friars of S. Marco, no conclusive verdict was given at the trial: a trial attended by a large and potentially mutinous crowd of devotees, who waited outside the Archiepiscopal palace to hear the result.[129] There should be no need to emphasize, furthermore, that every sermon preached by committed Savonarolan friars could not but have been prophetic in intent, though the prophecies themselves might have remained implicit. There was also a staggering number of prophecies circulating in manuscript from among Piagnoni groups in the city, some of which undoubtedly originated from S. Marco.[130]

---

[127] Cf. e.g. Luca Landucci, *Diario fiorentino*, ed. I. del Badia (Florence, 1883; repr. 1969), 285; Giovanni Cambi, *Istorie*, ed. I. di San Luigi (4 vols.; Florence, 1785–6), ii. 256–7; Parenti, *Istorie fiorentine*, 290; Bartolomeo Cerretani, 'Ricordi storici fiorentini 1500–1523', MS BAV Vat. Lat. 13651, fo. 85ᵛ.

[128] Cambi, *Istorie*, ii. 168–9.

[129] Moriconi, *La venerabile Suor Domenica del Paradiso*, 238–9; Borghigiani, *Intera narrazione*, i. 209–10.

[130] For examples of manuscript prophecies, see MS BNF Magl., VII, 1179; VIII, 1081; XXXV, 116, fos. 42 ff. For an example of those issuing from S. Marco, see Silvestro da Marradi, 'Prophetia viri cuiusdam sancti f. Silvestri', MS BRF 2053, fo. 107ᵛ. Fra Silvestro's authorship of this prophecy (suggested by Weinstein, *Savonarola and Florence*, 342) is confirmed by the 'Dialogo acefalo', MS BNF Magl., XXXIV, 33, fos. 16ᵛ–17ʳ. Two additional copies of this prophecy are extant, one in BMLF Antinori 203, vol. ii, fo. 12ᵛ and in BNF Magl., XXXV, 116, fo. 165ʳ⁻ᵛ.

The import of a prophet's utterances, however, could alter in accordance with his or her changing aspirations. A case in point was Domenica Narducci, whose prophecies, after she fell out with the friars of S. Marco, took on a distinctly anti-Piagnone and in time also pro-Medicean flavour. All this raises a question which no discussion of Piagnoni prophecies can ignore. How far, we must ask, were these prophecies consciously designed to further the changes which they foretold? To what extent, in other words, were the Piagnoni who voiced them endeavouring to persuade their audience to enter upon a course which would bring about the events which they described as imminent and inevitable?[131] There can be no doubt that, for the Piagnoni, prophesying was a powerful tool of persuasion. This is most apparent in the courses of action which they advocated. The individual Piagnone's understanding of the contemporary situation influenced his view of how best to usher in the coming millennium, and so dictated the content of his prophecies. The anonymous compiler of the so-called Albert of Trent prophecy, for example, striving to advance an anti-French policy, was thus moved to predict, against the whole canon of Savonarola's teaching, that they would prove to be untrustworthy allies and, ultimately, enemies to Christianity.[132] In similar vein, Benedetto Luschino,[133] languishing in the dungeons of S. Marco for homicide, chose to prophesy, in an attempt to precipitate an open confrontation between the pro- and anti-Savonarolan forces within the Tusco-Roman Congregation, that the millennium would be ushered in by an imminent blood-bath in the Congrega-

[131] For discussions of the prophecies of the Piagnoni and their contemporaries, see the various works by C. Vasoli and D. Weinstein already cited; A. Chastel, 'L'Apocalypse en 1500: La Fresque de l'Antéchrist à la Chapelle Saint-Brice d'Orvieto', *Bibliothèque d'Humanisme et Renaissance* (Mélanges d'Augustin Renaudet), 14 (1952), 124–40; M. Reeves, *The Influence of Prophecy in the Later Middle Ages* (Oxford, 1969), part IV.

[132] D. Weinstein, 'The Apocalypse in Sixteenth-Century Florence: The Vision of Albert of Trent', in A. Molho and J. A. Tedeschi (eds.), *Renaissance Studies in Honor of Hans Baron* (Florence, 1971), 321, 328.

[133] See F. Patetta, 'Fra Benedetto da Firenze compagno ed apologista del Savonarola, al secolo Bettuccio Luschino', *Atti della Reale Accademia delle Scienze di Torino*, 60 (1924–5), 623–59; D. Weinstein, 'A Lost Letter of Fra Girolamo Savonarola', *Renaissance Quarterly*, 22 (1969), 1–8.

tion, from which the Piagnoni would emerge victorious on all fronts.[134] A blood-bath was envisaged too by Fra Silvestro Marradi, caused by the obduracy of the leaders of Christendom and their determination to destroy the truth preached by Savonarola. Savonarola and his two martyred companions had appeared to him and enjoined him to forewarn the Elect of the imminent schism and persecution. For a while, however, the Elect had to remain silent, pray, and give no cause to their enemies to act against them.[135]

The most notable instance of all, however, is Giorgio Benigno's *rifacimento* of the original text of the *Apocalypsis Nova* by Amadeus Menez de Sylva, founder of the Amadeites.[136] Accomplished while Benigno was a member of the household of Cardinal Bernardino Carvajal in 1502, his reworking of this famous millenarian text brought into prominence the mystical themes and eschatological expectations which he himself favoured and to which he had already given expression in his *Propheticae solutiones*[137] and *De angelica natura*.[138] The role of the French as the instruments of God, the privileged status of Florence as the elect city, the prospect of converting the Turk to Christianity and of reuniting the Eastern and Western Churches under an Angelic Pope, all dear to Benigno's heart, were each underlined in the revised *Apocalypsis*

---

[134] Benedetto Luschino, 'Fons Vitae', MS BNF Magl., XXXV, 90, fo. 50$^v$.

[135] Silvestro da Marradi, 'Prophetia viri cuisdam sancti f. Silvestri', MS BRF 2053, fo. 107$^v$. The vision is said to have occurred on 30 May 1505, but the content would suggest that it referred to the Franco-Papal rivalry and to the *Conciliabolo* of Pisa.

[136] The major study on the *Apocalypsis Nova* is A. Morisi, *Apocalypsis Nova: Ricerche sull'origine e la formazione del testo dello pseudo-Amadeo* (Istituto Storico Italiano per il Medio Evo: Studi Storici, 77; Rome, 1970), see esp. 27–41 and n. 56. As 'Maestro Giorgio', Benigno's name was associated with the *rifacimento* as early as 1540 by the Piagnone Lorenzo Violi, and one Antonio, an Amadeite friar (possibly Fra Antonio da Cremona): see their letters in the appendix to 'Apocalypsis Amadei seu Revelationes', MS BNF Magl., XXXIX, 1, fos. 290–4. For C. Vasoli's comments on Benigno's role, see his 'Notizie su Giorgio Benigno Salviati (Juraj Dragisic)', *Studi storici in onore di Gabriele Pepe* (Bari, 1969), 495–8; 'A proposito di Gabriele Biondo, Francesco Giorgio Veneto e Giorgio Benigno Salviati', *Rinascimento*, 2nd ser. 9 (1969), 325–30; 'Sul probabile autore di una *profezia* Cinquecentesca', *Il Pensiero Politico*, 2 (1969), 464–72.

[137] See above, pp. 80–1.

[138] Giorgio Benigno, *Opus de angelica natura* (Florence, 1499) (*GW* 3843), sigs. e3$^r$, e4$^r$.

*Nova*.[139] It was incontestably, as Professor Vasoli has said, a prophecy based on a specific programme of ecclesiastical policy and designed to strengthen the campaign against Julius II orchestrated by pro-French cardinals who in 1511 championed the *Conciliabolo* at Pisa.[140] But it was other things besides, as his letters to the Piagnone Ubertino Risaliti indicate.[141] It was an attempt to obtain the Piagnoni's support for the programme; and also a means for him to return to the Piagnone fold after the abjuration of Savonarola in *De angelica natura*;[142] and it was, finally, a crass attempt to turn the Savonarolan vision into an instrument of self-aggrandisement.

All in all, however, it must be borne in mind that, in the context of apocalyptic expectations, some degree of consciously hortatory prophecy was inevitable. Unless it was to be entirely passive, belief in the prospect of the coming millennium necessarily involved a commitment to advancing it as far as was humanly possible. Whether the divine promises of a renewed world were to be indefinitely postponed, on the one hand, or speedily fulfilled, on the other, depended, according to this view, upon Christian endeavour. In promoting their earthly realization by prophecy, as by other means, Piagnoni preachers were at one with millenarians in general. Nor was the impulse to hasten the longed-for changes confined to the religious sphere alone. It was equally powerful in the realm of politics. If the imminent reign of Christ on earth could be brought closer by political means, then, the Piagnone believed, he must do his utmost in that direction as well. No less than their clerical brethren, therefore, lay Piagnoni had a duty actively to advance the Savonarolan cause. In the next section of this chapter, we see how they set about fulfilling their role.

---

[139] Morisi, *Apocalypsis Nova*, 15–19, 24–5, 30–1, *et passim*.
[140] Vasoli, 'Sul probabile autore di una *profezia* Cinquecentesca', 465. Since the *rifacimento* was largely complete by Oct. 1502, however (cf. Morisi, *Apocalypsis Nova*, 29–32 and n. 56), the Pope in question must have been Alexander VI, not Julius II.
[141] Morisi, *Apocalypsis Nova*, n. 56 on pp. 29–32.
[142] Vasoli, 'Notizie su Giorgio Benigno Salviati', 472–3.

## III

The course which the lay activists were to follow in the period from Savonarola's death to the return of the Medici in 1512 had been laid down by the prophet himself. It was to safeguard the Florentine Republic at all costs and to ensure against its overthrow. As we have seen, transmuted by his teaching, the new Republic became at once the concrete proof of the city's divine election and at the same time the essential prerequisite for the reform which she would lead. The realization of Florence's destiny was indissolubly linked to the fortunes of the Republic. This was Savonarola's legacy, a legacy which the Piagnoni worked assiduously to preserve.

At the end of May 1498, their political fortunes were at their lowest ebb. In the short space of two months, they had lost their popularly acknowledged political leader, Francesco Valori, murdered on 8 April,[143] and Savonarola himself, executed on 23 May. Arrest and proscription, moreover, had thinned their ranks. Their most influential supporters in governmental circles were fined and deprived of all political rights for terms of up to five years;[144] Piagnoni officials were removed from the Chancery and even from minor administrative posts;[145] and Piagnoni *Ottimati* who, because of their connections, were protected from harsher reprisals, had

---

[143] Villari, *La storia di Girolamo Savonarola*, ii. 168.

[144] ASF Signori e Collegi, Deliberazioni Ord. Aut. 100, fos. 39$^v$, 41$^r$, 44$^r$, 45$^{r-v}$, 55$^v$, 57$^r$; for examples of the variant lists which have been published of the Piagnoni condemned by the *Signoria*, see L. Passerini, 'Nuovi documenti concernenti a Frate Girolamo Savonarola e ai suoi compagni', *Giornale storico degli archivi toscani*, 3 (1859), 49–113; Cambi, *Istorie*, ii. 129–34; Parenti, *Istorie fiorentine*, 275–6. For an unpublished list, manifesting interesting variations, see ASM Pot. est., Firenze, 947, busta 3.

[145] D. Marzi, *La cancelleria della Repubblica Fiorentina* (Rocca S. Casciano, 1910), 28–89; N. Rubinstein, 'The Beginnings of Niccolò Machiavelli's Career in the Florentine Chancery', *Italian Studies*, 11 (1956), 80–2; Passerini, 'Nuovi documenti concernenti a frate Girolamo Savonarola', 55; Piero Parenti, 'Istorie fiorentine', MS BNF II.II.131, fos. 83$^{r-v}$. For a revisionist view see R. Black, 'Florentine Political Traditions and Machiavelli's Election to the Chancery', *Italian Studies*, 40 (1985), 1–16.

forced loans imposed upon them.[146] Given the bitterness of the political struggle of the previous three years the reprisals against the Piagnoni were severe but not exceedingly so. The policy of moderation advocated by such adversaries as Bernardo Rucellai, Giovanvettorio Soderini, and Tanai de' Nerli had its effects.[147] So also did the fear that continued civil unrest could easily degenerate into the crowd violence witnessed on 8 April, when S. Marco was besieged and attacked, the prisoners in the city gaol released, and the houses of the Valori and Cambini fired and pillaged with the death of at least two members of the Valori household.[148] Class interest came immediately to the fore as demonstrated by the bans forbidding the wearing of arms and demanding the restitution of all goods taken from the houses of Francesco and Niccolò Valori and of Andrea Cambini.[149] Indeed a special contingent of guards was posted to guard the Valori houses from any further such outrages.[150] A virtual state of martial law was imposed for the succeeding three weeks. Only on 30 April was the situation sufficiently stable for the government to issue a general amnesty for all crimes committed on 8 and 9 April.[151]

Now that they had the upper hand, and despite the tense situation, the anti-Savonarolans were not about to forgo the chance to retaliate against their opponents. The *Signoria* and Colleges passed decrees lifting all bans imposed on Francesco Cei in January 1497

[146] ASF Signori e Collegi, Deliberazioni Ord. Aut. 100, fo. 60ᵛ; Francesco Guicciardini, *Storie fiorentine dal 1378 al 1509*, ed. R. Palmarocchi (Bari, 1931; fac. repr. 1968), 155–6, 284; Parenti, *Istorie fiorentine*, 268, 275–6.

[147] Ibid. 266; Giovanvettorio Soderini ['Ricordanze'], MS ASF Signori, Dieci di Balìa, Otto di Pratica, Legazioni e Commissarie, Missive e Responsive, 36, fos. 80ᵛ, 81ʳ and 81ᵛ, where Paolantonio Soderini, who had fled from Florence fearing reprisal for his advocacy of Savonarola and cited to appear before the *Signoria*, asked to be escorted there by Tanai de' Nerli.

[148] Parenti, *Istorie fiorentine*, 260–5; ASF Provvisioni, 189, fo. 21ᵛ.

[149] ASF Signori e Collegi, Deliberazioni Ord. Aut. 100, fos. 34ᵛ, 35ʳ⁻ᵛ; Parenti, *Istorie fiorentine*, 266, where he states: 'E' primati ogni diligentia missono in salvare e' capi frateschi, sichome equali et simili a loro (et molto per male ebbono la morte di Francesco Valori)', and p. 271.

[150] ASF Signori e Collegi, Deliberazioni Ord. Aut. 100, fo. 34ᵛ.

[151] Ibid., fo. 41ʳ.

during Francesco Valori's gonfaloniership for a poem he had written against Savonarola. On the same day the *Signoria* formally freed
Giovanni Benizzi, Filippo Corbizzi, and Giovanni da Tignano
from prison, in which they had been confined in perpetuity for
conspiring against the Republic in April 1496.[152] A number of
Piagnoni who, during the gonfaloniership of Francesco Valori, had
won the privilege of membership to the Great Council were now
ejected and banned from all offices of state for two years.[153] On the
day in which the new *Signoria* was to be elected, fifty Piagnoni were
ordered not to attend the meeting of the Great Council.[154] Similar
discriminatory decrees were issued regularly for the remainder of
1498. More spitefully, an annual grant of money was made for
twenty-five years to the Franciscans of S. Salvatore al Monte for
their role, through the trial by fire on 7 April, in ridding the city of
the danger posed by the troublesome Dominicans.[155] The *Signoria*
also formally invited them to celebrate mass in the Palazzo della
Signoria in place of the friars of S. Marco.[156] Similarly, it confiscated the library and other goods once belonging to the Medici but
legally purchased by the friars of S. Marco and ordered closed the
recently constructed subterranean passage between the convent
and the *Sapienza* building.[157] Finally, it ensured that the *Piagnona*
would never be replaced by laying down that in future no bell in
S. Marco was to weigh more than 120 pounds.[158]

Equally significant was the attempt made to dismantle the charitable edifice so painstakingly erected at Savonarola's behest. The
attempt had two main thrusts. First, it was sought to undermine
the *Monte di Pietà* by forcing through legislation enabling the Jews
to lend money once again in Florence. Though the proposal was
presented to the Council of Eighty on six occasions it managed to
obtain a majority of votes on only two. Nevertheless, the Great
Council rejected the legislation in both instances.[159] Secondly, and

---

[152] ASF Provvisioni, 189, fos. 21ʳ–22ʳ.
[153] Parenti, 'Istorie fiorentine', MS BNF II.II.131, fo. 83ᵛ.
[154] Ibid., fo. 84ʳ; see also the shocked reaction of Giovanni Cambi, *Istorie*, ii. 132.
[155] ASF Provvisioni, 189, fo. 18ᵛ.
[156] ASF Signori e Collegi, Deliberazioni Ord. Aut. 100, fo. 68ʳ.
[157] Ibid., fos. 44ᵛ, 52ʳ, 53ᵛ, 57ᵛ, 58ʳ, 132ᵛ–133ʳ.        [158] Ibid., fo. 70ᵛ.
[159] ASF Libri fabarum, 71, fos. 104ʳ, 105ʳ, 106ʳ, 110ʳ, 111ʳ, 113ᵛ, 114ʳ⁻ᵛ; ibid.,

almost exactly at the same time, the *Signoria* moved against the *Buonuomini di S. Martino* and the other charitable organizations. On 18 May it decreed that henceforth the confraternity's officials were to be elected by the Great Council and were to be responsible to it for the duration of their term of office which was not to exceed one year.[160] At one stroke the confraternity lost its independence and the Piagnoni officials who had steered it through the last difficult years. Two days later another decree transferred to the new *Buonuomini* the responsibility of administering the *Ospedale del Ceppo*, which had hitherto been administered by Piagnoni officials.[161]

What lay behind this rash of punitive legislation became evident on 26 June, when the *Signoria* and Colleges decreed that all the documents pertaining to the *Buonuomini* were to be handed to the newly elected officials and that the collection box which the confraternity had placed in S. Marco be removed forthwith.[162] While undoubtedly successful in destroying all the traces of Savonarolan influence and in cutting all existing ties to S. Marco, the legislation was also responsible for a decline in the *Buonuomini*'s and the *Ospedale del Ceppo*'s ability to care for the sick and the poor. In the long run, as we shall see, this was to redound to the Piagnoni's credit and ensure that the administration of both charitable institutions was relinquished to them by successive governments without further interference.

Earlier in the year, on 17 March, at the first signs of unrest and in accordance with Florentine practice all confraternities including

---

Signori, Carteggi, Missive Ia Cancelleria, 51, fo. 82ʳ, in which Francesco Gualterotti, Florentine ambassador in Rome, is asked to obtain a licence from the Pope to allow Jews back into Florence in order to 'provedere a tante necessità del popolo'.

[160] ASF Provvisioni, 189, fos. 28ᵛ–29ᵛ; L. Passerini, *Storia degli stabilimenti di beneficenza* (Florence, 1853), 506–7; ABSM Capitoli e indulgenze dei Procuratori della Congregazione dei Buonuomini di S. Martino, fo. 13ᵛ, for list of the first eight *Procuratori* elected, amongst whom there is not one single Piagnone.

[161] ASF Provvisioni, 189, fo. 38ʳ⁻ᵛ. The decree was justified by the argument that 'buona parte degl'uomini di decta compagnia interveniano al governo et cura dello spedale del Ceppo', all of which demonstrates how closely Piagnoni activities had been watched.

[162] ASF Signori a Collegi, Deliberazioni Ord. Aut. 100, fo. 65ᵛ.

that of S. Michele Arcangelo were closed.[163] Whereas most other confraternities were permitted to reopen shortly after the arrest and execution of Savonarola, S. Michele Arcangelo was prevented from doing so until 24 February 1499.[164] It was a blow from which S. Michele Arcangelo had great difficulty recovering. Perhaps because of the fear induced by the recent persecution of Piagnoni or perhaps because of the onerous weekly contribution required of all members coupled with the unremitting round of duties and the ban on all activities which might have lightened the burden of membership, the confraternity, as we shall see, had difficulty obtaining a quorum at its meetings.

It was a time of doubt and despondency. Something of the aims and ideals which even at this time inspired and directed these Piagnoni can be gleaned from the sole treatise of substance composed by a politically qualified Piagnone which has come down to us from their period, the *Breve compendio e sommario della verità predicata e profetata dal R.P. fra Girolamo da Ferrara*, by Bartolomeo Redditi.[165] A doctor *in utroque iure* and a notary,[166] Redditi had held the post of ambassador at the Papal Court in 1489–90.[167] He had frequently been invited, also, to attend the meetings of the *pratiche*: a sure sign of political standing.[168] His partisanship of Savonarola, and especially his intriguing to persuade Archbishop Rinaldo Orsini to reinstate the Savonarolan Pietro Maria da Perugia as Vicar in Florence, led to his temporary eclipse;[169] but he was soon back on the political scene. He composed the *Breve compendio* in 1500, was appointed *Podestà* of Modigliana (a position

---

[163] ASF Compagnie Religiose Soppresse, 1430, fo. 9ʳ; see above, Ch. 1, n. 87.

[164] ASF Compagnie Religiose Soppresse, 1430, fo. 9ʳ. The company del Gesù, for instance, was permitted to resume its meetings on 2 May 1498: ibid., Otto di Guardia, Ep. Rep. 110, fo. 2ᵛ.

[165] Bartolomeo Redditi, *Breve compendio e sommario della verità predicata e profetata dal R.P. fra Girolamo da Ferrara*, ed. J. Schnitzer, *Quellen und Forschungen zur Geschichte Savonarolas*, i (Munich, 1902).

[166] L. Martines, *Lawyers and Statecraft in Renaissance Florence* (Princeton, NJ, 1968), 495.

[167] BNF Ginori Conti 29, 64, fo. 52.

[168] Bartolomeo Redditi, 'Libro di debitori, creditori e ricordi', ASF Conv. Sopp. 111: 152, fos. 65ʳ–66ᵛ.

[169] Villari, *Storia di Savonarola*, vol. ii, app., pp. cclxix–cclxx.

from which he was, however, excused) in 1504,[170] and resumed his attendance at the meetings of the *pratiche*.[171]

Like the Piagnoni friars whom we studied in the previous part of this chapter, Redditi too confronted the Savonarolans' problems directly in his *Breve compendio*. Everything, he admitted, seemed to be conspiring against Savonarola's innovations, both religious and political. The faith of his followers had been sorely tried, not only by the trials and subsequent persecution but also by the gulf between the promises which the prophet had held out to Florence and her immediate situation, in which her difficulties in retaining her territories and in recapturing those already lost—Pisa especially— loomed largest.[172] Again like his clerical counterparts, Redditi came to the conclusion that these tribulations were intended by God to strengthen the Florentines' resolve, purify their ambitions, and complete the reforms initiated back in 1494.[173] Whereas Domenico Cecchi, writing three years earlier, had been emboldened by Savonarola's triumphs to present a detailed programme of political and social changes, designed to bring Florence into full conformity with Savonarola's idea as he conceived it,[174] Redditi, sobered by his experiences, was under no illusions as to what might be achieved at the time. Leaving specific reforming measures aside until a more auspicious time, he adjured the Florentines simply to repair their divisions and to serve God by just and lawful expedients, as Savonarola had directed. In return, Redditi assured his readers, they would be granted all that had been promised. Voicing the sentiments of a God who had favoured Florence above all other nations, Redditi wrote, in a most expressive passage:

I am jealous of my bride Florence, saith the Lord. I would gladly have restored Pisa to her, but I fear lest she be stolen from me by another (and that she may become enamoured of earthly things) and forget me and her true salvation. But tell her that she must remain united in charity; and

---

[170] Redditi, 'Libro di debitori, creditori e ricordi', ASF Conv. Sopp. 111: 153, fo. 55ᵛ.

[171] See e.g. ASF Consulte e Pratiche, 70, fos. 80ᵛ–81ʳ.

[172] Redditi, *Breve compendio*, 37–8, 61–78.     [173] Ibid. 38–40, 49–50, 53.

[174] Domenico Cecchi, *Riforma sancta et pretiosa*, ed. in U. Mazzone, *'El buon governo': Un progetto di riforma generale nella Firenze Savonaroliana* (Florence, 1978).

when she is thus quite united, I shall give her the joys befitting a bride . . . and I shall give her a great kingdom. Tell her, however, that at this time she must be totally united, and that I love her dearly and will give her all things, as I have promised, and I shall not fail her one jot.[175]

Despite the loss of their leaders and the severity of the repression, the Piagnoni recovered with a speed which astounded their adversaries. Like their ecclesiastical counterparts, they turned the recent reverses to advantage. They now believed that the cause for which they stood had four martyrs to inspire and protect it: Savonarola, his two fellow Dominicans, and Francesco Valori. For, just as Savonarola and his two companions had died in order to fulfil the mission God had entrusted to them, so Francesco Valori, in the words of his nephew Niccolò, had given his life for the 'popular government' (*governo popolare*), 'justice', and 'liberty'.[176] These lofty principles, however, were not as yet to the fore in the activities which marked their re-emergence on the Florentine political scene. Their first show of strength was in fact to institute proceedings for sodomy against Doffo Spini, the leader of their most insolent opponents, the youthful *Compagnacci*, in November 1499. They failed to secure a conviction, but they were by now so well entrenched as to be able to forestall any attempt at retaliation.[177] They bided their time and when the occasion presented itself they moved against another enemy, Canon Giovanni Francesco Poggio Bracciolini, who had written an extremely damaging anti-Savonarolan pamphlet in the crucial early months of 1498.[178] Bracciolini was denounced for having publicly reviled the French alliance and the Florentine efforts to regain Pisa by force of

---

[175] Redditi, *Breve compendio*, 58–9: 'Io sono geloso della mia sposa Firenze, dice il Signore. Io gli harei ben reso Pisa, ma io ho paura, che la [i.e., Firenze] non mi fusse rubata da un altro (et che non si inamorasse di cose terrene) e dimenticassi di me e della sua vera salute. Ma digli, che stia unita in charità insieme e quando ella starà così tutta unita, io gli darò le gioie della sposa . . . e darogli un gran regno. Ma digli, che in questo mezzo stia unita insieme, e che io gli voglio bene e gli darò ogni cosa, come ho promesso, e non fallirò un iota.'

[176] Niccolò Valori [*et al.*], 'Ricordanze', BNF Panc. 134, fos. 13ᵛ, 17ʳ; see also Pseudo-Burlamacchi, *La vita*, 48, 239.

[177] Parenti, *Istorie fiorentine*, 291, and also MS BNF II.II.131, fo. 204ʳ.

[178] See above, pp. 92– 3.

arms: charges on which he was brought before the *Otto di Guardia* in July 1500 and sentenced to five years' exile.[179]

The Piagnoni's enemies swiftly retaliated. In the same month as Bracciolini was tried, the *Arrabbiati* denounced Giovanni Caccini to the *Otto di Guardia* for having stated, at the height of the French successes in northern Italy, that the time had come to avenge Savonarola's death and to execute the most prominent supporters of Lodovico il Moro in Florence.[180] Later in 1500, they moved also against Tommaso Tosinghi,[181] allegedly for a minor infringement of office but in reality because he had been one of Francesco Valori's henchmen and also a member of the *Otto di Guardia* on the occasions in which it had condemned to death the five pro-Medicean conspirators in 1497 and, more recently, sentenced Bracciolini to exile.[182] Despite the Piagnoni's efforts on their behalf, both were punished: Caccini being sentenced to a year's exile and Tosinghi deprived of his post of *Podestà* of Pistoia and disqualified from holding office for two years.[183] By then, however, the tide had turned. Within two months, and despite two previous attempts that had failed, the Piagnoni succeeded in obtaining the legal majorities in both the Council of Eighty and the Great Council to repeal the sentences against Tosinghi.[184] Furthermore, already by June 1500, a Piagnoni-dominated *Signoria*, acting with the complicity of the *Otto di Guardia*, apparently in contravention of the procedural requirements, revoked the proscriptions which had

---

[179] ASF Otto di Guardia, Ep. Rep. 117, fos. 151ᵛ–152ᵛ. Amongst the members of the *Otto* there were three Piagnoni, including Tommaso Tosinghi: ibid., fo. 1ʳ. See also Parenti, *Istorie fiorentine*, 294–5 and also in MS BNF II.II.132, fo. 55ᵛ. For Bracciolini's unsuccessful appeal against the sentence see ibid., fo. 62ʳ⁻ᵛ and Martines, *Lawyers and Statecraft*, 275 and n. 66.

[180] Parenti, 'Istorie fiorentine', MS BNF II.II.132, fos. 55ᵛ–56ʳ.

[181] On him see Guicciardini, *Storie fiorentine*, 139–45; Cambi, *Istorie*, ii. 106–7, 133–4; and below, pp. 256, 275–6, 313.

[182] Tommaso Tosinghi ['Vita'] MS BNF II.II.325, fo. 127ᵛ. These are strictly speaking *Ricordanze* but lack the opening folio and have been given a later, inappropriate title. See also Parenti, *Istorie fiorentine*, 295; Cambi, *Istorie*, ii. 151, and n. 179 above.

[183] Parenti, 'Istorie fiorentine', MS BNF II.II.132, fo. 63ʳ⁻ᵛ; Cambi, *Istorie*, ii. 151.

[184] ASF Libri fabarum, 71, fos. 151ᵛ, 152ʳ, 159ᵛ, 160ʳ; Tommaso Tosinghi ['Vita'], fo. 127ᵛ.

been imposed upon clerical and lay Piagnoni two years before. The manner in which this decree was issued and implemented was promptly challenged by their opponents, but to no effect.[185] With the return of their exiled brethren, for which they had been campaigning since October 1499, the Piagnoni were at full strength and ready for the political battles ahead.

This record of mutual enmity and petty spite, which was also enlivened by cruel pranks and public displays of mockery (*baie*) and scurrilous anonymous libels (*polizze*) directed at the leaders of the two factions,[186] should not be taken as evidence that the Piagnoni and their longest-standing opponents, the *Arrabbiati*, stood firm in mutual enmity at all times and on all issues. This was patently not so, despite the fact that such cases of discord were singled out by chroniclers for particular attention. At about this time political alignments began to undergo revolutionary changes, which in turn shaped the whole subsequent course of Florentine politics. The most significant change was the *rapprochement* of Piagnoni and *Arrabbiati*, which led, in turn, to the increasing isolation of the Mediceans, who were despised by both groups. Moves in this direction had been instituted as early as July 1498 by a *Signoria* desperately seeking the Piagnoni's co-operation in order to overcome one of the recurrent financial crises.[187] Nothing had come of it. The memory of Savonarola's death was too bitter and the enmities it had aroused too strong for it to have been otherwise. More concerted, though uncoordinated, efforts were made by the leaders of both factions the following year, again without immediate results.[188] Their hands were finally forced in December 1500 by rumours of an impending attack on Florence by Piero de' Medici. With a *Signoria* already downcast (*invilita*) by the threats of Cesare Borgia and thus incapable of acting decisively in the matter, with

---

[185] Parenti, 'Istorie fiorentine', MS BNF II.II.132, fos. 41ᵛ–42ʳ.

[186] See e.g. ibid., II.II.131, fos. 114ᵛ–115ʳ.

[187] S. Bertelli, 'Embrioni di partiti alle soglie dell'età moderna', *Per Federico Chabod (1901–1960), i. Lo Stato e il potere nel Rinascimento* (Perugia, 1980–1), 30–1, citing Giovanvettorio Soderini ['Ricordanze'].

[188] Parenti, *Istorie fiorentine*, 287–8. Parenti here asserts that the *Bigi* were also involved in the compact; but, in the list of names he provides it is impossible to recognize a notable *Bigio* name.

their own and the survival of the popular government at stake, Piagnoni and *Arrabbiati* decided that the time had come to act.[189] In time-honoured Florentine fashion the representatives of the two factions organized a number of 'dinners' at the homes of Jacopo de' Nerli, Alfonso Strozzi, Martino di Francesco Scarfi, Tommaso di Paolantonio Soderini, Cappone di Gino, and others. These dinners were attended by twenty-five to thirty men at a time, who entered into a compact 'not to desert each other and to stand against Piero de' Medici and, were the need to arise, to take up arms in their own and in the city's defence'.[190]

Some of the effects of the agreement were immediately felt. Almost miraculously, the petty public squabbles ceased forthwith, although individuals, especially amongst the Piagnoni, continued to harbour hate for their opponents, sought to damage them, and gathered evidence against them for future retribution.[191] The compact did not, however, lead to a policy of co-operation on all issues and at all levels. The foundations for such concerted action were laid, but their realization was as yet a distant dream. The problem here was twofold. First, both factions lacked social homogeneity. Substantial disagreements on individual policies between *Ottimati* and the rank and file were bound to arise within each faction. Secondly, neither grouping could count on an undisputed leader who possessed the authority to reconcile differences and decide on the policies which were to be pursued by the whole membership.

The Piagnoni were particularly vulnerable on both counts. With the death of Savonarola they lost not only their religious leader but

---

[189] Parenti, 'Istorie fiorentine', MS BNF II.II.132, fo. 86ᵛ.

[190] Parenti, *Istorie fiorentine*, 295–6: 'di non si abandonare e d'essere contro a Piero de'Medici e piglare l'arme bisognando in difensione loro e della città'. See also 298 and II.II.132, fos. 86ᵛ–87ʳ.

[191] See e.g. the various lists of opponents later appended to Savonarola's biographies such as BNF Conv. Sopp., G.5.1209, fos. 190ᵛ–192ᵛ; ibid., Baldovinetti, 115, pp. 262–3; ASF C. Strozz., ser. III, 267, ch. 22. An interesting example of the way in which revenge on enemies was sought is the notarized deposition before the Piagnone notary Ser Filippo Cioni by Ulivieri Guadagni of 22 Aug. 1508 in which Guadagni, 'zelo domini ductus', relates how the friars of the Dominican Conventual convent of S. Jacopo at S. Miniato al Tedesco were engaged in sexual trysts with nuns of nearby convents: ASF Not. Ant. C.555 (1508–11), fos. 14ʳ–15ᵛ.

also the single, most important unifying force within the party. Not even the disappearance of Francesco Valori had brought more cohesiveness. No undisputed leader emerged. A number of eminent individuals like Giovanbattista Ridolfi, Jacopo Salviati, Lorenzo Lenzi, and Lanfredino Lanfredini—all of them strong personalities with different political styles and with their own power bases—continued to vie for supremacy. To complicate matters further a small splinter group was formed, headed by the relatively youthful Antonio Canigiani, Pierfrancesco Tosinghi, and Niccolò Valori. Known as the Valori faction (*setta valoriana*) because its members had all been followers of Francesco Valori, this group was not amenable to advice from the putative older leaders of the movement and when necessary it pursued radical policies of its own.[192]

Social differences, too, though no more marked than in other political groupings, were perhaps of greater moment amongst the Piagnoni. There were two major reasons for this. In the first place, the group of Piagnoni notables *active* in politics was larger, wealthier, and, in some respects, socially more eminent than equivalent groups amongst the *Arrabbiati* and the Mediceans.[193] In the second place, these Piagnoni notables played a more prominent public role than their counterparts. As a consequence, their policy statements and political activities could be more easily scrutinized and contrasted to those of the rank and file. There are no doubts that on certain issues, taxation in particular, Piagnoni notables gave the impression of acting more in accordance with class than factional interests. A case in point was a private meeting of January 1501 in which twelve *Ottimati*, most of them leaders of the Piagnoni and *Arrabbiati* factions but including also a few non-aligned individuals like Piero Soderini, discussed the advisability of transferring control of all financial and fiscal matters from the Great

---

[192] Guicciardini, *Storie fiorentine*, 327–8.

[193] This is especially true after 1502, when many *Ottimati*, the best known of whom was Bernardo Rucellai, withdrew from politics in protest against Pier Soderini: Filippo de' Nerli, *Commentari dei fatti civili occorsi dentro la città di Firenze dall'anno 1215 al 1537* (2 vols.; Trieste, 1859), i. 112, 158–9; F. Gilbert, 'Bernardo Rucellai e gli Orti Oricellari: Studio sull'origine del pensiero politico moderno', *Machiavelli e il suo tempo* (Bologna, 1972), 22.

Council to an enlarged but still aristocratically controlled Council of Eighty.[194]

Disagreement surfaced also on other occasions. Thus, to cite but two examples, in the tortuous constitutional struggles which preceded the election of a *Gonfaloniere a vita* in 1502, Piagnoni *Ottimati*, led by Giovanbattista Ridolfi and Jacopo Salviati, took a distinctive stand. Believing that the future of the Republic—and, no doubt, their own interests—were best assured if important decisions were placed in the *Ottimati*'s hands, Ridolfi and Salviati advocated the establishment of a small, select council which could take over some of the functions of the Great Council, especially those connected with finance.[195] When this proved unacceptable, and the compromise of the *Gonfalonierato a vita* was decided upon, these *Ottimati* once again set themselves apart: giving their support to the candidature of Piero Soderini, whereas the majority of the Piagnoni would seem to have favoured Giovacchino Guasconi.[196]

Another matter on which the Piagnoni divided was the marriage of Filippo Strozzi to Clarice de' Medici, daughter of Piero, in 1508. Jacopo Salviati, brother-in-law of Giovanni de' Medici, and Giovanbattista Ridolfi, both now antagonistic towards Soderini, who opposed the match, gave it their support. With other *Ottimati*, they actively advanced Filippo Strozzi's suit.[197] Other Piagnoni,

[194] Parenti, 'Istorie fiorentine', MS BNF II.II.132, fos. 91ᵛ–92ʳ. The proposal was formally put to a *pratica*: H. C. Butters, *Governors and Government in Early Sixteenth-Century Florence, 1502–1519* (Oxford, 1985), 44.

[195] ASF Consulte e Pratiche, 66, fos. 219ᵛ–223ʳ; F. Gilbert, *Machiavelli and Guicciardini: Politics and History in Sixteenth Century Florence* (Princeton, NJ, 1965), 67–74; R. Pesman Cooper, 'L'elezione di Pier Soderini a Gonfaloniere a Vita', *ASI* 125 (1967), 145–57; L. F. Marks, 'La crisi finanziaria a Firenze dal 1494 al 1502', *ASI* 112 (1954), 40–72.

[196] Parenti, 'Istorie fiorentine', MS BNF II.II.133, fo 60ʳ⁻ᵛ; Guicciardini, *Storie fiorentine*, 251; Pesman Cooper, 'L'elezione di Pier Soderini a Gonfaloniere a Vita', esp. 161–5: but for a different view of Soderini's basis of support, S. Bertelli, 'Petrus Soderinus Patriae Parens', *Bibliothèque d'Humanisme et Renaissance*, 31 (1969), 93–8, and 'Pier Soderini "Vexillifer Perpetuus Reipublicae Florentinae" 1502–1512', in A. Molho and J. A. Tedeschi (eds.), *Renaissance Studies in Honor of Hans Baron* (Florence, 1970), 333–6. On Guasconi, see Villari, *La storia di Girolamo Savonarola*, vol. ii, app., pp. cclxiv–cclxvi; de' Nerli, *Commentari*, i. 137–8.

[197] Guicciardini, *Storie fiorentine*, 327. The whole episode has been exhaustively

however, took the opposite stand. Like other republican loyalists, they saw the marriage, which was contracted in open violation of the laws forbidding marriage association with the Medici and other Florentines outlawed by the Republic,[198] as an attempt by Cardinal Giovanni de' Medici to prepare the way for a Medici restoration by enlisting the support of *Ottimati* malcontents. The Piagnone opposition was led by the members of the Valori faction whose reading of the situation was not distorted by personal animosity towards Soderini.[199]

Once again, one should guard against placing too great a significance on these instances of disagreement in the movement. For, lapses of judgement aside, it is clear that the Piagnoni sought to the best of their abilities to advance the cause of the *governo popolare* even though they might have differed on how best to accomplish it. Evidence both of their common purpose and of the continued source of their ideological inspiration is provided by their approach to the election of the first *Gonfaloniere a vita*. On the eve of the election, according to Parenti,[200] 300 Piagnoni met in the convent of S. Marco, perhaps only to seek divine guidance concerning which candidate they should support, but also perhaps to discuss amongst themselves and with the friars whether they could arrive at a definite decision.

The strength of the Piagnoni's commitment towards the Republic accounts for the pivotal role they were enabled to play in it till its overthrow in 1512. They became, as a group, Soderini's staunch supporters and indefatigable allies in defending the Republic from internal and external enemies. So appreciative were they of Soderini's endeavours for the *governo popolare* and of the policies

---

analysed by M. M. Bullard, 'Marriage Politics and the Family in Florence: The Strozzi–Medici Alliance of 1508', *American Historical Review*, 84 (1979), 668–87. Amongst the *Ottimati* working against Pier Soderini was the Piagnone Raffaello di Alfonso Pitti, a member of the *Signoria*: ASF MAP, 108, 86.

[198] Lorenzo Strozzi, *La vita di Filippo Strozzi figlio di Filippo*, App. to Benedetto Varchi, *Storia fiorentina*, in J. G. Graevius (ed.), *Thesaurus antiquitatum et historiarum Italiae*, viii (2) (Leiden, 1723), col. 2; Guicciardini, *Storie fiorentine*, 325–6.

[199] Ibid. 328: cf. 327–8.

[200] Parenti, 'Istorie fiorentine', MS BNF II.II.133, fos. 57ᵛ–58ʳ.

he pursued to this end that they paid him the highest compliment: they spoke of him as one of their own, a man of genuine religious principles, who came to venerate Savonarola and who drew inspiration from his teaching.[201] Three of them, Alessandro Braccesi, Castellano Castellani, and Paolo Orlandini dedicated a number of poems to him and to his wife Argentina, in which he is spoken of in terms normally reserved for Savonarola.[202] He was, they maintained, sent by God to revive the moribund Florence. From him there issued the 'holy laws' which ensured God's protection and brought virtue, success, and happiness to Florence.[203] Not to be outdone, Soderini in turn fostered their belief in his veneration of Savonarola by, amongst other things, advocating the preferment of some of his followers to high ecclesiastical position.[204] In addition, as we shall see, he relinquished to them the administration of

---

[201] See e.g. Pseudo-Burlamacchi, *La vita*, 18, 179; Cambi, *Istorie*, ii. 248–9, 301–2, 310.

[202] Alessandro Braccesi, *Carmina*, ed. Alessandro Perosa (Florence, 1944), 125–6 (Nos. LXII, LXIII); Castellano Castellani, *Evangelii della quaresima*, in *Laude spirituali di Feo Belcari, di Lorenzo de' Medici, di Francesco d'Albizzo, di Castellano Castellani e di altri* (Florence, 1863), unnumbered pages following p. 287 and prefacing the *Evangelii* beginning with a new Roman pagination; Paolo Orlandini, *Carmina*, in 'Epythoma super universam bibliam', MS BNF Conv. Sopp., D.5.827, fos. 339ʳ–343ᵛ.

[203] The quotation occurs in Castellano Castellani, *Evangelii della quaresima*, in sonnet beginning 'Solida pietra'; see also Alessandro Braccesi, *Carmina*, 125 (No. LXIII); Paolo Orlandini, *Carmina*, esp. fos. 339ʳ⁻ᵛ; 341ʳ–343ᵛ. Orlandini's contribution as well as other poems praising Soderini are discussed in H. C. Butters, 'Piero Soderini and the Golden Age', *Italian Studies*, 23 (1978), 56–71. The most sanguine expression of the hopes pinned on Soderini by the Piagnoni is to be found in the letter—undated but written shortly after Soderini's election as *Gonfaloniere a vita*—from Matteo di Giovanni Bigazzi da Cascia, Canon of S. Lorenzo, to Marco di Matteo Strozzi, where he is said to have been appointed by God as 'suo substituto principe et pastore' in Florence against the powers of darkness: ASF C. Strozz., ser. III, 138, fos. 59ʳ–62ʳ.

[204] Pseudo-Burlamacchi, *La vita*, 18. It is in this context that one should view not only the commissioning of Fra Bartolomeo della Porta in 1510 to paint the altarpiece for the *sala* of the Great Council, but also the subject chosen for it and other decorative elements planned for the *sala*, like the statue of Christ the Redeemer; see J. Wilde, 'The Hall of the Great Council in Florence', *Journal of the Warburg and Courtauld Institutes*, 7 (1944), 78–81; R. M. Steinberg, *Fra Girolamo Savonarola, Florentine Art, and Renaissance Historiography* (Athens, Ga., 1977), 100–5.

two of the most important Florentine charitable institutions, the *Buonuomini di S. Martino* and the *Monte di Pietà*. Finally, he ensured that the government pass a number of legislative decrees long demanded by the Piagnoni.

It should be strongly emphasized that the relationship between the Piagnoni and Soderini was not forced upon them by weakness, but by their realistic appreciation of each other's strengths. The new office of *Gonfaloniere a vita* was to the Piagnoni a guarantee of institutional permanence for the Republic: indeed, all the more so since its creation as a means of overcoming recurrent political crises had been suggested by Savonarola before his death.[205] The Piagnoni, on the other hand, brought to Soderini not only a categorical ideological commitment to the Republic, but also unquestionable evidence of their newly regained and growing strength in Florentine politics. For their compact with the *Arrabbiati* had already begun to pay handsome dividends. In February 1502, during the term of a *Signoria* composed almost exclusively of Piagnoni and *Arrabbiati*, two significant pieces of legislation were passed.[206] First, the Great Council finally approved a law on the *ornamenta mulierum*, which had eluded successive Piagnoni-dominated *signorie* in 1496–7, including one headed by Francesco Valori.[207] As it stood, the provision of 11 February was unremarkable. It was a decree regulating the dress and ornaments of women and bore little or no resemblance to the reform proposal first mooted by Savonarola on 18 March 1496.[208] In view of the opposition such legislation had aroused in the past, it was, none the less, a signal victory. Above all, it was an intimation of the way in which Piagnone ideology began to pervade and then influence the decisions of the republican government.

Second, the Great Council passed on 23 February a provision which reversed the legislation promulgated in May and June 1498

---

[205] Villari, *La storia di Girolamo Savonarola*, vol. ii, app., p. clv.

[206] The exception being the Medicean Chimenti di Cipriano Sernigi. The full list in Giovanni Cambi, *Istorie*, ii. 175.

[207] ASF Provvisioni, 192, fos. 53r–54r. The legislation was passed in the *Ottanta* on 11 Feb. by 67:21 votes and in the Great Council on 22 Feb. by 788:290 votes: ibid., Libri fabarum, 71, fos. 170r, 171v.

[208] See above, pp. 40–2.

concerning the *Buonuomini di S. Martino* and the *Ospedale del Ceppo*.[209] It was admitted that the previous legislation had been a mistake and had led to the decline of the confraternities and to the consequent suffering of the poor. The provision of 23 February handed back to both confraternities control over their own affairs, especially in the selection of officials. For the *Buonuomini*, these were no longer to be elected by the Great Council for the term of one year but were to be appointed for life by the members of the confraternity, as had been the case in the past.[210] The confraternity was also relieved of all responsibilities towards the *Ospedale del Ceppo*, which was now given its independence and reverted to Piagnone control.[211] The composition of the twelve procurators to the *Buonuomini* appointed in accordance with the newly re-established procedure is most instructive. All but four, who either cannot be identified or whose political allegiance is not known, were Piagnoni.[212]

By this time the confraternity of S. Michele Arcangelo had fully resumed its activities. Though it had difficulty obtaining a quorum for its meetings and though its officials on occasions berated the members for their negligence, its charitable activities seem not to have experienced any decline.[213] The friars of S. Marco saw to that. It is clear, in fact, that members were continuously berated in order to obtain greater effort and single-minded commitment. This was

[209] ASF Provvisioni, 192, fo. 55ᵛ. On 11 Feb. it was passed in the *Ottanta* by 73:11 and on 22 Feb. in the Great Council by 866:212: ibid., Libri fabarum, 71, fos. 170ᵛ, 171ᵛ. The full text of the legislation is given in Passerini, *Storia degli stabilimenti di beneficenza*, 932–3; see also ABSM Capitoli e indulgenze dei Procuratori della Congregazione dei Buonuomini di S. Martino, vol. i, fos. 14ᵛ–15ʳ and vol. ii, fo. 6ʳ⁻ᵛ.

[210] ASF Provvisioni, 192, fo. 55ᵛ.

[211] Passerini, *Storia degli stabilimenti di beneficenza*, 193.

[212] ABSM Capitoli e indulgenze dei Procuratori della Congregazione dei Buonuomini di S. Martino, vol. i, fos. 14ᵛ–17ʳ. These were: Giovacchino Guasconi, Domenico di Bernardo Mazzinghi, Ser Pagolo di Amerigo Grassi, Jacopo Salviati, Piero del Rosso Ferranti, Piero d'Anfrione Lenzi, Leonardo di Benedetto Strozzi, Alessandro di Leonardo Mannelli. There were many Piagnoni, too, amongst the minor officials. Here, however, it is difficult to assess the proportions given the obscurity of many of the names: ibid., fos. 22ʳ–26ʳ.

[213] ASF Compagnie religiose soppresse, 1430, fos. 9ʳ, 41ʳ, 55ʳ; ibid., 1421, *passim*.

especially the case after Fra Cipriano di Pietro Cancelli da Pontassieve, one of the young friars who had received the habit from Savonarola, took over as *correttore*.[214] In a letter sent to the members on 14 November 1506 and read out at a meeting of the confraternity, Fra Cipriano stated that they were approaching the fullness of time.[215] And yet, he continued, the Holy Ghost had revealed that iniquity was on the increase whereas charity, the most perfect of guiding virtues, had disappeared from the world. For these reasons, it was beholden on the members to multiply their efforts. To ensure that this was done it was necessary to alter the company's statutes, which were, he averred, not sufficiently severe to instil into the confraternity the charity required in those harsh times.[216] Under his wardship, apart from extending the statutes and thus enlarging the range of activities, the confraternity drew still closer to S. Marco and to other foundations under Piagnone control.[217] With these developments the whole Piagnone charitable network became fully operational once again and was to remain so, undisturbed, until the final restoration of the Medici in 1530.

Such a demonstration of regained Piagnoni strength and prominence could not be lost on Soderini, a consummate politician still feeling his way in a controversial office. Nor could he have failed to draw the obvious lessons from the fact that, apart from himself, the two other candidates for the position of *Gonfaloniere a vita*, selected from an original list of 208 names, were Piagnoni. Giovacchino Guasconi might have been, as Parenti asserts, the Piagnoni candi-

---

[214] On him see Convento di S. Marco, 'Liber vestitionum', fo. 2ʳ, and the obituary in Ubaldini, 'Annalia', fo. 161ᵛ where, apart from being praised for his virtues and for his assiduous work for the good of men's souls especially in hearing confessions he is also credited with the foundation of the confraternity of the Assumption of the Virgin Mary popularly known as the Society of Contemplatives. I have not been able to identify this company since there were no fewer than eight confraternities dedicated to the Assumption in Florence: L. Del Migliore, *Zibaldone*, MS BNF Magl., XXV, 418, index.

[215] ASF Compagnie religiose soppresse, 1430, fo. 31ʳ.

[216] Ibid.

[217] Ibid., fos. 33ʳ⁻ᵛ, 34ʳ, 36ʳ⁻ᵛ, 38ᵛ, 46ᵛ, 53ʳ, *et passim*. Contacts were established with the nunneries of Sta Caterina and S. Giuseppe—not otherwise specified—and with the company of the Purification of the Virgin Mary and S. Zanobi. As late as 23 May 1518 its statutes were changed under the direction of four friars of S. Marco, including Fra Jacopo da Sicilia.

date because of his trustworthiness and partiality, but these were the very characteristics which would have frightened many voters away.[218] Antonio Malegonnelle's commitment to the cause might have seemed, perhaps, somewhat suspect because of his Medicean past; of his loyalty to Savonarola and to the movement which he inspired, however, there was never any doubt.[219] Although he could not have hoped to defeat Soderini, who in the second-last scrutiny obtained 300 votes more than he did, it is clear that Malegonnelle's chances were damaged by the split in the Piagnone vote,[220] as also, of course, were Guasconi's.

Soderini could not afford to ignore this evidence of Piagnone resurgence in the day-to-day running of government. There are no reasons to assume, however, that he even contemplated doing so. By all accounts a religious and devout man, devoid of vices and belonging to a family with strong Savonarolan connections, Soderini shared many ideals with the Piagnoni, including perhaps a genuine veneration for their leader. On taking up office, Soderini's first major piece of legislation was the far-reaching reform of the administration of justice which entailed both a speeding up of the judicial process and the creation of a new appeal court, the *Quarantia*.[221] To the Piagnoni's gratification, these 'holy laws' called for by Savonarola seemed to hold out the promise of more effective results in the fight against the 'unmentionable vice' of

[218] Parenti, 'Istorie fiorentine', MS BNF II.II.133, fos. 60$^{r-v}$; Cerretani, 'Istoria fiorentina', MS BNF II.III.74, fo. 300$^{r-v}$; id., 'Ricordi storici fiorentini', fo. 33$^r$.

[219] On him see Villari, *La storia di Girolamo Savonarola*, vol. ii, app., pp. ccxxviii, cclxxi, where he is stated to have signed the petition of 1497 though his name does not appear in any of the surviving lists; see also Guicciardini, *Storie fiorentine*, 123.

[220] Parenti, 'Istorie fiorentine', MS BNF II.II.133, fo. 60$^{r-v}$. There is no evidence in any of the sources that I have consulted that he was the Medicean candidate as H. C. Butters, among others, asserts: *Governors and Government*, 46. Perhaps this misconception derives from the dubious interpretation placed on the word 'statuali' used by Parenti to denote his supporters. To my knowledge, Parenti uses this term to describe *Ottimati* accustomed to govern or to hold 'lo stato'. Mediceans are not specifically excluded from this definition, but neither is it restricted exclusively to them.

[221] ASF Provvisioni, 193, fos. 85$^r$–88$^r$; A. Zorzi, *L'amministrazione della giustizia penale nella Repubblica Fiorentina: Aspetti e problemi* (Florence, 1988), 103–4.

sodomy and blasphemy.[222] On that same day the Great Council passed a resolution authorizing the expansion of the activities of the *Monte di Pietà* and conferring greater independence upon it by enhancing the powers of its officials.[223] As Professor Pampaloni has already remarked, the elevation of Soderini to the most eminent political position in Florence marked the beginning of an unprecedented period of prosperity for the *Monte di Pietà*.[224] The number and size of the endowments to the *Monte* increased to such an extent that it became necessary to decide how best to use the sums accrued while still fulfilling the original charitable intentions of the institution. At Soderini's behest, a special theological commission, comprising the priors of the convents of S. Marco, of the Badia, and of S. Salvatore al Monte, was formed to consider the matter. The commission made a recommendation to the government, which duly adopted it as law on 30 November 1505, that all profits from the *Monte di Pietà*, after expenses had been met, should be devolved to the *Buonuomini di S. Martino*.[225]

At recurrent intervals thereafter, Soderini steered through the Councils a series of legislative measures that could not but have enhanced his standing amongst the Piagnoni. Now that the resistance to sumptuary legislation had been overcome, the government pursued the advantage. On 1 August 1504, after obtaining comfortable majorities in the Council of Eighty and the Great Council, a law was promulgated setting out in a great wealth of detail the new regulations applying to the dress and ornaments of women, youths, and children.[226] In April 1511, in a climate of mounting exasperation at the evidence of continuing moral corruption and fear of approaching divine punishment,[227] a number of laws were enacted

---

[222] These were, according to the Piagnoni, the major aims of the judicial reform, see e.g. Landucci, *Diario fiorentino*, 251–2, where quotations occur, and n. 1 on p. 252.

[223] ASF Provvisioni, 193, fo. 88ʳ.

[224] G. Pampaloni, 'Cenni storici sul Monte di Pietà di Firenze', *Archivi storici delle Aziende di credito* (2 vols.; Rome, 1956), i. 537.

[225] Ibid. 537–8; Passerini, *Storia degli stabilimenti di beneficenza*, 742–3; ASF Provvisioni, 196, fo. 39ʳ. Though instituted only for an initial period of three years, the statute was renewed regularly thereafter and made permanent by a bull of Leo X in 1519: Passerini, *Storia*, 743, and ASF Libri fabarum, 72, fos. 95ᵛ–96ʳ.

[226] Ibid., fo. 35ᵛ; ibid., Provvisioni, 195, fo. 40ʳ⁻ᵛ.

[227] Cambi, *Istorie*, ii. 252–4, 256–7.

seeking to redress the situation. On 11 April an upper limit of 1,600 florins was imposed on all dowries.[228] It was the sort of enactment vainly sought by Savonarola even though he and his followers would have regarded the sum set as too high. On the same day, prostitutes were compelled to wear a distinctive veil in order to distinguish them from honest women.[229] Three days later a law was passed regulating the dress of women under 30 years of age.[230] On 28 April, in order to discourage the insolent behaviour of street-walkers (*cantoniere*), new and harsher penalties were instituted against them.[231] Finally, on the same day, a law similar in intent to the one issued on 14 April, was passed regulating in minute detail the dress of men under 30 years of age.[232]

The promulgation of these laws cannot be attributed exclusively to Piagnoni demands. Legislation of this kind was not confined to any particular regime nor was it the preserve of a specific political party. None the less, as the vicissitudes of such legislation in Savonarola's heyday clearly demonstrate, in Florence and for the period under investigation it was primarily associated with the Piagnoni. Whether a party or an individual supported it or opposed it depended on relationships with the Piagnoni rather than on the perceived merits of the legislation. At the very least, the promulgation and implementation of these laws at this juncture was a concession made to the Piagnoni by a grateful government for contributing to its achievements and prosperity.

In no field was this contribution more public and more welcome than in foreign affairs. For most of the period of Soderini's gonfaloniership two issues monopolized the government's energies on diplomatic matters: the war to recover Pisa and the French alliance. On neither issue were the Piagnoni in the mood to tolerate doubts or opposition, as Canon Giovanni Francesco Poggio Bracciolini had found to his cost.[233] The war to regain Pisa, supported by the majority of Florentines, became for the Piagnoni an

---

[228] ASF Provvisioni, 201, fos. 12ᵛ–13ᵛ; ibid., Libri fabarum, 72, fo. 127ᵛ.

[229] Ibid., Provvisioni, 201, fo. 14ʳ⁻ᵛ.

[230] Ibid., fos. 15ʳ–16ᵛ; ibid., Libri fabarum, fos. 127ᵛ, 128ʳ.

[231] Ibid., fo. 128ʳ⁻ᵛ; ibid., Provvisioni, 201, fo. 19ʳ⁻ᵛ. See Cambi, *Istorie*, ii. 254 for lamentations on their behaviour.

[232] ASF Provvisioni, 201, fos. 20ʳ–22ʳ; ibid., Libri fabarum, 72, fo. 128ʳ⁻ᵛ.

[233] See above, pp. 212–13.

obsession. For them, it had assumed the dimensions of a holy war. At stake was not only their pride as Florentines, but, more specifically, the veracity of their prophet who had often foretold it, and thus, by implication, the validity of their beliefs. The concept of a Florentine *imperium*, central to their millenarian expectations was, moreover, threatened by the obdurate resistance of an ungodly city. In their eyes, the Pisans' refusal to submit themselves to the Florentine yoke was nothing short of a blasphemous rebellion against God's revealed will. Piagnone speaker after speaker in the *pratiche* gave vent to their feelings. To recover Pisa, argued Giovanbattista Ridolfi, was tantamount to giving Florence back her soul.[234] No expense should be spared, no sacrifice rejected, and no alliance spurned to achieve this end whose attainment, they believed, was inevitable.[235] Not surprisingly, they had the lion's share of all discussion on Pisa and related diplomatic affairs. Indeed, so high was the proportion of Piagnoni participants in some of the key *pratiche* of the period, that one cannot but conclude that the meetings had been purposely stacked by a government wishing to receive the kind of advice it knew the Piagnoni would provide.[236] When Pisa at last capitulated, in June 1509, the event was marked by the return of the great bell, the *Piagnona*, to its rightful place in the belfry of S. Marco.[237] Its restoration after only ten years' exile, instead of the stipulated fifty, indicates how greatly the Florentine government valued the Piagnoni's support in the Pisan campaign.

[234] ASF Consulte e Pratiche, 68, fo. 41ʳ; the image was taken up by non-Piagnoni speakers such as Bernardo da Diacceto and Piero Popoleschi and by the Piagnone Bernardo Nasi: ibid., fo. 42ʳ, and 69, fos. 15ᵛ–16ʳ.

[235] See e.g. ibid. 66, fos. 61ᵛ–62ʳ for the opinions of Tommaso Tosinghi and Giovanbattista Ridolfi; ibid. 68, fos. 37ʳ–41ᵛ for the opinions of Antonio Malegonnelle, Francesco Gualterotti, Giovanbattista Ridolfi, Antonio Canigiani, Bernardo Nasi, Jacopo Salviati, Niccolò Valori; 'Diario con il verbale di tutti i consigli tenuti dalla Repubblica Fiorentina sì di guerra come di stato dal XXIII di maggio dell'anno MDV infino al XV agosto MDXII', MS BAV Ottob. Lat. 2759, fos. 29ʳ–30ʳ.

[236] See e.g. ibid., fos. 17ᵛ–28ʳ; ASF Consulte e Pratiche, 66, fos. 360ᵛ–362ᵛ; 68, fos. 40ʳ–44ᵛ, 45ʳ–47ʳ.

[237] Gherardi, *Nuovi documenti*, 322–3; Landucci, *Diario fiorentino*, 294. The *Signoria* also successfully petitioned the Pope to have the convent of Sta Caterina at Pisa returned to the 'Congregation of S. Marco': BMLF S. Marco, 925, fo. 87ʳ.

The obsession with Pisa placed under great strain the Piagnoni's commitment to the alliance with France. At first they had been heartened by the accession of Louis XII, who, they hoped, would assume the role of reforming prince for which Charles VIII had proved unfit. Similarly encouraging was France's successful campaign against Savonarola's arch-enemy, Lodovico il Moro, and the dispatch of a new French contingent to assist in the war against Pisa.[238] But, as the hoped-for success did not materialize and as evidence of French unreliability and greed mounted, despondency set in. In the *pratiche*, some Piagnoni joined their unaligned colleagues in demanding more tangible evidence of French goodwill before acceding to further requests for money or for political acquiescence.[239] At no stage, however, did the Piagnoni seriously contemplate abandoning the alliance.[240] Not even after the battle of Ravenna in April 1512, when the French were forced to withdraw from Italy, and the Holy League, led by Julius II, threatened spiritual and military sanctions unless Florence did so, did the Piagnoni relent. To comply with these threats, argued Bartolomeo Redditi, would have been a sinful violation of a solemn oath given to the most Christian King.[241] Despite momentary doubts and impatience, nothing could destroy their conviction that the twin destinies of Florence and France were divinely interwoven.

This admixture of political and religious devotion to France determined also their attitude to the Council of Pisa, proclaimed in

[238] Cambi, *Istorie*, ii. 146–7, 150, 240; Parenti, *Istorie fiorentine*, 294 and n. 1 and MS BNF II.II.132, fo. 41ᵛ; Landucci, *Diario fiorentino*, 208–9. Because of his opposition to Savonarola, Lodovico il Moro was among the Piagnoni's most hated figures: being called by Benedetto Luschino, for example, 'il biscion venenoso', 'Cedrus Libani ossia vita di Fra Girolamo Savonarola Scritta da Fra Benedetto da Firenze l'anno 1510', ed. V. Marchese, *ASI*, app. 7 (1849), 94.

[239] ASF Consulte e Pratiche, 66, fo. 10ᵛ (Niccolò Valori), fo. 84ʳ (Giovanbattista Ridolfi), fo. 244ʳ⁻ᵛ (Antonio Malegonnelle), fo. 381ʳ (Domenico Bonsi), fos. 382ᵛ–383ᵛ (Pierfrancesco Tosinghi, Piero Lenzi, and Lorenzo Lenzi); ibid. 68, fos. 147ᵛ–148ᵛ (Giovanbattista Ridolfi and Pierfrancesco Tosinghi).

[240] Although Lorenzo Lenzi, for instance, advised that an alliance with the Emperor should be considered in case the French did not come to their senses: ibid. 66, fo. 383ᵛ.

[241] Ibid. 70, fo. 81ʳ.

May 1511 and officially opened in November.[242] Convened at the behest of the French King, its ostensible purpose was Church reform: a necessity made even more pressing by the worldly pursuits of Julius II.[243] Its real object, however, was to weaken Julius II's authority and to oblige the Florentines to commit themselves more wholeheartedly to the French cause. As usual, opinion in Florence was divided. To the protests of those who, having never favoured the alliance with France, had no wish to support anything designed to strengthen it, were added the cries of others who regarded as ill-judged the choice of Pisa as a site for the Council. Soderini and his closest advisers were similarly perturbed. Discomfited by the likely repercussions, both political and religious, they did their best to temporize. When Julius II imposed an interdict on Florence and her territories on 23 September 1511, their resolve to change the site of the Council was increased.[244] Helped by the cool reception which the Pisan clergy gave the arriving cardinals and also by a riot which broke out on 9 November between the Pisan populace and the French and Spanish members of the cardinals' entourage, they succeeded in persuading the cardinals to transfer the Council to Milan.[245]

Years later, the Piagnoni were to claim that they, and the friars of S. Marco in particular, had never been conciliarists and had fought tooth and nail against the Council of Pisa—a claim subsequently enshrined in Piagnone historiography—but this was not the case.[246] The chroniclers Giovanni Cambi and Luca Landucci, for

---

[242] A. Renaudet, *Le Concile Gallican de Pise-Milan: Documents Florentins (1510–1512)*, (Bibliothèque de l'Institut Français de Florence, 1st ser. 7; Paris, 1922), 30–1, 449 ff.; R. C. Trexler, *The Spiritual Power: Republican Florence under Interdict* (Leiden, 1974), esp. 178–86. Most of the Florentine documents pertaining to the Council have been published by Renaudet, *Le Concile Gallican de Pise-Milan*.

[243] H. Jedin, *Il Concilio di Trento* (4 vols. in 5; Brescia, 1973–81), i. 123 ff.

[244] The interdict was repeatedly lifted and then reimposed: see Trexler, *The Spiritual Power*, 180 ff. For a chronology of events and for observations on the Florentines' response to the interdict, see MS BNF Magl., XXV, 378 (*Priorista e Ricordi*), fo. 199ʳ; Cambi, *Istorie*, ii. 279.

[245] Renaudet, *Le Concile Gallican de Pise-Milan*, 502, 504, 558 ff.

[246] First put forward by Tommaso Neri in 1564, this interpretation was afterwards elaborated by historians of the Dominican Order: see Tommaso Neri, *Apologia del reverendo padre Fra Tommaso Neri fiorentino dell'ordine de' frati*

example, had no hesitation in listing the Council's spiritual and political advantages. They saw it as a means to assuage the ills of the Church by remedying the depredations of its prelates.[247] Since Savonarola's day, moreover, the role of the French King in initiating ecclesiastical reform and the necessity for that reform to be achieved by a Church council had been a recurrent element in Piagnone agitation. Back in 1502, Giorgio Benigno had used the *Apocalypsis Nova* to prepare the ground for such a council;[248] and Bartolomeo della Fonte, while inveighing against the fiasco at Pisa in a letter to Antonio Pucci late in 1511, nevertheless expressed the hope that the renovation of the Church might still be accomplished under the aegis of a true council.[249] And although Jacopo Salviati opposed it,[250] the Council of Pisa as well as the French policy of which it was part, were defended by other prominent Piagnoni such as Tommaso Tosinghi, Giovanbattista Ridolfi, Jacopo Nardi, and Bartolomeo Redditi, all of whom spoke in their favour at the

---

*Predicatori in difesa della dottrina del R.P.F. Girolamo Savonarola da Ferrara del medesimo ordine* (Florence, 1564), 39–41; cf. Serafino Razzi, 'Cronica della Provincia Romana dell'ordine de' frati predicatori', MS BMLF S. Marco 873, fo. 8ᵛ; id., *Istoria degli Huomini illustri così nelle Prelature come nelle Dottrine del sacro ordine de gli Predicatori* (Lucca, 1596), 169–70; id., 'Defensione generale dell'opere e predicazioni del padre fra Ieronimo', MS BNF Magl., XXXVII, 44 fo. viiʳ; V. M. Fontana, *Monumenta Dominicana breviter in synopsim collecta* (Rome, 1675), 410–13; Quétif and Echard, *Scriptores*, ii. 66–7; Mortier, *Histoire des Maitres généraux*, v. 194–7; Ridolfi, *Vita*, ii. 37–8. One element in this interpretation has, however, been questioned by Renaudet, *Le Concile Gallican de Pise-Milan*, 495 n. 98, but see also 469 n. 58, where the interpretation as a whole is accepted. That the friars of the Tusco-Roman Congregation were not as hostile to the Council as Piagnoni historians maintain is also indirectly confirmed by a circular letter by Card. Tommaso de Vio Gaetano, dated 6 Sept. 1511, ordering all Dominicans not to have anything to do with the *Conciliabolo* and to support the rightful council convoked by Julius II on 9 Apr.: BMLF S. Marco 920, fos. 44ᵛ–45.

[247] Cambi, *Istorie*, ii. 187, 240, 251, 256, and esp. 265–6, 277; Landucci, *Diario fiorentino*, 208.

[248] See above, pp. 204–5.

[249] Bartolomeo della Fonte, *Epistolarum Libri III*, ed. L. Juhász (Bibliotheca Scriptorum Medii Recentisque Aevorum; Budapest, 1931), 53, 55, 57. Antonio Pucci was the nephew of the Papal Datary, Lorenzo Pucci, then acting as papal representative in the negotiations with Florence: Renaudet, *Le Concile Gallican de Pise-Milan*, 642.

[250] Filippo de' Nerli, *Commentari*, i. 159.

meetings of the *pratiche*.[251] The last word may be left to the anti-Savonarolan, Filippo de' Nerli. In his *Commentari*, he described how, on the issue of the Council of Pisa, opinion in Florence had been divided equally. In this situation, he maintained, the influence of the Piagnoni had been decisive. Of Soderini's decision to accede to France's wish for a council, Nerli wrote:

Perhaps this resolution would not have been passed as it was, if it had not been for one-third of the citizens who, moved by the great faith they placed in Savonarola's prophecies, by sectarian interests, or blinded by their superstitious credulity rather than by other and better reasons . . . put aside all other considerations and closed ranks with those who championed the Council and French policy.[252]

The standing of the Piagnoni in Florence cannot be measured solely in terms of their influence on governmental decisions. Less conspicuous, perhaps, but equally as important as a gauge of their strength were the enterprises and activities they engaged in or organized to further the aim of the Piagnone movement. In some respects, these 'unofficial' activities give a clearer indication of their ideological concerns and of their cohesiveness. They make it possible, in fact, to trace the personal connections, the networks joining small groups and individuals together, and, finally, the means contrived to lend each other support, which are impossible to detect in the specifically political sphere.

The reasons why the Piagnoni failed to cultivate more visible personal ties in political activity, even in these favourable times, are to be attributed to their fear of the laws on illegal political association. The state's ingrained dread of political *frondes* and *intelligenze* had been plainly evident at the trials of Savonarola and of many fellow Piagnoni, in which they were repeatedly questioned as to

[251] ASF Consulte e Pratiche, 70, fos. 13ᵛ–14ᵛ; Renaudet, *Le Concile Gallican de Pise-Milan*, 440–1, 554–5, 669.

[252] Filippo de' Nerli, *Commentari*, i. 166: 'Forseché tale deliberazione non si sarebbe fatta come si fece, se non fosse stata una terza parte di cittadini i quali mossi più dalla fede grande che avevano nelle profezie del Savonarola, che da altre migliori ragioni, o dagl'interessi delle loro sette, acciecati da quella loro superstiziosa credulità . . . posta da parte ogni altra considerazione, concorsero con quelli che favorivano il Concilio e le parti di Francia.'

whether they had conspired to support specific legislation or to nominate members of their faction for office and to vote for them in the subsequent elections.[253] This recent experience had taught the Piagnoni to be more circumspect than ever before while fulfilling their public political duties. Indeed, an exhaustive examination by Dr Butters of the nominees and nominators to public office in the years 1502–12 of such well-known Piagnoni[254] as Lanfredino Lanfredini, Giovanbattista Ridolfi, Jacopo and Alamanno Salviati, Tommaso Soderini and by such erstwhile *Arrabbiati* and neutrals as Giovanvettorio Soderini and Piero Soderini, has revealed that there was an absence of factional solidarity on the part of all concerned.[255] The Piagnoni did not seem to have been unduly favoured by their brethren either as nominees or nominators; nor shunned by their alleged enemies, who courted their support by nominating them or having themselves in turn nominated to office.

Besides prudence, other factors could account for this fragmentation. By this time, as we have seen, there was a *rapprochement* between the two groups which could not but have been reflected in the patterns of nominations. Moreover, these were experienced and astute politicians who were not about to leave evidence of collusion in the very records kept by the government to check whether such collusion was occurring. Means were found to manipulate the system without leaving incriminating traces; and Jacopo Salviati was accused in later years by an exasperated Galeotto de' Medici of being well adept at the art.[256]

Much greater freedom to express solidarity with fellow Piagnoni or to act in concert for the common cause existed outside the highly regulated world of politics. The private papers, letters, and *ricordanze* of such well-known Piagnoni as Niccolò Valori, Tommaso Tosinghi, Jacopo Salviati, Lanfredino Lanfredini, and Bartolomeo Redditi show that, when possible, they relied on each other for

[253] Villari, *La storia di Girolamo Savonarola*, vol. ii, app., pp. ccxxiii–ccxxiv, ccxxxviii, ccxlv, *et passim*.

[254] The identification is mine and not necessarily Dr Butters's.

[255] Butters, *Governors and Government*, 68 and appendices.

[256] Letter of Galeotto de' Medici to Lorenzo de' Medici, 21 Nov. 1514, ASF MAP 116, No. 516.

professional advice or business transactions or tended to favour one of their number when it came to dispensing patronage. To give but a few examples, Niccolò Valori had business interests of various kinds with Francesco Gualterotti, Andrea Cambini, and Antonio Canigiani, who had been a business partner of Francesco Valori.[257] In rebuilding his houses partly destroyed by fire on the night of 7 April 1498, he availed himself of wood supplied by Tommaso Tosinghi, to whom he sent a handsome gift in thanksgiving.[258] He was also in close contact throughout these years with Lanfredino Lanfredini, to whom he was related by marriage, Andrea Cambini, and Jacopo Salviati, to whom on at least one occasion he lent his precious porcelain vases when the latter was entertaining important guests.[259] Similarly, the account books and *Ricordi* of Bartolomeo Redditi show him to have numbered among his business associates and friends Domenico Benivieni, Giovanni Cambi, and Ser Paolo d'Amerigo Grassi.[260] The business and personal contacts between Jacopo Salviati and Lanfredino Lanfredini were complex and extensive, as attested by the correspondence between the two. They were also joined by ties of godparenting (*comparatico*) and by genuine admiration for each other's qualities.[261] Spiritual bonds of *comparatico* existed also between Niccolò Valori, Jacopo Salviati, and Andrea Cambini.[262] The Piagnoni sense of mission, their belief that they were serving a higher cause—revealed also by their determination to have subject cities like Pistoia accept the spirit of the

[257] ASF Not. Ant. V.357 (1504–10) (Ser Lorenzo Violi), fos. 77ᵛ–78ʳ; ASF Dono Panciatichi, Patrimonio Valori, Libri d'azienda, 2, fos. 3ᵛ–4ʳ; ibid. 3, fo. 144b.

[258] Ibid., fo. 150b.

[259] Letters of Niccolò Valori to Lanfredino Lanfredini, 'Carteggio Lanfredini', MS BNF II.V.21, fos. 31ʳ–39ᵛ, 42ʳ, 45ʳ, *et passim*; ASF Dono Panciatichi, Patrimonio Valori, Libri d'azienda, 3, fo. 163b.

[260] Bartolomeo Redditi, 'Libro di debitori, creditori e ricordi', ASF Conv. Sopp. 111: 152, fos. 19ᵛ, 35ᵛ; 153, fo. 58ʳ.

[261] Letters from Jacopo to Lanfredino in 'Carteggio Lanfredini', BNF II.V.21, fos. 154ʳ⁻ᵛ, 160ʳ–161ᵛ, 164ʳ, 168ʳ, *et passim*; ibid., II.V.22, fos. 6ʳ, 17ᵛ, *et passim*. Many letters in both *filze* also from Alamanno Salviati and Piero Guicciardini, exhibiting the same mutual respect. Ties of *comparatico* existed also between Alamanno Salviati, Lanfredino, and Francesco del Pugliese: Alamanno Salviati, 'Ricordi', MS ASP, ser. II, 22, fos. 79ʳ, 83ᵛ.

[262] Niccolò Valori, 'Ricordanze', fo. 11ᵛ.

*governo popolare*[263]—were reinforced by the way they invited their brethren's prayers and support on the assumption of an important political office.[264] They also circulated freely amongst themselves news of the latest miracles, worked either by Savonarola, posthumously, or by his disciples, as well as information about the most recent signs portending the fulfilment of his prophecies.[265]

Another important indicator of the complex network of mutual interdependence that had been established is provided by the Piagnoni's approach to death.[266] In drawing up their wills the Piagnoni, men and women alike, favoured Piagnoni notaries like Ser Filippo Cioni, Ser Lorenzo Violi, Ser Giuliano di Domenico da Ripa, and Ser Paolo d'Amerigo Grassi. Beside their own close relatives, they chose other Piagnoni as lay witnesses and executors. The convent of S. Marco and its church were the favourite places in which to draw up their wills and, unless other factors came into play, to receive burial. The friars of the convent helped them to prepare for this important spiritual task and provided the highest proportion of ecclesiastical witnesses and executors. Finally, they continued to assign their alms and endowments overwhelmingly to Savonarolan-controlled or Savonarolan-inspired institutions, thereby ensuring their prosperity and continued influence in the

---

[263] ASF Consulte e Pratiche, 66, fo. 427ᵛ (Giovanbattista Ridolfi) but see also fos. 419ᵛ, 422ᵛ–425ʳ.

[264] Letters of Niccolò Valori to Lanfredino Lanfredini on the latter's election to the post of *Gonfaloniere di Giustizia*, Oct. 1501, 'Carteggio Lanfredini', BNF II.V.21, fos. 46ʳ, 48ʳ, 68ʳ, 69ʳ, 73ʳ; R. Ristori, 'Un mercante savonaroliano: Pandolfo Rucellai', in *Magia, astrologia e religione nel Rinascimento* (Convegno, Warsaw, 1972; Florence, n.d.), 43.

[265] See the letter of Ugolino Verino to Fra Bartolomeo da Faenza, regarding the life and death of the Camaldolese Piagnone Girolamo Novati, in G. B. Mittarelli and A. Costadoni, *Annales Camaldulenses Ordinis Sancti Benedicti*, vii–ix (Venice, 1762–73), vii. 393–5, and partially translated into Italian in B. Ignesti, 'I Camaldolesi e il Savonarola', *Camaldoli*, 6 (1952), 144–6; see also the letter of Bartolomeo della Fonte to Fra Simone Cinozzi, regarding the signs portending Antichrist's coming, in Bartolomeo della Fonte, *Epistolarum Libri III*, 47–9. Various accounts of miracles related by Piagnoni to one another are appended to the contemporary biographies of Savonarola: see 'Vita Beati Hieronymi, martiris, doctoris, virginis, ac prophetae eximii', MS BNF Conv. Sopp., J.VII.28; Pseudo-Burlamacchi, *La vita*; Giovanfrancesco Pico, *Vita Reverendi Patris F. Hieronymi Savonarolae*. For a further discussion of this subject, see below, pp. 325–8.

[266] On what follows see my '*Dell'Arte del Ben Morire*'.

religious life of Florence. Over and above this, will-making became for the Piagnoni a spiritual and political activity through which they could publicly attest to their beliefs and earn salvation in the process.

How much could be achieved by these informal networks in both the spiritual and temporal spheres is demonstrated by the operation of the *Monte di Pietà* and of its whole dependent system of poor relief. We have already seen how the *Monte di Pietà* had begun to prosper through the intervention and protection of the government led by Piero Soderini. Over and above the favourable legislative measures, the government gave the surest indication of its goodwill by allowing the *Monte di Pietà* full independence in its internal operations. With the exception of the eight *Ufficiali del Monte*, who were to be elected in the normal way from the politically qualified citizens in the Great Council, all other minor officials were to be appointed from within.[267] This liberality allowed the *Ufficiali* almost unlimited scope, and since from the *Monte*'s very inception they were in the majority Piagnoni, the consequences are easily imagined. Apart from the *Ufficiali* which in any one triennium would never number fewer than two or three Piagnoni notables in its ranks,[268] even the minor salaried posts like the *massari* and *camerlinghi* were often assigned to Piagnoni like Giovanni di Lorenzo Scolari, Giovanfrancesco Lapaccini, and Lorenzo di Piero Mascalzoni.[269] Since these salaried officials were required by law to be vouched for by guarantors, a large number of wealthy Piagnoni stepped in to fill this need. Indeed, it is amongst these guarantors—who were often also past and future *Ufficiali*—that the proportionately highest number of Piagnoni is to be found, men such as Lorenzo di Anfrione Lenzi, Francesco del Pugliese, Leonardo Cambini, Bartolomeo di Pagnozzo Ridolfi, and Adovardo Canigiani.[270] Some of the sums vouched by these guarantors

---

[267] ASF Provvisioni, 187, fos. 5ᵛ–11ᵛ; in some cases, however, the *Signoria* reserved the right to ratify the appointments of minor officials.

[268] Such as e.g. Domenico di Bernardo Mazzinghi, Piero Guicciardini Francesco del Pugliese, and Jacopo Salviati for the triennium 1509–12: ASF MP, Registro 13, unfoliated.

[269] Ibid., Registro 14, fos. 4ʳ, 5ᵛ, 12ᵛ.     [270] Ibid., fos. 2ᵛ, 11ʳ⁻ᵛ, 23ᵛ.

are staggering, such as, for example, the 8,000 florins by Francesco del Pugliese for Domenico Lapaccini and by Girolamo d'Antonio Gondi for Giovanni Scolari.[271] There was undoubtedly a spirit of emulation at work whereby individual Piagnoni sought to demonstrate, both to their brethren and to society at large, the strength of their commitment to the cause. That to act as guarantor was not merely a matter of form was to be demonstrated by the defalcation in 1529 of one of these officials, Andrea di Silvestro Nardi, when his guarantors were forced to make good the embezzled money.[272] Apart from these commitments, the Piagnoni were also regular donors to the *Monte di Pietà*, especially at a time when the institution was experiencing problems accumulating a working capital.[273] Another major source of income was the alms-box the *Monte* was permitted to keep in S. Marco.

This whole Piagnone charitable network, to which belonged the *Buonuomini di S. Martino*, the *Ospedale del Ceppo*, and the confraternity of S. Michele Arcangelo, was the best possible embodiment of Savonarola's teaching on the subject. Before this period, charity at both the individual and the institutional levels had been characterized by notions of reciprocity, that is alms in exchange for prayers. Now, with the establishment of these institutions this element was played down, and charity was given to the poor, referred to as 'Christ's poor' (*poveri di Cristo*) out of the love one had for Christ, who like them, had been poor and outcast.[274] Because charity had thus become an act of love given gratuitously and anonymously to strangers, it became much more meritorious in the eyes of God. Even greater merit was accrued because in addition to alms and other donations, they also gave freely of themselves, showing their love for God through service to their Christian

---

[271] Ibid., fos. 23ᵛ, 26ᵛ, 24ᵛ; Scolari was vouchsafed a similar amount by Andrea Cambini, fo. 28ᵛ.

[272] Ibid., Registro 23, fos. 18ᵛ–19ʳ, 33ᵛ, 44ʳ: see also the letter of Jacopo Nardi to Luigi Guicciardini, 8 Oct. 1530: ibid., C. Strozz., ser. I, 59, n. 118.

[273] See e.g. ibid., MP, Registro 721, fos. iʳ, viiiᵛ, amongst the donors the Canon Marco di Matteo Strozzi, Giovanni Minerbetti, Messer Giorgio di Antonio Vespucci.

[274] On this new philanthropy see the invaluable study by B. Pullan, *Rich and Poor in Renaissance Venice* (Oxford, 1971), part II.

neighbours. All this explains why these institutions and the *Monte di Pietà* in particular became throughout these years and beyond a magnet for lay Piagnoni, who, by aiding the poor and the sick, acquired merit for themselves and for their city in the eyes of God.

In promoting the welfare of the Republic in all possible ways, the Piagnoni were moved by a consuming desire not only to fulfil Savonarola's instructions but also to avert the oncoming disaster with which he had threatened them. Early in 1498, disgusted by the Florentines' refusal to heed his admonitions, Savonarola had come to the reluctant conclusion that the city's apotheosis was likely to be delayed. He feared, as he preached to its inhabitants in March, that a tyranny of unprecedented cruelty and oppression would interpose itself between Florence and her destiny.[275] The events of 1512 were to endow his words with the authority of a divine prophecy. Despite all their efforts, the Piagnoni were unable to prevent the fall of the Republic: a catastrophe for which, ironically, the French alliance they favoured was in the end responsible. Far from sustaining the Florentine regime, as they had hoped, the pro-French policy was, as Nerli astutely observed, 'the chief cause of the downfall of that government'.[276] Soderini's inability to adjust to a changed situation, in which, following their Pyrrhic victory at Ravenna in April 1512, the power of the French in Italy was for the time being in eclipse, resulted in his downfall. At the Diet of Mantua in mid-August, the members of the Holy League, under the influence of Julius II and with the incitement of Medici gold, decided to oust Soderini from Florence and to restore the Medici.[277] With the sack of Prato by a Spanish contingent, Soderini was forced to resign and Florence capitulated.

---

[275] Girolamo Savonarola, *Prediche sopra l'Esodo*, ed. P. G. Ricci (ENOS; 2 vols.; Rome, 1956), 174–5; cf. 202–3. Two years before, he had hinted fleetingly at this possibility: *Prediche sopra Ruth e Michea*, ed. V. Romano (ENOS; 2 vols.; Rome, 1962), 359.

[276] Filippo de' Nerli, *Commentari*, i. 166: 'cagione principale della rovina di quel governo'.

[277] Cerretani, 'Storia in dialogo della mutatione di Firenze', MS BNF II.I.106, fo. 148ʳ.

The Piagnoni came to view the return of the Medici as the latest
and most severe test of their endurance, designed by God to
strengthen their devotion to Savonarola and his cause. 'For the sake
of a greater good' was their explanation of why this disaster had
been allowed to befall them. 'For the sake of a greater good', stated
one of the two Savonarolan interlocutors, the aptly named
Girolamo, in Bartolomeo Cerretani's *Storia in dialogo*, replying to a
Medicean sceptic who enquired as to God's purpose in permitting
the Medici to resume power:

in order that men may once more believe His servants, and anyone who
was warm-hearted in doing His work may be set on fire, and that those
who have refused to execute justice may perform their task—and that all
may realize how terrible the consequences would be if God had unleashed
his hounds and set up a wicked leader, as had been illustrated and told in
many places.[278]

Confronted, now, with a ruling power which was the antithesis of
all they had hoped and struggled for, the Piagnoni's interests
ceased to be aligned with those of the Florentine government.
Their situation thus came, at last, to resemble that of their clerical
counterparts, who, since the time of Savonarola's death, had felt
that they no longer owed any allegiance to their superiors. Fra
Cipriano di Pietro Cancelli da Pontassieve, who comforted Pietro
Paolo Boscoli, a ringleader in the Boscoli–Capponi conspiracy of
1513 against the Medici, in the last hours before his execution,
maintained that in this situation tyrannicide itself became a spiritually meritorious act. Against rulers like the Medici, who seized
power 'by force, all of a sudden, and despite the people', Fra
Cipriano asserted, tyrannicide did not merely cease to be sinful, but
became positively praiseworthy in the sight of God. 'I firmly believe that he is in heaven', he said of Boscoli after his death, 'and

---

[278] Ibid., fo. 156ᵛ: 'A fine di maggior bene . . . perchè li huomini credino
un'altra volta a' sua servi, et che chi era caldo alla sua opera sia di fuoco, et che chi
non ha voluto fare iustitia, la facci, et che si conosca che se Dio scioliera i cani, et
havessi dato un cattivo capo, quanto mal seguiva come era stato dipinto e detto in
più d'un luogo'. See also Landucci, *Diario fiorentino*, 329.

that he has not had to endure purgatory. And to tell you what I think . . . I believe that he was a martyr without any shadow of doubt.'[279] It was not only the promise of a heavenly crown which spurred the Piagnoni activists on. Although Savonarola had foretold a tyrant, he had also held out a promise of hope. The tyranny would be dire, but it would be brief. 'He will be the wickedest man in the world', he said of the coming usurper, 'and he will last but a little while.'[280] This prediction was to exercise a profound effect upon Piagnoni politics in the years of Medici rule. They could not simply sit by and endure the hated regime. Encouraged by Savonarola's assurances that it would not last long, they worked to ensure that it did, indeed, end as quickly as possible.

---

[279] Luca della Robbia, *Recitazione del caso di Pietro Paolo Boscoli e di Agostino Capponi scritta da Luca della Robbia l'anno MDXIII, ASI*, 1st ser. I (1842), 309: 'a forza, in un tratto, a dispetto del popolo'; 'Io credo al fermo ch'e' sia beato e che non abbia avuto purgatorio. E a dirti la mia oppenione . . . io credo che lui sia stato martire senza dubbio alcuno.' I have found no evidence to support the contention expressed, amongst others, by D. Cantimori that Boscoli was a Savonarolan: 'Il caso del Boscoli e la vita del Rinascimento', *Giornale critico della filosofia italiana*, 8 (1927), 251. On the execution of the two conspirators see also D. Weinstein, '*The Art of Dying Well* and Popular Piety in the Preaching and Thought of Girolamo Savonarola', in M. Tetel, R. G. Witt, and R. Goffen (eds.), *Life and Death in Fifteenth-Century Florence* (Durham, 1989), 88–104 and R. Trexler, *Public Life in Renaissance Florence* (New York, 1980), 198–205, 209–10.

[280] Savonarola, *Prediche sopra l'Esodo*, i. 174–5: 'Sarà el più cattivo uomo del mondo e durerà poco.'

# 6

# 'In Sodom and Gomorrah':
# The Piagnoni in Adversity and
# the Espousal of Radicalism

I

Giuliano de' Medici entered Florence on 1 September 1512, the day after Soderini had been seized and forcibly removed from office.[1] He returned ostensibly as a private citizen but, in reality, as the head of a faction dedicated to the restoration of the Medici regime.[2] In the same month, with the calling of a *parlamento* and the appointment of a *Balìa* after prolonged conflict with the republican *Ottimati*, the first steps were taken towards the realization of this aim.[3] Thus began a process which eventually resulted in the de-

[1] Bartolomeo Cerretani, 'Storia in dialogo, della mutatione di Firenze', MS BNF II.I.106, fo. 149[r]; Giovanni Cambi, *Istorie*, ed. I. di San Luigi (4 vols.; Florence, 1785–6), ii. 308–10; Iacopo Nardi, *Istorie della città di Firenze*, ed. A. Gelli (2 vols.; Florence, 1858), i. 428–30; Francesco Vettori, *Sommario della storia d'Italia*, in *Scritti storici e politici*, ed. F. Nicolini (Bari, 1972), 143–4. For details of the revolution of 1512, see R. Devonshire-Jones, *Francesco Vettori, Florentine Citizen and Medici Servant* (London, 1972), ch. iv, esp. pp. 66 ff.; F. Gilbert, *Machiavelli and Guicciardini: Politics and History in Sixteenth Century Florence* (Princeton, NJ, 1965), 131–6; H. C. Butters, *Governors and Government in Early Sixteenth-Century Florence, 1502–1519* (Oxford, 1985), 167–85.

[2] The best account of the aims and activities of this faction is to be found in Cerretani, 'Storia in dialogo', fos. 149[r] ff.

[3] Ibid., fos. 150[v]–154[r]; Lorenzo Strozzi, *La vita di Filippo Strozzi, figlio di Filippo*, in J. Graevius (ed.), *Thesaurus antiquitatum et historiarum Italiae*, viii (2) (Leiden, 1723), cols. 14–15; Filippo de' Nerli, *Commentari dei fatti civili occorsi dentro la città di Firenze dall'anno 1215 al 1537* (2 vols.; Trieste, 1859), i. 185–8; Luca Landucci, *Diario fiorentino*, ed. I. del Badia (Florence, 1883; repr. 1969), 328–9.

struction of every element in the republican system of government which the Piagnoni held dear. The *parlamento* was called in direct contravention of a law passed in August 1495 at Savonarola's instigation; the appointment of the *Balìa* signalled the end of the Great Council, which had been the hub of the Savonarolan system.[4] In little over a year's time, under the leadership of Lorenzo de' Medici, who had taken over from Giuliano,[5] the constitutional changes were brought to their conclusion with the creation of the Council of the Hundred and the Council of Seventy.[6] The period which witnessed the gradual tightening of Medici control in Florence also saw their rise to power in Rome. After the death of Julius II, Giovanni de' Medici was elected Pope, taking the title of Leo X, on 11 March 1513. Soon after, on 9 April, there followed the death of Cosimo de' Pazzi, Archbishop of Florence, due, purportedly, to sorrow for the Medici's great good fortune.[7] The Florentine See thus left vacant was immediately bestowed by Leo X on his cousin Giulio, whom he also created a cardinal later in the same year.[8] From 1512 onwards, therefore, the Piagnoni had to come to terms with erstwhile enemies who were not only entrenched in power in the civil government of Florence but also controlled the highest echelons of the Church.

The disappearance of the last vestiges of Savonarola's Florence was evident no less in matters of policy than in governmental structure. Jewish money-lenders were allowed by the Medici to return and to resume their trade.[9] The traditional carnivals and

---

[4] P. Villari, *La storia di Girolamo Savonarola e de' suoi tempi* (2 vols.; Florence, 1930), i. 311–12; Nardi, *Istorie della città di Firenze*, ii. 7.

[5] Cerretani, 'Storia in dialogo', fo. 158[r–v] and esp. fo. 163[v]; Vettori, *Sommario della storia d'Italia*, 152–3.

[6] Cerretani, 'Storia in dialogo', fo. 166[r]; Cambi, *Istorie*, iii. 33–7. For details of these constitutional changes, see Devonshire-Jones, *Francesco Vettori*, 77–83; Butters, *Governors and Government*, chs. VII, VIII.

[7] Cerretani, 'Storia in dialogo', fo. 162[v].

[8] Ibid., fo. 165[r]; Landucci, *Diario fiorentino*, 338–9; L. G. Cerracchini, *Cronologia sacra dei Vescovi e Arcivescovi di Firenze* (Florence, 1716), 175–6.

[9] Piero Parenti, 'Istorie fiorentine', MS BNF II.IV.171, fo. 109[r]; Landucci, *Diario fiorentino* 348 and n. 1; C. Roth, *The Last Florentine Republic* (London, 1925), 63–4. The decision enraged Marco di Matteo Strozzi, who in vain petitioned the Medici to rescind the order; see his 'Vita scritta da se stesso', MS ASF C. Strozz., ser. III, 138, fo. 49[v].

festivals, which Savonarola had transformed into religious celebrations, were restored to their original form: becoming once again, as
Giovanni Cambi mourned, revels of Sodom and Gomorrah.[10] In
the sphere of foreign affairs, moreover, the Medici were obliged by
political expediency to abandon the pro-French policy, to which
Savonarola had given his blessing, and to ally themselves with the
hated Spaniards.[11]

But what most aroused the Piagnoni's fury was the desec-
ration of the hall of the Great Council. As Giovanni Rucellai, the
Medicean interlocutor in Cerretani's *Storia in dialogo*, recounted
with relish, the hall was turned into a barracks, in one corner
of which a tavern was set up, in another gambling tables, in another a brothel. Rucellai freely admitted that this had been done to
spite the Piagnoni.[12] Thus was the visible embodiment of the
Savonarolan state—the *sala di Cristo*,[13] which, as Piagnone legend
had it, the angels themselves had laboured to build[14]—finally
violated, as the concept underlying it had been destroyed. Appalled
at this most heinous of deeds, the Piagnoni contented themselves with the reflection that vengeance, though it might be delayed, would nevertheless be certain. Divine retribution lay in wait
for all those who had contributed to the fall of the republican
government.

Like other Piagnoni who kept careful note of the invariably
gruesome deaths which, sooner or later, seemed to befall each and
every one of Savonarola's persecutors, Giovanni Cambi dutifully
recorded the premature end of the Florentine Archbishop, Cosimo,
son of Guglielmo de' Pazzi, who had played a prominent part in the
downfall of the Republic. Guglielmo de' Pazzi, wrote Cambi with
grim satisfaction, had been punished by God through his son for

---

[10] Cambi, *Istorie*, iii. 24; cf. pp. 2–3, 25, and 47. The likening of Florence under
the Medici to Sodom and Gomorrah was to become a commonplace in Piagnone
polemic.

[11] Ibid. ii. 329; see also Landucci, *Diario fiorentino*, 327, 329.

[12] Cerretani, 'Storia in dialogo', fo. 157$^r$; see also Landucci, *Diario fiorentino*,
333.

[13] Savonarola, *Prediche sopra Ruth e Michea*, ed. V. Romano (ENOS; 2 vols.;
Rome, 1962), i. 412.

[14] Villari, *La storia di Girolamo Savonarola*, i. 436.

his part in the overthrow of the *governo popolare*.[15] For the Medici
themselves, however, the worst fate of all was in store. Not content
to have betrayed their promise to live as private citizens, they had
also given full scope to their base tyrannical ambitions. 'Because of
this', Fra Benedetto Luschino commented some years later, after
the deaths of Giuliano and Lorenzo de' Medici, 'no one should be
surprised if God, within a short lapse of time, has sent Death's
scythe into that house and has utterly destroyed the legitimate
male line. For, perjury and the breaking of one's word are sins far
too displeasing to the Lord.' 'From this therefore', he summed up,
'one can demonstrate with the evidence of Holy Scripture, there
originated the ruin and the destruction of the above-mentioned
noble house of the Medici.'[16] By 1519, when Fra Benedetto wrote
these words, the Piagnoni could find some consolation in such
manifest proofs of God's displeasure as the deaths of Giuliano and
Lorenzo: proofs redoubled by the early death of Leo X in 1521.
Before this, however, there had been little indication of precisely
how God wished them to proceed in this hostile climate. In the
absence of direct guidance, they had to act as they thought best;
and, in the main part of this chapter, we shall examine which of the
various courses now open to them they took.

## II

Throughout all the constitutional turmoil, the Piagnoni were never
far from the Medici's thoughts. Unlike the more extreme of their

[15] Cambi, *Istorie*, iii. 14; cf. e.g. Pseudo-Burlamacchi, *La vita*, ed. P. Ginori
Conti and R. Ridolfi (Florence, 1937), 224–31; Giovanfrancesco Pico, *Vita
Reverendi Patris F. Hieronymi Savonarolae*, ed. J. Quétif (Paris, 1674), 134–7; and
also Bartolomeo Cerretani, 'Ricordi storici fiorentini, 1500–1523', MS BAV Vat.
Lat. 13651, App. entitled 'Nota d'huomini che morirono di mala morte, e' quali
furono ministri al piglar [*sic*] Fra Girolamo e amazarlo et piglare S. Marcho per
forza', fo. 235ʳ⁻ᵛ.

[16] Benedetto Luschino, 'Vulnera diligentis' (in three parts: parts I and II: MS
BNF Magl., XXXIV, 7; part III: MS BRF 2985), part III, fos. 51ᵛ–52ʳ: 'Per la qual
cosa nessuno si debbe maravigliare se Dio in breve tempo ha missa la falce della
morte in quella casa, et spento al tucto la legittima linea masculina. Imperò troppo
dispiace al Signore il peccato del periurio et frangimento di fede.' 'Di qui adunque

supporters—*amici* like Paolo Vettori, for example, and Giovanni Rucellai, who saw no alternative to a policy of total repression[17]— the Medici themselves, in this period at least, evidently acted in the belief that some measure of consent was essential if the regime were to prosper. At the same time, however, they were well aware that, in certain situations, repression was the only answer. They pursued, therefore, a twofold course: on the one hand, weeding out both declared enemies and persons of doubtful loyalty from vital government posts and, on the other, ingratiating themselves with the major forces in Florentine politics by permitting them to take part in running the government. As one of these forces, the Piagnoni were the object of both policies; and in this part of our chapter, we chart their varying responses.

In the experiences of the Piagnoni Giovanbattista Ridolfi and Ser Giuliano da Ripa, we have key examples of the Medici's repressive policy. On 8 September 1512 Ridolfi had been elected *Gonfaloniere* for the term of one year.[18] The Medici could not afford, however, to allow such an important post to remain in the hands of a prominent Piagnone. As Giuliano de' Medici was to advise his nephew Lorenzo, in an *Instructione* prepared for him at Leo X's behest when he was about to take up the reins of government in Florence, the candidate for the position, as well as being a man of standing, had also to be completely loyal to the family. He had, in Giuliano's words, to be numbered among the *amici*.[19] It was essential, therefore, that Ridolfi should be removed; and he was forced to resign after only two months in office.[20] The situation of

si pruova col testimonio della Sacra Scriptura essere nata la ruina et lo extinguimento della prefata nobil casa de' Medici.' See also Parenti, 'Istorie fiorentine', MS BNF II.IV.171, fo. 125ᵛ: 'Lo universale acceptò volentieri la morte predecta [of Giuliano], ricordandosi che tre anni avanti lui in persona haveva condocto el parlamento et tolto la libertà al popolo.'

[17] Paolo Vettori, 'Ricordi di Paolo Vettori al cardinale de' Medici sopra le cose di Firenze', in R. von Albertini, *Firenze dalla repubblica al principato* (Turin, 1970), app., pp. 357–9; Cerretani, 'Storia in dialogo', fos. 155ʳ, 159ʳ, 160ʳ.

[18] Ibid., fo. 150ᵛ.

[19] 'Instructione al Magnifico Lorenzo', in T. Gar (ed.), 'Documenti risguardanti Giuliano de' Medici e il Pontefice Leone X', *ASI*, app. I (1842–3), 300.

[20] Cerretani, 'Storia in dialogo', fo. 157ʳ.

Ser Giuliano da Ripa was equally unacceptable to the Medici. Though not a major office, his post in the Chancery, where he served as archivist and, more importantly, as notary for acts pertaining to Florentine dependent territories, was nevertheless a significant one.[21]

Notaries had long been a means of enabling the Medici to keep abreast of proceedings in the various magistracies to which they were attached and, further, to influence the decisions of these bodies. Advising Lorenzo to make good use of such officials, Giuliano de' Medici recalled how he himself had been greatly aided in this way by Ser Zanobi Pace, Chancellor of the *Otto di Guardia*, 'who reported to me and kept me informed about every deliberation in that office, and more often than not also those which were about to be taken'.[22] Ser Giuliano da Ripa, however, was manifestly unsuited to this role in a Medicean government. His rise in the Chancery had begun with the fall of Piero de' Medici in 1494, when he had ratified the *Signoria*'s acts of 9 November, a deed hardly destined to endear him to Piero's heirs.[23] A grateful government, mindful of his role and of the personal risks he had incurred on that day on behalf of freedom, conferred upon him for life a post in the Chancery as notary for the acts concerning the Florentine dominion.[24] In subsequent years his name was connected with some Piagnoni foundations; he is known to have attracted, moreover, a great number of Piagnoni clients in his private notarial practice.[25]

[21] D. Marzi, *La cancelleria della Repubblica Fiorentina* (Rocca S. Casciano, 1910), 305.

[22] 'Instructione al Magnifico Lorenzo', in Gar (ed.), 'Documenti risguardanti Giuliano de' Medici e il Pontefice Leone X', 301: 'el quale mi referiva et teneva ragguagliato d'ogni deliberatione che ne lo officio si faceva, et il più de le volte di quelle che far si dovevano'. See also pp. 302, 304. Paolo Vettori also stressed the importance of the Chancery: 'Ricordi di Paolo Vettori al cardinale de' Medici sopra le cose di Firenze', in Albertini, *Firenze dalla Repubblica al principato*, 358–9.

[23] Cambi, *Istorie*, ii. 89; Benedetto Varchi, *Storia fiorentina* (2 vols.; Florence, 1963), i. 103; Marzi, *La cancelleria della Repubblica Fiorentina*, 264.

[24] ASF Signori e Collegi, Deliberazioni Ord. Aut. 96, fo. 128ᵛ.

[25] He was connected, for instance, with the confraternity of the Purification of the Virgin and S. Zanobi; his protocols in ASF Not. Ant., G.527–532 (17 vols.) (1483–1546). Since the patronymics are not always stated, it is often difficult for us, as it was for contemporaries, to distinguish him from Ser Giuliano di Lorenzo

He was a follower of Pietro Bernardino[26] and may well have followed him to Mirandola since he disappears from view between 1500 and 1502. In 1512, after the return of the Medici, he was so incautious as publicly to advertise his allegiance to Pietro Bernardino.[27] Inevitably, after this rash act, he was dismissed from his post on 26 December, and thereafter was kept under close surveillance.[28]

At the same time, however, as Giuliano de' Medici emphasized in his *Instructione*, every effort had to be made to win leading citizens to the family's support: even to the extent of turning to them for advice. For such advice—which could, on occasion, prove more trustworthy than that proffered by pro-Medicean hotheads—Giuliano suggested that Lorenzo should consult Jacopo Salviati and Lanfredino Lanfredini, especially on matters of finance.[29] Because of their wealth, standing, and reputation, these were, in fact, the very men whom the Medici had been most concerned to win over during the early months of consolidation. Other Piagnoni, too, were encouraged to overcome their distaste for the regime. Giovanbattista Ridolfi, for instance, while too risky a *Gonfaloniere*, was nevertheless considered valuable as one of the twenty *Accoppiatori* and as a member of the Council of Seventy.[30]

---

da Ripa 'homo loquax et male vite' and a notary at the Archiepiscopal Curia, who in June 1496 attacked prominent Piagnoni, including Domenico Bonsi and when arraigned before the *Otto di Guardia* took refuge in S. Marco, seeking the friars' protection. At length he gave himself up and was sentenced to two years' exile which he does not, however, seem to have served. He became thereafter, a self-styled Piagnone, but, if his protocols are an indication, shunned by them. On him see ASF Signori e Collegi, Deliberazioni Ord. Aut. 98, fos. 50ʳ–51ʳ, 52ʳ⁻ᵛ, where the quotation occurs. See also Piero Parenti, *Istorie fiorentine*, ed. J. Schnitzer, *Quellen und Forschungen zur Geschichte Savonarolas*, iv (Leipzig, 1910), 124–6, 128; his protocols in ASF Not. Ant., G.535 (3 vols.) (1475–1525).

[26] Pandolfo de' Conti to Francesco Guicciardini, 13 Nov. 1512, in R. Palmarocchi (ed.), *Carteggi di Francesco Guicciardini*, i (Fonti per la Storia d'Italia, 3; Bologna, 1938), 123 (hereafter cited as Francesco Guicciardini, *Carteggi*).

[27] Ibid.

[28] ASF Signori e Collegi, Deliberazioni Ord. Aut. 114, fo. 137ʳ; Marzi, *La cancelleria della Repubblica Fiorentina*, 305.

[29] 'Instructione al Magnifico Lorenzo', in Gar (ed.), 'Documenti risguardanti Giuliano de' Medici e il Pontefice Leone X', 303–4.

[30] Cerretani, 'Storia in dialogo', fo. 157ᵛ; Filippo de' Nerli, *Commentari*, i. 202.

His right to sit on the *Balìa*, moreover, which should theoretically have been relinquished when he ceased to be *Gonfaloniere*, was never questioned, and he remained a member until his death in 1514. While Filippo de' Nerli states that the most rabid Piagnoni were excluded from the newly created councils of the state[31], this must not be allowed to obscure the fact that the moderates were well represented. Of the fifty-five original members of the *Balìa*, excluding the eleven *arroti*, ten, Giovanbattista Ridolfi among them, were Piagnoni.[32] Among the *Accoppiatori*, upon whom the future of the regime largely depended, were five prominent Piagnoni, including Giovanbattista Ridolfi.[33] There was no alternative to the policy of appeasement. As the Medici realized, to have done otherwise would have alienated from the regime some of the most important political figures in Florence. The Piagnone interlocutor in Bartolomeo Cerretani's *Storia in dialogo* saw through this policy and remarked upon it to his Medicean counterpart, Giovanni Rucellai, 'one can see that you were very frightened because, out of fear, you abandoned your friends and appointed the leading partisans of Savonarola'.[34]

The Piagnoni in general also benefited from this policy. Already at the time of the Medici's entry into Florence, Cardinal Giovanni had personally intervened to stop the populace from attacking S. Marco.[35] He had also backed the friars of S. Marco against a further attempt to assign the convent to the Lombard Congregation; and even gave his tacit support, or so it seems, to the friars' endeavours to prevent an enraged Julius II from discussing the whole

[31] Ibid., 190.

[32] They were: Giovanbattista Ridolfi, Roberto di Pagnozzo Ridolfi, Niccolò di Roberto degli Albizzi, Pandolfo Corbinelli, Piero di Iacopo Guicciardini, Lanfredino Lanfredini, Francesco di Chirico Pepi, Giuliano Salviati, Jacopo Salviati, Alessandro d'Antonio Pucci. The full list in ibid. 186–8.

[33] They were: Giovanbattista Ridolfi, Pandolfo Corbinelli, Piero Guicciardini, Francesco Pepi, Jacopo Salviati.

[34] Cerretani, 'Storia in dialogo', fo. 157ᵛ: 'vedesi che voi temevi forte perchè per paura voi lasciasti li amici vostri, e togliesti le prime lancie del frate'.

[35] Vincenzo Mainardi, 'Sermones et epistolae', MS BNF Magl., VI, 166, fo. 62ᵛ: letter of 26 Nov. 1512 to Fra Niccolò Schomberg, here mistakenly referred to as Procurator of the Dominican Order, a position he had not held since 1509–10.

Savonarolan question at the next session of the Lateran Council.[36] Later, following the public taunting of the Piagnoni during the Florentine celebrations of the news of Leo X's election,[37] the *Otto di Guardia* issued a ban on 12 March 1513, commanding that they be left in peace.[38] Giovanni de' Medici both as cardinal and then as Pope gave employment to Piagnoni. In Florence he engaged Fra Stefano Moldei da Castrocaro of S. Marco as his secretary.[39] Upon his election, he received Piagnoni into his household, appointed them to offices within the Curia, and sponsored their projects. Giovanni degli Albizzi, for example, and Amerigo de' Medici, the controversial Canon of Sta Maria del Fiore who had been a follower of Pietro Bernardino, became members of the household, as did Fra Zanobi Acciaiuoli, who was later appointed librarian at the Vatican, and the much maligned Fra Mariano Fetti on whom he later conferred the office of keeper of the papal seal ( *plumbator*).[40] Fra Santi Pagnini, too, was encouraged and materially assisted in translating for publication a new Latin version of the Bible.[41] Giulio de' Medici

---

[36] Ibid., fo. 63ʳ.     [37] Landucci, *Diario fiorentino*, 336.

[38] ASF Otto di Guardia, Ep. Rep. 223 (Minute di bandi emanati dagli Otto: 19 Feb. 1512/13–6 May 1527), fo. 10ʳ.

[39] Roberto Ubaldini, 'Annalia Conventus Sancti Marci', MS BMLF, S. Marco 370, fo. 165ʳ.

[40] A. Ferrajoli, 'Il ruolo della corte di Leone X (1514–1516)', *Archivio della R. Società Romana di storia patria*, 34–40 (1911–17), 34: 11, 15. Amerigo de' Medici was later to join the household of Cardinal Giulio de' Medici: see letter of Baldassarre Turini da Pescia to Lorenzo de' Medici, 7 Aug. 1515, ASF MAP 117, No. 195; S. Salvini, *Catalogo cronologico de' Canonici della Chiesa Metropolitana fiorentina* (Florence, 1782), 67; C. Vasoli, 'L'attesa della nuova era in ambienti e gruppi fiorentini del Quattrocento', *L'attesa dell'età nuova nella spiritualità della fine del medioevo* (Todi, 1970), 409 n. 58. Zanobi Acciaiuoli, *Theodoriti Cyrensis Episcopi de curatione Graecarum affectionum* (Paris, 1519), Ep. Ded. to Leo X, fo. 2ʳ; W. Roscoe, *Vita e Pontificato di Leone X* (10 vols.; Milan, 1816–17), x. 27–30; *DBI*; on fra Mariano Fetti see A. Zucchi, *Roma Domenicana* (4 vols.; Rome, 1938–43), ii. 198–203, and letter of Baldassarre Turini to Lorenzo de' Medici, 12 Apr. 1514, ASF MAP 107, No. 4.

[41] Roscoe, *Vita e Pontificato di Leone X*, iv. 144; T. M. Centi, 'L'attività letteraria di Santi Pagnini (1470–1536) nel campo delle scienze bibliche', *AFP* 15 (1945), 11–12; and esp. two letters from Giovanfrancesco Pico to Santi Pagnini, in Giovanfrancesco Pico, *Opera omnia* (Basle, 1573), ii. 1371–6. See also I. Taurisano, *I Domenicani in Lucca* (Lucca, 1914), 103–4, and R. Creytens, 'Les Actes capitulaires de la Congrégation Toscano-Romaine O.P. (1496–1530)', *AFP* 40 (1970), 161.

was to adopt a similar policy when he took over the government at Lorenzo's death. In the words of the historian Iacopo Pitti, 'he began to gather together and preserve the relics of Savonarola's disciples'.[42] Among these devotees, Pitti singled out Girolamo Benivieni,[43] who had celebrated Leo X's election by composing his *Frottola pro Papa Leone in renovatione ecclesiae*.[44]

Girolamo Benivieni readily responded to these overtures, and a warm and enduring friendship developed between the two men. Their mutual affection remained equally strong after Giulio de' Medici became Pope in 1523 and survived even the bitterness engendered by the expulsion of the Medici and the siege of Florence later in the decade.[45] Nor was Girolamo Benivieni alone in responding favourably to the Medici attempts to win Piagnoni allegiance. Whether because they were oblivious to the political and religious implications of their stance, or because they saw the Medici as a source of boundless patronage — or, again, because they devoutly hoped that Leo X would prove to be the long-awaited reforming Pope, or *Pastore Angelico*, of Savonarolan legend[46]—a number of Piagnoni responded as Benivieni had done.

---

[42] Jacopo Pitti, *Dell'Istoria fiorentina*, in *ASI*, 1st ser. 1 (1842), 123: 'cominciò a raccorre e trattenere le reliquie dei devoti del Frate'.

[43] Ibid., cf. Iacopo Nardi, *Istorie della città di Firenze*, where Giulio de' Medici is said to have cultivated the friendship also of Carlo del Benino, another Piagnone: ii. 63. A third Piagnone thus attracted, Francesco d'Antonio de' Ricci, will be dealt with in detail below.

[44] See above.

[45] For testimonies to their friendship, see the letter of Giulio de' Medici to Girolamo Benivieni, 25 June 1523, in BMF B.III.66, fo. 52ʳ; the letter of same (as Pope Clement VII) to same, 31 July 1524, in ASV Arm. XLIV, 9 (Clemens VII: Brevia ad Principes), fo. 26ʳ; Girolamo Benivieni, *Epistola . . . mandata a Papa Clemente VII* in *Storia fiorentina*, ed. G. Milanesi (3 vols.; Florence, 1858), iii. 307–9.

[46] e.g. Girolamo Benivieni, *Frottola pro Papa Leone in renovatione ecclesiae*, in *Opere* (Florence, 1519), esp. fo. 197ᵛ; Zanobi Acciaiuoli, 'Leonis X Laudes, Carmina', MS BMF A.LXXXII, fos. 237ʳ–240ʳ. The conceit was also popular outside Savonarolan circles: cf. Guglielmo de' Nobili, 'Scritti e canzoni in lode di Papa Leone X', MS BNF Landau–Finaly 183, fos. 2ᵛ, 35ᵛ, 55ᵛ; Naldo Naldi, *Ad Sanctissimum D.N. Leonem X Pont. Max.*, in *Carmina illustrium poetarum Italorum*, vi (Florence, 1720), 447; Anon., 'Poems in praise of Leo X', MS BNF Palatino–Baldovinetti 230, esp. fos. 4ᵛ, 14ʳ⁻ᵛ. Although this last work bears the inscription 'Hic liber est mei Petri Criniti', it cannot, as D. Weinstein has pointed out, be attributed to Pietro Crinito, since he died no later than 1507: *Savonarola and*

Giorgio Benigno, for example, had no sooner heard of Leo X's election than he dusted off a couple of treatises for presentation to him, taking care to remind him of his own long-standing services to the Medici, in recognition of which he ought, he felt, to be made a cardinal.[47] Ugolino Verino, who, after the publication of his invective against Savonarola, had returned to the Piagnone fold, went even further, dedicating to Leo X all the religious works he had composed in the previous twenty years and expressing the hope that he would finance the publication of his *Vetus et Novum Testamentum*.[48]

How, in view of all Savonarola's fulminations against tyrannies in general and that of the Medici in particular, did his followers feel able to collaborate with those whom he had most abhorred? Giulio de' Medici himself was much struck by this apparent paradox, and was moved to question Girolamo Benivieni on the seemingly untenable nature of his position. 'Girolamo,' he asked, 'you profess to believe in Savonarola; how do you reconcile that with being wholly our affectionate friend and companion?'[49] How indeed? In what way could these outwardly contradictory factors be reconciled? One hostile observer had a ready answer. 'The Piagnoni have completely disowned the Friar', was the priest Pandolfo de' Conti's sweeping announcement in a letter to Francesco Guicciardini in November 1512. 'The fierce ardour in many of them has been reduced to a flicker, since the greater light has been dimmed', he sarcastically went on, 'the friars of San Marco's have utterly lost the true light.'[50] For Pandolfo de' Conti, here was the explanation.

---

*Florence: Prophecy and Patriotism in the Renaissance* (Princeton, NJ, 1970), 351 n. 109.

[47] C. Vasoli, 'Notizie su Giorgio Benigno Salviati ( Juraj Dragisic)', *Studi storici in onore di Gabriele Pepe* (Bari, 1969), 480–1.

[48] A. Lazzari, *Ugolino e Michele Verino: Studi biografici e critici* (Turin, 1897), 206–7. For Ugolino Verino's resumption of Piagnoni ideals, see above, Ch. 5, n. 265.

[49] Antonio Benivieni, 'Vita di Girolamo Benivieni', MS BNF II.I.91, p. 258: 'Girolamo voi fate professione di credere al Frate, come può stare l'essere intieramente amico et affezionato nostro?'

[50] Francesco Guicciardini, *Carteggi*, i. 123: 'Li Piagnoni al tutto hanno rinnegato el frate. Ecci assai che di lume di torchio sono diventati lumicini quia maius lumen occupat minus, e' frati di Santo Marco hanno perso affatto el vero lume.'

The Piagnoni's association with the Medici was possible because they had forsworn all allegiance to Savonarola and his teaching. Girolamo Benivieni's view, however, was quite otherwise. When he answered Giulio de' Medici, he gave no indication that he had renounced any aspect of Savonarola's doctrine. 'Your Excellency,' he began, 'should not fear anything from the friends and followers of the Friar, because since they are awaiting the miracle and for God to intervene, they do not cause trouble.'[51] In his opinion, the Piagnoni's chief duty was to wait upon God. While certain aspects of Medici rule may have been reprehensible to him, positive action against them was nevertheless out of the question. Nothing remained for the Piagnoni, therefore, but to stand by passively and await the turn of events, secure in the conviction that God would decide. In Iacopo Pitti's version of the exchange between Giulio de' Medici and Girolamo Benivieni, the latter's mood emerges even more plainly: 'I do not deny, Your Excellency, that I am one of the Friar's followers or that I—like all good men in this city—desire freedom for the commonwealth; but neither I nor any of them will commit a felony on that account, nor will they ever take up arms against the state: we shall fervently pray God and yourself to grant it to us.'[52]

Although this view must have been widely shared, it was not, as Girolamo Benivieni assumed, universal. Other Piagnoni refused to accept that adversity was to be passively endured. They embodied another strain in Piagnone ideology: the view that the Christian had an active role to play in creating the conditions conducive to reform. They understood from Savonarola's teaching that the individual was responsible for the situation in which he found himself; and responsible, also, for remedying its defects. Thus impelled, they reacted to the Medici in a manner completely different from

[51] Antonio Benivieni, 'Vita di Girolamo Benivieni', 258–9: 'V.S. Illustrissima non tema già mai delli amici et devoti del Frate, essi aspettando il miracolo e che Dio Operi, quieti se ne stanno.'

[52] Jacopo Pitti, Dell'Istoria fiorentina, 123: 'Io non niego, monsignore illustrissimo, di non essere de' seguaci del Frate, ed insieme con tutti gli uomini dabbene di questa città, desiderare la libertà comune; ma nè io, nè coloro faranno per tal conto fellonia, nè verranno con le armi contro allo stato giammai: pregheremo bene Dio e voi, che ne la conceda.'

Girolamo Benivieni's. Refusing to allow that the present regime was immutable, they worked actively to reform it. Their response took one of three forms. Some accepted office in the new government and sought to reform it from within; others refused to have any truck with the Medici; still others took the course of open rebellion.

Among the Piagnoni who took office in the regime, there were many who saw their duty as either to modify its more extreme aspects or, at the very least, to prevent it from becoming an open tyranny. In their view, accepting the Medici's overtures did not entail a total, or even a partial, commitment to their rule. Their outlook is epitomized in the policies of the two most eminent Piagnoni office-holders of the time: Jacopo Salviati and Lanfredino Lanfredini. The motives of these two men were undoubtedly mixed. They received considerable financial benefit from their connections with the Medici, especially after the election of Leo X, when Salviati, for instance, was given important concessions for the farming of papal taxes.[53] Although by no means averse to an oligarchy, in which they could hope to exercise some sway, they nevertheless had no wish to see the Medici's power further strengthened. Having tried, and failed, to prevent the calling of a *parlamento* in September 1512,[54] they continued undeterred thereafter, attempting to restrain the Medici and to lessen the influence of the more extreme Mediceans while in the meantime advancing the interests of their fellow Savonarolans. Even though he was their relative by marriage (*cogniato loro*), as the Medicean interlocutor, Giovanni Rucellai, pointed out in Cerretani's *Storia in dialogo*, Salviati did his utmost to subvert Medici rule. 'Jacopo Salviati, their brother-in-law, did very little during their return', Rucellai commented indignantly; adding, moreover, that 'afterwards, he did all in his power to reintroduce and keep alive Savonarola's party, since he was such a devoted follower of the

[53] J. N. Stephens, *The Fall of the Florentine Republic, 1512–1530* (Oxford, 1983), 128–9 *et passim*; P. Hurtubise, *Une famille-témoin: Les Salviati* (Vatican City, 1985), 147 ff. Both Salviati and Lanfredini were appointed *Riformatori del Monte* in 1513: Cambi, *Istorie*, iii. 12, cf. Cerretani, 'Storia in dialogo', fo. 162ᵛ.

[54] Cerretani, 'Storia in dialogo', fos. 150ᵛ, 151ʳ, 152ʳ⁻ᵛ, 153ʳ.

Friar. And he was successful in this thanks to the bad way in which the *Balìa* had been set up; something which was very frequently discussed by us and brought us to the verge of despair because we could see how efficiently that party was being revitalized.'[55] In the opinion of Filippo de' Nerli, the Mediceans were well aware that, by these means, Salviati was preventing them from consolidating their precarious hold on the government.[56] Accordingly, they took action. They got Salviati out of the way while the consolidation of the regime was taking place, by having him appointed ambassador to Rome. Despite his repeated requests to be relieved of his post, he was not permitted to return to Florence until August 1513.[57]

Once back, he strove to make up for lost time. Abetted by Lanfredino Lanfredini, he did his best to obstruct those of Lorenzo de' Medici's activities which he understood to be despotic in aim. In February 1515, speaking on Lanfredini's behalf as well as his own, Salviati came out strongly against Lorenzo's rumoured plan to make himself sole ruler of Florence, threatening that he and Lanfredini would rally the populace against such a move. Galeotto de' Medici, acting as Lorenzo's deputy, relayed this information to Lorenzo in Rome, adding the further intelligence, a month later, that the same men were behind the attempt to have the *Otto di Pratica* give a full account of the financial transaction it had undertaken with the Spaniards at Lorenzo's behest.[58] In May, Salviati opposed the plan to make Lorenzo Captain-General of the Floren-

---

[55] Cerretani, fos. 158ᵛ–159ʳ: 'Jacopo Salviati, cogniato loro, operò molto poco nella lor tornata, di poi non attese mai ad altro che rintrodurre e tener viva la parte del frate, di chi e' fu sì divoto, et riusciavi rispetto al mal getto della balìa, di che moltissime volte fumo tra noi insieme et disperavaci perchè vedevamo risuscitare ma destramente quella parte.'

[56] Filippo de' Nerli, *Commentari*, i. 192; cf. 191–2.

[57] Devonshire-Jones, *Francesco Vettori*, 96–7 and n. 77. The diary he kept while on this mission is in ASP ser. III, libro 10.

[58] Stephens, *The Fall of the Florentine Republic*, 94. As early as Nov. 1514, a mere two months after Lorenzo moved to Rome, Galeotto was already warning him of Lanfredini's dissatisfaction with the regime: see R. Devonshire-Jones, 'Lorenzo de' Medici, Duca d'Urbino "Signore" of Florence?' in M. P. Gilmore (ed.), *Studies on Machiavelli* (Florence, 1972), 310 and n. 75.

tine forces.[59] And yet again, in 1518, he and Lanfredini opposed another scheme which they considered to be tyrannical in its implications. Strenuously maintaining that Lorenzo, a citizen like any other, should receive no special treatment, they condemned a proposal that, upon his return to Florence from France with his bride, Madeleine de la Tour d'Auvergne, he should be formally received by ambassadors.[60] Lorenzo could no longer ignore this defiance. In the past his deputies, including his mother Alfonsina Orsini and Goro Gheri, had often alerted him to the danger posed by both men but by Jacopo in particular.[61] It was also common knowledge that other members of Jacopo's family had openly criticized him for his despotic aims.[62] Though he had heeded these warnings, there was little Lorenzo could have done given Jacopo's standing in Leo X's eyes.[63] But now he was sufficiently in control to act. In retaliation, he excluded both Jacopo Salviati and Lanfredino from the inner circle of his advisers; whereupon Lanfredini retired from public life altogether and Salviati prudently withdrew to Rome, not to return until after Lorenzo's death.[64] Thereafter he took up where

[59] A. Anzilotti, *La crisi costituzionale della Repubblica Fiorentina* (Florence, 1912), 63; Devonshire-Jones, *Francesco Vettori*, 112; cf. the indignant reaction of another Piagnone, Giovanni Cambi, to this appointment, which he regarded as totally 'contro agli ordini della Ripubricha': *Istorie*, iii. 66.

[60] Ibid. 150–1; see also Filippo de' Nerli, *Commentari*, i. 208–9.

[61] See e.g. Letters of Galeotto to Lorenzo, 3 Feb. 1514, 11 Oct. 1514, 17 Oct. 1514, 21 Oct. 1514, 21 Nov. 1514 in ASF MAP 116, Nos. 94, 364, 392, 417, 516; Letters of Goro Gheri to Lorenzo, 26 Oct. 1517, 1 Nov. 1517 in ASF Copialettere di Goro Gheri (5 vols.), ii. fos. 523$^{r-v}$, 531$^{r-v}$.

[62] See e.g. letter of Giovanni di Poppi, one of Lorenzo's representatives in Rome, to Lorenzo, 5 June 1515 where he relates that 'Madonna Lucretia . . . exclama al cielo per havere vostra Signoria prese le arme [i.e. of Captain-General of Florence], dicendo che è stata cosa mal consigliata' ASF MAP 117, No. 107. For a later and more serious attempt by Jacopo's son, Card. Giovanni, to destabilize the regime, see Cerretani, 'Ricordi storici fiorentini', fo. 208$^v$.

[63] Goro Gheri, 'Copialettere di Goro Gheri', ASF, vol. iv, fos. 178$^r$–180$^r$; Letters of Baldassarre Turini to Gheri, 27 Mar. 1518 and 1 Apr. 1518: ASF MAP 144, Nos. 88, 74.

[64] Cambi, *Istorie*, iii. 151; Filippo de' Nerli, *Commentari*, i. 209. The anonymous author of the *Vita latina* that is 'Vita Beati Hieronymi, martiris, doctoris, virginis, ac prophetae eximii', MS BNF Conv. Sopp., J.VIII.28—who inexpli-

he had left off: his opportunities for successful obstruction being much enhanced by the prominent role which Giulio de' Medici accorded him in government. 'The Cardinal was generous in granting audiences and in expediting the affairs of state, and Jacopo Salviati was the one in whom he placed all his trust and counsel', said Giovanni Rucellai in Cerretani's dialogue. Salviati, he went on, took advantage of his position and, 'began to infiltrate both the Otto di Pratica and the Gonfaloniership of Justice and other offices with men of the faction hostile to us'.[65] Thus, the Medici's encouragement of the participation of rival parties in government—a policy dictated originally by the insecurity of their position but also as both enemies and supporters admitted by their kindness and inexperience[66]—worked, in the long run, to their disadvantage.

Naturally, the course adopted by Salviati and Lanfredini was not open to everyone. But nor was it universally attractive. For some, the degree of latitude enjoyed by the two most prominent Piagnoni office-holders was not sufficient. For them, there was no possibility of co-operating, either in religious affairs or in government, with a regime which they held to be inimical to the advancement of true religion. So uncompromising was their attitude that they found the idea of a Medici in S. Peter's Chair intolerable. At first, Giovanni Cambi could not conceal his pride at the news of the election of a Florentine to the papacy. It was not long, however, before he lost all pious illusions as to the reforming zeal of Leo X.[67] Girolamo, Cerretani's Piagnone interlocutor, on the other hand, had never had any doubts as to Leo X's true nature. In the *Storia in dialogo*, he graphically depicted him as one who, by his nepotism, profli-

cably holds that by this time Lanfredino had abandoned Savonarola for the Medici—reports that Lorenzo was so incensed by the opposition that he had Lanfredino beaten causing him to become insane and to die: *Vita latina*, fo. 91ʳ⁻ᵛ.

[65] Cerretani, 'Storia in dialogo', fo. 181ʳ: 'Il Cardinale non mancava delle udienzie e spedire tutto, et Jacopo Salviati era quello in cui tutto si fidava e consigliava, il quale cominciò a rintrodurre huomini della fatione nemici a noi et nelli Otto di Pratica e nel Gonfaloniere di Giustitia et altre dignità.'

[66] See e.g. Niccolò Valori, 'Ricordanze', MS BNF Panc. 134, fo. 17ᵛ, where he states that the Medici 'da natura invero erano benigni'.

[67] Cambi, *Istorie*, iii. 6, 13, 48–9, 73–4, 121.

gacy, and utter disregard for the spiritual needs of Christianity, had brought the Church to the edge of ruin.[68] Jaundiced, perhaps, by his long term of incarceration in S. Marco, Fra Benedetto Luschino offered an even harsher judgement. According to his reading of Scripture, he said, Leo X was that Pope 'of whom it has been written: And the Lion shall die at the fifth roar; the Son of Sodom shall wander through the waste land, and the Flower [Florence] shall no longer give forth its perfume.'[69]

For those who saw the world as such a desolate place, there were only two possibilities. Since the loathed regime was, in their eyes, totally irreclaimable, they had either to forsake it altogether or to work for its overthrow. Amongst those who took the former course were several friars of S. Marco,[70] including Fra Tommaso Caiani. 'Caiano has gone to preach to bumpkins', was Pandolfo de' Conti's derisive comment on Fra Tommaso's departure from the scene of the Medici's triumph. While in voluntary exile in the convent of S. Domenico in Lucca, Fra Tommaso continued to work against the regime. With the collaboration of another exiled friar of S. Marco and of a layman, he composed a treatise against Lorenzo de' Medici, recently created Duke of Urbino.[71]

---

[68] Cerretani, 'Storia in dialogo', fos. 163ʳ, 174ʳ.

[69] Benedetto Luschino, 'Vulnera diligentis', part I, fo. 1ʳ: 'de quo scriptum est: Et Leo in quinto rugitu morietur: Filius Sodomae per loca arida perambulabit, et Flos non dabit odorem'; and also part III, fo. 52ᵛ.

[70] Fra Luca Bettini was one of them. He was in Bologna from at least early 1515 onwards; and, while there, saw two editions of Savonarola's sermons through the press: see Girolamo Savonarola, *Prediche sopra i Salmi* (Bologna, 1515), prefatory letter of Bartolomeo di Francesco Gualterotti to Domenico di Antonio Bruni, sig. a1ʳ; R. Ridolfi, *Vita di Girolamo Savonarola* (2 vols.; Rome, 1952), ii. 40.

[71] Francesco Guicciardini, *Carteggi*, i. 123: 'El Caiano è ito a predicare a' porri'. See also Francesco Onesti da Castiglione, 'Persecutiones exagitate contra . . . S. Dominicam de Paradiso', MS ACDC Codice F, fo. 25ᵛ. Fra Tommaso's career as an itinerant preacher began at about the time of the Medici's return to Florence. With another friar from S. Marco, Bartolomeo Soderini, as his companion, Fra Tommaso travelled as far afield as Sicily, and even journeyed outside Italy: R. Creytens, 'Les Actes capitulaires', 170, 183; G. Meersseman and D. Planzer (eds.), *Magistrorum ac Procuratorum Generalium O.P. Registra Litterarum Minora (1469–1523)* (Monumenta Ordinis Fratrum Praedicatorum Historica, 21; Rome, 1947), 76, 183; Ubaldini, 'Annalia', fo. 169ʳ; J. Quétif and J. Echard, *Scriptores Ordinis Praedicatorum recensiti* (2 vols.; Paris, 1719–21), ii. 77; BMLF S. Marco

Lay Piagnoni, on the whole, could not take refuge in flight and give vent to their hostility from the haven of exile. Family and business ties forced them to remain in Florence and, despite the risks, make their opposition known by refusing either to accept the constitutionality of the regime or to abide by its dictates. The attitude of such men is best expressed by Tommaso Tosinghi. In a most revealing statement in his *Ricordanze*, he maintained that since the return of the Medici in 1512, apart from imprisonment and exile, he had been subjected to:

most grievous imposts, forced loans beyond all reason, dishonest taxes: in effect, I was in everything dealt with as an enemy of the state. And as for the scrutinies, neither I nor my sons have ever been selected for any office. I pay taxes, so as not to be at the mercy of public officials and bailiffs. And, in order to have the means to feed the 26 mouths in our household, I have had to rent my house to Jews and with my family I have had to go and live very poorly in the country house. And should someone say: 'Why have your companions not been treated like you', I reply, that had I wanted to go cap in hand and sought to accommodate myself to today's rule, as some others have done, I believe I should have found a place, as they have; but, since I deem this rule to be totally against my taste, I have never been able to come to terms with it and . . . I believe and indeed I have firm hope that in so doing I will be rewarded by God. And therefore I leave as a maxim to my sons rather to direct their attention to those things which are to the honour of God than to favour regimes which come to power by violent means.[72]

'884 [Processo per la canonizzazione di S. Antonino], fos. 18ᵛ–19ʳ: Letter of Tommaso Caiani to Fra Jacopo da Sicilia from Ragusa, dated 1 Dec. 1519.

[72] Tommaso Tosinghi ['Vita'] MS BNF Fondo Principale II.II.325, fo. 129ᵛ: 'albitrii disonestissimi, acchatti fuori d'ogni dovere, gravamenti disonesti, e in effetto in ogni chosa trattato come nimicho dello stato. E quanto alli squittini, nè io nè mia figliuoli mai fumo tratti a nulla. E per non essere preda di messi e chavallari pago le gravezze, et per aver le spese de 26 bocche che nnoi siamo in chasa, m'è bisogniato apig[i]onare la chasa a G[i]udei e ridurmi cholla mia brighata in villa assai miseramente . . . E chi diciessi: "Perchè non sono istati trattati gli altri tua chonpagni come te?" Rispondo che se io avessi voluto ciercare venia e achomodarmi al vivere d'oggi chome [h]anno fatto degli altri, chrederrei avere trovato lato chome loro; ma parendomi questo vivere totalmente chontro al gusto mio, non mi sono mai potuto achordare e . . . chredo e [h]o ferma speranza mi sarà giovato appresso a Dio. E chosì lascio per ricordo ai figliuoli mia che più presto e' dirischino a quelle chose che sono l'onore di Dio, che favorire stati violenti.'

Immediately after the restoration of the Medici, Niccolò Valori had also been determined not to have any truck with what he too characterized as regimes which had come to power by violent means (*stati violenti*) and had even contemplated leaving Florence, thinking better of it only for the sake of his wife and daughters.[73] His involvement in the anti-Medicean Boscoli–Capponi conspiracy, for which he received a sentence of two years' imprisonment in the fortress of Volterra to be followed by perpetual exile—a sentence which was never executed because he benefited from the amnesty declared at the election of Cardinal Giovanni to the papacy—persuaded him to adopt a more conciliatory stance towards the regime.[74]

Other prominent Piagnoni who made their opposition known were Tommaso Soderini, Luca degli Albizzi, and Girolamo Buonagrazia. They did not merely withdraw from politics—a course of action which, though distressing to the Medici who genuinely wanted consensus, would have pleased their more extreme partisans who had often sought this very end—but actively set out to damage the regime by all available means. Thus, Tommaso Soderini, from his villa at Scandicci where he had taken refuge, refused to pay the forced loan imposed upon him and refused also to provide an explanation for his default.[75] In addition, it seems that he and other members of his family sought to precipitate a financial crisis or at least a crisis in confidence by trying to sell all their holding of *Monte* stock until prevented by Gheri.[76] Luca degli Albizzi resorted to a more novel method of expressing his opposition. He voiced his fears that the Medici's policies would cause the ruin of the city and then advertised his belief in the

[73] Valori, 'Ricordanze', fo. 17ᵛ.

[74] Ibid., fos. 17ᵛ–18ᵛ; Parenti, 'Istorie fiorentine', MS BNF II.IV.171, fo. 84ʳ; see also his letter to Lorenzo de' Medici, dated 22 Oct. 1514, in which he thanks Lorenzo and especially his mother for their clemency and places himself at his disposal 'come fattura et creatura sua': ASF MAP 166, No. 420.

[75] Goro Gheri, 'Copialettere', vol. ii. fo. 302ʳ. On Tommaso Soderini, see Villari *La storia di Girolamo Savonarola*, vol. ii. app., pp. clxxviii, cciv; Pseudo-Burlamacchi, *La vita*, 210; J. Schnitzer, 'Il Burlamacchi e la sua "Vita del Savonarola"', *ASI*, 5th ser. 28 (1901), 272.

[76] Goro Gheri, 'Copialettere', vol. ii, fo. 304ʳ.

hopelessness of the situation by making a last will and testament at the Badia. When taken to task by Alfonsina Orsini, who accused him of seeking to cause a crisis in confidence, he admitted as much and justified his action on the grounds that he needed to put his affairs in order the better to concentrate on saving the state.[77]

Girolamo Buonagrazia's approach was both more subtle and more direct. On Jacopo Salviati's advice, he relayed to Lorenzo's deputy, Goro Gheri, the conversation which had allegedly taken place between a Carlo Marucelli and the Queen Mother of France, the tenor of which was that the Queen was horrified at how badly Florence was governed and wondered why the Florentines put up with it.[78] It was a singularly inappropriate approach to employ with Gheri, who was not a man to be either shamed or frightened into making political concessions, even if he had been in a position to do so. Nor was Niccolò Valori more successful in obtaining political reform with the presentation of his *Vita del Magnifico Lorenzo Vecchio de' Medici* to Leo X.[79] Niccolò may have intended the *Vita* to bring him reconciliation with and rehabilitation in the regime, but it was also a lesson in political ethics to the Medici masters and as such it was a variation of Buonagrazia's approach. In implied contrast to the present, the *Vita* posited an idealized version of Lorenzo il Magnifico's rule, when 'Virtue was held in high esteem; the people enjoyed freedom, the nobility honour, and the city an

---

[77] Letter of Filippo Strozzi to Giulio de' Medici, n.d. but Aug.–Sept. 1516: ASF MAP 105, No. 222.

[78] Goro Gheri, 'Copialettere', vol. iv, fos. 58ʳ–60ʳ.

[79] Prefacing Biagio Buonaccorsi, *Diario de' successi più importanti seguiti in Italia e particolarmente in Fiorenza dall'anno 1498 in sino all'anno 1512* (Florence, 1568; repr. 1973). On the *Vita* see M. Martelli, 'Le due redazioni della Laurentii Medicei Vita di Niccolò Valori', *La Bibliofilia*, 66 (1964), 235–63; N. Rubinstein, 'The Posthumous Image of Lorenzo de' Medici', in E. P. Chaney and N. Ritchie (eds.), *Oxford, China and Italy: Writings in Honour of Sir Harold Acton on his Eightieth Birthday* (Oxford, 1984), 94–107; C. Kovesi, 'Niccolò Valori and the Medici Restoration of 1512: Politics, Eulogies and the Preservation of a Family Myth', *Rinascimento*, 2nd ser. 27 (1987), 301–25; R. Pesman Cooper, 'Political Survival in Early Sixteenth-Century Florence: The case of Niccolò Valori', in P. Denley and C. Elam (eds.), *Florence and Italy: Renaissance Studies in Honour of Nicolai Rubinstein* (London, 1988), 73–90.

abundance of every good'.[80] Few concrete and immediate effects could be expected from these tactics. None the less, if the reactions of Alfonsina Orsini and Goro Gheri are any guide, recourse to them was most unsettling and served to undermine confidence in, and therefore the stability of, the regime.

The last course, of open rebellion, was fraught with dangers. Despite this, certain Piagnoni, having little care for their own safety, adopted it. They did so in the spirit of Fra Benedetto Luschino, who declared that because, with Leo X, the Church had reached the nadir of corruption, God had repudiated the papacy and would shortly bring about its ruin. Everywhere, Fra Benedetto saw portents foretelling 'that God has decided to take the government of the Church out of the hands of the wicked, and to ruin and destroy the churches, convents, and dwellings of Babylonian Rome, to turn everything upside-down and to annihilate it for all time; merely preserving its name pro forma, without any supreme pontiff normally residing there'.[81] The Piagnoni rebels took heart from their conviction that God's wrath against the Medici regime in Florence was no less, and that He would thus bless their endeavours to unmake it. Theirs was the philosophy of Boscoli's confessor, Fra Cipriano da Pontassieve, who attested that rebellion against an unjust ruler was not only the Christian's right, but also his bounden duty.[82] Mindful of Savonarola's prophecy that the threatened tyranny would be of short duration, these Piagnoni bent themselves to the task of speeding its end.

Discounting the Boscoli–Capponi conspiracy in which Niccolò Valori was unwittingly implicated, there were three instances of a

[80] Valori, *Vita del Magnifico Lorenzo Vecchio de' Medici*, sig. fo. 4ᵛ: 'Era la virtù in pregio, il popolo in libertà, la nobiltà in honore & la città abbondantissima d'ogni bene'.

[81] Luschino, 'Vulnera diligentis', part III, fo. 58ʳ: 'che Dio vuol torre il governo ecclesiastico dalle mani de' captivi, et che vuole ruinare et disfare le chiese et conventi et habitationi della Romana babillonia et mandare ogni cosa sotto sopra et spegnerla per sempre, excepto che conservare pro forma il titulo di quella, senza che in epsa ordinariamente habiti più sommo pontefice alcuno'. Cf. fos. 52ᵛ–54ᵛ, 56ᵛ–57ᵛ, 58ᵛ.

[82] See above, pp. 237–8.

Piagnoni challenge to the power of the Medici in 1513. The men involved were Martino di Francesco Scarfi (or, dello Scarfa), Bartolomeo Redditi, and Francesco del Pugliese. Martino di Francesco Scarfi was the scion of a prominent Piagnone family which was well known for its anti-Medicean activities. His father had been *Gonfaloniere di Giustizia* in the *Signoria* which had turned against Piero de' Medici in November 1494, and was chosen as one of the twenty *Accoppiatori* on 2 December.[83] So notorious were Francesco Scarfi's sympathies that his family was among those which Piero de' Medici had planned to exterminate, had his plot of 1497 succeeded;[84] and Savonarola's arrest cast a temporary cloud over his political future.[85] His son Martino had carried on the family tradition. In 1500, as we have seen, together with another Piagnone, Tommaso di Paolantonio Soderini, he had conferred with leading *Arrabbiati* in the hope of devising a joint policy against the common Medicean enemy.[86] Now, on 22 January 1513, Martino came on trial before the *Otto di Guardia*.[87] Proceeded against 'in order to preserve the present excellent and peaceful government and regime of the Florentine people and for other just and compelling reasons',[88] he was punished by a severe fine and five years' exile: his return to Florence being conditional upon a unanimous vote by the *Otto di Guardia*.[89] The harshness of his sentence suggests that his infringement had not been a minor one. It may, in fact, have amounted to actual conspiracy: a possibility which is strengthened by the fact that on the day he was tried, two

[83] Francesco Guicciardini, *Storie fiorentine dal 1378 al 1509*, ed. R. Palmarocchi (Bari, 1931; fac. repr. 1968), 96, 106.

[84] Villari, *La storia di Girolamo Savonarola*, vol. ii. app., p. xxi.

[85] Ibid., pp. clvii, clix, cclxxvii, cclxxviii–xxix, cclxxxii; Parenti, *Istorie fiorentine*, 266; Francesco Cei, 'Cronaca', MS BNF II.V.147, p. 155.

[86] See above, p. 215.

[87] ASF Otto di Guardia, Ep. Rep. 155, fos. 15ᵛ–16ʳ; 230, fo. 99ʳ. See also Landucci, *Diario fiorentino*, 334 (where the date of condemnation, however, is incorrectly given as 24 Jan.).

[88] ASF Otto di Guardia, Ep. Rep. 155, fo. 15ᵛ: 'pro conservatione presentis optimi pacifici status et regiminis populi florentini et pluribus aliis iustis et rationalibus causis moti'.

[89] Ibid., fos. 15ᵛ–16ʳ. His fine was set at 3,000 florins, with the proviso that, if paid within eight days, it would be reduced by half. Martino took advantage of this: ASF Otto di Guardia, Ep. Rep. 230, fo. 99ʳ.

other men were also condemned by the *Otto di Guardia* on the same grounds.[90]

The plot engineered by Bartolomeo Redditi, whose dissemination of Savonarola's ideas brought him and his accomplices before the *Otto di Guardia* in June 1513,[91] caused much more of a stir. The trouble began on 6 June, when two friars of Ognissanti, Niccolò di Matteo d'Agostino and Lorenzo di Eugenio da Cigoli, together with one Giusto di Piero della Badessa, were seized by the *Otto di Guardia*.[92] They must have revealed, under torture,[93] the existence of a plot in which Bartolomeo Redditi and the Provost of Ognissanti, Fra Marco da Milano,[94] were implicated, since five days later, when next the *Otto di Guardia* met to deliberate upon the case, both were sentenced, along with those who had already been arraigned.[95] The terms were much the same as those of Martino Scarfi's condemnation, but with an additional charge of spreading inflammatory rumours detrimental to the well-being of the government.[96] Redditi's treatment was more severe than that of the others. While all were sentenced to exile, he alone was denied the option of having this punishment commuted to the payment of a fine instead. He was banished beyond the borders of the Florentine archdiocese, the period of exile being fixed at one year and its termination being dependent, as in the case of Martino Scarfi, upon the unanimous decision of the *Otto di Guardia*.[97]

'Under the guise of prophecy', Piero Parenti said of the participants in the Redditi plot, 'they foretold revolution in the city and

---

[90] Ibid. These men, with Martino Scarfi, were pardoned under the general amnesty which was declared when Leo X became Pope: see Cambi, *Istorie*, iii. 8, 13.

[91] Parenti, *Istorie fiorentine*, 301.

[92] ASF Otto di Guardia, Ep. Rep. 156, fo. 20ᵛ; Parenti, *Istorie fiorentine*, 301. Although Parenti gives della Badessa's Christian name as Michele, the archival sources are agreed in calling him Giusto di Piero.

[93] Parenti, *Istorie fiorentine*, 301.

[94] Almost certainly to be identified with Marco Bossio: see G. Tiraboschi, *Vetera Humiliatorum monumenta* (3 vols.; Milan, 1766), i. 284–5. On Bossio, formerly an anti-Savonarolan, see above, p. 150.

[95] ASF Otto di Guardia, Ep. Rep. 156, fos. 22ᵛ–23ʳ; 230, fo. 108ʳ⁻ᵛ.

[96] Ibid. 156, fo. 22ᵛ.

[97] Ibid., fos. 22ᵛ–23ʳ. The friars availed themselves of the option but Giusto di Piero della Badessa did not, and was thus exiled: ibid. 230, fo. 108ᵛ.

elsewhere.'[98] His view, that they concealed political aims under a religious guise, points to the factor which, more than any other, was to prove crucial in the Medici's eventual decision to take definitive action against the Piagnoni extremists: their distinctive combination of political and religious motives. That this combination was also present in the Redditi conspiracy is apparent even from the sparse evidence which has come down to us. Parenti's accusation recalls the official charge against the participants and suggests that the inflammatory rumours there mentioned may have been utterances of a prophetic sort. The involvement of ecclesiastics in the plot is another significant element, as is the fact that the geographical limits of Redditi's exile were defined by an ecclesiastical, and not a civil, boundary. The *Otto di Guardia*'s own awareness of the religious dimension is further attested by two other directives which they issued to the conspirators. On 4 July 1513, having apparently paid his fine, Fra Marco da Milano was ordered to remain in Florence to await the arrival of the new Archbishop, Giulio de' Medici, and Lorenzo de' Medici: an instruction which indicates that the highest ecclesiastical powers in Florence, no less than the civil,[99] had a concern in his case. On 10 May 1514, moreover, when Redditi's sentence of exile was due to be reviewed, he was told to hold himself in readiness for an appearance in June before the Archiepiscopal Curia, where he was to give an account of the facts of his case:[100] an order suggesting that the decision whether to end his period of banishment may actually have rested with Cardinal Giulio, Archbishop of Florence, and the ecclesiastical authorities. Since, on 3 July 1514, the *Otto di Guardia* voted unanimously against extending his term of exile, it would seem that he had agreed to meet whatever requirements may have been imposed upon him.[101]

---

[98] Parenti, *Istorie fiorentine*, 301: 'Sotto nome di profetie anuntiavano mutamento nella città et altrove.'

[99] ASF Otto di Guardia, Ep. Rep. 156, fo. 38ʳ⁻ᵛ.     [100] Ibid. 159, fo. 6ᵛ.

[101] Ibid., fo. 58ᵛ. The conflict of jurisdiction this reveals or at the very least the interference of members of the Medici family in Lorenzo's running of the government is emphasized by Leo X asking Lorenzo to release Giusto della Badessa from exile: Letter of Baldassarre da Pescia to Lorenzo, 18 Apr. 1514, ASF MAP 107, No. 10.

The case of Francesco di Filippo del Pugliese came before the *Otto di Guardia* later in 1513.[102] A rich merchant, he was undoubtedly one of the most committed Piagnoni activists of his day. In the 1490s, he had been a close confidant of Savonarola and an eager participant in every scheme afoot to strengthen the Piagnoni's position in government.[103] Such was his standing, both among the Piagnoni and in the wider world of international trade, that in March 1498 he had been entrusted by Savonarola with the delicate task of writing to the English King to solicit his support for Savonarola's proposed Church council, designed to depose Alexander VI.[104] At the time of Savonarola's fall, and notwithstanding the efforts on his behalf of his father-in-law, Domenico Bonsi, Florentine ambassador in Rome,[105] Francesco del Pugliese was tried along with the other prominent Piagnoni. He was sentenced to a heavy fine and disqualified from holding office for two years.[106] The fact that in 1513 he was once again up before the authorities shows that he had refused to be daunted by his earlier sufferings. For having uttered words dishonouring the Medicean state and government,[107] he was sentenced by the *Otto di Guardia* on 3 September to ten years' exile.[108] For the substance of these words,

---

[102] ASF Otto di Guardia, Ep. Rep. 157, fo. 3ʳ; see also Landucci, *Diario fiorentino*, 341, where the fact is reported with some inaccuracies; and Cambi, *Istorie*, iii. 28.

[103] Villari, *La storia di Girolamo Savonarola*, vol. ii, app., pp. cvi, clvii, clxxi, clxxxiii, ccii, ccxxii–ccxxx; and esp. p. ccxxii.

[104] Ibid. ii. 135.

[105] A. Gherardi, *Nuovi documenti e studi intorno a Girolamo Savonarola* (Florence, 1887; fac. repr. 1972), 254.

[106] Parenti, *Istorie fiorentine*, 275; but see also ASM Potenze estere, Firenze, 947, busta 3: where the fine is stated to be 1,500 florins and not 500, as mentioned by Parenti; and where, in addition, Francesco is forbidden to leave Florence for ten years. For further information on his later pro-Savonarolan activity see my '*Dell'Arte del Ben Morire*: The Piagnone Way of Death 1494–1545', *I Tatti Studies: Essays in the Renaissance*, 3 (1989), 58–9, 63–4 and appendix.

[107] ASF Balie, 43, fo. 198ʳ. On 7 Dec. 1515 the reasons for this sentence were restated by the *Balìa*, when reviewing his case prior to setting him free and absolving him from all liabilities.

[108] ASF Otto di Guardia, Ep. Rep. 157, fo. 3ʳ. For an interesting comment on Francesco del Pugliese's subsequent career, see O. Tommasini, *La vita e gli scritti di Niccolò Machiavelli* (2 vols.; vol. i: Rome, Turin, Florence, 1883; vol. ii: Rome, 1911), ii. 324 n. 1.

which had brought down the wrath of the authorities so heavily upon his head, we must turn to the chronicler Giovanni Cambi, who recounts of Francesco del Pugliese that

one day, whilst he was talking with some others, it happened that during their discussion one of them chanced to mention Lorenzo de' Medici, who was then, as a young man of 23, the city's leading citizen, and he said: 'Lorenzo the Magnificent', whereupon Francesco del Pugliese said: 'the Magnificent, my arse'; his comment was overheard by a nearby soldier who reported him to the *Otto*.[109]

With his foolhardy riposte, Francesco del Pugliese had not merely poured scorn upon Lorenzo's assumption of the title which had sat so well upon the shoulders of his illustrious predecessor and namesake, but had also called into question the Medici's right to rule.

From the treatment meted out to him and to the other malcontents, it is clear that the Medici were by now fully alert to the radical implications of Piagnone activity. Although eager to conciliate those who were willing to work alongside them, they were prepared to deal firmly, not to say ruthlessly, with any who proved recalcitrant. They were becoming increasingly conscious, furthermore, that public statements which were purportedly confined to religious issues could also have an underlying political significance, boding ill for the peaceful continuance of the regime. This was especially true of prophecies of the imminent chastisement and renovation of Christendom. As the centre from which such utterances had traditionally emanated, the convent of S. Marco was naturally a focus of official concern. Already, at the time of the

---

[109] Cambi, *Istorie*, iii. 28: 'essendo un dì a ragionare chon altri, acchadde, che ne' ragionamenti uno ebbe a nominare Lorenzo de' Medici, che in questo tenpo era il primo della Ciptà, giovane di 23 anni, et cholui disse: "el Magnifico Lorenzo"; et Francesco del Pugliese disse: "el Magnifico merda"; di che uno soldato ch'era quivi presso udì, et raportollo agli Otto'. The insult to his pride may explain why Lorenzo de' Medici, repeatedly asked by his mother to intervene with the *Otto di Guardia* on Francesco del Pugliese's behalf, protested his inability to influence the *Otto*: a rare instance of resistance, on his part, to her wishes: Alfonsina to Lorenzo, 16 Feb. 1514, and 23 Mar. 1514, ASF MAP 114, Nos. 57 and 82; and Letters of Lorenzo to Alfonsina 15 and 20 Feb. 1514 and 4 Mar. 1514; ibid., C. Strozz., ser. I, 3, fo. 43ʳ and ibid., MAP 141, fo. 40.

Boscoli–Capponi conspiracy, the friars there had been said to be under great suspicion.[110] The degree of this suspicion becomes apparent once we learn that Cardinal Giulio de' Medici had taken the extreme step of cultivating a spy there. A certain Fra Francesco kept him informed of the goings-on both within S. Marco itself and in the Florentine religious community at large.[111] Shortly afterwards, in a move much resented by the friars, Cardinal Giulio obtained the right for himself or his Vicar to conduct a visitation of the convent whenever they saw fit.[112] It was an unprecedented move—permission for which must have been granted by Leo X—which violated the convent's privileges and immunities and which could only have been set in train by the Medici's determination to discourage subversive religious and political activities within its walls. A further effect of the initiative was to frighten off Piagnoni supporters who had looked to S. Marco for spiritual and political inspiration and who, in exchange, had rewarded the convent with alms and endowments.[113] Cardinal Giulio replied to the remonstrances of Fra Giovanni Maria Canigiani, Vicar-General of the Tusco-Roman Congregation, with the insidious argument:

Be sure that we love your Order and the preservation of your privileges as though they were our own, because we have always felt a special love and zeal for your house and we wish to increase and augment it. However, we feel that you have no cause to resent this, since it is done for your good and for your good name; moreover, we and our Vicar are carrying out this visitation as special apostolic legates and not as Ordinary and Archbishop of Florence—so that you and yours will always be able to use this argument with future archbishops should they wish to conduct such a visitation.[114]

[110] Luca della Robbia, *Recitazione del caso di Pietro Paolo Boscoli e di Agostino Capponi, ASI*, 1st ser. 1 (1842), 287.

[111] Letter of Giulio de' Medici to Lorenzo, 20 Dec. 1513, ASF MAP 66, No. 303. Almost certain to have been the erstwhile Piagnone Fra Francesco de' Medici, who also kept Goro Gheri informed and who advised him not to appoint Fra Filippo Strozzi as Master-General of the Dominican Order because he was an opponent of the Medici: Goro Gheri, 'Copialettere', vol. iv, fo. 225$^{r-v}$.

[112] Letter of Giulio de' Medici to Fra Giovanni Maria Canigiani, 10 Aug. 1514, BMLF S. Marco 920, fo. 111$^{r-v}$.

[113] Polizzotto, '*Dell'Arte del Ben Morire*', 67 and n. 102.

[114] BMLF S. Marco 920, fo. 111$^r$: 'Che possiate esser certi che noi amiamo la religione vostra et la conservatione dei vostri privilegi come cosa propria perchè

On the very day that Francesco del Pugliese was condemned, moreover, a ban on religious confraternities was promulgated.[115] Unlike previous legislation on the subject, this ban forbade the meetings of *all* confraternities, not merely those which lacked government authorization. It excepted only boys' confraternities: and stipulated, even here, that their members must not be over 16 years of age.[116] Unprecedented, too, were the penalties prescribed for transgressors. From a fine for a first offence, these rose sharply to five years' exile, together with additional punishments left at the discretion of the *Otto di Guardia*, for a second.[117] This ban was to be the first of many. Identical prohibitions were promulgated and renewed at regular intervals until 6 March 1527: the eve of the fall of the regime.[118] Both the promulgation of these bans and the punishment of the Piagnoni malcontents which preceded them plainly demonstrate how alive the Medici had become to the possibility that religion could function as a political weapon. It was inevitable that, in their new mood, they would act swiftly and decisively against any and all utterances which appeared to endanger the stability of their regime.

To this extremely unsettled situation, a further irritant was now added: Fra Francesco da Montepulciano, one of twelve Franciscan Conventuals who, having joined the stricter Amadeite rule, decided to spread word throughout Italy of the impending chastisement of the Church.[119] After visiting Florence in September 1513,

sempre havemo portato peculiare affectione et zelo ad questa casa et siamo per accrescerla et ampliarla. Tutta volta ne pare che di questo non vi havete da risentire perchè si fa pro bono vostro et splendor vite vostre et noi e nostro vicario facciamo tal visita come speciali commissarii apostolici et non come Ordinario et Archiepiscopo di Firenze et così poterete et poteranno li vostri sempre rispondere alli futuri archiepiscopi che presumessero fare simile visita.'

[115] ASF Otto di Guardia, Ep. Rep. 223 (Minute di bandi: 19 Feb. 1512/13–6 May 1527), fo. 26ʳ.

[116] Ibid.

[117] Ibid. To find an earlier prohibition of such severity, it is necessary to go as far back as the decree against confraternities which was issued on 19 Oct. 1419 and is published in L. Mehus, *Dell'origine, progresso, abusi e riforma delle confraternite laicali* (Florence, 1785), 141ff., and esp. 146–9.

[118] ASF Otto di Guardia, Ep. Rep. 223, fos. 41ʳ⁻ᵛ, 89ʳ, 100ʳ, 198ʳ.

[119] On Fra Francesco da Montepulciano, see Parenti, *Istorie fiorentine*, 302–3; Cambi, *Istorie*, iii. 37–9; Cerretani, 'Storia in dialogo', fo. 166ʳ⁻ᵛ; [id.], 'Ricordi

he returned in November to preach a series of sermons for Advent.[120] Delivered in the Franciscan church of Sta Croce, these sermons proved highly inflammatory. While their substance was undoubtedly Amadeite in origin,[121] Fra Francesco was influenced also by the Piagnone strain of apocalyptic thought. The prophecies of Amadeus Menez de Sylva, on which he drew, had been extensively reworked by Giorgio Benigno.[122] In addition, Fra Francesco placed himself in the Savonarolan tradition. When castigating Florence for her sins in the course of his sermons, he made particular reference to the previous eighteen years, implying that her citizens had taken no notice of the adjurations to reform which Savonarola had then voiced.[123] To his mind, this made their error all the worse; and would result, he declared, in a heavier punishment than any hitherto conceived. 'Would that you had never been born, Florence', he cried in his final sermon, 'would that you had never been born. O my beloved people, I have told you many times: those who say you are blessed lead you astray.'[124]

This last sermon, which caused the greatest stir of all, has survived in a number of versions. The many manuscript copies and

---

storici fiorentini', fos. 173ᵛ–174ʳ; Pitti, *Dell'Istoria fiorentina*, 112–13 (derived, in the main, however, from Bartolomeo Cerretani's 'Storia in dialogo'); Landucci, *Diario fiorentino*, 343–4; J. Schnitzer, *Savonarola* (2 vols.; Milan, 1931), ii. 441, 445; Weinstein, *Savonarola and Florence*, 348–9; Vasoli, 'L'attesa della nuova era', 406–7.

[120] Cerretani, 'Ricordi storici fiorentini', fo. 173ᵛ.

[121] A fact recognized by contemporaries: cf. Cerretani, 'Storia in dialogo', fo. 166ᵛ; 'Ricordi storici fiorentini', fo. 173ᵛ.

[122] See above, pp. 204–5.

[123] Francesco da Montepulciano, *Predica*, in *Profetie certissime, stupende et admirabili dell'Antichristo, et innumerabili mali al mondo (se presto non si emenderà) preparati, et donde hanno da venire, et dove hanno da cominciare* [Venice? 1530?], fo. 39ʳ. The volume was dedicated to the Venetian Doge, Andrea Gritti, and edited by Paulo Angelo, on whom see M. Reeves, *The Influence of Prophecy in the Later Middle Ages* (Oxford, 1969), 264 n. 3; and 432 and F. Secret, 'Paulus Angelus descendant des Empereurs de Byzance et la Prophétie du Pape Angélique', *Rinascimento*, 2nd ser. 2 (1962), 211–24. The *Predica*, which occupies fos. 32ʳ–40ʳ, has a preface by the Franciscan Fra Francesco da Lanciuole, then Inquisitor in Florence.

[124] Francesco da Montepulciano, *Predica*, fo. 38ʳ: 'O Fiorenza non fusti mai nata, non fusti mai nata. Io ti ho detto altre volte popule meus qui te dicunt beatum, te seducunt.' See also fo. 39ʳ⁻ᵛ.

two printed editions which have come down to us—one of them publishing the sermon as it was taken down by Lorenzo Violi, the transcriber of Savonarola's sermons—attest to the amount of attention the sermon received.[125] In it, with considerable daring, Fra Francesco applied the well-known apocalyptic themes of chastisement and tribulation to the contemporary scene. Concentrating especially upon Florence and Rome, which, he predicted, would suffer most of all, he painted a terrifying picture of the divine punishment about to be visited upon an erring world. 'That ordeal will be such that no greater has been seen since the world began', he warned.[126] 'I tell you that the first trial will be the sentencing of your city of Florence to be destroyed by fire.'[127] Such sentiments were unlikely to commend themselves to a ruling power striving at all costs to bring stability to a newly won state. When combined, as they were, with precise references of a highly circumstantial sort, the mixture became explosive.

'I say unto you, rulers,' Fra Francesco declaimed, not mincing matters, 'I say unto you whom it concerns: order processions to be made, and make good the errors which you can make good. Otherwise, I tell you that God has sworn to destroy palaces and to bring all things to ruin.'[128] As this final, desperate appeal indicates, he had no hesitation in placing the blame for the oncoming tribulation on the present heads of state, both spiritual and temporal. Three signs, he said, would usher in the divine visitation: first, the near-collapse

---

[125] For examples of manuscript versions, see BNF Magl. XXXV, 136; BRF 1251; BRF 2606; BRF 2620; BMF A.LXXXII. The printed version of Violi's transcription is entitled *Predica di F. Francesco da Monte Pulciano de' Frati Minori Conventuali di San Francesco. Fatta in S. Croce di Firenze, a dì XVIII di Dicembre 1513. Raccolta dalla viva voce del Predicatore, per Ser Lorenzo Vivuoli notaio Fiorentino, mentre che predicava* (Florence, 1590). Because this version would appear to have undergone various alterations before printing, it has been used only for purposes of comparison.

[126] Francesco da Montepulciano, *Predica*, fo. 34[r]: 'El sarà tale questa tribulatione, che non fu mai udita la maggiore dal principio del mondo, infin' ad hora.'

[127] Ibid., fo. 35[r]: 'Io vi annontio per la prima, che la città vostra di Fiorenza è sententiata al fuoco.'

[128] Ibid., fo. 39[v]: 'A voi capi dico, a voi che si appartiene dico, fate far processioni, et emendate gli errori che potete emendare. Altrimenti vi dico che ha giurato Iddio, di mandare a terra palazzi, et rovinar ogni cosa.'

of the power of the French King;[129] secondly, the rise of the house
of Aragon and the success of a descendant of the Emperor
Frederick;[130] and thirdly, the creation by that descendant of an
antipope who would cause a great schism in Christendom.[131] The
allusion to recent events in Italy, the aspersions cast on the
Medici's foreign policy as administered from Florence and from
Rome, were unmistakable. Since Florence and the papacy had
abandoned the French, favouring instead an alliance with Spain
and the Empire, it followed that both had contributed in no small
way to bringing about the chastisement of Christendom. In the
sight of God, therefore, they were especially blameworthy; and
none more so than their leaders. The faithful had been left to fend
for themselves, Fra Francesco lamented; adding, in a clear allusion
to the recent banning of confraternities in Florence, that 'we no
longer care about brotherhoods and confraternities; we have forgotten how to perform charitable acts'.[132] 'Lady Simony governs all
things', he went on, condemning the spiritual ministrations of the
Church.[133] For true believers, there could be only one course. 'Flee
unto the mountains', was his advice to each of them.[134] Evoking an
image which Savonarola had popularized two decades before, he
went on to warn his hearers that already 'God has placed a sharp
sword in the hands of one who will pierce the mountains as well as
men's bodies. And He has told him: "Go on your way, and do
not spare anyone, neither friars nor priests, neither women nor
children."'[135]

---

[129] Ibid., fo. 35$^v$.

[130] Ibid. In the other printed version of the sermon, from Violi's transcription,
these two points have been combined into one, namely: 'quando vedrete quello
che sarà della casa d'Aragona, e di Federigo Imperadore dominare quasi per tutto',
so that the scion thus identified tallies exactly with Charles V: an interesting
instance of the reworking of the Violi version: *Predica di F. Francesco da Monte
Pulciano . . . Raccolta dalla viva voce del Predicatore, per Ser Lorenzo Vivuoli*, 8.
For a discussion of the prophecies concerning the Emperors Frederick, see
Reeves, *The Influence of Prophecy in the Later Middle Ages*, 333–46.

[131] Francesco da Montepulciano, *Predica*, fo. 35$^r$.

[132] Ibid., fo. 38: 'non si curiamo più di fraternita, nè di compagnie, si è
dimenticato ogni ben fare'.

[133] Ibid.: 'Madonna simonia tira ogni cosa'. See also fos. 36$^{r-v}$, 39$^r$.

[134] Ibid., fo. 36$^{r-v}$: 'Fuggi ai monti.'

[135] Ibid., fo. 39$^v$: 'Iddio ha dato la spada in mano a uno tagliente da ogni banda,

There was nothing the Florentines liked more. 'There is in this city of ours, which is a magnet for all the charlatans in the world,' wrote Machiavelli to Francesco Vettori, reporting the news of Fra Francesco, 'a Franciscan friar who is a half-hermit and who, to gain greater influence with his preaching, claims to be a prophet.'[136] While we need not share Machiavelli's cynicism as to Fra Francesco's motives in assuming the prophet's mantle, it is nevertheless true that his prognostications were eminently suited to the Florentines' passion for fire and brimstone. To Vettori, the fault lay in the city's stars. 'Florence is under the influence of a planet which makes those kinds of men flock there', he commented resignedly to Machiavelli in his reply, 'where they find a ready audience.'[137] For whatever reason, thousands flocked to hear Fra Francesco's sermons, which, as Iacopo Pitti said, awakened memories of 'Savonarola's prophecies in all his disciples'.[138] But they did more than merely listen. Faced with the prospect of imminent destruction, as delineated by Fra Francesco, they saw little point in continuing their daily toil. 'The people were terrified', wrote Parenti, 'and they virtually ceased all activity at the thought of so much destruction about to befall them.'[139] For the opponents of the regime, the prophecies were a particular boon. They applied them directly to the existing regime, understanding Fra Francesco's words to portend the Medici's fall from power.[140] From the sermons, many deduced that some new fate was about to befall

che passerà i monti non che i corpi. Et gli ha detto: Va via, et non haver rispetto ad alcuno, nè a frati, nè a preti, nè a donne, nè a fanciulli.' Cf. with Villari, *La storia di Girolamo Savonarola*, i. 202–3; Ridolfi, *Vita*, i. 84.

[136] Niccolò Machiavelli to Francesco Vettori, 19 Dec. 1513, in Niccolò Machiavelli, *Lettere*, ed. F. Gaeta (Milan, 1961), 308: 'E' si trova in questa nostra città, calamita di tutti i ciurmatori del mondo un frate di S. Francesco, che è mezzo romito, el quale, per haver più credito nel predicare, fa professione di profeta.'

[137] Francesco Vettori to Niccolò Machiavelli, 24 Dec. 1513, in Machiavelli, *Lettere*, 313: 'Firenze è fondato sotto un planeta che simili huomini vi corrono e sonvi uditi volentieri.'

[138] Pitti, *Dell'Istoria fiorentina*, 112: 'le profetie del Savonarola in tutti i suoi divoti'. See also Cerretani, 'Storia in dialogo', fo. 166ᵛ.

[139] Parenti, *Istorie fiorentine*, 303: 'Isbigottinne il popolo et le faccende quasi allentavano pensandosi, che tanta rovina dovessi venire.'

[140] Pitti, *Dell'Istoria fiorentina*, 112.

Florence: 'an outcome', as Parenti observed, 'desired by many, if by such means the government which did not please them was overthrown'.[141]

Here was matter more than sufficient to arouse the concern of the Medici. As Pitti succinctly put it, the various responses occasioned by the sermons 'gave the rulers much food for thought'.[142] Although Lorenzo, in Florence, was to remain convinced, throughout the brief duration of the crisis, that he was fully in control of the situation and that his elders were overstating its importance,[143] they were in no doubt as to its gravity. Cardinal Giulio de' Medici and Leo X, both in Rome at this time, reacted promptly and with great earnestness. Only two days after Fra Francesco had preached his last, climactic sermon on 18 December, Cardinal Giulio was aware that something untoward had occurred in Florence. On 20 December, having already received an outline of the case from his informer in S. Marco, he wrote to him, via Lorenzo, requesting further information and urging him to confer with Lorenzo on what had best be done.[144] Before he had received a reply, he was apprised of the highly controversial content of the sermons by worried Miceans in Florence,[145] and wrote again to Lorenzo, on 22 December, expressing indignation that he had told him nothing of all this and warning of the potential dangers. In a passage which reveals an acute awareness of the threat which religious radicals could pose to political stability, Giulio stated,

and if it were not that we have seen what trustworthy men have written and heard the exact words which the said friar has used, we should be incapable of believing them, since they strike us as so scandalous and grave. Such things, which can generate confusion both in the spiritual and

---

[141] Parenti, *Istorie fiorentine*, 303: 'la quale cosa molti haveano cara, se per tale mezzo lo stato, quale non piaceva loro, si mutassi'.

[142] Pitti, *Dell'Istoria fiorentina*, 112: 'davano assai che pensare ai reggenti'.

[143] Lorenzo de' Medici to Giulio de' Medici, 24 Dec. 1513, ASF C. Strozz., ser. I, 3, fo. 29r; partially published in O. Tommasini, *La vita e gli scritti di Niccolò Machiavelli*, vol. ii. app., p. 987.

[144] Giulio de' Medici to Lorenzo, 20 Dec. 1513, ASF MAP 66, No. 303.

[145] Cf. Parenti, *Istorie fiorentine*, 303; and Cambi, *Istorie*, iii. 39.

temporal spheres, must always be observed and properly dealt with at the very beginning, because they often cause trouble as they increase.[146]

Adjuring Lorenzo to keep his hand on the bridle in future, Giulio informed him that Leo X was in the process of drafting a brief to the *Signoria* on the question.[147]

In fact, the brief was issued on the same day. Addressed to the Florentines, it condemned Fra Francesco's sermons and all those who had aided him in delivering them. The Archiepiscopal Vicar was requested to arrest their author and see to it that he was sent to Rome under good guard; the *Signoria*, to give the Vicar every assistance in fulfilling this command.[148] Before it could be carried out, however, Fra Francesco died. He had apparently been ill when preaching the sermons, and, weakened by the effort, and especially by the last sermon, he died a fortnight later, on 31 December.[149] This episode thus ended on an inconclusive note. Far from inconclusive, however, was the mass demonstration which accompanied the exequies accorded to Fra Francesco. As he lay in state, Cerretani recounts, all the people rushed to kiss the body and venerate it. Finally, because the situation was threatening to get out of hand, his body was removed and buried by stealth.[150] After such a display, there could be no doubt about how the Medici would react on another occasion.

In the ensuing two years, the unpopular pro-Spanish policy to which Fra Francesco had alluded in the sermon of 18 December 1513 remained a lively issue in Florentine politics. Much to the dismay of the majority of Florentines, and even some Mediceans,

---

[146] Giulio de' Medici to Lorenzo, 22 Dec. 1513, ASF MAP 66, No. 303: 'et se non fusse che habbia visto le lettere di homini di fede et inteso le parole formali che il decto frate ha usate non potremo crederle, tanto ci paiono scandalose e gravi. Queste simil cose che possono ne lo spirituale et nel temporale generare confusione si vuole sempre ne' principi observarle et curarle bene, perchè spesso, quando pigliono augmento, danno qualche fastidio.'

[147] Ibid.

[148] ASV Arm. XXXIX, 30 (Leo X: Brevia ad Principes), fo. 161ʳ.

[149] Cerretani, 'Storia in dialogo', fo. 166ᵛ; cf. Cambi, *Istorie*, iii. 39, for confirmation that the date of death was indeed 31 Dec. and not, as stated by Landucci, 18 Dec. (the date of the last sermon): *Diario fiorentino*, 343.

[150] Cerretani, 'Storia in dialogo', fo. 166ᵛ; L. Wadding, *Annales Minorum seu Trium Ordinum*, xiv (Rome, 1735), xv. 448.

the government continued to follow Leo X's lead in foreign affairs. Because it flew in the face of the traditionally pro-French Florentine attitude, this policy was a constant source of discontent.[151] Feeling was intensified when Florence joined the anti-French league in February 1515 and exacerbated by the resurgence of French power in Italy which followed the accession of Francis I.[152] Since it was hoped that Francis I's Italian expedition would result in the overthrow of the Medici, his progress was greeted with rejoicing by the anti-Mediceans in general and the Piagnoni in particular.[153] Both Lorenzo and the *Otto di Pratica* attempted to alert Leo X to the dangers which the prosecution of his policy represented to the security of the Florentine regime.[154] Anti-Mediceans in Florence were even said to be in contact with the French king and to be encouraging him to emulate his predecessor in freeing the city from tyranny.[155] The parallel with the situation as it had obtained in 1494 was too close for comfort. As Giovanni Rucellai, the anti-Savonarolan spokesman, remarked in Cerretani's *Storia in dialogo*, the prospect of a French invasion filled the Mediceans with terror.[156] Such was the unrest and the fear generated that the Mediceans were forced to tighten security measures and to strengthen the city guard. In addition, they secretly introduced men-at-arms to defend the Medici from possible attack, billeting them in S. Lorenzo and in Pierfrancesco de' Medici's palace.[157] It is not surprising, therefore, that the regime reacted

---

[151] Cerretani, 'Storia in dialogo', fo. 167ʳ, where, speaking of the projected Italian expedition of Louis XI in Dec. 1514, Giovanni Rucellai states, 'udivasi questa passata in Firenze molto volentieri sperando un altro moto, come dal Re Carlo'.

[152] Devonshire-Jones, *Francesco Vettori*, 109 ff.; ead., 'Lorenzo de' Medici, Duca d'Urbino "Signore" of Florence?', 301–4.

[153] Cerretani, 'Storia in dialogo', fos. 170ᵛ, 172ᵛ; cf. Cambi, *Istorie*, iii. 51.

[154] Devonshire-Jones, *Francesco Vettori*, 113–15; ead., 'Lorenzo de' Medici, Duca d'Urbino "Signore" of Florence?', 302–3; see also the letter of the *Otto di Pratica* to Leo X printed in H. Reinhard, *Lorenzo von Medici, Herzog von Urbino 1492–1515* (Freiburg, 1915), app., Doct. II, pp. 89–90.

[155] Letter of Pietro Ardinghelli to Alfonsina Orsina de' Medici, 22 Aug. 1515, in ibid., app., Doct. III, pp. 90–1; Parenti, 'Istorie fiorentine', MS BNF II.IV.171, fo. 119ᵛ.

[156] Cerretani, 'Storia in dialogo', fo. 170ᵛ.

[157] Letter of Bernardus Fiamminghus to Lorenzo de' Medici, 3 Sept. 1515, ASF MAP 105, No. 159.

with great severity to the report that the Piagnone Bartolomeo Pandolfini had added to the unrest by arguing, on the strength of letters received from his brother Francesco, who was then Florentine orator in France, that the French invasion was imminent.[158] For having criticized governmental policy, Bartolomeo was barred from public office for five years.[159]

The religious sphere was equally unsettled. Taking—albeit with greater circumspection—the same line as Fra Francesco da Montepulciano, various preachers helped to keep Florence in a state of constant turmoil. In July 1514, for instance, the Tuscan Provincial of the Carmelite Order, no less, proclaimed that the promised reform of the Church was imminent and endeavoured to demonstrate that Leo X was the Angelic Pope: a suggestion which was greeted, however, with open incredulity.[160] Meanwhile, other preachers were voicing similar views: most of them with greater caution than a certain friar of Sta Maria Novella who, having foretold the impending punishment of the Church in the customary manner, was ordered by the Archiepiscopal Vicar in December 1514 to stop preaching forthwith.[161]

While the authorities kept a watchful eye on these preachers, their chief interest lay with the Piagnoni, whom they held accountable for the political and religious turmoil which constantly afflicted Florence. From late 1514, it is clear that they were taking a progressively harder line with them. For this intensification of anti-Piagnoni feeling, Galeotto de' Medici and later Goro Gheri, who acted as Lorenzo's deputies in Florence, were in large part responsible. Whereas Lorenzo was unconvinced, if not totally unaware, that the Piagnoni constituted a serious threat to Florentine stability, as his seniors in Rome and his supporters closer to hand insisted, Galeotto and Gheri were far more receptive to the adjura-

[158] Letters of Galeotto de' Medici to Lorenzo, 27, 29 Dec. 1514, ASF MAP 116, Nos. 627 and 629; Letter of Zanobi Pace, chancellor to the *Otto di Guardia*, to Lorenzo de' Medici, 1 Jan. 1515, ibid., No. 12. The printed catalogue mistakenly attributes the letter to Zanobi di Nofri degli Acciaiuoli. On Bartolomeo, who had signed the petition of 1497, see Villari, *La storia di Girolamo Savonarola*, vol. ii, app., p. ccxxviii.

[159] ASF Otto di Guardia, 230, fo. 155ʳ.

[160] Parenti, *Istorie fiorentine*, 304–5.          [161] Ibid. 305.

tions of the *amici* and were thus prepared to take a far more uncompromising stand. The difference between them is reflected in
their respective attitudes towards Girolamo Benivieni's candidature for the post of *Officiale di Studio* in early December iber 1514.
Writing to Lorenzo on 2 December, Galeotto signified his and the
*amici*'s disapproval of Benivieni's 'piangnoneria' and of his connections with Jacopo Salviati:[162] considerations of little account to
Lorenzo, who replied that the appointment would nevertheless
meet with his full approval.[163] With Lorenzo absent in Rome,
however, Galeotto's view prevailed, and Benivieni was not appointed.[164] For his firm stand on such matters, Galeotto was
warmly praised by the Medicean stalwarts, who spoke highly of his
conduct in office.[165] During his period as deputy, the Piagnoni's
activities came under much closer scrutiny. In July 1514 Domenico
Cecchi was arraigned before the *Signoria* to give an account of his
activities.[166] Later in the year it was the turn of Ubertino Risaliti,
Giorgio Benigno's Florentine friend and correspondent. Dismissed
from his position of *Provveditore dell'Arte della Lana*, Risaliti was
subsequently accused of embezzlement and, despite the entreaties
of highly placed relatives, was condemned on 15 January 1515 to
have his hand cut off and to be imprisoned in the *Stinche* and
barred from public office for life.[167]

By far the most sinister case of manipulation of the judicial
process to ruin prominent Piagnoni occurred the following year
during the governorship of Goro Gheri. On this occasion, the
chosen victim was Tommaso Tosinghi, who, as we have seen, had
earned the Mediceans' undying hatred for his part in the execution

---

[162] Galeotto de' Medici to Lorenzo, 2 Dec. 1514, ASF MAP 116, No. 501.

[163] Lorenzo de' Medici to Galeotto, 6–8 Dec. 1514, ASF MAP 141, fo. 82[r].

[164] Cambi, *Istorie*, iii. 53; Scipione Ammirato, *Istorie fiorentine*, ed. L.
Scarabelli, vi and vii (Florence, 1853), vi. 302.

[165] Cerretani, 'Storia in dialogo', fo. 171[r]. It is further indicative of Galeotto's
more suspicious attitude towards the Piagnoni that he began at this time to warn
Lorenzo of the machinations of Jacopo Salviati and Lanfredino Lanfredini against
him: see above, pp. 252–3.

[166] ASF Signori e Collegi, Deliberazioni Ord. Aut. 116, fo. 77[r].

[167] Ibid., Arte della Lana, Partiti, atti e sentenze, 250, fos. 3[v]–5[r]; ibid., MAP
116, No. 56: Letter of Galeotto to Lorenzo, 15 Jan. 1515. See also Cambi, *Istorie*,
iii. 59–60; Ammirato, *Istorie fiorentine*, vi. 303.

of the five conspirators against the Republic in 1497.[168] Accused of having unlawfully taken possession of land rightfully belonging to his wards, Tommaso was forced, first, into a highly damaging agreement and later, by a decree of the *Otto di Guardia*, was deprived of the disputed possession and fined a total of 400 florins.[169] Tommaso's indignation at this sentence was justified.[170] We now know that Gheri had been behind the whole attack. Acting in accordance with his stated principle that to strengthen the regime, the supporters (*amici*) must be favoured and the enemies ruined,[171] Gheri had not only pressed the charges, but had also seen to it that Tommaso's adversaries were encouraged to proceed with them and were assured of the regime's assistance.[172] The outcome was all the more pleasing in that the *Otto di Guardia* had reversed a legal decision issued by the equally hated anti-Medicean Giovanvettorio Soderini and, above all, had caused a break between Tommaso and Jacopo Salviati, one of the members of the *Otto di Guardia*, who, though reluctant to find against Tommaso, had been urged by Gheri to pass sentence against him.[173] Boasting of his success, Gheri revealed to both Lorenzo and Alfonsina that he was planning another and even more damaging attack against Tommaso.[174] That nothing came of this was perhaps due to the fact that Jacopo Salviati and the Medici themselves intervened to stop him, as Gheri had feared throughout.[175]

The person who most alarmed the Medici in this period was the self-styled friar, Don Teodoro.[176] And in his case, they were able to

[168] See above, pp. 213, 256.

[169] Goro Gheri, 'Copialettere', vol. i, fos. 209ʳ, 210–211ʳ; Tommaso Tosinghi ['Vita'], fos. 128ᵛ–129ʳ.

[170] Ibid., fo. 129ʳ.

[171] Goro Gheri, 'Copialettere', vol. i, fo. 168ʳ; but cf. also fo. 187ʳ.

[172] Ibid., fos. 178ʳ, 187ʳ⁻ᵛ.

[173] Ibid., fos. 209ʳ, 210ʳ; Tommaso Tosinghi ['Vita'], fo. 129ʳ, where Tommaso relates how he had not been able to restrain himself from approaching Jacopo and asking for an explanation.

[174] Ibid., fos. 209ʳ⁻ᵛ, and 224ʳ.  [175] Ibid., fos. 211ʳ, 211ᵛ–212ʳ.

[176] On Don Teodoro, who gave his full name as Teodoro di Giovanni, see Parenti, *Istorie fiorentine*, 305–7; Landucci, *Diario fiorentino*, 349; Cerretani, 'Storia in dialogo', fos. 168ʳ–169ᵛ; 'Ricordi storici fiorentini', fo. 179ʳ⁻ᵛ; Cambi, *Istorie*, iii. 60–2; Letter of Pietro Delfin to Iacobo di Oderzo, 9 Mar. 1515, printed in J. Schnitzer, *Peter Delfin* (Munich, 1925), app. I, pp. 364–5; D. Moreni,

bring to bear upon him all the spiritual and temporal weapons which the premature demise of Fra Francesco da Montepulciano had deprived them of using a year before. Don Teodoro had entered the Camaldolese convent of Sta Maria degli Angeli at the age of 12 and had later moved to the Olivetan convent of S. Miniato al Monte, where he made his profession and remained for eight years. At this point, his career, which had so far been unexceptionable, abruptly changed direction. Tiring of monastic seclusion, he abandoned the Olivetan habit and fled his convent, proceeding to lead a wandering life which led him all over central Italy and involved him in a variety of secular occupations ranging from tailor to mercenary soldier. Eventually finding his way back to Florence, he unlawfully assumed the habit of a Camaldolese friar and spent his time in various convents of his adopted Order, remaining, ultimately, at the convent of S. Felice in Piazza. Here he began preaching in a prophetic vein and gathered round him a substantial number of followers. His teaching quickly aroused the concern of the authorities, who were keeping him under close surveillance from the beginning of 1514. When his activities became intolerable, he was arraigned before the Archiepiscopal Tribunal. This occurred on 12 January 1515. After several days of examination by the Archiepiscopal Vicar and the Canons of Sta Maria del Fiore, Don Teodoro broke down and confessed. He was thereupon forced to sign a written confession and to make a public abjuration of his sins. This abjuration took place on 11 February, before an immense crowd, in the cathedral of Sta Maria del Fiore. So enraged was the populace, we are told, by the confession of his manifold sins that the armed guards of the *Otto di Guardia* were able to protect him only with great difficulty. He was sentenced to ten years' imprisonment: to be

---

*Continuazione delle memorie istoriche dell'Ambrosiana R. Basilica di S. Lorenzo* (2 vols.; Florence, 1804–17), ii. 511 n. 2 (but the work from which a long extract is printed here, which Moreni considered to be an anonymous dialogue, is in fact Bartolomeo Cerretani's 'Storia in dialogo'); Cosimo Favilla, 'Flagellum pseudoprophetarum', MS BAV Vat. Lat. 3636, fos. 41ʳ, 64ʳ–70ʳ. See also the excellent study by A. Prosperi, 'Il monaco Teodoro: Note su un processo fiorentino del 1515', *Critica storica*, 12 (1975), 71–101, who also publishes the text of the *Processo* and the additional fifteen charges levelled at Don Teodoro after his escape. In my discussion, however, I will cite from the original documents.

served in the gaol of S. Miniato al Monte, the convent from which he had originally fled.[177] Immediately after his abjuration, his confession, witnessed by a long list of persons both ecclesiastical and lay, was rushed into print, together with a lengthy preamble explaining why it had been necessary to proceed against him and a series of prohibitions promulgated by the Archiepiscopal Vicar and intended to prevent a recurrence of the errors into which Don Teodoro and those who followed him had fallen.[178]

From these records, the substance of Don Teodoro's teaching can be readily ascertained. It was, inevitably, prophetic in content and was founded, moreover, on the teaching of Savonarola, to whom Don Teodoro publicly professed indebtedness and whose sanctity and divine inspiration he upheld. He claimed, in fact, to be directed by revelations from Savonarola.[179] In his printed confession he was made to recall how he told his followers that Savonarola 'had appeared to me and revealed to me great things concerning the Church's renewal . . . namely, that the princes would come forth from all four corners of the world, from the East, West, North, and South, and they would slaughter all priests and friars, together with the Pope and every Christian, except for those who followed this Angelic Pope, since God had decided to save the latter and use them for the renewal of this Church; which Church I said would no longer hold temporal dominion'.[180] As well as expounding the familiar themes of chastisement and renewal, however, Don Teodoro dared to develop arguments of an extremely radical sort, which

---

[177] *Processo di don Theodoro Monacho che si faceva chiamare Papa Angelico* [Florence, 1515], fos. [2]ᵛ–[6]ᵛ. The existence of this pamphlet was revealed by L. von Pastor, *Zur Beurtheilung Savonarolas († 1498)* (Freiburg, 1898), 63 n. 2; and id., *Geschichte der Papste*, iii (Freiburg, 1899), 168 n. 1, cf. *Storia dei Papi* (2nd Italian edn.), tr. A. Mercati, iii (Rome, 1959), 193. I have used the copy in the British Library.

[178] For the preamble, see *Processo di don Teodoro*, fos. [1]ᵛ–[2]ᵛ; for the confession, ibid., fos. [2]ᵛ–[7]ʳ; and for the prohibitions, ibid., fos. [7]ᵛ–[8]ᵛ.

[179] Ibid., fos. [2]ᵛ, [4]ʳ⁻ᵛ, [5]ʳ, [6]ʳ.

[180] Ibid., fos. [4]ʳ–[5]ʳ: 'mi era apparso et havevami revelate gran cose di questa renovatione della Chiesa . . . cioè che si moverebbono li principi di quattro parte del mondo ab oriente occidente et septentrione ac meridie et amazeriano tucti e' preti et frati con el papa et tutti li christiani excepti quelli che aderivano a questo papa angelico imperochè Dio voleva salvare quelli et di epsi rinovar questa chiesa; la quale chiesa dicevo che non haverebbe più dominio temporale'.

hitherto had been no more than implicit in Piagnoni polemic. He contended, for example, that the Church, once renewed, would be stripped of its wealth and would return to the saintly poverty and simplicity of the apostolic Church: an assertion which carried with it a strong condemnation of the present worldly estate of the Church and its ministry.[181] He claimed that he was himself that Angelic Pope who was to play a leading role in the coming changes: thus calling into question not only the credentials of the present incumbent of S. Peter's Chair but also his continued tenure of that exalted position.[182] Teodoro's prophetic message was surrounded with all the trappings which had come to be characteristic of such apostolates as his. He claimed to have received revelations from Heaven, as well as from Savonarola, and to be able to perform miracles; he asserted that he was gifted with powers of healing and that he was assisted, in his mission, by none other than the Archangel Michael.[183]

The manner in which Don Teodoro's confession was disclosed is more interesting even than the nature of the theories he admitted disseminating. The fact of its publication is an illuminating comment on the stage which the authorities had reached in their dealings with the Piagnoni. They had decided not simply to break those who would not bend to Medici rule but had set about doing so with care and foresight, embarking on a complex programme in which the treatment of Don Teodoro was a key element. The proceedings against him were conducted with a wary eye to public opinion. His abjuration, for example, became a public spectacle; his confession, a printed document, preceded by a blistering preamble and followed by bans upon a repetition of his practices, made it abundantly clear that a serious danger had been averted by timely intervention. In the *Processo di Don Teodoro*, the allegedly reprehensible nature of his activities was underlined, as was the threat which he had posed to the peace and security of Florence. He was represented as a self-confessed rogue, who had been prompted, in his every action, by the basest of desires. He had used his privileged

---

[181] Ibid., fos. [2]$^r$, [5]$^r$.    [182] Ibid., fos. [2]$^v$, [4]$^v$, [5]$^r$, [6]$^r$.
[183] Ibid., fos. [4]$^r$, [5]$^{r-v}$, [6]$^r$.

clerical status, so his confession ran, as a means to satisfy his inordinate sexual appetite;[184] he had encouraged the giving of alms and the performance of additional devotions at S. Felice in order to acquire a reputation for saintliness.[185] Most interesting of all, however, was the revelation of the ruse by which he had attracted and secured his Florentine following. For in the *Processo* Don Teodoro confessed or was made to confess, that he had no true allegiance to Savonarola at all. His professed devotion to the friar, his visions and miracles, had been no more than a pretence, designed to draw to his side all those Florentines who remained faithful to Savonarola and his teaching.[186]

The significance of this admission lies not only in its revelation of Don Teodoro's alleged hypocrisy but also in its demonstration that, in Florence, Savonarolan teaching retained a large number of staunch supporters who were convinced of its truth and eager to hear it reaffirmed. According to the *Processo*, these devotees were so closely knit as to form a sect in their own right: conducting their religious observances among themselves and refusing to accept that outsiders, whether clerics or laymen, were to be accounted true Christians.[187] The gullibility of these well-meaning, but credulous, Florentines was a theme of the *Processo*. A charlatan like Don Teodoro, so the authorities emphasized, had only to feign devotion to the cause to find himself at their head. As Don Teodoro stated, in reviewing the situation in retrospect, 'In other words, since I arrived at San Felice, my whole purpose has been to deceive the people by making out that I was a saint; and I chose to pretend to believe Savonarola because I saw that many simple, stupid persons were so taken up with that fantasy that they refused to confess their sins to anyone, except to those who believed such nonsense; and even if they do go to confession, they do not confess their sins in a satisfactory manner, nor do they consider their confessors to be good religious. Hence, in order to gain credit and for my own personal gain, I joined in this folly, pretending to obtain revelation from God and threatening men with the chastisement that I said

---

[184] Ibid., fos. [3]ᵛ–[4]ʳ.     [185] Ibid., fo. [5]ᵛ; cf. fo. [2]ᵛ.
[186] Ibid., fo. [4]ʳ; cf. fos. [2]ᵛ, [4]ʳ⁻ᵛ, [5]ʳ, [6]ʳ.          [187] Ibid., fos. [4]ʳ⁻ᵛ, [6]ʳ.

would surely come.'[188] Equipped, in this way, with a ready-made following, Don Teodoro could deceive these Savonarolans as he wished and lead them where he willed. Herein lay the danger to Florentine security. The substance of Don Teodoro's preaching, like that of his predecessors, was inflammatory and disruptive. As the authorities stated, it was intolerable that a large body of citizens should be susceptible to the lures of such swindlers (*ciurmatori*)[189] who, proclaiming allegiance to Savonarola, preached the overthrow of society. They had every reason to fear that Don Teodoro 'sowed . . . a seed of discord that was enough to bring ruin to your city'.[190]

This was by no means an alarmist viewpoint. By all accounts, the extent of Don Teodoro's support was indeed considerable. An opportunist who pleaded for donations to bribe the Archiepiscopal Vicar and secure Don Teodoro's release was able to collect quite a large sum, and then made off with it. This story comes from Parenti's *Istorie fiorentine*.[191] Bartolomeo Cerretani was another contemporary who underlined the significance of Don Teodoro's following. It was, in his opinion, one of the chief reasons for the prohibitions promulgated at the time of his trial and published in the *Processo*. Hitherto reluctant to antagonize the Piagnoni in general, the authorities, according to Cerretani, were now forced by the strength of Don Teodoro's support to enact measures directed specifically against them. 'These prohibitions', said the Medicean interlocutor, Giovanni Rucellai, 'were made because there was always some friar who would come forth, preaching and foretelling renewal and the calamities to be visited on the Church; and every

---

[188] Ibid., fo. [6]ʳ: 'In somma, di poi che io venni in San Felice, tucto el mio intento è stato di ingannare el popolo con fingere io di esser sancto; et presi questa via di fingere di credere a Fra Hieronymo perchè vedevo che molti semplici et sciocchi erano involuti in quella fantasia in tanto che non si volevano confessare se non da chi crede a tali insomnii et se si confessano non li dicono e' suoi peccati a satisfaction nè credono che siano buoni religiosi. Onde io per acquistarmi credito et roba intrai in questo farnetico, fingendo haver revelation da Dio et minacciando li huomini per li flagelli che diceva dover venire.'

[189] Ibid., fo. [2]ᵛ.

[190] Ibid: 'seminava . . . un seme di discordia tale che era sufficiente a rovinar la tua ciptà'.

[191] Parenti, *Istorie fiorentine*, 307.

day there rose up young girls, nuns, bigots, and peasants who forecast renewal and chastisement. This', he went on,

gave rise to two scandals: the one, that the universality of the common people, because they had liked what the friar had predicted and awaited its fulfilment, would prick up their ears and rush forth; while the citizens whose minds were full of all that he had said regarding the popular form of government and the Great Council, rose up at the first knell, convinced that the friar's prophecy was about to be fulfilled and the former government restored.[192]

The result, as Cerretani saw, was disruption in the civil sphere. Politically qualified citizens responded to these upstart prophets with as much vigour as did the populace in general. The problem was not only that the politically qualified Florentines (*cittadini*) were in a position to influence the government, but that Savonarola's doctrine obliged them to do so. The Piagnoni, in Cerretani's phrase, 'were utterly convinced that what the friar had foretold was destined to come about'.[193] Belief in Savonarola's prognostications entailed a commitment to ensuring that they were fulfilled. His devotees had therefore to work for the overthrow of the present regime and the restoration of the Savonarolan system of government. Both in the *Storia in dialogo* and in his *Ricordi*, Cerretani showed himself keenly alert to the dangers of this situation. In his *Storia in dialogo*, he had Giovanni Rucellai say, 'and so, every day their spirit would rise up in expectation'.[194] 'They were

---

[192] Cerretani, 'Storia in dialogo', fo. 169ʳ: 'Queste proibitioni se ferno perchè del continuo usciva qualche frate, predicava e prenuntiava rennovatione, flagelli sopra la chiesa; e tutti dì insurgeva fanciulle, monache, pinzochere, contadini, che prenuntiavano la rennovatione e flagelli. Il che faceva due scandoli: l'una che l'università della plebe, havendo le cose del frate amate, le aspettavono, e subito levavono l'orecchi e correvono; e' cittadini che l'havevono stampato nel'animo rispetto al vivere populare e quel gran consiglio, al primo tocco si destavono, pensando che si havessi adempire la profetia del frate e ritornare il passato stato.' See also id., 'Ricordi storici fiorentini', fo. 179ᵛ. Cerretani's view concerning the object of the prohibitions was expressed also by Giovanni Cambi, *Istorie*, iii. 61–2.

[193] Cerretani, 'Ricordi storici fiorentini', fo. 179ᵛ: 'si persuadevano a ogni modo che quello che haveva deto il frate havesse a essere'.

[194] Cerretani, 'Storia in dialogo', fo. 169ʳ: 'et a questo modo, tutti l'animi si sollevavono ogni dì'.

honoured',[195] he goes on. 'Nevertheless, they looked back, since they felt they had lost a form of government where they were utterly in control and from which they had obtained both advantage and honour. Whenever they met one another, they would exchange slogans and thereby continue to nourish their old fantasies, keeping together and helping each other with their votes.'[196] In the *Ricordi*, this point was made even more forcefully. The Piagnoni, Cerretani wrote, 'always kept their attention riveted on the past, and whenever there was a vote to be taken they would help each other immensely without any regard for the government and totally without fear of the Medici; and the truth of the matter can be seen from the fact that on a certain vote in the *Mercanzia* Nic[col]ò Valori received more support than L[orenzo] de' Medici, while in the very Council of One Hundred they were more influential than the Medici supporters'.[197] With these examples he made it plain that the Piagnoni were not merely a potential threat. Steadfast to their ideals, they were already undermining the Medici's hold on government in Florence.

The prohibitions promulgated after Don Teodoro's trial were designed, so the authorities claimed, to remove the incentive to subversive action which prophets of his ilk provided.[198] It was decreed that, with the sole exception of the cathedral Canons, no one in the Florentine archdiocese was to preach, to hear confession,

---

[195] In his 'Ricordi storici fiorentini', fo. 179ᵛ, Bartolomeo Cerretani adds that the Piagnoni were respected, 'riveriti', by the Medici.

[196] Cerretani, 'Storia in dialogo', fo. 169ʳ: 'niente di manco, si riguardavono adreto, parendo haver perduto uno stato dove eron Sig[no]ri affatto e dove e' traevono utile et honore et vedendosi in viso con qualche motto andavono nutricando le fantasie vecchie aiutando con le fave l'un l'altro, usando insieme'.

[197] Cerretani, 'Ricordi storici fiorentini', fo. 179ᵛ: 'sempre havevan l'ochio adietro et dove s'aveva adoperare le fave s'aiutavano forte senza respetto alchuno dello stato o paura alchuna de' Medici; e che sia il vero, nell'arte de' merchanti a un certto partito Nic[col]ò Valori hebbe più favore che L[orenz]o de' Medici, nel Consiglio del Cento stesso havevono più favore che e' palleschi'. See also id., 'Storia in dialogo', fo. 169ʳ⁻ᵛ, where the concluding passage is given as 'e che questo fussi vero, nel'arte de' Mercatanti hebbe più voti un cittadino che Lor[en]zo de' Medici, nel consiglio del Cento, che era scelto dello stato, et i frateschi havevon più favore di noi'. On this, see also Parenti, *Istorie fiorentine*, 307. For confirmation of this election see Niccolò Valori, 'Ricordanze', fo. 20ʳ.

[198] *Processo di don Teodoro*, fo. [7]ʳ.

or to undertake any cure of souls without licence from the Archbishop, under penalty of excommunication and a fine. Anyone who essayed to divine the future in unacceptable ways—whether by prophesying and by interpreting Scripture in a manner unsanctioned by the doctors of the Church, or by astrological or mathematical means—was to consider himself *ipso facto* excommunicated and forbidden to preach in perpetuity. Anyone who asserted, untruthfully, that he had received visions from God or from His angels was, with the assistance of the civil authority, to be publicly degraded and imprisoned for life. Any preacher who foretold the renovation of the Church in such a way that he attacked its privileges or any dogmas relating to them was to be accounted a heretic and punished accordingly, as were any persons who fostered the same attitude or declared their belief in it. Further, anyone possessing or venerating images, clothing, bones, or writings belonging to persons condemned as heretics and schismatics was himself to be adjudged a heretic and schismatic and therefore excommunicated. All such objects and writings were to be surrendered up to the Archiepiscopal Curia within a fortnight. In an attempt to prevent the display of spurious relics for financial gain, moreover, provision was made for all dubious relics to be authenticated and licensed before being put on show. Strict precautions were also taken against the continuation of private religious meetings of the sort which Don Teodoro had fostered. All those who joined together in conventicles for the purpose of conducting novel religious ceremonies, or who met in the presence of any person, lay or ecclesiastic, who claimed to be divinely inspired and thus able to place their own construction on scriptural texts, were condemned as schismatics and enemies to the Church. In consequence, it was decreed that no religious meetings of any sort were to be held, either in public or in private, without the express permission of the Archbishop, anyone who attempted to establish a conventicle being at once excommunicated and, if he or she did not desist, declared a heretic.[199]

To all intents and purposes, these prohibitions made it impossible for another preacher to do what Don Teodoro had done and get

---

[199] Ibid., fos. [7]ᵛ–[8]ᵛ.

away with it. Unable to testify with impunity to the truth, as he saw it, concerning the impending scourging of the Church—unable, indeed, to preach at all without permission—the Piagnone preacher was severely hampered in any attempt to kindle the fires of pro-Savonarolan sentiment in Florence. Even in the comparative privacy of a meeting of devotees, he could not touch upon the forbidden subjects or regale the faithful with visible symbols of Savonarola's apostolate. For, since Savonarola had been condemned by the Church as a heretic and schismatic, all the strictures against possessing the images, relics, or writings of heretics or schismatics, much less revering them, applied to him in full measure. By the same token, private individuals were unable to call Savonarola to mind by any outward observance of this sort.

As the prohibitions suggest, Don Teodoro's trial was the first step in a concerted plan to rid Florence and the Church of the problem which the Piagnoni posed by condemning them root and branch. Although implicated in the prohibitions, Savonarola and his followers were not specifically denounced in them; nor were they openly criticized in the other documents relating to Don Teodoro's trial. In the *Processo*, nevertheless, the groundwork was laid for these and other moves against the Piagnoni. Among the witnesses to Don Teodoro's confession, for instance, were three prominent Piagnoni: Fra Paolo da Fucecchio, Bartolomeo Redditi, and Marco di Matteo Strozzi. Since Fra Paolo da Fucecchio was Florentine Inquisitor at the time, his position may account for his involvement in the trial, but neither Bartolomeo Redditi nor Marco Strozzi held any such indispensable post. While their motives in putting their names to Don Teodoro's confession must remain a matter for speculation,[200] the presence of their signatures, following a precedent established at Savonarola's trial,[201] evinces a concern on the part of the authorities to show that some Piagnoni acquiesced in the proceedings against Don Teodoro: their presence would cause

---

[200] It may be, for example, that Redditi was obliged to co-operate in order to keep on the right side of the authorities, who had permitted him to return from exile in the previous year; or it may be that he and the other two had been convinced by Don Teodoro's confession of his guilt.

[201] Villari, *La storia di Girolamo Savonarola*, vol. ii, app., pp. clxxiv–clxxv.

Don Teodoro's followers to doubt both their judgement and their leader's sincerity, ensuring thereby their acceptance of the authorities' decisions. In addition, it could later be argued that the Piagnoni were divided amongst themselves: some being conscious of the dangers which an extremist like Don Teodoro presented and others remaining adamant that they would follow unquestioningly anyone who directed them along Savonarola's path.

Significantly, the name of another prominent Piagnone, Fra Sante da San Casciano,[202] also occurs in the trial records: not as a witness, however, but as one of Don Teodoro's accomplices.[203] His was the sole exception to the authorities' decision that, in the best interests of all concerned, the names of Don Teodoro's followers should not be revealed.[204] The exception is significant because it too gave a hint of what was to come. Fra Sante was a friar of S. Marco, which, together with the entire Tusco-Roman Congregation it dominated, was shortly to be the subject of stringent legislation, designed to purge the Congregation of all Piagnone influence.[205] Even Fra Sante, however, was not condemned in the same terms as Don Teodoro. Instead, he was described as having been led astray: a description also applied, as we have seen, to Don Teodoro's followers in general.[206] The emphasis on their gullibility was in itself extremely ominous. While, for the present, the fact that the Savonarolans were easy prey for such deceivers as Don Teodoro exonerated them from the blame attached to him, it boded no good. Since, on the evidence of Don Teodoro's trial, the Savonarolan following in Florence could be transformed, however unwittingly, into a force inimical to the peace of the city and the unity of Christendom, so it was essential that their enthusiasm should be curbed. The necessity for Florence and the Church to be protected from the Florentines' 'innate disposition'[207] to run after what the authorities referred to as rabble-rousers like Don Teodoro was only

---

[202] See Convento di S. Domenico, Fiesole, 'Chronica Conventus Sancti Dominici de Fesulis', MS Archivio del convento di S. Domenico (no location number), fo. 98ᵛ; Pseudo-Burlamacchi, *La vita*, 180, 188; Schnitzer, *Savonarola*, ii. 533.

[203] *Processo di don Teodoro*, fo. [5]ʳ.          [204] Ibid., fo. [7]ʳ; cf. fos. [4]ʳ⁻ᵛ, [5]ʳ.

[205] See below, pp. 305–6.          [206] See above, pp. 280–1.

[207] *Processo di don Teodoro*, fo. [1]ᵛ: 'ingenita inclinatione'.

partly met by the prohibitions which followed his trial and was afterwards to be reasserted by the authorities as more severe measures were thought to be necessary. Yet another foretaste was the emphasis on Don Teodoro's moral turpitude. His manipulation of the Piagnoni for his own ends was constantly reiterated in the *Processo*. Here, too, a foundation was laid for subsequent, even harsher measures, designed to blacken Savonarola's name for ever. His reputation could not but be stained by the supposedly base character of one who purported to be carrying on his mission. If Savonarola's cause was so attractive to such charlatans as Don Teodoro, so the authorities argued, must it not be intrinsically evil, and its original leader no less of a hypocrite than his self-appointed successor? The question was not long to remain unanswered.

By the time Don Teodoro was condemned, the programme which the proceedings against him had initiated was already under way. One of its earliest victims was Ser Giuliano da Ripa, long a scapegoat for Piagnoni wrongs, whom we last saw being dismissed from the Chancery in 1512.[208] By December 1513 he had been called before the *Signoria* no fewer than three times.[209] Now, at the beginning of February 1515, he was referred to the *Otto di Guardia* by the Archiepiscopal Curia on the charge of having kept an image of Savonarola in his house and having held it 'in that veneration in which one must hold the image of Christ'.[210] On 7 February, in a letter conveying this news to Lorenzo, who was still in Rome, Galeotto de' Medici put forward the opinion that Ser Giuliano was to be punished severely so as to serve as an example to the other Piagnoni.[211] It must be borne in mind that, although the practice of which Ser Giuliano had been accused was to be outlawed in the prohibitions appended to Don Teodoro's confession, these were not promulgated until 11 February, four days later. The hapless Ser Giuliano was thus the chosen victim of a concerted campaign

---

[208] See above, pp. 244–5.

[209] ASF Signori e Collegi, Deliberazioni Ord. Aut. 115, fos. 133ᵛ, 139ʳ, 140ʳ. The reasons for the summons, however, are not made clear.

[210] Galeotto de' Medici to Lorenzo, 7 Feb. 1515, ASF MAP 116, No. 119: 'in quella venerazione che s[i] [h]a a tenere quella di Cristo'. See also letter of Zanobi Pace to Lorenzo, 10 Feb. 1515, ibid., No. 118.

[211] Ibid., No. 119.

against the Piagnoni. In the same letter, moreover, Galeotto asked Lorenzo whether there was any truth in the rumour that Leo X had denounced the writings of Savonarola and forbidden their publication.[212] On 10 February Lorenzo de' Medici wrote two letters whose import was to prove far-reaching. To Galeotto he addressed a temporizing reply, stating that he would tell him later whether Leo X had forbidden the publication of Savonarola's books.[213] To Luigi della Stufa, a staunch Medicean, he issued an instruction to convey forthwith to the Florentine Archiepiscopal Vicar the records of Savonarola's trial.[214] Clearly, a fresh move in the campaign was afoot; and it was directed from Rome.

It came two months later, in the form of a papal brief, dated 17 April 1515 and addressed to the Florentine Archbishop and the Chapter of Canons at Sta Maria del Fiore.[215] For moving against Don Teodoro, that instrument of perdition who had dared to usurp the title of Angelic Pope, Leo X wrote, the Florentine ecclesiastical authorities deserved high praise.[216] They were to be commended, further, for all that they had done against Savonarola himself and against Pietro Bernardino: both of whom, it was emphasized, had already been condemned by the Church as heretics and schismatics.[217] The accusation against Savonarola of guilt by association, implicit in the proceedings against Don Teodoro, was thus carried a stage further. In a public statement by the Church, Savonarola's

[212]   Galeotto de' Medici to Lorenzo.

[213]   Lorenzo de' Medici to Galeotto, 10 Feb. 1515, ASF MAP 141, fo. 96ᵛ. The passage continues, 'Et se Ser Giuliano da Ripa ha errato, puniscasi'.

[214]   Lorenzo de' Medici to Luigi della Stufa [10 Feb. 1515], ASF MAP 141, fo. 97ʳ. It proved impossible, however, to get hold of the original copy since it had been previously borrowed by Filippo Buondelmonti, who had then lent it to Marcello Adriani, who had passed it on to Giovanni Corsi, who in turn had given it to Cardinal Giulio, who had apparently lost it: letter of Galeotto to Lorenzo, 13 Feb. 1515 and of Luigi della Stufa to Lorenzo, 14 Feb. 1515, ibid. 116, Nos. 126 and 127.

[215]   Printed from the original, apparently now lost, in Moreni, *Continuazione delle memorie istoriche dell'Ambrosiana R. Basilica di S. Lorenzo*, vol. ii, app., pp. 511–15. Useful only for purposes of comparison is the incomplete and imperfect copy in MS BRF 2053, fos. 58ᵛ–59ʳ.

[216]   Moreni, *Continuazione delle memorie istoriche dell'Ambrosiana R. Basilica di S. Lorenzo*, vol. ii, app., pp. 511–12.

[217]   Ibid. 512–13.

name was now linked not only with that of Don Teodoro, but also
with Pietro Bernardino. Because the private lives of both acolytes
had been severely calumniated,[218] the connection was a threat to
Savonarola's reputation, and was seen as such by the Piagnoni, who
were subsequently to make strenuous efforts to divorce him from
them.[219] Leo X's brief went on to praise the authorities' efforts to
suppress conventicles, pseudo-prophets, and other self-seeking
persons who, under the veil of prophetic utterances and with the
ostensible purpose of reforming the Church, attempted to destroy
its unity and to turn the faithful against the Apostolic See.[220] The
proceedings against the Piagnoni in Florence were thus endowed
with the highest ecclesiastical authority: the sanction of the Pope
himself.

But Leo X did not confine himself to praising the authorities'
action in retrospect. He also encouraged them to renew their efforts
in the same direction, by stamping out any surviving spark of
Piagnone activism. With this object, he granted plenipotentiary
powers to the Florentine ecclesiastical authorities.[221] The brief
went on to emphasize that no regard should be paid to status or
privilege but that all suspects, whether laymen or clerics, whether
claiming special dispensation or not, should be proceeded against
to the full extent of the law. To facilitate this, two extraordinary
measures were recommended: one, that a theological commission
should be appointed to judge matters of heresy;[222] the other, that a
lay organization, on the lines of the Bolognese *Confraternitas
crucesignatorum*, should be established to crusade against heretics:
seeking out any manifestation of astrology, necromancy, witchcraft, or any other practice condemned by the Church.[223] The latter
proposal was clearly designed to fight fire with fire. It reveals an
awareness, on Leo X's part, of the use which the Piagnoni had
made of the confraternal structure as a means of strengthening
Savonarolan loyalties. The sort of confraternity which he had in
mind as a retaliatory measure had already been established in Flor-

---

[218] See above, p. 137.      [219] See below, p. 298.
[220] Moreni, *Continuazione delle memorie istoriche dell'Ambrosiana R. Basilica di
S. Lorenzo*, vol. ii, app., p. 514.
[221] Ibid.      [222] Ibid.      [223] Ibid.

ence, under the influence of S. Peter Martyr, in the thirteenth century. It had been revived in Bologna in 1450 and, under Dominican control, had since spread throughout northern Italy, where it served as an arm of the Inquisition.[224]

In looking ahead to determine what might best be done to forestall a resurgence in Piagnone activity, the papal brief of April 1515 represented a new departure in official policy. Previously, the authorities had looked no further than to suppress an outbreak which had already occurred. Only the prohibitions promulgated on the day of Don Teodoro's public abjuration had been designed to prevent a repetition of the situation which had enabled Don Teodoro to gain his following. In Leo X's brief this forward-looking approach was taken up and extended. Whereas the prohibitions had done little more than fulminate against certain spiritual practices and prescribe penalties for those who indulged in them, Leo X made provision for special machinery to be set up to enforce a policy of prevention. Hereafter, this object was to underlie every procedure relating to the Piagnoni's suppression. For, important as it was in investing the decisions of the Florentine ecclesiastical hierarchy with full papal authority, the brief of April 1515 was not the final blow to the Savonarolans. Nor was it intended to be. Plans aimed at disarming them by other means were shortly to be in operation.

## III

In *Vulnera diligentis*, a treatise in dialogue form by the imprisoned Piagnone friar Benedetto Luschino, these plans are described succinctly and with great vividness. The treatise describes a fictitious encounter eighteen months after Leo X's brief.[225] Various allegorical figures, who have met to discuss Savonarola and his

---

[224] Examples are the Compagnia Maggiore della Vergine Maria (or, del Bigallo) and the Compagnia di S. Agnese: see G. M. Monti, *Le confraternite medievali dell'alta e media Italia* (2 vols.; Florence (Venice), 1927), i. 150–3, 160–1; and esp. G. Meersseman, *Ordo fraternitatis: Confraternite e pietà dei laici nel medioevo*, (3 vols.; Rome, 1977), ii. 754–95.

[225] Benedetto Luschino, 'Vulnera diligentis', part II, fo. 67ᵛ.

apostolate, are interrupted in their discourse by one 'Gaspar venetiano', now known to have been Gasparo Contarini.[226] On a journey from Pieve di Sacco to Camaldoli, Gaspar pauses to acquaint the disputants with his mission. He is engaged to meet Paolo Giustiniani at Camaldoli, in order to defend in person the thesis which he has already advanced in a letter to him: that the teaching of Savonarola contains nothing whatsoever of heretical import. His mission is of the greatest urgency, Gaspar explains, because a plot is afoot to condemn this doctrine: 'For as I understand, many ecclesiastics would like once again to condemn this doctrine as heretical by means of a synod in Florence while the Lateran Council is still in session.'[227] The synod to which the treatise refers was the Synod of Florence, due to begin in October 1516; the Lateran Council had been in session since 1512. Having mulled over Gaspar's news, Agricola, Savonarola's bucolic champion in the dialogue, realizes its underlying purpose. The grand design, he perceives, was to issue, through the medium of the Synod of Florence, a renewed denunciation of Savonarola and his doctrine, which would then be sent to and automatically confirmed by the Lateran Council.[228] The worthy Agricola could not restrain himself from condemning, on the Piagnoni's behalf, the duplicity of the opponents of Savonarola.[229]

As it transpired, it was decided to issue a fresh denunciation of Savonarola and his teaching because neither his excommunication by Alexander VI in 1497 nor his trial and execution as a heretic and schismatic in 1498 had succeeded in dissuading his followers from the conviction that he was innocent. His excommunication, they believed, was null and void; his trial and execution, a travesty of justice. The case for the defence was first advanced in 1497, when Giovanfrancesco Pico contended that the decree of excommunication contravened divine and human law and that Savonarola was therefore justified in ignoring it.[230] In the remaining years of the

[226] See below, pp. 294– 5.

[227] Luschino, 'Vulnera diligentis', part II, fo. 67ᵛ: 'imperò molte persone ecclesiastiche, secondo che intendo, vorriano vedere per via di qualche sinodo dannarla nuovamente in Firenze come cosa heretica, mentre è in piedi el concilio laterano'.

[228] Ibid.    [229] Ibid.    [230] See above, pp. 90–1.

fifteenth century and the first decade of the sixteenth, when the reasons for Savonarola's trial and execution came under intense and hostile scrutiny from such Piagnoni apologists as Fra Simone Cinozzi, Fra Giovanni da Pescia, and Fra Silvestro da Marradi, this case was further developed. The proceedings against Savonarola, these polemicists maintained, had been undertaken in order to prevent the successful accomplishment of much needed ecclesiastical reforms, and had been carried out by corrupt prelates who calculated that, by executing Savonarola, they would effectively silence all calls for change.[231]

By the beginning of 1516, it was evident that the force of pro-Savonarolan sentiment, which had proven so resistant to previous onslaughts, had to be quelled at its source. This need was expressed in the strongest of terms by none other than Paolo Orlandini, whom we last saw as a prominent Piagnone.[232] By now, however, he had cast aside his loyalty to the Savonarolans and had become one of their most formidable opponents. In January 1516 he composed the *Expugnatio Miletana*,[233] a treatise dedicated to Pietro Andrea Gammaro, the Florentine Archiepiscopal Vicar, and denouncing the prophetic writings of Francesco da Meleto,[234] who, although he cannot be conclusively identified as a Piagnone, was certainly seen as such by Orlandini.[235] While devoting most of his attention in the

[231] See above, Ch. 5.    [232] See above, pp. 149–53.

[233] Paolo Orlandini, 'De scolastica scripturarum sanctarum interpretatione, contra prophetas vanos quae alio nomine de Expugnatio Miletana', part III of his 'Eptathicum', MS BNF II.I.158, fos. 122ᵛ–147ᵛ. For a discussion of this attack, see E. Garin, 'Paolo Orlandini e il profeta Francesco da Meleto', in *La cultura filosofica del Rinascimento italiano* (Florence, 1961), 213–23.

[234] See S. Bongi, 'Francesco da Meleto un profeta fiorentino a' tempi del Machiavello', *ASI*, 5th ser. 3 (1889), 62–70. Francesco da Meleto can perhaps be identified with the Procurator, of the same name, of the convent of SS. Annunziata in Florence: Bartolomeo Masi, *Ricordanze di Bartolomeo Masi calderaio fiorentino dal 1478 al 1526*, ed. G. O. Corazzini (Florence, 1906), 145.

[235] Orlandini, 'Expugnatio Miletana', fos. 123ᵛ, 140ʳ, 144ʳ. While Francesco da Meleto cannot be said to have derived his teaching on ecclesiastical reform from Savonarola, they saw alike on many issues. Francesco moved, moreover, in Piagnoni circles: being chosen by Girolamo Benivieni as an interlocutor in his *Dialogo di Antonio Manetti cittadino Fiorentino circa al sito, forma, et misure dello inferno di Dante Alighieri poeta excellentissimo*, and himself selecting two well-known Piagnoni, Benedetto Manetti and Francesco Baroncini, as spokesmen in his own *Convivio de' secreti della Scriptura Sancta*. On this, see C. Vasoli, 'La

*Expugnatio* to refuting Francesco da Meleto's teaching, Orlandini also offered some extremely pertinent comments on the Savonarolan tradition: directing attention to precisely those aspects of the Piagnone movement which required suppression, if the movement itself was to be overthrown.

The example of Savonarola, he asserted, was the movement's life-force. Despite his execution and the various condemnations issued against him, his doctrine continued to inspire his followers and thus to promote schism, both in the Church and in the world.[236] Orlandini was even more alarmed by the millenarian aspect of Savonarola's teaching, which threatened the security of the existing hierarchy and encouraged lay upstarts such as Francesco da Meleto to meddle in affairs which were not their concern.[237] He took special care to underline the importance of Florence as a focus for this kind of religious upheaval. Since Savonarola's death, he argued, Florence had never been free from the clutches of pseudo-prophets, to whose enticements her citizens were uncannily susceptible.[238] For the measures which had so far been taken against the Piagnoni, Orlandini had scant praise. Even the recent action of the Florentine ecclesiastical authorities against Don Teodoro and the brief of commendation issued by Leo X, he argued, had failed to stem the tide.[239] What was needed were redoubled efforts of an unprecedented sort. Reviewing the dangers of the present situation, to which the popularity of Francesco da Meleto bore eloquent witness, Orlandini concluded his treatise with an appeal to Pietro Andrea Gammaro to suppress the Piagnoni once and for all, by proceeding against them with stronger measures than ever before.[240]

Almost immediately, the scheme which Fra Benedetto Luschino was to denounce was under way. It was designed to meet precisely

---

profezia di Francesco da Meleto', *Umanesimo e Ermeneutica (Archivio di Filosofia)* (Padua, 1963), esp. 29 and n. 12; and 40 ff. Included in this essay are substantial extracts from the *Convivio* and Francesco's two other surviving works. A detailed refutation of all Meleto's 'errors' is in Cosimo Favilla, 'Flagellum pseudo-prophetarum', fos. 41ᵛ–42ʳ, 73ᵛ–86ᵛ.

[236] Orlandini, 'Expugnatio Miletana', fo. 123ᵛ.
[237] Ibid., fos. 123ʳ⁻ᵛ, 128ʳ, 129ᵛ, 140ʳ, 144ʳ, 145ᵛ–146ʳ.
[238] Ibid., fos. 123ᵛ, 124ʳ, 140ʳ.     [239] Ibid., fo. 123ʳ⁻ᵛ.
[240] Ibid., fo. 147ʳ.

those objections which Orlandini had voiced against existing legislation: being aimed at exorcising Savonarola's memory and finally curing the Florentine populace of its addiction to radical religious teachers. Although the Synod of Florence did not open until October 1516,[241] preparations for it had been under way for some time before then. They are thought to have been set in motion, in fact, as far back as late 1515 or early 1516, when Leo X passed through Florence on his way to and from Bologna to treat with Francis I.[242] The plan to have Savonarola condemned by the Synod got off to an early start. In February 1516 the Florentine Archiepiscopal Vicar entrusted its direction to the renowned theologian, Paolo Giustiniani, then in the convent of Camaldoli.[243] By early March Giustiniani had received a copy of the *Expugnatio Miletana* from Orlandini; and shortly afterwards he was in correspondence with Francesco da Meleto himself.[244] Collecting information against this prophetic writer was part of his task, but it was to the proposed condemnation of Savonarola that he gave most attention. Among the items of evidence which he drew together for this purpose was a copy of Delfin's *Dialogus in Hieronymum Ferrariensem*, and he wrote also to Gasparo Contarini, soliciting his opinion on whether Savonarola had been justified in disregarding Alexander VI's sentence of excommunication and in prophesying the renovation of the Church. Contarini replied with the *Copia di un consiglio facto sopra le cose del Reverendo padre Fra Hieronimo Savonarola:*[245] the

[241] Cambi, *Istorie*, iii. 102.

[242] Parenti, *Istorie fiorentine*, 309; Ridolfi, *Vita*, ii. 39, quoting A. Giorgetti, 'Fra Luca Bettini e la sua difesa del Savonarola', *ASI* 7/2 (1919), 189 ff.

[243] Letter of Paolo Giustiniani to Pietro Andrea Gammaro, Feb. 1516, in Paolo Giustiniani, *Trattati, lettere e frammenti dai manoscritti originali dell'Archivio dei Camaldolesi di Monte Corona nell'Eremo di Frascati*, ed. E. Massa (Rome, 1967), 112. The beginnings of the scheme can be deduced from this admirable catalogue of Giustiniani's works and letters. Unfortunately, I have not been able to obtain access to the documents themselves.

[244] Letters of Paolo Giustiniani to Paolo Orlandini (2 Mar. 1516) and to Francesco da Meleto (undated): Giustiniani, *Trattati, lettere e frammenti*, 113.

[245] Gasparo Contarini, *Copia di un consiglio facto sopra le cose del Reverendo padre Fra Hieronimo Savonarola Ferrarese per Messer Guasparre Vinitiano in Pieve di Sacco addì XVIII di Septembre MDXVI. Ad instantia di Fra Paolo Vinitiano Monaco dell'eremo Camaldulense*, in F. Gilbert, 'Contarini on Savonarola: An Unknown Document of 1516', *Archiv für Reformationsgeschichte*, 59 (1968), 147–9.

letter to which he, in the persona of 'Gaspar venetiano', was made to refer in Fra Benedetto Luschino's *Vulnera diligentis*.[246] Contarini's piece, like Delfin's, was dispatched to Giustiniani in September.[247]

The *Copia di un consiglio* reveals how widespread the belief in Savonarola's innocence had become. Although not a Savonarolan, Contarini was uncompromising in Savonarola's defence. Alexander VI's decree of excommunication, he argued, had been invalid, so that Savonarola had been right to carry on his apostolate and to refuse to seek absolution. While the truth of his prophecies could be judged only by God, it was nevertheless undeniable, so Contarini concluded, that the Church, as Savonarola had taught, was in urgent need of reform.[248]

At about the same time, Piagnoni pamphleteers, incensed by the plan to issue a new condemnation of Savonarola, were voicing even more radical arguments. In the treatises composed by two Piagnoni friars of S. Marco, Zaccaria di Lunigiana[249] and Luca Bettini,[250] the events of 1497–8 were no longer regarded as merely unacceptable evidence of Savonarola's guilt and became, instead, evidence of his innocence. The excommunication, trial, and execution, argued Fra

In an incomplete form the *Copia di un consiglio* had previously been published in A. Giorgetti, 'Fra Luca Bettini e la sua difesa del Savonarola', 213–14. The identification of Messer Guasparre Vinitiano and Fra Paolo Vinitiano as Gasparo Contarini and Paolo Giustiniani respectively was first made by E. Massa in his catalogue of Giustiniani's works: Giustiniani, *Trattati, lettere e frammenti*, pp. cxxiii–cxxiv. The original letter of Paolo Giustiniani, requesting Contarini's advice, has apparently not survived. It does not appear in the correspondence between the two men which H. Jedin has published: 'Contarini und Camaldoli', *Archivio italiano per la storia della pietà*, 2 (1953), 59–117.

[246] See above, p. 291.

[247] Letter of Pietro Delfin to Paolo Giustiniani, 12 Sept. 1516, in Schnitzer, *Peter Delfin*, app. I, p. 365; see n. 245 above.

[248] Gasparo Contarini, *Copia di un consiglio*, in Gilbert, 'Contarini on Savonarola', 149; cf. 147–9.

[249] See Ubaldini, 'Annalia', fo. 171ᵛ; Serafino Razzi, *Istoria degli Huomini illustri . . . del sacro ordine de gli Predicatori* (Lucca, 1596), 282–3; and also below, pp. 305–6, 374–5, 380–1, 405–6.

[250] See his 'Prohemio . . . ad tutti li electi di Dio amatori della verità', in Savonarola, *Prediche sopra i Salmi* (Bologna, 1515), sig. a1ᵛ; Ubaldini, 'Annalia', fo. 168ᵛ; F. Bonaini (ed.), 'Chronica antiqua Conventus Sanctae Catharinae de Pisis', *ASI*, 1st ser. 6/2 (1848), 624.

Zaccaria's *Defensio*[251] and Fra Luca Bettini's *Opusculum*,[252] had not been in accordance with the procedures prescribed for dealing with heretics and schismatics. The bull of excommunication had not specified the religious crimes which Savonarola was alleged to have committed; and his arrest and trial had been conducted with scant regard for the legal processes attendant upon the indictment of a member of the regular clergy on such serious charges. These inconsistencies, the apologists went on, were more than ever apparent in Savonarola's sentence and the manner in which it was carried out. Death, which should be imposed only after obstinate persistence in error, was not the correct punishment for a first offence of either sort. Neither had Savonarola been called upon to make the public abjuration of his sins which was normally required of heretics and schismatics. Finally, before his execution he had been permitted to receive the last rites: which demonstrated, if further proof were needed, that he had remained to the end a faithful son of the Church.[253]

As well as refining and elaborating the case which their predecessors had presented in vindication of Savonarola, Fra Zaccaria and Fra Luca Bettini levelled against Alexander VI accusations of an unequivocally *ad hominem* nature: thus reiterating and enlarging the doubts which Savonarola had first cast on his claim to the papacy. According to them, Alexander VI had not been a worthy Pope. He had not, in fact, been a Christian at all. This had been rumoured during his lifetime, and confirmed, they explained, by a

---

[251] Zaccaria di Lunigiana, 'Defensio Fratris Zachariae Lunensis qua tuetur Hieronymum Savonarolae sociosque ab haeresi', MS BNF Conv. Sopp., J.1.46, fos. 1ʳ–18ᵛ. A short extract from another copy, in MS BRF 2053, fos. 50ʳ–58ʳ, has been published by Giorgetti, 'Fra Luca Bettini e la sua difesa del Savonarola', 215–16.

[252] Luca Bettini, 'Opusculum Fratris Luce Bectinis florentini, Ordinis praedicatorum de observantia, in defensionem fratris Hieronymi Savonarolae ferrariensis ejusdem Ordinis ... tempore Synodi compositum florentinae MDXVI', MS BRF 2053, fos. 1ʳ–21ᵛ, of which there is a substantial extract in Giorgetti, 'Fra Luca Bettini e la sua difesa del Savonarola', 217–28. Except for the sections here published, the MS version has been used throughout. In citing the MS, folio references are used; in citing the published extracts, page references.

[253] Zaccaria di Lunigiana, 'Defensio', fos. 2ᵛ–3ᵛ, 8ᵛ–9ʳ, 14ʳ, 17ʳ; Luca Bettini, 'Opusculum', fos. 10ʳ–11ʳ; and pp. 221–8.

member of his household, who had revealed that Alexander VI had not been baptized until after Savonarola's execution. It had, furthermore, been corroborated by the present Pope, Leo X, who had confided to two members of his entourage, Fra Bonifacio Landino and Fra Mariano Fetti, both of S. Marco, that, in his opinion, Alexander VI had lacked all Christian faith. The result was to invalidate every act which Alexander VI had performed. More particularly, as the polemicists triumphantly pointed out, his decisions against Savonarola lost all weight.[254] With Alexander VI cast in the role of enemy to Christianity, Savonarola emerged without a stain upon his reputation: emerged, indeed, as a champion of Christianity.

Such arguments were not confined to the proceedings of 1497–8. Skilfully used, they could be directed also against subsequent denunciations of Savonarola. Having contended that the original indictment had been illegal and that the Pope who authorized it had been no Pope at all, Fra Zaccaria di Lunigiana and Fra Luca Bettini turned their attention to Leo X's brief of 1515. Since it commended a decision now shown to have been invalid, they argued, it too was to be dismissed.[255] At the same time, in emphasizing that so heinous a decision as that of Alexander VI against Savonarola could not be justified on any grounds whatsoever, they pointed to a highly pertinent question. Why, when he believed that Alexander VI had not even been a Christian, had Leo X commended that decision in his brief of 1515? As a Medici Pope, who took an active part in directing the Florentine government, Leo X was extremely vulnerable to attacks upon his motives, since the Piagnoni threatened not only his spiritual leadership, but also his family's hold on

---

[254] Zaccaria di Lunigiana, 'Defensio', fos. 15ᵛ–17ʳ; Luca Bettini, 'Opusculum', fos. 12ʳ⁻ᵛ, 13ʳ. The citation of the two S. Marco friars, especially Fra Mariano Fetti, as witnesses to Leo X's statement, suggests that they may possibly have served as spies in the papal household. This would be a useful corrective to the view of Savonarola's biographers, who have universally given Fra Mariano a bad press, claiming that he was the 'buffone di corte del papa': Schnitzer, *Savonarola*, ii. 439. His contemporaries did not dismiss him so lightly. For another instance of the amassing of evidence in support of the contention that Alexander VI was not a Christian, see MS BRF 2053, fo. 107ʳ.

[255] Zaccaria di Lunigiana, 'Defensio', fos. 10ʳ⁻ᵛ, 17ʳ–18ᵛ; Luca Bettini, 'Opusculum', fos. 1ᵛ, 6ᵛ; and pp. 220–1.

Florence. In this way, the calumnies upon Alexander VI's character cast a long shadow. Once the decisions of a Pope had been questioned on these grounds, there was nothing to stop the same argument being used against his successors. Neither were Fra Zaccaria and Fra Luca Bettini even momentarily discountenanced by Leo X's coupling, in his brief, of Savonarola's name with those of Pietro Bernardino and Don Teodoro. Faced with the threat to Savonarola's good name which his association with Pietro Bernardino implied, both polemicists abandoned the latter without compunction. Maintaining that they had seen the records of his trial, they contended that Bernardino had been condemned not for heresy and schism, but for sodomy: arguing that no connection, therefore, could be established between Savonarola's religious teaching and Bernardino.[256] The case of Don Teodoro was too recent to admit of such ready dismissal but Fra Luca Bettini had no hesitation in tackling it. The proceedings against Don Teodoro, he asserted, had been illegal, and because his confession had been extorted from him, it was not a reliable testimony to his actions.[257] Fra Zaccaria's *Defensio* and Fra Luca Bettini's *Opusculum* demonstrate how radical Piagnone argumentation had now become, that it could sweep aside a recent papal brief no less than a decision of twenty years' standing. By the time the Synod of Florence was under way, therefore, Paolo Orlandini had been proved correct. The previous anti-Savonarolan measures had indeed, as he contended in the *Expugnatio Miletana*, been inadequate against the driving force of Piagnone sentiment.

Only too well aware of what he was up against in endeavouring to secure Savonarola's condemnation once and for all, Paolo Giustiniani prepared a formidable array of arguments for presentation at the Synod in which he accused him of being a schismatic,

[256] Zaccaria di Lunigiana, 'Defensio', fo. 17ᵛ; Luca Bettini, 'Opusculum', p. 222. This argument concerning Pietro Bernardino, according to which his reputation was sacrificed in the interest of Savonarola's, was almost immediately enshrined, with appropriate elaboration, in Savonarolan apologetic: *Vita latina*, fo. 43ʳ; Pseudo-Burlamacchi, *La vita*, 241–2.

[257] Luca Bettini, 'Opusculum', p. 222.

a heretic, and a false prophet.[258] Because the minutes of the meetings have not survived, it is impossible to be certain that Giustiniani actually presented his case.[259] The procedure adopted at the
Synod, however, makes it entirely possible that he did. Whereas on
past occasions proposed enactments had been drafted in advance
and had simply been put to the vote of the assembled clerics, the
Florentine Synod of 1516–17 broke new ground in adopting a
conciliar method of procedure, whereby certain participants
pleaded the case for a particular item of legislation. If accepted by
the majority, the measure passed into the records of the Synod,
together with the arguments used to support it.[260] From these
records, it is nevertheless clear that, despite all Giustiniani's
groundwork, no condemnation of Savonarola was issued. While
Francesco da Meleto and others like him were denounced in the

[258] In Ignazio Manardi, *Apologeticus pro Frate Hieronymo Savonarola Ordinis
Praedicatorum, adversus ei obiecta a Venerabili Paulo Iustiniano Eremita
Camaldulensi*, in I. Taurisano, 'Fra Girolamo Savonarola (Da Alessandro VI a
Paulo IV)', *La Bibliofilia*, 55 (1953), 35. Fra Ignazio (in the world, Timoteo)
Manardi da Ferrara, who collaborated with Giovanfrancesco Pico in his *Vita
Reverendi Patris F. Hieronymi Savonarolae*, entered the Convent of S. Marco in
1519. After 1536, he joined the Camaldolese Order and entered the hermitage of
Montecorona, where, coming across Paolo Giustiniani's notes for his attack on
Savonarola, he considered it his duty to refute them. His *Apologeticus* was written
in 1539 and was inserted amongst the Giustiniani papers. On Fra Ignazio, see
Convento di S. Marco, 'Liber vestitionum', MS ACSM (no location number), fo.
10ʳ; Ubaldini, 'Annalia', fo. 179ᵛ; Taurisano, 'Fra Girolamo Savonarola', 21 n. 1;
id., *I Domenicani in Lucca* (Lucca, 1914), 90–3, 240.

[259] A copy of his case in ACSM Miscellanea P. Benelli, inserto L. This copy
was taken from the original in the Camaldolese Archives of Monte Corona at
Frascati and conforms to the description given by E. Massa in Paolo Giustiniani,
*Trattati, lettere e frammenti*, 111–12.

[260] *Concilium Florentinum Provinciale ... Constitutiones seu Ordinationes*, in J. D.
Mansi (ed.), *Sacrorum Conciliorum nova et amplissima collectio*, xxxv (Paris, 1902),
cols. 215–318. For examples, cf. e.g. cols. 220, 223–4, 226, 227; and also
Paolo Giustiniani, *Trattati, lettere e frammenti*, 114: 'Verba habita in sinodo
Metropolitana Florentina contra opera Meleti'. In the opinion of R. C. Trexler,
however, this method of procedure was merely a formality, resulting from a desire
to emulate the great councils of the past; and those who addressed the Synod
spoke 'for an already fixed body of law': *Synodal Law in Florence and Fiesole,
1306–1518* (Vatican City, 1971), 10.

synodal constitutions, promulgated in 1518, Savonarola himself remained untouched.[261]

Why such carefully laid plans should have failed to come to fulfilment can only be explained by the strength of Piagnone opposition. Of its existence, we have evidence from Giustiniani himself. Writing to Contarini, who, in a letter of 15 November 1516, requested news of how the matter of Savonarola was faring at the Synod and asked whether a decision had yet been reached,[262] Giustiniani made an equivocal reply, in which one can detect his irritation at the failure to secure Savonarola's condemnation.[263] From Piagnoni writings of the time, we may gain some notion of the likely form which their opposition took. The treatises by Fra Zaccaria di Lunigiana and Fra Luca Bettini, for example, were part of the Piagnoni's counter-attack. Composed with the Synod specifically in mind, and designed to sway the opinion of the participants in Savonarola's favour, they put the case for the defence in such exhaustive detail that they may even have been intended as briefs for sympathetic spokesmen at the Synod. If it is true, furthermore, as Professor Weinstein has argued, that the Ferrarese priest, Francesco Caloro, forwarded to the Synod a copy of his *Defensione contro gli adversarii de Frate Hieronymo Savonarola*, which had been published, together with a collection of Savonarola's sermons, in 1513,[264] then the news of the impending condemnation had prompted even comparatively remote Piagnoni to

[261] *Concilium Florentinum Provinciale . . . Constitutiones seu Ordinationes*, cols. 269–74.

[262] Letter of Gasparo Contarini to Paolo Giustiniani, 15 Nov. 1516, in Jedin, 'Contarini und Camaldoli', 113.

[263] Quoted by E. Massa in his Introduction to Paolo Giustiniani, *Trattati, lettere e frammenti*, p. cxxiii.

[264] Francesco Caloro, *Defensione contro gli adversarii de Frate Hieronymo Savonarola prenuntiatore delle instanti calamitade et renovatione della Chiesa*, in Appendix to Girolamo Savonarola, *Prediche devotissime et piene di divini mysterii* (Ferrara, 1513). Caloro's *Defensione* was included in many subsequent editions of Savonarola's sermons: cf. e.g. Savonarola, *Prediche . . . sopra Amos propheta* (Venice, 1528). Extracts of the *Defensione* published in I. Farneti, 'Giovanni Manardo e gli ambienti savonaroliano a Mirandola e Pichiano a Ferrara', *Ferrara viva*, 4 (1965), 312–13.

spring to the prophet's aid at this time of trial.[265] By far the most pertinent contribution, however, came from another friar of S. Marco, Lorenzo Macciagnini.[266] There survives, in point form, the draft of a speech in Savonarola's defence, which he prepared for delivery at the Synod.[267] In recognition of the needs of an audience not necessarily familiar with the details of Savonarola's career, Fra Lorenzo included in his draft background information which would, to a Savonarolan assembly, have been superfluous. While he presented much the same arguments as Fra Zaccaria and Fra Luca Bettini, he did so in moderate vein. Conscious of the learning of his audience, he took pains to base his defence on an appeal not to the emotions but to the intellect. Under twenty-seven heads, his argument led inexorably to the conclusion that there were no grounds on which the assembled clerics could justifiably condemn Savonarola.[268]

Whether the Synod ever had the opportunity to assess Fra Lorenzo's case is unlikely. Sadly for his precisely argued defence, but fortunately for the greater cause which he espoused, it seems there was no need for his speech to be delivered. A rubric is appended to the draft to the effect that there had, in the end, been no call for it since Savonarola's adversaries had desisted from their attack.[269] Evidently, the Piagnoni had been able to muster a great deal of support and had found themselves commanding a considerable following at the Synod. Realizing the weight of this opinion and fearful, perhaps, of the consequences, the anti-Savonarolans had to relinquish their former goal. Since they had failed in the first stage of their plan, the second stage, too, was doomed. It may be

---

[265] Weinstein, *Savonarola and Florence*, 359; and see also 84 n. 37. Weinstein does not, however, give a source for this information.

[266] Convento di S. Marco, 'Liber vestitionum', fo. 3[r]; Ubaldini, 'Annalia', fo. 163[r].

[267] Lorenzo Macciagnini, 'Sermo venerabilis Patris fratris Laurentii de Macciagninis de Florentia O.P. observantia in defensione R.P. fratris Hieronimi Savonarolae de Ferraria eiusdem ordinis. Instante Concilio sive Synodo Florentino post falsum Leonis brevem contra eundem Reverendum Patrem', MS BRF 2053, fos. 103[v]–106[r]. The *Sermo* must have been completed before 13 Nov. 1516, the date of Macciagnini's death: Ubaldini, 'Annalia', fo. 163[r].

[268] Lorenzo Macciagnini, 'Sermo', fos. 103[v]–106[r].     [269] Ibid., fo. 106[r].

that Savonarola's doctrine did come up for discussion at the Lateran Council. Piagnone tradition has it that an attempt was indeed made to condemn Savonarola there, but that it was forestalled by Giorgio Benigno, who delivered an impassioned address in his defence.[270] The planned attack had turned into a rout; the Piagnoni did not hide their satisfaction.[271] The time of danger had passed without the feared condemnation being issued.

But the Piagnoni were not to enjoy an unqualified victory. Although they succeeded in preserving Savonarola's reputation from further besmirching, they lost much of the freedom which they had hitherto enjoyed. Certain decisions taken by the Synod of Florence and the Lateran Council, while they did not specifically mention the Piagnoni, deeply affected them, being designed to impede their activity no less than that of other religious radicals.[272] In commanding all friars and priests to adhere strictly to the prescribed regulations concerning clerical dress, for example,[273] the Synod of Florence struck particularly at Piagnoni clerics, whose custom it was to attire themselves in very simple vestments as a way of demonstrating their fervour for the friar.[274] As part of a general tightening up of discipline, it was decreed that all prospective candidates for the priesthood should have witnesses to their character. Other stipulations, that no Florentine ecclesiastic was to hear confession without licence from the Ordinary and that no cleric ordained outside Florence was to take up a cure of souls

[270] Ridolfi, *Vita*, ii. 39 and 239 n. 55, following Schnitzer, *Savonarola*, ii. 476 and 497 n. 65, citing an unpublished version of the Pseudo-Burlamacchi *Vita* in BNF, G.5. 1209, fo. 221ʳ.

[271] Benedetto Luschino, 'Vulnera diligentis', Part II, fo. 68ʳ.

[272] One such was a certain Fra Bonaventura, active in Rome in 1516, who announced himself to be the Angelic Pope and promptly excommunicated Leo X and the rest of the ecclesiastical hierarchy, with the result that he was arrested and imprisoned in May: von Pastor, *Storia dei Papi*, iii. 196–7; iv (I). 100 n. 7, and 569. Although von Pastor maintains that Fra Bonaventura was influenced by Savonarola, the connection between the two does not appear to be convincing.

[273] *Concilium Florentinum Provinciale . . . Constitutiones seu Ordinationes*, cols. 220–1.

[274] Schnitzer, *Quellen und Forschungen zur Geschichte Savonarolas*, iii. 75. It had been to stop just these displays of loyalty that Fra Vincenzo Bandelli and Fra Malatesta Sacramoro laid down strict regulations regarding dress in the Tusco-Roman Congregation in 1502: see above, pp. 185–6.

within the city without the Ordinary's permission, were intended to strengthen episcopal control over regular as well as secular clergy.[275]

From the Piagnoni's point of view, the most damaging decrees were those relating to preaching and prophesying. A revered cleric, in a polemical speech to the Synod, criticized modern preachers for their unwarranted scriptural interpretations.[276] In so doing, the cleric argued, these preachers were undermining the faith of their charges and leading them on to error and schism.[277] His words were recorded in the preface to the series of acts which end with the condemnation of Francesco da Meleto. He was not, however, its sole subject. The decree was aimed at suppressing the dissemination, whether by the written or the spoken word, of unauthorized scriptural expositions.[278] To this end, it authorized the Ordinary to make the final decision on whether a book might be published: a regulation which applied to Florence the provisions of the papal bull *Inter sollicitudines*, promulgated on 4 May 1515 at the tenth session of the Lateran Council.[279] Concerning preaching, the synodical decrees stipulated that in the whole province of Florence no one was to preach without having first obtained letters patent from the Ordinary. In this, the Synod of Florence would seem to have anticipated, rather than followed, the Lateran Council.[280] The

---

[275] *Concilium Florentinum Provinciale . . . Constitutiones seu Ordinationes*, cols. 244, 255–7.

[276] 'Venerabilis senex': ibid., col. 269. On the strength of his *Expugnatio Miletana*, historians have conjectured that Paolo Orlandini was the cleric in question: Bongi, 'Francesco da Meleto', 69–70, and, following Bongi, Vasoli, 'La profezia di Francesco da Meleto', 37; cf. Weinstein, *Savonarola and Florence*, 362. It is no less likely, however, to have been Paolo Giustiniani, who had gathered an imposing body of evidence against Francesco da Meleto and who spoke against him at the Synod: Giustiniani, *Trattati, lettere e frammenti*, 114–15. A final decision must, however, await the publication of the text of this speech by E. Massa.

[277] *Concilium Florentinum Provinciale . . . Constitutiones seu Ordinationes*, col. 269.

[278] Ibid., cols. 272–4.

[279] Ibid., cols. 274–5; cf. vol. xxxii, cols. 912 ff.

[280] *Concilium Florentinum Provinciale . . . Constitutiones seu Ordinationes*, cols. 272–3. This assumption is based on the fact that the decree cites no precedent from the Lateran Council, when this was generally the practice for a decree on the subject of which the Lateran Council had already pronounced. For a dif-

delegates at the Lateran Council, alarmed, as the Florentine clergy had been, by the increasing currency of prophetic utterances, took action themselves, and succeeded in obtaining clear guidelines from the Pope in the bull *Supernae majestatis praesidio*, which required all intending preachers to be examined first by their immediate superiors and then by the Ordinary in the diocese where they wished to preach. No one, furthermore, was permitted to preach in a prophetic vein without the approval of the Apostolic See or, at least, of the local bishop.[281]

Piagnoni preachers in general, not to mention their followers, were hampered by these decrees; but for Piagnoni friars in the Tusco-Roman Congregation the situation was even grimmer. The lack of definition in the extent of episcopal jurisdiction over the regular clergy, upon which they had been able to rely for a considerable measure of freedom, was largely remedied by the Lateran Council. This was done in response to a concerted move by the Ordinaries, both before and after the tenth session, to increase their powers over the regular clergy by having some of their privileges and exemptions withdrawn, and despite a desperate rearguard action led by the Masters-General of the Augustinian and Dominican Orders, Egidio da Viterbo and Tommaso de Vio Gaetano.[282] With the bull *Regimini universalis Ecclesiae*,[283] promulgated at the tenth session, some of the regulars' privileges were rescinded; and at the eleventh session, they lost more. The bull *Supernae majestatis praesidio*, mentioned above, imposed severe re-

---

ferent view, however, see D. Cantimori, *Eretici Italiani del Cinquecento* (Florence, 1939), 11.

[281] Mansi, *Sacrorum Conciliorum nova et amplissima collectio*, vol. xxxii, esp. cols. 946–7; C. J. Hefele, J. Hergenröther, and H. Leclercq, *Histoire des Conciles* (Paris, 1917), viii. 525–7; Paride de' Grassis, 'Diarium sive annales pontificatus Leonis X', MS BNF II.III.141, fos. 229$^{r-v}$.

[282] Hefele, Hergenröther, and Leclercq, *Histoire des Conciles*, viii. 451–64, 517–24. In the original German edition of this work, the petition of the Ordinaries and the counter-petitions of the regular clergy are also published: Hefele, Hergenröther, *Conciliengeschichte*, viii. 813–31. See also Paride de' Grassis, 'Diarium sive annales pontificatus Leonis X', fos. 152$^v$–153$^r$, 213$^r$–215$^r$, 227$^{r-v}$; von Pastor, *Storia dei Papi*, iv (i). 535–6.

[283] Mansi, *Sacrorum Conciliorum nova et amplissima collectio*, vol. xxxii, cols. 907–12; Hefele, Hergenröther, and Leclercq, *Histoire des Conciles*, viii. 468–71.

strictions upon their freedom to preach;[284] and another bull, *Dum intra mentis arcana*, forbade them to hear confession without episcopal sanction.[285] Piagnoni friars were further impeded by legislation directed specifically against them. On 23 February 1515 a papal brief, aimed at silencing dissension within the Congregation and preventing the formation of parties and pressure-groups, had laid down stricter regulations for the election of officials;[286] and, in the following year, these regulations were augmented by others concerning discipline.[287]

In 1517 the new policy was put to the test. At the Provincial Chapter of the Congregation, held at S. Marco on 1 May, Fra Luca Bettini, his defence of Savonarola not long completed, was elected Prior of the convent of Sta Caterina at Pisa.[288] The authorities did not allow this to pass unremarked. Fearful of what might occur if S. Marco itself were to fall under the control of such a radical Piagnone, the Master-General, Tommaso de Vio Gaetano, now Cardinal, wrote to the Vicar-General of the Congregation, Fra Girolamo de' Rossi, forbidding him to confirm any Piagnone as Prior of S. Marco.[289] Following the death of Girolamo de' Rossi later in the same year, a direct confrontation finally occurred. Holding Cardinal Gaetano's instructions in unqualified contempt, the Priors of the Congregation elected Luca Bettini as the new Vicar-General.[290] This renewed manifestation of Piagnoni loyalties was intolerable. Acting at Leo X's behest, Cardinal Gaetano at once quashed the election. Claiming that Luca Bettini was too young

---

[284] See above, p. 304.

[285] Mansi, *Sacrorum Conciliorum nova et amplissima collectio*, vol. xxxii, cols. 970–4; Hefele, Hergenröther, and Leclercq, *Histoire des Conciles*, viii. 532–5.

[286] T. Ripoll and A. Brémond (eds.), *Bullarium Ordinis Praedicatorum* (8 vols.; Rome, 1729–40), iv. 316.

[287] Ibid. 325, 329–30. In the Provincial Chapters of 1517 and 1518, moreover, some of the regulations laid down by the Synod of Florence and the Lateran Council, pertaining to ordination and preaching, were adopted by the Tusco-Roman Congregation: Creytens, 'Les Actes capitulaires', 167, 169.

[288] Ibid. 166; Bonaini (ed.), 'Chronica antiqua', 624; see also *DBI* under Luca Bettini.

[289] Gherardi, *Nuovi documenti*, 337.

[290] Creytens, 'Les Actes capitulaires', 167; Bonaini (ed.), 'Chronica antiqua', 624; G. Benelli, 'Di alcune lettere del Gaetano', *AFP* 5 (1935), 363–72.

and—which was more to the point—that he had composed a treatise in Savonarola's defence,[291] Gaetano appointed Fra Matteo di Marco in his place. The new appointee followed this up by removing Luca Bettini from his post of Prior of Sta Caterina as well.[292] In the resulting furore, Cardinal Gaetano was so hard-pressed by pro-Piagnoni sympathizers that he was forced to reassert his authority. In a letter to Matteo di Marco, dated 8 February 1518, he told the friars with ill-repressed fury that he had every right to intervene in an election.[293] Four days later, in another letter, he empowered Matteo di Marco to quash any further attempt by the friars of Sta Caterina to restore Luca Bettini to his post, as they were threatening to do.[294] Gaetano was clearly not one to leave anything to chance. In March he forced Bettini to give an undertaking that he would not so much as read aloud, let alone publish, any of his works, without special licence from the Master-General.[295] Understandably, Luca Bettini, accompanied by his brother Domenico, fled the Congregation shortly afterwards. Taking refuge at Mirandola, at the court of Giovanfrancesco Pico, he resumed his composition of pro-Savonarolan tracts.[296] For their joint act of insubordination, he and his brother were formally expelled from the Congregation in 1526.[297]

[291] Creytens, 'Les Actes capitulaires', 167–8. Luca Bettini was 28 years old at the time.

[292] Ibid.; Bonaini (ed.), 'Chronica antiqua', 624.

[293] Benelli, 'Di alcune lettere del Gaetano', 368–72.

[294] Ibid. 372–3.      [295] Ibid. 373–4.

[296] He became, in fact, one of Giovanfrancesco Pico's administrators; and composed, during these years, his painstaking list of Savonarola's prophecies on reform, which he entitled *Oracolo della renovatione della Chiesa secondo la dottrina del Riverendo Padre Frate Hieronimo Savonarola da Ferrara* and which his brother published in Venice in 1536. He also aided in the composition of the second version of Giovanfrancesco Pico's *Vita Reverendi Patris F. Hieronymi Savonarolae*. See also Ubaldini, 'Annalia', fo. 168ᵛ; F. Ceretti (ed.), *Biografie pichensi*, vol. ii (Memorie storiche della città e dell'antico ducato della Mirandola, 18; Mirandola, 1909), 68.

[297] Creytens, 'Les Actes capitulaires', 186. Luca Bettini died in Alba, a feudal possession of the Pico in Piedmont, on 22 July 1527: Ubaldini, 'Annalia', fo. 168ᵛ; Bonaini (ed.), 'Chronica antiqua', 624. Giovanni Maria Bettini, another brother of the five in S. Marco, also left the Congregation and joined Giovanfrancesco Pico's household staff at about this time: Ubaldini, 'Annalia', fo. 169ᵛ.

As this confrontation demonstrates, whereas some individuals might have been frightened into flight, the Piagnoni friars in the Congregation were, on the whole, far from cowed. Deaf to entreaties, unmoved by threats, favours, and blandishments, they continued to pose a serious threat to the regime. The point was appreciated by Goro Gheri, who, shortly after taking office as Lorenzo's deputy and acting perhaps as a spokesman for the *amici*, revived the project to transfer S. Marco to the Lombard Congregation in order, as he put it, to confound the Piagnoni.[298] However, far too many interests were at play for him to succeed and his plan, like all previous ones, was abandoned. The friars of S. Marco, meanwhile, despite the suspicion in which they were held, continued in their aggressive and expansionist ways. When Leo X asked Gheri to explore the possibility of reforming the convent of Sta Maria Novella,[299] the Piagnoni, both lay and ecclesiastic, came immediately to the fore. The first to do so was Lanfredino Lanfredini, who presented himself to Gheri and warmly supported the proposal, even suggesting that the reform be extended to all other Conventual convents of the city.[300]

Shortly afterwards, the friars of S. Marco, having got wind of the likelihood that Sta Maria Novella would be assigned to the Lombard Observant Congregation, made their appearance. Their spokesman, Fra Stefano Moldei da Castracaro, sought an audience with Gheri. To Gheri's amazement, Fra Stefano, while supporting the proposed reform, roundly condemned the very notion of calling the hated Lombards to Florence in order to implement it.[301] Arguing that the friars of S. Marco were at the very least the Lombards' equals, he let it be known that they should therefore be entrusted with the task of reforming Sta Maria Novella. He also pointed out that the proposed introduction of the Lombard friars would have made the religious situation in Florence much more volatile because of the animosity they would have aroused and

[298] Gheri, 'Copialettere', vol. i, fos. 148ʳ, 186ᵛ.
[299] Ibid., vol. iv, fos. 194ʳ, 197ᵛ; letter of Baldassarre Turini to Gheri, 4 Mar. 1519, ASF MAP 114, No. 121; see also nos. 125, 126.
[300] Gheri, 'Copialettere', vol. i, fo. 194ʳ.    [301] Ibid., fos. 200ᵛ–201ʳ.

because the Lombards were themselves divided into two hostile factions. More pointedly, Fra Stefano stated unequivocally that the friars of S. Marco could not but interpret such a decision, if carried out, as evidence of the Pope's hatred of them and as an overt attempt to harm them. By revealing to Gheri that the successes enjoyed by the Medici, especially in the war of Urbino, had been due to their prayers, Fra Stefano made it clear that these prayers could be just as easily and efficaciously turned against them.

Gheri was quick to notice the implied threat. While in his letter he inveighed against the friars' ambitions and Fra Stefano's effrontery, he was none the less as conciliatory and as reassuring as he could be.[302] By the following day he had made most of Fra Stefano's arguments his own and was advising the Pope not to proceed with the planned introduction of the Lombard friars into Sta Maria Novella.[303] Within a week, the whole city seemed to have turned against the proposal. Deputations of citizens impressed upon Gheri their opposition to the scheme, arguing that if it was proceeded with regardless of their wishes the Lombards would be deprived of alms and would soon be forced to leave the city.[304] One can detect in this dramatic development the hand of the friars of S. Marco, who, not satisfied with the turn of events, sought to make sure of the outcome by dispatching a high-powered deputation consisting of Fra Filippo Strozzi, Fra Cosimo Tornabuoni, and Fra Cherubino Primerani to Rome.[305] In view of the almost unanimous opposition it is not surprising that it was finally decided to abandon the whole project. The friars of S. Marco might have rued the lost opportunity to take over the despised, rival convent of Sta Maria Novella but could not but have drawn satisfaction from the fact that they had prevented the Lombards from re-establishing a bridgehead in Florence.

Emboldened, perhaps, by this partial victory, the friars of S. Marco next turned against Suor Domenica Narducci del Paradiso by resorting to the very machinery put in place by Leo X to combat them. Since the restoration of the Medici, Domenica's convent had

[302]  Ibid., fos. 201ʳ–202ʳ.          [303]  Ibid., fo. 205ʳ.
[304]  Ibid., fos. 218ᵛ–220ᵛ.          [305]  Ibid., fo. 221ʳ.

thrived; in the intervening years her own reputation, following, and prestige had also grown steadily, to the annoyance of the friars of S. Marco, who had not forgiven her for rejecting their wardship. During one of his visits to Florence, Fra Tommaso Caiani brought formal charges of heresy against her before the Archiepiscopal Curia. It was a particularly unwise move given Fra Tommaso's notorious anti-Medicean sentiments, Suor Domenica's popularity, the flimsiness of the evidence on which the charges were based, and given also the likely composition of the commission and, finally, the Medici's new awareness of the political and religious dangers posed by S. Marco.[306] A large and eminent theological commission was convoked, headed by Cardinal Giulio de' Medici as Archbishop of Florence, Antonio Pucci, Bishop of Pistoia, and Leonardo de' Medici Bishop of Forlì, but including also Pietro Andrea Gammari, Vicar of the Archbishop of Florence, Fra Paolo da Fucecchio, Florentine Inquisitor, and Fra Benedetto da Foiano, Regent of Sta Maria Novella, as well as representatives from the major monastic institutions in Florence excepting S. Marco: in all some twenty theologians.[307] The commission met in the Medici palace on 20 August 1519.[308] Little is known of the proceedings. In the circumstances, however, there could not have been any doubt as to the outcome, especially in view of the fact that Francesco Onesti da Castiglione, Canon of S. Lorenzo, and also Suor Domenica's confessor and most vocal defender, had made it known that the charges of heresy had been levelled against her by vengeful friars of S. Marco who could not tolerate her defiance of their command to plot against the Medici and against the government.[309]

---

[306] The charges are to be found in 'Transumptum sententiae super disputatione epistolae Venerandae matris sororis Dominicae', MS ACDC Codice M, fo. 66ᵛ.

[307] Ibid., fos. 64ᵛ–65ʳ, 67ʳ⁻ᵛ. It should be remembered, however, that at this time Fra Benedetto da Foiano was described by Goro Gheri as 'Huomo da bene et litterato et amico della casa': 'Copialettere', vol. ii, fo. 543ᵛ.

[308] 'Transumptum sententiae', fo. 74ʳ.

[309] Francesco Onesti da Castiglione, 'Persecutiones exagitate contra Venerabilem sponsam Jesu Christi S. Dominicam de Paradiso', fo. 25ᵛ. See also his 'Difesa di una lettera di Suor Domenica del Paradiso', MS ACDC Epistole Morali, Codice I, fos. 398ʳ–429ʳ, where, however, the copyist has mistakenly transcribed the date as 1516.

The commission found in favour of Suor Domenica. Fra Tommaso, once again, took himself off into exile.[310]

Meanwhile, the Florentine ecclesiastical authorities had not heard the last of that indomitable prophetic preacher, Don Teodoro. In 1519 he escaped from S. Miniato al Monte and withdrew with some of his followers to the island of Polvese in Lake Trasimeno.[311] He thus brought himself forcibly to the attention of the very same theological commission which Leo X, in his brief of April 1515,[312] had recommended that the Florentine Archiepiscopal Curia should establish and which, as we have seen, was convoked in August 1519 to examine Caiani's charges against Suor Domenica. As well as Giustiniani, its members on this occasion apparently included Paolo Orlandini.[313] From a letter sent by Orlandini at Pietro Andrea Gammaro's instigation to Giustiniani on 25 April 1519, it is evident that Don Teodoro had returned to his old ways.[314] This letter, in which a meeting was arranged at the archiepiscopal palace to discuss Don Teodoro, makes it clear that since his earlier brush with officialdom he was said to have adopted certain innovations, the most scandalous being the doctrine that sexual relations between the members of his sect were an act of divine praise.[315] Don Teodoro's period of freedom was, however, short-lived. The authorities were ruthless in proceeding against him; and he who had rejoiced in the title of Angelic Pope was consigned to the papal galleys for life.[316]

---

[310] 'Transumptum sententiae', fos. 74$^{r-v}$, 76$^r$–77$^r$.

[311] MS BNF Magl., VIII.1398, fos. 35$^r$–36$^r$. From a comparison of this document, which contains fifteen charges against Don Teodoro, with the *incipit* and *explicit*, as given by E. Massa, of the report on Don Teodoro's errors which was enclosed in a letter of Paolo Orlandini to Paolo Giustiniani, dated 25 Apr. 1519 and concerning Don Teodoro, it is clear that the document is a copy of the original report. Its title, as given by E. Massa, is *Articuli de erroribus cuiusdam Theodori, qui pro pappa angelico se gerrebat; contra quos frater Paulus in quadam congregatione in archiepiscopali palatio Florentie pauca verba habuit anno MDXIX; qui ad triremes perpetuas damnatus est*: Giustiniani, *Trattati, lettere e frammenti*, 116.

[312] See above, p. 289.      [313] See above, p. 292.

[314] Giustiniani, *Trattati, lettere e frammenti*, 116.

[315] MS BNF Magl., VIII.1398, fos. 35$^v$–36$^r$. Rumours to this effect had however been current even at the time of Don Teodoro's trial in 1515: see Cerretani, 'Storia in dialogo', fo. 168$^v$.

[316] Giustiniani, *Trattati, lettere e frammenti*, 116.

From now on, the Piagnoni had to contend with ecclesiastical authorities who were both more alert and better armed than ever before. In the next chapter we shall see how they responded to the challenge. A comment by Niccolò Machiavelli bears eloquent witness to the changed situation in which they now found themselves. On 14 May 1521, while at Carpi as special Florentine envoy to the General Chapter of the Franciscan Order, he was commissioned to secure the services of Fra Giovanni Gualberto, known as 'il Rovaio', to preach at the cathedral of Sta Maria del Fiore in the coming Lenten season;[317] and was confronted by an obduracy surprising in one who had served the Medici well and had nothing to fear from the Florentine government.[318] Writing to Francesco Guicciardini on 18 May, Machiavelli explained why Fra Giovanni Gualberto was refusing to have anything to do with the offer because he no longer knew what was expected of a preacher and feared he might end up in the galleys like Don Teodoro.[319] The latter's fate was long to remain a disquieting reminder of the perils attendant upon the pursuit of a preacher's calling in Florence.

And yet it is clear that the Medici had failed to rid the Church and Florence of Piagnoni trouble-makers. At best, given their inexperience, their international ambitions with concomitant diminished interest in Florence, their tendency to interfere with each other's decisions, they could only hope to deal effectively with men who had drawn attention to themselves by imprudent behaviour. There is no evidence to suggest that they appreciated the full extent of the problem. The Piagnoni's formal and informal networks were permitted to operate undisturbed. Throughout this period of Medici ascendancy, such organizations as the *Monte di Pietà*, the *Buonuomini di S. Martino*, the confraternities of S. Michele Arcangelo and of the Purification of the Virgin and of S. Zanobi, the male and female Observant Dominican convents, enabled the Piagnoni to keep in contact with one another and to engage in

---

[317] Niccolò Machiavelli, *Legazioni e commissarie*, ed. S. Bertelli (3 vols.; Milan, 1964), iii. 1555.

[318] Tommasini, *La vita e gli scritti di Niccolò Machiavelli*, ii. 448.

[319] Machiavelli, *Le lettere*, 411. This cannot but be a reference to Don Teodoro, as Prosperi, 'Il monaco Teodoro', 90, No. 41 has pointed out.

activities which gave meaning and purpose to their lives in expectation of the long-awaited deliverance. Furthermore, when the
need arose, they rallied to the support of brethren who had fallen
foul of the authorities. Thus Niccolò Valori was protected and
assisted by Jacopo Salviati and by Fra Filippo Strozzi and his five
brothers in the convent of S. Marco;[320] the priest Baldassarre da
Pescia, one of Pietro Bernardino's more compromised supporters,
was moved out of harm's way and given the rectorate of a country
church by the Benivieni, who held patronage rights over it;[321] Ser
Giuliano di Domenico da Ripa found it possible to survive after his
removal from the Chancery because his Piagnoni brethren rallied
round him and provided him with work.[322] Similarly, it had proved
impossible to cleanse the Florentine political system of Piagnoni.
The leniency shown to them after the restoration of 1512—which
had so alarmed Medicean partisans[323]—had now come to haunt the
Medici. Those Piagnoni who served in government continued to
afford protection to their brethren and to work towards the implementation of Savonarola's ideals, despite the hostile climate.[324] In

[320] ASF C. Strozz., ser. I, 336, fos. 174ʳ, 178ʳ–182ʳ, 188ʳ: Letter of Jacopo
Salviati to Niccolò, 12 July 1521; five letters of Fra Filippo and Fra Tommaso
Strozzi to same, 24 Aug.–14 Sept. 1525.

[321] AAF Visite Pastorali, 34 (Visita di P. A. Gammaro), fo. 26ʳ.

[322] ASF Not. Ant. G.532, Nos. 76, 89, 111, 151, 158, 186, 251, 253, 255, and
refer to index prefacing the volume.

[323] See above, p. 246.

[324] Tommaso Tosinghi ['Vita'], fo. 129ʳ, where Jacopo Salviati tried to pacify
Tommaso by assuring him that he had been on his side and defended him, though
unsuccessfully, during the meetings of the *Otto di Guardia* held to decide the
ownership of the land which, at Gheri's instigation, was finally taken from him; he
also assured him that he would see to it that he would not have any more trouble
in the future: cf. above, p. 276. See also ASMO Cancelleria Ducale, Ambasciatori
(Firenze), filza 14, dispatch, of 15 May 1529, by Alessandro Guarini, Este Orator
in Florence, to the Duke in which he relates how Jacopo Salviati had ensured that
the Piagnone Bernardo Gondi was made *Gonfaloniere di Giustizia* for the period
July–Aug. 1525. See also letter of Galeotto de' Medici to Lorenzo de' Medici, of
Jan. 1515, where he relates how Lanfredino Lanfredini advised that money from
the *Monte comune* should be employed to provide dowries for poor girls: ASF
MAP 116, No. 33. Finally, see Goro Gheri's frustrated comments on the opposition some of the regime's proposals were receiving in the *Balìa* and attributing this
to the fact that 'in quel principio che la fu facta vi furono messi huomini d'ogni
sorte. Bisogna per lo advenire separare el loglio dal grano': 'Copialettere', vol. ii,
fo. 542ʳ. Some of these issues are discussed in my 'The Medici and the

addition, some of their more prominent representatives, such as Niccolò Valori and Tommaso Tosinghi, who had been ostracized after the restoration of the Medici, began to enjoy a success of sorts and were elected to minor offices. One suspects, however, that their success was due as much to their opponents as to their brethren. By voting them into office, the anti-Savonarolans sought to convince the Medicean leadership that Piagnone radicalism was on the increase and that sterner measures were needed to combat it.[325] It was soon realized even by the Medici themselves that the best way to contain the Piagnoni's political influence was to ensure that the important offices of the state were reserved for the *amici*. It was essential to know, therefore, who they were, and conversely who their opponents were and who among them could be enticed to change sides. Florentine politics became a time-consuming and to a large extent futile exercise in political divination, with the major exponents of the regime vying with each other to provide reliable and continuously updated lists of *amici*, would-be *amici*, uncommitted individuals and opponents, irreducible or otherwise.[326] In the indefatigable compiling of these lists the Mediceans came to resemble the Piagnoni, who were just as obsessively engaged in recording the names of Savonarola's persecutors for future retribution.[327]

Savonarolans, 1512–1527: The Limitations of Personal Government and of the Medicean Patronage System', in F. W. Kent and P. Simons (eds.), *Patronage, Art and Society in Renaissance Italy* (Oxford, 1987), 135–50.

[325] For Niccolò Valori see 'Ricordanze', fo. 20ʳ where, however, he also mentions his appointment to the major post of *Podestà* of Arezzo; for Tommaso Tosinghi, see ['Vita'], fo. 129ʳ, 130ʳ, where he also relates the persecution he was subjected to as a result. Some hints of the anti-Savonarolans' strategy can be obtained from Cerretani, 'Storia in dialogo', fo. 181ʳ.

[326] A sampling of these ubiquitous lists in BNF Capponi (Mobile), Cassetta I, No. 20; cf. ibid., Nuovi Acquisti, 988, where the categories are most comprehensive ranging from 'amici', 'confidenti allo stato', and 'nimici', to 'non-amici', 'dubii', and 'ultimi'; see also ASF Cart. Strozz., ser. I, 9, fo. 176ʳ⁻ᵛ.

[327] For examples of these Piagnoni lists almost invariably appended to the biographies of Savonarola, see ASF C. Strozz., ser. III, 267, chs. 22–3 not foliated; BNF Baldovinetti, 115, pp. 262 ff.

# 7

# 'The New Jerusalem':
# The Last Florentine Republic

### I

In the early 1520s Bartolomeo Cerretani's Girolamo, the Savon-arolan spokesman in his *Storia in dialogo della mutatione di Firenze*, gazed ahead upon a prospect unclouded by any doubt or fear. The measures recently enacted against Piagnoni ecclesiastics left him undaunted. Weighted against the premature deaths of Lorenzo and Giuliano de' Medici, the misrule of the Mediceans and the new stirrings of reform beyond the Alps, these set-backs were to him of little moment. Filled with hope by the direction which events now appeared to be taking, he looked forward to a future of unprec-edented achievement.[1] The ensuing decade was in fact to prove the most momentous in the Piagnoni's history. In these years, they were to achieve successes which fell only a little short of Girolamo's wildest dreams; but their fortunes were also to sink to an ebb from which they would never recover. The fall of the Medicean govern-ment in 1527 was the long-awaited answer to their prayers. With the establishment of the last Florentine Republic, they were of-fered, for however short a time, the opportunity to put into effect all the dreams and plans which they had nurtured for so long. In this chapter we shall see how far they succeeded; and to what extent the heady experience of an unaccustomed freedom wrought its own changes upon them in turn. All too soon, however, and not least because of the Piagnoni's unwillingness to compromise, the

---

[1] Bartolomeo Cerretani, 'Storia in dialogo, della mutatione di Firenze', MS BNF II.I.106, fos. 140ᵛ–143ᵛ, 166ʳ, 169ᵛ.

Republic was overthrown. With the fall of the Republic, the Piagnoni's last chance to fulfil Savonarola's dream of a Florence triumphant was gone forever, although many of them refused to accept the evidence that lay before them.

In the years of rule which yet remained to them, the Mediceans continued steadfast in the conviction that the Piagnoni must be suppressed at all costs. Despite the legislation enacted by the Synod of Florence and the Lateran Council, not to mention the measures taken within the Tusco-Roman Congregation, the Piagnoni were still, in the eyes of the *amici*, a powerful threat to the stability of the regime. Their outlook was that of Cerretani's Giovanni Rucellai, who, far from ridiculing Girolamo's hopes for the future, felt that they were all too likely to be realized.[2] He was no less struck than Girolamo by the deaths of Giuliano and Lorenzo de' Medici: fearing that this could indeed prove to be the turning-point for which the Piagnoni were waiting.[3] To Rucellai, the leadership of Giulio de' Medici, who took over the reins of government in Florence at Lorenzo's death, left much to be desired. As a prince of the Church, his interest had necessarily to be divided between Florence and Rome, while Rucellai considered that Florence needed all the attention she could get. Giulio's policy, moreover, was for some time conciliatory. Rucellai abhorred, for example, his propensity to ingratiate himself with leading Piagnoni. Those so favoured would, in Rucellai's opinion, use the opportunity to advance their own cause and ultimately to take over the government completely.[4] To such Mediceans as Cerretani's spokesman, therefore, Giulio's was not the strong hand Florence so desperately needed.

All too soon, their doubts concerning him were shown to be fully justified. In December 1521, when Leo X died and Giulio was called to Rome, the Mediceans took the opportunity afforded by his absence to prosecute the policy which they wished him to implement in Florence. They arrested seventeen prominent opponents of the government, amongst whom were the Piagnoni Tommaso Tosinghi and his nephew, Francesco di Pierfrancesco

---

[2] Ibid., fos. 177ᵛ–178ʳ, 179ᵛ–180ʳ.      [3] Ibid., fos. 175ᵛ, 180ᵛ.
[4] Ibid., fo. 181ʳ; and see above, p. 248.

Tosinghi, and Niccolò Valori and his sons.[5] Upon his return to
Florence at the end of the month, however, Giulio de' Medici made
no secret of his disapproval of this high-handed action, and at once
ordered the victims' release.[6] Much to the Mediceans' dismay, he
compounded what they saw as a consummate error of judgement
by actively encouraging the speculation, earlier permitted by Leo
X, that the Florentine government would shortly be reformed
along more 'popular' lines and by soliciting, for this purpose, the
opinions of leading citizens of diverse political affiliations.[7] According to Cerretani, the Piagnone Francesco de' Ricci responded
in a manner which can have done little to alleviate the *amici*'s
misgivings.[8] Cerretani, who knew Francesco well, speaks of him in
laudatory terms. Apart from his exemplary religious and moral
conduct—he took communion almost every week and engaged
assiduously in prayer, meditation, and contemplation—Francesco
was learned in religious works and always associated with saintly
men.[9] The constitutional discussions initiated by Cardinal Giulio
prompted him to ask Cerretani to arrange a meeting with the
Cardinal. Granted an audience, Francesco told Giulio that God
wanted him to reform the government of Florence in order to
render it more 'popular'; if he failed to do so, he too would be

[5] Giovanni Cambi, *Istorie*, ed. I. di San Luigi (4 vols.; Florence, 1785–6), iii.
189–90; Tommaso Tosinghi ['Vita'], MS BNF Fondo Principale II.II.325, fo.
129[r]: he had already been sent into precautionary exile in 1518 and was to be
exiled again in 1525.

[6] Cambi, *Istorie*, iii. 190; Jacopo Pitti, *Apologia de' Cappucci, ASI*, 1st ser. 4/2
(1853), 325.

[7] Ibid., 325–6; Jacopo Nardi, *Istorie della città di Firenze*, ed. A. Gelli (2 vols.;
Florence, 1858), ii. 69; Filippo de' Nerli, *Commentari dei fatti civili occorsi dentro la
città di Firenze dall'anno 1215 al 1537* (2 vols.; Trieste, 1859), ii. 10–12. On the
response occasioned by this overture, and the various plans submitted to Giulio
de' Medici, see R. von Albertini, *Firenze dalla repubblica al principato* (Turin,
1970), 78–83; J. N. Stephens, *The Fall of the Florentine Republic, 1512–1530*
(Oxford, 1983), 113–15.

[8] Bartolomeo Cerretani, 'Ricordi storici fiorentini 1500–1523', MS BAV Vat.
Lat, 13651, fo. 215[r–v]; on all this see my 'Prophecy, Politics and History in Early
Sixteenth-Century Florence: The Admonitory Letters of Francesco d'Antonio
de' Ricci', in P. Denley and C. Elam (eds.), *Florence and Italy: Renaissance Studies
in Honour of Nicolai Rubinstein* (London, 1988), 107–31.

[9] Cerretani, 'Ricordi storici fiorentini', fo. 215[r].

struck down, as the other Medici leaders had been.[10] Cardinal Giulio, by all accounts an impressionable man,[11] listened for two hours, telling Cerretani later that he was struck by Francesco's goodness and by his unequivocal words.

Francesco elaborated on these matters to Cerretani himself, providing 'proofs' of the genuineness of his illumination. He asserted that if Florence were not reformed there would ensue great scandals and much harm for the city. If, on the other hand, Cardinal Giulio were to heed and execute God's commands he would become the most eminent man in the world. In corroboration, Francesco displayed letters from two deceased Piagnoni friars of S. Marco, Fra Silvestro da Marradi, whom we have already met, and Fra Raffaello del Cappucciaio, latterly Prior of the convent of Sta Caterina at Pisa and Master of Novices at S. Marco just before his death in 1518.[12] These he had received through the agency of an angel, who would also transmit a reply. These matters and others, Francesco concluded, had been prophesied to him by three angels of God.[13]

Though Cardinal Giulio expressed some doubt concerning Francesco's mental state,[14] he none the less, according to Cerretani, continued to respect his saintliness and to grant him a hearing when requested. He also heeded Francesco's advice and sought to act upon it whenever possible. Thus, in the aftermath of the Buondelmonti–Alamanni conspiracy, whose members had plotted to assassinate Cardinal Giulio and to overthrow the regime, Cardinal Giulio sent for the miraculous image of Our Lady of Impruneta and decreed three days of prayers, fasting, preaching, and proces-

[10] Ibid.

[11] D. Cantimori, 'Note su alcuni aspetti della propaganda religiosa nell'Europa del Cinquecento', in H. Meylan (ed.), *Aspects de la propagande religieuse* (Travaux d'Humanisme et Renaissance, 28; Geneva, 1957), 341.

[12] On Fra Silvestro, who had died in 1517, see above, pp. 198–9. On Fra Raffaello, who was a close companion of Fra Silvestro and who had died in 1518, see Roberto Ubaldini, 'Annalia Conventus Sancti Marci', MS BMLF S. Marco 370, fos. 96[v] and 164[v] and F. Bonaini (ed.), 'Chronica antiqua Conventus sanctae Catharinae de Pisis', *ASI*, lst ser. 6/2 (1848), 125.

[13] Cerretani, 'Ricordi storici fiorentini', fo. 215[v].

[14] Speaking to Cerretani he referred to him as a 'santo huomo, non so se un pocho manichonichetto', Cerretani, 'Ricordi storici fiorentini', fo. 215[v].

sions as Francesco had advised. Francesco's calls for reform had by this time gained in precision and scope. In addition to constitutional reform, Francesco now wished the Cardinal to introduce true Christian living in his household, in Florence, and in the whole Church. Throughout, Francesco held out the promise that, should Giulio initiate these reforms, God would raise him above all other men and appoint him as His minister.[15]

It is extremely unlikely that Cardinal Giulio at any time seriously considered liberalizing the government of Florence along the lines suggested by Francesco and other Savonarolans. His election to the papacy in 1523, as Clement VII, would in any case have put an end to such a notion. His elevation, incidentally, confirmed Francesco's prophecy. Certainly Francesco took it as a sign that he should not only continue in his divinely sanctioned task of guiding and admonishing Clement VII in his new office, but should also extend this favour to other leaders of Christendom. To this end, he wrote numerous admonitory letters, of which seven, written between 1527 and 1533, have survived: five addressed to Clement VII and two to the Emperor Charles V.[16] They will be discussed later, at their appropriate places.

Even before Giulio's election to the papacy the tide in Florence had begun to turn. In an extremely volatile situation in which, according to Cerretani, discontent was rife and three-quarters of the citizens were hostile to the regime,[17] a series of events was to play into the hand of the die-hard *amici*. On 21 December 1521 a Fra Spirito from the convent of S. Spirito—who had already been arrested the previous year for preaching, at the command of Savonarola, who had appeared to him in a vision, that the popular government had to be restored and the Church renewed—made his way to the Piazza della Signoria and there caused a near riot

---

[15] Ibid., fos. 215ᵛ, 218ʳ⁻ᵛ, 219ʳ.

[16] All of them are to be found in ASF C. Strozz., ser. I, 14. A summary description of them is given in C. Guasti, *Le Carte Strozziane del R. Archivio di Stato in Firenze* (2 vols.; Florence, 1884–91), i. 86–7. Since the compilation of this catalogue, however, the foliation has been changed. I will use the new foliation.

[17] Cerretani, 'Ricordi storici fiorentini', fos. 211ʳ, 213ʳ, 225ʳ, 231ᵛ; on fo. 214ʳ, the percentage is assessed as two-thirds.

by crying out: 'popolo, popolo e libertà'.[18] He was seized by the guards, beaten, silenced with great difficulty, and taken to the *Bargello*, where he was tortured before being committed to prison.[19] Another, more serious riot occurred shortly afterwards when a rumour was circulated that Giulio had been created Pope. The populace rose, bonfires were lit, all the shops in the Mercato Vecchio were sacked, and only with great difficulty was it possible to prevent a similar fate from befalling the Medici palaces and those of their relatives.[20] The *amici* were convinced that the rumour had been maliciously circulated so as to cause the riot as a preliminary to the overthrow of the government. Their enemies were equally convinced that the whole commotion had been planned by the Mediceans to justify sterner measures against the opponents of the regime.[21]

The *amici*'s fears concerning the opposition to the regime were shortly to prove well founded and official policy was forced to swing round to their view and become, in the end, every bit as uncompromising as they had desired. This transformation was brought about by the discovery in May 1522 of a plot against Giulio de' Medici. The conspirators, it was revealed, who were in contact both with Cardinal Soderini and with the French, had planned to assassinate Giulio and to reappoint Piero Soderini as *Gonfaloniere a vita*.[22] Two of the plotters, Luigi di Tommaso Alamanni and Jacopo da Ghiacceto, were seized and executed, while those who managed to escape, or who were already in a safe place, including the Piagnone Battista della Palla[23] in Lyons, were condemned *in*

---

[18] Ibid., fo. 206ʳ.    [19] Ibid., fo. 207ʳ.

[20] Ibid., fo. 207ʳ.    [21] Ibid.

[22] Most of the documents relating to the conspiracy are published in C. Guasti, 'Documenti della congiura fatta contro il cardinale Giulio de' Medici nel 1522', *Giornale Storico degli Archivi Toscani*, 3 (1859), 121–232 and 239–67. See also Stephens, *The Fall of the Florentine Republic 1512–1530*, 120–22.

[23] On him see H. Hauvette, *Un exilé florentin a la cour de France au XVIᵉ siècle: Luigi Alamanni (1495–1556): Sa vie et son œuvre* (Paris, 1903), index. On his Savonarolan sentiments see letter of Lorenzo Violi to him, 18 Mar. 1528, in BNF Cappugi, 124, fos. 1ʳ⁻ᵛ; Jacopo Nardi, *I due felici rivali*, ed. A. Ferrajoli (Rome, 1901), p. XXIV; L. Polizzotto and C. Elam, '*La unione de'gigli con gigli*: Two documents on Florence, France and the Savonarolan Millenarian Tradition', *Rinascimento*, 31 (1991), 239–59.

*absentia* and had their goods confiscated.[24] Further Piagnone involvement in the scheme was revealed during the proceedings against another participant, Niccolò Martelli, who was caught and brought to trial in 1524.[25] In the records of his trial, accusations against the Piagnoni loom large. Martelli accused Jacopo Salviati, Niccolò Valori, and Tommaso di Paolantonio Soderini, together with other noted anti-Mediceans, of having master-minded the plot.[26] Whether these accusations were genuine, or whether they were engineered by the *amici* in order to justify the policy of unremitting harshness which was adopted after the conspiracy was unveiled, cannot now be determined. It remains true, nevertheless, that, with the discovery of the plot, Giulio de' Medici's programme of conciliation was brought to an abrupt end; and the Piagnoni, no less than any other opposition group, suffered from this changed climate.[27] The harsh policy thus instituted was pursued with even more vigour after Giulio became Pope in 1523 and, under the guiding hand of his deputy in Florence, Silvio Passerini, Cardinal of Cortona, continued in force until the collapse of the Medici regime. The anti-Medicean Piero Orlandini was executed for having cast doubt on the legitimacy of Giulio de' Medici's election as Pope and two Piagnoni, Martino di Francesco Scarfi and Francesco Torrigiani, were arrested and then exiled for criticizing the regime.[28] Inevitably Tommaso Tosinghi too fell foul of the authorities and, for allegedly speaking out of turn in a meeting of the

[24] Guasti, 'Documenti della congiura fatta contro il cardinale Giulio de' Medici', 122–42.

[25] Ibid. 213–15.

[26] Ibid. 216–32, 239–67 collated with: '[Primo] Processo di Niccolò Martelli . . . Die 14 octobris 1524' and 'Secondo Processo di Niccolò Martelli facto a Civitavecchia sotto dì 17 di giugno 1526', MS ASF Miscellanea Repubblicana, 8, inserto 4, no foliation.

[27] Jacopo Pitti, *Dell'Istoria fiorentina*, in *ASI*, lst ser. 1 (1842), 129; Filippo de' Nerli, *Commentari*, ii. 14.

[28] Cerretani, 'Ricordi storici fiorentini', fos. 232$^v$–233$^v$. According to Cerretani, beginning at this time with Giulio's deputies, one of the first of whom was Fra Niccolò Schomberg of S. Marco and by now Bishop of Capua, 'le deliberationi dello stato erano più strette che le fussino mai perché non achopiatori, non otto di praticha non 70 non cento, ma solo si risolveva per deliberatione di tre o quattro ciptadini il che rechava loro invidia a' cieli e odio': ibid., fo. 222$^v$.

Council of the *Arte dei Mercanti*, he was exiled for two years despite his advanced age.[29]

Not all Piagnoni represented as dire a threat to the government as the Mediceans believed. Many, as we have seen, were convinced that the truth as Savonarola had seen it could be served only by advancing his cause in defiance of the authorities. Others, however, thought differently. The Piagnoni's mixed response to those in power was due partly to the fluctuations in official policy, but also to their long-standing differences over how best to promote their divine mission. For example, at the opposite end of the spectrum from the radicals were those who reached a compromise with their rulers and remained willing to follow the Medici's leadership. As in the past, Girolamo Benivieni, close friend and adviser to Giulio de' Medici, was one of the more notable exponents of this policy.[30] With his intimate friend and fellow Piagnone, the priest Francesco Fortunati, Girolamo Benivieni was in close contact with the cadet branch of the Medici family. Having looked after the financial interests of Giovanni delle Bande Nere for some time, in 1524 he was invited by Jacopo Salviati and Giulio de' Medici, now Clement VII, to undertake the tutelage of the young Cosimo, afterwards Duke of Florence. Although he declined it, on grounds of ill-health, the offer is an indication of the position of trust which he enjoyed among the members of the Medici family.[31] A similar position was held by another Piagnone, Lorenzo Violi, who became Second Chancellor on 11 July 1520. Holding this appointment

---

[29] Tosinghi ['Vita'], fos. 129$^{r-v}$, 130$^{r}$; he was then 77 years old.

[30] See above, pp. 248–9.

[31] ASF MAP 7, 443; Antonio Benivieni, 'Vita di Girolamo Benivieni', MS BNF II.I.91, p. 247; C. Re, *Girolamo Benivieni fiorentino* (Città di Castello, 1906), 130–1; *DBI*; A. Pelizzari, *Un asceta del Rinascimento (Della vita e delle opere di Girolamo Benivieni* (Genoa, 1906), 53. Jacopo Salviati was of course Cosimo's grandfather. On the subject of the connections of Girolamo Benivieni, Francesco Fortunati, and Jacopo Salviati with the cadet branch of the Medici family, see C. Milanesi (ed.), 'Lettere inedite e testamento di Giovanni de' Medici detto delle Bande Nere, con altre di Maria e di Jacopo Salviati', *ASI*, NS 7/2 (1858), 3–48; A. Gherardi, *Nuovi documenti e studi intorno a Girolamo Savonarola* (Florence, 1887; fac. repr. 1972), 259–60; id., 'Due lettere di un'antica gentildonna', in I. del Badia, *Miscellanea fiorentina di erudizione e storia* (2 vols.; Florence, 1902), ii. 122–5.

without a break throughout the remaining years of Medici rule, Violi was frequently entrusted with the task of conducting negotiations of an especially delicate nature within the Florentine territories.[32] Carlo del Benino, too, finally responded to Medici overtures and was rewarded, being made *Gonfaloniere di Giustizia* for March–April 1521.[33] Even Niccolò Valori, his bona fides now attested by his highly placed patrons and by the *Vita del Magnifico Lorenzo Vecchio de' Medici*, was suitably rewarded with the prestigious post of *Podestà* of Arezzo.[34]

How fruitful the policy of co-operation could be for the Piagnoni is clearly apparent from the success of two of its undertakings. One was the foundation in Florence of a hospital for the incurably ill. First mooted by Fra Callisto da Piacenza, an Augustinian Canon Regular from the Badia of Fiesole, when he was preaching at Sta Maria del Fiore, this project was at once taken up by Fra Cherubino Primerani of S. Marco. On 23 March 1520 a meeting of 150 citizens, acting with Giulio de' Medici's blessing, drew up the constitution for a confraternity to build and maintain the hospital. The confraternity's officers, who were appointed on the same occasion, included a considerable proportion of Piagnoni. The Prior himself, Alessandro d'Antonio Pucci, was one; and of the twelve *consiglieri* chosen to assist him, Marco di Simone del Nero, Marco Strozzi, and Bartolomeo Redditi were all Piagnoni. Given the name of the Arciconfraternità della SS. Trinità, the confraternity had its constitutions approved by Leo X, who also issued a plenary indulgence to encourage the giving of alms for the scheme. Having benefited greatly from the donations of an enthusiastic populace, and from a sizeable contribution by Cardinal Giulio himself, the

---

[32] D. Marzi, *La cancelleria della Repubblica Fiorentina* (Rocca S. Casciano, 1910), 314, 317 and n. 4. C. Vasoli, 'Note sulle "Giornate" di Ser Lorenzo Violi', *Memorie Domenicane*, NS 3 (1972), 21.

[33] Cambi, *Istorie*, iii. 183; Francesco de' Gaddi, 'Priorista', MS BL Egerton 3764, fo. 256ʳ.

[34] Niccolò Valori, 'Ricordanze', fo. 20ʳ. I have found no evidence to support F. Gilbert's contention that he was made Florentine ambassador in Rome in 1522: 'Guicciardini, Machiavelli, Valori on Lorenzo Magnifico', *Renaissance News*, 11 (1958), 112 n. 21. He did indeed move to Rome at about this time, or shortly afterwards, but exclusively in a private capacity.

work of the hospital was begun within the month, even though permanent premises were not yet ready. Thus, unwittingly, the Medici had enabled the Piagnoni to add to their network of institutions which provided them with shelter and with the means of fulfilling their Christian duties.[35]

Equally rewarding was the Piagnoni's involvement in the canonization of S. Antonino. This had been an initiative launched by Leo X in 1516 partly to pacify the friars of S. Marco, whose convent had been founded by S. Antonino, and partly to enhance the standing of the Medici at a time when their popularity was at a very low ebb.[36] It proved impossible, however, to obtain the approval of the College of Cardinals for the canonization. The whole process had come to a standstill when in 1520 the friars of S. Marco stepped in. Led by Fra Roberto Ubaldini, who co-ordinated activities, they obtained the finances needed and instituted another trial to gather more evidence of Antonino's sanctity. Piagnoni, lay and ecclesiastic, including even Fra Tommaso Caiani, dominated the proceedings. From this trial there emerged a much altered image of S. Antonino: a S. Antonino who prefigured Savonarola and who, by his actions and pronouncements, validated the apostolate of Savonarola and of his followers and condemned, at the same time, the activities of the Medici in Florence and in the Church. When, in 1523, Clement VII brought the whole tortuous process to a close

---

[35] ASF Spedale degli Incurabili, I, fos. 2ʳ–17ᵛ (first folio is missing); 'Origine e fondazione della Venerabile Confraternita della Santissima Trinita e Arcispedale degli infermi incurabili', MS BNF Gino Capponi, 205, esp. fos. 8ʳ ff.; letter of Angelo Marzi to Bishop Bernardo de' Rossi, Governor of Bologna, 22 Apr. 1522, ibid., II.VI.51, fos. 85ʳ⁻ᵛ; Cambi, *Istorie*, iii. 159–61; L. Passerini, *Storia degli stabilimenti di beneficenza e d'istruzione elementare gratuita della città di Firenze* (Florence, 1853), 203–9; G. Conti, *Fatti e anedotti di storia fiorentina* (Florence, 1902) 450–1. Until the new premises were ready, the hospitals of Sta Caterina dei Talani and S. Rocco were used by the new confraternity.

[36] The original acts of the trial are in BMLF S. Marco, 883–5; they are to be supplemented with the *transumptum*, partly printed and partly in MS, in BNF Conv. Soppr., J.1.51. See also S. Orlandi, 'La canonizzazione di S. Antonino nella relazione di Fra Roberto Ubaldini da Gagliano', *Memorie Domenicane*, 81 (1964), 85–115 and 131–62 and my 'The Making of a Saint: The Canonization of St. Antonino, 1516–1523', *Journal of Medieval and Renaissance Studies*, 22 (1992), 353–81.

with the publication of the formal bull of canonization,[37] he could not have been aware of how thoroughly the original aims had been subverted and how useful S. Antonino was to prove for S. Marco and for the Savonarolan tradition.

Meanwhile, other Piagnoni refused to countenance this degree of compromise with the Medici regime and pursued a different course. Their project was to write the definitive life of their martyred leader. The delicate and painstaking task of composing Savonarola's biography was undertaken at two separate centres, one at Mirandola and one in Florence. First off the mark was Giovanfrancesco Pico, ever loyal to the Piagnone cause and ever ready to devote his energies to its advancement. In 1520 or thereabouts, he produced the first version of his *Vita Reverendi Patris F. Hieronymi Savonarolae*, in twenty-two chapters.[38] This was subsequently enlarged to thirty chapters to include accounts of recent miracles worked by Savonarola and his acolytes.[39] Yet a third version, in thirty-two chapters, was to follow before Giovanfrancesco died in 1533.[40] The other biography of Savonarola, known as the *Vita latina*,[41] got under way rather more slowly than Giovanfrancesco's. Various dates have been assigned to its completion,[42] but the absence of any mention either of the fall of the

---

[37] T. Ripoll and A. Brémond (eds.), *Bullarium Ordinis Praedicatorum* (8 vols.; Rome, 1729–40), iv. 417–26.

[38] MS BRF 2053, fos. 65ʳ–90ʳ.

[39] Giovanfrancesco Pico, *Vita Reverendi Patris F. Hieronymi Savonarolae*, ed. J. Quétif (Paris, 1674).

[40] MS BNF Conv. Sopp., J.VII.31, with additions by Fra Ignazio Manardi. Examples of other copies in Florentine libraries are: MS BNF Magl., XXXV, 288; MS BNF Magl., XXXVII, 65; MS BNF Conv. Sopp., J.VII.26. On the various versions of the Giovanfrancesco Pico life, see J. Schnitzer, 'La vita del Savonarola scritta dal Conte Giovanfrancesco Pico della Mirandola', *Ricerche religiose*, 5 (1929), 429–34. For an indication of the profusion and diffusion of these versions in various Italian and European libraries, see the admirable inventory in C. B. Schmitt, *Gianfrancesco Pico della Mirandola (1469–1533) and his Critique of Aristotle* (The Hague, 1967), app. A, sect. III, pp. 217–26.

[41] 'Vita Beati Hieronymi, martiris, doctoris, virginis ac prophetae eximii', MS BNF Conv. Sopp., J.VII.28.

[42] J. Schnitzer assigns it to 1527, but on the grounds of his mistaken hypothesis that its author was Fra Luca Bettini, who died in that year: *Savonarola* (2 vols.; Milan, 1931), ii. 531. R. Ridolfi assigns it to 1528: *Vita di Girolamo Savonarola* (2 vols.; Rome, 1952), ii. 81–2.

Medicean government or of the establishment of the new Republic would suggest a *terminus ad quem* of May 1527. While only one copy of the *Vita latina* is known to have survived, there are countless copies of the *Vita italiana*, a liberal Italian translation of the Latin life which was made shortly afterwards and was until recently attributed to Fra Pacifico Burlamacchi.[43] Copies of the later versions of Giovanfrancesco's life survive in similar profusion. The extent to which these copies, as well as those of the Pseudo-Burlamacchi *Vita*, were dispersed is remarkable. There was scarcely a religious foundation in central Italy which did not boast one or both; and their catalogues are a valuable way of assessing the spread of Piagnone influence later in the sixteenth century, when direct evidence of Piagnoni activity can no longer be found.[44]

In the past, attempts had been made to sketch the high points in Savonarola's career but even the most comprehensive of them, Placido Cinozzi's *Epistola de vita et moribus Savonarole*,[45] had done no more than outline certain key events in his apostolate. Giovanfrancesco Pico's *Vita* and the *Vita latina*, on the other hand,

---

[43] Examples are: MSS BNF Conv. Sopp., G.5.1207–9; G.9.1885; J.VII.43; J.VIII.5–6; BNF Magl., XXXVII, 281; BMLF Fondo S. Marco 427. A version of this life, attributed to Pacifico Burlamacchi, was first published by J. D. Mansi in his App. to S. Baluze, *Miscellanea novo ordine digesta . . . opera ac studia* (Lucca, 1761), i. 530 ff.; and was subsequently reissued several times separately. Another version has been published by P. G. Conti [and R. Ridolfi] (eds.), *La vita del Beato Ieronimo Savonarola scritta da un anonimo del sec. XVI e già attribuita a Fra Pacifico Burlamacchi* (Florence, 1937); and this is the copy which, with certain exceptions, and cited as Pseudo-Burlamacchi, *La vita*, has been used throughout the book. On the relationship between the *Vita latina* and the Pseudo-Burlamacchi *Vita*, see R. Ridolfi, 'La questione dello Pseudo-Burlamacchi e della "Vita Latina"', in *Le lettere di Girolamo Savonarola: Nuovi contributi con un'appendice sulla questione dello Pseudo-Burlamacchi e della 'Vita Latina'* (Florence, 1936), 19–34.

[44] For the part played by the friars of S. Marco in the diffusion of these works after the suppression of the Tusco-Roman Congregation, see S. Razzi, 'Cronica della Provincia Romana dell'Ordine de' frati predicatori', MS BMLF S. Marco 873, *passim*.

[45] Placido Cinozzi, *Estratto d'una epistola Placidi de Cinozis Ordinis Praedicatorum S. Marci de Florentia, De vita et moribus reverendi patris fratris Hieronimi Savonarole de Ferraria, fratri Iacobo Siculo, eiusdem Ordinis vicarius generalis* [sic] *post mortem dicti Prophete*, in P. Villari and E. Casanova (eds.), *Scelta di Prediche e scritti di Fra Girolamo Savonarola, con nuovi documenti intorno alla sua vita* (Florence, 1898), 3–28.

represented a concerted endeavour to recount his history in all its detail. In this, they were the products of the newly hostile climate which followed the attacks levelled against Savonarola and his followers from 1515 onwards. Their immediate purpose was to defend Savonarola and his ideals against the official calumnies. To this end, they recorded the events of his life and apostolate in exhaustive detail, combing them for proof both of his personal sanctity and of the divine nature of his mission. To these truths, the accounts of miracles performed after his death, supposedly through his agency, added further testimonies. Because the object of the authorities' recent moves against Savonarola had been to discredit him by demonstrating the unworthy character of those, such as Pietro Bernardino and Don Teodoro, who had professed allegiance to him, the authors of the new lives strove to demonstrate the opposite. Either by prudently refraining from mentioning Pietro Bernardino or Don Teodoro, thus refusing to acknowledge that they belonged to the Savonarolan movement, which was the course Giovanfrancesco Pico took, or by openly condemning and rejecting them both, as the author of the *Vita latina* had no compunction in doing,[46] the biographers endeavoured to prove that the mainstream of the tradition which owed its origins to Savonarola was without equal both in the purity of its reforming ideals and in the moral rectitude of its leadership.[47]

This was not the only way in which Giovanfrancesco's *Vita* and the *Vita latina* reflected the changing times. They had also a long-term purpose which was unlike anything hitherto attempted. They were written, in a crucial sense, for posterity. Whereas Cinozzi's narrative of Savonarola's life had been intended for the edification of one person only, the recently converted Jacopo da Sicilia,[48] these biographies were designed to influence present and future generations of Piagnoni activists. Composed partly to circumvent the authorities, now that preaching of a radical sort could no longer be

---

[46] 'Vita latina', fos. 43$^r$, 72$^v$; cf. Pseudo-Burlamacchi, *La vita*, 241–2.

[47] See e.g. 'Vita latina', fos. 21$^r$–23$^v$; 68$^v$–74$^v$; Giovanfrancesco Pico, *Vita Reverendi Patris F. Hieronymi Savonarolae*, 159–201; Pseudo-Burlamacchi, *La vita*, 97–101, 118–27.

[48] See above, p. 174.

undertaken with impunity, the lives were also an attempt to ensure that what had so far been achieved should not be lost to acolytes too young to have experienced it. In this respect, their composition marked a new departure in Piagnoni attitudes. While their immediate aim was to vindicate Savonarola and his followers, their overriding purpose was hortatory, not hagiographical, in nature: succeeding generations were to be spurred on to complete the mission which Savonarola had begun.[49] Their composition was thus a way of coming to terms with the bans instituted against the cult of Savonarola and the dissemination of his doctrine. After a hard-headed appraisal of the limited opportunities now open to Piagnoni reformers under Medici rule, the biographers had come to the decision that, in these reduced circumstances, the best way of furthering Savonarola's cause was to see that succeeding generations were fully informed of the true temper of the tradition to which they were heir.

How many had come to this decision can be seen from the number of Piagnoni who assisted in the production of the lives. Both were collaborative efforts: Giovanfrancesco Pico being aided by Fra Luca Bettini and Fra Ignazio Manardi,[50] and the anonymous compiler of the *Vita latina* acknowledging debts to Placido Cinozzi, Fra Sante da S. Casciano, Giovanfrancesco Pico, and Girolamo Benivieni.[51] Much was owed, further, to the contributions of other Piagnoni who supplied accounts of miracles performed by Savonarola and his followers, either directly to the biographers, or through the agency of Fra Bartolomeo da Faenza, who took upon himself the task of gathering this information together.[52] Additions

---

[49] The prologues to both works make this plain: see 'Vita latina', fo. 1$^r$; Pico, *Vita Reverendi Patris F. Hieronymi Savonarolae*, 1–3; cf. Pseudo-Burlamacchi, *La vita*, 3–4. See also Schnitzer, 'La vita del Savonarola scritta dal Conte Giovanfrancesco Pico della Mirandola', 429; Ridolfi, *Vita*, ii. 82; I. Taurisano, *I Domenicani in Lucca* (Lucca, 1914), 88, 92.

[50] Pico, *Vita Reverendi Patris F. Hieronymi Savonarolae*, 185; see also MS BNF Conv. Sopp., J.VII.31.

[51] 'Vita latina', fo. 94$^r$.

[52] All three biographies acknowledge Fra Bartolomeo as a source: 'Vita latina', fo. 73$^r$; Pico, *Vita Reverendi Patris F. Hieronymi Savonarolae*, 160–2, 175; Pseudo-Burlamacchi, *La vita*, 18, 105, 138, 221, 226–7. See also MS BNF Palatino-Baldovinetti, 115: 'Visione di fra Bartolomeo da Faenza', fos. 365$^r$–369$^r$; and *DBI*.

to this list of collaborators are provided by the Pseudo-Burlamacchi *Vita*, which made mention of the assistance of Fra Jacopo da Sicilia, Iacopo Mannelli,[53] Canon of Sta Maria del Fiore, and Fra Tommaso Caiani.[54] In the light of the subsequent history of the Piagnone movement, the decision by so many of its notables to devote their energies, whether fully or in part, to this activity (complemented also when possible with the publication of Savonarola's works)[55] takes on an even greater importance. Their decision was based on an assessment of their situation which, in the short term, was to be proved wrong, since the establishment of the last Florentine Republic provided unprecedented opportunities for the Piagnoni to accomplish even their most radical aims. But, in the long run, the movement was driven underground, much as Giovanfrancesco Pico and the other biographers had anticipated; when that occurred, the biographies proved their worth in keeping alive the memory of Savonarola.

For the moment, however, there were many Piagnoni who, while endorsing the value of the first biographies, saw no reason to allow the quietistic approach favoured by their authors to dominate their own work for the Savonarolan cause. Believing that a more active commitment was required of them, even in the present inauspicious times, but sobered, at the same time, by the experience of Don Teodoro, they followed the example of many of their brethren and underwent voluntary exile from Florence in order to work unimpeded for the cause. Among those who took this step were the three Bettini brothers, Luca, Domenico, and Giovanni Maria. Having renounced the Tusco-Roman Congregation, where Luca Bettini's opportunities for advancement had been effectively thwarted by the intervention of Tommaso de Vio Gaetano, they all made new lives for themselves in Mirandola.[56] Another exile was

---

[53] On him see E. Sanesi, *Vicari e canonici fiorentini e il 'caso Savonarola'* (Florence, 1932), 26, 29, 30–6; P. Villari, *La storia di Girolamo Savonarola e de' suoi tempi* (2 vols.; Florence, 1930), vol. ii, app., p. ccxxx.

[54] Pseudo-Burlamacchi, *La vita*, 192, 210, 213, 232.

[55] AGOP, IV, 16, fo. 351$^{r-v}$: for difficulties incurred in obtaining official permission, but of course, unofficially, his works were being published throughout these years.

[56] See above, p. 306.

Fra Santi Pagnini, who, after the death of Leo X, attached himself to the household of Cardinal François de Clermont in Avignon and Lyons, where he became a leading light in the local Florentine communities.[57] Here with another, but unknown, Piagnone—possibly Fra Iacopo da Sicilia, who had also made his way to Lyons by about this time[58]—Fra Santi welcomed the fugitive conspirators Zanobi Buondelmonti and Luigi di Piero Alamanni, who had escaped from Florence after the discovery of their plot against Giulio de' Medici.[59]

Something of the constructive work undertaken by Piagnoni exiles can be seen in Pistoia, where they took part in the organization of a youth confraternity which had been founded in 1516. Although established to end the internecine feuds between the Cancellieri and Panciatichi factions, the Compagnia della Purità quickly came under Piagnone influence. Among its officials were Fra Girolamo Giannotti, who was to translate and publish Savonarola's sermons on the Psalm *Quam bonus* which appeared in Venice in 1528, and his brother Alessandro.[60] The confraternity was closely associated with the local Dominican convent of S. Domenico. Indeed, some of the Dominican friars referred to the confraternity as a school (*scuola*) and looked upon it as a vocational training centre for their Order. Their expectations were not disappointed: the Compagnia della Purità, which by August 1517 numbered seventy-two members, was to become an important source of vocations, at least in the years immediately following its foundation. In other respects, however, the confraternity was a

[57] T. M. Centi, 'L'attività letteraria di Santi Pagnini', *AFP* 15 (1945), 16, 19–20; Taurisano, *I Domenicani in Lucca*, 104–8.

[58] R. Creytens, 'Les Actes capitulaires de la Congrégation Toscano-Romaine', *AFP* 40 (1970), 176.

[59] Guasti, 'Documenti della congiura fatta contro il cardinale Giulio de' Medici', 201, 211–12.

[60] P. Vigo (ed.), *Una confraternita di giovanetti pistoiesi a principio del secolo XVI (Compagnia della Purità): Cronachetta inedita* (Scelta di curiosità letterarie inedite o rare dal secolo XIII al XVIII: Dispensa CCXX; Bologna, 1887), 3, 111. On Fra Girolamo and Fra Alessandro Giannotti, see Ridolfi, *Vita*, ii. 31, 49. Fra Girolamo Giannotti's edition of the *Prediche del Reverendo Padre Fra Girolamo Savonarola sopra il Salmo 'Quam bonus Israel Deus'* (Venice, 1528), was subsequently published again in Venice in 1539 and 1544.

failure. It did not put an end to factionalism—it appears, rather, to have exacerbated it—and was greatly troubled by litigations and defections encouraged by another confraternity which had been specifically founded to spite the Compagnia della Purità.[61]

Shortly afterwards, in 1521, another group of Piagnoni friars from S. Domenico reformed the Pistoiese convent of Sta Caterina. Till then Sta Caterina, founded in 1477, had been one of the numerous loosely organized communities of Dominican tertiaries. At the urging of Fra Cherubino Primerani, Prior of S. Domenico, the tertiaries took the vows of chastity, poverty, and obedience in his presence and adopted the strict rule of the Dominican Observants. They also reformed their habit and abandoned worldly comforts for the harsh life of Observant nuns.[62] In 1526, after repeatedly petitioning the Dominican hierarchy, they secured the support of Fra Timoteo de' Ricci and of Fra Simone Strada and were permitted to make their formal, solemn profession as Dominican nuns. By this time they had also evinced a determination to place their convent even more squarely in the mainstream of the Savonarolan religious tradition. They beseeched the Dominican authorities to appoint over them two nuns from the convent of Sta Caterina in Florence. Refusing to be discouraged by the hierarchy's denials, they persisted with their requests until the newly appointed Vicar-General of the Congregation, Fra Niccolò Michelozzi, complied with their wishes by appointing Suor Paola Pescioni as Prioress and Suor Margherita del Cittadino as Teacher of Novices. The Pistoiese convent of Sta Caterina became an important prize both for the Savonarolan cause and for the Tusco-Roman Congregation as a whole.[63]

[61] ASPI Corporazioni Religiose Soppresse, XXXII-442B: 'Libro di ricordanze del Convento di S. Domenico 1516–1732', separately and erratically foliated section at the end on the Compagnia della Purità of 7 folios numbered from fo. 160ʳ–201ᵛ. The statement occurs on fo. 161ᵛ. See also Vigo, *Una confraternita di giovanetti pistoiesi*, 96, and R. C. Trexler, 'Ritual in Florence: Adolescence and Salvation in the Renaissance', in C. Trinkaus and H. A. Oberman (eds.), *The Pursuit of Holiness in Late Medieval and Renaissance Religion* (Leiden, 1974), 249 *et passim* for an illuminating discussion of the confraternity's religious practices.

[62] ASPI Corporazioni Religiose Soppresse, XXII-257B: 'Cronache del Convento delle Monache di S. Caterina 1477–1646', fos. 3ʳ–4ᵛ.

[63] Ibid., fos. 5ᵛ–6ᵛ, 44ʳ–47ʳ.

The most valuable recruit to the scattered band of Piagnoni exiles was Fra Benedetto da Foiano from Sta Maria Novella. Early in 1520 Fra Benedetto, who till recently had been closely identified with the Medici[64] and who had held some of the most important posts in the convent, including that of Prior, voiced strong criticism of his Order and of individual members within it, declaiming, in characteristically Savonarolan language, against their religious indifference (*tiepidità*). On 26 May 1520 the Master-General of the Order, Garcia di Loaysa, visited the convent of Sta Maria Novella specifically to deal with the case; and on 1 June, after a special meeting, issued a condemnation of Fra Benedetto. Fra Benedetto decided to abandon the convent and flee to Venice, where he remained until the collapse of the Medici regime.[65] From the fact that he was recalled to Florence by the first *Dieci di Libertà* to take office after the Medici's fall, it would appear that the anti-Medicean stance for which he was later to become famous was already known during his exile.[66] It was evidently no news to the friars of S. Marco, for instance, who received him as an honoured guest in their convent upon his return, until he was created Prior of the convent of Sta Maria Novella.[67]

To the incorrigible radical, however, none of these alternatives to direct action was remotely feasible. Even under the present government, Piagnoni extremists remained convinced that, by deserting the Florentine political and religious scene, they would be renouncing their allegiance to Savonarola and their birthright. Although they appear to have been largely successful in concealing from the Medici their subversive activity and the complex ramifications of their personal and institutional networks, Niccolò

---

[64] See above, Ch. 6, n. 307.

[65] Convento di S. Maria Novella, 'Ricordanze 1507' [and following], MS ASF Conv. Sopp. 102, 89, fo. 88^{r–v}; Convento di S. Maria Novella, 'Libro de' Consigli segnato A', MS Archivio di S. Maria Novella (no location number), fo. 26^r. On Fra Benedetto's early career, see D. M. Sandrini, 'Vite dei Frati di S. Maria Novella celebri in santità', MS Archivio di S. Maria Novella (no location number), 663–72; I. G. da Hemso (ed.), 'La vita di Giovanni da Empoli', *ASI*, app. III (1846), 31; L. Neretti, *Fra Benedetto da Foiano* (Florence, 1894), *passim*; *DBI*.

[66] Benedetto Varchi, *Storia fiorentina* (2 vols., Florence, 1963), i. 433; C. Roth, *The Last Florentine Republic* (London, 1925), 202.

[67] Ibid.; and *DBI*.

Martelli was in no doubt of what they were up to. As well as accusing leading Piagnoni of complicity in the plot against Giulio de' Medici at his trial in 1524,[68] Martelli uttered repeated denunciations against the Piagnoni in general.[69] He depicted them as a group irreconcilably hostile to the Medicean government and gave, as the explanation for their stance, the removal of the Great Council, in which they had placed all their trust.[70] His proposed solution reveals how closely the political and religious affiliations of the Piagnoni were associated in the Florentine mind. To silence them, he adjured the government, it was necessary only to cultivate with assiduity the friars of S. Marco. Once they were won over to the regime, there would be no more trouble from the Piagnoni.[71]

A similar indictment, though confined specifically to the religious sphere, was made by Fra Cosimo Favilla,[72] a Servite friar from SS. Annunziata in Florence, a convent contiguous to S. Marco. Proximity, however, had not bred neighbourliness; on the contrary, on 8 April 1498, the friars of SS. Annunziata led the mob's charge against S. Marco and provided the grappling ladders used to scale the convent's wall. Much of the venom which had characterized relations in those distant days is present in Favilla's treatise *Flagellum pseudoprophetarum*, presented to Clement VII in 1526.[73] In many ways, the treatise is a throw-back to the polemic of the pamphlet war in both the subjects it raises and the way Favilla chose to deal with them. Its main purpose was to defend the integrity of the Church and the authority of the Pope by confuting what he describes as the new errors and the perverse doctrines which had defiled the Church of God for the past thirty years.[74] Favilla traced the destructive Protestant schism then afflicting the

[68] See above, p. 320.

[69] '[Primo] Processo di Niccolò Martelli', MS ASF Miscellanea Repubblicana, 8, inserto 4.

[70] Ibid.    [71] Ibid.

[72] Biographical details in M. Poccianti, *Catalogus scriptorum Florentinorum* (Florence, 1589), 43; L. G. Cerracchini, *Fasti Teologali* (Florence, 1738), 220; and in particular L. M. Magi, 'Elementi ecclesiologici nel *Flagellum Pseudoprophetorum* di Cosimo Favilla', unpubl. thesis (Facoltà Teologica Marianum, Rome, 1967), 4–8. Favilla entered the convent of SS. Annunziata in 1496–7.

[73] MS BAV Vat. Lat. 3636.    [74] Ibid., fo. 4$^v$, but see also fos. 8$^r$, 43r$^{r-v}$.

Church back to Savonarola's apostolate of thirty years before, to his false prophecies and to his heretical denial of papal authority.[75] Savonarola had inspired a succession of other heretics and pseudo-prophets, beginning with Pietro Bernardino and his *Unti*, continuing with Don Teodoro, Francesco da Meleto, an Aretine priest named Bernardino, Pietro Pomponazzi, and ending with Martin Luther.[76] These heretics had presented Christianity with an intractable problem: like the poisonous heads of the hydra to which they were likened, no sooner were they struck off than others grew in their place. Favilla believes that they had been treated too leniently and that far too much latitude had been given them to spread their poison. All this would come to an end if Christians were made to realize that the Pope was God's representative in the Church Militant, and as such infallible; that he had the plenitude of power in all matters of doctrine and discipline and that, above all, there could not be any salvation without him.[77] Ultimately, therefore, there was no alternative but to punish these heretics whose doctrines had found a particularly fertile soil in Tuscany. No mercy should be shown to them; no opportunity provided for them to air their views. They should be condemned immediately and punished as cruelly as their crimes deserved.[78]

Martelli's and Favilla's assessments of the strength and importance of the Piagnoni received confirmation from a disinterested observer, the Venetian ambassador, Marco Foscari. The report which he submitted to the Venetian Senate in 1527, after a year or so in Florence, argued that the Piagnoni played a key role in Florentine affairs, being the largest and most influential of the three parties there.[79] While it is likely that Foscari was influenced in his assessment by the events of 1527, which may have led him to attribute a greater role to the Piagnoni than they had actually played before the Medici's fall, his is none the less a useful vantage-

[75] Ibid., fos. 40ʳ, 44ʳ–62ᵛ.      [76] Ibid., fos. 62ᵛ–100ᵛ.
[77] Ibid., fos. 23ᵛ–26ᵛ, 155ᵛ.      [78] Ibid., fos. 31ʳ, 35ʳ⁻ᵛ.

[79] *Relazione di Firenze del clarissimo Marco Foscari tornato ambasciatore di quella Repubblica l'anno 1527*, in E. Alberi (ed.), *Relazioni degli ambasciatori veneti al Senato*, ser. 2, vol. i (Florence, 1839), 69. To the sect of the Piagnoni, Foscari maintained, belonged 'quasi tutti li primi uomini di Firenze per prudenza, bontà, parentado, ricchezza, ed ogni altra sorta di estimazione': ibid.

point from which to look back over the preceding years. The sharp contrast between the Piagnoni's apparent inertia in the years immediately preceding 1527 and their amazing resurgence immediately afterwards is inexplicable unless it is assumed that it indicates not inactivity on their part but rather the successful concealment of subversive activities. Their prompt reappearance as a fully fledged radical party in 1527 would suggest that the course of resistance had been espoused by more and more Piagnoni as time went on. As the repressive policy of the Medicean government gained momentum, the paths of compromise and moderation must rapidly have lost their attractiveness, so that the Piagnoni, instead of being forced into compliance or apostasy, were driven to test the limits of their devotion to the Friar. They thus provided an example to other Florentines disenchanted with Medici rule, and the dramatic collapse of Medici power in Florence attests to the success of their stand. After the fall of the Medici, for a while at least, they were to reap their reward. The republican regime then established enabled them to bring into being the system of godly rule which Savonarola had foretold.

II

Their opportunity came early in 1527, when the Florentines, outraged by Clement VII's policies both domestic and foreign, drove Cardinal Passerini and the two Medici minors in his custody from the city. Clement VII's cavalier conduct in leaving Florence to be ruled by an outsider whose maladministration had become notorious while at the same time demanding her resources to help finance his own ill-advised schemes angered the Florentines. They were further antagonized by Clement's failure to ensure the adequacy of the defences of the city, which his disastrous foreign policy was rendering more and more vulnerable to attack, and by his failure to provide relief from a famine which afflicted them. It was Clement VII's abandonment of the imperial alliance and espousal of a pro-French stand, by joining the League of Cognac, which finally precipitated the Medici's overthrow. Even the fact that he had now committed Florence to his alliance with the French, whom the

Florentines traditionally favoured, did little to rob them of the conviction that he had little concern for the city, seeing it merely as a source of income.[80] Accordingly, in April 1527, when the imperial forces penetrated as far south as Tuscany and were encamped near Florence, the citizens' panic was fuelled by extreme resentment of their treatment by the Pope. There ensued the uprising known as the Friday riot (*tumulto del venerdì*), which, although short-lived, was in effect a rehearsal for the overthrow of the Medici in the following month.

On 26 April the youths of Florence, who had for weeks past been clamouring for arms to enable them to defend the city, gathered in the Piazza della Signoria, demanding the formation of a citizen militia.[81] By this time the danger which threatened the city had been considerably eased, since the forces of the League of Cognac had drawn near to Florence, thus making it unlikely that the imperial troops would attack. The incipient riot in the city none the less gained momentum until it was completely out of hand, a development facilitated by the absence of the Florentine garrison, which, with Cardinal Passerini at its head, had gone out to meet the League's forces. The Piazza della Signoria became packed with a rebellious crowd, to whose original demands had now been added a cry for the expulsion of the Medici. When the pleas of the *Gonfaloniere*, Luigi Guicciardini, had failed to quell the rioters, the *Signoria* agreed to accede to their wishes. To the time-hallowed cries of 'popolo' and 'libertà', it voted—unanimously, we are told—to oust the Medici, to lift all sentences which had been imposed upon the advocates of a popular regime, and to restore the constitution as it had existed before the Medici's advent in 1512.[82]

The Piagnoni played a prominent part in the 'tumulto' itself and also in preparing the ground for it. Already, on 12 April, Battista

---

[80] Pitti, *Apologia de' Cappucci*, 332–7; de' Nerli, *Commentari*, ii. 14–19; Varchi, *Storia fiorentina*, i. 50–2, 87–90; Roth, *The Last Florentine Republic*, 9–17; Stephens, *The Fall of the Florentine Republic 1512–1530*, 194–6.

[81] Varchi, *Storia fiorentina*, i. 99 ff.; Pitti, *Dell'Istoria fiorentina*, 135 ff.; Roth, *The Last Florentine Republic*, 23–5; Stephens, *The Fall of the Florentine Republic 1512–1530*, 198–9.

[82] Varchi, *Storia fiorentina*, i. 102–3; Nardi, *Istorie della città di Firenze*, ii. 114–15; Cambi, *Istorie*, iii. 305–7; Roth, *The Last Florentine Republic*, 26–7.

della Palla, together with Zanobi Buondelmonti, had sent an open letter to the members of the *Signoria*, which they caused to be printed for distribution throughout the city, urging them to rebel against the Medici and restore the government of 1512. As an inducement to the Florentines they mentioned that Siena had put aside 96,000 bushels (4,000 *moggia*) of wheat for them at a convenient price were they to expel the Medici.[83] On the day of the riot, prominent Piagnoni distinguished themselves by their actions. Girolamo Buonagrazia worked assiduously to ensure that the Medici be banned from Florence.[84] In the unaccountable absence of the notary who usually served the *Signoria*, the decrees were ratified by Ser Giuliano di Domenico da Ripa, who thus secured himself a place in Florentine history yet again.[85]

The attempt to overthrow the Medici on 26 April proved abortive. Later in the day, when Cardinal Passerini returned with the garrison, the situation altered dramatically. As the troops entered the square, a magical transformation seemed to overtake the rioters, who, changing their cry in mid-voice, according to Benedetto Varchi, from 'popolo' to 'palle' (the balls on the Medici coat of arms), hastily dispersed.[86] A small group of die-hards, led by another Piagnone, the historian Iacopo Nardi, put up a show of resistance by barricading themselves in the Palazzo della Signoria, but were eventually forced to lay down their arms, which they did on condition that those who had participated in the revolt would not be punished.[87] Despite this agreement, some who had been directly implicated were dealt with: Ser Giuliano da Ripa, for example, being gaoled in the *Bargello* until he could pay the very

---

[83] Varchi, *Storia fiorentina*, i. 121, 236.

[84] The broadsheet is to be found in BNF II.III.433, fo. 8ʳ; Roth, *The Last Florentine Republic*, 22, where, however, *moggia* are taken to be equivalent to bushels.

[85] V. Fiorini (ed.), 'Una lettera di Iacopo Nardi sulla mutazione dello Stato nel 1527', *Miscellanea fiorentina di erudizione e storia*, i. 136, Cambi, *Istorie*, iii. 307; Varchi, *Storia fiorentina*, i. 103; Pitti, *Dell'Istoria fiorentina*, 139.

[86] Varchi, *Storia fiorentina*, i. 107.

[87] Ibid. 108–16; Nardi, *Istorie della città di Firenze*, ii. 115 ff.; Roth, *The Last Florentine Republic*, 28–30.

steep fine of 1,000 florins. A fine of 800 florins was imposed on Buonagrazia, who had by then made good his escape.[88]

Although the risk of revolt had been temporarily averted, the period of respite for the Medici government was to prove brief. Once the imperial forces had moved on, to sack Rome on 6 May, leaving Clement VII's representative in Florence without direction or support, the citizens had no reason to remain in subjection to them. When the news of the calamity reached Florence on 11 May, the events of 26 April were repeated, and this time there was no turning back. Bands of youthful hotheads began once again to roam the city, calling for decisive action against the government; and even the principal citizens were by now openly advising Cardinal Passerini to leave Florence.[89] The tide of change was further swelled by the return to Florence of Filippo Strozzi and his wife Clarice de' Medici, who settled a number of old scores with Clement VII by encouraging the popular movement against his regime: making it plain to Cardinal Passerini that he could expect no help from them either.[90] On 16 May Passerini agreed to depart; and the following day, accompanied by the two Medici youths and their most compromised supporters, he left the city amid scenes of wild rejoicing.[91]

With this departure long-awaited and prophesied events had finally come to pass. Both the sack of Rome and the expulsion of the Medici vindicated the Piagnoni's faith in Savonarola's prophecies and silenced those opponents who had derided them for their credulity. There were, however, additional reasons for rejoicing.

[88] ASF Signori e Collegi, Deliberazioni Ord. Aut. 129, fos. 68ᵛ–74ᵛ. Cambi, *Istorie*, iii. 309–10; Varchi, *Storia fiorentina*, i. 121. See also the decree of the *Balìa* on 16 May 1527, absolving and freeing from prison the participants in the *tumulto del venerdì*, published in Roth, *The Last Florentine Republic*, app. p. 351. Amongst those who had been fined or arrested were Bardo Altoviti, Giovanni Rinuccini, and Canon Antonio de' Nerli.

[89] Cambi, *Istorie*, iii. 313 ff.; Varchi, *Storia fiorentina*, i. 127–33; Pitti, *Dell'Istoria fiorentina*, 140–1; Roth, *The Last Florentine Republic*, 40–3.

[90] Varchi, *Storia fiorentina*, i. 133–5; Lorenzo Strozzi, *La vita di Filippo Strozzi*, in J. Graevius (ed.), *Thesaurus antiquitatum et historiarum Italiae*, viii (2) (Leiden, 1723), cols. 24–6; Roth, *The Last Florentine Republic*, 42–5.

[91] Varchi, *Storia fiorentina*, i. 136–7; Roth, *The Last Florentine Republic*, 45.

As revealed in a letter sent by Francesco de' Ricci to Clement VII, the scourging of Rome and the ending of Medici tyranny were seen as the prelude to the millennium and to the apotheosis of Florence. The letter, ostensibly written in the early months of 1527, is a not-too-subtle attempt to use the sack of Rome—or the Judgement of God as Cambi described it[92]—to force Clement VII to free Florence from the Medicean yoke.[93] Francesco's argument is founded on a novel reworking of Florence's recent history in millenarian terms. Combining prophetic elements drawn from both the civic and the Savonarolan traditions, he casts the Medici family of the post-1512 period in a messianic role, thereby seeking to reconcile the two most inimical forces in Florentine society. According to Francesco, the restoration of the Medici to Florence in 1512, their subsequent elevation to the rank and honour which they had formerly enjoyed, and the election of Leo X to the papal throne had been willed by God. The Medici's mission was therefore to free Florence, the chosen city of which God had appointed Himself King and the Virgin Mary Queen. Leo X's subsequent refusal to initiate the reform had angered God, who had demonstrated His displeasure by striking down the equally remiss Giuliano and Lorenzo. When Leo failed to respond to these warnings, he too was struck down.

All this and more, Francesco continues, he had relayed to Clement before his election to the papacy in the course of their three meetings in Florence. At the last of these Francesco had shown Clement six letters from various servants of God, together with numerous angelic missives, bidding him, Francesco, to pray for the future Angelic Pope. Francesco had then made it clear that Clement was to be the person so singled out by God as long as he reformed the city of Florence. Francesco goes on to recount how, in letters written subsequently to Clement, he had also outlined for him the role he was to play in leading Christendom to the mystical Jerusalem. Finally, he had explained to Clement the reasons for the troubles he was experiencing and

[92] Cambi, *Istorie*, iii. 315.
[93] Published in my 'Prophecy, Politics and History in Early Sixteenth-Century Florence', 121–3.

their eventual outcome should he delay any further the fulfilment of God's will.

By subtly adapting the prophecy in Jeremiah 49: 14–15 to suit Clement, Francesco warns of the gathering of heathens against him, of the war that will ensue, and of the humiliation that awaits him. On the basis of his reading of Revelation he explicitly prophesies that the coming month of May (marking the conclusion of forty-two months since Clement's election) will be a climacteric. The inevitability of these prophecies, Francesco continues, is confirmed by Revelation 17 and 18. Here it is made clear that the reformation of the Church is dependent on the destruction of both the present ecclesiastical establishment and of the city of Rome. He ends by declaring that Clement, like King Hezekiah, can avoid retribution by beseeching God and the Virgin for mercy and by undertaking to fulfil the task assigned to him for the well-being of the Florentines, the spread of Christianity, and, last but not least, his own glory.

The exact chronological coincidence of the prophesied chastisement of Rome by a heathen army and the actual sack of the city on 6 May 1527 puts it beyond doubt that Francesco's is a prophecy *post eventum*. Even the retrospective account of past prophecies which have been fulfilled, though interspersed with verifiable events which could be corroborated by other participants such as Clement VII and Cerretani, gives the distinct impression of having been glossed over, especially in those passages where interpretations of the original utterances are proffered. By such manipulations Francesco was bringing pressure to bear on Clement to act on Florence's behalf and thus speed the millennium on its way.[94]

In the event, as we have seen, the Florentines did not have to wait on Clement's decision: they regained their freedom through their own efforts alone and despite the presence in Florence of more than 3,000 soldiers posted at key points throughout the city, including, significantly, the Piazza of S. Marco.[95] No time could be lost. On the very day Passerini agreed to leave, the *Balìa* had set out the structure of the new government: taking care to absolve from

[94] Ibid. 122–3.   [95] Cambi, *Istorie*, iii. 316–17.

blame all those who had been punished for their anti-Medicean activity and also for their part in the *tumulto del venerdì* of the previous month.[96] In line with the essentially aristocratic temper of its members, as also of those who had directed the changes so far brought about, the *Balìa* devised a constitution which was designed to retain power in the hands of the *Ottimati*.[97] Within days, however, the protests of the dissatisfied radicals, who had expected much more in return for their support, forced through further changes. On 18 May the *Signoria* was obliged to dismiss the *Otto di Guardia e Balìa*, which was identified in the radical mind with the rule of the Medici, and to promise that the Great Council, which the *Balìa* had planned to convene in a month's time, would meet instead on 21 May.[98] Much to the Piagnoni's delight,[99] work was at once begun to clean up the hall of the Great Council, which the preceding regime had desecrated. With immense satisfaction, Giovanni Cambi recorded how its reopening was marked by the celebration of a mass to the Holy Ghost and by its new religious consecration.[100] At its first meeting the Great Council appointed new members to the *Otto di Guardia e Balìa*, dismissed the *Otto di Pratica*, and replaced it with the *Dieci di Libertà e Pace*.[101] Even these measures, however, were not enough for the extremists. Antonfrancesco degli Albizzi, who in 1512 had been one of the

[96] Published in Roth, *The Last Florentine Republic*, app., pp. 349–51; but for individual decisions, including the liberation of the Piagnone Marco di Giovanni Strozzi (not to be confused with the other Piagnone the Canon Marco di Matteo Strozzi) condemned to two years' exile, see ASF Signori e Collegi, Deliberazioni Ord. Aut. 129, fos. 82$^r$–87$^r$, 89$^r$, 96.

[97] Roth, *The Last Florentine Republic*, app., pp. 349–51. The details of this plan are succinctly set out in Stephens, *The Fall of the Florentine Republic 1512–1530*, 208–11, and in R. Devonshire-Jones, *Francesco Vettori, Florentine Citizen and Medici Servant* (London, 1972), 198–9.

[98] Roth, *The Last Florentine Republic*, app., pp. 351–3; Varchi, *Storia fiorentina*, i. 140–4; Cambi, *Istorie*, ii. 320.

[99] They apparently went about the city and 'allegri dicievano e' ci fu promesso': letter of P. Giugni to Benedetto Varchi, n.d., MS BNF II.III.433, fo. 67$^{r-v}$.

[100] Cambi, *Istorie*, iii. 321; see also Pierfilippo d'Alessandro Pandolfini, 'Sermone sopra l'elezione del gonfaloniere . . . alla fine dell'anno MDXXVII avanti fusse raffermo Niccolò Capponi', BL MS Add. 28630, fo. 115$^r$.

[101] Varchi, *Storia fiorentina*, i. 147–8; Pitti, *Dell'Istoria fiorentina*, 114; Roth, *The Last Florentine Republic*, 50.

leaders of the revolt against Piero Soderini, now decided to force the *Signoria* to resign *en masse*. He was aided not only by his youthful following, but also by Piagnoni led by Fra Bartolomeo da Faenza, who was entrusted with the delicate task of suborning the guards of the Palazzo della Signoria.[102] On 28 May the *Signoria* yielded; and on 31 May new members were elected, Niccolò Capponi being appointed *Gonfaloniere*, but not *a vita*. According to new regulations drawn up in the preceding three days and harking back to the constitution which had enjoyed a brief life in September 1512, the *Gonfaloniere* was now to hold office for a fixed term of one year.[103] The elections on 31 May brought to a conclusion the series of constitutional changes which had been enacted in the previous two weeks and which were to remain in force, without substantial alteration, until the fall of the government in 1530.

Piagnoni involvement in the events of April and May 1527 was a foretaste of the part which they were to play in the running of the newly formed government. Their position of prominence was due to the strength of the following which they commanded and the power of the tradition to which they were heir, as well as to their indubitable talents. It is not insignificant, for example, that, while Iacopo Nardi took it upon himself to defend the Palazzo della Signoria in the latter stages of the *tumulto del venerdì*, Ser Giuliano da Ripa and Fra Bartolomeo da Faenza were both singled out for their respective roles. No one was better qualified than Ser Giuliano to notarize the constitutional changes which the *Signoria* attempted to bring about on 26 April. In November 1494 he had performed the same function for the newly enacted laws which had ushered in the Savonarolan state and had been suitably rewarded for it. He was also the man who, because of his Piagnoni sympathies, had since then been most consistently baulked in his attempts to be true to his beliefs and to pursue his career: becoming, in the process, a symbol not only of Piagnone political radicalism but also

---

[102] de' Nerli, *Commentari*, ii. 45, cf. 41–5; Varchi, *Storia fiorentina*, i. 190–1; Roth, *The Last Florentine Republic*, 52–3.

[103] Varchi, *Storia fiorentina*, i. 164–70; de' Nerli, *Commentari*, ii. 49–50; Nardi, *Istorie della città di Firenze*, ii. 127–8; Roth, *The Last Florentine Republic*, 53–4.

of anti-Medicean resistance.[104] Fra Bartolomeo da Faenza represented other, no less valuable elements in the Piagnone tradition. After Savonarola's death, the mantle of the martyred leader had fallen upon his shoulders, and by gathering information concerning Savonarola's miracles, he had actively fostered the cult. No friar within S. Marco commanded more respect and devotion than he; and no man outside it could exert a greater influence upon the Piagnoni at large.[105] For the task of supporting Antonfrancesco degli Albizzi in his attempt to force the *Signoria*'s resignation in May, therefore, there could have been no better choice.

It was of paramount importance that, in the various constitutional reforms, there should be seen to participate persons who, as well as symbolizing the spirit of Piagnone resistance to tyranny, were able to command its allegiance. That such a man as Antonfrancesco degli Albizzi, who had in his youth been associated with the Piagnoni's adversaries and who had earned their hatred for his part in the overthrow of Piero Soderini,[106] should nevertheless have called upon Fra Bartolomeo da Faenza's assistance, shows how acute was this sense of the Piagnoni's value.[107] In a series of letters written later in that year while on an official mission to Piacenza he makes clear, moreover, that the experience of the Medici tyranny had turned him into a convinced republican. In particular, this experience had had the effect of inducing him to adopt a militant religious stance characterized by strong anti-clerical, or to be more precise, anti-papal sentiments akin to those espoused by many Piagnoni.[108] Like them, he expressed his admiration for that brand

---

[104] See above, pp 244–5, 287.

[105] For comments by contemporary historians concerning his reputation, see Varchi, *Storia fiorentina*, i. 190; Pitti, *Dell'Istoria fiorentina*, 190; Bernardo Segni, *Storie fiorentine* (3 vols.; Milan, 1834), i. 266.

[106] Francesco Guicciardini, *Storie fiorentine dal 1378 al 1509*, ed. R. Palmarocchi (Bari, 1931; fac. repr. 1968), 324, 327; Cambi, *Istorie*, ii. 308; Cerretani, 'Storia in dialogo', fo. 149$^r$.

[107] de' Nerli, *Commentari*, ii. 41, 45; Varchi, *Storia fiorentina*, i. 190–1.

[108] Antonfrancesco degli Albizzi, 'Copialettere', MS BRF 4133, fos. 15$^v$, 19$^r$, 21$^{r-v}$, where he even questions the legality of Clement VII's pontificate arguing, further, that the Pope and the Curia, 'per li exempli scelerati' had ensured that 'non solamente questa nostra provincia ma tutto il resto di Christianità ha perduto quasi in tutto et la devotione et la religione, causa principalissima della nostra ruina'.

of Christianity represented by Gasparo Contarini, but unlike them he had few illusions as to what the future held in store and was already planning to remove his family from Florence in fear that it too would be sacked like Rome.[109]

Other leading political figures also did their utmost to ingratiate themselves with the Piagnoni. Alfonso Strozzi, for instance, who with Doffo Spini had led the *Compagnacci* in Savonarola's heyday,[110] was now making overtures to the Piagnoni.[111] An even more striking example is provided by the conduct of Niccolò Capponi, whose election as *Gonfaloniere* was said to have been due in no small measure to his having captured the Piagnone vote by cultivating Fra Bartolomeo da Faenza and by promoting the memory of Savonarola.[112] After his election, Capponi was to cultivate the Piagnoni even more. Although never closely connected with them or with the religious ideals for which they stood, he took pains to be seen in the company of the friars of S. Marco, and especially Fra Bartolomeo da Faenza.[113] Not a man to miss a likely opportunity, Capponi also patronized Suor Domenica del Paradiso, who advised and protected him and also kept him informed of God's wishes.[114]

All this, however, is not to suggest that the Piagnoni had become a marginal group, content to play a purely supporting role. Far from it. They had been preparing for the establishment of a new Republic since the fall of Soderini. The intervening years had

[109] Ibid., fos. 9ᵛ, 25ᵛ, 34ʳ.

[110] Piero Parenti, *Istorie fiorentine*, ed. J. Schnitzer, *Quellen und Forschungen zur Geschichte Savonarolas*, iv (Leipzig, 1910), 262; Ridolfi, *Vita*, i. 296–7; Schnitzer, *Savonarola*, i. 238, 446; ii. 83–5, 507. Alfonso Strozzi had also been an examiner in Savonarola's trial: see Villari, *La storia di Girolamo Savonarola*, ii. app., pp. cxlv, cxlviii.

[111] Francesco Cei, 'Cronaca', MS BNF II.V.147, pp. 159–60.

[112] de' Nerli, *Commentari*, ii. 50; see also Varchi, *Storia fiorentina*, i. 187.

[113] de' Nerli, *Commentari*, ii. 60–1; Varchi, *Storia fiorentina*, i. 199, 297, 359, 463; Cei, 'Cronaca', 160. Both in his *Storie fiorentine* and in his biography of his uncle, Niccolò Capponi, the historian Bernardo Segni glossed over these connections with the Piagnoni, while giving a detailed account of his legislation and its religious content: *Storie fiorentine*, i. 69–70; id., *Vita di Niccolò Capponi*, in App. to vol. iii of *Storie fiorentine*, pp. 314–15.

[114] *Sacra Rituum Congregatione . . . canonizationis ven. ancillae Dei Sor. Dominicae* (Rome, 1755), Part i, p. 38; B. M. Borghigiani, *Intera narrazione della vita . . . della Venerabile . . . Suor Domenica del Paradiso* (2 vols.; Florence, 1719–1802), ii. 98.

undoubtedly taken their toll. Blandishment and persecution had caused some to defect; old age and mortality had thinned their ranks. The spirit of the group as a whole, however, had not waned. In those years a new generation of Piagnoni had grown up, nurtured by their elders, inured to adversity and hardened by persecution. Defections and deaths had been more than compensated for by new converts to the cause. This younger generation, moreover, had all the militancy and few of the social and political inhibitions of their elders. They were not about to waste the opportunity, so long prophesied and dreamed of, through meekness or through lack of purpose and determination.

Among the Piagnoni most assiduously courted was one Pieruccio, a lowly linen carder. Nothing is known of Pieruccio before this period: an anonymity due, one suspects, to his youth and low status. Earlier in that year, he had founded the conventicle of the *Capi rossi* and was soon to dedicate himself to the care of the city's poor, becoming known throughout Florence as Pieruccio 'dei poveri'.[115] Though undoubtedly the early undisputed leader of the conventicle, Pieruccio was aided in his manifold activities by another linen carder, Rinaldo by name, and by one Giuliano di Cipriano, whose trade has not been recorded.[116] The occupation and, by implication, the social position of the leaders were representative of the membership of the whole conventicle. The *Capi rossi*, in fact, consisted of forty to fifty members, most of whom were labourers or lowly artisans and, as such, disenfranchised

---

[115] On Pieruccio and his conventicle see MS BNF Magl., VIII, 1398, fos. 32ʳ–34ʳ. (This consists of two documents, the first, on fo. 32ʳ, entitled 'Gabriello Pallottolaio vive ancora', the second, on fos. 33ʳ–34ʳ [Incipit] 'La Compagnia de' capi rossi trovata da Pieruccio de' poveri'); Cei, 'Cronaca', 158–61; Varchi, *Storia fiorentina*, i. 518; ii. 154; de' Nerli, *Commentari*, i. 125; Giambattista Busini, *Lettere . . . a Benedetto Varchi sopra l'assedio di Firenze*, ed. G. Milanesi (Florence, 1860), 33, 52–3, 68; Segni, *Storie fiorentine*, i. 165–6. See also my 'Confraternities, Conventicles and Political dissent: The case of the Savonarolan *Capi Rossi*', *Memorie Domenicane*, NS. 16 (1985), 258–82 and ibid., 17 (1986), 285–300 for all relevant documents. Some of these documents have also been published by C. Vasoli, 'Il notaio e il "Papa Angelico". Noterella su un episodio fiorentino del 1538–1540', in V. Lanternari *et al.* (eds.), *Religioni e civiltà: Scritti in memoria di Angelo Brelich* (Bari, 1982).

[116] BNF Magl., VIII, 1398, fo. 33ʳ.

*sottoposti* in the Florentine guild structure.[117] Some individual members of the *Capi rossi* could count on powerful patrons and sympathizers amongst the Florentine aristocracy. It seems clear, however, that none of these Florentine aristocrats was formally a member of the *Capi rossi* and they may, indeed, have ignored the existence of the conventicle.

The aristocrats' reluctance is not surprising. The conventicle had no official sanction—and could not have had since it was formed in the period of Medici rule—and therefore held its meetings illegally. The exclusive working-class composition of the *Capi rossi* rendered it even more suspect because it contravened not merely the legislation against the unlawful foundation and meetings of religious confraternities but also guild ordinances banning unauthorized workers' associations.[118] Their own awareness of the potential dangers of their position was probably instrumental in determining the peculiar formation and development of the *Capi rossi*. Instead of forming an independent confraternity which, because of the illegality of its foundation and the composition of its membership, could not have escaped detection for long by ecclesiastical or civil authorities, the *Capi rossi* sought cover by infiltrating two established and highly respected religious confraternities: the Compagnia of S. Benedetto Bianco and the Compagnia of S. Benedetto Nero, both meeting in the convent of Sta Maria Novella.[119]

Even after the expulsion of the Medici and the restoration of the republican regime, the *Capi rossi* could not afford to relax their vigilance. They well knew that the new government was as suspicious of confraternities and of *intelligenze* as the preceding Medicean regime had been.[120] A commitment to the religious and

---

[117] Ibid.

[118] G. Gandi, *Le arti maggiori e minori in Firenze* (Florence, 1929), 17 and n. 2; S. K. Cohn, *The Laboring Classes in Renaissance Florence* (New York, 1980), 15, 68–9, 127, *et passim*.

[119] L. Polizzotto, 'Confraternities, Conventicles and Political Dissent', 260–2, for some information on both companies.

[120] Compagnia della Purificazione della Vergine e di S. Zanobi, 'Libro di Ricordi', 2 vols.; MS ASF Comp. Sopp. 1646, vol. ii. fos. 279ᵛ, 280ᵛ, 281ʳ–282ʳ; ASF Otto di Guardia, Ep. Rep. 205, fo. 2ʳ.

political ideals of the Republican government was no guarantee of protection and immunity, especially in a polity where, with the single exception of the *Gonfaloniere di Giustizia*, rapid rotation of office-holders was the norm. Accordingly, throughout the Republican period, the *Capi rossi* observed strict secrecy and the only evidence we have of the conventicle's activities is through the action of some of its most important members, Pieruccio in particular. Pieruccio's career is well documented and allows us to gain an insight into the ideals and concerns of the small group of people he led.

He first came to public notice early in 1527, a short time after the formation of the *Capi rossi*. Plying his trade of itinerant linen carder and moving from house to house throughout Florence with his companion and assistant, Pieruccio had ample opportunity to initiate his apostolate and to fulfil his mission.[121] Advocating and spreading the Savonarolan message, he consequently strengthened by words and deeds the newly instituted Republican government.[122] It is clear that at the beginning Pieruccio's apostolate was confined to the humble people whom he visited as a linen carder. At first he seems to have concentrated on reiterating Savonarola's doctrines with little personal embellishment and with few references to the present situation. In time, however, his message became more personal, even though it was still firmly rooted in Savonarola's arguments, and began to acquire more immediate relevance. This new orientation was accompanied by the gift of prophecy.[123] Thereafter, there were few issues or events of importance which Pieruccio did not address, although he was to be best remembered for his view that the whole male population of Florence should be armed, a view which he also personally put to the *Gonfaloniere* Niccolò Capponi.[124]

---

[121] Cei, 'Cronaca', 159.

[122] Ibid. 159–60; Segni, *Storie fiorentine*, i. 165–6.

[123] Cei, 'Cronaca', 159.

[124] Ibid. 160; Varchi, *Storia fiorentina*, i. 518; Segni, *Storie fiorentine*, i. 165–6; Busini, *Lettere*, 68. Two other prophecies without attribution, but undoubtedly by Pieruccio, are in MS BNF II.III.343, fo. 55$^{r-v}$. The first of these prophecies, dated 4 Dec. 1528, begins by promising speedy recovery from sickness of an unnamed prelate, if he were to give alms to the poor and turn to God, and ends with dire

Pieruccio's following grew in both size and importance. Now, in addition to his humble followers, he could count on the support of such well-known aristocratic Piagnoni as Giuliano Capponi, Marco di Giovanni Strozzi, Ulivieri Guadagni, and Pietro Bernardino's erstwhile supporter, Amerigo de' Medici.[125] The *Gonfaloniere di Giustizia* himself, Niccolò Capponi, now considered it politic to be seen to be deferring to Pieruccio's opinions.[126] Even well-known Miceans, impelled, no doubt, by the need to avert inevitable retribution, began to seek Pieruccio's company and advice. Others again, most notably Lionardo Bartolini and Alfonso Strozzi, feigned belief in his prophecies and protected him in order to advance their political careers.[127] There are no doubts that Pieruccio's exemplary conduct and obvious religious sincerity contributed to his widening popularity. Not even his most rabid detractors, writing at a time when wholesale condemnation of Pieruccio could be expressed with impunity, could find fault with him in this regard. They could accuse him of religious credulity, of political innocence, and of levity, but at no stage did they imply that his behaviour, both in private and in public, was less than exemplary.[128]

Recognition for Pieruccio came in 1528, when, as a result of the plague and widespread famine, the number of poor in Florence, and deaths from starvation, increased alarmingly. The *Signoria* tackled the problem by appointing a *Balìa* of five citizens to whom were given almost unlimited powers to deal with the poor themselves and to requisition food and buildings for their maintenance

---

prognostications regarding the city of Viterbo. The second, dated 19 Jan. 1528/9, promises to Francis I the return of his sons, a resounding victory, and a glorious future if he turns away from the pleasures of the flesh and follows the commands of God. In this latter prophecy, the prophet refers to himself as 'fiorentino' and 'poverello'. See also two letters of Nofri Busini in Florence to Filippo Strozzi in Lyons, dated 10 and 19 May 1529, relating further prophetic utterances by Pieruccio: ASF C. Strozz., ser. V, 1209, Filza Iª, letters 46 and 52.

[125] Busini, *Lettere*, 33, 53. BNF Magl., VIII, 1398, fo. 33; letter of Filippo Strozzi to Migliore Covoni, 23 Mar. 1529/30 in ASF C. Strozz., ser. V, 1209, Filza Iª, inserto 29.

[126] Cei, 'Cronaca', 159–60.          [127] Ibid.; Busini, *Lettere*, 33.

[128] See e.g. ibid. 53.

and shelter.[129] The *Balìa* found no better solution than to remove them forcibly from the streets and to confine the *fanciulli* amongst them in the *Sala del Papa* in Sta Maria Novella, where they were to be fed and cared for at public expense.[130]

Pieruccio and his companion were charged to minister to them: a task which, witnesses are agreed, they fulfilled admirably, caring as much for their bodily as for their spiritual needs.[131] The scheme proved so effective that it was set up on a permanent basis and lasted throughout the siege and until the fall of the Republic.[132] Pieruccio and his companion could not by themselves have undertaken and carried through such a daunting task, especially since the number of indigenous poor was swelled by the influx of refugees from the surrounding *contado*. The government may have provided additional help. It is far more likely, however, that Pieruccio and his companion relied on the combined assistance of the confraternities of S. Benedetto Nero and S. Benedetto Bianco or at least of the *Capi rossi* within these confraternities. The religious as well as the charitable nature of the ministration to the poor, not to mention the place chosen to confine the destitute *fanciulli*, lend weight to this conjecture. In fact, it is possible that the *Balìa* chose the *Sala del Papa* as the assembly point for the destitute *fanciulli* of Florence only after Pieruccio had signified his willingness and his ability, supported by the confraternities of S. Benedetto Nero and S. Benedetto Bianco, to look after them.

Pieruccio's career demonstrates how the decision to court the Piagnoni's favour was to exercise a profound effect upon the character of the new regime. From the very first, the Piagnoni took full

[129] ASF Signori e Collegi, Deliberazioni Ord. Aut. 130, fo. 42ʳ, decree of 1 Mar. 1527/8. These officials were later to be known as *Ufficiali di Sanità*.

[130] Varchi, *Storia fiorentina*, i. 433. More detail on the arrangements made to cater for the poor in Borghigiani, *Intera narrazione della vita . . . della Venerabile . . . Suor Domenica dal Paradiso*, ii. 96, where it is stated that the indigent women were taken to the Medici stables next to S. Marco. The *Sala del Papa* had already been used for the purpose, see Luca Landucci, *Diario fiorentino*, ed. I. del Badia (Florence, 1883; repr. 1969), 150 and n. 2 for a decree of 21 May 1497 charging the *Buonuomini di S. Martino* to take the poor there.

[131] Cei, 'Cronaca', 160; Busini, *Lettere*, 53.

[132] ASF Signori e Collegi, Deliberazioni Ord. Aut. 131 fo. 36ᵛ, decree of 28 Mar. 1529; see also Roth, *The Last Florentine Republic*, 123, 131 n. 56.

advantage of the opportunities set before them. The ceremony which Ser Giuliano da Ripa made of his task on 26 April is a notable case in point. Carried into the signorial chamber upon the shoulders of an ecstatic populace, Ser Giuliano performed his function with immense bravura, losing no chance to point the Savonarolan moral. To sign the instrument expelling the Medici and restoring the republican regime, he knelt down upon the floor, saying, as he did so, that the *Signoria*'s decision was to be hailed as a holy decree (*un partito santo*).[133] When the constitutional changes then attempted were successfully accomplished in the following month, the Piagnone chronicler Giovanni Cambi took equal pains to endow his description of the event with an aura of holiness. The Medici, he wrote, 'had been expelled by Christ'.[134]

The theocratic colour which imbued the new regime was immeasurably enhanced by the endeavours of non-Piagnoni politicians to cloak their every action beneath what contemporaries described as the mantle of religion.[135] Once again, Niccolò Capponi provides us with the most telling examples. In one of his speeches before the Great Council, delivered on 9 February 1528, he voiced sentiments so closely identifiable with Savonarola's that both Filippo de' Nerli and Benedetto Varchi remarked upon it.[136] Capponi followed this up by proposing, as Savonarola had done in 1495, that Christ and the Virgin should be elected King and Queen of Florence respectively, and had a plaque proclaiming this affixed to the main entrance to the Palazzo della Signoria. Finally, and again as Savonarola had decreed in 1495, he caused a tablet carrying Savonarola's verses against the calling of a *parlamento* to be placed in the hall of the Great Council.[137]

---

[133] Varchi, *Storia fiorentina*, i. 103.

[134] Cambi, *Istorie*, iv. 1: 'furno chacciati da Cristo'. See also iii. 318.

[135] de' Nerli, *Commentari*, ii. 45. Exactly the same phrase was used by Varchi, *Storia fiorentina*, i. 190; and by Donato Giannotti, *Della Repubblica Fiorentina*, in *Opere politiche e letterarie di Donato Diannotti*, i, ed. F. L. Polidori (Florence, 1850), 233.

[136] de' Nerli, *Commentari*, ii. 60; Varchi, *Storia fiorentina*, i. 297.

[137] de' Nerli, *Commentari*, ii. 60–1; Varchi, *Storia fiorentina*, i. 297–8; Segni, *Storie fiorentine*, 16–17; Pitti, *Dell'Istoria fiorentina*, 152; Scipione Ammirato, *Istoria fiorentina*, ed. L. Scarabelli, vi and vii (Florence, 1853), vii. 40–2. The full text of this law establishing Christ and the Virgin as King and Queen has not

The influence of Piagnone ideology upon the regime was not confined to ceremonial trappings of this kind. For the politicians' association with leading Piagnoni was not merely a show. According to Donato Giannotti, at that time serving in the Florentine Chancery, the convent of S. Marco became a centre of unparalleled importance for the exchange of ideas and policies and even for political lobbying and scheming. The convent's new-found prominence contrasted markedly, he observed, with its former political isolation.[138] The implication of Giannotti's comment, that the friars of S. Marco were acquiring a decisive say in the conduct of political affairs, is borne out by Benedetto Varchi.[139] The resulting combination of political expertise and clerical direction was, as Giannotti ruefully acknowledged, unbeatable. The citizens and friars thus became so arrogant that no one had the courage to contradict them.[140]

The inevitable result was that the Piagnoni vision of the new Republic as the realization of the Savonarolan dream dominated its government from the beginning. The politicians set to work to make of Florence a city morally and spiritually regenerate, and so fit to assume her divinely appointed role as harbinger of the coming millennium. The newly elected *Signoria* celebrated its inauguration with a procession of the sort dear to Piagnoni hearts—led by Niccolò Capponi as *Gonfaloniere*, it not only passed by S. Marco on its route but actually wended its way through the convent's cloisters[141]—and then promptly settled down to enact the legislation

survived; the gist of the decree, however, is to be found in ASF Libri fabarum, 72, fo. 234ᵛ, where voting figures are also given; see also above, Ch. 1, n. 66.

[138] Giannotti, *Della Repubblica Fiorentina*, 235, see also 233–4.

[139] Varchi, *Storia fiorentina*, i. 190.

[140] Giannotti, *Della Repubblica Fiorentina*, 233. Francesco Baldovinetti expressed identical opinions regarding the influence exercised by the friars of S. Marco, especially Fra Zaccaria di Lunigiana (whom he mistakenly called Fra Zanobi) and Fra Benedetto da Foiano, on Florentine politics, but stated that they were incited by politically motivated citizens: 'e per certo si crede che i cittadini che governavano detto stato stessero con loro spesso e facessero dire loro quello che volevano i detti cittadini', E. Londi (ed.), *Appunti di un fautore dei Medici durante l'assedio di Firenze* (Florence, 1911), 52.

[141] Cambi, *Istorie*, iii. 328–9; Varchi, *Storia fiorentina*, i. 192–3; M. Lupo Gentile, 'Studi sulla storiografia fiorentina alla corte di Cosimo I de' Medici', *Annali della R. Scuola Normale Superiore di Pisa*, 19 (1906), app. XIII, p. 157.

which such a ceremony promised. On 6 June it was decreed that as a first step towards the purification of Florence, Jews, as Savonarola had ordained in 1495, should be forbidden to continue their trade as usurers and, having been given a year in which to wind up their affairs, should be expelled from the city.[142] As the law's preamble makes abundantly clear, the prevailing concern was to reawaken the spirit of the Savonarolan Republic as it had existed before the Medici return in 1512.[143]

In this, the first law of the new *Signoria*, the programme of social and religious reform which the government was to undertake was plainly intimated. The contribution of 'wise ecclesiastics' in the drafting of this legislation is admitted; this contribution is no less strongly in evidence in subsequent legislation. Sumptuary laws, regulating the clothing and ornamentation of men as well as women, were followed immediately by the prescription of strict penalties for sodomy and blasphemy.[144] These crimes were now punished with exemplary harshness. While in the past sodomites and blasphemers had frequently succeeded in having their sentences commuted to fines, they now found themselves, more often than not, condemned to mutilation and even death. Piero di Giovanni Altoviti, for example, who under the Medici had twice been tried for sodomy and had been able to purchase his freedom on both occasions, was executed, despite the entreaties of his relatives, when convicted of the same offence under the Republic.[145] Ordinary citizens were forbidden to discuss matters of religion except under the guidance of clerics,[146] just as censorship had already been imposed upon printers, who were now forbidden to publish new books without a licence.[147] Prostitutes were placed

---

[142] ASF Provvisioni, 206, fo. 5ʳ; published in full in U. Cassuto, *Gli Ebrei a Firenze nell'età del Rinascimento* (Florence, 1918), app., pp. 383–4. See also Roth, *The Last Florentine Republic*, 63–4.

[143] ASF Provvisioni, 206, fo. 5ʳ.

[144] Ibid., fos. 14ʳ–18ᵛ; Cambi, *Istorie*, iv. 19; Varchi, *Storia fiorentina*, i. 198; Roth, *The Last Florentine Republic*, 64.

[145] Busini, *Lettere*, 35–6. For examples of similarly severe sentences for blasphemy, see ASF Otto di Guardia, Ep. Rep. 205, fo. 93ʳ⁻ᵛ; Roth, *The Last Florentine Republic*, 64. See also von Albertini, *Firenze dalla repubblica al principato*, 125 n. 1.

[146] Varchi, *Storia fiorentina*, i. 198; Roth, *The Last Florentine Republic*, 64.

[147] Ibid. 64, and, for the text of the provision, 78–9 n. 18.

under more rigorous controls than they had been hitherto;[148] gambling was prohibited, as was the manufacture of playing cards;[149] and far more stringent regulations were applied to taverns.[150] At the instigation of the Archiepiscopal Vicar, who had entered into the spirit of things by suggesting that, at the sounding of the bell for the *Ave Maria*, the entire population of the city should genuflect to the ground, reciting not only an *Ave* but also a *Paternoster*, this too became law.[151]

It now became a recurring task of the government, moreover, to decree religious feasts and processions. The city's festivals, which the Mediceans had stripped of the spiritual significance invested in them by Savonarola, were restored to their former glory; and every major occasion was graced by the solemnities of religious pomp and ceremony.[152] The government also took pains to ensure that the Florentines would be instructed by preachers who could be relied upon to support the present regime. As early as 21 May 1527, the *Signoria* was pleading with Fra Bernardino da Vicenza to come to Florence to preach;[153] and the first *Dieci di Libertà e Pace* called upon Fra Benedetto da Foiano, no less, to return from Venice to preach in Florence.[154] How theocratic the government had become is especially apparent in its assumption of the duty of regulating the

[148] ASF Signori e Collegi, Deliberazioni Ord. Aut. 129, fo. 88[r–v]; see also Varchi, *Storia fiorentina*, i. 198; Stephens, *The Fall of the Florentine Republic 1512–1530*, 215. For an example of the punishment of a prostitute who infringed the new regulations, see ASF Otto di Guardia, Ep. Rep. 205, fo. 9[r].

[149] Cambi, *Istorie*, iv. 12; Roth *The Last Florentine Republic*, 64.

[150] Ibid.; see also Stephens, *The Fall of the Florentine Republic 1512–1530*, 215.

[151] ASF Signori e Collegi, Deliberazioni Ord. Aut. 129, fo. 139[r] (15 Aug. 1527).

[152] Cambi, *Istorie*, iv. 12; Roth, *The Last Florentine Republic*, 64.

[153] Letter of *Signoria* to Fra Bernardino da Vicenza, 21 May 1527, printed in Roth, *The Last Florentine Republic*, 78 n. 10. Fra Bernardino must have made a good impression, since the *Signoria* afterwards requested his services on two further occasions. On 21 Jan. 1528 it was asked whether he could come to Florence to preach during Lent, 'havendo visto per experientia di quanta efficacia sieno le sue predicazioni ad indurre gli huomini et disporli al bene et honesto vivere, conoscendo maxime quanto e' sia da tutti desiderato, et in quanta fede sieno le parole sue appresso questo popolo', letter to Master-General of Franciscan Order, ASF Signori, Carteggi, Minutari, 18, fo. 598. On 4 Oct. 1528 it was decreed that he should again be invited to come and preach, this time for Advent: ASF Signori e Collegi, Deliberazioni Ord. Aut. 130, fo. 178[v].

[154] Varchi, *Storia fiorentina*, i. 433.

discipline and daily life of religious foundations and the conduct of individual members. Whereas previous regimes had all been careful to act in this connection only after authorization from the ecclesiastical authorities, even in cases where clerics had committed civil crimes, the new Republic acted without prior consultation even in matters which were unquestionably of a religious nature.[155] Significantly, those friars who supported the regime, the Piagnoni most prominent among them, were immune from these untoward attentions, and in fact received the government's full protection.

Throughout its brief existence, the Republic of 1527 presented a rigid and uncompromising face to the world. Its treatment of those associated with the preceding regime gave all too clear a warning of the course which it was unwaveringly to follow. Despite the usual solemn undertaking not to proceed against the members and supporters of the old order,[156] the government took action very promptly and with unprecedented harshness. As was customary, the chanceries were purged of supporters of the previous government[157] and assaults were made on the careers and property of its key figures. What was new was the thoroughness of these reprisals. Extra machinery was devised to dispense retributive justice: the *Quarantia*, a specially instituted tribunal, being revived for the purpose, and five syndics being appointed to review all business deals relating to the government since 1512.[158] The judicial memory proved to be exceedingly long, and no one, however highly

[155] ASF Signori e Collegi, Deliberazioni Ord. Aut. 130, fos. 142$^r$, 144$^v$: appointment of *Quarantia* to try Fra Ludovico dei Guglielmi of Sta Croce. See also the letter of the *Signoria* to the Master-General of the Franciscan Order, acquainting him of the arrest of certain friars of Sta Croce and urging him to come to Florence to reform the convent: ASF Signori, Carteggi, Minutari, 18, fo. 593$^r$. It would appear that one of these friars was Fra Vittorio de' Franceschi, who was accused of plotting to betray the city to the besiegers and was, after a trial by the *Quarantia*, sentenced to death: ASF Signori e Collegi, Deliberazioni Ord. Aut. 131, fos. 219$^r$, 220$^v$, 221$^v$–222$^r$; see also Roth, *The Last Florentine Republic*, 206.

[156] Decree of *Balia* on 16 May 1527, printed in Roth, *The Last Florentine Republic*, app., p. 351.

[157] Marzi, *La cancelleria della Repubblica Fiorentina*, 318–19 ff.

[158] Busini, *Lettere*, 142–4; Roth, *The Last Florentine Republic*, 65–7. Stephens, *The Fall of the Florentine Republic 1512–1530*, 220 ff. gives the fullest and best account of the *Quarantia*'s and of the syndics' policy of revenge: an account to which I am greatly indebted.

placed, was exempt from prosecution. The resulting list of victims reads like a Medicean *Who's Who*: Chiarissimo de' Medici was constantly arraigned and heavily fined for decrying the government, committing bigamy, practising usury, and evading customs duties in the export of grain since 1512;[159] Alfonsina Orsini de' Medici suffered a similar penalty for defrauding the city of Florence with her speculations in the marshes of Fucecchio;[160] and a swelling number of adherents of the old regime, beginning with Benedetto Buondelmonti, were proceeded against for maladministration or for financial offences of the same sort.[161] In addition, Ippolito and Alessandro de' Medici, together with Cardinal Passerini, were denounced to the *Otto di Guardia* and cited to appear before it.[162] The wave of vindictive action against people in high places reached ludicrous extremes when first his treasurer, and then Clement VII himself, were cited to appear before the syndics to give an account of the money which the Pope had drawn from Florence in order to finance his activities.[163]

Another line of attack was to prosecute transgressors of the dowry laws; and here, too, the list of offenders is impressive. Piero Ridolfi, Luigi Ridolfi, Galeotto de' Medici, and Averardo d'Antonio de' Medici were all proceeded against for this offence.[164]

---

[159] ASF Otto di Guardia, Ep. Rep. 200, fos. 24$^v$, 36$^r$, 40$^r$, 47$^r$, 56$^r$; ASF Signori e Collegi, Deliberazioni Ord. Aut. 130, fos. 23$^v$–24$^r$; Stephens, *The Fall of the Florentine Republic 1512–1530*, 230–1; Roth, *The Last Florentine Republic*, 89–90.

[160] Stephens, *The Fall of the Florentine Republic 1512–1530*, 223–4; see Giovanni Cambi's rejoicing at the news that the marshes of Fucecchio were to be appropriated by the government: *Istorie*, iv. 28.

[161] Busini, *Lettere*, 14, 145; Varchi, *Storia fiorentina*, i. 227–8; Roth, *The Last Florentine Republic*, 67, 89. For a most thorough discussion of this aspect of the Republic's policy, see Stephens, *The Fall of the Florentine Republic 1512–1530*, 220–33.

[162] ASF Otto di Guardia, Ep. Rep. 200, fos. 160$^r$, 171$^r$, 192$^v$; ASF Signori, Carteggi, Minutari, 21, fos. 175$^r$–176$^r$; Roth, *The Last Florentine Republic*, 89–90.

[163] Stephens, *The Fall of the Florentine Republic 1512–1530*, 229–30. Later Clement VII and the four Florentine cardinals at his court were secretly denounced (*tamburati*) as traitors. The *Otto di Guardia* was reluctant to proceed, however, and referred the matter to the *Signoria*. Two *pratiche* were convened to discuss whether to proceed with the charges, but on both occasions it was decided to let the matter drop: Varchi, *Storia fiorentina*, ii. 33–5; Roth, *The Last Florentine Republic*, 243.

[164] Stephens, *The Fall of the Florentine Republic 1512–1530*, 225.

Where no crime, real or imagined, could be found, the government adopted the old Florentine stand-by of discriminatory taxation: levying exorbitant sums upon erstwhile members of the Medici regime, such as Francesco Guicciardini, Francesco Vettori, and Roberto Acciaiuoli.[165] The government's desire to suppress all memory of the Medici led to a decree that their arms, the distinctive *palle*, should be obliterated from places both public and private; and even the Latin epitaph in the church of S. Lorenzo, praising Cosimo de' Medici as *Pater Patriae*, came under attack.[166] Similarly, any unfavourable comparison between the present regime and the preceding one met with an unequivocal response. One Carlo Cocchi was executed for daring to maintain that Florence was still Medicean at heart: a punishment which even Filippo del Pugliese's injudicious remark concerning Lorenzo de' Medici had failed to provoke under the old order. Ficino Ficini, nephew of Marsilio, was condemned to death for asserting that the city had been better governed under the Medici.[167] The better to prosecute its policy of retribution, the new regime became as adept as the old one in drawing up lists of suspect individuals.[168]

An even more insidious note, and one which clearly indicated the direction which the last Florentine Republic was taking, was the prosecution not only of persons indissolubly linked with the

[165] Ibid. 214; Devonshire-Jones, *Francesco Vettori*, 203–4.

[166] For these and other examples of intolerance towards the symbols of the Medici in Florence, see Roth, *The Last Florentine Republic*, 96–7, 110–11. By then the practice of demanding the removal of the symbols of the vanquished regime from all public and private buildings had become so recurrent—and expensive—that some had hit upon novel ideas to bypass the legislation while at the same time seemingly abiding by it. See e.g. the anonymous denunciation against Palla Rucellai 'che ha corrispondenti il nome con e' facti' for having covered the Medici arms on his palace 'con un telo di pannolino et di poi impiastrato di sopra di gesso, in modo che l'arme resta di sotto accesa e pulita': ASF Otto di Guardia, Ep. Rep. 201, fo. 121ʳ, published by R. Ridolfi, 'Tamburazione fatta contro Palla Rucellai', *Rivista storica degli Archivi Toscani*, 1 (1929), 131–2.

[167] Busini, *Lettere*, 36; Varchi, *Storia fiorentina*, i. 670–2. These are but two, if the harshest, of many examples of the punishment meted out to opponents of the Republic. For an excellent assessment of the extent and virulence of these repressions, see Stephens, *The Fall of the Florentine Republic 1512–1530*, 220–41.

[168] An example in BNF II.III.433, fo. 50ʳ, where all the names of the men who in 1512, on the day the *parlamento* was held, had taken over the Palazzo della Signoria, *armata mano*, are listed.

Medicean government but also of others who, although ideologically opposed to it, had nevertheless seen fit to reach a compromise
with its leaders. Thus two Piagnoni moderates came within the
scope of the programme of vengeance: Jacopo Salviati, who was
accused of having both evaded customs duties and violated the
dowry laws;[169] and Carlo del Benino, who, after receiving overtures
from Giulio de' Medici,[170] had become reconciled to the Medici
regime, eventually being appointed *Gonfaloniere di Giustizia*, was
now prosecuted for failing to repay a government loan made to him
when he held that post.[171] Even Girolamo Benivieni was adjudged
'as not too well-disposed' towards the Republic and was punitively
taxed accordingly.[172] That the Piagnoni had a hand in the persecution of their moderate brethren whom they adjudged to have betrayed the common cause by their association with the Medici is
made unequivocally clear by the terms of the anonymous denunciation levelled against Carlo del Benino. The anonymous accuser
charged him with being a 'decrepit, evil man, an enemy of this
republican form of government', but, above all, of being totally
untrustworthy presumably because by his decision to collaborate
with the Medici he had 'renounced Christ'.[173]

As time went on, even those *Ottimati* who, so far from having
supported the Medici, had actually helped to overthrow them,
found themselves coming under suspicion. Nothing more clearly
illustrates the republican government's steady swing towards radicalism than the fact that, as its leaders became increasingly extreme, some of its original champions should eventually have come

---

[169] ASF Balìe, 46, fos. 104$^r$, 107$^r$. Later, after the fall of Niccolò Capponi, it was
twice proposed that Jacopo Salviati should have his goods confiscated for collabo-
rating with the Pope; and later still, a house he owned at Montughi was deliberately burned and he was declared a rebel: de' Nerli, *Commentari*, ii. 109; Roth, *The
Last Florentine Republic*, 135, 191.

[170] See above, p. 248 n. 43.          [171] ASF Balìe, 46, fos. 107$^{r-v}$, 108$^r$.

[172] Letter of Girolamo Benivieni to Jacopo Salviati, Sept. 1530, in C. Re,
*Girolamo Benivieni fiorentino*, app., p. 348. 'come poco amico'. Girolamo also
recounted how, in the last year of the Republic, 'me toccò a pagare in comune, tra
balzelli, accatti, sale, stime di casa, lotti, decime e arbitrii, dugento ducati d'oro o
più di mia proprietà': ibid.

[173] ASF Balìe, 46, fo. 108$^r$: 'decreptio, cattivo uomo, nimicho di questo stato
politicho'; 'rinegato Christo'.

to appear too conservative to be trusted. This backlash struck at Filippo Strozzi and Antonfrancesco degli Albizzi, both of whom had contributed in no small way to the success of the revolt of May 1527.[174] Oppressed either by heavy taxation or by finding their efforts at advancement baulked at every turn, some of these men had no recourse but to flee Florence, and some were ultimately driven to cross over to the enemy camp.

The same vengeful spirit manifested itself within the confines of the Tusco-Roman Congregation. With the Piagnoni now very much in the ascendancy within the convents of the Congregation,[175] their opponents had little hope of surviving unscathed. Fra Bonaventura da Castelfranco, for example, was denounced to the *Signoria* for having praised Clement VII and for having stated, on more than one occasion, that the present regime could not last. On 24 April 1529 his case was referred to the *Quarantia*, which handed it on to the *Otto di Guardia*.[176] By 7 May, when the *Otto* passed sentence, Fra Bonaventura had, whether willingly or under duress, left S. Marco.[177] He was condemned to be imprisoned in the *Stinche* for one year, his release being dependent on a unanimous vote by the *Otto di Guardia*.[178] Not even the most highly placed clerics were immune from such measures. Later in 1529 Fra Zanobi Pieri, the Vicar-General of the Congregation, who was known to be a supporter of Clement VII, was exiled by the *Signoria* for two years. With him were also exiled two other friars of Sta Maria Novella,

---

[174] Lorenzo Strozzi, *La vita di Filippo Strozzi*, col. 28; Roth, *The Last Florentine Republic*, 68, 205. Of these men, Filippo de' Nerli commented dryly 'che furono capi e principali autori di render lo stato e la libertà al popolo furono poco tempo dipoi di tal sorte da quello stato popolare riconosciuti e ristorati, e furono di tale e sì fatta maniera trattati, e in tanti modi, e con tanta qualità d'ingiurie offesi, che potettero largamente dipoi piagnere quello che vollero': *Commentari*, ii. 34.

[175] In the three years of the Republic, an unprecedented number of Piagnoni were elected to the highest positions in the Congregation. In 1527 Fra Zaccaria di Lunigiana and Fra Timoteo Ricci were chosen Priors of S. Spirito at Siena and S. Domenico at Pistoia respectively; in 1528 Fra Cherubino Primerani was elected Prior of S. Marco; in 1529 Fra Timoteo Ricci became Prior of S. Spirito of Siena in his turn, Fra Zaccaria di Lunigiana became Prior of S. Romano in Lucca, Fra Raffaello Risaliti became Prior of Sta Caterina at Pisa: Creytens, 'Les Actes capitulaires', 187–92.

[176] ASF Signori e Collegi, Deliberazioni Ord. Aut. 131, fos. 69^{r-v}, 72^r.

[177] ASF Otto di Guardia, Ep. Rep. 205, fo. 6^r.          [178] Ibid.

Fra Vincenzo Chelli and Fra Arcangelo di Giovanni.[179] Judging by
the records of the meetings of the friars of Sta Maria Novella, the
atmosphere in that convent, now that Fra Benedetto da Foiano had
returned in triumph, was not a happy one. Fra Benedetto seems to
have lorded it over the other friars and monopolized the convent's
more remunerative positions.[180]

This desire for vengeance was matched by a lofty intolerance.
Now that the Piagnoni friars were in an unassailable position *vis-à-
vis* the Florentine government, they had no hesitation in denying to
others the toleration which they had hitherto sought so desperately
for themselves. Of those towards whom the friars of S. Marco now
became especially antipathetic, Pieruccio dei Poveri, flourishing
under the government's indulgent eye, was one of the most prominent.[181] They suspected Pieruccio's arrogation of prophetic powers
and the independent stance this entailed as they had once suspected
Pietro Bernardino, one of the men from whom Pieruccio drew his
inspiration. It is evident, too, that they resented the increasing
popularity of an upstart who was after all competing with them for
influence and for alms. This was probably the case with Suor
Domenica also. But, by now she had acquired a vast following and
a great reputation for sanctity, so that the friars, while no doubt
resentful of her, could do nothing to overset her.[182]

Against Antonio Brucioli, however, the friars were successful, as
they could not be against Pieruccio dei Poveri, in venting their
wrath against lay persons who took part in religious affairs. Their
volte-face on this question is a most telling instance of the intolerance which now characterized their public demeanour. All along

[179] ASF Signori e Collegi, Deliberazioni Ord. Aut. 132, fos. 13ʳ, 19ᵛ; MS
BMLF S. Marco 920 (Miscellanea di documenti relativi a San Marco), fo. 247ʳ.
This took place early in the siege: Fra Zanobi was sentenced on 8 Nov. 1529 and
the order of expulsion was dated the following day.

[180] Convento di Sta Maria Novella, 'Libro de' Consigli segnato A', MS
Archivio del convento di S. Maria Novella (no location number), fos. 26ʳ, 31ʳ, 33ʳ.

[181] Varchi, *Storia fiorentina*, ii. 154–5.

[182] Busini, *Lettere*, 33, 53; Segni, *Storie fiorentine*, i. 192; Luigi Guicciardini,
*Del Savonarola, ovvero dialogo tra Francesco Zati e Pieradovardo Giachinotti il
giorno dopo la battaglia di Gavinana*, ed. B. Simonetta (Florence, 1959), 72; *Sacra
Rituum Congregatione . . . Canonizationis Ven. Ancillae Dei Sor. Dominicae*, part I,
p. 38.

it had been one of the distinguishing marks of the Piagnoni, and
also one of their strengths, especially in times of adversity, that they
had not only permitted laymen to discuss religious subjects but
also—as with Pietro Bernardino, for example—to lead such discussions and even to preach.[183] Now that they had the ear of the
government all this changed. In May 1529 Antonio Brucioli, who
had been connected with the plot against Giulio de' Medici and had
been in exile in Venice until the restoration of the Republic,[184] was
arrested by order of the *Signoria*.[185] It was rumoured that Brucioli
had gathered a following of youths, to whom he had publicly read
the works of Martin Luther.[186] While this may have been the ostensible reason for the proceedings against him, the real cause is
likely to have been his prolonged controversy with the friars of S.
Marco and also with Fra Benedetto da Foiano at Sta Maria Novella.
Brucioli had made no secret of his opinion that the friars should be
prevented from playing the role in Florentine politics which they
had now assumed and, further, that, if left unchecked, they would
have the same divisive effect upon the city as Savonarola had had.
The friars, he contended, should stick to their monkish chores. Not
surprisingly, the friars thus rebuked turned against Brucioli, as did
the Piagnoni in general.[187] They began to attack him publicly,[188] Fra
Benedetto da Foiano going so far as to make an ominous pun, in a
sermon, in which he threatened Brucioli with burning at the
stake.[189] Brucioli's fate, although not as grim as Fra Benedetto had
hinted it ought to be, was nevertheless severe. This may have been
partly due to the fact that he was rumoured to have written to his
friend Luigi Alamanni, in France, that the republican government,
being administered by the radical rabble (*ciompi*), could not last

[183] See above, Ch. 3.

[184] Guasti (ed.), 'Documenti della congiura fatta contro il cardinale Giulio de'
Medici', 122 *et passim*; G. Spini, *Tra Rinascimento e Riforma: Antonio Brucioli*
(Florence, 1940), 36 ff.

[185] Letter of Ottaviano Ciai to Ceccotto Tosinghi, 29 May 1529, in Guasti, *Le
Carte Strozziane del R. Archivio di Stato in Firenze*, i. 369–70.

[186] Ibid. 370. See also ASMO Cancelleria Ducale, filza 14, letter of Alessandro
Guarini to the Duke, 5 June 1529, no foliation.

[187] Guasti, *Le Carte Strozziane del R. Archivio di Stato in Firenze*, i. 370; Busini,
*Lettere*, 33–4; Varchi, *Storia fiorentina*, i. 487–90.

[188] Busini, *Lettere*, 34; Varchi, *Storia fiorentina*, i. 488.          [189] Ibid.

long.[190] In any case, the *Signoria*, composed entirely of Piagnoni who were sufficiently advanced in years to remember Savonarola, directed the *Otto di Guardia* to exile him from Florence for two years.[191]

The explanation for the progressive radicalization of the regime lies with the Piagnoni. Both through their participation in government and their influence upon its policies, they succeeded in bringing it into total conformity with their ideals. In this they were closely aided by their erstwhile enemies, the *Arrabbiati*. Locked in mutual enmity during Savonarola's heyday, the two groups had nevertheless been united, even then, by their fervent devotion to republican principles and, more importantly, by their implacable hatred of the Medici. We have already seen how, in 1500, the leaders of the two factions had sunk their differences and made common cause against Piero de' Medici's threatened return to power.[192] The decades of wary partnership which had cemented an alliance based on political expediency had also gone far towards eroding their ideological differences. To some extent, a distinction remained. When it came to the election to the *Gonfalonierato* in 1527, for example, Alfonso Strozzi's overtures towards the Piagnoni, and especially Pieruccio dei Poveri, did not outweigh his past as a leading *Arrabbiato*, and he lost to Niccolò Capponi.[193] Nevertheless, the two groups were becoming, to all intents and purposes, indistinguishable. More important, from the point of view of the future course of the Republic, was the fact that it was the Piagnone ideology which came to dominate them both.

The *Arrabbiati*'s refusal to accept that Savonarola and his teaching should be accorded the devotion which was the Piagnoni's *raison d'être* had all along been the main difference between the two parties. This refusal, they now gradually withdrew. Whether because of force of circumstances or because of an actual change of heart, the rationale of the *Arrabbiati*'s stand became difficult to

---

[190] Busini, *Lettere*, 34–5.

[191] ASF Signori e Collegi, Deliberazioni Ord. Aut. 131, fo. 93; ASF Otto di Guardia, Ep. Rep. 205, fo. 33[r-v]: both directive and sentence were dated 5 June 1529.

[192] See above, pp. 214–15.          [193] de' Nerli, *Commentari*, ii. 50.

distinguish from that of the Savonarolans. Outstanding evidence of this elision of their ideological differences is provided by the orations delivered to the Florentine militia by Luigi di Piero Alamanni,[194] Pier Filippo Pandolfini,[195] Piero Vettori,[196] Bartolomeo Cavalcanti,[197] and Filippo Parenti[198] in the period 1528–30. None, as far as one can tell, was recognized as a Piagnone; and yet their speeches expressed sentiments which were unmistakably Savonarolan. The belief that virtue was best fostered in a republican regime and most threatened under a tyrannical one; the assumption of a moral perspective from which political issues must be judged; the stress on the individual's responsibility for shaping the conditions under which he lived and the conviction that the great *renovatio* was possible only in a socially just polity ruled by charity:[199] all were prominent and all were Savonarolan. Most striking of all is the conviction, most forcefully expressed in Pandolfini's oration, that the present Republic was a gift from God, and one of which the Florentines must prove themselves worthy.[200] Once they had done so, there could be no doubt that Christ, their King, would

---

[194] Luigi Alamanni, *Oratione . . . al popol fiorentino sopra la nuova sua militar disciplina*, in G. Canestrini (ed.), 'Documenti per servire alla storia della milizia italiana', *ASI*, 1st ser. 15 (1851), 342–9.

[195] Pier Filippo Pandolfini, *Oratione . . . al popolo di Firenze nel tempio di San Lorenzo a dì XXVIII di gennaio MDXXVIII*, in G. Canestrini (ed.), 'Documenti per servire alla storia della milizia italiana', 350–76.

[196] Piero Vettori, *Oratione . . . fatta alla militare ordinanza fiorentina l'anno MDXXIX il dì (5 Febbraio)*, in von Albertini, *Firenze dalla repubblica al principato*, app., pp. 418–24; but see also pp. 428–35 for his later, alleged, disenchantment with the Savonarolan stance as reported by Luigi Guicciardini.

[197] Bartolomeo Cavalcanti, *Orazione . . . al popolo e alla milizia fiorentina* in P. Dazzi, *Orazioni politiche del secolo XVI* (Florence, 1866), 405–37.

[198] Filippo Parenti, *Orazione . . . a' soldati della nuova milizia fiorentina*, ibid. 438–65. All these orations are discussed in von Albertini, *Firenze dalla repubblica al principato*, 130–6, and in C. C. Bayley, *War and Society in Renaissance Florence: The 'De Militia' of Leonardo Bruni* (Toronto, 1961), 296–8.

[199] Alamanni, *Oratione*, 343, 345, 346, 348; Pandolfini, *Oratione*, 350–2, 354–6; 370; Vettori, *Oratione*, 418, 420–1, 422–3; Cavalcanti, *Orazione*, 409, 419, 422; Parenti, *Orazione*, 454–5.

[200] Pandolfini, *Oratione*, 355–6. A little further on in the *Oratione*, in an unmistakable allusion to Savonarola, Pandolfini referred to 'quell'uomo quasi divino ministro di Dio a spargere il seme, et raccendere il lume della vita cristiana, et ordinare et piantare il principio della vostra libertà': ibid. 357–8.

always defend His people and would ensure that it was exalted 'victorious and triumphant above all other peoples'.[201]

The most dyed-in-the-wool Piagnone could not have put it better. This peculiar combination of religious outlook and political activism, which had once been the exclusive property of the Savonarolans, was now the ideology of the two most influential parties in the Florentine government. While in certain areas, most notably concerning the role to be given to religion and the weight accorded to prophecy, some degree of dissension may have remained, on the central issues of the course which the Republic should follow and the policies which it should adopt, Piagnoni and *Arrabbiati* were in full agreement.[202] The lack of substantial differences between them, now that the *Arrabbiati* had adopted a Savonarolan viewpoint, is reflected in the changing language of contemporary politics. Amongst the devotees of the Republic, the terms *Arrabbiati* and Piagnoni fell into disuse. The sole distinction now made was in terms of extremism: the most radical republicans being designated *Fedeli*, *Adirati*, or *Libertini*, in a method of categorization which effaced the former division between the parties.[203] To those in opposition, however, such subtle contrasts were

---

[201] Cavalcanti, *Orazione*, 422; 'vittorioso e trionfante sopra gli altri populi'; but see also Parenti, *Orazione*, 465.

[202] For a contemporary assessment of the similarities and contrasts between the exponents of the respective traditions, two dialogues by Luigi Guicciardini are extremely valuable. *Gonfaloniere* at the time of the *tumulto del venerdì*, Luigi Guicciardini had, by the time he composed these dialogues, turned decisively against the Republic. See Luigi Guicciardini, *Dialogo*, in which the two disputants are the Piagnone Francesco Capponi and the staunch republican Piero Vettori, published in von Albertini, *Firenze dalla repubblica al principato*, 428–35; and Guicciardini, *Del Savonarola*, in which the disputants are the Piagnone Francesco Zati, and the republican Pieradovardo Giachinotti.

[203] Busini, *Lettere*, 25; Pitti, *Dell'Istoria fiorentina*, 153, 168; Segni, *Storie fiorentine*, 18; id., *Vita di Niccolò Capponi*, 207. While continuing to postulate a division between Piagnoni and *Arrabbiati*, Benedetto Varchi does so solely on the grounds of their belief or otherwise in the prophecies of Savonarola, and not because of any political distinction: *Storia fiorentina*, i. 183–5, 651. Some of these factions were, in turn, known by alternative names—the *Adirati*, for instance, being known also as *poveri* in apposition to the *ricchi*—or subdivided into further groupings, such as *giovani* and *vecchi*: ibid. i. 651–2. Foreigners found these divisions totally incomprehensible in terms of social composition and political ideology; see, e.g. the confused assessments of the Este ambassador in Florence:

unimportant. To them what mattered was that the republicans were now united by their ideology as well as by their political affiliations; and it was a mark of this ideology's significance that they now classed them all as Piagnoni.[204]

The fact that, with the *Arrabbiati*'s adoption of a Piagnone stance, the republicans were now generally Savonarolan in outlook had a decisive effect upon the subsequent history of the regime. More than any event in their brief reign, this alliance was to bring Florence to her knees. Conducting the city's affairs with the blind assurance of men who believed themselves possessed of a divine mandate, they ensured, through their merciless policy of revenge, that Clement VII, denied any clemency for his family or its adherents, would be driven to make common cause with the Emperor in declaring war on Florence. Stubbornly persisting in a foreign policy which, although aligned with Savonarolan sentiments, was totally at odds with the exigencies of contemporary European politics, they continued the alliance with France, whose King Savonarola had marked out for a primary role in the imminent changes,

---

letters of Alessandro Guarini to the Duke, 20 Feb. and 15 May 1529, ASMO Cancelleria Ducale, filza 14, unfoliated.

[204] Already, just after the *tumulto del venerdì*, the Mediceans were referring to all those involved as Piagnoni: Varchi, *Storia fiorentina*, i. 122. The anonymous compiler of the *ricordanze* of Sta Maria del Carmine, moreover, complaining about the republican government's requisitioning of the convent's treasure, considered the members of the government to be Piagnoni to a man: 'quella setta pessima de' piagnoni e' quali non potendo reggere che già le borse de' cittadini erano di pecunia exauste et vote si dettono alli beni della chiesa', ASF Conv. Sopp. 113, 19, 'Ricordanze 1453–1647', fo. 69. Similarly, the poetaster Lorenzo di Santi de' Buonafedi, looking back on the years 1529–30, referred to them as 'A tempo che reggevono i Piagnoni': M. Rastrelli, *Storia d'Alessandro de' Medici primo duca di Firenze* (2 vols.; Florence, 1781), i. 190; see also 192–3. Finally, Francesco Vettori speaking of Fra Benedetto da Foiano calls him 'capo . . . delli ostinati et arrabbiati', von Albertini, *Firenze dalla repubblica al principato*, app., p. 442; and see below, Ch. 8, n. 47. The most illuminating comment on the alliance between the Piagnoni and the *Arrabbiati*, however, was made by Malatesta Baglioni, Captain-General of the Florentine forces during the siege. Determined to come to terms with the besieging forces, he is said to have remarked, 'Firenze non è stalla da muli: io la salverò ad agni modo a dispetto de' traditori'—by whom he meant, according to Benedetto Varchi, who recounts this, the Piagnoni and the *Arrabbiati*—'volendo intendere non di sè, ma de' Piagnoni e degli Arrabbiati': *Storia fiorentina*, ii. 203.

notwithstanding the fact that, since France could not assist them, their chosen course was suicidal. Finally, faced with the siege which inevitably resulted from their actions, they remained so convinced of God's support that they would brook no compromise with the enemy. Certain that victory would ultimately be theirs, they insisted, despite their vastly inferior resources, upon war *à outrance*, and brought their beloved Republic to ruin. For the belief that the regime had been instituted by God for His purpose, and that therefore nothing occurred which was not willed by Him, obviated any need for *realpolitik*. Convinced that they were the children of the promise, the members of the government believed that their policies were endowed with divine authority. Consequently, they saw no reason to assess any situation in terms of human potential and disability, human achievement, and human error. Cushioned against reality, they drifted further and further from the practical problems of diplomacy and defence which should have engaged their attention, pursuing their chosen courses in the absolute assurance that God would preserve them. Thus, in the absence of the divine intervention upon which they had relied, the Republic moved inexorably towards certain doom.

The fanaticism which was increasingly to characterize the actions of the Florentine government had not always been a republican failing, however, and, before the war became inevitable, the moderates had done their utmost to avert disaster. They were led by Niccolò Capponi, who, while he had taken care to ingratiate himself with the Piagnoni, as with other influential groups and individuals, had failed to be dazzled by their rhetoric, and had retained a clear-headed grasp of political realities. Aware of Florence's vulnerability, the moderates made strenuous efforts to secure an agreement with Clement VII, but were constantly thwarted by an opposition party under the leadership of the arch-Piagnone, Tommaso Soderini.[205] In the latter half of 1527 the Pope became

---

[205] Busini, *Lettere*, 13, 48, 53; Varchi, *Storia fiorentina*, i. 267–73; Segni, *Storie fiorentine*, i. 26, 31; id., *Vita di Niccolò Capponi*, 328–9. See also the dispatch of Carlo Capello, Venetian ambassador to Florence, in Alberi (ed.), *Relazioni degli ambasciatori veneti al Senato*, 174–7. On Florentine foreign policy and relations with Clement VII in general, see Roth, *The Last Florentine Republic*, 68–77, 86–9, 95–6, 100–8; Stephens, *The Fall of the Florentine Republic 1512–1530*, 241–55.

more and more angered by the actions of the Florentine government in not only proceeding so rigorously against the Mediceans
but also taxing the Florentine clergy. Although he was originally
not averse, it would seem, to coming to some sort of agreement
with the new government, these actions made it virtually impossible for him to do so, and by December 1527, when he regained his
freedom after the sack of Rome, it was plain that he was ready to
come to an understanding with the Emperor Charles V.

At this crucial time, there took place a Florentine embassy to the
Pope at Orvieto. Necessitated by Clement VII's threat to excom-
municate the Florentines in retaliation for their taxation of the
clergy, the embassy was entrusted to Fra Tommaso Caiani.[206] The
choice of this rabid Piagnone, one of the Medici's most implacable
opponents, to negotiate with Clement VII shows the powerlessness
of the moderates in the government, and the determination of the
extremists to steer a collision course with the Pope. Caiani, who as
he averred was prepared to shed his blood for his beloved city,
carried out his mission in April 1528.[207] In an audience with the
Pope, by restraining himself, he succeeded in having the threat of
excommunication lifted.[208] His duty done, however, he then proceeded to live up to the expectations of those who had selected him
for the task by delivering an impassioned address against papal
power and privilege, choosing as his venue the cathedral church of
Orvieto.[209] Even after this incident, which can have done little to
endear Florence to the Pope or his advisers and which was, in fact,
followed within days by the death of Caiani, in suspicious circumstances,[210] the moderates might still have brought about an agree-

---

[206] Segni, *Storie fiorentine*, i. 111; id., *Vita di Niccolò Capponi*, 336. Some of the
documents pertaining to this embassy have been published in Roth, *The Last
Florentine Republic*, app., pp. 356–8 and by R. Ridolfi, 'Gli ultimi anni della
Repubblica Fiorentina', *ASI*, 7th ser. 12 (1929), 282–3, where, however, the
dispatch of Caiani is seen as a conciliatory measure by Capponi, p. 281.

[207] Ibid. 282–3, Roth, *The Last Florentine Republic*, app., p. 357.

[208] Ridolfi, 'Gli ultimi anni della Repubblica Fiorentina', 282, where quotation
occurs, and ASF Signori, Carteggi, Responsive, 42, fo. 102ʳ.

[209] Serafino Razzi, *Istoria degli Huomini illustri così nelle prelature come nelle
dottrine del sacro ordine de gli Predicatori* (Lucca, 1596), 281; J. Quétif and J.
Echard, *Scriptores Ordinis Praedicatorum recensiti* (2 vols.; Paris, 1719–21), ii. 77.

[210] He was, in fact, said to have been poisoned: Razzi, *Istoria degli Huomini
illustri*, 281; Quétif and Echard, *Scriptores*, ii. 77. His death is reported as having

ment which would have prevented the opening of hostilities. As late as the spring of 1529, there were apparently opportunities for this, and Capponi did his utmost to take advantage of them. However, when his secret negotiations with the Pope, via Jacopo Salviati, became known, he was at once dismissed from the *Gonfalonierato*, being succeeded by Francesco Carducci, one of the most radical republicans and a leading advocate of the French alliance. Shortly after the fall of Capponi, the agreement between Clement VII and Charles V was concluded on 29 June 1529 in Barcelona. This was followed on 5 August by the Treaty of Cambrai between Charles V and the King of France. Florence's fate was sealed.[211]

Once it became known that the papal–imperial alliance was within days of being concluded, the government redoubled its efforts to make the city morally impregnable. While military preparations were not neglected—the service of the *condottiere*, Malatesta Baglioni, being secured, for example, as Captain-General of the Florentine forces—they were regarded as a secondary consideration. Believing that the purification of Florence was all-important in the eyes of God upon whom their safety rested, they set about the task of strengthening the laws against blasphemers and criminals, paying particular attention to moral crimes.[212] The clearest expression of the temper in which the city approached the looming storm is provided by the law of 26 June 1529.[213] This piece of legislation is undoubtedly the most militant statement of Savonarolan principles ever incorporated in the city's statutes. The law has none of the directness of governmental legislation since it is partly an apology and partly a rallying call to action. The whole document is, moreover, predicated on the assumption that the Florentines were the children of the promise. God's injunction as uttered through the mouth of Moses, that 'if you heed my voice

---

occurred on 2 May 1528: Ubaldini, 'Annalia', fo. 169[r]. It should be remembered, however, that Fra Tommaso was already ailing with tertian fever on 8 Apr.: ASF Signori, Carteggi, Responsive, 42, fo. 102[r].

[211] Roth, *The Last Florentine Republic*, 120–8, 138–9, 142–5.

[212] ASF Provvisioni, 207, fos. 58[v]–59[r].

[213] Ibid. 208, fos. 24[v]–28[r] but I shall use the copy in BRF Moreniano, 332, fos. 20[r]–24[r].

and keep my covenant and obey my commandments, then you shall be my favoured people above all others', was taken as referring specifically to the Florentines.[214] On the basis of this unique relationship the *Signoria* reaffirmed the city's subjection to the Lordship of Christ and of the Virgin, pledged to observe the Christian faith, and to preserve at all costs 'the present popular government and most holy liberty as the most singular gifts of His Divine Majesty'.[215]

From these premises, the *Signoria* went on to make the most aggressive claims regarding Florence's position *vis-à-vis* her enemies. The claims were made in the most forceful way possible, by resorting that is, to typological arguments. In the first place, the *Signoria* decreed that henceforth the Crown of Thorns should become the main emblem of the Florentine people. It was to be added to the Cross in the Florentine shield and was also to be placed above the entrance door of the Palazzo della Signoria. The emblem, so the *Signoria* stated, would make clear the Florentines' will to reject all other servitudes but that to their true immortal King.

The choice of what the *Signoria* itself referred to as the 'figura' of the Crown of Thorns was extremely significant.[216] As the symbol of the Messiah's martyrdom, the Crown of Thorns marked the end of the Old Dispensation and the beginning of the New. It thus also set in opposition, as type and antitype, the Jews—the Elect Nation of old—and the Florentines—the Elect Nation under the New Dispensation. To ensure that the argument was properly understood, the *Signoria* added the explanation that in failing to recognize the Messiah and his martyrdom the Jews had been justly punished, forfeiting, moreover, the election as God's chosen people. The argument was employed not merely to establish the rightfulness of Florence's claim to the Messianic role as promised to her by God through Savonarola her prophet, since the Jews had proved

---

[214] Ibid., fo. 20ʳ: 'se voi udirete la mia vocie et osserverete il mio pacto et obedirete a mia comandamenti voi sarete il mio popolo peculiare intra li altri popoli'.
[215] Ibid., fo. 20ʳ⁻ᵛ: 'il presente popular vivere et sanctissima libertà come dono singularissimo della Divina Maiestà'.
[216] Ibid., fo. 20ᵛ.

unworthy of the election. Rather, it enabled the Florentines to claim this role exclusively under the New Dispensation and to reject the pretension of any who, by arrogating to themselves an authority they did not possess, dared to impose their will on Florence or to interfere in her special relationship with God. More importantly, by extension, the typological argument also allowed the Florentines to cast all their enemies in the role of the Jews. In failing to recognize Florence's election and her Messianic role, in fact, these enemies, including the Pope, were, like the Jews, disobeying God's mandate and attempting to interfere with His plans for Christianity. Like the Jews, therefore, they would be scattered and punished.[217]

The *Signoria* next set out to ensure that words would be followed by deeds. To cement the special relationship between God and Florence, the Florentines had to fulfil the two most important precepts of divine law: to love God and to love one's neighbour as oneself. Penalties against blasphemers were strengthened. The law also made it much more difficult for murderers to obtain an amnesty or a pardon and decreed that in future vendettas were no longer to be regarded leniently and that, indeed, new judicial procedures were to be instituted to remove them from God's city.[218] Having thus demonstrated the citizens' love for God, the *Signoria* turned next to their love for one another, legislating for unity amongst the citizens along the lines of the universal peace (*pace universale*) preached by Savonarola in 1494–5. It also decreed that all crimes committed before 16 May 1527 were to be pardoned, unless they had already been judicially dealt with or unless the crime was murder or illegal appropriation of the Republic's property.[219] The better to ensure the fulfilment of these decrees, the *Signoria* further stipulated that the Great Council be assembled and every member, beginning with the *Gonfaloniere*, be asked to swear an oath to observe the law 'as proof and attestation that this just, republican state and popular government had been built on the solid foundation of Jesus Christ, the immovable rock'. Each member should record this solemn pledge for posterity by signing

---

[217] ASF Provvisioni, 207.    [218] Ibid., fos. 21r–22r.
[219] Ibid., fos. 22v–23r.

a specially prepared parchment roll, the original of which was to be preserved in the chapel of the *Signoria* and a copy in the cabinet holding the statutes of the Republic.[220]

Finally, to remind Florentines of God's mercy towards them, the *Signoria* decreed that the feast day of 9 December, instituted in remembrance of the expulsion of the Medici in 1494, should in future be celebrated as a solemn religious festival. Two additional solemn religious festivities were instituted: 16 May, on which day in 1527 'it pleases our Immortal Lord to restore us to Christian liberty and to free us from the very harsh yoke of tyranny', and 9 February, the day in which Christ had been declared King of Florence. All were to be celebrated in a typically Savonarolan manner with prayers, processions, and the distribution of alms to the poor.[221]

There is no need to emphasize the apocalyptic and millenarian import of the law of 26 June, highlighted in particular by the appropriation of the Crown of Thorns and by the declaration of the universal peace. There should be no need either to insist on the legislation's hortative and cautionary aims. The law was meant to prepare the Florentines for the struggle which was to usher in the promised millennium and to intimidate enemies and convince them to desist from their ungodly machinations against the Elect Nation. What should be stressed is the vision of politics which the legislation provides. At a time when the recurrent political crises had induced many Florentine political thinkers, from Machiavelli and Guicciardini to Lodovico Alamanni and Francesco Vettori,[222] to abandon the belief in the superiority of a republican system of government in favour of the security and stability promised by princely rule, many other Florentines, drawing inspiration from Savonarola, believed still in the citizens' right to shape their destiny. The active participation of the citizens in politics, so they

---

[220] Ibid., fos. 23ʳ–24ʳ: 'in segnio et testimonio della sancta fundatione di questo iusto, politico vivere et popolare governo sopra lo stabil fondamento della immobil pietra, Christo Iesu'.

[221] Ibid., fo. 24ʳ: 'piacque al nostro Re immortale restituirci alla christiana libertà et liberarci dal durissimo giogho della tirannide'.

[222] On this whole topic see von Albertini, *Firenze dalla repubblica al principato*, 22–38 *et passim*; Stephens, *The Fall of the Florentine Republic 1512–1530*, 160–3; Devonshire-Jones, *Francesco Vettori*, 156–7.

believed, had an ennobling spiritual effect; it engendered virtue and civic responsibility and, therefore, alone assured that decisions were taken for the common good rather than for personal or factional interest. This belief is expressed in the very political terminology employed in the legislation. The present form of government is variously described as legitimate (*legittimo*), just, republican state and popular government (*iusto politico vivere et popolare*), Christian liberty (*christiana libertà*), and so on. Princely government, on the other hand, cannot but be a human tyranny (*humana tyrannide*) and devilish servitude (*diabolica servitù*).[223] Almost identical sentiments were expressed in the *pratiche*, attesting to their currency and pervasiveness.[224] This defence of republicanism, of freedom, and of the individual's right and duty to be involved in politics, was all the more forceful for its presentation in a religious context.

Thus prepared, the Florentines believed themselves ready to face events. The long-threatened arrival of the Emperor Charles V in Italy in August 1529 occasioned a last flurry of diplomatic activity, but these eleventh-hour negotiations were opposed by the radicals.[225] At a *pratica* convened to discuss the question of what powers should be given to the newly created ambassadors to the Pope, the Piagnone die-hard, Bernardo da Castiglione, reminded those present of Savonarola's promise that, though the whole world should take up arms against her, Florence would never again fall under a tyranny.[226] The negotiations were at best half-hearted, and were eventually to break down irretrievably on the vexed question of the restitution of Medici rights and property.[227]

---

[223] BRF Moreniano, 332, fos. 20$^v$, 23$^{r-v}$, 24$^r$.

[224] Ibid., fos. 16$^r$ (Bernardo da Castiglione), 46$^v$–47$^r$ (Giovanni Canacci, Matteo Tanagli, and Filippo del Nero); ASF Consulte e Pratiche, 72, fos. 21$^v$ (Alfonso Strozzi), 23$^v$ (Tommaso Soderini), 73$^v$ (Battista della Palla), 90$^v$ (Antonio Giugni), 92$^v$ (Lorenzo Segni and Ulivieri Guadagni); but see esp. the long peroration by Antonfrancesco degli Albizzi on fos. 49$^r$–54$^r$ with its radical social and political message, and the statement of Andrea Niccolini relating the opinion of the men of his *gonfalone* who advised the government 'che si prepari alla difesa et offeronsi et vogliono più presto morire liberi che vivere in servitù', fo. 103$^r$.

[225] Roth, *The Last Florentine Republic*, 146–51.

[226] Segni, *Storie fiorentine*, i. 183.

[227] Varchi, *Storia fiorentina*, i. 634–5, 644–5; Pitti, *Apologia de' Cappucci*, 355–

Typical of the Florentines' attitude towards the Pope is the speech reportedly given by a member of this embassy, the Piagnone Iacopo Guicciardini, in his presence. Guicciardini drew a highly uncomplimentary comparison between the infinite mercy of God and the all-too-finite limits to the compassion of His viceregent upon earth. In no uncertain terms, he drew Clement VII's attention to the fact that the Florentines, in defending their city, were defending a divinely bestowed gift, of which not even the Pope could deprive them.[228] Guicciardini's and Bernardo da Castiglione's speeches indicate that the Piagnoni, with governmental encouragement, fostered the notion of total resistance to papal pretensions. Since God would eventually come to Florence's rescue, civil liberty should not on any account be compromised, as it would be by dealings with Clement VII.

Throughout these desultory negotiations, the Florentines drew courage from the assurances of the various Piagnoni preachers and prophets, lay and ecclesiastic alike, such as Pieruccio dei Poveri, Francesco de' Ricci, Fra Benedetto da Foiano, and Fra Zaccaria di Lunigiana. Pieruccio had long prophesied that the Emperor would not dare to move against Florence; but, were he to do so, he would come to certain ruin.[229] A similar assurance, though far more moderately expressed, was proffered by Francesco de' Ricci in two letters addressed to the Emperor, dated 15 and 18 August 1529.[230] Writing in the immediate aftermath of Charles V's landing at Genoa with a strong army, Francesco cannot hide his bewilderment at the foolhardiness of the Emperor. Though saddened by the prospect of war, he is convinced that Florence will emerge victorious from the encounter. God—who had made Himself King of Florence, after all—is on the city's side. Having chosen Florence to lead the reform of mankind and then to be the centre of His Kingdom, He will not desert His elect. At His bidding angels and

66; Roth, *The Last Florentine Republic*, 171–2; and also, for further discussion of Bernardo da Castiglione, 173–4; Devonshire-Jones, *Francesco Vettori*, 212–19.

[228] Segni, *Storie fiorentine*, i. 217; Devonshire-Jones, *Francesco Vettori*, 219.

[229] Busini, *Lettere*, 68; Varchi, *Storia fiorentina*, i. 518–19.

[230] ASF C. Strozz., ser. I, 14, fos. 2ʳ–4ᵛ, 12ʳ–14ᵛ, 144ʳ–145ᵛ; see also my 'Prophecy, Politics and History', 113–14.

saints will join the struggle. In defence of God's law and of their own liberty, and for the sake of their dear ones, the Florentines will undergo any sacrifice and continue the struggle until final victory. With God's help, like Gideon they will overcome all odds and thus provide the ultimate proof of their election.[231] By moving against Florence, the new Zion, Charles V is disregarding God's will and committing a grave sin that will lead to his and his followers' ruin and spiritual perdition. Not content with these warnings, Francesco proceeds to give the Emperor a lesson in ethics. He reminds him of the obligations inherent in his position, of his responsibility to the faithful and, above all, of his Christian duty to respect the rights and possessions of others. By seeking to impose his will on Florence, Charles is committing the very sin for which Lucifer and his accomplices had been banished to hell.[232] He is also exacerbating the divisions of Christendom to the advantage of its enemy, the Turk, against whom the Emperor's might should be turned if he is to fulfil God's commands and contribute to the great work of universal reform by converting the Infidel. Finally, appealing to personal ambition, Francesco assures Charles of greater power, wealth, and glory if he follows these instructions.[233]

Now that Florence enjoys the freedom from tyranny essential for the true religious and spiritual life, even the Medici can be dispensed with. And yet, Francesco does not relinquish his former saviours without regrets. As he tells the Emperor, during his long and close association with Clement, he had often entreated him to give back to the Florentines the liberty of which they had been deprived by force. Had Clement listened, Francesco goes on, he would have been spared the reverses, including the devastation of S. Peter's see, which he, Francesco, had prophesied. Nor are Clement's tribulations at an end. On the basis of his reading of Revelation 18, Francesco prophesies that before the end of 1531 Rome will be razed to its foundations by the heathen, becoming a godless waste and losing forever its religious primacy.[234]

---

[231] ASF C. Strozz., ser. I, 14, fo. 2[r–v].          [232] Ibid., fos. 2[v]–4[r], 144[v].

[233] Ibid., fos. 3[v]–4[r], 144[v]. Assistance for a crusade against the Turks had been promised to Charles V by the Pope at Barcelona: L. von Pastor, *Storia dei Papi* (2nd Italian edn.; Rome, 1959), iv. 340.

[234] ASF C. Strozz., ser. I, 14, fos. 3[r], 143[v].

Piagnoni friars daily reiterated this message from the pulpit to much larger audiences. They assured the Florentines that Savonarola's prophecies had mapped out the course which the Republic would follow. He had predicted that her miraculous re-vivification would be preceded by a time of tribulation, and this was what the city was now experiencing.[235] Contemporaries were well aware that the influence of the friars had soared to unprecedented heights;[236] and the enemies of the Republic did their best to subvert it. In September 1529 the Prior of S. Marco was so intimidated by Giovanni Baldi de' Tebaldi as to order Fra Zaccaria di Lunigiana to stop preaching. In great indignation the *Signoria* set up a committee of inquiry with orders to leave no stone unturned in its search for the source of this intimidation.[237] When identified, Giovanni Baldi de' Tebaldi had already fled the city. He was nevertheless fined *in absentia*, declared a rebel, and exiled for life.[238]

The experiences of Michelangelo reveal the various forces at play in Florence and the pressures brought to bear on individual citizens. While he was working on the fortifications of S. Miniato, a man whispered in his ear that, in order to save his life, it was best for him to leave the city.[239] No sooner had he acted on this advice and taken refuge in Venice than the *Signoria* did its utmost to have him return. Battista della Palla, to whom Michelangelo had turned for help and advice regarding a proposed flight to France, added his voice to that of the government to persuade him to return to Florence. He allayed Michelangelo's fears regarding his likely re-

---

[235] Varchi, *Storia fiorentina*, i. 739; ii. 39, 75; Guicciardini, *Del Savonarola*, 66–8, 131–5; id., *Dialogo*, in von Albertini, *Firenze dalla repubblica al principato*, 428–30.

[236] Varchi, *Storia fiorentina*, ii. 74.

[237] ASF Signori e Collegi, Deliberazioni Ord. Aut. 131, fos. 190ʳ, 201ʳ. Although it has been generally assumed that the Prior of S. Marco at this time was Fra Bartolomeo da Faenza (see e.g. Roth, *The Last Florentine Republic*, 202–3), this was not the case. During the Last Florentine Republic, Fra Bartolomeo did not hold any official position in the Congregation; and the Prior of S. Marco in 1529 who was intimidated into compliance was Fra Niccolò Michelozzi: see Creytens, 'Les Actes capitulaires', 192.

[238] ASF Signori e Collegi, Deliberazioni Ord. Aut. 131, fos. 238ʳ–239ʳ.

[239] Letter of Michelangelo to Battista della Palla, n.d., but end of Sept. or beginning of Oct. 1529, in *Il carteggio di Michelangelo*, ed. G. Poggi, P. Barocchi, and R. Ristori (5 vols.; Florence, 1965–83), iii. 280–1.

ception and, above all, impressed upon him that by returning he would have the opportunity of enjoying and benefiting from 'those times which you have so long waited and yearned for'.[240] The gathering enemy armies, instead of inducing in him despair, fill him with joy since they signal the apotheosis of Florence. The city cannot fall, it will last forever and is about to rise to heaven. Everywhere one could see, so Battista assured Michelangelo:

a universal and admirable fervour to preserve freedom: a unique fear of God; a reliance on Him and on the justice of our cause and [on] innumerable other benefits, which can be promised with certainty at least here, to our city: the renewal of the world and the golden age which, I hope you, together with other friends of yours, will have occasion to enjoy.[241]

Such entreaties proved remarkably effective and by the following month Michelangelo had made his way back to Florence.

In its reaction to the intimidation of both Fra Zaccaria di Lunigiana and Michelangelo, the government showed how much it relied on religious and more specifically, millenarian arguments to justify its stand against the Pope. To this end, it encouraged Piagnoni friars to deliver hortatory sermons to keep up the Florentines' morale. Indeed, this was to be their most vital function during the siege, as the Medicean Francesco di Giovanni Baldovinetti recognized.[242] From Sta Maria del Fiore, where Fra Zaccaria di Lunigiana preached, and from Sta Maria Novella, whence the fulminations of Fra Benedetto da Foiano issued forth, this was the constant refrain: that the enemy both without and within the gates must be overthrown.[243] Above all, it was increasingly emphasized that, as long as the citizens did their utmost for Florence, they could not but be victorious in the end, and should

---

[240] Letter of Battista della Palla to Michelangelo, ibid. 282–3: 'quelli tempi già da voi aspettati et desiderati'.

[241] Ibid.: 'una unione et ardore mirabile alla conservatione della libertà, uno timore solo di Dio, una confidentia in lui et nella giustitia della causa et inumerabili altri beni, da promettersi al certo, almeno qua drento, renovatione di secolo et età aurea, la quale confido, insieme con altri amici vostri, vi habbiate a trovare a godere'.

[242] Londi (ed.), *Appunti di un fautore dei Medici durante l'assedio di Firenze*, 51.

[243] Ibid. For an example of the insults levelled at Clement VII from the pulpit by Fra Benedetto da Foiano, see Pitti, *Apologia de' Cappucci*, 370–1.

someone die in the struggle he would receive a martyr's heavenly rewards.[244]

The government resorted to other means too of maintaining the citizens' morale. From the beginning of 1530, the reinstated religious processions became a permanent feature of Florentine life. On 14 February 1530 the *Signoria* decreed that, in order to gain God's mercy and to move Him to aid Florence, on the seven succeeding Fridays the miraculous crucifix of S. Pier del Murrone should be carried in procession through the city.[245] Fra Benedetto da Foiano organized the first of these processions, in which the members of the *Signoria* and of the Florentine magistracies also took part.[246] Meanwhile, Fra Zaccaria di Lunigiana recommended from his pulpit that, on every Wednesday during the Lenten season, there should be another procession of the same kind, led by the Holy Sacrament.[247] All these processions, which were held by order of the *Signoria* until the very eve of the Republic's fall,[248] were attended by immense pomp and ceremony. Besides the populace in general, members of the government and the priests and friars, dressed in sackcloth, participated as well as the youth companies and, on occasion, the members of the militia.[249] The Piagnoni friars played a leading role in the direction of such demonstrations, and were also active in other capacities. On 24 February 1530, for example, Fra Benedetto da Foiano preached before the Great Council. In a ceremony conducted with a sharp eye for dramatic effect, he blessed a standard proclaiming Christ to be King of

[244] Londi (ed.), *Appunti di un fautore dei Medici durante l'assedio di Firenze*, 51; see also p. 52.

[245] ASF Signori e Collegi, Deliberazioni Ord. Aut. 132, fo. 151ᵛ.

[246] Cambi, *Istorie*, iv. 52; 'Diario d'incerto del 1529 e 1530 dell'assedio di Firenze', MS BNF Magl., XXV, 555, fo. 139ᵛ.

[247] Cambi, *Istorie*, iv. 52; 'Diario d'incerto del 1529 e 1530 dell'assedio di Firenze', fo. 143ʳ⁻ᵛ. Once again, this was done at the behest of the *signoria*: ASF Signori e Collegi, Deliberazioni Ord. Aut. 132, fo. 178ʳ.

[248] ASF Signori e Collegi, Deliberazioni Ord. Aut. 133, fos. 96ᵛ–97ʳ.

[249] Cambi, *Istorie*, iv. 52–3, 60–1; 'Diario d'incerto del 1529 e 1530 dell'assedio di Firenze', fos. 139ᵛ, 143ʳ⁻ᵛ, 169ʳ, 170ᵛ; ASF Consulte e Pratiche, 73, fos. 54ʳ–55ʳ; Marino Sanuto, *I diarii*, lii (Venice, 1898; fac. edn. Bologna, 1970), cols. 215–16. The most detailed descriptions of some of these processions are to be found, however, in 'Appunti e notizie storiche degli anni 1527–1533 a Firenze', MS BMLF Antinori 136, fos. 3ʳ–4ᵛ.

Florence, presented it to the *Gonfaloniere*, and informed the assembled throng that when all seemed lost, they should unfurl the standard and venture out against the enemy, in the certain knowledge that God would give them victory.[250] One who tried to secure the same result, but by more practical means, was Fra Santi Pagnini, who wrote to Henry VIII of England imploring him to come to Florence's aid.[251]

The tide of religious fervour, so evident in the processions during Lent, was also manifest in other decisions and deliberations of the governing bodies of the city. In November 1529, shortly after the siege had begun, it was decreed that, whenever the Florentine forces were engaged in action, at the sound of the bell of the Palazzo della Signoria tolling the *Ave Maria* every non-combatant, whether priest or layman, woman or child, should genuflect where he or she stood, and pray for victory.[252] Enactments of a morally uplifting kind came with increasing frequency, and culminated on 28 June 1530 with the expulsion of prostitutes, who had previously only been restricted to certain areas of the city.[253] Some months previously, moreover, on 3 March, the *Signoria* had decreed that, since the tribulations Florence was suffering must be due in no small measure to the sins of her inhabitants, the whole population should seek God's forgiveness through penances, fasts, prayers, and alms.[254] And on 29 July a proclamation was issued by the *Signoria* declaring that on the following Sunday every man should confess and take communion before holding another solemn propitiatory procession.[255]

---

[250] Varchi, *Storia fiorentina*, ii. 39; 'Diario d'incerto dell'assedio di Firenze', fo. 139ᵛ; Alberi (ed.), *Relazioni degli ambasciatori veneti al Senato*, 275–6; Pitti, *Apologia de' Cappucci*, 371.

[251] Letter of Santi Pagnini to Henry VIII, 22 Apr. 1530, published in C. Roth, 'L'inghilterra e l'ultima Repubblica Fiorentina', *Rivista storica degli archivi toscani*, 1 (1929), 38.

[252] ASF Signori e Collegi, Deliberazioni Ord. Aut. 132, fo. 4ʳ⁻ᵛ.

[253] ASF Signori e Collegi, Deliberazioni Ord. Aut. 133, fos. 66ʳ–67ʳ. But it would seem that, in the end, only a few elderly prostitutes were actually expelled: 'Diario d'incerto del 1529 e 1530 dell'assedio di Firenze', fos. 128ʳ, 170ᵛ; Varchi, *Storia fiorentina*, ii. 145–6; Roth, *The Last Florentine Republic*, 267.

[254] ASF Signori e Collegi, Deliberazioni Ord. Aut. 132, fo. 177ᵛ.

[255] ASF Signori e Collegi, Deliberazioni Ord. Aut. 133, fos. 96ᵛ–97ʳ; 'Diario d'incerto del 1529 e 1530 dell'assedio di Firenze', fo. 120.

With this legislation the government reveals its increasing reliance upon the intervention of a suitably placated Almighty. The same trust is even more clearly apparent in the deliberations of the *pratiche*. While human aids were not entirely dispensed with, as can be seen from the conduct of the war, there is little evidence of much attention to practicalities. A telling example of the way in which religious principles interfered with practical considerations is provided by the government's attitude towards the large number of the indigent and of refugees, many of them from the *contado*, who had flocked to the city once hostilities had begun. In the *pratiche* held on 7 December 1529 and 2 June 1530 to discuss whether these 'useless mouths' should be ejected from the city as the Florentine military commanders demanded in order the better to withstand the siege, the majority of speakers could not bring themselves to approve a proposal which, though they acknowledged it as essential, they deemed cruel and against all tenets of Christian charity.[256] Displaying typically Savonarolan principles, they argued that the poor—referred to by one speaker as the soldiers of Christ (*soldati di Christo*)—should be given shelter, preferably in Florence, in order not to provoke God's wrath.[257] As Tommaso Soderini advised, only those useless mouths not acceptable to God, namely prostitutes, should be expelled; all the others should be permitted to stay, unless prepared to leave of their own volition.[258] Indeed, in the six months separating the two *pratiche* held on this issue, months which had witnessed the almost total blockade of the city with attendant increase in the number of deaths by starvation, there had been a hardening of attitudes against expulsion.[259] Though a census

---

[256] ASF Consulte e Pratiche, 71, fos. 129$^r$–132$^r$; ibid. 73, fos. 51$^v$–54$^r$. A copy of the first meeting is also available in BRF Moreniano, 332, fos. 77$^r$–80$^r$; see esp. the opinions of Simone Gondi, Tommaso Soderini (in both *pratiche*), Giovanni Girolami, Bernardo da Castiglione (in both *pratiche*).

[257] ASF Consulte e Pratiche, 71, fos. 129$^{r-v}$, 131$^r$, where quotation occurs; ibid. 73, fos. 51$^{r-v}$, 54$^r$.

[258] Ibid. 73, fos. 52$^v$–53$^r$.

[259] Cf. in particular the advice proffered by Bernardo da Castiglione, who in the *pratica* of 7 Dec. 1529 had argued that the city should behave towards the poor like sailors who got rid of useless ballast 'perché la prima charità è salvare la patria', whereas in the second meeting he had counselled discretion and the expulsion only of prostitutes, ibid. 71, fo. 130$^v$: cf. 73, fo. 53$^v$.

of the refugees was authorized, nothing more substantial was done, the government proving as reluctant as the *pratiche* to countenance such an uncharitable solution.[260] God would provide.

In the same vein, at meetings in February, April, and May 1530, when the *pratiche* discussed whether additional funds should be raised by taxing the clergy and other normally immune charitable organizations, there was no question of diplomatic compromise. By declaring that their policy must be dictated by the exigencies of the times, speaker after speaker betrayed an intensely Savonarolan concept of the Church as an institution dedicated to spiritual and moral welfare and so in no need of earthly wealth.[261] The most radical view was voiced by Giovanbattista Cei, who counselled that the goods not only of religious institutions, but also of certain wealthy citizens, should be collected with the utmost vigour.[262] Throughout these meetings, there was an absolute determination not to come to humiliating terms with the Pope and an unswerving commitment to the preservation of freedom and of the Great Council.[263] In one of the last *pratiche* held before the capitulation, Antonfrancesco Davanzati, speaking for the *Gonfalonieri*, expressed their wish to fight and die rather than suffer themselves to be enslaved and thus relinquish the freedom conferred upon them by God and enshrined in the constitution with the election of Christ as King of Florence.[264] Equally prevalent was the conviction that, so long as prayers and good works were encouraged, all would be well.[265] As

---

[260] ASF Signori e Collegi, Deliberazioni Ord. Aut. 132, fo. 161ʳ; Varchi, *Storia fiorentina*, ii. 145–6.

[261] ASF Consulte e Pratiche, 74, fos. 36ʳ–39ʳ, 39ᵛ–46ʳ, 62ʳ–66ʳ. Fairly typical was the opinion of Francesco Carducci, who stated 'questi beni hanno origine da i nostri, che hanno pensato che se ne vaglino ad pias animas et causas, delle quali nessuna più pia causa è che questa': fo. 64ʳ⁻ᵛ; cf. the opinion of Giuliano Ciai on fo. 62ᵛ. For earlier advice on taxing the clergy, see ibid. 71, fos. 18ᵛ–22ʳ.

[262] Ibid. fo. 65ʳ.

[263] Ibid. 71, fos. 76ʳ–77ʳ, 90ʳ–93ᵛ, esp. the opinions of Lorenzo Segni, Ulivieri Guadagni, and Bernardo da Castiglione; and fos. 101ᵛ–104ʳ, esp. opinions expressed by Alessandro Pieri, Marco degli Asini, Andrea Niccolini; ibid. 73, fos. 2ᵛ–18ʳ; BRF Moreniano, 332, fos. 31ᵛ, 47ʳ, 55ʳ, *et passim*.

[264] ASF Consulte e Pratiche, 73, fo. 56ᵛ.

[265] Ibid. 71, fos. 61ᵛ–64ʳ, esp. opinions of Ulivieri Guadagni and Zanobi Carnesecchi; and fos. 78ᵛ–79ʳ, 92ᵛ, esp. opinions of Giovanbattista Cei and Lorenzo Segni; ibid. 72, fos. 45ʳ, 59ʳ, 65ʳ, 141ʳ–144ᵛ; ibid. 73, fos. 58ʳ⁻ᵛ, 62ʳ⁻ᵛ; ibid. 74, fos. 43ʳ⁻ᵛ, 45ᵛ, *et passim*.

late as 30 May, when a *pratica* was held to discuss what emergency measures should be adopted after the fall of Empoli, Raffaello Lapaccini, speaking for the *Dodici Buonuomini*, could but counsel, 'to turn to God with all our means . . . being of the opinion that alms will avail us more than 500 soldiers'.[266]

'The atmosphere', in the words of Cecil Roth, 'was that of a revivalist camp.'[267] Religion had become so intrinsic a part of the deliberations of the *pratiche* that its members no longer considered their discussion complete without recourse to a higher authority. On 20 April they considered the question whether, since their mere human endeavours had as yet borne little fruit, a *pratica* of clerics should be convened to advise them how better they might proceed. This unusual proposal was received by the assembly as though it had been divine in origin.[268] The preachers had made such important contributions to the Republic that they should indeed be encouraged to do even more than they were already doing, enthusiastically declared Bastiano Canigiani on behalf of the *Dodici Buonuomini*.[269] The Piagnone Lorenzo Ridolfi, speaking for the quarter of S. Spirito, made a series of pronouncements which indicate very clearly the pervading spirit of this and other meetings. Having duly given thanks to Christ, in His capacity as King of Florence, for having inspired the proposal, Ridolfi went on to attest that he and the other *richiesti* for S. Spirito would be prepared to support whatever suggestions the clergy might make as to how God's wrath could best be assuaged. He had only one observation to offer; and, predictably, it concerned Savonarola. Since 'what had been done against Savonarola in the past had been done against God', he suggested, would it not be wise for the *Signoria*, if truly bent upon placating the Almighty, to remove from the governmental archives, where they were still held, the slanderous records of Savonarola's trial?[270]

With the conviction that Florence was in God's care went the belief that her enemies were His, and that the Florentines were

---

[266] Ibid. 74, fo. 86ʳ: 'che si ricorra a Dio con tutte le opere . . . giudicando che l'elemosine faccino più che 500 fanti'.

[267] Roth, *The Last Florentine Republic*, 203.

[268] ASF Consulte e Pratiche, 74, fos. 60ʳ, 62ʳ.          [269] Ibid., fo. 60ᵛ.

[270] Ibid., fo. 61ʳ: 'quello si è fatto contra lui si è fatto contra Dio'.

thus engaged upon a holy war against the forces of evil. How these
attitudes militated against an objective assessment of the city's
circumstances is apparent in the sermon preached by Fra Zaccaria
di Lunigiana in January 1530.[271] The sole sermon preached by a
cleric closely involved in the religious life of Florence during the
siege of which a complete text survives, it supplemented the usual
prophetic arguments concerning Florence's future with those of a
more practical kind. Taking a leaf from Savonarola's book, Fra
Zaccaria sought to convince by scriptural and logical arguments
those doubters who would not be swayed by spiritual means.[272]
Against the contention that Florence could not hope to emerge
victorious from an encounter with the Pope and the Emperor, Fra
Zaccaria asserted that the Florentines had right and justice on their
side.[273] If the city were not victorious, then the standard of normal
Christian values would be overthrown, and so, he maintained,
somewhat ingenuously, God would assuredly save Florence. Otherwise many would doubt His existence, or the truth of the faith.[274]

As others had done, Fra Zaccaria attributed the fact that Florence was still enduring tribulations to the sinfulness which yet
survived within her walls, but contended that, none the less, no city
could compare with her for Christian virtue.[275] Nowhere else in
Christendom was there so much charity towards the poor and to
the peasants who had sought refuge in the city. Nowhere else were
there as many just men or as many good works performed. No city
had received as much divine grace and illumination. Many sinners
had been converted and in the whole city many good deeds had
been done, through penance, prayers, processions, and alms.[276] For
all these reasons, the city could not fall. Fra Zaccaria accepted that
human remedies could play a part in overcoming present difficul-

[271] Zaccaria di Lunigiana, *Predica fatta l'ottava domenica fra l'ottava della Epifania da Fra Zaccheria da Lunigiana*, ed. C. Gargiolli, *Il Propugnatore*, 12/1 (1879), 417–43. The sermon is analysed in O. Niccoli, *Profeti e popolo nell'Italia del Rinascimento* (Bari, 1987), 155–8: I cannot agree, however, with the author's proposition that it marked the end of the 'moduli della predicazione profetica'.

[272] In this sermon, Fra Zaccaria follows the method employed by Savonarola in his famous sermon on the renovation of the Church, preached on 13 Jan. 1495: *Prediche sopra i Salmi*, ed. V. Romano (ENOS; 2 vols.; Rome, 1969–74), i. 37–62.

[273] Zaccaria di Lunigiana, *Predica*, 427, 428–9.

[274] Ibid. 429.   [275] Ibid. 430–2.   [276] Ibid. 432, 436.

ties, but the substance of his sermon was the argument that the Florentines must place their trust in God alone.[277] Florence would be tried to the limits of her endurance, in order that the few evil men who remained within her walls could be destroyed by God. Fra Zaccaria foretold that she would, in the end, be saved, where-upon, as a community of just men, her citizens would enter into the glory and happiness long promised them by their prophet, Savonarola.[278]

The Piagnoni view of Florence's military situation was distorted by this absolute trust in God. Both the discomfort of non-combat-ants within the city and the reverses suffered by her troops outside were seen, not as evidence that she was unlikely to recover, but as the trials which were a necessary prelude to her ultimate triumph. Every instance of hardship or defeat thus came to be greeted by the Piagnoni with rejoicing, as further proof of Florence's divinely appointed destiny.[279] As the reverses mounted, moreover, so did their reiteration of Savonarola's assurances that no army would ever prevail against Florence.[280] Unfortunately for the safety of the city, their increasing emphasis upon God's imminent intervention meant that debate was stifled, that human endeavour was increas-ingly undervalued, and that erstwhile allies who did not share their faith in Savonarola's prophecies of deliverance were alienated.[281] According to Donato Giannotti, these Piagnoni attitudes caused a paralysis in government which its enemies exploited to bring about the Republic's downfall.[282]

As the situation grew steadily worse, the Piagnoni developed the further argument that each defeat not merely hastened the ultimate victory but would make it all the more miraculous since God would have to resurrect the city from a situation which was, in human

---

[277] Ibid. 438–42.     [278] Ibid. 433, 436–7, 442–3.

[279] Giannotti, *Della Repubblica Fiorentina*, 233.

[280] Savonarola, *Le lettere*, ed. R. Ridolfi (Florence, 1933), 115; see Varchi, *Storia fiorentina*, ii. 154.

[281] The best description of this deterioration is provided by Guicciardini, *Dialogo*, in von Albertini, *Firenze dalla repubblica al principato*, 428–32, in which the interlocutors are the Piagnone Francesco Capponi and the disenchanted re-publican Piero Vettori, who three months earlier in a public speech to the militia, with 'potente ragioni humane et divine' had defended the Republic's stand.

[282] Giannotti, *Della Repubblica Fiorentina*, 233.

terms, irretrievable.[283] By the time of the battle of Gavinana on 3 August 1530, which immediately preceded the capitulation of Florence on 12 August, the Piagnoni had been forced to stretch credulity even further with their explanation for Christ's non-appearance on the scene. Far from admitting the collapse of all their hopes, they simply incorporated this latest disaster into the Savonarolan scheme. They now argued that only when all human endeavour had been exhausted and the enemy had breached the walls would the heavenly legions manifest themselves. 'Then, I say, and not before the Angels will visibly appear, our holy prophet in their midst', declared Francesco Zati, Luigi Guicciardini's Piagnone interlocutor in his dialogue *Del Savonarola*, 'and, with bloody swords in their hands, they will easily take the lives of our bold and so far victorious enemies; and with angelic fury they will destroy them and instantly repulse them from our blameless walls.'[284] But these pathetic, if bloodthirsty, appeals went unheard. Staunch to the last, the Piagnoni—or most of them—stood firm as Florence fell: mercifully unaware, perhaps, of how much they had contributed to the Republic's destruction.

## III

Despite the Piagnoni conviction that God would intervene to save His elect, despite also the brave words in the *pratiche* and in the other organs of government, more and more Florentines were becoming convinced that something needed to be done to stop the city's slide into ruin. Already on 23 April the committee of clerics convened[285] to advise the government on how best it could proceed

---

[283] Guicciardini, *Del Savonarola*, 132.

[284] Ibid. 131: 'Alhora dico, et non prima, appariranno visibilmente li Angeli, con la presenza del nostro sancto propheta togliendo facilmente, con le spade sanguinose in mano, alli arditi et già vittoriosj inimici la vita; et con tanto angelico furore consumandoli, et subbito discostandoli dalle nostre innocentissime mura.' See also Varchi, *Storia fiorentina*, ii. 193–4; Ambrogio Caterino Politi, *Discorso del Reverendo P. Frate Ambrosio Catharino Polito, Vescovo di Minori contra la dottrina et le profetie di Fra Girolamo Savonarola* (Venice, 1548), fos. 21ʳ, 26ᵛ, 48ᵛ [*bis*], 61ᵛ.

[285] See above, p. 379.

to speed God's intervention on the city's behalf had given a far from comforting reply. In a report preserved for us by Francesco da Castiglione, a member of the commission and also the current confessor of Suor Domenica, the clerics attributed the present tribulations of Florence to the lack of genuine religious spirit, to the absence of unity amongst the citizens, and to the private enmities and vendettas that continued to characterize the life of the city.[286] They hinted strongly at the fact that many of the decisions taken by the government in the recent past had been motivated not by concern for the common good, but by these private enmities. God's wrath could only be placated, they continued, if justice was fairly and rigidly administered, if the recently introduced laws and penalties against blasphemers, sodomites, prostitutes, and transgressors of the sumptuary regulations were applied with draconian severity.[287]

Having thus presented their credentials, the commission felt free to attack the course upon which the government had embarked. It condemned the inflexible and indiscriminate requisitioning of stores, especially from monasteries and convents. The results had been famine and untold suffering among the male and female religious, whose afflictions they pointedly observed, would undoubtedly call down God's vengeance upon Florence.[288] Even more blameworthy in the eyes of God, they continued, was the Republic's disregard for the traditional privileges enjoyed by the clergy, its presumptuous extension of jurisdiction to cover ecclesiastical and spiritual affairs. What to the Piagnoni was the unmistakable sign of divine election and of the imminent fulfilment of long-awaited promises, was to the commission of clerics both proof of the Republic's wrongfulness and the explanation for the present tribulations; it was, in addition, the clearest intimation of impend-

[286] 'Caritativo, buono e prudente consiglio dato da i religiosi e sacerdoti al Gonfaloniere di Iustitia del Popolo fiorentino l'anno 1530', in *Libro de' conti della fabbrica fatta a tempo della B.M. Suor Domenica dal Paradiso*, MS ACDC Codice segnato lett. R, fos. 36ʳ–41ʳ (dated at end 23 Apr. 1530), fos. 37ᵛ, 38ʳ. See also Varchi, *Storia fiorentina*, ii. 74–8. The committee consisted of twenty clerics: unfortunately, apart from Francesco da Castiglione, their names are not recorded.
[287] 'Caritativo, buono e prudente consiglio', fos. 38ʳ–39ʳ.
[288] Ibid., fo. 39ᵛ.

ing doom.[289] Finally, the commission averred that, in order to reconcile God with Florence, the government had no alternative but to sue the Pope for peace since, so they argued, it was well known that the city had been insolent to the Holy See. An embassy should be sent to the Pope to sue for pardon and, as long as liberty was guaranteed, accepting his spiritual jurisdiction over Florence.[290] It was the very sort of advice the government did not seek. The members of the *pratica* convened to discuss the report made plain their displeasure at the insolence of the clerics. None the less, the report was such an unusual and damaging expression of dissent and had such ominous implications that the *Signoria* insisted that an oath of secrecy be taken by all members of the *pratica*.[291]

Further evidence of dissatisfaction with the government's extremism is provided by records of attendance and voting in the Council of Eighty and the Great Council. During this period two major trends can be detected in both sets of figures. There was, first, a tendency towards higher absenteeism amongst the members of the Great Council. Secondly, and more importantly, as the effects of the siege began to be felt, opposition to the government's measures increased, especially but not exclusively in matters pertaining to taxation and to the requisitioning of ecclesiastical goods.[292]

To these expressions of opposition and exasperation was added the intention of the Florentine army to come to terms with the

---

[289] 'Caritativo, buono e prudente consiglio', fo. 40ʳ.     [290] Ibid., fo. 40ᵛ.

[291] ASF Consulte e Pratiche, 74, fos. 62ᵛ–66ʳ. Secrecy was normally required, but seldom it seems was it specifically requested.

[292] ASF Libri fabarum, 72, fos. 255ʳ, 256ʳ, 257ᵛ, 258ᵛ. A few examples of these trends will suffice. Whereas in June 1527 the Council of Eighty and the Great Council had decided by 86 to 14 votes and by 1,120 to 190 votes respectively to proceed with the sale of ecclesiastical goods, in June–July 1530 a similar piece of legislation obtained a majority of 76:36 in the Council of Eighty, was then rejected when first presented to the Great Council, and only accepted by it on the second attempt by 529 to 479 votes: ibid., fos. 229ʳ⁻ᵛ, 260ʳ, 261ʳ. Legislation imposing an extraordinary *accatto* in June 1527 received a majority of 95:5 votes in the Council of Eighty and of 812:418 in the Great Council; in Apr. 1530 a similar *accatto* was passed by 84:22 votes in the Eighty and by 677:535 votes in the Great Council: ibid., fos. 229ʳ, 259ʳ.

besieging forces. With the defeat of the relieving army at the battle
of Gavinana and with the death there of their military leader
Francesco Ferrucci, looked upon by many Piagnoni as the new
Gideon who with God's help would defeat Florence's enemies,
many lost heart. Malatesta Baglioni demanded a cessation of hostilities and, despite the insistence of the Florentine government
upon continuing the fight, entered openly into negotiations with
the Pope. The rift between the government and its military leader
produced extreme tension within Florence. Rather than risk a civil
war, on the one hand, or a totally defenceless city, on the other, the
*Signoria* eventually, on 8 August, acceded to Malatesta's demands
that negotiations be opened in order to reach a settlement.[293] Even
so, in a *pratica* held on the following day, despite the general agreement that Florence could not stand alone, many speakers, including Bernardo da Castiglione, Antonio Giugni, Lorenzo Giacomini,
and Scolaio Spini, argued against negotiations and for the continuation of hostilities, citing as evidence the experience of 1512 and the
bad faith of princes.[294] Meanwhile, on the same day on the other
side of the river, a body of about 400 citizens, most of them young
men, assembled in the Piazza di S. Spirito to signify their approval
of Malatesta's intention to capitulate. Nor were they all Medicean
sympathizers. The throng included some of the most ardent advocates of republicanism, such as Pier Filippo Pandolfini, Bartolomeo
Cavalcanti, and Piero Vettori; and even certain well-known
Piagnoni, who had also experienced a change of heart: the moderates Girolamo and Lorenzo Benivieni, and the radical Giuliano
Capponi.[295] Clearly, with the enemy now within and without,
there was no alternative to capitulation and Piagnoni radicals were
to be deprived of the purifying holocaust that was to precede the
apotheosis of Florence.

[293] Varchi, *Storia fiorentina*, ii. 194–206; Busini, *Lettere*, 175–83; Roth, *The
Last Florentine Republic*, 315–19.

[294] BRF Moreniano, 332, fos. 30ʳ–33ᵛ. But, on the other hand, the Piagnoni
Bernardo Gondi and Ulivieri Guadagni, though insisting quite illogically, like
most speakers, on the preservation of the city's freedom, were in favour of negotiations.

[295] Varchi, *Storia fiorentina*, ii. 206–7; Busini, *Lettere*, 184; Roth, *The Last
Florentine Republic*, 319.

On 12 August the document of capitulation was signed. It guaranteed an immunity to all those who had supported the republican government, but, in return, the city was forced to pay heavily. The Medici and their supporters were to be recompensed and reinstated in Florence; Florence was to pay the costs of the war; and its form of government was left to the discretion of Charles V.[296]

[296] Roth, *The Last Florentine Republic*, 320.

# 8

# 'By the Waters of Babylon':
# The Death of a Movement

The capitulation of Florence was followed by a short period of respite. For a while at least, Bartolomeo Valori, who ruled Florence almost single-handed, as Clement VII's deputy, was able to maintain a semblance of normality, despite an atmosphere charged with fear, hate, and despondency and a desultory attempt by the mob to attack and sack S. Marco.[1] Indeed, the first major decisions taken to dismantle the republican political structure were characterized by punctilious legality and by the determination to preserve a degree of continuity between the old and new regime. As in 1512, a *parlamento* was called in order to appoint a *Balìa* with full powers to reform the government. On this occasion, however, to remove any doubt on the legality of the *parlamento*, the law of 13 August 1495 was specifically abrogated before proceeding to the creation of the *Balìa*.[2] Amongst the twelve members of the *Balìa*, moreover, were Raffaello Girolami, the last *Gonfaloniere di Giustizia* elected by the republican regime, and Zanobi Bartolini, who had played an important political and diplomatic role during the last Republic.[3] Bartolomeo Valori, however, was the only Medicean counselling

[1] The atmosphere in Florence at the time is best captured by Giambattista Busini, who concludes his description with the words 'Quella città era proprio un inferno', *Lettere . . . a Benedetto Varchi sopra l'assedio di Firenze*, ed. G. Milanesi (Florence, 1860), 185. For the attack on S. Marco see Francesco Onesti da Castiglione, 'Persecutiones exagitate contra venerabilem sponsam Jesu Christi S. Dominicam de Paradiso', MS ACDC Codice F, fo. 23 [*bis*]ʳ.

[2] ASF Provvisioni, Registri, 209, fo. 31ʳ⁻ᵛ; ibid., C. Strozz., ser. I, 12, fos. 200–205.

[3] List of names of the twelve members of the *Balìa* in Filippo de' Nerli, *Commentari* (2 vols.; Trieste, 1859), ii. 170 and ASF Balìe, 51, fo. 93ʳ⁻ᵛ.

moderation. As more and more exiled aristocrats and Mediceans made their way back to Florence and as Clement VII was able to take a more active part in government, Bartolomeo found himself more isolated and increasingly suspect as a weak, venal, and therefore unreliable Medicean representative.[4] The returning exiles, to a man, wanted vengeance on their defeated enemies and were not unduly concerned about the methods employed. Most insistent in demanding a policy of wholesale retribution was Clement VII, partly to avenge himself for the humiliation he and his family had been forced to undergo over the previous three years but partly also in a conscious attempt to engender enmities and to harden divisions in Florentine society so as to convince the Florentines that the only solution lay in relinquishing all power to the Medici.[5] That the most humane member of the Medici family—the only member in fact who in the past had shown a genuine concern for Florence's interests and had actively worked to reconcile its destructive opposing factions—should have encouraged so vindictive and divisive a policy is the clearest indication of how dramatically the political situation had deteriorated during the last Republic. Nor were there any doubts in Clement's mind as to who should be primarily blamed for the polarization of Florentine politics and society: it was the Piagnoni and the ideology they had espoused, the very ideology with which the Republic had justified its extremism. Regardless of the terms of the capitulation, they had

---

[4] See in particular 'Sustanzia di lettere ricevute da Mr. Pietropaolo Marzi nel tempo si ritornò in Firenze doppo l'assedio nel 1530 ricevute da Roma d'ordine di Papa Clemente VII', MS ASF C. Strozz., ser. II, 149, fo. 39$^{r-v}$, where Clement VII writing to Francesco Guicciardini and Francesco Vettori states 'come gli è venuto ad notitia che loro assai si dogliono che Bartolomeo Valori li impedisce la resolutione loro con accennarli Sua Santità non se ne contentare che alli tre, cioè Gio. Battista Cei, Luigi Soderini et Piero Adovardo [Giachinotti] fussi facto il medesimo che alli altri, et il segretario Aldobrandino fussi messi nel fo[n]do della torre a Pisa'. Clement denies angrily ever having given such instructions and demands that the four be punished like the others. See also Bartolomeo's letter of 16 Sept. 1530 to Luigi Guicciardini on behalf of Paolantonio Soderini: ibid., C. Strozz., ser. I, 59, No. 55. On his 'natura graziosa' and venality see, amongst others, Busini, *Lettere*, 39, 183, 186; see also Benedetto Varchi, *Storia fiorentina* (2 vols.; Florence, 1963) ii. 249.

[5] The clearest evidence of Clement VII's policy is to be found in 'Sustanzia di lettere ricevute da Mr. Pietropaolo Marzi', *passim*; but see also de' Nerli, *Commentari*, ii, 180 and Varchi, *Storia fiorentina*, ii. 265.

to be punished as had also the major exponents of the republican regime. Above all, a political settlement had to be imposed on Florence which would both prevent extremists from regaining control and guarantee Medici ascendancy. There could be no return to the political system in force between 1512 and 1527 and to the relatively moderate policies pursued in those years. Both had been found wanting and, as the man most responsible for their adoption, Clement was not about to repeat the same mistakes.[6] Consequently, while encouraging discussions on the form of the future government of Florence, he began to lay the foundations for a Medicean principate.[7]

Clement VII's inflexible and punitive approach won the day, despite the continued opposition of Bartolomeo Valori and of a few other highly placed individuals, such as Jacopo Salviati and Cardinal Ippolito de' Medici.[8] To facilitate the payment of old scores, the newly elected *Balìa* prohibited everyone from leaving the city. Arrests and interrogations of the more influential representatives of the republican regime began in earnest.[9] A curfew was imposed and bans were promulgated against the wearing or keeping of arms.[10] The by now predictable purges of government magistracies and officials, attendant upon every change of regime, were set in train once again. In this instance, however, the process was not only more ruthless and systematic than on previous occasions but was extended into institutions and positions which had never in the past experienced such direct governmental interference. On 22 August the incumbent members of the *Otto di Guardia* were dismissed and new officials appointed in their place.[11] Three days later the two magistracies of the *Nove di Milizia* and *Dieci di Balìa* were quashed,

[6] See above, Ch. 5.

[7] R. von Albertini, *Firenze dalla repubblica al principato* (Turin, 1970), 187. The underlying intentions of Clement VII are best expressed in a letter to Filippo de' Nerli cited in G. Capponi (ed.), 'Discorsi intorno alla riforma dello stato di Firenze', *ASI*, 1st ser. 1 (1842), 416.

[8] And to a lesser extent also Filippo Strozzi. The better to pursue this policy, Bartolomeo Valori was deprived of his office as *Commissario* in favour of Fra Niccolò Schomberg: von Albertini, *Firenze dalla repubblica al principato*, 188. See also de' Nerli, *Commentari*, ii. 188.

[9] See, e.g. ASF Balìe, 51, fo. 12$^{r-v}$; Varchi, *Storia fiorentina*, ii. 246.

[10] Ibid. ii. 235; see also 'Appunti e notizie storiche degli anni 1527–1533 a Firenze', MS BMLF Antinori 136, fo. 16$^r$.

[11] ASF Provvisioni, 209, fo. 35$^r$.

the latter being replaced by a Medicean *Otto di Pratica* on 26 September.[12] Even such relatively minor offices as the *Sei di Mercanzia*, the *Provveditori delle arti*, *Ufficiali della Torre*, *Capitani di Parte Guelfa*, and *Consoli di Mare* were purged of all members elected by the republican regime and new officials appointed; as was also the case with politically more sensitive magistracies and officials such as the *Ufficiali del Monte*, Vicars and Governors of the various towns and territories subject to Florentine rule, the five syndics empowered to review the activities of the past regime.[13] In all applicable cases, new scrutinies were authorized to ensure that such purges were institutionalized and that only partisans of the Medici were to be rendered eligible for office.[14] Not surprisingly, given their importance in the day-to-day running of government, there occurred the usual replacement of notaries in the chanceries and in other government magistracies; once again, in keeping with the prevalent spirit of retaliation, no exceptions were made. The notaries appointed by the Republic were ejected and new ones appointed in their places, while all officials in government employment who had been deprived of their posts by the previous regime were now, by executive decrees, reinstated in office.[15]

Such instances of high-handed political imposition—which, despite the thoroughness with which they were applied, followed patterns established in previous Florentine political upheavals—could be multiplied indefinitely. All that, however, would still fail to convey the essence and the full extent of the political revolution. Unlike the previous regime, which even at its most radical and revengeful had observed certain well-established conventions, the restored Mediceans did not shrink from unprecedented, highly questionable, and unpopular, partisan decisions. For instance, the sentences and fines imposed by the previous regime

---

[12] ASF Balìe, 49, fo. 27[r], and 51, fo. 9[r].

[13] Ibid. 49, fos. 79[r]–80[r], 81[r], 85[r]–87[r], 134[r]–135[r], 161[r–v], 239[r–v]; see also 'Sustanzia di lettere ricevute da Mr. Pietropaolo Marzi', fos. 55[v]–56[v], for Clement's instructions as to who should be appointed to these offices.

[14] ASF Balìe, 49, fos. 81[r], 85[r], 87[r].

[15] Ibid., fo. 161[r–v] and ibid. 50, fos. 27[v], 32[r]; see also D. Marzi, *La cancelleria della Repubblica fiorentina* (Rocca S. Casciano, 1910), 325.

on its enemies were now annulled and all moneys and confiscated properties returned to them.[16] Even more resented was the decree by which all the goods and properties belonging to religious institutions, to guilds, and to the Medici sold at public auction by the republican regime should now be returned by the purchasers to the previous owners without compensation.[17] More ominous and equally unprecedented was the decision to waive constitutional restraints and allow *amici* who had been drawn for the *Signoria* to take up office despite being in arrears with their taxes.[18] Finally, in a move which deeply shocked the Piagnone chronicler Giovanni Cambi and which convinced him that the Mediceans had embarked on a policy of gradually restricting eligibility to government in order to create a seigneurial regime, the *Accoppiatori* appointed the new *Signoria* without proceeding at the same time with the customary election of the *Gonfalonieri delle compagnie*.[19] When the transition to a full seigneurial regime was finally consummated in 1532 with the creation of Alessandro de' Medici as Duke of Florence and with the removal of the system of government which had endured since the thirteenth century, few were surprised, though some, such as Jacopo Salviati, could not contain their sorrow.[20]

As the Medici moved inexorably towards tyrannical rule, other measures were taken to weaken or destroy opposing factions and individuals. Though financial needs dictated that all Florentines of means should be forced to advance loans to the government, well-

---

[16] See e.g. ASF Balìe, 49, fos. 323[r–v], 328[r–v].

[17] Ibid. 54, fo. 285[r–v]. So unprecedented and generally resented was the decision that all contemporary historians remarked upon it, see e.g. de' Nerli, *Commentari*, ii. 178–9; Giovanni Cambi, *Istorie*, ed. I. di San Luigi (4 vols.; Florence, 1785–6), iv. 90–1; 'Appunti e notizie storiche degli anni 1527–1533', fo. 18[v].

[18] ASF Balìe, 49, fo. 327[r].

[19] Cambi: *Istorie*, iv, 106; in ASF Balìe, 54, fo. 195[r–v], a lame justification of the practice on grounds of the restraints imposed by the law on the *divieto* is given.

[20] Busini, *Lettere*, 89. A foreshadowing of this trend is provided by the 'decision' of 17 Feb. 1531 by which the *Balìa* in thanksgiving appointed 'Duca' Alessandro de' Medici a member of the *Balìa*, and rendered him eligible to all offices he wanted without the limitations decreed by the laws on *divieto*, and in them to exercise full authority: ASF Balìe, 49, fo. 379[r–v] and ibid. 50, fos. 92[r]–93[r]; see also ibid. 52, fo. 17[r].

known enemies of the Medici, renowned republicans, and die-hard Piagnoni were in addition so punitively assessed and taxed as to suggest that the primary aim was to ruin them.[21] Many, unable to comply and fearing arrest as a consequence, sought salvation in flight, thus playing into the hands of their enemies. All the while arrests of the representatives of the republican regime continued apace. Even those highly placed moderates who, like Raffaello Girolami, seemed at first to have survived the transition unscathed were now arrested. The chance survival of the abridged transcripts of the interrogation by the *Otto di Guardia* of two eminent exponents of the republican regime, Iacopo Gherardi and Francesco Carducci, enables us to obtain some indication of the thoroughness with which the policy of retribution was pursued, regardless of the terms of the capitulation. These two prisoners, in fact, were forced to implicate in major, if imaginary, crimes other anti-Mediceans, who were subsequently arrested, banished, and even executed.[22] When, as in the case of Raffaello Girolami, it proved impossible to attribute to opponents past misdeeds, present or potential crimes were imputed to them.[23] In the majority of cases, however, it was not necessary to go to all this trouble. It was sufficient for the *famigli* of the *Otto di Guardia* to claim that prohibited arms had been found at an opponent's house for arrest and imprisonment to follow.[24] Few pleas for mercy were entertained or granted, regardless of the eminence or trustworthiness of the persons making them. Indeed, whenever it seemed that the traditional Florentine tendencies towards moderation and compromise were on the point of asserting themselves, Clement VII would intervene from Rome,

---

[21] Busini, *Lettere*, 51, fos. 21ᵛ–23ᵛ. See also the already cited letter of Bartolomeo Valori to Luigi Guicciardini (n. 4 above) where the former insists that the second *accatto* imposed on Paolantonio Soderini be waived as unjust since Paolantonio had already paid his dues.

[22] ASF Miscellanea Repubblicana, 8, inserto 239, unfoliated.

[23] ASF Balìe, 52, fo. 12ʳ⁻ᵛ, where in a letter to Alessandro de' Medici, the *Balìa* states: 'Raffaello non è ritenuto per cose seguite avanti la capitolazione, ma per suspecti et inditii di nuove machinationi . . . Et [da] quando è suto facto lo accordo non ha mancato di nuove pratiche contro a questo stato et è verisimile che sempre habbi a fare così.'

[24] 'Appunti e notizie storiche degli anni 1527–1533', fos. 16ᵛ–17ʳ.

urging the indiscriminate arrest of all opponents of the regime and insisting upon their exemplary condemnation.[25]

The blood-letting continued unabated. The radical leaders of the Republic, Francesco Carducci, Iacopo Gherardi, Bernardo da Castiglione, Luigi Soderini, Gianbattista Cei, and Pieradovardo Giacchinotti were all executed. A score of other anti-Mediceans were also executed or condemned to death *in absentia*. Approximately two hundred more were either imprisoned or sent into exile from which the majority was never to return. Among the victims were some of the greatest names in Piagnone history. Bernardo da Castiglione, as we have seen, was executed, and his sons Dietisalvi, Vieri, and Francesco were exiled. Iacopo Nardi, Martino di Francesco Scarfi, Tommaso Soderini, and his son Paolantonio were also exiled. Leonardo Bartolini and Battista del Bene were condemned to death *in absentia*, having managed to escape from Florence before the *Balìa* had circumscribed movement to and from the city. Battista della Palla was imprisoned for life in Pisa and there assassinated. Marco Strozzi, who had died during the siege, was formally damned and his goods were confiscated.[26] Girolamo Buonagrazia, who had played such a prominent part in the *tumulto del venerdì*, was brought before the *Otto di Guardia* on two separate occasions. On the first, he was tried and condemned to a fine for possession of prohibited arms. On the second instance, he was

---

[25] 'Sustanzia di lettere ricevute da Mr. Pietropaolo Marzi', fos. 39ᵛ, 41ᵛ–43ʳ, 53ʳ⁻ᵛ, 133ʳ, *et passim*. Typical of Clement's intransigence was his refusal to heed a *raccomandazione* to release Lamberto Cambi from prison, where he was held for his part in the sale of ecclesiastical goods: 'Dice sua Santità che per lei si farebbe fussi mendico et stessi peggio non sta et così li altri della sorte sua per averlo per un perfido et crudelissimo inimico di casa sua, et che per ciò non vuole fare nulla', ibid., fo. 66ʳ. On only one instance did Clement accede to a request for mercy; this was made by Ormanozzo Deti on behalf of Salvestro Aldobrandini, who was thus spared his life but was exiled none the less. It seems, however, that in addition Salvestro had promised to collaborate with the new regime: ibid., fos. 101ʳ, 122ʳ.

[26] A fairly comprehensive list of the victims in Varchi, *Storia fiorentina*, ii. 247–65. The full list, which includes also 'middling' men not mentioned by Varchi, is to be found in ASF Otto di Guardia, Ep. Rep. 209 and 231. Girolamo Benivieni attempted unsuccessfully to intercede through Jacopo Salviati for Iacopo Nardi and Donato Giannotti: C. Re, *Girolamo Benivieni fiorentino* (Città di Castello, 1906), app., pp. 349–52.

charged with heresy for having corresponded with Martin Luther and for having subscribed to some of his doctrines. This charge was also extended to cover his activities against the Pope during the *tumulto del venerdì* and during the years of the last Republic. Condemned to death, he had his sentence commuted to perpetual exile and a fine of 2,000 florins as a result of his recantation before an especially convened ecclesiastical tribunal which also included Angelo Marzi, Bishop of Assisi.[27]

The roll-call of Piagnoni victims could be extended much further. Few eminent families with a tradition of Savonarolan loyalty escaped unscathed: the Rinuccini, Tosinghi, Bettini, Cambini, Guidotti, and Zati, to mention some of the more prominent names, were grievously weakened by the loss of one or more members through imprisonment and exile. Only a handful of families, notably the Valori, Guadagni, and Capponi, managed to weather the transition without losses, despite the fact that some of their members continued publicly to profess belief in Savonarola's doctrines. The immunity of the Valori was guaranteed, for a while yet, by Bartolomeo. Almost impossible to explain was the survival and the continued political prominence enjoyed by the Capponi and the Guadagni. This is particularly mystifying when it is considered that two of the most prominent members of these families, Giuliano Capponi and Ulivieri Guadagni, had publicly aligned themselves with the radical exponents of the Piagnone movement. Indeed, Ulivieri Guadagni was one whose blood was most insistently clamoured for by Clement VII after the fall of Florence.[28] Whatever the explanation, these were

---

[27] L. Passerini, 'Il primo processo per la riforma luterana in Firenze', *ASI*, 4th ser. 3 (1879), 337–45; *DBI*, s.v.; S. Caponetto, *Aonio Paleario (1503–1570) e la riforma protestante in Toscana* (Turin, 1979), 43, 180 n. 6. See also P. Simoncelli, *Evangelismo italiano del Cinquecento* (Rome, 1979), 386–7 where, however, on the basis of Buonagrazia's recantation the author argues for his anti-Savonarolan position.

[28] On Giuliano Capponi see P. Litta, *Famiglie celebri italiane* (10 vols.; Milan, 1819–74), x, table xiii; on Ulivieri Guadagni see L. Passerini, *Genealogia e storia della famiglia Guadagni* (Florence, 1873), 76–7; Busini, *Lettere*, 33, 43, 149; 'Sustanzia di lettere ricevute da Mr. Pietropaolo Marzi', fos. 53$^r$, 133$^r$.

among the dozen or so prominent Piagnoni who managed to avoid retribution.[29]

The persecution of Piagnoni was accompanied by a concerted effort to undo their achievements. Not unexpectedly, the first moves were made against the moral and sumptuary legislation of the last Republic. On 5 October 1530 the *Balìa* repealed the law enacted on 3 April 1528 which had in effect placed the taverns of the city out of bounds to Florentines because they endangered the spiritual welfare of the people and thus prevented Florence from entering into her Kingdom.[30] On 8 November 1530 it was the turn of the sumptuary legislation passed on 15 June 1527. Criticizing it as too severe and therefore unenforceable and even counter-productive, the *Balìa* removed its most severe and controversial provisions.[31] In little over one year's time, however, it was forced to reverse the decision, which had been taken purely out of spite and with utter disregard for the perilous economic conditions. Accordingly, on 27 November 1531 it promulgated on purely economic grounds a piece of legislation more severe in its provisions than the recently diluted law of 15 June 1527.[32]

A similar disregard for consequences seems to have characterized the Mediceans' intervention in the Piagnone-controlled system of public welfare. The confraternity of the *Buonuomini di S. Martino* was undoubtedly the most leniently treated of the Piagnoni foundations. Suffering from a shortage of funds and consequent reduction of its charitable activity and placed under the control of the redoubtable Giovanni de Statis, the papal deputy

[29] Amongst these, one should mention Lorenzo Violi, Girolamo Benivieni, Iacopo Morelli, Bernardo Gondi, Gherardo Taddei. However, they were one and all minor and harmless figures who could be easily tolerated even though they could not be allowed to play just as yet a prominent political role; thus the rejection of Lorenzo Violi's candidature for the post of Chancellor of the *Otto di Pratica*: ibid., fo. 2[r].

[30] ASF Balìe, 50, fos. 11[r]–12[r].

[31] Ibid. 49, fo. 220[r–v] where it is stated that the promulgation of the law 'ha ridocto le cose in tanta strecteza che la observantia di quella è stata non solamente cosa difficilissima ma ancora reputata più presto al vivere civile cosa indecente'; see also ibid. 50, fos. 55[v]–56[v].

[32] Ibid. 54, fos. 240[r]–242[r] and ibid. 55, fos. 52[r]–55[r].

over ecclesiastical matters in Florence, the confraternity seemed destined to an imminent demise. That it was spared and given the means to continue its activity was due to the good offices of Jacopo Salviati. Though unable to intercede successfully for individual fellow Piagnoni, Jacopo pleaded the confraternity's case with Clement VII, who, in turn, restrained Giovanni de Statis and authorized him to make over to the confraternity a sum of 300 ducats which it needed for its operations.[33] The confraternity of S. Michele Arcangelo also received relatively lenient treatment. It was closed in November 1530 and, if its records are to be trusted, it remained closed until 16 February 1539. Thereafter, it seems to have been permitted to operate almost undisturbed and was to have a later flourishing period under the spiritual guidance of Fra Alessandro Capocchi of Sta Maria Novella, a fervent admirer of Savonarola.[34]

No such reprieve was granted to the *Ospedale del Ceppo*. Not even the long-standing friendship that had existed between Clement VII and Girolamo Benivieni, one of the governors of the *Ospedale del Ceppo*, could prevent the hospital from being requisitioned by Giovanni de Statis to house the displaced Benedictine nuns of Sta Maria whose convents on S. Miniato had been razed to the ground in preparation for the siege. Despite the fact that Girolamo Benivieni and his fellow governor and Piagnone Bernardo di Carlo Gondi had agreed to surrender the hospital only for one year, it proved impossible for the confraternity to regain control over it. After the stipulated year had passed, the nuns petitioned Clement VII and succeeded in having the hospital and surrounding property assigned to them in perpetuity. The

---

[33] On Giovanni de Statis and on his ruthlessness in demanding the restitution of ecclesiastical property see Varchi, *Storia fiorentina*, ii. 276; ABSM, Filza 51, letters of 27 May 1531 and 27 June 1531 from Jacopo Salviati in Rome to the *Procuratori dei Buonuomini*. Though in Rome throughout this period, Jacopo had been made a *Proposto* of the *Buonuomini* late in 1530: ibid., Libro di Entrata e uscita segnato F, fo. 44ᵛ.

[34] ASF Compagnie Religiose Soppresse, 1430, fos. 69ᵛff.; G. Richa, *Notizie istoriche delle chiese fiorentine* (10 vols.; Florence, 1754–62), viii. 268–9; F. Marchi, *Vita del Reverendo Padre Frate Alessandro Capocchi fiorentino* (Florence, 1583), 40.

confraternity was permitted to retain only its meeting-place in one of the buildings but soon abandoned it and moved elsewhere, ceasing meanwhile its charitable activities. In 1544 its remaining assets were assigned to the hospital of the *Incurabili*.[35] This latter hospital, too, did not emerge unscathed from the political turmoil. Though by now too important an element in the Florentine welfare structure to be treated in such a cavalier fashion, it was none the less forced to make changes in its personnel and to accept closer governmental control. Within a few years the government had to assume financial responsibility for its operations, a move which was rendered necessary by the ensuing reluctance of private donors to fund it to the necessary level.[36]

Paradigmatic of the Medicean approach to the Savonarolan welfare system was undoubtedly the fate of the *Monte di Pietà*. On 18 November 1530, in a meeting held in the Medici palace, an unspecified group of Mediceans proceeded to dismiss the recently elected officials of the *Monte di Pietà* and to appoint new officials. Of the eight appointed, seven were trusted Medici servants, including Bartolomeo Valori and Filippo Strozzi; only one, the 68-year-old Bernardo di Carlo Gondi, was a Piagnone.[37] The reasons for his choice are obscure, though his age, moderation, and wealth might have been factors in his favour. Only another Piagnone, Ulivieri Guadagni, was to be appointed to the board of the *Monte di Pietà*, for the triennium 1536–9.[38] In this case, too, wealth was undoubtedly a factor. One cannot discount the possibility, however, that the appointment of these two Piagnoni was an overture by the Medici both to them personally, to overcome their opposition to the regime, and to the many uncommitted Florentines who might thus have been convinced that the *Monte di Pietà* had not

[35] 'Ricordanze del Ceppo di Firenze', ASF Ospedale di S. Maria Nuova, Spedale degli Incurabili, 10, fo. 65ʳ; L. Passerini, *Storia degli stabilimenti di beneficenza e d'istruzione elementare gratuita della città di Firenze* (Florence, 1853), 193–4.

[36] Ibid. 209–11; ASF Ospedale di S. Maria Nuova, Spedale degli Incurabili, 11, fo. 99ᵛ *et passim*.

[37] ASF MP, Registro 23, fo. 101ʳ⁻ᵛ; see also ibid., Registro 13, unfoliated.

[38] Ibid. From 1533 the officials of the *Monte* were elected by the *Senato dei Quarantotto*.

become an exclusively Medicean organization bereft of religious ideals and purpose and that as the appointment of such upright men demonstrated, it still abided by the principles under which it had been founded, and deserved, therefore, their support and patronage.

The operational changes which the new masters forced the *Monte di Pietà* to introduce lend weight to this interpretation. For the remainder of 1530 and for at least the early months of 1531, the *Monte* officials continued to meet in the Medici palace.[39] On 13 July 1532, moreover, the newly established *Senato dei Quarantotto* decreed that all loans secured by pledge should attract an interest of at least 2 *denari* per *lira* per month, which was not only double the rate set in 1496 but, by providing more money than required to run the institution, could be construed to represent a usurious rate of interest.[40] Worse was to come. On 27 February 1538 the interest rate was doubled again to 4 *denari* per *lira* per month.[41] By then, as authorized by the decree of 10 June 1533, the *Monte di Pietà* was permitted to accept deposits from public bodies and private citizens and to pay depositors an interest of 5 per cent. Later still, on 12 May 1544, it was accorded the right to lend money to private citizens and to public institutions.[42]

Some, if not all these changes, were dictated by the need to render the *Monte di Pietà* solvent after the loans it was forced to make to the government during the last Republic. These loans had been exceptionally high and had drained it of reserves, threatening

---

[39] ASF MP, Registro 23, fos. 102ᵛ, 106ᵛ, 116ᵛ.

[40] Ibid., Registro 2, fos. 12ᵛ–13ᵛ; G. Pampaloni, 'Cenni storici sul Monte di Pietà di Firenze', *Archivi Storici delle Aziende di credito* (2 vols.; Rome, 1956), i. 539. The legislation establishing the *Monte di Pietà* had allowed for the possibility, only in the most extreme of circumstances, to charge 1½ *denari* per *lira* per month: ASF Provvisioni, Registri, 187, fo. 9ᵛ. The whole question of the rate of interest and the spiritual dangers inherent in it being set too high was addressed by all contemporary preachers, including Savonarola, on whom see M. Ciardini, *I banchieri ebrei in Firenze nel secolo XV e il Monte di Pietà* (Borgo S. Lorenzo, 1907; repr. Florence, 1975), 95–9.

[41] Pampaloni, 'Cenni storici sul Monte di Pietà di Firenze', 539; ASF MP, Registro 2, fo. 14.

[42] Pampaloni, 'Cenni Storici sul Monte di Pietà di Firenze', 541.

its future viability.[43] None the less, the solutions implemented by
the *Monte di Pietà* represented a radical departure from the spirit of
the enabling law of 21 April 1496. From a charitable institution
fulfilling the twofold spiritual function of improving the lot of the
poor while at the same time allowing individuals to acquire merit
by contributing their substance and services to it, the *Monte di
Pietà* had become a public bank, closely supervised by the Medici
and providing all the services and benefits of a bank, including
profits for its depositors. It still played an important role in the
Florentine system of public welfare, but, as some would have argued, it did so almost by default and at an intolerable spiritual cost.
If the appointments of Bernardo Gondi and Ulivieri Guadagni to
the board of the *Monte di Pietà* were indeed designed to offset the
impression created by these changes, then the ploy did not work.
Piagnoni and republicans did not flock back to its support; on the
contrary, no recognizable names can be identified amongst the
minor officials and guarantors. These positions were now monopolized by trusted Medici servants and career officials.[44] Thus, by
the end of the first year of Medicean government and with the
promulgation of the usual bans against unauthorized meetings
of confraternities,[45] hardly anything remained of the Savonarolan
system of public welfare and of mutual support.

Political considerations were obviously at the bottom of this
intervention. The Mediceans could no longer ignore the fact that
these organizations, in addition to being indissolubly linked with
Savonarola and serving to keep his memory alive, were also important centres of Piagnone political activity. In the past, especially in
times of adversity, they had enabled individual Piagnoni to keep in
touch with one another, work together, and, in the process, estab-

---

[43] Ibid. 538–40. Indeed, the financial problem caused by forced loans and by
the defalcation of some of the *Monte* administrators, including Andrea Nardi,
Jacopo's brother, greatly taxed the officials' ingenuity: ASF MP, Registro 23, fos.
42$^v$–43$^r$, 102$^v$–103$^r$.

[44] Ibid., fos. 106$^v$ ff.

[45] L. Polizzotto, 'Confraternities, Conventicles and Political Dissent . . . Documents' *Memorie Domenicane*, NS 17 (1986), 292–3.

lish important social and political networks.[46] If permitted to survive or to operate undisturbed they could become focuses of opposition to the regime. They had, therefore, to be disbanded or, if this were not possible, taken over by the regime. Those Piagnoni who had managed to escape proscription or imprisonment were thus deprived of their last remaining possibility of engaging in political activity. Excluded from office, isolated and harassed by a regime which, by concentrating all power in the hands of the *signore*, had deprived them of all avenues of redress, the Piagnoni, as a political movement, ceased to be a force in Florence. But this was not yet evident to the leading men of the Medicean regime, who were still haunted by the events of 1527 and by the suddenness and fierceness of the Piagnone revival in that year. Events were to justify, partially at least, their caution.

Equally as thorough was the purge of the ecclesiastical standardbearers of the Piagnone movement. Of the three great religious leaders of the last Republic, Fra Benedetto da Foiano, who had been arrested by Malatesta's men and handed over to the Pope even before the capitulation was signed, was incarcerated in Castel S. Angelo and there starved to death. Fra Bartolomeo da Faenza sought safety in flight.[47] Fra Zaccaria di Lunigiana also managed, albeit with great difficulty, to escape,[48] and found refuge in Venice, where as we shall see, he continued to be a thorn in the side of the ecclesiastical authorities.

---

[46] See above, Ch. 6.

[47] Varchi, *Storia fiorentina*, ii. 235–6. See also Cambi, *Istorie*, iv. 71. Francesco Vettori, for one, considered that Fra Benedetto, even while incarcerated in Castel S. Angelo, was still being treated too leniently since, although in prison for two months to date, he had not been tortured to give an account of the part he had played in the siege. He was, according to Vettori, 'capo, guida et corona delli obstinati et arrabbiati, quello che ha tirato la scriptura sacra al senso suo, ribaldo che è stato causa principale della morte almeno di cento mila anime': letter of Francesco Vettori to Bartolomeo Lanfredini, 16 Nov. 1530, in von Albertini, *Firenze dalla repubblica al principato*, app., 442. Fra Bartolomeo died in the Convent of S. Romano in Lucca on 29 July 1532: Roberto Ubaldini, 'Annalia Conventus Sancti Marci', MS BMLF S. Marco 370, fo. 171ʳ; Serafino Razzi, *Vita dei santi e beati del sacro ordine de' Frati Predicatori* (Palermo, 1605), 325.

[48] Varchi, *Storia fiorentina*, ii. 236–7; P. Tacchi-Venturi, *Storia della Compagnia di Gesù in Italia*, i. (Rome and Milan, 1910), 45; 'Appunti e notizie storiche degli anni 1527–1533', fo. 20ᵛ.

By far the greatest blow, however, was the suppression of the Tusco-Roman Congregation. Its destruction as a corporate entity, which had been threatened since the time of Alexander VI,[49] was finally carried out, with no forewarning, by Clement VII in a bull issued on 27 October 1530.[50] The convents which had previously made up the Congregation were incorporated into a new and larger body, to be known as the Roman Province. Later Dominican apologists, not wishing perhaps to draw attention to their Order's conflicts with the papacy and basing their arguments on the abridged transcription of the bull of suppression published in the *Bullarium Ordinis Praedicatorum*, have attempted to justify Clement VII's decision for organizational reasons.[51] Had they consulted the complete version of the bull they would have found no grounds for such a generous interpretation. Clement VII had no compunction in laying the blame for the suppression of the Congregation on the scandals caused by Savonarola 'of damned memory'. On his example, the bull avers, the friars of the Congregation had treated the Pope with contempt and had led the Florentines into open rebellion against the papacy and against the Church it represented. Almost inevitably, the bull drew the damaging parallel between Savonarola and his Congregation and those who had led Germany and other parts of Christendom into heresy: Martin Luther and his followers. For these reasons, the Tusco-Roman Congregation could not be tolerated any further and had to be abolished.[52] Piagnoni friars failed to be convinced by these arguments. They

---

[49] See above, pp. 76–7.

[50] BMLF S. Marco 925, fo. 108ʳ; an abridged version of this bull, 'Quia nonnumquam', in T. Ripoll and A. Brémond (eds.), *Bullarium Ordinis Praedicatorum* (8 vols.; Rome, 1729–40), viii. 470–1. Excellent discussion of the dissolution, within the limits to be mentioned presently, in R. Creytens, 'Les Actes capitulaires de la Congrégation Toscano-Romaine', *AFP* 40 (1970), 136–8.

[51] This, in fact, is the traditional Dominican view: see e.g. I. Taurisano, *I Domenicani in Lucca* (Lucca, 1914), 35–6; and D. A. Mortier, *Histoire des Maîtres généraux de l'Ordre des Frères Precheurs* (Paris, 1911), v. 287–91. It receives some support from the fact that the Lombard Congregation also was turned into a Province by Clement VII on 2 Sept. 1531; but despite this, Creytens, for one, remains unconvinced that this interpretation is valid, notwithstanding the fact that he had not consulted the original copy of the bull: 'Les Actes capitulaires', 136–8.

[52] BMLF S. Marco 925, fo. 108ʳ.

attributed the abolition partly to Clement VII's desire to avenge himself upon the Congregation as a whole, and especially upon its leading convent, S. Marco, for their roles in the events of the preceding three years, and partly to his determination to sap their reforming spirit by merging the member convents with lax Conventual, that is unreformed, convents of the Order.[53]

The Piagnoni friars suffered a further set-back. The first Provincial of the new Roman Province was Zanobi Pieri, who, having been exiled from Florence in 1529, had little reason to view the Piagnoni in a favourable light.[54] With great enthusiasm, Zanobi Pieri took in hand the purging of S. Marco. As two of his letters to Luigi Guicciardini, dated 23 November and 18 December 1530, make clear, he intended to follow Clement VII's instructions to the letter.[55] He would punish the guilty friars with exemplary harshness, transfer them to other convents of the Order, and exile them if necessary. He attributed all the troubles issuing from the Congregation to certain friars who were leading the younger men astray.[56]

---

[53] Ubaldini, 'Annalia', fo. 31ᵛ; F. Bonaini (ed.), 'Chronica antiqua Conventus Sanctae Catharinae de Pisis', *ASI* 1st ser. 6/2 (1848), 628, where the indignation at the destructiveness of this order comes through very clearly: 'Eo autem anno 1530, . . . finito bello quod contra Florentinos Clemens VII gesserat, quia eo belli tempore quidam ex nostris Florentiae praedicaverat, reputans Pontifex ejus predicationibus bellum protelatum; adepta victoria, in omnes nos ulcisci voluit; et Congregationis vocabulum, jus provinciae nobis tribuens, suppressit. Et licet tunc Conventualibus, quos appellamus, junxisset, mox tamen, saniori usus consilio, ut antea nos ab illis separatos esse jussit . . .'. This sentiment was shared by Fra Ignazio Manardi at this time in Lucca, where he was compiling the chronicle of the convent of S. Romano: 'Cronica del Convento di S. Romano di Lucca', Biblioteca governativa di Lucca, 2572, fos. 49ᵛ–50ʳ, and again in 'Annalium divi Romani praedicatorum ordinis conventus Lucensis civitatis', ibid. 2636, fo. 11ʳ.

[54] Ripoll and Brémond (eds.), *Bullarium Ordinis Praedicatorum*, viii. 470. See also the brief of Clement VII to the Florentine *Signoria*, dated 30 Oct. 1530, enjoining its members to give Fra Zanobi Pieri whatever assistance he might require to fulfil his task of 'reforming' the new Province, and the letter of the *Signoria* to Luigi Guicciardini, now *Commissario Generale* of Pisa, dated 23 Nov. 1530, both in C. Guasti, *Le Carte Strozziane del R. Archivio di Stato in Firenze* (2 vols.; Florence, 1884–91), i. 299–300, 309–10. In its letter, the *Signoria* freely admitted that Clement VII had committed to Zanobi Pieri 'la castigatione et correptione di quelli frati che havessino errato o che errassino', ibid. 299–300.

[55] For the letter of 23 Nov., see ibid. 303–4; for that of 18 Dec., see ASF C. Strozz., ser. I, 59, fo. 204ʳ.

[56] Ibid., fo. 204ʳ.

'In the future', he wrote, determined that this should not recur, 'and for as long as I have the duty to govern, I will be so vigilant that no such abuses will occur and should someone (may God forbid) dare to behave insolently he shall be punished so harshly as to serve as an example to the others.'[57]

While the hitherto tightly knit community was dismembered, directives from Clement VII in Rome to his representatives in Florence sought to bring about the demise of S. Marco as both the well-spring of Savonarolan spirituality and the source of anti-Medicean opposition. Apart from removing or transferring suspect individuals from the convent, Clement VII insisted that friars with a proven history of loyalty to the Medici should now receive preferential treatment in selection for office and even in the settlement of private disputes.[58] Fra Niccolò Schomberg, Archbishop of Capua, a trusted Medici servant of long standing despite his distant Savonarolan connections, was placed in control of S. Marco regardless of the fact that he no longer held any official position in the Order.[59] Clement was also determined to ensure that S. Marco's spiritual influence be curtailed. He was particularly disturbed by the close connections existing between S. Marco and the children's confraternity of the Purification of the Virgin Mary and of S. Zanobi, which had its meeting-place in the grounds of the convent. Fra Tommaso Strozzi had told him that the friars were in the habit of selecting from amongst the children of the confraternity suitable recruits for the Order. To prevent this, Clement instructed that the confraternity be deprived of its meeting-place and be removed from S. Marco. The failure, perhaps, to find alternative accommodation meant that neither command was enforced. The lesson, however, was not lost on the guardians of the confraternity. Slowly they distanced it from S. Marco, placing it more and more under the jurisdiction of the Archiepiscopal authorities. This dissociation

---

[57] Ibid. 'Per il tempo futuro insino che tocherà a me el ghoverno, starò in tal modo vigilante che non achaderanno simili inconvenienti, et se pure (quod Deus avertat) qualcuno ardissi di portarsi insolentemente se ne farà tal iustitia che darà examplo alli altri.'

[58] 'Sustanzia di lettere ricevute da Mr. Pietropaolo Marzi', fos. 15$^v$, 52$^v$, 85$^{r-v}$.

[59] Ibid., fo. 42$^v$; see also n. 8 above.

was also reflected in the decline in the number of youths who decided to become novices in S. Marco: by the end of the decade the confraternity had ceased to be the reliable source of recruits that it had been in the past.[60]

Once again, as in the period after 1512 but in this instance as a result of deliberate policy, S. Marco became isolated and was even ostracized. Its influence on the political, social, and religious life of Florence began dramatically to decline. The first effects were felt on its intake of novices. In the past, novices had come primarily from Florence and to a lesser extent from the *contado*. More pertinently they had also included a substantial proportion of representatives from the most influential Florentine families. After 1530 this was no longer the case. More and more novices came now from outside the Florentine dominions, from the distant reaches of the now expanded Congregation and from as far afield as Flanders, Germany, and France. Some *Ottimati* names like Strozzi, Frescobaldi, Bonaccorsi, can still be found, but far more rarely now and almost lost amid the profusion of obscure, outlandish names.[61]

From 1530 onwards the number of novices seeking admission to S. Marco began to decline. This decline continued until 1537–8.[62] After that year the decline in both the number and the Florentine provenance of novices was arrested and indeed partially reversed; but by then the harm had been done. Many years were to pass before S. Marco was to regain a semblance of its former prominence and prestige. Proscription and exile of Piagnoni and also the fear of becoming identified with the religious and political tradition

---

[60] 'Sustanzia di lettere ricevute da Mr. Pietropaolo Marzi', fos. 27ᵛ, 63ᵛ, 127ᵛ; Compagnia della Purificazione della Vergine e di S. Zanobi, 'Libro di ricordi', 2 vols.; ASF Comp. Sopp. 1646, vol. ii, fos. 200ʳ–202ᵛ, 290ʳ, 291ᵛ–292ʳ. Between 1531 and 1540 only six boys chose to enter S. Marco or one of its associated convents.

[61] Convento di S. Marco, 'Liber vestitionum', MS ACSM (no location number), fos. 16ʳ–23ᵛ; Ubaldini, 'Annalia', fos. 108ʳ–111ʳ. Indeed for the years 1530–4, the majority of newly professed friars came from outside Florence and its *contado*.

[62] Convento di S. Marco, 'Liber vestitionum', fos. 16ʳ–23ʳ. In these years the number of friars making their professions were: 1530–1: 1; 1531–2: 6; 1532–3: 8; 1533–4: 8; 1534–5: 4; 1535–6: 10; 1536–7: 11; 1537–8: 13; slightly different figures given by Ubaldini, 'Annalia', fos. 108ʳ–111ʳ.

of S. Marco meant that fewer and fewer people from outside the parish sought the ministrations of its friars for such important and lucrative occasions as the drawing up of wills and funerals. Fewer still sought to be buried in S. Marco or left endowments to its friars for the celebration of commemorative services, anniversary masses, and offices. For a community living almost exclusively on alms and on the income derived from such endowments, these trends signalled that hard times were ahead.[63]

The Medicean policy of containment and isolation would seem to have been successful. From being one of the most active centres of Florentine political and religious life, S. Marco became, in a few short months, a backwater which had little opportunity or indeed inclination to play a more active religious and political role. Its depleted community, struggling to make ends meet and undoubtedly eager not to antagonize the city's new political masters, eschewed prominence and controversy. At all events, no murmurings of discontent, much less of opposition to the new religious and political status quo, were to reach the outside world for the next fifteen years.

This is not to say that the friars whom S. Marco had once nurtured and who were now scattered throughout Christendom had been cowed into quiescence. Far from it. As already mentioned, Fra Zaccaria di Lunigiana, from the haven of Venice and under the protection and patronage of the Venetian government, resumed his religious apostolate. Though the time and place dictated that he abandon obvious millenarian themes positing Florentine glory, he none the less continued to work towards the realization of the dream which had sustained him and his brethren

---

[63] On this whole argument see my article '*Dell'Arte Del Ben Morire*: The Piagnone Way of Death', *I Tatti Studies: Essays in the Renaissance*, 13 (1989), 66–8. The extent of S. Marco's indigence and vulnerability became apparent in 1545 when Cosimo attempted to expel the Dominicans from the convent. By then with a community numbering 80 friars, the annual revenues from endowments amounted to 300 florins. In the circumstances, any suspension or discouragement of additional alms, as Cosimo attempted to bring about, spelled disaster for the friars who, as Paul III charged, 'si morivano di fame': ASF Mediceo, Minute, 1, inserto 2, lettera del Duca Cosimo scritta al Cardinale, undated, unfoliated; ibid. 6, fos. 572^r–573^r; A. Amati, 'Cosimo I e i Frati di S. Marco', *ASI* 81 (1923), 263–7; see also below.

in the past and whose restatement now, in however muted a fashion, justified their past endeavours and rendered bearable the present sufferings. This dream took the following forms. It was expressed, first, in Fra Zaccaria's resumption of the polemic against Clement VII and against the ecclesiastical hierarchy in general.[64] Secondly, and more constructively, it received embodiment in the introduction of an essential element of the Savonarolan programme of reform to Venice. In fact, with the enthusiastic support of the Venetian ecclesiastical and lay authorities, Fra Zaccaria took over an abandoned church and convent in the island of S. Secondo and proceeded to found there the first Observant Dominican community.[65] So strictly was the rule observed and so exemplary was the life of the community that the government, which had already provided the site and also the moneys for the reconstruction of the convent, afforded it every protection especially after the buildings were destroyed by a fire set alight by a secular priest resentful of the Dominicans' success. Despite these set-backs the community prospered, its prestige and reputation enhanced by the calibre of the many novices it attracted from the Venetian nobility.[66] In the third place, the dream was sustained by the ministry of the word on which Fra Zaccaria's fame had thrived.

Unfortunately none of his sermons from this period have come to light, though we possess contemporary circumstantial accounts of some of them. Apart from his attacks on the ecclesiastical hierarchy and on Clement VII in particular, he seems to have taken upon himself the task of confuting Lutheran heresy. From the pulpit he expounded and thus reclaimed for orthodoxy the Pauline epistles which the Lutherans had made their own and engaged in debate with Lutheran members of his audience.[67]

[64] L. von Pastor, *Storia dei Papi* (Rome, 1959), iv (2). 500.

[65] D. Codagli, *Historia dell'isola e monasterio di S. Secondo di Venetia* (Venice, 1609), fos. 23$^r$–25$^v$.

[66] Ibid., fos. 27$^v$–31$^r$; J. Quétif and J. Echard, *Scriptores Ordinis Praedicatorum recensiti* (2 vols.; Paris, 1719–21), ii. 110.

[67] F. Gaeta (ed.), *Nunziature di Venezia*, i (Rome, 1958), 74, 104–5, 178–9. Much of this information, not strictly of an official nature, was conveyed by the papal nunzio Girolamo Aleandro to the papal secretary and Savonarolan of long-standing Jacopo Salviati, who had asked for information on Fra Zaccaria.

Most revealing, and ominous as to his future relations with the Venetian lay and ecclesiastical authorities, was the fact that his audience was composed primarily of humble, unlettered people.[68] Another potential cause of attrition was the renewed interest in some of Savonarola's more controversial doctrines, which is undoubtedly to be attributed to Fra Zaccaria's apostolate and which is attested by the publication at about this time of many of his works, including the *Compendio di rivelazioni* and the influential selection of his prophecies compiled by Luca Bettini.[69] What specific directions his apostolate would have taken, however, it is impossible to know for he had little time to build upon these early successes. He died in 1535 in Pesaro in suspicious circumstances. Dominicans and republican exiles alike had no doubt that he had been poisoned by the Medici, partly to silence him and partly to exact revenge finally upon him.[70] So favourable was the impression that Fra Zaccaria had created that, for the next few years, the Venetian authorities requested and obtained the services of other Piagnoni friars of S. Marco, like Fra Niccolò di Domenico and Fra Zanobi de'

---

[68] Ibid. 104, where Aleandro states that his audience consists 'più assai di ignoranti et di idioti che di dotti: cosa che a me certo pocco è piaciuta perciò che la dottrina sacra non è subietto da mettere in mani dil vulgo et di persone idiote, massime sappiendo che la heresia lutherana è pullulata et cresciuta in Alemagna solo per questa via'.

[69] A comprehensive listing of the works published in Venice at this time in *Short-title Catalogue of Books Printed in Italy and of Italian Books Printed in Other Countries from 1465 to 1600 now in the British Museum*, 611–15. The selection of Savonarola's prophecies compiled by Luca Bettini is the already cited *Oracolo della renovatione della chiesa secondo la dottrina del Riverendo Padre Frate Hieronimo Savonarola*. It was first published in Venice in 1536 and republished there in 1542; it was placed in the Index of prohibited books in 1558: A. Giorgetti, 'Fra Luca Bettini e la sua difesa del Savonarola', *ASI* 7/2 (1919), 202–3.

[70] Busini, *Lettere*, 188; BMLF S. Marco 903, 'Ricordanze B del Convento', fo. 169ᵛ of last section of MS entitled 'Principio e progressi del convento di S. Marco' which is also separately foliated; ASF C. Strozz., ser. V, 1207, Filza 3, letter 112, undated and unaddressed, in which are enumerated the crimes of Alessandro de' Medici to be presented to Charles V. He had just been made Procurator of the convent of San Secondo and given permission to return to his old province to preach: 'Registrum primum actorum et litterarum Procuratorum et Vicariorum Ordinis', AGOP, IV. 24, fo. 33ʳ.

Medici, to come to Venice and preach there during important liturgical seasons.[71]

Other friars of the Diaspora reacted in a similarly constructive manner in seeking, despite their own personal distress at the turn of events, to work towards the fulfilment of their prophet's programme of reform. Such was the decision of Fra Santi Pagnini, whom we last saw trying to mobilize Henry VIII on behalf of Florence.[72] In Lyons, where he still resided, Fra Santi stepped up his already hectic activity as if to compensate for the reverses suffered in Florence by his brethren. In addition to his scholarly and editing activity in the field of biblical studies and to his campaign fought mainly from the pulpit against Lutherans and other Protestant Reformers, he worked tirelessly to establish a comprehensive system of poor relief.[73] Beginning in 1532, when the Lyonnais clergy refused to fund poor relief at the level of previous years, Fra Santi preached daily on the individual Christian's duty towards the poor.[74] At his instigation and that of his friend Jean de Vauzelles, a system of poor relief was instituted which, though larger in scope, resembled closely in its operations and especially in its method of distribution of charity, the Florentine *Buonuomini di*

[71] See e.g. the letter of Andrea Gritti, Doge of Venice, dated 23 Mar. 1537, to Fra Giuliano Mazzeo, Provincial of the Roman Province, requesting an extension of Fra Zanobi's stay in Venice, where he was preaching the Lenten season. The petition was motivated by his and the Venetian nobles' desire 'che qui si habbia a seminare dottrina approbata et veramente christiana': BMLF S. Marco 925, 'Index diplomaticus conventus et congregationis S. Marci', fo. 122. Fra Niccolò di Domenico, in fact, died in Venice on 28 Jan. 1536 after preaching there a cycle of sermons in Advent. Some Savonarolan influences were to last for many years and can be detected as late as 1556 in the 'Statuti della Fraternita e compagnia dei fiorentini in Venezia dell'anno MDLVI' (ed. A. Sagredo), *ASI*, app. 9 (1853), 441–97, partly composed by Iacopo Nardi.

[72] See above p. 376.

[73] On his literary activity in Lyons see T. M. Centi, 'L'attività letteraria di Santi Pagnini', *AFP* 15 (1945), 17 ff.; see also E. Wind, 'Sante Pagnini and Michelangelo: A Study of the Succession of Savonarola', *Gazette des Beaux Arts*, 26 (1944), 243–6.

[74] J.-P. Guitton, *La Société et les pauvres: L'Exemple de la généralité de Lyon 1534–1789* (Paris, 1971), 263–87; Natalie Zemon Davis, *Society and Culture in Early Modern France* (Stanford, Calif., 1979), 29–34.

*S. Martino.*[75] That the resemblance was not fortuitous is suggested by the fact that Fra Santi, during his periods as Prior of S. Marco, had an ex officio role as an elector of the governors of the confraternity. Fra Santi urged the construction of additions to the existing hospital of Saint-Laurent in order to accommodate indigent victims of the plague.[76] One cannot but point to specific Florentine precedents for such measures, in particular to the foundation of the hospital of the *Incurabili*, which, as we have seen, was undertaken primarily by Piagnoni and was subsequently administered by an especially created confraternity in which they were in the majority.[77] When the additions to the hospital of Saint-Laurent were built, the project's major benefactor was Tommaso Guadagni, a brother of the radical arch-Piagnone Ulivieri Guadagni.[78]

Few Dominicans from S. Marco, even those transferred away from Florence, could have hoped for Fra Santi's and Fra Zaccaria's sympathetic reception, freedom of action, and subsequent success. Fearing retaliation by the papacy or by Florence, the host cities would have demanded moderation from the friars, who, in turn, would have complied to avoid censure and expulsion. None the less, however grudgingly, they were afforded more freedom in the performance of their duties than was the case in Florence. The sermons and devotional treatises by some of these Savonarolan friars have come to light. Originating predominantly in Lucca, they

[75] Ibid., esp. 39, where the practice of examining individuals and of issuing tickets to the poor entitling them to relief was identical to the practice of the *Buonuomini*: the tickets too were identical in the way they were set out and in the procedure they established to receive assistance. More striking, however, is the underlying concept common to both systems which ensured that poor relief was a civic responsibility and that therefore its administration should be in lay hands. Whether this was an innovation to be attributed to the Christian humanism of Pagnini and Vauzelles, as Prof. Davis suggests, is, however, open to question.

[76] Ibid. 279 n. 54; Guitton, *La Société et les pauvres*, 271.

[77] See above, p. 322.

[78] Guitton, *La Société et les pauvres*, 271 n. 269. I have not been able to find any evidence to confirm Natalie Zemon Davis's statement in *Society and Culture in Early Modern France*, 279 n. 54, that Tommaso Guadagni's wife was related to Pagnini. On Tommaso Guadagni see Passerini, *Genealogia e storia della famiglia Guadagni*, Table III and pp. 73–6.

cover the years 1530–48 and are by such renowned friars as Niccolò Michelozzi, Ignazio Manardi, Angelo Bettini, Matteo Lachi. These homilies reveal the responses of committed Savonarolan friars to the changed political and religious realities.[79]

The fact that all these sermons and devotional treatises were addressed to nuns may account in part for their rarefied spiritual atmosphere, for their lack of location in either time or place. But only in part, for these traits were seldom in evidence in earlier collections of sermons preached primarily to nuns and already examined. The explanation lies, I believe, elsewhere. By abstracting the religious message from the historical context these friars may have sought to avoid controversy and the intervention of lay authorities. The absence of the polemical framework and the abandonment of overt millenarian allusions which since Savonarola's days had been constant features of these sermons, endowing them with a distinctive style and accounting also, as Caroli had remarked,[80] for their popularity, did not entail a dilution of the religious message. Indeed, one could argue that this message gained in strength and currency because of its wider application.

The problem of salvation is viewed in these sermons and devotional treatises from the perspective of the individual. The focus shifts dramatically away from the Elect and the apotheosis of a city to the constant and immense efforts required of every Christian to earn salvation. The message is one of struggle and of single-minded dedication. It is, moreover, almost invariably expressed in traditional terms, as a gradual ascent on the ladder of perfection to God.

---

[79] These are the collections consulted: Angelo Bettini, 'Preparatione al glorioso padre nostro S. Domenico fatta . . . alle sue figliuole in Christo monache di S. Domenico in Lucca, l'anno . . . 1544', MS BNF Magl., XXXV, 72; Niccolò Michelozzi, Matteo Lachi [et al.], 'Prediche di diversi nostri reverendi predicatori', MS BPP Pal. 836; Ignazio Manardi, 'Esposizione dei Salmi e Sermoni', MS BRF Ricc. 1483; id., 'Prediche XXXI dell'amore di Dio', MS BMLF Redi, 78; id., 'Opere spirituali', MS BNF Magl., XXXV, 243; id., 'Opuscoli', MS BNF Pal. 14; id., 'Prediche e scritti', MS BPP Pal. 259. On the religious and specifically Savonarolan situation in Lucca at the time see M. Trigari, 'Momenti e aspetti del Savonarolismo a Lucca', *Critica storica*, 5 (1967), 590–624; R. Ristori, 'Le origini della Riforma a Lucca', *Rinascimento*, 3 (1952), 269–92; M. Berengo, *Nobili e mercanti nella Lucca del Cinquecento* (Turin, 1974), *passim*.

[80] See above, p. 79.

The themes of divine love and of the expression of this love through a life led in imitation of Christ reappear.[81] As we saw with Domenico Benivieni, this inward-looking impulse is a sign of despondency, a dejected reaction to the collapse of hopes that seemed on the point of realization.

In one instance at least in these homilies, there is a fiery, if generic indictment, reminiscent of Benivieni's condemnations, of the leaders of the Church, likened by Fra Matteo Lachi to ravenous wolves and devils incarnate.[82] Now and again, too, there are allusions, little more than asides, to the harmful effects of worldly learning on the individual's striving for salvation.[83] But, unlike Domenico Benivieni, these friars with the benefit of hindsight could not but be aware of the dangers inherent in condemning learning and the *magisterium* of professed religious, as revealed not only by the excesses of their brethren the *Unti*, but also by the activities of reformed groups beyond the Alps. Accordingly, they ensured that the affective elements in the struggle for salvation were balanced by cognitive ones. They stressed, too, the individual's need for guidance, for moderation, and for constant watchfulness lest he or she fall prey to pride. This concern was also expressed by their insistence that the individual should cultivate, throughout the gradual ascent to God, the virtues of obedience, patience, and humility. Finally, they sought to forestall dangerous enthusiasm and false optimism by arguing that, because of human frailty, illumination and perfect union with God were seldom achieved on earth.[84]

[81] See e.g. Bettini, 'Preparatione al glorioso padre nostro S. Domenico', fos. 13ʳ–20ʳ; Manardi, 'Esposizione dei Salmi e Sermoni', fos. 25ᵛ–31ʳ; Lachi, 'Predica . . . in die exaltationis Sancte Crucis', in 'Prediche di diversi nostri reverendi predicatori', fos. 63ʳ–66ᵛ.

[82] Ibid., fo. 44ᵛ.

[83] See e.g. Michelozzi, 'Predica', ibid., fo. 4ʳ; Manardi, 'Prediche e scritti', fo. 25, where there occurs the strongest condemnation of worldly learning: 'Più sa di Dio uno contadino che mai seppe Aristotile, più una vechiarella che Platone'.

[84] See e.g. ibid., fo. 68ʳ⁻ᵛ; id., 'Prediche XXXI dell'amore di Dio', Predica Prima (not foliated); Michelozzi, 'Predica', in 'Prediche di diversi nostri reverendi predicatori', fos. 1ʳ–12ᵛ; Bettini, 'Preparatione al glorioso padre nostro S. Domenico', fos. 40ᵛ–41ʳ, 124ʳ⁻ᵛ, where the most positive assertions of the soul's capacity to unite with God are given.

As Lachi's outburst against the ecclesiastical leaders suggests, these friars were not always able to contain their anger and to draw a veil over the past. Even less were they capable of forgetting the Savonarolan teaching they had absorbed in S. Marco during their novitiate and beyond. Though Savonarola is never mentioned by name, allusions to him and to his fate are not uncommon.[85] More importantly, despite the fact that millenarianism and in particular millenarianism of the specific Florentine variety was now anathema, the subject is never far from these friars' thoughts. Now and then, in unguarded moments, they revealed that acceptance of their religious message, ultimately traceable to Savonarola, denoted election. These utterances were never elaborated, but rather were immediately invested with an exclusive spiritual significance to which no one could take exception.[86] Fra Angelo Bettini, in particular, seemed incapable of refraining from controversial millenarian allusions because he temperamentally relished confrontation and danger. For the good of the cause, and like his more moderate brethren, he reined in his natural instincts and chose the safe way out by elaborating these allusions spiritually. On one occasion, however, he induced his wailing audience to join him in singing Psalm 136 and thereby express, like the captive Israelites, their anguish at the loss of the spiritual and earthly Zion.[87]

In Florence, too, despite the arrests and proscription of the best-known, radical Piagnoni and despite also the continuing Medicean vigilance, the Savonarolan reforming and millenarian vision made its appearance once again. Not surprisingly, however, the first Piagnoni to propound this vision were moderate men who had once

[85] See e.g. Manardi, 'Opuscoli', fo. 38, where in the course of expounding the Psalm 'Salvum me fac, Deus', and speaking of Christ's execution, he goes on to say in a clear allusion to Savonarola: 'Habbiamo veduto un exemplo a' giorni nostri molto simile ad quello di Iesu . . .'; Lachi, 'Predica della providentia divina', in 'Prediche di diversi nostri reverendi predicatori', fos. 44$^v$–45$^r$.

[86] Id., 'Predica . . . in die exaltationis Sancte Crucis', ibid., fos. 64$^v$–65$^r$, where, employing terminology given currency beyond the Alps, he equates election with predestination; Niccolò Fabroni, 'Predica', ibid., fos. 130$^r$–131$^r$; Michelozzi, 'Predica', ibid., fos. 4$^v$–5$^r$; Manardi, 'Prediche XXXI dell'amore di Dio', Predica Quarta e Predica Ottava (unfoliated).

[87] Bettini, 'Preparatione al glorioso padre nostro S. Domenico', fos. 9$^{r-v}$, 16$^r$, 25$^v$–26$^r$, 124$^{r-v}$.

been close to Clement VII and who could still count, therefore, on his forbearance. Thus, on 6 October 1530, less than two months after the fall of the Republic, Lorenzo Violi wrote to Jacopo Salviati expressing his apprehension at the spread of the Lutheran heresy in Germany and urging Salviati to use his influence with the Pope to persuade him to initiate a thorough reform of the Church. This, he believed, would have the effect of destroying the Lutherans' *raison d'être*.[88] Shortly afterwards, on 1 November, Girolamo Benivieni, always an optimist, wrote to Clement VII in an attempt to convince him not only of the truth of Savonarola's doctrine, but also of the advisability of instituting in Florence a system of government conducive to internal peace and prosperity.[89] The next Piagnone moderate to propound this vision was Francesco d'Antonio de' Ricci, whom we last saw trying to dissuade Charles V from moving against Florence.[90] Francesco now resumed his one-sided correspondence with Clement VII. Four of his letters have survived: the first dated 22 February 1532, with a long addendum of 4 March, the last three on or about 13 September 1533 on the occasion of the imminent meeting of Clement VII and Francis I at Marseilles.[91] The four letters are almost identical in content, even to the extent of relying on identical scriptural and literary texts. In all four letters, from slightly differing perspectives, Francesco raises his vision of Florentine election. The experiences of the last few years and in particular the fall of the Republic could not, however, but have left their mark on Francesco and on his vision. Gone are his categorical statements that brooked no doubts or qualifications; gone, too, is his trenchant optimism. The vision, as now proffered, has been modified in some important respects and it is shrouded with sadness.

The most striking effect of the fall of Florence on Francesco's prophecy was the enlargement of his historical perspective. Already, in the first surviving letter after the siege, his prophecies on

---

[88] Lorenzo Violi to Jacopo Salviati, 6 Oct. 1530, ASF C. Strozz., ser. I, 137, fo. 166ʳ.

[89] Girolamo Benivieni, *Epistola . . . mandata a Papa Clemente VII*, in App. to Benedetto Varchi, *Storia fiorentina*, ed. G. Milanesi (3 vols.; Florence, 1858), iii. 307–30; see esp. 308–9, 325.

[90] See above, p. 371.  [91] ASF C. Strozz., ser. I, 14, fos. 186ʳ–193ʳ.

the future of Christianity and of his beloved city are predicated on a far more comprehensive view of Florentine history than he had expressed before. Instead of arguing that the Medici's eschatological role had begun after their restoration in 1512, Francesco now contends that they had been divinely chosen as far back as 1433–4. In that year God had placed Florence under the protection of Cosimo and his successors for a hundred years, on condition, however, that they reform the city and prepare her for the great mission ahead.[92]

Because neither Cosimo nor his descendants, as Francesco ruefully points out, had obeyed God's commands, they had been punished in their persons by disease and death, and in their office by continuous dissension and factionalism. Francesco pinpoints the years of worst strife: 1433–4, 1466, 1478, 1493–4, 1512, 1529, and 1530, showing that he no longer differentiates between Florence and the Medici, and their respective trials.[93] According to his new historical vision, the interests and destinies of both have been and will continue to be inextricably bound together until either the end of the allotted century or the fulfilment of God's promises to Florence. Viewed in this light, the fall of Florence in 1530—and 1512 for that matter—lose their unique significance as momentous set-backs for the Savonarolan cause, to become merely two more of the trials suffered by the city and the Medici alike in punishment for their failure to institute God's reforms.

In this new vision of the past no room remains for divisive political issues. That the enmity which in the past divided Savonarolans and Mediceans had also been political, having its origins in two totally contrasting ideologies of government, is forgotten. Whereas in his earlier letters Francesco had taken pains to declare that the apotheosis of Florence would be conditional on the Medici's restoration of her political freedom, such a condition is no longer stipulated.

The decision to omit references to Florentine liberty could be attributed to Francesco's desire not to antagonize Clement VII. But it is as likely to have resulted from a disillusionment with political

---

[92] ASF C. Strozz., ser. I, 14, fo. 189[r].    [93] Ibid.

forms, born of the Florentines' inability, despite favourable political circumstances, to initiate a lasting reform during the recent
republican interlude. Realizing the inevitability of Medici control
in Florence, Francesco may have decided to come to terms with it.
Whatever the case, the Medici are now presented as having a much
more vital role to play in the realization of Florence's Savonarolan
heritage. Since 1434, Francesco now argues, the Medici and the
Florentines have been jointly entrusted by God to lead Florence
into her kingdom.

Francesco now enjoins Clement to demonstrate his trust in Florence. More importantly, Francesco continues, Clement must ensure that he does not alienate the Florentines by appointing
overbearing governors. He impresses upon Clement that he must
not repeat the error committed in the past when the unsuitable
Silvio Passerini, Cardinal of Cortona, had been entrusted with the
delicate task of overseeing the running of the Florentine government. A more flexible, prudent, and provident person is needed,
Francesco suggests, and Angelo Marzi is one such. With his prudence and benevolence Marzi could ensure that Florence remained
loyal and united until she came to her spiritual inheritance after
1534.[94]

The content of Francesco's message did not change substantially
in the subsequent eighteen months. The three letters he wrote to
Clement VII in September 1533, on the occasion of the Pope's visit
to Marseilles, are none the less of some significance.[95] Francesco's
mounting frustration is immediately apparent. He is exasperated
by the absence of tangible events portending the fullness of time,
and by the procrastination, bickering, and self-serving egotism of
the leaders of Christendom. Seeking to allay his disquiet, he re-
views his calculation and the scriptural bases for them. The emphasis now is on tribulation, the milestone being the sackings of Prato
and Rome in 1512 and 1527 respectively. As for the future,
Francesco's calculations demonstrate once again that the great

[94] Ibid., fo. 190ᵛ.
[95] On the meeting and its preliminaries see von Pastor, *Storia dei papi*, iv (2),
448–52; E. Rodocanachi, *Histoire de Rome: Les Pontificats d'Adrien VI et de
Clément VII* (Paris, 1933), 255–62.

tribulations will end in 1534—perhaps in September of that year—and will be followed immediately afterwards by God's bestowal of the promised blessings on Florence and on mankind.[96]

Francesco then proceeds to restate the familiar message of Florentine election and glory, though it is now more stridently and polemically expressed. Ignorant of the agenda for the meeting in Marseilles, Francesco suspects the motives of the two protagonists and even implies that they have come together to advance their dynastic interests rather than the interest of Christendom. He fears that their meeting will have the effect of exacerbating the divisions of Christendom, even suggesting in one letter that the resulting strife, which he likens to the catastrophic civil war between Caesar and Pompey, will form part of the last great tribulation.[97] His fear that Clement and Francis, through pride and short-sighted selfishness, will reach decisions harmful to Florence as well as to Christianity move him to remind Clement of what is at stake for him personally. He warns Clement also of the punishment reserved by God for rulers who ignore His commands as uttered through His prophets and act against the interests of their charges, especially charges who are God's elect.

For the first time in his letters, Francesco cautions against the false pride afforded by rank and worldly learning. Echoing the sentiments of earlier Savonarolan popular prophets, he too now suggests that only the humble and the ignorant are worthy of illumination.[98] In so doing Francesco reveals his awareness of his impotence, that he is unable any longer to influence the course of events in Florence's favour. Though loath to admit it, he knows that Florence has been left behind by events and that he will not live to enter the promised land. The dream of Florence as the New Jerusalem, which had sustained him and generations of Florentines in the past and had seemed so close to fulfilment in his youth, now recedes further into the future. The dream must, however, be kept alive for the sake of future generations. Accordingly, in a hastily written last note to Clement, Francesco begs him to cultivate Francis's son Henry, and to win him to the cause. For it

---

[96] ASF C. Strozz., ser. I, 14, fos. 186ʳ, 192ʳ.        [97] Ibid.        [98] Ibid.

is certain that Henry has been chosen by God to be an instrument of reform.[99]

The Savonarolan millenarian vision was also propagated by other Piagnoni. All of them paid dearly for their foolhardiness. They were arrested and seem to have been sentenced without trial. Among them was a member of the Carucci family who was accused of having used Savonarola's prophecies to conspire against the state and was deprived of all his privileges and property and sent to the galleys of Andrea Doria.[100]

In those visions we are able to examine we find the same despondency already witnessed in Francesco de' Ricci's last letters. In Bartolomeo Rinuccini's *Visio*,[101] written down on 9 December 1534 but relating a series of events and mystical visions that had taken place between 20 September, as news of Clement VII's fatal illness began to spread, and 15 October of that same year, Bartolomeo set out his plan for a new reformed order of priests which would devote itself to spreading Savonarola's message of reform. Those whom he approached to join him in this mission, however, refused to do so out of fear.[102] Then Savonarola appeared to him and comforted him in his distress. He assured Bartolomeo that God's punishment of unworthy prelates, princes, and ecclesiastics who had betrayed His trust in them or their vows to Him was imminent and would be exemplary.[103] Those who, despite the persecutions and the collapse of religious and moral standards, had lived by Savonarola's words would be spared and allowed to enter His kingdom here on earth and then in heaven. In particular, all God's promises to His Florentines as conveyed by Savonarola would be fulfilled. Their steadfastness in adversity as demonstrated by their continued entreaties to Him to save them, His people, would soon be rewarded.[104] Though small in number and though severely tried by persecution and suffering, they were to be God's instruments for the imminent renewal of the Church and for the conversion of the whole world to Christianity. Patience and prayer would ensure

---

[99] Ibid., fo. 193ʳ.

[100] 'Appunti e notizie storiche degli anni 1527–1533', fo. 38ʳ.

[101] G. Dotti (ed.), *Visione di un Piagnone (1534)* (Florence, 1868).

[102] Ibid. 1–2.    [103] Ibid. 3–5.    [104] Ibid. 6–7.

that they would soon come to their inheritance and enjoy full happiness in a world ruled by the Spirit through an Angelic Pope.[105]

The discrepancy between the opening pessimism of the *Visio* and its concluding optimism reflects the dissonance between the present harsh reality and the blessings of the hoped-for outcome. It reflects, further, Bartolomeo Rinuccini's reactions to the death of Clement VII, which occurred on 26 September and which could not but be interpreted as a boost to Piagnoni hopes. Moreover, one must not forget the primarily hortative purpose of the *Visio*. As Bartolomeo admits, it was written down and, one assumes, disseminated 'for the consolation of God's elect',[106] to comfort them in their present plight by reminding them of their prophet's promises now that Clement VII's sickness and death seemed to signal their imminent fulfilment.

In the absence of other favourable signs, while the Medici ruled supreme and they themselves were decimated by proscriptions, deprived of influence, and constantly watched, the Piagnoni were increasingly forced to look to such portents to keep their faith alive. Thus, in 1537, when Alessandro de' Medici, Duke of Florence, was assassinated by his distant relative and boon companion Lorenzino de' Medici, Piagnoni reactions were much as one would have expected. In this event, surely, they had a portent. In an unguarded moment, Lorenzo Violi described the event to a sympathetic Cardinal Roberto Pucci as 'the resurrection of our affairs';[107] and the Piagnoni in general, too, according to the historian Varchi, were hopeful that the new era prophesied by Savonarola had dawned.[108]

But nothing came of these hopes. The anti-Medicean *Ottimati* both in Florence and in exile were too divided and too inept to profit from this event. Admittedly, they were not in a position to prevent the relatively smooth transfer of power to Cosimo. None the less, by their bickering and by their naïve belief that they could

---

[105] G. Dotti (ed.), *Visione di un Piagnone (1534)* (Florence, 1868).

[106] Ibid. 7: 'per consolatione degli eletti di Dio'. A typically sarcastic assessment of the *Visio* is given by F. Cordero, *Savonarola*, iv (Bari, 1988), 703–5.

[107] Letter of Lorenzo Violi to Roberto Pucci, 13 Jan. 1537, ASF C. Strozz., ser. I, 339, fo. 286ʳ: 'la ressurrectione de' casi nostri'.

[108] Varchi, *Storia fiorentina*, ii. 561–2.

negotiate their way back into the city and its government, they ensured Cosimo time to consolidate his control over Florence. When finally, in exasperation, the exiles decided to sink their differences and to move against him, they did so too late, with insufficient planning and in such a half-hearted fashion that the catastrophe at Montemurlo was inevitable.[109] However, it should be stressed that the battle for control of Florence was not lost at Montemurlo. Rather, Montemurlo was the last in a long series of defeats suffered by the anti-Mediceans on the battlefield and at the diplomatic table.

Military and diplomatic failure was further compounded by a failure of nerve. As friends and foes alike realized, the anti-Medicean leaders had no alternatives, either ideological or political, to offer. The Piagnone ideology which the majority of anti-Mediceans had adopted in the past was no longer deemed acceptable in view of its failure to deliver victory and a lasting political settlement in the years 1527–30. Only the Piagnoni continued to subscribe to it. But they counted for little in an opposition whose leadership was now monopolized by men like Filippo Strozzi and Bartolomeo Valori who had only lately fallen out with the Medici. All the anti-Mediceans could offer was a variation of the system under which Florence had been ruled between 1494 and 1512, with attendant dissensions, weakness, and isolation. Indeed, till the very end, the anti-Mediceans were bitterly divided over the hoary issue of whether the republican system of government to be introduced was to be given a 'popular' or 'aristocratic' cast. As intimated by these squabbles what the aristocratic leadership offered was a form of oligarchic government without the Medici.[110] These considera-

---

[109] The best treatments of the exiles and of their bickerings and divisions are to be found in I. Nardi, *Istorie di Firenze*, ed. A. Gelli (2 vols.; Florence, 1858), ii. 231–332; Varchi, *Storia fiorentina*, ii. 545–642; Busini, *Lettere, passim*. Most enlightening in this context is the anonymous report sent to the Florentine government which counselled against assassinating Filippo Strozzi on the grounds that he was much more useful to the Medici regime alive than dead: ASF C. Strozz., ser. V, 1221, fos. 87$^r$–88$^v$.

[110] According to Benedetto Varchi, they were prepared to go even further than that: 'Arebbono i principali de' fuorusciti, ancorachè fussono confusi e discordanti tra loro, acconsentito ad uno stato di ottimati con un capo a vita, e si sarebbono contentati di Cosimo . . .', *Storia fiorentina*, ii. 635.

tions, together with war-weariness and the frightening prospect of another unequal struggle against the Medici and their international allies, engendered a wait-and-see attitude within Florence, and debilitating doubts, even defeatism, among the exiles outside. This was as true of the anti-Medicean *Ottimati* in general as it was of the Piagnoni amongst them in particular; and it all helps to explain not only the fiasco of Montemurlo, but also the unreal calm that reigned in Florence throughout this emergency and which cannot be explained simply in terms of the strict security instituted there by Cosimo and his advisers.[111]

Amongst those who kept aloof from events, but not for the reasons previously outlined, were members of the conventicle of the *Capi rossi*. The conventicle, last seen fulfilling, under the leadership of Pieruccio, the important social role of ministering to the poor during the last Republic, had managed to survive unscathed its fall and the subsequent purges and proscriptions. Only Pieruccio now thought it prudent to abandon his prophetic and public welfare missions and to fade into the background. The *Capi rossi* began to meet once again as soon as the prohibitions against confraternities were lifted in 1533 and the confraternities of S. Benedetto Nero and S. Benedetto Bianco, on which they relied for cover, resumed their activities.[112] Pieruccio, however, seems not to have attended any of the *Capi rossi*'s meetings and even to have shunned contact with the members of the conventicle.[113] Unofficial leadership of the *Capi rossi* was consequently assumed by the notary Ser Cristoforo da Soci.[114] The two members of the conventicle on whom Ser Cristoforo relied most for assistance were Gabriele di Antonio dei Piselli, a shot-maker, and Nigi di Ruggero, a milliner from Flanders. The social composition of the conventicle does not seem to have undergone significant change even though it seems

[111] See my 'Confraternities, Conventicles and Political Dissent', 272–4.

[112] ASF Conv. Sopp. 102, 96, 'Nota depositionum testium pro parte Societatis Sancti Benedicti Bigi', fos. 2$^{r-v}$, 3$^r$.

[113] BNF Magl., VII, 1398, fo. 34.

[114] Ibid., fo. 33$^v$. For this second stage of the *Capi rossi*'s activities see also C. Vasoli, 'Il notaio e il "Papa angelico": Noterella su un episodio fiorentino del 1538–1540', in V. Lanternari *et al.* (eds.), *Religioni e civiltà: Scritti in memoria di Angelo Brelich* (Bari, 1982), 615–40.

that some of its aristocratic sympathizers now took a more active part in its affairs. This is especially true of Amerigo de' Medici, who now not merely lent support to individual members of the conventicle, but also protected it and took part in its activities.[115]

For the whole of their second period of activity, the *Capi rossi* eschewed social welfare and other charitable ministrations, partly, no doubt, because the government arrogated to itself a policing and supervisory role over the field. It seems, however, that the decision was also prompted by the conventicle's resolve to concentrate on more specific religious activities. What form these activities took is not always clear because they have been summarily and unfavourably described in later accounts and trial records.[116] In some respects, the activities of the *Capi rossi* closely resembled those of *compagnie di disciplina*,[117] differing only in the intensity of their commitment and dedication. The frequency of their meetings is a case in point. With the lifting of prohibitions against confraternities in 1533, the *Capi rossi* began to meet regularly on Sundays and on all major religious feast days.[118] Since the confraternities of S. Benedetto Nero and S. Benedetto Bianco are known to have met less frequently, this indicates that the *Capi rossi* were no longer timing their meetings to coincide with those of the two confraternities they had infiltrated.[119] This change is surprising and must have increased the chances of detection.

In other respects, also, the *Capi rossi* seem to have cast caution to the winds. Believing their meeting-place to be safe, behind closed

---

[115] BNF Magl., VIII, 1398, fos. 33ʳ–34ʳ.

[116] Thus, for instance, ibid., fo. 33ʳ, mention is made of the purchase by Amerigo de' Medici of red, green, and white ribbons 'per appiccare a' corni', but no further explanation is given.

[117] These consisted of 'uffizii, discipline et orationi': ibid.

[118] Ibid., ASF Conv. Sopp. 102, 96, 'Nota depositionum testium pro parte Societatis Sancti Benedicti Bigi', fo. 2ʳ.

[119] At this time, the confraternity of S. Benedetto Bianco met regularly on the first and third Sunday of the month. Only later in the century were the statutes changed, decreeing that meetings should be held every Sunday: Archivio Parrocchiale di S. Lucia sul Prato, 'Capitoli di S. Benedetto Bianco' (no location number), fo. 11ʳ, and part II, fo. 11ʳ. Though no specific information on the *tornate* of S. Benedetto Nero has survived, it seems certain, given the close relationship between the statutes of the two confraternities, that they corresponded with those of S. Benedetto Bianco.

doors,[120] they embraced a range of activities which were to bring them to public notice. While continuing to pursue such unexceptionable activities as self-flagellation and individual and collective prayers and devotions, they invited some sympathetic friars of Sta Maria Novella to come to their meeting-place to celebrate mass, to confer the sacrament of the Eucharist, and to recite the divine office, often to the memory of Savonarola and of his two martyred companions.[121] For their trouble and complicity the officiating friars were given alms in money and kind which the *Capi rossi* referred to as the 'panellini' for S. Benedict.[122] All members of the *Capi rossi*, moreover, were required to preach, at various times, to the assembled congregation.[123] In itself this was not a novelty: lay preaching had become a normal feature of Florentine confraternal life.[124] With few exceptions, however, this privilege had been reserved for particularly learned and devout persons, and only amongst the followers of Savonarola had there been a tendency to disregard this convention.[125] By resuming and indeed widening the practice, the *Capi rossi* were increasing the risk of discovery and, therefore, of ecclesiastical censure.

Were all this not sufficiently incriminating, the *Capi rossi* also embarked on a course of action guaranteed eventually to bring them into open confrontation with the government and with the Church. They began increasingly to rely on prophecy, divine revelation, and mystical visions as means to regulate the con-

---

[120] ASF Conv. Sopp. 102, 96, inserto with title, in later hand, on cover 'S. Benedetto Biancho 1538', and with another title, in contemporary hand, on the following, facing folio: 'Testes examinati in causa fratrum S. Marie Novelle contra societatem S. Benedicti', fo. 3ᵛ. (I shall cite the later title to identify this inserto.)

[121] Ibid., fos. 1ʳ, 2ʳ⁻ᵛ, 5ʳ, 6ᵛ, 11ᵛ, *et passim*; see also ibid., 'Nota depositionum testium pro parte Societatis Sancti Benedicti', fos. 2ʳ⁻ᵛ, 3ᵛ; BNF Magl., VIII, 1398, fos. 33ʳ, 34ʳ.

[122] ASF Conv. Sopp. 102, 96, 'Testes examinati in causa fratrum S. Marie Novelle contra societatem S. Benedicti', fos. 1ʳ, 3ʳ, 15ʳ; ibid., 'Nota depositionum testium pro parte Societatis Sancti Benedicti Bigi', fos. 2ʳ, 3ʳ.

[123] BNF Magl., VIII, 1398, fo. 33ʳ.

[124] G. M. Monti, *Le confraternite medievali dell'alta e media Italia* (2 vols.; Florence (Venice), 1927), i. 187 ff.; see also P. O. Kristeller, 'Lay Religious Traditions and Florentine Platonism', in id., *Studies in Renaissance Thought and Letters* (Rome, 1956), 104–6.

[125] As, for instance, in Pietro Bernardino's conventicle, on which see above.

venticle's activities and to bring about the desired millennium.[126] Again it might seem that these activities did not constitute a radical departure from previous practice in the Savonarolan movement. After all, Pietro Bernardino and their own former leader, Pieruccio, had prophesied publicly and had been the recipients of divine revelation. What was new was the fact that these activities or gifts were no longer confined to the leaders of the group but shared by all, or most, members of the conventicle. Prophecy, revelation, and mystical vision became, in short, group experiences which, as far as the *Capi rossi* were concerned, were both a sign and a seal of divine election.[127] Secure in this conviction, the *Capi rossi* drifted inexorably towards the propagation of prophecies which they believed would help to bring about the millennium and towards the public witnessing of their cause.

At first this activity took the form of attacks, couched in prophetic terms, against real and imagined opponents of their apostolate. Both Suor Domenica del Paradiso and the nuns of the Dominican convent of S. Vincenzo at Prato were the subjects of dire prophecies: Suor Domenica being told that the convent she had worked so long and so assiduously to found would be destroyed and the nuns of S. Vincenzo that soon they would all die in the convent.[128] That prophecies of this kind were not meant exclusively for internal edification but also for public consumption is attested by the fact that Suor Domenica was apprised by someone of the tenor of the prophecy relating to her and replied in kind, accusing Ser Cristoforo of being inspired by an evil spirit.[129] It is strange that the government remained for so long unaware of the prophetic accusations and counter-accusations being flung back and forth among the various lay and religious groups in Florence. It seems to have been ignorant, too, of the mystical activities of the *Capi rossi*. Or perhaps it had been informed but had decided not to act on the information since it did not perceive the political implications of these activities: a not unlikely occurrence in the chaotic last years of Alessandro de' Medici's rule.

---

[126] BNF Magl., VIII, 1398, fo. 32ʳ.     [127] Ibid., fos. 32ʳ, 34ʳ.
[128] Ibid., fos. 33ʳ, 34ʳ.     [129] Ibid., fos. 34ʳ.

With the assassination of Alessandro, however, the situation both within the conventicle and in the Florentine government changed radically. The *Capi rossi*, like many other Savonarolans, interpreted the assassination as the first sign of the inevitable realization of the millennium and, accordingly, altered their activities to bring about its speedier fulfilment. The stage was thus set for confrontation. They began by ignoring the ban on confraternities which was promulgated and strictly enforced shortly after Cosimo's assumption of power.[130] There could be no question of abandoning their meetings, especially since the elect had now, given the signs portending the imminence of the millennium, to provide concrete proof of their election. They were emboldened also, no doubt, by many years of successful clandestine activity. Despite their now boundless optimism, they could not but realize, however, that it was impossible to meet in Florence with safety and that some caution had to be exercised until such time as they received the final revelation that the millennium was at hand. Accordingly, while continuing to live in Florence, they thought it prudent to hold their weekly meetings in Fiesole.

Every Sunday and on major festival days from February 1537, when the ban on confraternities was promulgated, until 1538, when they were finally discovered, the *Capi rossi* would make their way to Fiesole. Meeting in a chapel of the church of Sta Maria Primerana or in the oratory of S. Ansano, they endeavoured, through their prophetic utterances, to speed the millennium on its way.[131] From now on one detects a significant change of emphasis in their prophecies. Whereas before, as we have seen, they had concentrated on condemning opponents of the Savonarolan cause, they now began at last to attack and to seek to overthrow the existing political system. Only this, they believed, prevented Florence from enjoying the blessings promised by Savonarola. When Florence had rid herself of the tyranny of the Medici and had instituted a 'popular'

---

[130] Polizzotto, 'Confraternities, Conventicles and Political Dissent', 252, 272–4.

[131] BNF Magl., VIII, 1398, fo. 32ʳ; ASF Conv. Sopp. 102, 96, 'Nota depositionum testium pro parte Societatis S. Benedicti Bigi', fo. 3ʳ.

form of government in which virtue could flourish, they prophesied, the millennium would come to pass.[132]

According to the *Capi rossi*, the time had come for the elect to
take a more active part in the unfolding of events. They should no
longer confine themselves to prayers and devotion but should strive
to disseminate throughout Florence the revelations of God's intentions.[133] At first sight there appears to be nothing new in the *Capi
rossi*'s prophecies in which a causal connection was posited between
a popular form of government and the unfolding of the millennium. This belief was, as we have seen, one of the central tenets of
the whole Savonarolan movement. Identical statements had been
made by Savonarola and by the great majority of his followers.
What was new was the radical interpretation which the *Capi rossi*
placed on the term 'popular'.

No longer prepared to posit a general contrast between the
Medicean and republican forms of government, they now argued
that a really *popular* government (that is, a true republic), should
have no aristocratic members at all. The *Ottimati*, they contended,
were as harmful to the Florentine cause and, therefore, to the
Florentine destiny as the Medici. The elect should eschew contact
with both.[134] It is clear that the *Capi rossi*'s political strictures were
loosely derived from Savonarola's condemnation of oligarchic governments,[135] but recent events, most notably the siege and the
capitulation of Florence, which had demonstrated all too clearly the
aristocrats' ability as a class to survive and even to benefit from
political turmoil,[136] were just as important in the formulation of
their anti-aristocratic belief. Needless to say, the *Capi rossi*'s almost
exclusively proletarian origins may also have contributed to this
bias in their prophecies.

---

[132] ASF Otto di Guardia, Ep. Grand. 19, fos. 15$^v$–16$^r$.

[133] BNF Magl., VIII, 1398, fo. 32$^r$.

[134] ASF Otto di Guardia, Ep. Grand. 19, fos. 15$^v$–16$^r$.

[135] See above, Ch. 1.

[136] A lesson which had also been learnt by an exasperated Clement VII, who set
out to ensure that in future the Medici would not be the only victims of political
revolution: see his letter to Nerli in Capponi (ed.), 'Discorsi intorno alla riforma
dello stato di Firenze', 416 n.

This exclusion of the *Ottimati* from the *Capi rossi*'s vision of the future had some immediate practical effects. It meant, first, that the *Capi rossi* did not take part in the ill-fated attempts of the exiles to overthrow Cosimo and to restore a republican form of government. They could not but have been aware that the exiles' military and political campaigns were directed and financed by *Ottimati* and that, had they been successful, they would have instituted a political system in which power was concentrated in their hands.[137]

Refusal to be drawn into the exiles' schemes meant, further, that the *Capi rossi* were not caught up in the widespread executions, imprisonments, and proscriptions which followed the defeat of Montemurlo. Rather, the ensuing political confusion and the continuing precariousness of Cosimo's position enabled the *Capi rossi* to intensify their activities in expectation of the last revelation portending the beginning of the millennium.[138] The long-awaited sign came early in 1538.[139] In a meeting in Sta Maria Primerana, Ser Cristoforo was inspired to prophesy that on Saturday 18 May the city of Florence would finally be liberated from the Medicean yoke.[140] The liberation, he averred, would be heralded by famine, plague, fire, and a bloody struggle, involving great slaughter, between the Mediceans and the *Ottimati*. The *Ottimati* would emerge victorious; but the elect should avoid contact with them because they wanted to institute an aristocratic government.[141] They should, instead, prepare for these portentous events by prayer, confession, and communion and, above all, by abiding with the

---

[137] See n. 110 above. Most instructive is also the letter by an anonymous informer in Venice to Cosimo, dated 22 July 1537 in ASF Mediceo, Carteggio Universale, Filza 333, fo. 97$^r$: 'Della voluntà di questi fuorusciti grandi è chiaro che non vogliono stato di Republica populare, et Filippo [Strozzi] parlandone col Duca d'Urbino a questi giorni passati lo disse chiaramente; sicché questo è chiaro, che lo stato che cercono è uno fatto come il vostro o poco dal più al manco.'

[138] Again, unfortunately, it is not possible to understand the full meaning of some of these activities, which seem, however, to have been of a propitiatory kind, see BNF Magl., VIII, 1398, fo. 32$^r$.

[139] ASF Otto di Guardia, Ep. Grand. 19, fo. 15$^v$.

[140] Ibid.; the prophesied date is given as 20 May in BNF Magl., VIII, 1398, fo. 32$^r$.

[141] ASF Otto di Guardia, Ep. Grand. 19, fo. 16$^r$.

*popolo* on whom the apotheosis of Florence depended.[142] Ser Cristoforo concluded by citing the prophet Habakkuk. The time was at hand when the elect could not passively stand by and let events take their course. Instead it was incumbent upon them to make their way back to Florence and there, by spreading the word, contribute to the deliverance of the city.[143]

It was unfortunate that one of the persons Ser Cristoforo contacted with the good news was one Migliore Guidotti, who immediately reported it to the *Otto di Guardia*.[144] The political situation in Florence and Cosimo's own insecurity, fed by alarming reports from Ser Bastiano Bindi, the chancellor of the *Otto di Guardia*, ensured that the members of the government would take Guidotti's information seriously.[145] In fact they acted upon it with great urgency. That very day Ser Cristoforo was arrested and examined under torture. Those of the *Capi rossi* who had not been sufficiently prudent to make good their escape as soon as they heard of Ser Cristoforo's arrest were rounded up by the *Otto di Guardia*.[146] There then began a series of examinations, depositions, and trials which were to take almost the whole of 1538.

It was to be expected that the *Otto di Guardia* would deal with the *Capi rossi* swiftly and with exemplary severity. But from the moment their prophecies became publicly known, the government moved with extreme circumspection, not wishing to lend credence to these prophecies by appearing to react too strongly to them. At the same time it did not dare to disregard them entirely and by so

---

[142] Ibid.          [143] BNF Magl., VIII, 1398, fo. 32[r].

[144] Ibid.; ASF Otto di Guardia, Ep. Grand. 19, fo. 15[v]. Migliore Guidotti had only recently been permitted to return to Florence, under the terms of a recently negotiated amnesty, after eight years' exile for his part in the last Florentine Republic: Varchi, *Storia fiorentina*, 264, 268.

[145] Ser Bastiano had a vested interest in making the situation appear worse than it, perhaps, was in reality. A sampling of his reports to Cosimo are in ASF Mediceo, Carteggio universale, Filza 335, fo. 183[r]; Filza 337, fos. 203[r-v], 297[r]–298[v]; Filza 338, fo. 123[r-v]; Filza 346, fos. 45[r-v], 131[r]–132[r], 256[r-v]. On him see also the revealing if highly critical, anonymous biography: 'Vita di Ser Bastiano Bindi', MS BNF II.II.325, fos. 120[r]–123[v]. See also my 'Confraternities, Conventicles and Political Dissent', 272–3.

[146] BNF Magl., VIII, 1398, fo. 33[v]. The interrogations were presided over by Ser Bastiano and by the second coadjutor to the *Otto*, Ser Pier Maria Lotti: a clear indication of the importance attributed to the case.

doing perhaps tempt fate and arouse God's wrath. Thus, when Ser Cristoforo was imprisoned in the *Stinche*, guards were placed outside his door to prevent a miraculous escape or deliverance. Most significantly, though examination of the conspirators continued apace, the three leaders were not condemned until 21 May: three days after the passing of the prophesied day of deliverance for Florence.[147]

While the failure of the *Capi rossi*'s prophecies to eventuate made the government's task somewhat easier, it did not remove all difficulties at a stroke. As past experience had shown, the basis of a prophet's standing and the loyalty of his following did not rest on mere dates, which could always be adapted to changing circumstances. Most important was the appeal of the prophetic message and the influence which this message had on the population. The persistently troublesome repercussions of Savonarola's prophecies on Florentine life for the past forty years left no room for doubt on either score. The government was thus confronted with the problems of discrediting the latest formulation of Savonarola's message and of punishing its perpetrators without giving fresh currency to the message or creating new martyrs who would in turn become the object of popular veneration.

A solution to both problems was finally found. It consisted of a subtly orchestrated campaign aimed at casting ridicule upon the *Capi rossi* and thus, by extension, discrediting their prophecies. The *Capi rossi*, and in particular their three leaders, were classified and dealt with as madmen, utterly deluded and therefore suitable objects of scorn and ridicule.[148] It seems to have been a matter of policy, moreover, not to raise publicly the issue of the *Capi rossi*'s links with Savonarola.[149] To have done so would have been coun-

---

[147] ASF Otto di Guardia, Ep. Grand. 19, fos. 15ʳ–16ᵛ.

[148] The whole anonymous account in BNF Magl., VIII, 1398, fos. 32ʳ–34ʳ conveys, in fact, this version of the *Capi rossi*. See also n. 149 below.

[149] Unlike previous practice when followers of Savonarola had been tried, no mention is made of Savonarola in the various trials of, or relating to, the *Capi rossi*. The connection, however, was not lost on even the most casual observer of events such as Bindaccio Guizzelmi da Prato, who witnessed on 22 May the public pillorying of the three leaders of the *Capi rossi*: 'Nota came a dì detto fu scopato in Firenze ser Crisofano di . . . da Soci, notaio, et co llui dua sua compatrioti, e' quali

ter-productive because it would have legitimized the *Capi rossi*'s prophecies to many Florentines. It could also have been taken as an admission of the persistent divisions which Savonarola's doctrines continued to cause in Florence at a time when the government, or rather Cosimo, wanted desperately to convey the impression that, apart from a few deluded individuals, the whole population was satisfied with the present status quo.

Discredited and isolated from all sources of sympathy, the *Capi rossi* could be dealt with in an exemplary fashion. This is demonstrated by the sentences passed on their three leaders on 21 May, after a trial in which they were charged with having conspired against the state. Ser Cristoforo was condemned to three years' imprisonment while Gabriele di Antonio dei Piselli and Nigi di Ruggiero to four months each respectively.[150] In addition, all three were condemned to the infamous *cerca maggiore*,[151] that is, to be paraded through the streets of Florence, Ser Cristoforo on a donkey and his two companions on foot, on a defined route and to be subjected to whipping and birching by the ministers of the *Otto di Guardia* and to the jeers, insults, and physical abuse of the throng. Further, to proclaim the nature of their crime, they were forced to wear mitred hats with attached inscriptions which, in Ser Cristoforo's case, stated that he was a false prophet and in the cases of Gabriele dei Piselli and Nigi di Ruggiero that they were followers of a false prophet.[152] Upon completion of their sentences they were to be exiled from Florence for an unspecified period.[153]

As they stand, these sentences seem unexceptional and hardly commensurate to the alarm caused by the discovery of the activities of the *Capi rossi*. And this was undoubtedly the impression the

---

erano inpazati nelle cose di Fra Girolamo e publicamente dicievano aver a venire per tutto a dì 20 di detto o 'l più lungho per tutto maggio gran sengni, e tutti discievano essere predetti dal detto frate, talmente che, esaminati e tormentati per e' signori Otto di guardia, furono sentenziati al suprizio predetto e in carcere, non possendo essere cavati se nonn'è per l'otto fave. É exenplo di chi volessi o vorrà tale eresie tenere o publichare e' nomi de' seguaci': 'Le "Ricordanze" di Bindaccio Guizzelmo da Prato (sec. XVI)', in *Rivista storica degli archivi toscani*, 5 (1933), 238.

[150] ASF Otto di Guardia, Ep, Grand. 19, fo. 16ᵛ.
[151] Ibid., fo. 16ʳ.          [152] Ibid., fo. 16ʳ⁻ᵛ.          [153] Ibid., fo. 16ᵛ.

sentences were meant to convey. However, the term of exile, being unspecified, could be indefinitely extended at the pleasure of the *Otto di Guardia*. Similarly unspecified was the fact that for their term of imprisonment they were confined not to the ordinary, criminal section of the *Stinche*, but to the *pazzeria*, the grisly lunatic asylum.[154]

Having dealt with the three leaders of the *Capi rossi*, the Florentine authorities took an inordinately long time to reopen the case against the conventicle. Only in November 1538 were proceedings resumed. Judging by the surviving evidence,[155] the major targets of the government's inquiry were by then no longer individual members of the conventicle but the institutions which had given it shelter: that is, the confraternities of S. Benedetto Nero and S. Benedetto Bianco and the convent of Sta Maria Novella. The reasons for the delay are obvious. Now forced to contend with powerful vested interests, the government was obliged to proceed slowly and to prepare a much tighter case than would have been necessary had it to deal with isolated individuals. Delay also enabled the government to play for time: defusing the issue and consolidating its position before tackling this potentially dangerous problem.

Despite the groundwork, however, it proved impossible to incriminate these institutions or the individuals within them. In their inquiry government officials met with an impregnable admixture of obstructionism, profession of ignorance, logical argument, and constant, if implied, appeals to ecclesiastical independence.[156] Any attempt at forcing the issue would have raised dangers which the Florentine government could not afford to face. Even had his position been more secure, Cosimo could not have hoped to deal successfully with the problem without the co-operation of the ecclesiastical authorities. This co-operation was not forthcoming.

---

[154] BNF Magl., VIII, 1398, fo. 33ᵛ.

[155] ASF Conv. Sopp. 102, 96: see nn. 120 and 121 above. All these documents have been published in my 'Confraternities, Conventicles and Political Dissent: The Case of the Savonarolan "Capi Rossi" Documents'.

[156] ASF Conv. Sopp. 102, 96, 'Testes examinati in causa fratrum S. Marie Novelle contra societatem S. Benedicti', fos. 3ʳ, 6ʳ⁻ᵛ, 8ᵛ, 11ᵛ, 13ᵛ, *et passim*; ibid., 'Nota depositionum testium pro parte Societatis Sancti Benedicti Bigi', fos. 2ᵛ–3ʳ.

Nor could he count on the support of the Curia, since his relations with Pope Paul III were extremely strained. There was no alternative, therefore, but to abandon the attempt.

This was not the end of the *Capi rossi*. As a result of a petition on his behalf, Ser Cristoforo was discharged from prison before he had fully served his sentence and begun his term of exile. The authorities did not release him, however, until he had given assurances that he would no longer prophesy or meddle in religious and political issues. This assurance he willingly gave. But his sense of duty for the cause was too strong and once out of the watchful eyes of the authorities he resumed his former activities and performed even more objectionable deeds than he had done before. He fled from his allotted place of exile, closely followed by an executioner, who had orders to kill him on sight, and took refuge in the Marches. There he joined a heretical sect, led by a hermit who believed himself to be the Angelic Pope. In a ceremony in the church of Sta Agata Feltria attended by the whole local population, the hermit was formally dressed in white papal robes and then proceeded to elect twelve cardinals for his Church.[157]

Ser Cristoforo was forced once again to flee from the Marches, where a price was put on his head and where he was condemned to be hanged. He made his way to Bologna, accompanied it seems by other members of the sect, including the Angelic Pope—prophesying, confessing, and expounding Scripture all the way. Dispatched, finally, to Florence, the five sectarians were tried and sentenced by the *Otto di Guardia*.[158] The nature of the crime for which they were tried on 1 June 1540 is not specified. Indeed, the records of the trial are so brief and cryptic that one cannot but conclude that the authorities wanted to deal with the matter as quickly and as secretly as possible. To have done otherwise would have been tantamount to alerting Ser Cristoforo's followers and thus would raise publicly, once again, the whole issue of Savonarola, Florentine election, and Medici rule at a time when Cosimo had not yet consolidated his hold over Florence. The harshness of

---

[157] ASF Magl., VIII, 1398, fos. 33ᵛ–34ʳ. For further details of this second stage of Ser Cristoforo's apostolate see Vasoli, 'Il notaio e il Papa angelico', 628–30.

[158] Ibid. 631–3, and 640 for the text of the trial of 1540.

the sentence lends weight to this interpretation. They were all condemned to imprisonment in the *Stinche* for an indefinite period at the discretion of the *Otto di Guardia*. Twenty-five years later Ser Cristoforo was still serving out his sentence in a hospital, as he had requested, and in complete silence.[159]

The *Capi rossi* made a lasting impression on Cosimo. The timing of the threat they posed, the nature and the persistence of this threat, and the difficulties experienced in dealing with it firmly and conclusively, influenced his response when next the problem presented itself. This occurred five years later, in 1545, when it came to Cosimo's notice that a friar of S. Marco, Benedetto di Bartolomeo Franceschi, had not only preached Savonarola's doctrine and expounded his writings but had also written a book which, apart from invoking God's wrath on Cosimo and on his family, called into question the legitimacy of both Medicean rule and of the papacy as then constituted.[160] The exact nature of the argument against the Medici contained in the book is not known since Franceschi's superiors took care to burn it before Cosimo could lay his hands on it.[161] The disappearance of the evidence suited Cosimo's purposes perfectly. It enabled him to charge the friars with collusion and thus to launch a far more wide-ranging attack than would otherwise have been possible. He claimed that the friars of S. Marco not only meddled continuously in the governmental process but had actually conspired against his state, seeking to overthrow it.[162] He argued, further, that their meddling

---

[159] ASF Magl., VIII, 1398, fo. 34[r].

[160] Ubaldini, 'Annalia', fo. 33[v], gives a short but balanced account of the controversy. The whole episode is discussed in A. Amati, 'Cosimo I e i Frati di S. Marco', 227–77; additional documents, including the passage from *Annalia* cited above, published by A. Gherardi, *Nuovi documenti*, 343–6. On Benedetto di Bartolomeo Franceschi, who died in Aug. 1545 at the onset of the 'storm' he had raised, see Convento di S. Domenico, Fiesole, 'Cronica Conventus Sancti Dominici de Fesulis', fo. 152[r], where he is described as 'vir . . . bonis litteris et moribus sed deficiens in iudicio'.

[161] Ibid.; ASF Mediceo, Minute, 6, fo. 282[r–v] (Letter of Cosimo I to Alessandro del Caccia, 14 Oct. 1545): Amati, 'Cosimo I e i Frati di S. Marco', 244–5.

[162] Ibid. 243; A. Gherardi, *Nuovi documenti e studi intorno a Girolamo Savonarola* (Florence, 1887; fac. repr. 1972), 345; ASF Mediceo, Minute, 6, fos. 258 [*tris*][v].

was not a recent development but, rather, had been a feature of Florentine politics since Savonarola's day.[163] Throughout this period, Cosimo averred, the friars had pursued two major aims: to ensure that Florence remained loyal to France and to work towards the establishment of a lasting popular government in the city.[164] He would have been remiss in his duties as a ruler, he maintained, had he not acted promptly and firmly in arresting and then expelling from his dominion the friars of S. Marco and of the associated convents of S. Domenico at Fiesole and of Sta Maria Maddalena in Pian di Mugnone. To ensure that the Savonarolan friars would never again threaten his rule, Cosimo handed the convent of S. Marco over to the Augustinians and asked that the two other convents be assigned to the Dominicans of the Lombard Congregation.[165]

Cosimo was by this time sufficiently well versed in diplomatic affairs to know that his actions would not go unchallenged, especially at the Vatican, where Paul III did not lose the opportunity to obstruct his plans. None the less, he considered the issue at stake of sufficient importance to warrant the risk. The attack of one friar, immediately disowned by his superiors, would not have elicited such an intemperate response had not recent precedents caused Cosimo to believe, or to feign to believe, that S. Marco still represented as much a threat to Medici rule as it had ever done. In reality, as he no doubt was aware, S. Marco, as an institution, had long ceased to be a danger to his rule. As we have seen, the *Capi rossi* had no links with S. Marco, though they drew their inspiration from the teaching of Savonarola as interpreted for them by Pieruccio and Ser Cristoforo. The purges and the reorganization which the convent had been forced to undergo after the siege,

---

[163] Ibid., fos. 257ᵛ–258ʳ (Cosimo to the General of the Dominican Order, undated); fos. 318ᵛ–319ʳ (Cosimo to Don Francesco di Toledo, 31 Oct. 1545); Amati, 'Cosimo I e i Frati di S. Marco', 242–3.

[164] ASF Mediceo, Minute, 6, fo. 389ʳ⁻ᵛ (Cosimo to Don Francesco di Toledo, 3 Dec. 1545); fo. 319ʳ (same to same, 31 Oct. 1545), where Cosimo succinctly states that since Savonarola's days the friars had conducted a campaign throughout Florence 'di stare sotto l'ombra et patrocinio della corona di Francia et di governare la città a populo'.

[165] Amati, 'Cosimo I e i Frati di S. Marco', 244–6.

moreover, had deprived it of its radical spokesmen and had placed it under close Medicean control. Friars who were either anti-Savonarolan or were at best indifferent to him but determined that his person or teaching should no longer disturb the peace of the convent, now had the upper hand.[166] Indeed, it was one of these friars who apprised Cosimo of Fra Benedetto Franceschi's activities and who thus helped to precipitate the crisis.[167] All this should not be taken to mean that S. Marco had turned its back on Savonarola. Far from it. His memory was still venerated in the convent and, when the need arose, the friars would brave hardship and censure publicly to defend him. As we shall see, however, it was not Savonarola, the political and religious reformer they were defending, but another Savonarola of their own devising, meek, apolitical, and an upholder of the religious status quo.

The convent's dire financial position, and its consequent dependence on the goodwill of the government and of its aristocratic supporters to survive, militated against the expression of dissent or opposition to the Medici and guaranteed swift containment and suppression were it to occur. To express dissent through prophecy, as the friars of S. Marco had usually done in the past, would have been extremely foolhardy in the current religious climate. For, after the challenge to its authority mounted by Protestant reformers, the ecclesiastical hierarchy had turned against prophecy as never before because of its essentially anti-authoritarian and hence disruptive nature.[168] Resort to prophecy now was bound not only to antagonize lay authorities but also to alienate the ecclesiastical hierarchy at a time when it would otherwise have welcomed any attack on Cosimo's rule.

[166] Ubaldini, 'Annalia', fo. 75[r-v] for a list of priors of S. Marco for the years 1530–46. The first Savonarolan to be appointed after the fall of Florence was Fra Vincenzo Ercolani, elected in May 1552.

[167] His name is given as Fra Maurizio, to be identified, perhaps, with Fra Maurizio di Francesco Tosinghi, on whom see Ubaldini, 'Annalia', fos. 33[v], 111[v]; P. Benelli, 'Catalogo dei Frati di S. Marco, secoli XV e XVI', MS ACSM Miscellanea P. Benelli, inserto P, unpaginated.

[168] O. Niccoli, Profeti e popolo nell'Italia del Rinascimento (Bari, 1987), 241–9; R. De Maio, Savonarola e la Curia Romana (Rome, 1969), 156–71; id., Riforme e miti nella Chiesa del Cinquecento (Naples, 1973), 85–91.

It is clear that Cosimo in attacking S. Marco was in fact seeking to exorcise the memory of Savonarola. By striking at the visible embodiment of that memory he sought to destroy the anti-Medicean tradition it had once come to represent, not fully realizing, perhaps, how thoroughly the task had been accomplished by Clement VII in 1530–1. Or, if he was aware of this, perhaps he regarded any veneration of Savonarola as having inherent political implications, as on previous evidence he was undoubtedly justified in doing, and therefore as warranting his intervention. Indeed, the fact that Cosimo had begun to attack the convent for the allegedly dubious methods it employed to recruit novices early in 1545, that is before the crisis over Fra Benedetto Franceschi, suggests as much. At about the same time, moreover, he also demanded—unsuccessfully as it turned out— that all convents and monasteries of the Dominican Order within his dominions be placed under the control of four lay overseers (*soprastanti*) appointed by him. At the same time the convent and friars of S. Marco were subjected to a humiliating and obviously organized campaign of vandalism, harassment, and sexual molestation. While it lasted, hooligans disrupted religious functions, manhandled and insulted the friars, made indecent proposals to them, fondled novices and young boys in the convent's charge, and went through the motions of committing sodomy with one another whenever the friars walked in procession through the streets of Florence.[169]

It is obvious that Cosimo had not anticipated the strength of ecclesiastical reaction. As well as burning the incriminating book he had written, Fra Benedetto Franceschi's immediate superiors transferred him to Orvieto and, following Cosimo's lead, repudiated him by letting it be known that Fra Benedetto was not in possession of his mental faculties and could not, therefore, be held

[169] ASF Mediceo, Minute, 6, fos. 2ʳ–3ʳ (letter of Cosimo to Averardo Serristori, Mar. 1545); ibid., Carteggio Universale, 375, fo. 503ʳ (Fra Francesco da Castiglione, Vicar-General of the Dominican Order, to Cosimo, 21 Mar. 1545), fo. 585ʳ (Bishop of Lucca to Cosimo, 25 Mar. 1545), fo. 582ʳ (Fra Francesco de' Medici to Cosimo, 25 Mar. 1545).

responsible for his actions.[170] First the Cardinal Protector and the Vicar-General of the Dominican Order, then an array of cardinals and other prelates pleaded and remonstrated with Cosimo.[171] Finally, when all these approaches failed, Paul III gleefully stepped in. Aware by now of Cosimo's isolation, the Pope adopted an intransigent attitude. Deaf to all entreaties, he was intent only on exacting a humiliating total capitulation from Cosimo. In vain did Cosimo try to placate him by arguing that he had acted also for the good of the Church. He reasoned, further, that the friars of S. Marco, apart from denying the legitimacy of all popes after Sixtus IV, were disciples of a friar who had been executed by the Holy See as a heretic and whom the Protestants themselves, including Luther, revered as a martyr and acknowledged as a precursor. But not even these arguments could induce Paul III to relent.[172] With ill-repressed rage Cosimo was finally forced to readmit the expelled Dominican friars, even though for a few years yet he tried to rid himself of them by various means, including the deprivation of the customary alms which were necessary for survival.[173]

[170]   Amati, 'Cosimo I e i Frati di S. Marco', 245, and see above, n. 160: ASF C. Strozz., ser. I, 123, unfoliated (Alessandro del Caccia to Cosimo, undated).

[171]   Amati, 'Cosimo I e i Frati di S. Marco', 245–6; ASF Mediceo, Carteggio Universale, 373, fo. 461[r] (Bernardino Duretti, Florentine representative at the Council of Trent, to Cosimo, Aug. 1545), fo. 504[r] (Fra Francesco da Castiglione, Vicar-General of the Dominican Order, to Cosimo, 16 Aug. 1545); ibid. 374, fo. 239[r–v] (Pandolfo Pucci to Cosimo, 7 Nov. 1545), fo. 302[r–v] (Bernardino Duretti to Cosimo, 15 Nov. 1545), where even Fra Ambrogio Caterino Politi—the archenemy of S. Marco—cautions the Duke against the course of action he had undertaken; ibid., C. Strozz., ser. I, 78, fo. 25[r–v] (Pier Filippo Pandolfini to Cosimo, 9 Dec. 1545).

[172]   ASF Mediceo, 6, fo. 282[r–v] (Cosimo to Alessandro del Caccia, 14 Oct. 1545), fos. 424[v]–425[r] (Cosimo to Pier Filippo Pandolfini, 30 Dec. 1545).

[173]   Ibid., fos. 572[r]–573[r] (Cosimo to Giovanni di Vega, 24 Mar. 1546). See also Cosimo's circular letter to individual members of the College of Cardinals, variously dated between 15 and 31 Mar. 1546, in which he disingenuously refutes these charges, published in Amati, 'Cosimo I e i Frati di S. Marco', 266–9. A slightly different version in M. Cresci, 'Storia delle cose d'Italia dall'anno 1525 all'anno 1546', MS BNF II.III.66, fos. 269[r]–272[v]. By this time, the only person unctuously approving Cosimo's actions was Pietro Aretino, who sought by these means to have some recompense for the portrait of himself painted by Titian which he had sent to Cosimo: ASF Mediceo, Carteggio Universale, 376, fo. 6 [bis][r], 6 [bis][v] (Pietro Aretino to Cosimo, 6 Apr. 1546).

The bogies of Savonarola and S. Marco were to be raised again in the future, often by interested parties who had something to gain by so doing. There was even less foundation for this than there had been in 1545 and thus, not surprisingly, nothing came of it. If anything had emerged from the crisis of 1545 it was S. Marco's quietism, its orthodoxy, its unquestioned acceptance by the hierarchy, but also its political weakness, its lack of support in Florence. Previously parishioners and highly placed sympathizers had rushed to its defence, but now no Florentine voice was raised on its behalf. Once it had been worth defending because it enshrined the Savonarolan promise of Florentine glory. It now no longer did so and, even worse, it had lost its hold over those Florentines who counted. Indeed, the well-intentioned modification of the Savonarolan dream by Francesco de' Ricci and the appropriation of this dream by the proletarian *Capi rossi*, with the frightening possibilities thereby adumbrated, could not but have accelerated the final unquestioning acceptance of the Medici by socially and economically prominent Florentines. As Bartolomeo Rinuccini in his heart of hearts had realized when in his *Visio* he had Savonarola assure him that God despite everything would save His people and lead them to glory, it had become wellnigh impossible for the elect to bring about with their own efforts the unfolding of the millennium. Only God, by His direct and gratuitous bestowal, in answer to their entreaties that He should intervene on their behalf, could now make possible the fulfilment of the Florentine dream. However reluctantly made, this was an admission of defeat. Even worse, it was the anguished and disconsolate acceptance of the fact that the apotheosis of the city as Savonarola had imagined it would no longer come to pass.

# 9

# *Epilogue*

Having weathered the crisis of 1545–6, the worst it had faced till then, S. Marco resumed its activities and continued on its slow road to recovery. Once the memory of the humiliating defeat had faded, Cosimo ceased troubling the convent and even began to single it out for special favour. After years of mutual enmity it became convenient once again to emphasize the connection between S. Marco and the Medici which had existed from the time of Cosimo *pater patriae*. For its part, S. Marco gave the Prince the obeisance and honour he regarded as his due and ensured that no criticism either of the Medici or of the political system imposed on Florence would ever again emanate from its precincts. Both had a great deal to gain from the establishment of peaceful relations and both accordingly ensured that nothing should interfere with their gradual *rapprochement*.

The establishment of harmonious relations was not achieved without compromises on S. Marco's part. The first and major casualty was the figure of Savonarola. Even if the superiors of S. Marco had wanted to, and this was by no means the case, it was impossible to disown the man with whom the convent had become so closely identified. To have done so would have called into question the good faith not only of the hierarchy in S. Marco but of the whole Dominican Order, both of whom had often in the past sprung to his defence. More importantly, given the large number of Dominicans who still followed Savonarola or sympathized with his views, such a move would have split the Congregation and would inevitably have led to its destruction. And yet, in this harshest of climates, characterized on the one hand by princely absolutism in Florence and on the other by the spirit of reaction in Rome, it was just as dangerous to leave things as they were in the hope that the issue of Savonarola would disappear of its own accord. Savonarola had become too powerful a symbol of political and religious dissent for this to be possible. Nor was it wise to ignore the fact that the figure of Savonarola, simply because of this symbolic significance, could be manipulated to damage the Dominican Order and to undermine its standing in the Church.

These were undoubtedly some of the considerations which influenced the process of reinterpretation of Savonarola and of his apostolate. There were three major components in this process. First, a concerted effort was made to rework, revise, and even to write anew, in line with Dominican aims but also prevailing fashions, the earlier biographies of Savonarola, in particular the Italian rendition of the *Vita latina*, that is the Pseudo-Burlamacchi *Vita*.[1] This activity peaked with the composition of two large-scale biographies of Savonarola: one by Fra Marco di Francesco della Casa and the other by Fra Serafino Razzi.[2] The biographical revision went hand in hand with, and was also influenced by, a campaign to collect and to write down in convenient, easily consultable lists, a representative selection of Savonarola's miracles.[3]

An examination of the resulting biographies and of the newly compiled collections of miracles discloses the effects as well as the underlying intentions of this process of reinterpretation. These exercises in piety lacked the missionary zeal which had permeated

---

[1] Versions, some of which display interesting local variations, are to be found in just about all large manuscript libraries in north and central Italy; but see e.g. MSS BNF II.II.407, 430; II.III.490; II.IV.504; MS BNF Magl., XXXVII, 44; MS BNF Palatino, 626; MS BNF Palatino-Baldovinetti, 168; MSS BLF Fondo S. Marco, 410, 417, 420, 424, 425, 426, 428, 429; MSS BRF 1905, 2039, 2746.

[2] Different versions of these biographies were also produced. I have used the following: for Della Casa, MS BNF II.II.430 and MS BRF 4071; for Razzi, MS BRF 2012.

[3] Each of the biographies listed above (nn. 2 and 3) has its own more or less formal list of miracles. Two additional biographies, MS BNF Conv. Sopp., G.5.1209 and MS ASF C. Strozz., ser. III, vol. 267, display most interesting variations. On occasion, independent lists, that is lists not appended to biographies, were compiled, the most interesting of which is undoubtedly the one written down by the secular priest Agostino Campi, MS BNF Conv. Sopp., J.VII.2. Such lists can occur, however, in the most unlikely places as, for instance, in Bartolomeo Cerretani's 'Ricordi storici fiorentini', MS BAV Vat. Lat. 13651, fo. 235$^{r-v}$.

the work of the first biographers. Above all, they displayed none of the hortatory quality and the passion which had distinguished the *Vita latina* and Giovanfrancesco Pico's *Vita Reverendi Patris F. Hieronymi Savonarolae*. Unfortunately but inevitably in the circumstances, the reworked lives sank to the level of hagiography above which their prototypes had so emphatically risen. From all this, Savonarola's character emerged profoundly modified. The qualities which had made him a religious leader who, whatever his human failings, could inspire men to give their lives for the cause of civic and religious reform, not only while he lived but long after his death, were replaced by others more befitting the saint which his devotees and Dominican brethren now sought to make of him. His belligerence and disobedience glossed over, Savonarola became the defender of orthodoxy, the very model of conformity and of the reforming zeal demanded by the Counter-Reformation Church. His prophetic mission, when not ignored altogether, was divested of its polemical and even revolutionary content to become purely an instrument of moral suasion. Similarly, the long appendices of miracles—almost invariably accompanied by the enumeration of Savonarola's supporters and opponents and of the contrasting fates reserved for them by the Almighty—extended and reinforced this new image.[4]

The process was completed by the pursuit of a policy of associating Savonarola with famous figures whose sanctity was beyond dispute. Direct spiritual links and even complete discipleship between Savonarola and S. Antonino, Sta Caterina de' Ricci, S. Filippo Neri, and on occasion encompassing other saints such

---

[4] These developments reached their climax with the works of Serafino Razzi, the most notable of which are 'Vita del Reverendo Padre Frate Girolamo da Ferrara', MS BRF 2012; id., 'Brevi risposte alle oppugnazioni di Frate Ambrosio Politi Catharino', MS BNF Palatino 906, fos. 1ʳ–40ʳ; id., 'Defensione della dottrina, delle profezie e della santità del Padre Fra Girolamo Savonarola', ibid., fos. 40ᵛ–64ʳ; id., 'Opere varie', MS ACSM (no location numbers), esp. fos. 154ᵛ–156ʳ. The only work that does not fit this mould and which displays still a great deal of belligerence is Lorenzo Violi's *Le Giornate* written, however, when Cosimo's persecution of S. Marco was still in progress. On this see the invaluable introduction by the editor of *Le Giornate* (Florence, 1986), Gian Carlo Garfagnini, and esp. pp. xxxi–xxxiii.

as S. Francesco da Paola and the blessed Caterina da Racconigi, were soon posited.[5] By the end of the sixteenth century Savonarola had thus been transformed into the cult figure which he was ever afterwards to remain, at least in Dominican circles. It is, perhaps, the saddest comment upon the slow demise of the Piagnone tradition that its last act was to make of the prophet and martyr who had inspired it a featureless and sedately tinted plaster saint.

The new Savonarola proved to be a useful and immensely resilient creation. In this new guise, the cult of Savonarola and of his two companions, which in lay circles had been driven underground by harsh governmental repression, could be tolerated, if not actively encouraged by Dominican authorities in those convents of the Order where he still had a faithful following.[6] It was an important concession which, by serving as a safety-valve, prevented the public witnessing to Savonarola's cause which in the past had proved so harmful to the Order. Savonarola also became much easier to defend from attacks launched by interested parties against him and through him against either S. Marco or the Order as a whole. The series of attacks was opened by the quarrelsome erstwhile Piagnone and Dominican from S. Marco, Ambrogio Catarino

---

[5] It was a policy pursued at various levels which would repay detailed study. On S. Antonino and Savonarola one should examine the Poccetti fresco of 'S. Antonino taking possession of the Cathedral of Florence' in the cloister of S. Antonino in S. Marco and also the 'Albero di religiosi morti in concetto di santità nel convento di S. Marco di Firenze' formerly in S. Antonino's cell. On Sta Caterina de' Ricci and Savonarola see S. Razzi, *Vita di S. Caterina de' Ricci*, ed. D. Di Agresti (Florence, 1965), *passim*; D. Di Agresti, *Sviluppi della riforma monastica savonaroliana* (Florence, 1980), esp. 74–102; on S. Filippo Neri and Savonarola see ibid. 80 ff. and references therein; on Savonarola and S. Franceso di Paola see the latter's *Centurie di lettere* (Rome, 1665), 295–324; on Savonarola and Caterina da Racconigi see Giovanfrancesco Pico, 'Compendio delle maravigliose cose di Catherina da Raconisi', MS BNF Conv. Sopp., B.8.1648, *passim* and id., *Vita Reverendi Patris F. Hieronymi Savonarolae* (Paris, 1674), 164.

[6] C. Guasti, *L'Officio proprio per Fra Girolamo Savonarola e i suoi compagni scritto nel secolo XVI* (Prato, 1863); A. Gherardi, *Nuovi documenti e studi intorno a Girolamo Savonarola* (Florence, 1887; fac. repr. 1972), 358–65. For repression of Savonarola's cult in lay circles, apart from instances provided in the previous chapter, see ibid. 338–9.

Politi, who in 1548 published a treatise against Savonarola.[7] More dangerous still was the campaign orchestrated by the Jesuits but launched by Paul IV in 1557. Convinced by them that Savonarola's doctrine was more scandalous and dangerous than the Lutheran heresy,[8] Paul IV determined to have his books consigned to the *Index librorum prohibitorum*.[9] The last concerted attack was made by the Florentine Archbishop Alessandro de' Medici, who, in two letters to the Grand Duke Francesco I of 26 August and 20 October 1583, warned him of the fact that Savonarola's cult continued to flourish in the convents of S. Marco and of S. Vincenzo at Prato

---

[7] A. Caterino Politi, *Discorso . . . contra la dottrina et prophetie di Fra Girolamo Savonarola* (Venice, 1548). An excellent discussion of the treatise in P. Simoncelli, *Evangelismo italiano del Cinquecento* (Rome, 1979), 19–24 *et passim*. Simoncelli's book raises, in addition, some important arguments on the connections between Savonarolism and Italian Evangelism.

[8] Vincenzo Ercolani, *Lettera del P. Fra Vincenzo Ercolani Perugino dell'Ordine de' Predicatori, quando era Priore nella Minerva di Roma, scritta ai suoi frati di S. Marco di Firenze, dove si racconta l'esamina fatta sopra la dottrina di Girolamo Savonarola ed altre cose accadute a ciò*, in B. Aquarone, *Vita di fra Jeronimo Savonarola* (2 vols.; Alessandria, 1857–8), vol. ii, app., p. xxvi. See, however, the more charitable interpretation provided by the Jesuit M. Scaduto, 'Lainez e l'Indice del 1559: Lullo, Sabunde, Savonarola, Erasmo', *Archivum Historicum Societatis Jesu*, 24 (1955), 3–32.

[9] Paolino Bernardini, *Defensione sopra la dottrina et opere del Rev. Padre fr. Hieronimo Savonarola da Ferrara fatta e ditta in presentia delli Reverendissimi Cardinali della inquisitione nel tempo di Papa Paolo IV*, in I. Taurisano, 'Fra Girolamo Savonarola (Da Alessandro VI a Paolo IV)', *La Bibliofilia*, 55 (1953), 47–53; Vincenzo Ercolani, *Lettera*, pp. xxii–li; a detailed 'official' rebuttal was also published shortly after by Tommaso Neri, *Apologia del reverendo padre Fra Tommaso Neri fiorentino dell'ordine de' frati Predicatori in difesa della dottrina del R.P.F. Girolamo da Ferrara del medesimo ordine* (Florence, 1564). This work, as Tommaso Neri admits, was written at the behest of the Master-General of the Dominican Order, the Genoese Stefano Usodimare, in the aftermath of the attack levelled at the Papal Curia by Paul IV and the Jesuits in 1557, who based their arguments against Savonarola on the book by Ambrogio Caterino Politi: see ibid., Ep. Ded. to Francesco da Diacceto, sig. a4$^{r-v}$. On this whole issue see the valuable works by P. Simoncelli, 'Momenti e figure del savonarolismo romano', *Critica storica*, 11 (1974), 47–82, and by P. Simoncelli and M. Firpo, 'I processi inquisitoriali contro Savonarola (1558) e Carnesecchi (1566–1567): Una proposta di interpretazione', *Rivista di storia e letteratura religiosa*, 18 (1982), 200–52; see also B. Carderi, 'Messe all'Indice le opere di Savonarola?', *Memorie Domenicane*, NS 36 (1960), 37–52; R. De Maio, *Riforme e miti nella Chiesa del Cinquecento* (Naples, 1973), 61–91.

and thus posed a threat to Medici rule unless firm steps were taken to suppress it.[10]

These attacks need not detain us for long. No sooner were they made than the Dominican Order formally undertook to repulse them. Some concessions had to be made;[11] on the whole, however, the Dominicans were successful in preventing an official, wholesale condemnation of Savonarola and of his writings which would have been extremely damaging to the Order. In the process, of course, they refined and elaborated on the evolving image of Savonarola as a Counter-Reformation saintly prelate. Indeed, apart from enabling the Order to withstand these attacks, the new Savonarola became the titular saint of a Dominican reforming and expansionist movement drawing its inspiration and personnel from S. Marco. Through the agency of friars like Fra Angelo Bettini, Fra Matteo Lachi, and Fra Paolino Bernardini, who had already given ample proof of their devotion to Savonarola, the programme of conventual reform was extended to convents as far afield as the Abruzzi and Calabria but also closer at hand in Florence to the refractory Sta Maria Novella and S. Domenico del Maglio.[12] Far from being an exclusively Dominican initiative, the reform was actively advocated and supported by ecclesiastical and civic authorities who, despite public pronouncements against Savonarola, appreciated his work for monastic reform and the principles underlying it, seeking

[10] Published in Guasti, *L'Officio proprio per Fra Girolamo Savonarola*, 26–30. An excellent treatment of the attack and of the religious context from which it was issued in A. D'Addario, *Aspetti della controriforma a Firenze* (Rome, 1972), 243–67.

[11] Ibid. 266–7; Ercolani, *Lettera . . . scritta ai suoi frati di S. Marco*, p. xxxvii; Simoncelli, 'Momenti e figure del savonarolismo romano', 66.

[12] Serafino Razzi, 'Cronica della Provincia Romana dell'Ordine de' frati predicatori', MS BMLF S. Marco 873, fo. 88$^{r-v}$; Taurisano, 'Fra Girolamo Savonarola', 27–8; G. L. Esposito, 'S. Domenico di Cosenza, 1447–1863', *Memorie Domenicane*, NS 5 (1974), 338; B. Carderi, 'La riforma domenicana in Abruzzo', *Memorie Domenicane*, 75 (1958), 72–125; P. T. Masetti, *Monumenta et antiquitates Veteris disciplinae Ordinis Praedicatorum* (2 vols.; Rome, 1864), ii. 18–19, 57–8; M. Biliotti, 'Venerabilis coenobii Sanctae Mariae Novellae de Florentia Chronica', *Analecta Sacri Ordinis Fratrum Praedicatorum*, 12 (1915–16), 634–40; F. Viviani della Robbia, *Nei monasteri fiorentini* (Florence, 1946), 186–90.

when possible to extend it. Thus, when the time came to reform Sta Maria Novella and S. Domenico del Maglio, the friars of S. Marco, anticipating trouble, were assisted by secular authorities including large contingents of men-at-arms made available by the *Otto di Guardia*. In both cases it became necessary to effect forcible entry to the convents.[13] There ensued some very unpleasant scenes, especially during the occupation of Sta Maria Novella when Fra Angelo Bettini, incensed by the opposition, lost his temper and turned on a recalcitrant Conventual friar.[14]

Not once, throughout these years, does the millenarian vision of Florentine election re-emerge. Even the arch-Piagnone Benedetto Luschino, now a secular priest and over 80 years of age, thought it wise not to raise this subject openly in his rebuttal written between 1549 and 1551 of Ambrogio Catarino Politi's attack on Savonarola.[15] Its absence from a work largely given over to a defence of Savonarola's prophetic mission—a work in which Benedetto Luschino also tried to enlist the support of another millenarian prophet attacked by Politi, Guillaume Postel—was undoubtedly due to the fact that it was revised at Luschino's request by the Dominican Egidio Foscarari, Maestro del Sacro Palazzo.[16] Even Luschino, despite his zeal and unshakeable belief in Savonarola's teaching, had come to appreciate the wisdom of restraint. He too, like his more illustrious former brethren, had realized that a defence of Savonarola's eschatology at that time would have been untimely and counter-productive. With the triumph of

---

[13] Ibid., 187–8; Biliotti, 'Venerabilis coenobii Sanctae Mariae Novellae di Florentia Chronica', 637–9.

[14] ASF Diplomatico, S. Maria Novella, 22 Aug. 1556: censure of Fra Angelo Bettini for the personal violence used when taking possession of Sta Maria Novella.

[15] Benedetto Luschino, 'Risposta . . . contra al mendace libello di Ambrosio Catarino', MS BAV Patetta 1845.

[16] Ibid., Pref. letter to Politi, fo. 1ʳ, but erased and therefore not transcribed by F. Patetta, 'Fra Benedetto da Firenze, compagno ed apologista del Savonarola, al secolo Bettuccio Luschino', *Atti della Reale Accademia delle Scienze di Torino*, 60 (1924–5), 646. Luschino's letters to Postel are in, 'Risposta . . . contra al mendace libello di Ambrosio Catherino', fos. 2ʳ, 4ʳ, 5ʳ. On Postel see W. J. Bouwsma, *Concordia Mundi: The Career and Thought of Guillaume Postel (1510–1581)* (Cambridge, Mass., 1957) and M. L. Kuntz, *Guillaume Postel Prophet of the Restitution of All Things: His Life and Thought* (The Hague, 1981).

Spain throughout Italy and with the imposition of conformity and uniformity on Catholic Christendom by the Council of Trent the premisses for Savonarola's millenarian vision had vanished.

Not that prophecy disappears completely from Florence. The city continued to be visited by prophets of various hues, at least one of whom claimed, in however vague a fashion, to have some affinity with Savonarola.[17] However, they were, one and all, prophets of doom, unable to comprehend the import of Savonarola's prophetic message and incapable, therefore, of reviving it even if the times had been favourable, which they undoubtedly were not. Savonarola's vision, and thus by extension the vision of his followers, was far more complex than they envisaged. Above all, it was predicated not on religious dictates alone, but on an admixture of political, social, *and* religious considerations. Both in theory and in practice, Savonarola had shown that the true Christian, as he defined him, could not properly fulfil his appointed role if he confined his activities to only one of these areas. Because spiritual regeneration could not be achieved in a hostile political climate or in an unjust society ruled by greed it followed that political and social reform were prerequisites for religious renovation and for Florence's final enjoyment of her divine destiny. Enshrined in his sermons and writings was the principle that political activism of a predetermined kind and altruistic social commitment were the duties of the men of God, of the Elect. This, first and foremost, was Savonarola's legacy to Florence and to his followers: a legacy which, as its subsequent history demonstrates, has proved to be most resilient and adaptable.[18]

[17] See e.g. 'Diario delle cose eseguite [*sic*] in Firenze dal 1532 al 1589', MS BNF II.III.274, fos. 92ᵛ–96ᵛ.

[18] D. Weinstein, *Savonarola and Florence: Prophecy and Patriotism in the Renaissance* (Princeton, NJ, 1970), 3 ff. The influence of Savonarolan millenarian ideology on the *Risorgimento* and on modern Italian history would repay further study given the identity of some of its principal proponents, the best known of whom were Massimo d'Azeglio (*Niccolò de' Lapi, ovvero i Palleschi e i Piagnoni*, 1841) and Francesco Domenico Guerrazzi (*Assedio di Firenze*, 1836); some preliminary observations in G. D. d'Oldenico, 'Massimo d'Azeglio e Girolamo Savonarola: Variazioni sul Risorgimento italiano', *Memorie Domenicane*, 67 (1950), 201–10. See also E. Guccione, 'Girolamo Savonarola nel pensiero politico-sociale dei cattolici italiani tra il xix e il xx secolo', *Atti dell'Accademia di Scienze, Lettere e Arti di Palermo*, 36 (1976–7), 253–305.

# APPENDIX

### Signatories of the Subscription List of 1497[1]

| Name | Guild affiliation[2] | Gonfalone[3] |
|---|---|---|
| ADIMARI Piero di Bernardo | M | SG Drago |
| AGNI Cristoforo (Agli?) | | |
| Degli ALBIZZI Antonio di Manno | M | Chiavi |
| Degli ALBIZZI Giovanni di Felice (as below?) | | |
| Degli ALBIZZI Giovanni di Tedici (P: father's name given as de Tadie) | M | Chiavi |
| Degli ALBIZZI Maso di Bartholomeo | M | Chiavi |
| Degli ALBIZZI Piero di Lucantonio | M | Chiavi |
| Degli ALBIZZI Piero di Paolo | M | Chiavi |
| Degli ALBIZZI Raffaello di Paolo | M | Chiavi |

[1] Based on the three published lists by P. Villari and E. Casanova (eds.), *Scelta di prediche e scritti di Fra Girolamo Savonarola, con nuovi documenti intorno alla sua vita* (Florence, 1898), 514–18 (F); P. Emiliani-Giudici, *Storia dei comuni italiani* (3 vols.; Florence, 1864–6), iii. 533–9 (G); A. Portioli, 'Nuovi documenti su Girolamo Savonarola', *Archivio storico lombardo*, 1st ser. 1 (1874), 341–5 (P); and collated with two manuscript lists, BNF II.II.437, fos. 10ʳ–11ʳ and ibid., Panc. 117, vol. i, fos. 382ʳ–387ʳ. See also above Introd. and Ch. I. Surnames have been rationalized by standardizing their spelling when variations were minor or when the possibility of error was minimal. On the whole, however, I have preferred to err on the side of caution and have listed separately even those names which on the face of it one may assume had been distorted by copyists and whose original correct form cannot be ascertained. I have also decided not to take for granted that signatories with the same surname belonged to the same family, or guild or *gonfalone*. Guild affiliation and *gonfalone* provenance have been assigned to individual signatories on the basis of specific attribution by the sources. Of a total of 503 names, 364 have been positively identified and their provenance noted. It has also been possible to trace their guild affiliation. Sources of information: Giovanni Cambi, 'Il libro degli abili al consiglio', MS BNF Passerini 39; ASF Tratte 1071; Priorista Gaddi, BL Egerton MS 3764; R. Pesman Cooper, 'The Florentine Ruling Group under the "Governo Popolare", 1494–1512', *Studies in Medieval and Renaissance History*, 7 (1985).

[2] M stands for affiliation to the Major Guilds; m for affiliation to the minor guilds.

[3] To distinguish between Drago, S. Spirito, and Drago, S. Giovanni, the latter is recorded as SG Drago.

| Name | Guild affiliation | Gonfalone |
|---|---|---|
| ALDOBRANDINI Aldobrandino di Brunetto (P: father's name given as Benv.) | M | Lion d'oro |
| ALDOBRANDINI Bernardo di Silvestro | M | Lion d'oro |
| ALDOBRANDINI Francesco di Giorgio | M | Lion d'oro |
| ALDOBRANDINI Piero di Salvatore (as below?) | | |
| ALDOBRANDINI Piero di Salvestro (P: without father's name) | M | Lion d'oro |
| Degli ALESSANDRI Alessandro d'Antonio | M | Chiavi |
| ALTOVITI Guglielmo di Bardo | M | Vipera |
| AMADORI Lorenzo di Francesco | M | Scala |
| AMBROGI Francesco | m | Unicorno |
| AMBROGINI Francesco | M | Unicorno |
| Dall'ANCISA Giovanni Battista di Jacomo | M | Chiavi |
| Dall'ANTELLA Thadeo di Bernardo | M | Carro |
| ARNOLDI Giovanni di Doffo (G: as Arnolfi) | M | Bue |
| ARNOLFI Nofri | M | Carro |
| AZZINI Stephano di Ghino (G: as Arzini) | M | Lion bianco |
| BAGNESI Rinieri di Francesco | M | Lion nero |
| BALDESI Antonio di Torino | M | Lion bianco |
| BALDINELLI Guido di Baldino (as Bandinelli below?) | | |
| BALDOVINETTI Alesso di Francesco | M | Vipera |
| BALDUCCI Piero di Francesco (P: as Baldusini) | | |
| BANDINELLI Guido di Baldino | | |
| BANDINI Corsino di Pietro | | |
| BANDINI Niccolò di Giovanni | | |
| BANDINI Nicolò di Goro (as above?) | | |
| De BARDI Jacopo di Bernardo di Jacopo | | |
| De BARDI Pandolfo di Berto | | |
| BARDINI Pier Francesco di Ser Giuliano | | |
| BARTOLI Bernard [in]o | M | Unicorno |
| BARTOLI Doffo di Marco | M | Unicorno |
| BARTOLI Lorenzo di Giovanni | M | Unicorno |
| BARTOLI Piero di Cosmo | M | Unicorno |
| BARTOLINI Antonio di Domenico (P: as Bertolini) | M | SG Drago |
| BARTOLINI Giovanni Battista di Niccolò | | |
| BARTOLINI Pierfrancesco di Ser Giuliano | | |
| BECCHI Giovanni di Francesco (P: as Bochi) | M | SG Drago |
| Del BECCUTO Felice di Deo (P: as Del Begutto) | M | SG Drago |
| BENAIUTI Domenico di Benvenuto | | |

| Name | Guild affiliation | Gonfalone |
| --- | --- | --- |
| BENCI Antonio di Francesco | M | SG Drago |
| BENCI Giovanfrancesco di Tommaso | m | SG Drago |
| (P: father's name given as Leonardo) | | |
| BENCI Girolamo di Bencio (P: as Bensi and | m | SG Drago |
| without father's name) | | |
| BENEDETTO di Bernardo di Conero | | |
| Del BENINO Carlo di Lionardo | M | Ferza |
| Del BENINO Carlo di Lodovico | | |
| (perhaps as the above) | | |
| Del BENINO Leonardo di Carlo | M | Ferza |
| BENINTENDI Paolo di Zanobi | M | Carro |
| BENIVIENI Antonio | M | Chiavi |
| BENIVIENI Girolamo di Ser Paolo | M | Chiavi |
| BENVENUTI Domenico di Benvenuto | M | Lion d'oro |
| BERLINGHIERI Antonio di Jacomo | | |
| BERTI Giovanni Battista di Bartolomeo | M | Scala |
| BERTI Piero di Matteo | M | Bue |
| BERTOLDI Pietro Pagolo | | |
| BETTINI Ser Antonio di Piero | | |
| BETTINI Francesco Antonio | m | Chiavi |
| BETTINI Piero di Francesco | m | Chiavi |
| Del BIADA Bernardo di Jacopo | M | Lion bianco |
| (P: as Del Hinda) | | |
| BIANCARDI Benedetto di Francesco | | |
| BIANCIARDI Benedetto di Giovanni | | |
| BILIOTTI Carlo di Aldigieri | M | Bue |
| BILIOTTI Matteo di Bernardo | M | Nicchio |
| BINDI Niccolò di Niccolò di Giunta | M | Chiavi |
| (P: grandfather's name given as Civita) | | |
| BISDOMINI Carlo di Francesco | M | Chiavi |
| BOCHAZI Benedetto | | |
| BONAGRAZIA Girolamo | | |
| BONCIANI Raffaello di Nicolò | M | Vipera |
| BONHOMINI Jeronimo di Paolo | | |
| BONI Andrea di Giovanni (P: as De Bono) | M | SG Drago |
| BONI Giovanni Batt [ist]a | M | SG Drago |
| BONI Lionello di Giovanni | M | SG Drago |
| BONI Raffaello di Lionardo | M | SG Drago |
| BONSI Antonio di Francesco | M | Ferza |
| BONSI Bernardo di Baldassar | M | Ferza |
| BONSI Domenico | M | Ferza |

| Name | Guild affiliation | Gonfalone |
|---|---|---|
| BONSI Piero di Cosimo | M | Ferza |
| BORANI Jacopo di Giovanni | | |
| BOTTI Benedetto di Matteo | | |
| BRACCI Jacopo di Giovanni | | |
| BRANDOLINI Cristofano di Anfrione (P: no father's name given) | | |
| BRANDOLINI Cristofano di Giuliano | M | Bue |
| BRUNACCI Bastiano di Lazzaro (P: as Burnati) | m | Drago |
| BRUNATTI Giacomo di Giovanni | | |
| BRUNELLI Bastiano di Lazzero (as Brunacci above?) | | |
| BRUNI Agnolo di Girolamo | | |
| BRUNI Antonio | M | Drago |
| Del BUGLIAFFA Bernardo di Francesco | M | Ferza |
| Del BUGLIAFFA Thomaso di Francesco (P: as Del Bugaffa) | M | Ferza |
| BUONANNI Benedetto di Niccolò (perhaps Buonvanni Benedetto below) | | |
| BUONANNI Carlo di Niccolò (perhaps Buonvanni Cambio below) | | |
| BUONCIANI Raffaello di Niccolò | | |
| BUONDELMONTE Bartholomeo del Rosso | M | Vipera |
| BUONDELMONTE Lorenzo | M | Vipera |
| BUONDELMONTI Theghiaio di Francesco (G: as Tegliaio) | M | Vipera |
| BUONINSEGNI Domenico di Piero | M | Lion bianco |
| BUONVANNI Benedetto di Nicolò (P: as Bonnanni) | M | Lion d'oro |
| BUONVANNI Cambio di Nicolò (P: as Bonnanni) | M | Lion d'oro |
| BUONVANNI Francesco di Nicolò (P: as Bonnanni) | M | Lion d'oro |
| BUTI Mariotto di Domenico (P: as Butti) | | |
| Del CACCIA Matheo di Nofri (P: Del Casia) | M | Ruote |
| CACCINI Alessandro di Francesco (P: as Casini) | M | Lion nero |
| CACCINI Giovanni di Francesco | M | Lion nero |
| Da CAIIANO Giuliano di Piero | | |
| CAIUBI Giovanni (Cambi?) | | |
| CAMBI Francesco di Guido | M | SG Drago |
| CAMBI Giovanni del Nero | M | Unicorno |
| CAMBI Giovanni di Nicolò | M | SG Drago |
| CAMBI Guido di Nicolò | M | SG Drago |

| Name | Guild affiliation | Gonfalone |
|---|---|---|
| CAMBINI Andrea di Antonio | M | Lion d'oro |
| CAMBINI Bernardo di Nicolò | M | Lion d'oro |
| CAMBINI Lionardo di Antonio | M | Lion d'oro |
| CAMBINI Nicolò di Francesco | M | Lion d'oro |
| CANIGIANI Adovardo di Simone | M | Scala |
| CANIGIANI Simone di Antonio | M | Scala |
| CAPELLI Piero di Lionardo | | |
| CAPPELLI Giovanni di Filippo | M | SG Drago |
| CAPPELLI Niccolaio di Bernardo | | |
| CAPPONI Girolamo di Gino | M | Nicchio |
| CARDUCCI Agnolo di Lorenzo | M | Vipera |
| CARLETTI maestro Zanobi di Daniello | m | Chiavi |
| CARNESECCHI Bernardo di Francesco | M | SG Drago |
| CARNESECCHI Giovan di Lionardo | M | SG Drago |
| CARNESECCHI Giovanni di Niccolò | | |
| CARNESECCHI Giovanni di Simone | | |
| CARNESECCHI Juliano di Simone | M | SG Drago |
| CARNESECCHI Zanobi di Francesco | M | SG Drago |
| Della CASA Aldighieri di Paolo | M | SG Drago |
| CAVALCANTI Guido d'Antonio | | |
| CEFFI Giovan Battista di Thomaso | M | Ruote |
| CENTELINI Lorenzo di Giovanni (P: as Centolini) | | |
| CENTELLINI Giovanni di Lorenzo | | |
| CHOESINI Bartolomeo (perhaps Corsini) | | |
| CIACCHI Jacomo di Scholaro | M | Carro |
| CIACCHI Thomaso di Scolaro | M | Carro |
| CIAI Bartolomeo | M | Lion d'oro |
| CIAI Lorenzo di Francesco | M | Lion d'oro |
| CIAMPELLI Niccolò · | M | Carro |
| CICIAPORCI Bernardo di Benedetto | M | Scala |
| CIESCI Piero di Lorenzo (perhaps Cresci below) | | |
| CINI Lorenzo di Francesco | m | Lion rosso |
| CINOZZI maestro Girolamo di ser Angelo (P: father's name given as Francesco) | m | Lion d'oro |
| CINOZZI Piero di M.o Simone | m | Lion d'oro |
| CINURI Niccolò | | |
| CIONI Domenico di Gabriello | | |
| Delle COLOMBE Raffaello di Corso | m | Nicchio |
| [Delle COLOMBE] Raffaele di Michele di Corso | m | Nicchio |
| COMPAGNI Cante di Giovanni | M | Unicorno |

| Name | Guild affiliation | Gonfalone |
|------|-------------------|-----------|
| COMPAGNI Piero di Giovanni di Cante | M | Unicorno |
| CORBINELLI Giovanni di Thomaso | M | Nicchio |
| CORBINELLI Piero di Thomaso | M | Nicchio |
| CORIDIANI Antonio | | |
| CORSINI Antonio di Bartholomeo di Bertoldo | M | Ferza |
| CORSINI Bartholomeo di Bertoldo | M | Ferza |
| CORSINI Bertoldo di Bartholomeo | M | Ferza |
| CORSINI Gerardo di Bartolomeo | M | Ferza |
| CORTIGIANI Adoardo di Simone | | |
| COSMO di Piero di mastro Bettino | | |
| CRESCI Piero di Lorenzo | M | Vaio |
| DAVANZATI Francesco di Francesco | M | Unicorno |
| DAVANZATI Francesco di Lorenzo | M | Unicorno |
| DAVIZI Paolo di Davizo | | |
| DAZI Paolo | M | Lion rosso |
| DAZZI Marchionne (P: as Dagi) | M | Lion rosso |
| DAZZI Piero di Daniello | M | Lion rosso |
| DEI PAGOLO di Sinibaldo (as Di Deo below?) | | |
| DELL'EREDE Jacopo | | |
| Da DIACCETO Gasparre di Jacomo | | |
| Da DIACCETO Gasparre di Lapo | M | Lion nero |
| Da DIACCETO Giovanbattista di Lapo | M | Lion nero |
| DI DEO Agnolo di Sinibaldo Buono | m | Bue |
| DINI Dino di Jacopo | | |
| DINO di Jacopo di messer Guccio | | |
| DONI Giovanni di Francesco | m | Vaio |
| Da EMPOLI Lionardo di Giovanni | | |
| FABBRINI Piero di Francesco | M | SG Drago |
| FACHINI Piero | | |
| FEDERIGHI Domenico (P: as Domenedio) | M | Lion rosso |
| FEDERIGHI Girolamo di Paolo | M | Lion rosso |
| FEDERIGHI Piero di Giovanni | M | Lion rosso |
| FEDINI Martino di Ser Nicolò | M | Unicorno |
| FERARETTI Andrea di Maretti | | |
| FERRANTI Piero di Francesco | m | Drago |
| Da FILICAIA Battista di Berto (P: father's name given as Battista) | M | Chiavi |
| Da FILICAIA M.o Berto | M | Chiavi |
| FILIPEPI Simone di Mariano (G: occurs as Filippi) (P: as Filipetri) | | |
| FILIPETTI Bonacorso | | |

| Name | Guild affiliation | Gonfalone |
|------|------------------|-----------|
| GADDI Girolamo d'Agnolo | M | Lion d'oro |
| GADDI Giuliano di Agnolo | M | Lion d'oro |
| GADDI Tadeo (P: father's name given as Agnolo) | M | Lion d'oro |
| GADDI Zanobi di Agnolo | M | Lion d'oro |
| GAETANI Filippo di Piero | M | Unicorno |
| Da GAGLIANO Giovanni di Roberto (P: as De Cayano) | | |
| GAGLIANO Giuliano di Piero | M | SG Drago |
| GALIANO maestro Giuliano di Martino | M | SG Drago |
| GALLI Domenico di Sandro (P: as Gani) | | |
| GERARDINI Ottaviano di Gerardino | M | Carro |
| GHERARDI Gherardo di Bernardo | M | Ruote |
| GHERARDINI Angnolo di Salvestro | | |
| GHIRARDINI Angelo di Lorenzo | | |
| GIANFIGLIAZZI Antonio di Niccolò | M | Unicorno |
| GINORI Alessandro di Gino (P: as Gironi) | M | Lion d'oro |
| GINORI Carlo (P: as Sinori) | M | Lion d'oro |
| GINORI Girolamo di Gino (P: father's name given as Agnio) | M | Lion d'oro |
| Del GIOCONDO Paolo di Antonio (P: as Giocondi) | | |
| GIOVANNI Battista di Lapo | | |
| Di GIOVANNI Giovanni Battista di Francesco | M | Nicchio |
| GIOVANNI di Jacopo di Dino (as below?) | | |
| GIOVANNI d'Jacopo di Dino di Guccio | | |
| GIROLAMI Geri di Zanobi del Testa | M | Lion rosso |
| GIUGNI Antonio di Giovanni | M | Ruote |
| GIULIANO di Martino | | |
| M.o GIULIANO di Martino di Giuseppe | | |
| GIUNTINI Filippo di Francesco | M | Unicorno |
| GONDI Alessandro di Antonio | M | Lion bianco |
| GONDI Benedetto di Bernardo | M | Lion bianco |
| GONDI Benedetto di Carlo | M | Lion bianco |
| GONDI Bernardo di Carlo | M | Lion bianco |
| GONDI Filippo di Bernardo | M | Lion bianco |
| GONDI Filippo di Carlo | M | Lion bianco |
| GONDI Giovanni d'Antonio | M | Lion bianco |
| GONDI Girolamo d'Antonio | M | Lion bianco |
| GONDI Simone di Antonio | M | Lion bianco |
| GORI Benedetto di Matteo | M | Lion d'oro |

| Name | Guild affiliation | Gonfalone |
|---|---|---|
| GRASSI Paolo Amerigo (Ser) | M | Chiavi |
| GRASSO Francesco Paolo Domenico | | |
| GUADAGNI Oliviero di Simone | M | Chiavi |
| GUADAGNI Piero di Gino di Cante | | |
| GUALTEROTTI Filippo di Lorenzo (P: as Filipozi) | M | Scala |
| GUALTEROTTI Francesco | M | Scala |
| GUARDI Bartholomeo di Gherardo | | |
| GUARDI Nicolò di Guardo (P: as Guarchi) | | |
| GUASCONI Bernardo di Beltramo | M | Lion d'oro |
| GUASCONI Francesco di Francesco | M | Lion d'oro |
| GUASCONI Gioachino | M | Lion d'oro |
| GUASCONI Giovanbattista di Carlo | M | Lion d'oro |
| GUASCONI Giovanbattista di Niccolò | M | Lion d'oro |
| GUASCONI Ser Lorenzo di Giovacchino (G: defined as Prete) | M | Lion d'oro |
| GUASINI Filippo di Francesco | | |
| GUCCI Neri di Piero | M | Lion nero |
| GUIDACCI Simone di Francesco | | |
| GUIDETTI Antonio di Michele | | |
| GUIDOTTI Andrea di Zanobi | M | SG Drago |
| GUIDOTTI Antonio di Migliore | M | SG Drago |
| GUIDUCCI Andrea di Biagio (P: as Guiduzi) | | |
| GUIDUCCI Andrea di Stagio (as above?) | | |
| GUIDUCCI Simone di Francesco | M | Unicorno |
| HENZI Giuliano di Girolamo (Benci?) | | |
| INGHIRAMI Baldo (G: Inghirlani) | M | Lion d'oro |
| INGHIRAMI Giovanni di Francesco | M | Lion d'oro |
| INGHIRAMI Girolamo di Francesco | M | Lion d'oro |
| INGHIRLANI Giovanni di Francesco (as Inghirami above?) | | |
| INGHIRLANI Girolamo di Francesco (as Inghirami above?) | | |
| JACOMO di Bartholomeo di Boccaccio | | |
| Del LANCIA Giovambatista d'Jacopo | | |
| LANFREDINI Antonio di Jacomo (G: as d'Jacopo) (F and G: as Lanfredi) | M | Drago |
| LANFREDINI Lanfredino di Jacopo (P: father's name given as Jacomo) | M | Drago |
| LAPACCINI Domenico di Benedetto | M | Lion bianco |
| LAPACCINI Giacomo di Alessandro | M | Lion bianco |

| Name | Guild affiliation | Gonfalone |
|---|---|---|
| LAPACCINI Giovanni Francesco di Benedetto | M | Lion bianco |
| LAPATAZI Giovanni Francesco (as above?) | | |
| LAPAZINI Domenico (as above?) | | |
| LAPI Bartolomeo di Apollonio | M | Vaio |
| Da LAPO Gaspare | | |
| LAPUCCI Giovanfrancesco di Benedetto (as Lapaccini above?) | | |
| LENZI Lorenzo di Anfrione | M | Unicorno |
| LENZI Piero di Anfrione | M | Unicorno |
| LEONARDO dec. di M.o Francesco | | |
| De' LIBRI Andrea di Nicolò | M | Bue |
| LIONI Domenico | m | Lion d'oro |
| LIPPI Stephano di Filippo | M | Ferza |
| LORINI Filippo di Antonio | M | SG Drago |
| LOTTI Bastiano | M | Nicchio |
| MACHIAVELLI Alessandro di Nicolò | M | Nicchio |
| MACHIAVELLI Nicolò di Alessandro | M | Nicchio |
| MAGALDI Domenico di Niccolò | M | Bue |
| MANCINI Niccolò di Taddeo | M | Bue |
| MANELLI Alesso di Lionardo | M | Scala |
| MANELLI Francesco di Bernardo | M | Scala |
| MANELLI Francesco di Lionardo | M | Scala |
| MANELLI Tommaso di Paolo | M | Scala |
| MANETTI Bernardo di Filippo | M | Scala |
| MANUNZI Jacopo di Lorenzo (actually Manucci) | m | Nicchio |
| MANZUOLI Ugolino di Giovanni | | |
| Del MARE Francesco di Bernardo | m | SG Drago |
| MARISCOTTI Messer Agamennone da Calvi, Podestà di Firenze | | |
| MAROZI Francesco | | |
| MARTELLI Raffaele | M | Lion d'oro |
| MARTELLI Thomaso | M | Lion d'oro |
| MARTINI Antonio di Thomaso | M | Chiavi |
| MARTINI Bernardo di (Ser) Giovanni | M | SG Drago |
| MASCALZONI Piero di Francesco | | |
| MASI Piero di Andrea | | |
| MAZZEI Lapo di Giovanni | m | Vaio |
| MAZZEI Lappo di Jacopo | m | Vaio |
| MAZZEI Mazzeo di Giovanni | m | Vaio |
| MAZZEI Mazzeo di Lapo | | |
| MAZZEI Piero di Bernardo | m | Vaio |

| Name | Guild affiliation | Gonfalone |
|---|---|---|
| MAZZEI Raffaello di Mazzeo (both F and G give surname as Mazzeo) | m | Vaio |
| MAZZINGHI Domenico di Bernardo | M | Lion bianco |
| MAZZINGHI Francesco di Bernardo | M | Lion bianco |
| MAZZINGHI Girolamo di Agostino | M | Lion bianco |
| MAZZINGHI Piero di Bernardo | M | Lion bianco |
| De' MEDICI Bernardo di Alamanno | M | Lion d'oro |
| De' MEDICI Bernardo di Alessandro | M | Lion d'oro |
| De' MEDICI Giovanni Battista di Bernardo | M | Lion d'oro |
| De' MEDICI Giovan Battista di Niccolò | M | Lion d'oro |
| MICHELOZZI Ser Nicolò | m | SG Drago |
| MIGLIOROTTI Antonio di Ser Piero (G: as Miglioretti) | m | Chiavi |
| MINERBETTI Giovanni di Antonio | M | Lion rosso |
| Da MODEI Bartolomeo di Alamanno | | |
| MONTE Giovanni di Francesco | m | Lion d'oro |
| MONTE Giovanni di Ser (G: as Sermonti) | m | Lion d'oro |
| MONTI Biagio di Michele (F: as di Monte) | m | Lion d'oro |
| MONTI Biagio di Nicolò | m | Lion d'oro |
| MORELLI Thomaso di Paolo | M | Lion nero |
| MORI Filippo di Nicolò | M | Unicorno |
| MOROZZI Francesco di Giuliano | m | Lion nero |
| NASI Alessandro di Francesco | M | Scala |
| NASI Filippo di Luthozzo | M | Scala |
| NELLI Francesco di Bartholomeo | M | Lion d'oro |
| NELLI Giovanni di Matteo | M | Lion d'oro |
| NERETTI Matheo di Francesco | m | Unicorno |
| NERETTI Neretto di Francesco | m | Unicorno |
| Del NERO Nero di Francesco | M | Scala |
| Del NERO Simone di Bernardo | M | Scala |
| NESI Giovanni di Francesco | M | Bue |
| NETI Giovanni di Francesco (as Nesi above?) | | |
| NICCOLÒ di Taddeo | | |
| NICHILOSI Francesco Nicolò | | |
| NICOLI Costanzo di Girolamo (P: as Nicolai) | M | Lion d'oro |
| NICOLI Pietro Pagolo | M | Lion d'oro |
| NOCETTI Matteo di Francesco (as Neretti above?) | | |
| ORLANDINI Bartholomeo di Giovanni | M | SG Drago |
| ORLANDINI Francesco di Giovanni | M | SG Drago |
| ORLANDINI G[h]ino di Lorenzo | M | SG Drago |

| Name | Guild affiliation | Gonfalone |
|------|-------------------|-----------|
| ORLANDINI Iacopo di Lorenzo (P: as Velandini) | M | SG Drago |
| ORLANDINI Orlandino di Bartholomeo | M | SG Drago |
| PAGOLO di Avizo di Avizo | | |
| PALESCIONI Gualterotto di Lionardo (i.e. Palancioni) | M | Ferza |
| PANCIATICHI Giuliano di Piero | M | SG Drago |
| PANDOLFINI Bartholomeo di Pandolfo | M | Chiavi |
| PANDOLFINI Giovanni di Pandolfo | M | Chiavi |
| PARENTI Stefano di Giovanni | M | SG Drago |
| PARENTI Stefano di Lorenzo | M | SG Drago |
| PARIANI Pariano di Giuliano | | |
| PARTICINI Particino di Giuliano (G: as Particeni) | M | Lion rosso |
| PASQUINI Thomaso di Paolo (P: as Pasconi) | m | Lion bianco |
| PERINI Giovanni di Agnolo (P: as Pirini) | m | Lion d'oro |
| PERUZZI Antonio di Domenico | M | Lion nero |
| PESCIONI Michele di Lionardo (P: as Pesuoni) | M | Lion bianco |
| PETRUCCI Alamanno di Cesare | M | Lion rosso |
| PIERO di Giovanni di Conte | | |
| PIETRO Paolo di Romolo di Bartolo | | |
| PITTI Alfonso di Mr Jannozzo | M | Nicchio |
| PITTI Carlo di Luigi (P: as Patti) | M | Nicchio |
| PITTI Francesco di Giovanni di Buonacorso (P: omits di Giovanni) | M | Nicchio |
| PITTI Raffaeleo di Alfonso | M | Nicchio |
| PLARNINI Gualterotto di Lionardo (as Palescioni above?) | | |
| PORTINARI Benedetto di Paolo | M | Vaio |
| PORTINARI Francesco di Giovanni | M | Vaio |
| PORTINARI Thomaso di Folco | M | Vaio |
| PUCCI Aless[andr]o di Antonio | M | Vaio |
| PUCCI Bartholomeo di Puccio | M | Vaio |
| PUCCI Francesco di Antonio | M | Vaio |
| PUCCI Giannozzo di Antonio | M | Vaio |
| PUCCI Priore di Saracino (G: where name is Piero) | M | Vaio |
| PUCCI Thomaso di Puccio | M | Vaio |
| PUCCINI Giannozzo di Antonio (perhaps as Pucci above) | | |
| PUCCINI Piero di Andrea | m | Chiavi |
| Del PUGLIESE Francesco di Filippo | M | Drago |

| Name | Guild affiliation | Gonfalone |
|------|------------------|-----------|
| Raffaello di Marco | | |
| Rasi Francesco di Andrea | | |
| Redditi Bartholomeo (P: as Devedito) | M | Ruote |
| Ricardi Bartholomeo di Giovanni | M | Lion rosso |
| De' Ricasoli Jacomo di Gasparo | M | Vipera |
| De' Ricci Francesco d'Antonio | M | Vaio |
| Ridolfi Bartholomeo di Pagnozzo | M | Ferza |
| Ridolfi Bernardo di Inghilese | M | Nicchio |
| Ridolfi Giovan Battista | M | Ferza |
| Ridolfi Niccolò di Guglielmo (as Nicolò di Giuliano below?) | | |
| Ridolfi Nicolò di Giuliano | M | Ferza |
| Ridolfi Pier Francesco di Giorgio | M | Ferza |
| Ridolfi Piero di Giuliano | M | Ferza |
| Ridolfi Ruberto di Pagnozzo | M | Ferza |
| Ridolfi Schiatta di Nicolò | M | Nicchio |
| Rinardi Bartolomeo di Luca (perhaps Rinaldi) | | |
| Rinucci Nicolò del Buono | M | Ferza |
| Rinuccini Francesco di Filippo (P: as Janucini) | M | Bue |
| Rinuccini Neri di Filippo | M | Bue |
| Risaliti Jacopo di Gasparre | M | Bue |
| Risaliti Ubertino di Geri (P: as Visalitti) | M | Bue |
| Risi Francesco d'Antonio | | |
| Da Romena Cristoforo di fr. Francesco | m | SG Drago |
| Rondinelli Aless [andro] di Giovanni | M | Lion d'oro |
| De' Rossi Giovanni di Matteo | | |
| De' Rossi Noferi di Piero | M | Nicchio |
| Del Rosso Agnolo di Renzo | | |
| Del Rosso Angelo di Perozzo | M | Chiavi |
| Del Rosso Domenico di Antonio | M | Chiavi |
| Del Rosso Domenico di Pierozzo (P: father's name given as Derozo) | M | Chiavi |
| Rosso di Piero di Domenico | | |
| Del Rosso Pierozzo del Rosso | M | Chiavi |
| Rucellai Adovardo | M | Lion rosso |
| Rucellai Alessandro di Carlo | M | Lion rosso |
| Rucellai Giovanni Battista di Mariotto (P: as Rusilalghi) | M | Lion rosso |
| Rucellai Lorenzo di Antonio | M | Lion rosso |
| Rucellai Mariotto di Piero (P: as Rusilalgli) | M | Lion rosso |
| Sacchetti Filippo di Niccolò | M | Bue |

| Name | Guild affiliation | Gonfalone |
|---|---|---|
| SACCHETTI Nicolò di Matheo | M | Bue |
| SALVIATI Alamanno | M | Ruote |
| SALVIATI Alessandro di Bernardo | | |
| SALVIATI Giannozzo di Bernardo | M | Ruote |
| SALVIATI Jacopo di Giovanni | M | Ruote |
| SALVIATI Lorenzo di Lotto | M | Ruote |
| SALVIATI Piero di Thomasso | M | Ruote |
| SAPITI Bernardo di Antonio (P: as Sapeti) | M | Nicchio |
| SAPITI Francesco di Giovanni | M | Nicchio |
| SAPITI Otto di Francesco | M | Nicchio |
| SCALI Anton Francesco di Bartholomeo | M | Vipera |
| SCALI Anton Francesco di Tommaso | | |
| SCHIASOSI Jacomo di Lorenzo (Schiattesi-Stiattesi?) | | |
| SCHIATTESI Giovanni di Ludovico | | |
| SCOLARI Giovanni di Lorenzo | M | Scala |
| SEGNI Bernardo di Stefano | M | Nicchio |
| SERDA Domenico di Gianozo (as Stradi below?) | | |
| SERESI Piero di Bernardo | | |
| SINGORI Ugolino d'Antonio | | |
| SODERINI Girolamo di Luigi | M | Drago |
| Da SOMMAIA Francesco | M | Unicorno |
| SPINA Francesco di Ghino (P: father's name given as de Zoan) | M | Carro |
| SPINI Thomaso di Silvestro | | Unicorno |
| STIATTESI Jacopo di Lodovico (i.e. Schiattesi) | M | Bue |
| STRADI Cesare di Gianozzo | M | Ferza |
| STRADI Domenico di Giannozzo | M | Ferza |
| STROZZI Andrea di Carlo | M | Lion rosso |
| STROZZI Carlo di Lorenzo | | |
| STROZZI Casocci di Zanobi (P: name as Carosio) | M | Lion rosso |
| STROZZI Giovanbattista di Lorenzo | | |
| STROZZI Leonardo di Benedetto | M | Lion rosso |
| STROZZI Marco di Giovanni | M | Lion rosso |
| STROZZI Michele di Carlo | M | Lion rosso |
| STROZZI Piero di Giovanni | M | Lion rosso |
| STROZZI Piero di Zanobi | M | Lion rosso |
| STROZZI Raffaello di Battista (P: father's name given as Soldo) | M | Lion rosso |
| Della STUFA Deifebo di Francesco | M | Lion d'oro |
| Della STUFA Enea | M | Lion d'oro |

| Name | Guild affiliation | Gonfalone |
|------|-------------------|-----------|
| Della STUFA Pandolfo di m. Agnolo | M | Lion d'oro |
| TAGLI Guglielmo (as Tanagli below?) | | |
| TALLANI Bartolomeo di Sandro | M | Ruote |
| TANAGLI Guglielmo di Francesco | M | Chiavi |
| TEBALDI Andrea di Jacopo (P: as Tedaldi) | M | Vaio |
| TEDALDI Jacopo di Pietro | M | Vaio |
| TEMPERANI Piero di Mr Manno | M | Lion rosso |
| TEMPERANI Temperano di Mr Manno | M | Lion rosso |
| TERINGHI Pierfrancesco di Francesco (Tosinghi?) | | |
| TOLOMEI Nerio | | |
| TORNABUONI Antonio di Filippo | M | Lion bianco |
| TORNABUONI Lorenzo di Giovanni | M | Lion bianco |
| TORNABUONI Simone di Filippo | M | Lion bianco |
| TORNAQUINCI Benedetto di Antonio | M | Lion bianco |
| TORNAQUINCI Giovanni di Antonio | M | Lion bianco |
| TORRIGIANI Antonio di Torrigiano | m | Nicchio |
| TORRIGIANI Francesco di Torrigiano | m | Nicchio |
| TOSINGHI Francesco di Pier Francesco | M | SG Drago |
| TOSINGHI Pier Francesco di Francesco | M | SG Drago |
| TOSINGHI Rinieri di Francesco (P: as Toseghi) | M | SG Drago |
| TRADI Cesare di Giannozzo (as Stradi above?) | | |
| UBALDINI Antonio di m. Brandino (G: father's name given as M. Bernardo) | | |
| UBALDINI Benedetto di Ser Antonio | M | Lion d'oro |
| UBALDINI Francesco Antonio di Benedetto | | |
| UBALDINI Raffaello di Antonio (P: as Tubaldino) | M | Lion d'oro |
| UGOLINI Bernardo (Brando) di Giovanni | M | Ferza |
| UGOLINI Nicolo di Giorgio | M | Ferza |
| UGUCCIONI Buonaccorso di Benedetto (P: as Ugononi) | M | Carro |
| VALARIANO di Piero Valariano | M | Lion d'oro |
| VALERIANO di Piero di Luca (F: father's name corrected in note to Prospero) | | |
| VALORI Francesco | M | Chiavi |
| VALORI Nicolò di Bartholomeo | M | Chiavi |
| VECCHIETTI Giacomo di Bernardo | | |
| VECCHIETTI Giovanni di Bernardo (P: Vecchiotti) | M | Lion bianco |
| VECCHIETTI Matteo di Nicolao (P: as Vichetti) | M | Lion bianco |
| VELLUTI Biagio di Bonacorso | M | Nicchio |

| Name | Guild affiliation | Gonfalone |
|---|---|---|
| VERBI Giovanbattista di Bartolomeo | | |
| VERNACCI Anton Francesco | M | Lion bianco |
| VERNACCI Marcello di Lionardo | M | Lion bianco |
| Da VERRAZZANO Antonio di Amerigo | M | Ruote |
| VESPUCCI Marco di Bernardo | M | Unicorno |
| VETTORI Bernardo di Francesco | M | Nicchio |
| VETTORI Giovanni di Gianozzo | M | Nicchio |
| VIERI Francesco Ugolino (as below?) | | |
| VIERI (Ser) Ugolino | M | Ferza |
| VIERINI ser Agnolino di Vieri de' Vieri (as above?) | | |
| VINISINI Raffaele (as below) | | |
| VIVIANI Raffaello di Giuliano | m | Vipera |
| VIVIANI Raffaello di Guglielmo (as above?) | | |
| ZATI Francesco di Andrea | M | Ruote |

*Distribution of Signatories by City Quarter and*
*District (Gonfalone)*

| City Quarter | District | Number |
|---|---|---|
| Sta Maria Novella | Unicorno | 24 |
| | Vipera | 10 |
| | Lion bianco | 31 |
| | Lion rosso | 27 |
| | Total | 92 |
| Sta Croce | Ruote | 13 |
| | Lion nero | 9 |
| | Carro | 8 |
| | Bue | 16 |
| | Total | 46 |
| S. Spirito | Drago | 6 |
| | Nicchio | 27 |
| | Scala | 17 |
| | Ferza | 26 |
| | Total | 76 |
| S. Giovanni | Vaio | 20 |
| | Lion d'oro | 57 |
| | Chiavi | 31 |
| | Drago | 42 |
| | Total | 150 |
| TOTAL | | 364 |

*Guild Affiliation of Signatories*

| | |
|---|---|
| Major Guilds | 324 |
| Minor Guilds | 40 |
| TOTAL | 364 |
| RATIO | 8.1 : 1 |

# SELECT BIBLIOGRAPHY

ALBERTINI, RUDOLF VON, *Firenze dalla repubblica al principato* (Turin, 1970).

BUTTERS, HUMFREY C., *Governors and Government in Early Sixteenth-Century Florence, 1502–1519* (Oxford, 1985).

CAMBI, GIOVANNI, *Istorie*, ed. Ildefonso di San Luigi (Delizie degli eruditi toscani, 20–3; 4 vols.; Florence, 1785–6).

CERRETANI, BARTOLOMEO, '*Ricordi storici fiorentini 1500–1523*', MS, Biblioteca Apostolica Vaticana, Vat. Lat. 13651.

——'Storia in dialogo della mutatione di Firenze', MS, Florence, Biblioteca Nazionale, Fondo Principale, II.I.106.

CORDERO, FRANCO, *Savonarola* (4 vols.; Bari, 1986–8).

CREYTENS, RAYMOND, 'Les Actes capitulaires de la Congrégation Toscano-Romaine O.P. (1496–1530)', *Archivum Fratrum Praedicatorum*, 40 (1970), 125–230.

DEVONSHIRE-JONES, ROSEMARY, *Francesco Vettori, Florentine Citizen and Medici Servant* (London, 1972).

GHERARDI, ALESSANDRO, *Nuovi documenti e studi intorno a Girolamo Savonarola* (Florence, 1887; fac. repr. 1972).

GINORI CONTI, PIERO [and Roberto Ridolfi], *La vita del beato Ieronimo Savonarola, scritta da un anonimo del sec. XVI e già attribuita a Fra Pacifico Burlamacchi* (Florence, 1937).

GUICCIARDINI, FRANCESCO, *Storie fiorentine dal 1378 al 1509*, ed. R. Palmarocchi (Bari, 1931; fac. repr. 1968).

HAY, DENYS, *The Church in Italy in the Fifteenth Century* (Cambridge, 1977; corrected repr. 1979).

PARENTI, PIERO, *Istorie fiorentine*, ed. in part by J. Schnitzer, *Quellen und Forschungen zur Geschichte Savonarolas*, iv (Leipzig, 1910).

——'Istorie fiorentine', MS, Florence, Biblioteca Nazionale, Fondo Principale, II.II.131–4; II.IV.171.

RIDOLFI, ROBERTO, *Vita di Girolamo Savonarola* (2 vols.; Rome, 1952).

ROTH, CECIL, *The Last Florentine Republic* (London, 1925; fac. repr. New York, 1968).

RUBINSTEIN, NICOLAI, *The Government of Florence under the Medici 1434 to 1494* (Oxford, 1966).

——'I primi anni del Consiglio Maggiore di Firenze (1494–99)', *Archivio storico italiano*, 112 (1954), 151–94, 321–47.

——'Politics and Constitution in Florence at the End of the Fifteenth Century', in E. F. Jacob (ed.), *Italian Renaissance Studies* (London, 1960), 148–83.

SAVONAROLA, GIROLAMO, *Compendio di rivelazioni e Dialogus de veritate prophetica*, ed. A. Crucitti (Edizione Nazionale delle Opere di G. Savonarola; Rome, 1974).

——*De Simplicitate christianae vitae*, ed. P. G. Ricci (Edizione Nazionale delle Opere di G. Savonarola; Rome, 1959).

——*Le lettere . . . ora per la prima volta raccolte e a miglior lezione ridotte*, ed. R. Ridolfi (Florence, 1933).

——*Lettere e scritti apologetici*, ed. R. Ridolfi, V. Romano, and A. Verde (Edizione Nazionale delle Opere di G. Savonarola; Rome, 1984).

——*Operette spirituali*, ed. M. Ferrara (Edizione Nazionale delle Opere di G. Savonarola; 2 vols.; Rome, 1976).

——*Prediche sopra Aggeo con il Trattato circa il reggimento e governo della città di Firenze*, ed. L. Firpo (Edizione Nazionale delle Opere di G. Savonarola; Rome, 1965).

——*Prediche sopra Amos e Zaccaria*, ed. P. Ghiglieri (Edizione Nazionale delle Opere di G. Savonarola; 3 vols.; Rome, 1971–2).

——*Prediche sopra l'Esodo*, ed. P. G. Ricci (Edizione Nazionale delle Opere di G. Savonarola; 2 vols.; Rome, 1955–6).

——*Prediche sopra Ezechiele*, ed. R. Ridolfi (Edizione Nazionale delle Opere di G. Savonarola; 2 vols.; Rome, 1955).

——*Prediche sopra Ruth e Michea*, ed. V. Romano (Edizione Nazionale delle Opere di G. Savonarola; 2 vols.; Rome, 1962).

——*Prediche sopra Giobbe*, ed. R. Ridolfi (Edizione Nazionale delle Opere di G. Savonarola; 2 vols.; Rome, 1957).

——*Prediche sopra i Salmi*, ed. V. Romano (Edizione Nazionale delle Opere di G. Savonarola; 2 vols.; Rome, 1969–74).

SCHNITZER, JOSEPH, *Savonarola* (2 vols.; Milan, 1931).

STEPHENS, JOHN N., *The Fall of the Florentine Republic, 1512–1530* (Oxford, 1983).

TREXLER, R. C. *Public Life in Renaissance Florence* (New York, 1980).

——'Ritual in Florence: Adolescence and Salvation in the Renaissance', in C. Trinkaus and H. A. Oberman (eds.), *The Pursuit of Holiness in Late Medieval and Renaissance Religion* (Leiden, 1974), 200–64.

UBALDINI, ROBERTO [*et al.*], 'Annalia Conventus Sancti Marci', MS, Florence, Biblioteca Medicea Laurenziana, S. Marco 370.

VASOLI, CESARE, L'attesa della nuova era in ambienti e gruppi fiorentini del Quattrocento', *L'attesa dell'età nuova nella spiritualità della fine del medioevo* (Convegno del Centro di Studi sulla Spiritualità Medievale III: 16–19 Oct. 1962; Todi, 1970), 370–432.

——'Giovanni Nesi tra Donato Acciaiuoli e Girolamo Savonarola: Testi editi e inediti', *Memorie Domenicane*, NS 4 (1973), 103–79.

——'Note sulle "Giornate" di Ser Lorenzo Violi', *Memorie Domenicane*, NS 3 (1972), 11–56.

——'Notizie su Giorgio Benigno Salviati (Juraj Dragisic)', *Studi storici in onore di Gabriele Pepe* (Bari, 1969), 429–98.

——'Pietro Bernardino e Gianfrancesco Pico', *L'opera e il pensiero di Giovanni Pico della Mirandola nella storia dell'Umanesimo* (Convegno internazionale, Mirandola, 15–18 Sept. 1963), ii (Florence, 1965), 281–99.

VERDE, ARMANDO, *Lo studio fiorentino 1473–1503: Ricerche e documenti* (Istituto Nazionale di Studi sul Rinascimento; 4 vols. in 7; Florence, 1973–85).

VILLARI, PASQUALE, *La storia di Girolamo Savonarola e de' suoi tempi* (2 vols.; Florence, 1930).

WEINSTEIN, DONALD, 'Machiavelli and Savonarola', in M. P. Gilmore (ed.), *Studies on Machiavelli* (Florence, 1972), 253–64.

——'Millenarianism in a Civic Setting: The Savonarola Movement in Florence', in S. L. Thrupp (ed.), *Millenarian Dreams in Action: Essays in Comparative Studies* (Comparative Studies in Society and History, Supplement II; The Hague, 1962), 187–203.

——'The Myth of Florence', in N. Rubinstein (ed.), *Florentine Studies: Politics and Society in Renaissance Florence* (London, 1968), 15–24.

——'Savonarola, Florence and the Millenarian Tradition', *Church History*, 27 (1958), 291–305.

——*Savonarola and Florence: Prophecy and Patriotism in the Renaissance* (Princeton, NJ, 1970).

# INDEX